Ex Libris

Gerald A. Brinsdon

London 12.02.09.

Wagner and Venice

Eastman Studies in Music

Ralph P. Locke, Senior Editor
Eastman School of Music

Additional Titles on Nineteenth-Century Music

A complete list of titles in the Eastman Studies in Music Series,
in order of publication, may be found at the end of this book.

Wagner and Venice

JOHN W. BARKER

UNIVERSITY OF ROCHESTER PRESS

First published 2008

University of Rochester Press
668 Mt. Hope Avenue, Rochester, NY 14620, USA
www.urpress.com
and Boydell & Brewer Limited
PO Box 9, Woodbridge, Suffolk IP12 3DF, UK
www.boydellandbrewer.com

ISBN-13: 978–1–58046–288–4
ISBN-10: 1–58046–288–X

ISSN: 1071–9989

Library of Congress Cataloging-in-Publication Data

Barker, John W.
    Wagner and Venice / John W. Barker.
        p. cm. — (Eastman studies in music, ISSN 1071–9989 ; v. 59)
    Includes bibliographical references and index.
    ISBN-13: 978–1–58046–288–4 (hardcover : alk. paper)
    ISBN-10: 1–58046–288–X (hardcover : alk. paper)
    1.   Wagner, Richard, 1813—1883–Travel—Italy—Venice. 2.   Wagner,
Richard, 1813–1883—Death and burial. 3.   Opera—Italy—Venice—19th
century.   I. Title.

    ML410.W12I8135 2008
    780.92—dc22
    [B]
                                                        2008037840

A catalogue record for this title is available from the British Library.

This publication is printed on acid-free paper.
Printed in the United States of America.

To MARGARET,

Who Is Hard Put to Decide

Which She Loves More:

the Music of Wagner

or the City of Venice

Richard Wagner, 1871 (Photo, Franz Hanfstaengl, Munich)

Contents

Part 4: Wagner and Venice Amalgamate

Part 5: Addenda

Illustrations

Preface

On the life and work of Richard Wagner, the literature is enormous—exceeded, it is said, only by that on Jesus Christ, William Shakespeare, Napoleon Bonaparte, and Abraham Lincoln. By now it may well be beyond one person's absorption within a single lifetime. By contrast, on the history and the cultural—especially musical—life of Venice in the latter half of the nineteenth century, there is pathetically little. There are scattered surveys and tidbits in Italian, but hardly much substantial in English-language treatments of Venice. In its post-1797 history few writers have shown much interest, save perhaps as a vague setting for the study of non-Italian artists, writers, and travelers who passed through the city.

As a specialist neither in Wagneriana nor in late Veneziana, I have come to the subject of this book simply as a result of the confluence of my love of music (Wagner's included) and my fascination with the history and culture of Venice. It was as an informally credentialed Venetianist, not as a music historian, that I was first drawn to the subject. Specialists in either realm might have done better with each aspect of what follows, and will surely find gaps and errors in what I have attempted. But neither camp has actually made any substantial effort at bringing the themes of Wagner and Venice together with the depth and fullness they deserve. My venture is offered, then, *faute de mieux*.

There has been, to be sure, some writing on Wagner's connections with Venice, as viewed entirely from the point of view of his life and mentality. Written within months of Wagner's death were two books directed respectively to German and to Italian readers, by "Henry" Perl, and Giuseppe Norlenghi, which will be given particular scrutiny below. Following also in Italian was Mario Panizzardi's two-volume study, *Wagner in Italia* (1914–23), excursive and episodic in character. There have also appeared numerous Italian vignettes of the composer's Venetian involvements, usually as sections of larger works or articles in diverse publications. Naturally, full-scale biographies of Wagner have alluded to his stays in Venice as a matter of course. The teasing title of a 1983 volume in German by Friedrich Dieckmann, *Richard Wagner in Venedig: Eine Collage*, only prepares us for disappointment, however. It is a short book that actually surveys Wagner's life broadly, through passages collected from writings by or about the composer, strung together by a shallow connecting text, with little time spent after all on the Venetian episodes.

Moreover, none of these publications deals with the Venetian aftermath of Wagner's death. To be sure, Angelo Neumann's breezy memoirs, culminating in his travels with his itinerant Wagner opera company, do report on the presentation of the *Ring* cycle in Venice two months after the composer's death there. But there has been no serious discussion of the ensuing Wagner commemorations and memorials in Venice. Despite some exploration of the role of Italian Wagnerites in the important cultural wars of postunification Italy, little has been done, even by Italians, about the place of Venice in that process. Above all, there has been no attempt to assemble all of these topics into the larger, overarching story of how the identity of a great cultural figure came to fuse with the identity of a remarkable city, and in very special ways. That multifaceted story is what I have endeavored to set forth. This book may offer no dramatic revelations, but it may add some interesting details for Wagnerian biography, while illuminating neglected areas of Venice's modern cultural history.

This is, then, not just another venture in Wagner biography, or some segment thereof. Nor is it just one simple story. Wagner's own involvements with Italy in general and Venice in particular are obviously a prime focus of attention. Not simply through one synthetic narrative, however, but through an intense exploration of sources, both known and neglected, and emphasizing use of the actual words of Wagner himself and of his contemporaries, as far as possible. The first two parts of the book offer parallel treatments of the same events, daring to risk repetition for purposes of viewing those events in turn through different eyes. We see how Wagner saw Venice, and we see how Venice saw Wagner. We assess the record of Wagner's visits to Venice and his death there, not only through a "standard" account, based primarily upon Cosima Wagner's diaries, but also in the differing pictures given us by Perl and Norlenghi, as well as by the local newspapers. Further, we are able to view afresh Wagner's *Der Ring des Nibelungen*: within the context of Italian efforts to come to terms with the composer's challenging work. We trace the landmark debut of the great tetralogy in Venice, only two months after the composer's death there, through the reports both of the production's impresario and of its Venetian critics. We trace this in the context of the contemporaneous "culture wars" Italy was undergoing, in which "Wagnerism" was a major factor. Finally, we see ways in which Wagner's posthumous mystique was incorporated into Venice's own mystique, in various media.

Neither a conventional narrative nor a simplistic sourcebook, this book is designed as something in between—an assimilative source study. As such, it aims to contribute to the literature on *both* Wagner and Venice.

I have pursued this project sporadically over a quarter-century. It originated in a paper, "Wagner and Venice" that I contributed to an elaborate colloquium in Chicago in 1983, which commemorated the hundredth anniversary of Wagner's death. Titled *Wagner in Retrospect: A Centennial Reappraisal*, its contents were published four years later. Part 1 of the present book is, in effect, a greatly extended expansion of that paper. Meanwhile, recognizing that there was much more to the subject, I explored it further during a series of visits to Venice, often as a sideline to other work. Two such visits involved the generous support of the Istituto Ellenico de Studi Bizantini e Neoellenici, to which I am greatly indebted, on many counts as well as this. As so often happens with research projects, what began as a passing sideline has swollen into an extensive and diversified project. Wagner has a way of taking over one's life, after all!

One of the most important categories of material I have utilized involves Venetian newspapers of the time. Newspapers can be problematical sources, of course, in terms of both accuracy in what they treat and omissions of what they do not treat. But their coverage is in itself an index to local attitudes. Above all, these journals provide rich troves of information and reactions entirely from Venetian perspectives, thus allowing us to view the interaction of Wagner and Venice clearly from the city's vantage point. That in itself, I believe, allows a totally new and more fully comprehensive view of our subject, and one only very rarely and sporadically drawn upon so far.

Specifically used were three newspapers whose various spans of publication covered our time period: *La Gazzetta di Venezia* (1812–1959), *La Venezia* (1876/77–94), and *Il Gazzettino* (1903–present). Unfortunately, individual issues of these journals have not always been available, resulting in some frustrating gaps in reporting.

Of the many text passages that are quoted in this book, all those taken from Italian or German (or even French) sources, are given in my own translations, unless otherwise identified. With no pretensions as a linguist, I have tried only to make these materials accessible to English-language readers in a way that preserves the style and flavor of the originals while presenting them in coherent English. The quirks of style, sentence structure, and punctuation fashionable in Italian and German journalism or literary writing can seem rather quaint and even perverse after a century and more. Writers in both languages often used ellipses in their style. I have tried to preserve these as unspaced periods (...), while marking my own excisions in quoted texts with spaced periods (. . .). Writers also were inconsistent and careless in spelling many names. Such inconsistency is part of the flavor, even the charm, of their writing, coming from a time when many foreign names were still strange and unfamiliar to Italians. By preserving many of their misspellings I do not wish to mock our writers but to respect their phases of assimilation. Thus, retaining the Italians' use of "Riccardo Wagner" reflects their comfort with the adaptation of "Richard" familiar to them, while, conversely, it suggests the degree to which Venetians were making him their own.

For access to the Venetian journals, and to so much other local material, I am greatly indebted to the staffs of the Biblioteca Nazionale Marciana and the Biblioteca del Museo Correr, who were generously patient in assisting a fumbling foreigner. I have also received invaluable help from the interlibrary loan department of the Memorial Library of the University of Wisconsin–Madison. I must also express great appreciation to Rich Worthington of the UW–Madison Cartography Lab for providing the map of Venice. For some special help in seeking photographic illustrations, I thank my colleague Cheryl Bensman Rowe, Simonpietro Cussino of Venice, and Chiara Pancino of the Venice Music Conservatory. Dr. Alan Walker has been exceedingly gracious in his advice and assistance with the Joukowsky portrait of Liszt. To George Tzougros of Madison I am indebted for setting the musical illustration used.

Several other individuals deserve particular thanks. I have benefited over the years from the recurrent advice and encouragement of Professor (now Emerita) Marion S. Miller, of the University of Illinois–Chicago Circle. I cannot imagine this book coming into being without her. I also must thank Suzanne Guiod and Katie Hurley at the University of Rochester Press, Ralph P. Locke, senior editor of the Eastman Studies in Music series, and copyeditor Therese Malhame, for their patience, supportiveness, and guidance, through the shoals of publication. Last but hardly least, I acknowledge both the encouragement and the direct assistance given me by my wife, Margaret, to whom it is utterly appropriate that I dedicate this book. Our mutual love of Wagner's music and our mutual delight in the city of Venice were among the factors that brought us together in the first place.

Madison, Wisconsin, July 31, 2008

Copyright Acknowledgments

I wish to thank the following for their kind permission to quote from their publications:

Harcourt, Inc. (Philadelphia/Orlando FL), for *Cosima Wagner's Diaries*, Vol. 2: *1878–1883*, translated by Geoffrey Skelton (1977); and for Martin Gregor-Dellin, *Richard Wagner: His Life, His Work, His Century*, translated by J. Maxwell Brownjohn (1983).

W. W. Norton and Company (New York), for *The Selected Letters of Richard Wagner*, translated by Stewart Spencer and Barry Millington (1987).

Carton Books/André Deutsch (London), for Rudolph Sabor, *The Real Wagner* (1987).

Faber and Faber (London), for Stewart Spencer, *Wagner Remembered* (2000).

Yale University Press (New Haven CT), for Joachim Köhler, *Wagner: The Last of the Titans*, translated by Stewart Spencer (2004).

I wish to thank the following for graciously making available to me photographic materials, with rights of reproduction:

Nationalarchiv der Richard-Wagner-Stiftung, Bayreuth, for the *frontispiece, figs. 2–5, 7–10, 13, 16, 21–24, 27, 29–34, 36–37, 40.*

Biblioteca del Conservatorio di Musica "Benedetto Marcello" di Venezia (Venice), photos by Mattia Mian, for *figs. 18, 19, 25, 26, 28.*

Münchner Stadtmuseum (Munich), for *fig. 46.*

Wittelsbacher Ausgleichsfonds, München (Schloss Nymphenburg), for *fig. 6.*

Art Resource (New York), for *figs. 11* (Réunion des Musées Nationaux), *35* (Scala).

Private Collection (Paris), for *fig. 12.*

New York Philharmonic Archives (New York), for *fig. 38.*

Alan Walker (Ancaster, ON.), for *fig. 20.*

Christopher N. Barker (Madison, WI), for *fig. 42.*

(Note: *figs. 1, 14, 15, 17, 41, 43, 44, 45* are by the author.)

Map by Rich Worthington, University of Wisconsin Cartographic Lab.

Prologue

A Letter to Ludwig

To His Majesty King Ludwig II of Bavaria—20 February 1883
On Saturday morning around 10 o'clock the [train from Venice] came from Kufstein and the most reverent undersigned could discharge your gracious instructions.

The Master's widow, scarcely still alive, who was reduced almost to a skeleton, completely oblivious to the outside world, was accommodated in a closed carriage. For the first time in five days she opened her eyes again upon the report of your most lofty good will and she awoke at that moment, called forth by the beam of the sunshine of royal grace, back to a new life.

The prior events at and following the Master's decease may most humbly be described in the following way:

On Tuesday afternoon February 13 about 1:23 o'clock the family was gathered in order to go to the table, when the Master gave word that he felt unwell and the family should eat without him. The Master had often before had presentiment of his heart-spasm attacks and he wished to be entirely alone until this had passed. However, since this time the heart spasm came on with quite special violence, he rang for the chambermaid, who therefore went into the family room and addressed to Frau Wagner the words "Come *immediately* to the gracious master." The stress on the word "immediately" struck everyone with the deepest terror.

Frau Cosima rushed into the Master's room and saw that he was struggling for breath amid a violent convulsion. She attempted to aid him in every way and sent for the physician. When the convulsion had subsided, the Master appeared to slip into a gentle sleep: he sat in an easy chair, his wife on a bench next to it. Suddenly there an artery in his heart must have burst, then he slumped over on his spouse as she was supporting him—she of whom he drew in his last glance and his last gasp—and he breathed out his life.

Upon arriving, the physician could only confirm the death.

Frau Cosima had sunk down at the feet of the departed Master and held his feet in an hours-long embrace.

Around evening the Master was laid on a bed and the poor wife insisted that she be left alone with him. She threw herself on the beloved corpse and passed twenty-five hours in convulsive embracing, without moving away, without a sound or a tear.

When at last on the night of the next day she was near to fainting, she had to be firmly pulled away from the corpse, so that the embalming could be done.

For this procedure the body would be treated with arsenic and any lingering in the vicinity itself is fatal. Therefore the wife was only allowed, on her urgent entreaties, to remain with him a minute. When that time was expired, Herr Gross and Dr. Keppler escorted the utterly shattered wife out of the room and led, or carried, her to a divan in a more distant room.

After that she went through a passage leading around outside and closed the door.

When after three to four hours Dr. Keppler wanted to look back in on Frau Cosima, he found the divan empty and, struck by a presentiment, he rushed into the death chamber, where he found, close beside the corpse, the unconscious wife, who, taking advantage of the brief moment of his absence, had returned to the death chamber and was then personally excluded by him.

On the next morning the coffin was sealed in the presence of the wife, who did not withdraw from its side during this task that lasted five hours; and, just before this, as a memorial to her husband, she had her long, full hair cut off and laid within the coffin.

The court physician of the city of Venice, who had to seal the coffin and complete the official death certificate, upon his departure from the house, said to banker Gross, "I do not know these people, but this I know, that no man was ever loved by a wife so much." When the coffin was closed, Frau Cosima, who wore on her head her husband's cap, threw herself onto the coffin and wanted to undertake the journey on it. She had determined that her life was finished. She deplored that her nature should be so terribly weak-willed: Isolde wanted to follow her Tristan. She reproached herself that her pain did not kill her, inasmuch as she knew that the Master would not have survived her death so long.

In this mood and these thoughts she confronted the royal message of the most gracious condolence. The most gracious letter was read to her by her daughter and, pleased with these most gracious gestures, she revived the will to live again.

She expressed to her daughter the overflowing sentiments of gratitude for Your Majesty's graciousness, and she begged, in the most earnest terms, to lay at your feet the feelings of her heart, spilling over with the most profound respect for Your Majesty.

Then success even attended the united appeals of the family and of its friends, to persuade her to accept a saucer of milk, after having taken no other nourishment for 4 days.

Ludwig von Bürkel, Hofsekretär

Part 1

Richard Wagner Absorbs Venice

Chapter One

The First Encounter

On the afternoon of February 13, 1883, some three months short of his seventieth birthday, Richard Wagner died in the Palazzo Vendramin-Calergi in Venice.

Why in Venice? Why should this paragon of German pride, this living legend of German cultural aspiration and achievement, have died in a city so removed from his Teutonic world? What did that city actually mean to him that he should have been resident in it when his fatal heart attack came? Two questions, the first fairly easy to answer, the second more difficult but also more stimulating to confront.

In the first place, Wagner was in Venice partly because of geography—because of the city's milder winter climate, as compared with that of Germany. As his years advanced, Wagner's temperament and health increasingly came to require escape from the cold and rain of northern winters. For all his involvement in the theatrical Valhalla he was creating for himself in Bayreuth, he had come to loathe the Franconian climate, considering its winters too clammy to endure.[1]

The perpetual lure of sunny Italy for Europe's northerners, and the longing for comfortable winter weather are, however, only part of the story. Italy itself represented still more than simple escapism in Wagner's life and outlook, while, within that context, Venice was something yet more special.

Part of Italy's meaning for Wagner was travel. He certainly came to think of himself as a cosmopolitan intellectual, a man of the world, and, among the expensive tastes he cultivated, travel became one of them. We who are accustomed to easy and frequent globe-trotting in present-day life must remember that, a century and a half ago, accessible touristic travel on a broad scale was only beginning to develop, and still for comparatively limited levels of society. Nevertheless, though extensive, Wagner's record of travel was not exceptional for musicians of his time. He was both a professional orchestra conductor and an ambitious composer of operas. Musicians of either category were normally obliged to travel widely and frequently to fulfill obligations and seek opportunities. In both these capacities Wagner moved about Europe actively in his middle years. He established a reputation as one of the pioneers of orchestral conducting for his time, while doggedly (if not always successfully) promoting his operas. Of course, for Wagner another important motivation for his travels, at least earlier on, was flight from creditors or from the police.

For these reasons, and not for pleasure, Wagner saw the various cities of the Germanies, along with such others as Vienna, Paris (which he hated), and London. Refuge or work—either or both—took him frequently to the cities of Switzerland, notably Zurich and Lucerne. Nevertheless, when it came to the pleasures of touring itself, and to the indulgence of agreeable settings for work, as well as a bit of refuge, it was to Italy, and only to Italy, that Wagner directed his steps, in no less than nine visits over thirty years.[2] Contemptuous of Italian musical life in general, Wagner was ambivalent about promoting his own music on the peninsula. Paramount for him were needs of work and health—plus, eventually, escape. Precisely as he became identified with Bayreuth, the more often did he seek refuge in the alternate clime and ambience of Italy, as if to give his life a needed balance.

Wagner's mature years also fell within a period of major social and economic change. They coincided further with the expanding availability of transportation, by means of rail or steamship. Those two factors gave tourism and travel for pleasure a new feasibility, on a scale far exceeding conditions of his earlier years. The old attraction to Italy of the Grand Tour, once restricted to the wealthy, could now appeal to a much wider clientele, Wagner among them. Gradually, he grew so addicted to pleasure-travel that he came to contemplate a wide range of it, though sometimes not without professional motivations. Nevertheless, from 1868 onward, the vacations and residences abroad that Wagner actually undertook involved no other country than Italy.

Wagner made his first brief venture into Italy in the summer of 1852. He was then thirty-nine years old, and behind him already were the operas of his emerging maturity: *Rienzi* (1842), *Der fliegende Holländer* (1843), *Tannhäuser* (1845), and *Lohengrin* (1850). Composition of his most majestic and defining operatic works still lay ahead of him. Since his involvement with the abortive revolutionary rising in Dresden in June of 1848, he was unemployed and subject to arrest in Germany. After some roving, he had been living as a political exile in Zurich, Switzerland.

The 1852 episode reflected his recurrent love for hiking. It might be called his first vacation: "the only [journey] I had ever undertaken solely for my recreation," as he put it. After a walking tour alone through the Swiss Alps, he visited the Borromean Islands of Lago Maggiore. Then, at Lugano, joined by his wife Minna Wagner, he completed what had been a brief but altogether enjoyable first encounter with Italy.[3] A second visit followed over a year later. It lasted a little longer, and it allegedly had more striking results. In December of 1852 he had completed the poetic text for his massive tetralogy, *Der Ring des Nibelungen*, but he supposedly suffered a mental block to beginning the musical composition of the work. In elusive pursuit of better health, as well as of renewed creativity, Wagner journeyed alone in late August of 1853, via Turin to Genoa. His first "genuine Italian city,"[4] Genoa quite delighted him, at least until illness and discomfort drove him to nearby La Spezia. There, according to his later account, he felt relieved of further torments, and in a dream he found his inspiration for the opening pages of *Das Rheingold*—the chord of E-flat major, associated with watery depths. With creative floodgates at last opened, Wagner could tear himself away from the loveliness he had come to perceive.[5]

More substantially momentous for Wagner's career and creativity was his next visit to Italy, the third, which not only brought him to Venice for the first time, but was almost exclusively focused on that city. It also provoked him into an avalanche of reactions to Venice, far beyond his response to any other city. His direct motive, in this instance, was to escape the impossible tangle of his personal life. For, his deteriorating marriage to Minna was explosively complicated by his awkward love affair with Mathilde Wesendonck, wife of his long-suffering Zurich benefactor, Otto Wesendonck.

The year was 1858. Having broken off work on the *Ring* for the time being, Wagner had plunged into the epochal creation of his *Tristan und Isolde*. He had completed composition of the music for Act I in Zurich. Life there having become unbearable, however, he had decided to separate from Minna and go somewhere in Italy to continue *Tristan*. In August 1858, Wagner had decided on Venice, and was in contact with his friend and benefactor, Franz Liszt, among others, to assure himself that, as a German in an Austrian-controlled city, he would be secure. On August 24, he clarified his choice in a letter to Liszt:

> . . . I feel the necessity of living in strict seclusion for some considerable period, in order to devote myself entirely to my work. The country will not, in the long run, do for this, and in an indifferent town I might, at last, be reduced to making acquaintance with commonplace people—the worst of all evils. One of the interesting, large cities of Italy is exactly what I want. In such surroundings one can most easily keep to oneself, for every walk presents objects of an important kind, and satisfies the want of men and things. But in large towns the noise of carriages is absolutely unbearable to me; it drives me wild. Venice is notoriously the quietest, *i.e.*, most noiseless city in the world, which has decided me in its favour. . . . Finally, Venice is more convenient for my frequent communications with Germany than any other Italian town would be; by way of Vienna my letters, etc., will reach the centre of Germany in no time. In short, I am obstinately fixed on Venice, and do not want to think of any other choice, because it is not travelling about, but settling down as soon as possible that I care for.[6]

Venice had been chosen also on the advice of his young friend and protégé Karl Ritter, the son of one of Wagner's benefactors, Frau Julie Ritter. This youth, with talents as writer and musician that were to lead him only to dead ends and a futile career, dearly loved the city and agreed to join Wagner for the journey. Caught up in the collapse of his own stormy marriage, Ritter's emotional state paralleled that of the likewise matrimonially challenged composer—though, in fact, Wagner says that they did not discuss such matters between them, but surrendered to the journey.

Thus did Wagner undertake his first encounter with Venice. On that he has left us an abundance of his impressions in his own words.

Departing Geneva, Wagner and Ritter set forth for Italy by train.[7] They stopped first at Lago Maggiore where Wagner was able again to relish the beauties and peace of the Isola Bella in the Borromean Islands. At a transfer stop in Milan, Ritter was so eager to proceed to Venice that Wagner had little time to see any sights. On August 29, 1858, they arrived in the Lagoon City: leaning out the train window on the rail causeway into it, Ritter lost his hat to the wind, and so Wagner impulsively threw his own away as a comradely gesture, and as a prelude to his first—not entirely happy—impressions of the city:

> . . . thus we both arrived bare-headed in Venice and immediately got into a gondola, to proceed along the entire Canale Grande to the Piazzetta beside San Marco. The weather had suddenly turned somewhat unpleasant, and the sight of the gondola itself had shocked me a bit; for despite all I had heard of these conveyances, painted black on black, the actual sight of one was still a rude surprise: when I had to go under the black awning, my first thought was a revival of a fear of cholera that I had previously mastered; it decidedly seemed to me as if I were taking part in a funeral procession during an epidemic. Karl assured me that this was how most people felt, but that one got used to it very quickly.[8]
>
> Now came an extremely long trip round the many bends of the Canale Grande: the impressions made by all this were not sufficient to dispel my anxious mood. Whereas Karl had eyes only for a Ca d'oro . . . or some other famous palace between the deteriorating walls, my melancholy glance fell solely on the crumbling ruins between these interesting buildings. At length I fell silent and offered no objection to getting out at the world-famous Piazzetta to be shown the Palace of the Doges, though I reserved the right to admire it until such time as I had freed myself of the melancholy mood which my arrival in Venice had produced.[9]

The two men found a room for the night at the Hotel Danieli—on the Riva degli Schiavoni overlooking the Bacino, just east of the Piazzetta—a popular stop for foreign visitors. Their rooms were dark, with only views of small canals in the rear, hardly anything acceptable beyond the moment:

> . . . I first hunted for a suitable place to live for my longer stay. I heard that one of the three Giustiniani palaces, not far from the Palazzo Foscari, was at present almost free of lodgers as a result of a location deemed not very suitable for the winter season: I found some exceptionally big and imposing rooms there, being told that they would all remain unoccupied; thus I rented a large and stately room, with a spacious adjoining bedroom, had my bags brought there quickly, and could tell myself by that evening of August 30th that I was now residing in Venice.

Wagner found the palace "utterly dilapidated," noting the "unworthy doors" with which the landlord, an Austro-Hungarian, had replaced "the valuable originals, which had probably been stolen." The composer quickly set about making his lodgings suitable on his own terms:

. . . I soon found the grayish walls of my main room distasteful, as they were ill-suited to the ceiling, which was painted with what I considered a rather tasteful fresco. I decided to have the large room completely hung with an admittedly very cheap dark red wallpaper: this caused a lot of commotion at first; yet it seemed worth the effort to go through with it, as I could gaze down from my balcony at the wonderful canal with a gradually increasing sense of well-being and tell myself that here was the place I would complete my *Tristan.*[10]

Red calico curtains and showy furniture were soon added. Wagner also felt the need for two familiar items, and ordered them sent from Zurich. One was his bed, since "I had a feeling I would learn in Venice what it is to freeze." The other was his Érard piano, which was delayed because it had been seized by his creditors. Eventually it arrived at the beginning of October.

Long before, Wagner had taken stock of his initial situation in a letter of September 1 to his wife:

. . . Do not ask me to tell you much about Venice today. I am dreadfully overwrought as a result of the journey and, especially, of looking for an apartment. I shall not recover my senses until I have established myself here as well and as comfortably as is necessary if I am to hold out; you know that where I live counts for a good deal with me; and I *must* now set my sights on settling down in one place in order to be able to continue my work. I am of course living in furnished accommodation: there is no other kind. My landlord, who is Austrian, was delighted to house such a famous name. All such apartments here are in large palaces that have been abandoned by their former aristocratic owners; speculators have now turned them into apartments for foreigners. But I shall tell you all about this next time. For today let me say only that I hope to be able to hold out in Venice; this town is exceedingly interesting, and the actual stillness—one never hears a carriage—is indispensable for me. I receive no visitors, and hope to live here totally withdrawn into myself. For the moment I am seeing Karl every day for [dinner], for which we always arrange to meet at a restaurant in St. Mark's Square. If ever this arrangement should no longer suit me, I can have the meal brought to my apartment. It really does not seem at all expensive; only the apartment is relatively not cheap.[11]

Two days later, on September 3, Wagner made the first entry written in Venice in an intermittent diary he had begun to keep of this journey, meant for and addressed to Mathilde Wesendonck. To some extent the entry anticipates the report he would later give in *Mein Leben,* but with nuances. After mentioning his "uplifting" reaction to the garden at Isola Bella, he notes his arrival in Venice:

. . . On the way down the Grand Canal to the Piazzetta, melancholy impressions and graveness of mood; grandeur, beauty and decay, in close array; yet comfort in the reflection that here no modernity flourished, and in consequence no bustling triviality. S. Mark's Square of magical effect. A wholly distant, outlived world, it admirably fits the wish for solitude: nothing to strike one as directly real life; everything objective, like a work of art. I *will* remain here,—and accordingly I shall.—

Next day, after long debate, apartments taken on the Grand Canal in a mighty palace where I am quite alone for the present; wide, lofty spaces, wherein I can wander at will. Since the question of Abode is so important to me, as the housing for my labour-mechanism, I'm devoting all possible care to arranging it after my wish. I wrote for the Érard at once; it ought to sound wonderful in my vast, high palace-salon. The peculiarly intense stillness of the Canal suits me splendidly. Not till 5 in the afternoon do I leave my abode, to dine; then promenade towards the public garden; brief halt in the square of S. Mark, which gives a thoroughly theatrical suggestion through its absolute uniqueness and its sea of utter strangers void of all concern to me, merely distracting one's fancy. Toward 9 return home in a gondola; find the lamp lit, and read a little till bedtime.

    Thus will my life flow outwardly on, and thus would I have it. Unfortunately, my stay here is already known; but I have given orders, once for all, to admit nobody. This solitude, possible wellnigh here alone to me—and so agreeably possible— caresses myself and my hopes. . . .[12]

Two days later, Wagner reported more impressions in the diary:

. . . Marvelously beautiful, the Canal by night; bright stars, last quarter of the moon. A gondola glides by; from the distance the chant of gondoliers calling to each other. This last is extraordinarily beautiful, sublime: Tasso's stanzas are recited to it no more, they say, but the melodies are in any case of hoary eld, as old as Venice; certainly older than Tasso's stanzas, which must simply have been fitted to them after. . . . These profoundly melancholy ditties, sung with full ringing voice, borne across the water from afar, and dying into still remoter distance, have sublimely moved me. Glorious![13]

And the following week, in an entry for September 16, Wagner was still addressing highly charged impressions to Mathilde:

. . . Meanwhile I have all manner of dreadful and tedious correspondence, that takes away my time; yet ever thou quicken'st me in midst thereof, and Venice gloriously assists thee to cheer me up. For the first time I breathe this pure, delicious, ever even air; the magic of the place enfolds me in a tender melancholy charm, which never ceases to exert its beneficial power. Of an evening, when I take a gondola trip to the Lido, it vibrates round me like one of those mellow long-drawn fiddle-notes I love so, and to which I once compared thee. Judge thence how I feel, in the moonbeams there on the sea![14]

Two days before that, on September 14, Wagner had written a long letter to his wife Minna, devoted largely to personal matters and to projecting his future plans. He promised to write in detail later about his situation in Venice, but for the moment he observed:

. . . I made a very lucky choice with Venice: . . . the singular melancholy-cheerful repose of this place, with the absolute retirement in which I'm able and intend to live here, already begins to strengthen and smooth me out, and in any case I hope to pass the winter here. By the winter's end I definitely hope to finish *Tristan* quite; till then I shall not stir. . . .[15]

Only at the end of the month did Wagner finally bring Minna up to date on his lodgings, in a letter to her of September 28:

. . . A small unfurnished lodging was out of the question; they are only to be found in the business quarter of the inner city, from which God preserve me! Apart from those, there are none but the furnished apartments in palaces bought from the impoverished old nobili and fitted up by speculators for foreigners who visit Venice for a shorter or longer time. After long search I had to think myself lucky to find something of the kind to suit me at last, and to submit to paying more than I had anticipated.

Like all such apartments, it is in a big ancient palace, with wide halls and spaces. For my living room I have an enormous saloon looking on to the Grand Canal; then a very roomy bedchamber, with a little cabinet beside it for a wardrobe. Fine old ceiling-paintings, splendid floors inlaid with magnificent mosaic; badly distempered walls (once richly tapestried, no doubt), antique furniture, very elegant in appearance, covered with red cotton-velvet, but very rickety and miserably stuffed; nothing quite in working order, doors not shutting properly, all somewhat the worse for wear. I had a big state-bed removed at once, and replaced by a smaller iron bedstead with spring mattress. Linen so-so; pillows stuffed with wool; for the colder season a foot-quilt weighing 3 hundredweight. The landlord, an Austrian [Austro-Hungarian], is delighted to have me in his house, and does all he can to satisfy me; I have contrived a few conveniences myself, arranged a passable divan, fanteuil, etc. Things now will do quite well, and the piano is sure to sound glorious in my big saloon. The want of air-tightness in windows and doors is said to be no serious drawback even in winter here. The climate and the air are really heavenly; a regard in which Venice is said to be one of the most favoured of places, far more so than Florence, Rome, or even Naples. An agreeably refreshing East wind constantly blows from the sea, moderating any excessive heat, keeping the sky always clear, and furnishing beautiful air. For a whole month we've only had two rainy days, and only one at a time. Of course, one never sees a trace of drought, as the sea keeps the air always moist. I still go about in full summer clothing, and that of an evening; not until then do I make my promenade.

My manner of life is as follows: The whole day till 4 I work—at whatever there has been to do yet—then I get ferried across the Canal, walk up S. Mark's piazza, meet Karl there at 5 in the restaurant, where I dine *à la carte*, well, but dear (I can never get off under 4 to 5 francs!—without wine, too); after dinner, so long as the fine season permits, out in a gondola to the Public Garden, promenade there, and return either afloat or on foot through the town; then another promenade on shore for the length of the Molo, a glass of ice at the pavilion there, and then home, where the lamp stands lit for me at 8; a book picked up, and finally to bed. So I have been living for 4 weeks now, and am not tired of it yet, even without real absorbing work. What affords the never-flagging charm, is the strange contrast of my dwelling with the part that serves me for a promenade: here all still, supremely tranquil, a broad track of lapping water from the sea, with ebb and flow; instead of carts and horses, gondolas moored to the houses' very doors; wonderful palaces in front and everywhere, all lofty, silent, melancholy. Then of a sudden, on one's stepping forth, mean alleys of the strangest twists and crossings, often scarcely wide enough for two to pass, all flanked with open shops and stalls in which one feels as if upon the pavement; continually flooded with a stream of people one only needs to join, when without the smallest notion of topography one either arrives at the Rialto—the business quarter—or the Square of St. Mark, where nobody does anything but promenade.

The amazing, unique, and quite unparalleled splendour of this Square, and every-thing connected with it down to the water's brink, is not to be described; each time I reach it from my house, the whole thing staggers me afresh. By all means I must send you some good pictures of it soon. One would never believe one was in the street, if only since it all—there being no horse traffic—is paved with slabs of mar-ble just like some great prince's court. (I've a bad foot, and for many days have been going out in my slippers.) Everything strikes me as a marvelous piece of stage-scenery. Here it is one continual surging up and down, everyone doing nothing but stroll and amuse himself. This peculiar gaiety never fails of its effect on the new-comer; one feels at ease, and the eye is perpetually entertained. For myself the chief charm consists in its all remaining as detached from me as if I were in an actual the-atre; I avoid making any acquaintances, and therefore still retain the feeling. The gondola trip out to sea always has an extremely soothing and beneficial effect: the battle in the sky twixt day and night is glorious; ever new isles in the distance to keep the fancy alert with their gardens, churches, palaces.

In brief, I believe the choice of Venice was the happiest I could have made; for there was everything to fear for me if I had not lit on such an element, if I had felt uncomfortable, not come to rest, lost patience, roved about, and never got to work—which in fine is the one and only thing to enthrall me sustainedly. . . .

At the outset my landlord spread the news of my arrival, and it got into the papers once; but I won't let him admit anyone, and am enjoying the most com-plete retirement. . . . I am only too glad to be left in peace here. True, they demanded my pass a second time, and I began to fear lest demurs would be raised to my remaining longer; but the police returned it to me—very flatteringly addressed, in fact, "to the renowned Herr R. W."—with the assurance that no objection had been discovered to my unmolested residence in Venice. Consequently I am now enjoying full asylum.[16]

On the following day, Wagner was drawing more mood pictures for Mathilde. In his diary entry for September 29, he reports how the moonlight at the Lido plunged him into a fit of self-pity, only somewhat relieved in the aftermath:

The waning moon now rises late: at its full it furnished me fine comfort through agree-able sensations which I needed. After sunset I regularly took a gondola to meet it, toward the Lido, for the battle twixt day and night was always an entrancing vision in this limpid sky: to the right, amid the dusk-rose aether, gleamed kindly bright the evening star; the moon in full splendour cast its flashing net towards me in the sea.

[. . .] Silent and at peace I reached the gaily-lighted, ever-lively Piazzetta. Then down we go the melancholy grave Canal: to left and right stand lordly palaces: without a sound: only the gentle gliding of the gondola, the plashing of the oar, broad shadows from the moon. At my dumb palace steps I disembark: wide halls and spaces, now inhabited by me alone. The lamp is burning; I pick up a book, read little, ponder much. All's still.—Music there, on the canal! An illuminated gondola with singers and musicians: more and still more boats with listeners follow in its wake: the flotilla spans the breadth of the canal, gliding all but moveless past. Fine voices, passable instruments, render songs. All is ear.—Then, scarcely perceptibly it curves round the bend, and vanishes still more imperceptibly. For long I still can hear the tones, ennobled and transfigured by the midnight stillness, tones that as art could hardly captivate me, but had here become part of nature. At last all ceases: the last one as if dissolves into the moonlight, which softly goes on shining as a visual remainder of the sound-world. . . .[17]

Paralleling what he had written to Minna two days before, Wagner drew a variant picture of his situation, with some further details, in part of a long letter that he wrote on September 30 to one Frau Eliza Wille, a neighbor of the Wesendoncks in Lucerne:

I am not leading an actual life as yet here; there can be no question of that till I'm at work once more: and I still am waiting for the piano! So rest content with a description of the terrain on which I have had to fix to live. . . . My palace lies about midway between the Piazzetta and the Rialto, close to the knee the Canal here makes, which is formed the sharpest by the Foscari palace (barracks now) at my side; right opposite is the Palazzo Grassi. . . . My landlord is an Austrian who received me enthusiastically for my famous name and shews himself extraordinarily obliging to me in every way. (He is also the cause of my arrival's getting into the newspapers at once.) . . .

I am still the solitary guest (lodger) in my palace, and occupy spaces that scared me at first. However, I could find little cheaper, absolutely nothing more convenient; so I moved into my big drawing-room . . . with a passable ceiling-picture, splendid mosaic floor, and what is bound to be glorious resonance for the Érard. I took some pains forthwith to overcome the stiff unhomeliness of the upholstery; the folding-doors between a huge bedroom and a little adjoining cabinet had to be removed at once, and portières took their place. . . . The colour had to be red this time, as the rest of the furniture was that already; only the bedroom is green. An immense hall gives space for my morning promenade; on one side it has a balcony over the canal, on the other it looks into the courtyard with a little well-paved garden. So here I pass my day till about 5 in the afternoon. Of a morning I make my own tea: I have two cups, one of which I bought here and Ritter gets to drink from, if I bring him back in the evening; out of the other I drink myself. . . .

About 5 the gondolier is called, for I'm so situated that whoever wants to get at me must cross the water (which also affords me a pleasant shrug-offness). Through the narrow alleys right and left, yet "sempre dritto" (as you know!) to the restaurant in S. Mark's square, where I find Ritter as a rule. Thence "sempre dritto" in the gondola to the Lido or the Giardino Pubblico, where I usually take my little promenade; then back by gondola to the Piazzetta for another saunter,

my glass of ice in the Café de la Rotunde, then to the traghetto, which returns me
through the sombre night of the Canal to my palace, where a lighted lamp awaits
me about 8!

The singular contrast of the still and melancholy grandeur of my abode and its
site with the constant mirth and glitter of the Square and its belongings, the pleasing sense of personal indifference towards this throng, the perpetual din of wran-
gling gondoliers, and finally the quiet transit in the twilight or as night
falls—hardly ever fails to make a grateful and at last an agreeably calming impression upon me. And at this I have stopped, for the present; as yet I have felt no crav-
ing for inspection of the art-treasures; I reserve that for the winter: I'm glad
enough, for now, to be able to taste this placid rise and setting of my day with
equable content.— My mouth I open to no one but Ritter, who is so taciturn as
never to disturb me; he likewise is alone, his wife having stayed behind. We part
on the traghetto every evening, and very seldom does he set his foot in my abode.

It would have been impossible for me to choose a spot better suited to my present needs. Utterly alone in an insignificant, uninteresting little place, a gregarious
hankering after company would have been bound in the end to make me seize
some opportunity of social intercourse; and an acquaintanceship sprung from
that sort of need, and finally consolidated, is just the thing to torture one at last.
On the contrary, I could nowhere lead a more retired life than here; for the interesting, theatrically absorbing spectacle that here renews for me its vivid contrast
day by day prevents the faintest wish arising to play a definite individual role
therein, since I feel I should then lose all the charm which the spectacle offer me
as a purely objective beholder. Thus my life in Venice until now is a perfectly faithful image of my whole bearings toward the world at large; at least as, in accord with
my knowledge and resignative need, they must and shall be. How I have to regret
it, every time I step beyond them!

When they've played pieces from Tannhäuser and Lohengrin in S. Mark's
Square—where we have a military band on Sunday evenings—it really seemed to
me, for all my anger at the dragging tempo, as if I had nothing whatever to do with
it. For that matter, I'm already known everywhere; in particular, the Austrian officers often astonish me with signs thereof in delicate attentions. It has got about,
however, that I wish to remain in most thorough seclusion, and after a few callers
have been persistently refused admittance people are leaving me in peace. With
the police I'm on excellent terms: certainly my pass was demanded again, after a
while, so that I began to think of measures commencing; but it was soon sent me
back with due ceremony, and the assurance that there was absolutely no objection
to my continued stay in Venice. Thus Austria decidedly vouchsafes me refuge,
which really is something worth acknowledgement.

This letter draws to an end with another flourish of self-pity wrapped in Venetian
imagery:

What gives my life from inside-out so peculiar, almost dreamlike a character, is its utter
lack of future. . . . When I go on the water of an evening, survey the mirror-bright
expanse of sea, which, stretching motionless to the horizon, there joins the sky with

absolutely no distinction to be noted, the evening red of the heavens completely wed to its reflection in the water—I have before me a faithful likeness of my present: what is present, past, or future, is as little to be distinguished as there the sea and sky. . . .[18]

A few weeks later, writing to Liszt on October 19, Wagner reported resumption of his work, while complaining about interruptions from visitors. Nevertheless, he reaffirmed his satisfaction with his location:

. . . Venice continues to be most sympathetic to me; my choice was guided by instinct, and has turned out well. This kind of retirement is most pleasant to me. I see just enough to occupy my fancy agreeably; nothing disturbs me.[19]

Wagner's reports of insistence on isolation blurred the fact that he did develop some small social circle in Venice. There was, of course, his daily dinner companion, Karl Ritter—who made a trip back to Germany from mid-November until the beginning of January. Not long after arriving in Venice, the composer met a charming Russian aristocrat, one Peter Vladimirovich Dolgoruki (or Dolgorukov), who had reacted enthusiastically just that August to *Lohengrin* in Vienna, and also claimed to be a friend of Liszt. Since Dolgoruki was staying in the same hotel (the Albergo San Marco) where Wagner and Ritter met every evening for dinner, the Russian soon joined with them, and Wagner came to like him. Through the same restaurant contacts, a Viennese painter called Rahl was added to the group. A pianist named Alexander Winterberger (1834–1914), who was one of Liszt's many acolytes, took up rooms also in the Palazzo Giustiniani. Wagner found him very congenial, as he did also a Venetian piano teacher named Tessarin, unusual among Italians in having a strong passion for German music.[20] For this circle Wagner eventually organized at least one musical soirée.

Otherwise, Wagner did his best to avoid distractions and kept other people generally at bay. Another noble Russian arrival in Venice was the pretentious Princess Gallitzin. Wagner fended off invitations to call on her. Then, needing the vocal scores of his *Tannhäuser* and *Lohengrin*, he was chagrinned to be told that this princess was the only person in Venice who had copies. With characteristic cheek, he succeeded in requesting and obtaining these from her without the necessity of actually visiting her.

Wagner had further contacts and associations, however, as he revealed in a letter of October 28 to Minna. It was written to accompany pictures of the city he had promised to send her:

. . . I have sent the chief views coloured, although they're not exactly works of art; only, with Venice the vivid colouring has so much to do with the effect, that one can really form no notion of it from mere black outlines. The Doge's Palace and church of St. Mark look just as bright and dazzling in reality, as in the pictures. I have marked the photographs on their backs; a portion of my palace comes into one of them, though unfortunately not the part in which I dwell: still, it will give you some idea. On the big bird's-eye view of Venice I have made a red cross where my palace stands; going up the Grand Canal you must keep to the left, and at the first big bend you'll find it.

I also have enclosed a folk-group that pleased me most; these are the feminine water-carriers, who really have a very original look. . . . Among the men, the sailors are often very interesting; striking physiognomies, with red caps *à la* Stumme von Portici. But your subscriber chiefly mixes with the gondoliers, who naturally play a big role in Venice; they try to overcharge you when they can, but I am already well known in my district and no longer treated by them as a foreigner, which makes it easier and cheaper for me. They all have fine, clear, powerful voices. Nothing is more thrilling, than when one hears a solitary gondolier on the Canal at night suddenly begin with plaintive accent "O Venezia!" etc.; it's quite unique. Then one hears them answering one another from the distance with a kindred chant, until it dies away; which has quite an indescribable effect. Moreover, there is a regular Gondoliers' Vocal Union, with a workman at the Arsenal for conductor and composer; the voices are wonderfully sonorous and robust. For the upper part they have altos, which lends their singing quite a novel character; and then they sing the most diverse kinds of ballads in the folk-style, all with incredible precision, purity of intonation, and nuance. They usually get hired by strangers to make a slow tour of the whole Canal on a gondola lit with coloured lanterns; which is followed by a lengthening train of boats and listeners, amid great silence, and actively applauded from the windows. They have often entertained me, on my balcony, very finely in this fashion.

. . . Already I am as well known to the Austrian officers as a spotted dog; they always make for Karl to get my news. Unfortunately I have been unable to avoid coming into contact with the local military bandmasters. Perhaps you know that the Austrian military bands are excellent? Well, there are *three* of them here, which take it in turns to play in S. Mark's square of an evening, when the whole of Venice is on its legs. One of these bandmasters got round my landlord, but I had him turned away. In the evening I heard the Tannhäuser march performed by him, however, and the dragging tempo vexed me; so I sent him word that the next time he gave anything of mine he must let me know first, that I might shew him the correct tempo etc. He promptly fetched me to a rehearsal of the Tannhäuser overture, for military band! That was in barracks, and all the officers dropped in. It really went quite well, against all expectations.—But then the bandmaster of the royal Marines got hold of Karl, and begged him to persuade me just to honour him as well: he wanted to perform the overture to Rienzi. What else could I do? I had to go off to the Marine barracks, where a regular high-ceremonial reception awaited me, all the officers *en masse*. The overture went very well; I heard it from the restaurant with Karl, over dessert and half a bottle of champagne.—Next day the bandmaster of the Hungarian regiment announced himself, with pieces from Lohengrin: but I dismissed him for the nonce.

There—those are about all my adventures; otherwise everything is going very uniformly. I am glad to be back at my work. . . .[21]

In his retrospective account in *Mein Leben*, Wagner included some variant details and alternate perspectives:

All my social life during the seven months I spent in Venice was restricted to these few relationships, while my daily routine was maintained with scrupulous regularity the whole time I worked until two o'clock, then stepped into a waiting gondola to voyage along the solemn Canale Grande to the bustling Piazzetta, whose unusually rich charms refreshed me every day anew. There I went to my restaurant on St. Mark's Square, took a walk after the meal along the riva, either alone or with Karl Ritter, to the Giardino Publico, the only place in Venice where there are any trees, and at nightfall I came back in the gondola down the canal, growing every more silent and sombre, until reaching the point at which I could see my little lamp shining out at me, the only point of light in the nocturnal facade of the Palazzo Giustiniani. After I had done some more work, Karl would arrive regularly at eight p.m., his approach announced by the splashing of the gondola, and we would take our tea and chat for an hour or two. I interrupted this routine only rarely to visit one of the theaters, among which I decidedly preferred the plays in the Camploi Theater, where works by Goldoni were very well performed. I paid the opera [i.e., the Teatro La Fenice], on the other hand, only transitory attention, enough to satisfy my curiosity. More frequently, and particularly when bad weather hindered our walks, we attended the popular plays produced every day at the Malibran Theater; there, for an entrance fee of six kreuzers, we could join a splendid audience (mostly in shirtsleeves), whose preference was for melodramas of knight-errantry. Yet one day I saw here to my amazement and utter delight the grotesque comedy *Le Baruffe Chiozziote*, which Goethe in his time had so much enjoyed at the same place, and which was given with greater verisimilitude than I have ever encountered anywhere else.

Beyond this there was little to attract my attention in the very oppressed and degenerate life of the Venetian populace, for as far as human activity in the glorious ruins of this wonderful city was concerned, the only impression I was able to form was that it was maintained as a bathing resort for tourists. Strangely enough, it was the thoroughly German element of good military music, so well represented in the Austrian army, that brought me here into a certain contact with public life. The bandmasters of the two Austrian regiments stationed in Venice got the idea of playing overtures of mine, such as those to *Tannhäuser* and *Rienzi*, and invited me to attend rehearsals at the barracks [in the converted church of the Gesuati]. Here I found the whole officer corps assembled, which on this occasion treated me very respectfully. The two bands took turns playing in the evening in the middle of a brilliantly illuminated St Mark's Square, which offered a truly superb acoustical setting for such music. Several times at the end of dinner I was surprised to hear my overtures all of a sudden; when I sat at the restaurant window abandoning myself to the impressions of the music, I did not know which dazzled me most—the incomparable square in its magnificent illumination filled with countless numbers of moving people, or the music which seemed to be wafting all these phenomena aloft in a resounding transfiguration. But there was one thing utterly lacking here which one would otherwise have certainly expected from an Italian audience: thousands of people grouped themselves around the band and listened to the music with intense concentration; but no two hands ever forgot themselves to the extent of applauding, for any sign of approbation for an Austrian military band would have been looked upon as treason to the motherland. All public life in Venice suffered from this strange tension between the populace and the authorities, and this was particularly obvious in the behavior of the people toward the Austrian officers, who floated about in public life in Venice like oil on water. The populace also behaved with equal reserve, and even hostility, to the clergy, whose members were in fact mostly of Italian descent. I once saw a procession of clerics crossing St Mark's Square in full ceremonial vestments to the accompaniment of unconcealed derision on the part of the people.

It was very difficult for Ritter to induce me to interrupt my daily routine even to visit a gallery or a church, although whenever we had to walk through the city I was always delighted anew by the untold manifold architectural peculiarities and marvels. But throughout my entire stay in Venice my principal recreation lay in the gondola trips to the Lido. Above all it was the homeward journey at sundown which invariably overwhelmed me by its incomparable impact. Right at the outset of our stay in September of that year we saw on such occasions the magical appearance of the great comet, which was at that time at its highest brilliance, and was generally held to be a portent of imminent catastrophe in war. Then there was the singing of a popular choral society, formed and directed by an official of the Venetian Arsenal, which sounded truly idyllic in the lagoon. These singers generally sang only three-part folksongs with simple harmonies. It was new to me to hear the top part not rising above the alto range, thus not touching the soprano at all and thereby imparting to the sound a quality of masculine youthfulness I had not know until then. On fine evenings they went along the Canale Grande singing in a big, illuminated gondola, stopping to serenade in front of certain palaces, no doubt prearranged and for pay, and usually attracting countless other gondolas as a retinue.

On a sleepless night that drove me out on the balcony of my apartment at about three o'clock in the morning, I heard for the first time the famous old folksong of the gondolieri. I thought the first call, piercing the stillness of the night like a harsh lament, emanated from the Rialto, barely a quarter hour's distance away, or thereabouts; from a similar distance this would be answered from another quarter in the same way. This strange melancholy dialogue, which was repeated frequently at longish intervals, moved me too much for me to be able to fix its musical components in my mind. Yet on another occasion I learned that this folksong had an indisputably poetic interest. When I was riding back late one evening along the dark canal, the moon came out and illuminated, together with the indescribable palaces, the tall silhouette of my gondolier towering above the stern of his gondola, while he slowly turned his mighty oar. Suddenly from his breast came a mournful sound not unlike the howl of an animal, swelling up from a deep, low note, and after a long-sustained "Oh," it culminated in the simple musical phrase "Venezia." This was followed by some words I could not retain in my memory, being so greatly shaken by the emotion of the moment. Such were the impressions that seemed most characteristic of Venice to me during my stay, and they remained with me until the completion of the second act of *Tristan,* and perhaps even helped to inspire the long-drawn-out lament for the shepherd's horn at the beginning of the third act.[22]

Wagner found it difficult to settle down to a consistent work routine at the very beginning of his stay in Venice. Soon after arrival, he was plagued by a severe bout of gastritis. The long-delayed shipment of his Érard piano, however, seems to have made a great difference. On October 6, he wrote to Mathilde rejoicing that the instrument had arrived, been set up, and tuned. With this resource, work on the second act of *Tristan* seems to have moved forward. On October 19, he wrote optimistically to Liszt:

> I have at last got my Érard. It stands in the large echoing hall which serves me as a study. There *Tristan* will be finished this winter. . . . In the completion of the second act, which I have only slightly sketched, I am continually interrupted by visits. I have just begun working at it again; it will be very beautiful, and is to be finished and printed by the end of this year at the latest. By March the last act will follow, and if all goes well I shall witness the first performance about Easter.[23]

But his moods continued to falter. Awakening before dawn on November 1, the day before All Souls' Day, Wagner went out on his balcony amid a storm and, peering down into the Grand Canal running black below, he seriously thought of pitching himself unseen into it, to end the torments he felt. At least, so he wrote to Mathilde in his diary entry for that day. Soon after, he was tormented by an ulcer on one leg, just at the time Ritter had left Venice. During his convalescence, he spent much time reading. Early along he had been delving into Buddhism and Eastern philosophy; now he turned again to Schopenhauer.[24] But he also found himself pursuing an appropriate line of historical investigation and illumination:

> . . . Unable to work, I sought diversion in reading the history of Venice by Count Daru,[25] and being on the spot there myself derived treat interest from it. In particular it made me lose some of my popular prejudices against the tyrannical mode of government in old Venice. The notorious Council of Ten and the State Inquisition now appeared to me in the light of a certain characteristic naïvety, though certainly of a grim kind; the open admission that in the secrecy of its methods lay the guarantee of the power of the state seemed to enlist the citizens of this unusual republic so decidedly in its cause that the suppression of knowledge of governmental activities was quite reasonably made a real republican duty. True hypocrisy was thus entirely foreign to this state, just as the ecclesiastical element, though respectfully wedded to the secular power, never managed to exert such a degenerate influence on the character development of its citizens as in other parts of Italy. The ruthless calculations underlying reasons of state were converted into maxims of a character completely at one with the ancient, pagan world, with nothing dark or ominous about them, and which vividly recalled the same maxims which the Athenians, as we read in Thucydides, quite openly acclaimed as the basis of manly morality.[26]

Wagner also found himself suffering from the cold. He had noted at the outset that his rooms in the Palazzo Giustinian-Brandolin faced north and were thus subject to "frequent gusts of wind," while the place had no heating. Later, in a letter to Mathilde written on January 19, 1859, Wagner interrupted nostalgic outpourings to observe:

... So I'll just go on complaining. My abode is big and beautiful, but horribly cold. Hitherto I've frozen—now I know it—in Italy alone. . . . Never in my life have I made such friends with the stove, as in lovely Venice. The weather is mostly bright and set fair, thank goodness!—but it's cold here, too, though perhaps colder where you are in Germany. The gondola merely serves as a hack conveyance now, for pleasure-trips no longer; for one freezes badly in it,—which comes of the incessant north-wind, which is just what gives such brilliant weather here. What I am getting to miss the sorest, are my rambles over hill and dale: nothing remains for me but the fashionable promenade from the Piazzetta along the Riva to the public gardens, half an hour's walk, with a fearful crush of people always. Venice is a wonder: but that's all it is.[27]

Wagner's sense of loneliness and even futility must have been unbearable at times. At one point in December he contemplated making a return to Switzerland for Christmas, but this idea aborted, and he was obliged to spend Christmas Day by himself. He faced the same prospect for New Year's Day 1859, save that on it Ritter suddenly returned, to Wagner's delight. Also, as the winter began to wane, the composer bethought himself of that favorite recreation, out-door walking. At some point during the winter he had taken the train for a quick visit to Viterbo. Again, at the beginning of March, he caught a train he hoped would take him to Vicenza but that went instead to Treviso. From there he began a walk toward the Alps. But, impeded by bad weather, he did not go far. Weary and dusty, he was glad to be back in Venice.[28]

The city itself, however, seems to have lost his attention as his stay progressed. After the bursts of fascination with it in the initial weeks, he had less and less to say about it in his diary entries (which ceased after January 8) and his letters. The latter he fills either with more romantic maunderings or else—especially in his numerous missives to Minna—with discussions of musical matters and promotion of his operas. All the while, *Tristan*'s second act was progressing, and he would play newly composed passages of it to enthusiastic audiences of Ritter, Winterberger, and Tessarin. In the early months of the new year he was sending bundles of score manuscript to Leipzig for engraving, to match what had already been done for Act I. On March 17, he sent the final packet, with Act II completed and fully orchestrated.

Meanwhile, Wagner was finding that the recently difficult weather was improving, as he reported in a letter of February 10 to Minna, with whom he was discussing choices of climate for their possible future residence locations:

... Venice, for instance, hasn't been precisely hot this winter, but I must say I've never enjoyed such clear, pure air, with blue and cloudless skies, almost throughout a whole winter before. November was stormy and raw, as everywhere; but since then, on an average, we have had bright clear weather nearly all the time, mild, yet often fairly fresh; and now we're also getting the beginning of Spring warmth. I almost think this climate would be bound to do you good: only I doubt if Venice itself and its canals would please you otherwise; also, I'm not exactly mad on passing another winter here so soon. Karl's not having needed a fire comes from his living on the Riva [degli Schiavoni, facing the

Bacino], where the sun beats from its rising to its setting; also from his room being [quite small]. It is a regular Venetian attic, and must be absolutely unbearable in summer. Moreover, Karl wasn't in Venice from November 20 to January 1, *i.e.* the coldest period, whereas it has been bright ever since, that is to say, sun in his room; which counts for a very great deal in Italy. It would never have occurred to myself to take rooms on the Riva, as in all this else so tranquil Venice it is the only spot where from morn til even cries, bagpipes, barrel-organs, Punch-and-Judy shows, and now at Carnival time even the music of rope-dancers etc., never cease. I take my daily promenade the length of it, and am as if in pieces when I've got through all the hubbub; so that I keep asking Karl, who always has his windows open for the sun, how he can stand it. He declares he has got used to it now, and indeed had done no work at first whatever. That's true: at the outset he rummaged Venice like a madman for pictures and art-treasures, and was never to be found at home; even now one mostly cannot catch him. But I, on the other hand, have my big room on the solemn, still Canal, and—for the winter alas!—no sun. Added to it, a bleak corner where the Messieurs Winds often come to quite terrible blows when they're changing. Then, miserable stoves, very badly fitting windows, and—with the exception of 2 to 3 hours—I'm all the time indoors. That makes a fearful difference. Indeed, I should have moved out in the end if I hadn't the Spring in front of me; which begins very early here, and precisely in this apartment, lying as it does, should compensate me richly for the winter. Already I'm stoking much less, and fancy I soon shall leave off altogether.[29]

Wagner had originally hoped he would complete *Tristan* before the end of 1858, but progress had fallen much behind that goal. He wondered if he should stay on in Venice to work on the opera's third and final act after all. By February 27, he had already concluded that such a work commitment would be too extended: "I neither could, nor should I care to, stay in Venice so long as that; so I'm already meditating leaving here by the end of this [next] month."[30] He seems to have concluded, also, that he would not want to remain into the hot weather of summer. In a subsequent letter to Minna (March 9), Wagner was reflecting on the advantages of the area around Lake Lucerne, where clearly he was contemplating relocation for the summer.

But the issue, or at least the timing, was decided for him as much by political shifts as by the weather. Venice was, of course, a possession of the Austrian monarchy at this time, and since Austria was not a part of the German Confederation, not subject to its rules of extradition, Wagner's status as a political fugitive there was not in jeopardy. Further, Wagner had a Swiss passport, which, as we have seen, was initially accepted by the Austrian authorities in Venice. Back in Dresden, Minna was agitating to have her husband restored to favor and to his old position there. Wagner also had further backing there from the powerful Grand Duke of Baden, though the idea of returning to Germany still held great risks. In Venice itself, some of the local officials were favorably disposed to Wagner. Notable among these was the Venetian police chief, Angelo Crespi, who genuinely admired Wagner's music. But, Crespi's superior in Vienna, Baron von Kempen, had been pressured by the Saxon government—

which still hoped to arrest and imprison Wagner—to expel him from Venice. Crespi had visited Wagner in the late autumn, when Wagner was laid low by his ulcerated leg, and warned him of the problem. Von Kempen was willing to accept the argument of ill health for the moment, but insisted that Wagner would have to leave as soon as he had recovered. Crespi had attempted stalling tactics, arguing ardently that Wagner was an artist of the highest stature and was in Venice purely to pursue artistic goals. But von Kempen was unmoved and by late winter he had overridden Crespi's protests. On February 3, Crespi informed Wagner, with the greatest personal regret, that the composer was to leave Venice as soon as possible. The only alternative was to make an appeal to the Hapsburg governor-general for Italy in Milan, the Archduke Maximilian. This step proved successful for the nonce, the archduke issuing emphatic orders that Wagner be left alone.[31]

By March, however, dramatic new international circumstances decisively defined Wagner's plans. In the making was a war that would pit the alliance of Cavour's Sardinia-Piedmont with Napoleon III's France against Austria that spring—to culminate in the successive Battles of Magenta and Solferino that June. Wagner realized that this upheaval could cut off his eventual passage to Switzerland. Accordingly, in mid-March the composer made plans to beat a strategic early retreat. He settled his affairs as best he could. The orchestration for the new Act II of *Tristan* completed, Wagner dispatched his precious Érard piano back over the Alps to Switzerland, and bade goodbye to his friends. In his last letter to Minna from Venice, on March 23, he announced his commitment to Lucerne, his impending departure from Venice the next day, and his plans to do some sightseeing in Milan en route. Winterberger had already left for Rome, and Ritter, who had decided to settle in Italy, was to join him. At the railroad station on March 24, Wagner embraced both Dolgoruki and Ritter. The former was devastated at the loss of this friend. The latter, despite their closeness, Wagner would never see again.

Notwithstanding some passport tangles at Milan, Wagner settled in there for three days. On March 25, he wrote to Mathilde:

> So I have taken leave in your name, Lady-friend, of my dreamy Venice. Like a new world the hum of streets surrounds me, a world of dust and dryness, and Venice already seems a fairy dream.

After recounting an actual dream of heated emotion, Wagner goes on to report some of his immediate sightseeing in Milan, notably the Brera Gallery, some of whose paintings he discusses. Then he adds: "I have also been into, and on to the roof of, the marble cathedral: but really that is imposing to tediousness!"[32] Clearly making up for the lack of time the previous August when he was with Ritter, Wagner now put the opportunity to full use, catching as many more sites as he could. Recollecting the visit in *Mein Leben*, he commented particularly on

Leonardo's *Last Supper* and his reactions to its decay. He also spent evenings at the theater, particularly the small Teatro Re, where he enjoyed a play by Goldoni. On the other hand, his visit to La Scala only prompted scorn for

> a production of an unbelievably worthless and incompetent operatic effort by a modern composer whose name I have forgotten. Yet I discovered on that same evening that the Italian public, reputed so passionately fond of the lyric art, already regarded the ballet as a preparation for a huge choreographic extravaganza with nothing less than Antony and Cleopatra as its subject. . . .[33]

Completing his stay in Milan, Wagner moved out of the Italian spring, with stops at Como and Lugano, and on to snowy Lucerne. There he set himself up in a hotel in order to compose the final act of *Tristan,* which he completed that July.

Chapter Two

From Visit to Vacation

If Venice faded momentarily from Wagner's thoughts, it had clearly made a deep impression on him, as a city and as a part of his life. His fourth visit to it followed soon after. It was extremely brief, almost a mere pendant to the previous one, but it had repercussions that suggested anew how much Venice meant to him. During the intervening years Wagner underwent his frustrating experiences in Paris (September 1859–spring 1861), focused on the tumultuous production there of the revised *Tannhäuser*; followed by a stay in Vienna, where he first heard his *Lohengrin* but failed in negotiations for a production of *Tristan*. It was in Vienna that he renewed acquaintance with the ebullient Winterberger, and from him had news of Ritter's sad situation in Naples at the time. And it was amid all this that Wagner's political proscription was ended and he was at last free to enter German lands once more.

Momentarily stalled in Vienna in the autumn of 1861, Wagner was desperate for any new prospects or support. He had been in contact with the Wesendoncks. About to leave for a vacation in Venice, they invited Wagner to join them there. Impulsively, he jumped at the offer.

. . . Heaven knows what I had in mind when I set off one gray November day to go by rail via Trieste, and from there with a steamboat, which made me sick, to reach Venice and proceed to my little room in the Hotel Danieli. My friends, whom I found in flourishing circumstances, were reveling in enjoyment of the paintings and seemed to have it in mind to dispel my depression by sharing these delights.

It quickly became clear to Wagner that the Wesendoncks were no longer moved by Wagner's tales of disaster and frustration, and were little inclined to play the grand role of patrons any further. But what made this brief and trivial visit to Venice significant, at least in Wagner's recollection, was a momentary encounter. To it the composer would attribute a significant impact:

. . . Wesendonck, who was always armed with a huge opera glass, ready to inspect works of art, managed to induce me only once to visit the Palace of the Doges, a building which I had known only from the outside on my former visit to Venice. I have to admit that despite all my apathy Titian's *Assumption of the Virgin* in the great hall of the Doges made a most exalting impression upon me, so that by this inspiration I found my old creative powers awakening within me with almost their original primordial power.

I decided to write *Die Meistersinger*.

After a frugal dinner with my old acquaintance Tessarin and the Wesendoncks, whom I had invited to the Albergo San Marco, and after exchanging friendly greetings with Luigia, my former attendant at the Palazzo Giustiniani, I suddenly left Venice, much to the amazement of my friends. I had spent four externally dreary days there [November 7–11, 1861], and now started my long and dismal trip back by train on the roundabout land route to Vienna. During this journey I first thought of the musical treatment of *Die Meistersinger*, the poem for which I had retained in my mind only in its earliest form; I conceived the main part of the overture in C major with the greatest clarity.[1]

Here Wagner's recollections are problematical. The muddled locating of Titian's great painting is a confusion in versions of *Mein Leben*, whose original (privately printed) text specified instead the Accademia degli Belli Arti, Venice's greatest gallery of its paintings. That the spectacular religious message of this painting should have in any direct way suggested or inspired Wagner's tribute to "holy German art," or to the cultural and social life of sixteenth-century Nurembergers, has long puzzled commentators. Perhaps the best that can be said for Wagner's retrospective account is some recollection that the encounter with the creative energy of another great artist stimulated his own into renewed productivity.[2]

It was, indeed, out of determination to establish the ascendancy of German art that Wagner plunged into the creation of *Die Meistersinger von Nürnberg*. He completed his writing of the text in 1862, and finished composing the music in 1867. In June of the following year, the opera's premiere in Munich was a triumph for the composer and his music. Along the way, too, Wagner consolidated his conservative nationalist ideas, his philosophical direction, and his deepening anti-Semitism. These were, meanwhile, the years of decisive upheaval in Wagner's personal life. A residence in Vienna left him ever deeper in debts, which were, however, liquidated by the sudden generosity of the new king of Bavaria, Ludwig II, who initiated his passionate sponsorship of the composer he idolized by bringing Wagner to Munich. Above all, during this period of the king's controversial patronage, Wagner—now entering his fifties and still womanizing—developed his crucial relationship with Cosima Liszt. Daughter of the famous pianist and composer Franz Liszt, Wagner's long-time champion, Cosima was then the wife of another Wagner supporter, the pianist and conductor Hans von Bülow—who, as it happened conducted the premieres of *Tristan und Isolde* in June 1865 and of *Die Meistersinger* three years later. This scandalous relationship, clandestine at first, was consolidated when the two arranged a shared household for themselves and family in the Villa Tribschen on Lake Lucerne.

Amid the working out of their personal lives, Wagner's fifth visit to Italy took place. Back in 1862, Wagner had resisted repudiating his marriage to the long-estranged Minna, and instead he had worked out a definitive separation. With Minna's death in January 1866, Wagner was maritally independent at last. For her part, Cosima, now living ever more openly with Wagner, was ready to consider the dissolution of her shredded marriage to Bülow and to devote herself totally to Wagner. This step she and Wagner discussed during their journey, from mid-September to early October 1868. The trip itself was a sentimental one for each of them. It included Cosima's return to her birthplace at Lake Como, and it allowed Wagner to enjoy again his beloved Borromean Islands, as well as to take renewed delight in Genoa. Adventure was added to the trip by a flood-menaced passage over the Ticino.[3]

Between that brief excursion and their next visit to Italy, nine years ensued and much happened. The last of the three children Cosima bore Wagner (while still married to Bülow) was born in 1869. Only a year later did Bülow agree to a divorce so that Wagner and Cosima could finally marry (August 1870).[4] Meanwhile, Wagner had in 1862 resumed the composition of *Der Ring des Nibelungen* that he had put aside in 1854. He completed the last two of its four operas in 1865–74, fulfilling the grandest of his musical visions. Dissatisfied with weak Munich productions of the first two of the *Ring* operas in 1869 and 1870, Wagner had conceived the correspondingly grand vision of creating his own theatrical venue for presentation of his works. For this he selected the modest town of Bayreuth in the Upper Franconian district of the Bavarian Kingdom. The foundation stone of his projected Festspielhaus was laid on his birthday (May 22) in 1872. Wagner and Cosima established residence there, eventually in the mansion named Wahnfried, built for them. Plans for the first Wagner festival, to offer the world premiere of the complete *Ring*, were plagued by delays and inadequate funds, but serious rehearsals began in 1785, and in August 1876 the tetralogy was given in three full cycles, under the baton of Hans Richter.

This first Bayreuth Festival was an event of international attention and significance in the world of music, as well as an artistic landmark for Wagner himself. Nevertheless, it left him not only deeply in debt but utterly exhausted. Responding to the latter issue with characteristic disdain for the former one, the Wagners chose to recuperate by vacationing in Italy. Wagner had already intended such a move two years before. By now, though, it may have served Cosima's purposes in taking him away from the attractive Judith Gautier, whom Wagner now fancied as his latest romantic interest. Richard and Cosima journeyed this time, too, as a superficially conventional family. Accompanied by their three children (Isolde, Eva, Siegfried), as well as the younger of Cosima's two daughters by Bülow (Blandine), plus a governess, they set out from Munich by train on September 14, 1876.[5] Their first stop, on the fifteenth, was in Verona, where they spent three days. His health uneven, Wagner had limited interest in sightseeing, but Cosima diligently led the children in a rigorous tour of churches, the art museum, and other sights.

On September 19, they proceeded to their next stop, for Cosima's first encounter with the city that seemed now to have displaced her husband's earlier affection for Genoa. In Venice, they settled into the Hôtel de l'Europe (on the Grand Canal, facing the Dogana) for a week. (It is said that the apartment of rooms they occupied had also been used at various times by Meyerbeer and by Verdi.) On their first evening there they were serenaded by workers at the dockyard. The following day, they connected with Wagner's old local comrade in the city, the piano teacher Tessarin, whom Cosima in her *Tagebuch* called "the earliest Wagnerian in Italy, a true Venetian." In the course of their stay they strolled about, took a few excursions, frequently attended the theater, and enjoyed evenings at the Piazza San Marco. But Wagner's health problems again weighed on him—"R. not well, the air does not much agree with him," Cosima noted on a rainy September 21. Nevertheless, her thirst for the sights would not be denied. Wagner did tour the Doge's Palace with her, and he joined her in a round through the Accademia di Belle Arti on their last day in Venice. But she regularly left him behind (to avoid tiring him) as she indefatigably scoured the churches and museums. The paintings at the Accademia greatly excited her, and she particularly noted encountering Titian's *Ascension of the Virgin* "as if I were hearing a Beethoven symphony for the first time" (September 23).[6] By the time of their departure on the afternoon of September 26, Cosima found it "as difficult to part from these divine things as from Venice itself. . . ."

> . . . How very sad a city in which those who dwell in it seem like worms, utterly alien to the noble, diversified body! But I did not contemplate this living element, seeing only the eternity; from few human beings have I found it harder to part than from this city, which went straight to my heart as I know no other will ever do.

That evening, as she completes her diary entries on the days in Venice, she is "melancholy that they were so fleeting." Clearly, Venice had cast its spell on Cosima, if not as a community, at least as a concept and a setting.

By the evening of September 26, the Wagners were in Bologna, which was apparently a particular focus of the journey. In November 1871, the performance of *Lohengrin* at its Teatro Comunale, under Angelo Mariani, had been Wagner's first significant breakthrough in Italy and had initiated a special relationship between the composer and this city. In May of the following year, the city's municipal council, on the recommendation of the syndic (*sindaco*, or mayor), Camillo Casarini, had awarded Wagner the status of honorary citizen of Bologna. Wagner had written his thanks for the honor and had vowed to visit his "fellow-citizens" there within the next year or two. Only now, in the autumn of 1876, was he fulfilling the pledge. The new sindaco, Conte Tacconi, gave Wagner a warm reception, but the stay was only a brief one. Of their two days in the city, Cosima had barely one day in which to survey the sights, devoting particular reactions to paintings there. At 2:00 a.m. on September 29, they took a train to Naples, arriving at 10:00 p.m. the same evening. Settling into the Hôtel Vittoria there for five days, they first needed to recover from the exhausting journey. Cosima again ranged through museums, and an excursion to Posilipo particularly pleased Wagner: "R. very much enjoys the hectic life here, and it really is the liveliest city imaginable; popular in the most extravagant sense of the word." Yet, Naples could not erase a lingering impression: "I think a lot about Venice the silent, the needy, where I should feel more at home" (October 2).

On October 5, the Wagners departed by ship for their next stop, Sorrento, where they set up first in a cottage beside the Hôtel Vittoria, and then in the hotel itself, for what would be the longest and most deliberately restful phase of the stay, some thirty-three days. There was little of art and monuments to concern them here. Of course, there were excursions to be taken: to Capri and to Pompeii. But much time was devoted to resuming lessons for the children, while evenings were often spent in joint reading (especially of Sismondi's *History of the Italian Republics*) or discussions of literature (Dante, Goethe, etc.). There were, as well, unhappy moments, as Cosima was racked by torments over Wagner's erratic emotions and over a dream he had of her being executed. For his part, Wagner was recurrently gloomy over the mountainous deficit that the Bayreuth *Ring* had generated.

Still, there was some social life and there were frequent visitors. One was a local resident, Malwida von Meysenbug, a friend of long standing to both Wagner and Cosima. Malwida was also a friend to the brilliant young philosopher, Friedrich Nietzsche (1844–1900), whose youthful intellectual admiration for Wagner, and personal devotion to him, was now waning. As it happened, and purely by coincidence, Malwida was already entertaining Nietzsche and his companion, Paul Rée, as her guests. When Malwida brought them all together socially, the viciously anti-Semitic Cosima discovered that Rée was Jewish, and promptly banned him from their company. Then, in private conversation, Richard tactlessly pressed upon Nietzsche some of his religious ideas in connection with his plans for *Parsifal.* The result was the deepening of a rift between them that was never to be resolved and that turned Nietzsche into a bitter anti-Wagnerian.[7]

These unhappy frictions may have prompted the Wagners' decision to leave Sorrento on November 7. They spent two nights back at the Hôtel Vittoria in Naples, the day in between spent in shopping, a little touring ("more delicious glimpses of folk life"), and a bit of theater. On the evening of November 9, they arrived in Rome and, after an unsatisfactory stay at the Hotel Constanzi they shifted to the Hôtel d'Amérique on the Via del Babuino, for a visit of some twenty-two days. This was the first visit to Rome for each of them. There were many social occasions, and some of Richard's time was spent in pursuing local contacts, while Cosima gingerly met with the long-hostile Princess Sayn-Wittgenstein, her father's ultimate *inamorata*, who lived nearby on the Via del Babuino. Along the way, Wagner encountered one of Liszt's disciples, the pianist–composer Giovanni Sgambati (1841–1914), whose focus on instrumental composition had cost him neglect in his native Italy. Wagner was very impressed by his music, promising to help promote and publish some of it. One of the participants in a Sgambati performance that Wagner attended was Luigi Mancinelli, of whom more will be heard later. At another musicale, the singer–composer Paolo Tosti (1846–1916) joined Sgambati. Another new acquaintance there was the young French diplomat and writer, Comte Joseph Arthur de Gobineau (1816–82). The two men immediately struck it off personally. Later on, the composer would immerse himself in the writings of Gobineau, especially his racialist studies, which influenced Wagner enormously, and which would only make their friendship closer. But, in fact, much of the Wagners' time in Rome was spent in sightseeing: strolling among sites and monuments, visiting churches, museums, and villas—Cosima sometimes on her own, but with Richard himself involved most of the time. She relished some of the great art, delighting particularly in the Sistine Chapel, though both she and Richard reacted to St. Peter's with a disgust they compared to Luther's.[8]

On December 3, 1876, the Wagners left Rome for Florence, where there was at least one shift in lodgings at the outset of their fourteen-day stay. Moreover, the first days (December 4–5) were devoted to a quick trip back to Bologna, where there were more ceremonial receptions and a local performance—apparently quite a good one—of his early opera *Rienzi*. At a banquet in his honor the next day, Wagner gave a speech with artfully crafted tributes to the city.[9] And at another point (December 12), they impulsively made an excursion from Florence to Pisa, "with whose history R. has great sympathy." They admired the cathedral—nothing being said about the notorious campanile!—but generally they had "a sad impression" of the city as a whole. In Florence itself there were some social calls and they were given some sightseeing guidance by one of Wagner's pre-Mathilde romantic interests, Jessie Taylor Laussot, and her soon-to-be new husband, the historian Professor Karl Hillebrand. An even more regular attendant was Hillebrand's friend, Baron Karl Eduard von Liphart, who regularly helped them see the sights. At that task they were quite diligent, taking in the important churches, palaces, villas, and museums, with the Uffizi a particular favorite. While no further nostalgia was expressed here for Venice, Cosima did record (December 10) that Richard could think seriously of settling in Florence—were it not for his sense of German identity and need to make a living.

After "a melancholy farewell" to Florence at the Uffizi, the Wagner family took a train on the evening of December 17; transferring at midnight in Bologna, they were graciously met by its syndic, Gaetano Tacconi. By evening on the eighteenth, they were in Munich for a two-night stay, in which Wagner endeavored to secure King Ludwig's relief of the Bayreuth debts. Late on the evening of December 20, they reached home in Bayreuth itself, ending the 1876 journey—Wagner's sixth to Italy.

During the next three years Wagner balanced his time between consolidating his philosophical and racialist ideas, on the one hand, and his composition of his last opera, *Parsifal*, on the other. Still plagued by debts, Wagner undertook in 1877 to lead a series of concerts in the new Albert Hall London, the last public display of his epochal talents as an orchestral conductor. It was an artistic success, and an interesting cultural experience, but not the financial bonanza for which he had hoped. Thanks, however, to a final agreement with King Ludwig as to the Bayreuth deficit (March 1878), Wagner could begin to make plans for a second festival to be built around the new opera. But the labor of its composition bore heavily on him and ravaged his health. In his mid-sixties by now, Wagner also found the cold and damp winter weather of Bayreuth particularly hard on him. So it was that Wagner's seventh visit to Italy was generated, though its gestation lasted a year.

When the idea of a winter escape to Italy was first raised is not clear, and, despite the musings in 1876 about removing to Florence, it was now on Naples that they focused attention. That was discussed in the middle days of January 1879. By March 6, the Villa d'Angri at Posilipo was being investigated. Along the way, they obtained the help of a young admirer, Professor Dr. Otto Schrön, then director of the University of Naples' Pathological Institute, as their intermediary. Negotiations must have become tangled, and fears of a lawsuit being made against them were relieved only as of July 7. For a while Schrön investigated another site, the Villa Maraval, only to reject it as too distant from Naples, reported Cosima (July 22). Only on September 22 did Cosima note the definite settlement of agreements for Naples, and in the months that followed, Dr. Schrön saw to detailed arrangements. (When on December 4, she received a letter from him asking if they would need stoves in the villa, Cosima reacted: "So it is cold there, too!")

It was none too soon for the ailing Wagner, suffering from the onset of Bayreuth's winter, that the journey finally commenced. With Daniela von Bülow added to the same five as before, the family set out on the last day of 1879 for Munich. There they spent New Year's Eve and the two days following. On January 3, 1880, they boarded the train for a long and exhausting overnight trip that brought them to Naples the following day. Here Wagner began the longest of his sojourns in Italy, and his longest stay (seven months) in a single locale there.[10] Within a hectic day or so, the Wagners settled into the Villa d'Angri, a splendid residence, adjacent to the celebrated Palazzo di Donna Anna on the northern shore of the Bay of Naples, to the southwest of that city itself. Its ample grounds ran down to the sea, with a vista reaching grandly across the bay, past the great presence of Mt. Vesuvius—then quite active—toward Sorrento and Capri to the south.

For some days Wagner still suffered serious health problems, but he began to hold court for visitors. Among them was the obliging Dr. Schrön, who lectured Wagner on "the talent of the Italian people," and then on the local criminal society, the Camorra—"with which he claims to be in touch," Cosima notes (January 12). A visitor of subsequent importance first appeared on January 18. This was the painter Paul von Zhukovsky or Joukowsky (1845–1912). His Russian father, a tutor of the future Tsar Alexander II, had been a poet and a translator into Russian of major works of German literature. From this father, and from his German mother, Joukowsky had inherited not only his artistic bent, but also a useful command of her native language. He had already met Cosima in 1876 and now, with his studio nearby in Naples, he came to meet Wagner. The latter quickly found him congenial and useful, and made him a regular visitor.

In this idyllic setting, Wagner began to improve in health, and relished a certain leisure, joining his family in local excursions. One of these (March 15) was, at his own impetus, to the Naples law courts where he found himself caught up in a criminal case involving an arrogant defendant ("the majesty of crime") and some poignant female witnesses. All of this he found "a fascinating experience" and "affecting proceedings" of "fine humaneness"—clearly the response of a dramatist.[11] The Wagners also spent much time in reading, regularly to each other in the evening, and having intense literary discussions, all as was Wagner's wont. He did a little essay writing, and at times continued the dictation of *Mein Leben* to Cosima. Supposedly, he was to resume work on *Parsifal*. He had finished the basic composition of it the previous April 25 (1879), but he now had to work out the orchestration, a slow process, and one in which he apparently progressed rather minimally at the Villa d'Angri.

Alternatively, from June 1 onward, Wagner began writing his long and important essay *Religion und Kunst*. Otherwise, however, he allowed himself regular distractions. A prime example of them came late in the spring, when the Wagners undertook a three-day excursion (May 25–27) that brought them first to Amalfi. Its cathedral displeased Wagner, but the overnight stay at the Albergo dei Cappuccini redeemed all that. The following day they drove to Ravello where the famous gardens of the Villa Rufolo were in full bloom. "Lovely beyond description," was Cosima's verdict, but for the enraptured Wagner, immersed as he was in completing *Parsifal* and in planning its production, the site was a revelation. "I have found Klingsor's enchanted garden," he wrote in the villa's guestbook, adding the date with his and his family's name. His exclamation may still be seen engraved on a plaque mounted on one of the garden walls. They went on to enjoy the view from Santa Chiara ("the loveliest, in my opinion," affirmed Cosima), and spent a second night at the Amalfi hotel. On a boat tour the following day, they visited the Grotto of Sant'Andrea and the pretty town of Vietri before returning by train. A few days later (June 1), Joukowsky could show Wagner his scenic design for Act II of *Parsifal*, based on the Ravello gardens.

The continuing procession of visitors to the Wagners at Villa d'Angri included the friend of long standing, Malwida von Meysenbug. Another familiar was Giovann[in]a Lucca, the Italian music publisher, who had met Wagner in years past and had acquired rights to the composer's music in Italy.[12] She was in the process of organizing a new production of *Lohengrin* in Rome at the time. In a personal visit to the Villa d'Angri on March 10, while indulging freely in nostalgia, she secured a virtual promise of the composer's assistance at rehearsals. But Wagner's recurrent doubts about involving himself in Italian productions of his works seems to have asserted itself, doubtless amplified by concerns about his health. On March 14, he wrote to "Frau Lucca" begging off his commitment. She was back again on March 25, this time with a formal invitation to the composer at least to attend the performance in Rome. According to Cosima, Lucca was "imprudently noisy" as Wagner explained his objection to "this turbulent woman," and the encounter left him wearied by "such nonsense." Nevertheless, Wagner was kept informed of the success of the production (April 3, at the Teatro Apollo): first by communications from Rome (April 5, 8, 9), and then (May 20) by a visit from the singer Stella Bonheur. That distinguished contralto had sung the role of Ortrud in the production: she gave a good report of it and of the efforts of its promoter, now recognized by Cosima as "our good, energetic Frau Lucca."[13]

To his habitual aloofness from Italian musical life, Wagner made one notable exception in an episode of contact with the Naples Music Conservatory. According to Cosima, the contact was initiated by Wagner on March 25, on an impulse following the trying encounter with Lucca. As it happened, this was Holy Thursday, and Wagner decided he wanted to attend the traditional *Miserere* service in the institution's chapel. He and Cosima were received there by the Duke and Duchess of Bagnara, the duke being president of the conservatory. Indeed, one wonders if Wagner's seeming impulse may have been in response to a prior invitation by the duke. The principal musical work of the service was an extended eight-voice setting of the *Miserere* psalm made in 1739 by the earlier Neapolitan master Leonardo Leo (1694–1744). This music deeply impressed Wagner.

At this point the data are confused. Though Cosima totally excludes the matter from her diary, other reports have it that on the next day, Good Friday, there was a choral concert of conservatory alumni, which Wagner and his wife also attended. Of its program Wagner was particularly impressed by Clément Jannequin's descriptive piece, *La Battaile de Marignan*, and by its performance as well. He was less pleased by both the quality and the performance of an operetta by a young local composer. Following this, Wagner is reported to have visited the conservatory's magnificent library. There, he and Cosima took particular pains to flatter its distinguished librarian, Francesco Florimo, who had established himself as a vociferously chauvinistic anti-Wagnerian. Since Florimo had been a friend of Bellini and had become his biographer, Wagner made a great point of praising Bellini's operas, while Cosima charmed Florimo personally. (She later wrote him a letter in which she characterized the aging savant as "the most courteous of librarians and the youthful octogenarian" (*le plus gracieus des bibliothécaires et le juvenile octogénaire*).[14]

The Duke of Bagnara chose to exploit this opening by leading a delegation of conservatory officials to visit Wagner two days later, on Easter Sunday (March 28). According to Cosima, Wagner urged them to create an opera school that would set new standards for performing more than just Italian opera. Following upon this meeting, and perhaps at the duke's invitation, Wagner addressed to him a letter (dated April 22, 1880, and written in French) conveying reactions to his encounters with the conservatory, its personnel, and its activities. Above all, he consolidated his advice for improvements, stressing the need for intensive cultivation of precision in performance and for sensitivity to dramatic values. He recommended the study of specific operas by Mozart, Gluck, and Spontini, as particular models of style.[15]

Of Italian musicians, Wagner was willing to receive composer Sgambati who came (June 20, 21), with his wife, to visit and to play some of his music. Most visits were focused on work. The young Engelbert Humperdinck (1854–1921), emerging among Wagner's army of talented assistants, was apparently brought onto the scene, perhaps as a copyist of the emerging score, but also in time (May 22) for an improvised trial run of *Parsifal* choruses, at which he joined the Wagner children and some friends. Humperdinck's presence was noted again (among the "Knights of the Grail") on the evening of May 17. Later, on July 6 and then on July 10, Wagner suffered through two twenty-minute sittings for the Swiss painter Edmond Jean, Baron de Pury, to do his portrait (fig. 9). A fortnight later, on July 24, another Swiss painter, the more celebrated Arnold Böcklin (1827–1901), arrived to discuss possible scenic designs for the new opera.

But the Neapolitan paradise had turned sour. Wagner was troubled by his recurrent erysipelas, and by heat rash. He and Cosima decided (August 6) that they would leave the Villa d'Angri, but would arrange for the children to stay behind for the time being. Their feelings about Naples were still mixed when, on August 8, the couple set out by train for Rome, which they reached that evening, to lodge for one night at the Hotel Quirinal. After minimal touring, they took the train again to arrive that next evening (August 9) in Pistoia, where they stayed at its Hotel London. Wagner's physical sufferings continued, but they took a carriage ride to the village of San Marcello where they found particularly uncomfortable accommodations.

An attempt the following day (August 11) to find something better at the town of Abbetone proved unsuccessful, and they returned for the night to Pistoia, where they spent a pleasant day before moving on to Florence. A night there at the Hotel di Roma was a prelude to the next stop that Wagner had chosen, Perugia. Friends there—the archaeologist Helbig and his wife, a student of Liszt—made a booking for them at its Hotel Perugia, and there they took up a week's residence (August 13–20). They were amused to find that Wagner was famous in Perugia: not for his own work, but because he had been, as music director in Dresden, a successor to a beloved local son, conductor–composer Francesco Morlachi (1784–1841), who had served in Dresden before him.[16]

The couple found Perugia relaxing, on the whole, allowing leisurely visits to some monuments—Cosima sometimes on her own—and carriage rides about the area. Wagner even talked again (August 14) about settling in Italy, though worrying that this would distract him from his goals: to finish writing *Parsifal*, "then symphonies, then I will complete various bits of my work." It does appear, though, that by this time (August 17) the drafting of *Mein Leben* had been finished.

There was discussion of reunion with the children, planned at first for Florence, to which Richard and Cosima traveled on August 20, and where they spent that night. But the rendezvous was then shifted to Siena, to which the two moved on the next day. Their main task there was to look for a villa in the area where they could settle again as a family. They were dispirited at first, but the mood changed when they took an intermission and visited Siena's famous cathedral. "R. moved to tears, the greatest impression he has ever received from a building," reported Cosima: "How I should love to hear the Prelude to *Parsifal* beneath this dome!" These reactions would prove prophetic, as will be seen. By the end of the day, however, they had achieved their purpose, to make their choice of a villa and to negotiate the terms. After a night at Siena's Grand Hotel, the following day (August 22) was devoted to meeting the children who, going first by train to Florence, finally arrived at the Siena station. Thereupon the reunited family spent their first night at their new lodgings.

These were at the Villa Torre Fiorentina, an impressive pile on the Via Fiorentina, about three kilometers outside Siena on the road to Florence. In this colorful and historic facility—in one of its beds Pope Pius VI had slept!—surrounded by lovely gardens, the Wagners spent the second-longest stay of the 1880 sojourn. Cosima took ample opportunity to visit the artistic and cultural sites, both with and without Richard. Indeed, when her father joined the family for a portion of the residence (September 16–25), she had that much more company with whom to share the art. For his part, Wagner seems to have returned to serious work on *Parsifal*: above all, just preparing the ruled score pages. In the process he remarked to Cosima "how remote orchestration now seems to him" (September 1). He did, though reserve time for some article writing as well.

Paul Joukowsky had accompanied the children on their train journey to Siena, and seems to have become a regular companion to them. At some point, then, he was allowed to take "Fidi"—Siegfried, the Wagner's youngest child, then eleven—on an art-and-architecture tour.[17] Wagner had decided that Siegfried should be trained as an architect, while daughter "Lodi" (Isolde) should become a painter (September 6). Mention is made of the boy's visits with Joukowsky to Perugia (September 8) and Orvieto (September 25, 26); though Wagner later resisted the idea that Joukowsky show Siegfried around Ravenna (September 30).

Apparently with Wagner's promptings, the artistic exercises of both children came early to focus on the Siena Duomo. Whether or not the idea came at the time of Wagner's first experiencing of the great cathedral, as Cosima recorded it, he soon imagined it as the model for the Grail Chapel in *Parsifal*. As early as September 2, he had at hand a sketch of the Duomo interior made as just such a scenic study: though not so stated, probably made for him by Joukowsky. On September 6, he and Cosima perused drawings that both children had made of the cathedral. Mention is made of further sketches of its interior made by Siegfried (September 13). It is thus as part of a family preoccupation, prompted by Wagner himself, that we should understand how Joukowsky's drawings of the Siena Duomo came to serve as the scenic designs for Act I of the impending opera production at Bayreuth, just as his drawings of the Villa Rufolo gardens provided the set design for Act II. In such manner were Wagner's 1880 experiences in Italy fused into the realization of his final German music drama.

The residence outside Siena was barely a month old (and perhaps the lease on the villa was running down) when Wagner began to feel new stirrings, with an old attraction reasserted. "The cool weather makes him wish increasingly for Venice," Cosima reported on September 18, suggesting that it may not have been the first such twinge. Symbolism intruded as the impulse strengthened: "R. enjoys the countryside, but also the prospect of going to Venice, particularly since there he will not see the leaves falling" (September 24). He was thinking of Venice again on September 28, and even more urgently as the family packed for departure two days later. But first there was an intermediary stop, back in Florence, meant to make up for depriving the children of a stay there in August. Lodged at the Hotel New York, they had two-and-a-half days to enjoy the high points of Florence's sites. A delay in securing proper railway reservations prefaced an uncomfortable trip on October 4, but that afternoon they arrived in Venice, for what would be a stay of twenty-six days (October 4–30, 1880).

Requiring long-term lodgings, they negotiated arrangements at the Palazzo Contarini delle Figure on the Grand Canal. The family did have to spend their first two nights at the Hotel Danieli on the Riva degli Schiavoni before moving into their full accommodations on October 6. Cosima had to conduct the negotiations, so that, in a reversal of the usual, it was Richard who took the children sightseeing on the fifth. The new setting brightened the atmosphere for Wagner, who was, Cosima immediately reported (October 5), "glad to be in Venice." And, after two days of rain, she again noted: "Glorious weather, which R. enjoys with all his heart; his delight in the city is unbounded, whether going by boat or on foot" (October 9). And, indeed, they employed their time extensively for sightseeing, visiting major monuments, enjoying art at the Accademia, taking a few excursions (e.g., Murano), and shopping. And there was socializing.

Not long after their settling at the palazzo, Joukowsky joined them, hereafter to become a continuing member of the Wagner household. Almost immediately, too, the Wagners renewed acquaintance with Richard's good old friend from 1858–59, Angelo Tessarin, with whom they visited several times. His livelihood by teaching had apparently collapsed, and Cosima found a way to blame this on

Jewish slanders and malice (October 28). Another visitor was Count Gobineau (October 22, 25), whose influential writings Wagner had not yet been able to read, but whose friendship with the composer now began to crystallize.[18] Wagner also worked: if not much for now on *Parsifal*, at least on one of his Schopenhauer-inspired essays on religion.

Return to Germany had become necessary, while the palazzo lease was ending, so on October 29, Wagner and Joukowsky went to the railroad station to reserve the saloon carriage the composer required. That evening they relished a final stroll through the Piazza San Marco. A touch of bad weather the next day prompted Wagner to deplore departing a warm land for a cold one, and to express explicit nostalgia for Naples. A group of local singers serenaded them on their gondola ride to the station, for a particularly Venetian conclusion to the family's longest sojourn in Italy. After a twenty-four-hour train ride they reached Munich on the evening of October 31. A stay of over two weeks in Munich included Wagner's last personal contacts with the deteriorating King Ludwig. Finally, on November 17, 1880, the family reached Bayreuth and Wahnfried after an absence of nearly eleven months.

Wagner was barely back in his German home than the dreary weather made his thoughts turn southward again, and specifically to Venice (November 19, 20; December 8, 1880). He was, at least, back to serious work on *Parsifal*. He would finish the scoring of its Act I the following April 25. And eventually he undertook more philosophical writings. Nevertheless, the year was scarcely ended before he was thinking of a new winter escape to the south. In the recent stay in Venice they had inspected with interest a Palazzo Loredan (which one is not clear). Now, on December 11, while strolling with Cosima, he announced that they would spend the winter next year at the Villa [*sic*] Loredan in Venice, going "via Seville and Palermo." The sudden attention to those two cities, neither of which they had visited before, was never explained, but may have been prompted by various elements of cultural and historical curiosity. Constant nostalgia for Venice continued to be expressed (December 23, 1880; February 11, 1881), but on May 19, the visiting Count Gobineau's description of Athens provoked discussion of spending the next winter there. On July 17, the idea of going to Palermo resurfaced, though without Seville.

A new composite scheme seemed to be emerging by August 6: "Yesterday R. worked out a plan to complete his score [i.e., *Parsifal*] by January and then to take us via Venice and Corfu to Athens, and from there to Palermo!" There seems, however, to have been a souring on Athens (September 7), although Wagner still "thinks longingly of Corfu" on September 18, and was thinking of it again on October 2, as he studied an atlas. The next day "R. thinks of Venice but is put off by thoughts of all his acquaintances there." On October 5: "We think of distant lands, of Palermo, he reads about it in Baedeker and then goes to work with a semblance of good cheer." Then, on October 11, he and Cosima are "imagining a journey up the Nile"; and the next day they discuss "the journey up the Nile and Palermo." On the day after that, it was nostalgia's turn again: "Memories of the Villa d'Angri, the night on the terrace, watching everyone come and go: 'One felt like God Almighty,' says R." Wagner was soon caught up in new excitement over the Nile journey plan (October 19, 20), in which he "serves at least to distract himself thoroughly from other thoughts," observed Cosima.

On October 20, Wagner completed the orchestration of *Parsifal*'s Act II, which he had begun on June 8. He awoke the next day concluding that "the thought of the Nile journey suddenly seemed like madness, let alone writing his 3rd act there." All of this vacillation was finally resolved on October 23. Cosima was advised by their physician that Richard's health—plagued for months by chest pains and spasms—required that he leave the damp air of Bayreuth soon, and so she immediately booked rooms in Palermo. By process of elimination, it would seem, the Sicilian capital had won out, and to this final arrangement Wagner raised no objection.

The stage was thus set for Wagner's eighth visit to Italy.[19] Together with only four of the children (Daniela being with her grandfather), Richard and Cosima took a night train on November 1, 1881, and arrived the next morning in Munich. Within an hour they were on the train south. Joukowsky joined them for the ride between Bolzano and Verona. A brief stop was made in Pesaro, where a festivity was held in Wagner's honor in front of the city's statue of Rossini. The Adriatic sunshine delighted him. Stops were also made at Ancona and Osimo, and the itinerary continued through Rimini and Foggia before arrival in Naples, where they lodged at the Hotel Bristol. The next morning (November 4) their friend from their previous visit, Dr. Schrön, greeted them and took them for a quick visit back to the Villa d'Angri, where they had a pleasant reunion with the staff. From there they went to the harbor to board their steamship. Wagner fretted and fussed until he could be given a cabin with a bunk on which to spend the night, while Cosima and the children had to settle down on the deck amid the motley cargo ("horses, oxen, chickens, convicts, soldiers, and other Italians"). Arriving at Palermo the next day (November 5), they were welcomed by Josef Rubinstein, a musician whose talent as player and arranger had long made him a "house pianist" at Bayreuth and at Naples—all that despite the fact that he was of Jewish background. Rubinstein had himself moved to Palermo that August. His glowing accounts of the place had been, if not the origin of Wagner's choice of the city, at least a strong encouragement.

Initial lodging was taken up at Palermo's elegant Grand Hôtel des Palmes, where Wagner and Cosima arranged for a suite of three rooms on the *primo piano*, while the children were settled in quarters on the ground floor. On an exploratory ride through the city, Cosima found it disappointing and much inferior to Naples: "this is hardly likely to become our permanent winter abode for the future." But she appreciated the greenery and, as the days passed, she and Richard found themselves enjoying this city in which they were to make one of their longer stays in Italy. Filled with historical fascination and nationalistic pride over the glorious era of Norman and Hohenstaufen rule in Sicily, Wagner was eagerly responsive to the island's wonderful cultural mix amid sunny Mediterranean climate and lush vegetation. (The Wagners were, however, annoyed by the mosquitoes.) Richard and Cosima hastened to relish, on repeated visits, such treasures as the great cathedral of Monreale and the glorious Cappella Palatina. They also explored the city itself in frequent walks, reacting either positively or negatively to sites they encountered, and they enjoyed local gardens and villas.[20]

They were shepherded to the Saracen-Norman palaces, La Zisa and La Cuba, by a new acquaintance, Count Tasca (or Almerita-Tasca), who took them on frequent carriage rides. He also introduced them to some of the local nobility, denizens of Lampedusa's world who were happy to pay court to this distinguished celebrity.[21] Nevertheless, with the exception of the loyal Rubinstein and the fondly regarded Joukowsky (who arrived on December 23), Wagner generally avoided visitors and, given the limited musical life, felt no distractions in that quarter. He and Cosima more than ever devoted their time together to discussions of literature. Above all, he found the location ideal for work and, aside from more essay writing, set back to work on the *Parsifal* score. While Wagner toiled on the instrumentation, Rubinstein prepared the piano arrangement under his supervision. The orchestration of Act III was not fully finished, and the score's final pages were ruled but still blank, when Wagner presented the manuscript to Cosima as a birthday gift on Christmas Day. The true completion followed on January 13, 1882.

It was exactly at this moment that Wagner was besieged by a new visitor. Auguste Renoir (1841–1919), already distinguished as a leader in the new Impressionist movement in France, had been in Naples, where a friend suggested he should try to do a portrait of Wagner. Renoir promptly took a ship to Palermo and, after some difficulties, tracked Wagner down to the Hôtel des Palmes. His initial approach to the Master was turned away through a servant. Apparently aware of the havoc his ill health played with his facial appearance, Wagner had long resisted such requests, even from Joukowsky himself. When Renoir returned the following day, fearing renewed rejection, he was met with encouragement by Joukowsky, and told to come back the next day. After more delays then, the weary composer (joined shortly by Joukowsky and Cosima) allowed Renoir an interview of about a half-hour's duration.

For whatever reason, Wagner abandoned his reluctance and agreed to sit for the French artist, which he did for about three-quarters of an hour the next day (January 15, 1882). According to Renoir (whom Cosima called "Renouard"), Wagner made boorish conversation, full of anti-Semitic bile. When shown the resulting sketch (made in oils; fig. 11), he told Renoir that the latter had made him look like a Protestant clergyman; while to Cosima, Richard said "that it makes him look like the embryo of an angel, an oyster swallowed by an epicure."

From the oil sketch Renoir subsequently made a pencil sketch the following year. In 1893, he made a full portrait in oils, whose characterization of Wagner's bloated face has been alternatively condemned as distortion or praised for psychological insight; and, around 1900, Renoir also produced a lithographic version. Meanwhile, two days after the Palermo sitting for Renoir, perhaps by way of making it up to Joukowsky, Wagner sat for that favored artist. But Joukowsky completed no more than an oil sketch, and he departed Palermo on January 22, and no finished portrait resulted at that point.[22]

By this time, Wagner seems to have developed mixed feelings about residing in the center of Palermo and particularly in the Grand Hôtel des Palmes. Already on January 9, with Count Tasca's help, Cosima spied out a villa (Airodi) for possible relocation, but it was found unsatisfactory. On January 23, one of their new acquaintances, Prince Gangi, offered Wagner the use of his country villa at nearby Piazza di Porrazzi, on the road to Monreale. The family had already visited it, back on December 26, and, after inspecting it anew, the agreement was made. Wagner immediately gave notice to the hotel manager, Sgr. Ragusa, of their intention to leave. They had been booked to stay there for two more months, and the manager expected payment for the unused portion of the reservation, which Wagner resented; but a grudging resolution was worked out. Misgivings soon arose about the villa's suitability. Since it was a summer refuge, it lacked stoves, for which the Wagners had to arrange at some expense. Two days after Daniela von Bülow joined them, the family finally made their transfer, on February 2. "What will you pay me for leaving?" Wagner tauntingly asked Sgr. Ragusa as they departed the hotel; "I'll pay you something to stay on," he replied.[23]

The new location did not work out well. Though Wagner tried to follow his regimen of work in the mornings, his health took some turns for the worse, and, on February 5, there was even a medical consultation about the advisability of staying on. Anxiety was expressed about the children's safety in the area, and Cosima's concern about confining the girls so rigidly provoked much tension. The children developed illnesses, especially Siegfried who, now twelve, had wandered freely around Palermo and had contracted a serious typhoid infection. Always cantankerous and irascible, Wagner had had enough by March 8. He rather tactlessly told his host how little he thought of the villa and its situation. "Since we are here dealing with a very well meant act of kindness," recorded Cosima the next day, "it pains me to think that our departure might take place in a spirit of vexation." Delayed only by doubts about Siegfried's readiness to move, preparations were under way by March 14, with Acireale, a resort town on the island's eastern coast, the next destination selected.

The departure was fraught with upheaval. On the next day, March 15, Count Tasca informed Cosima that the hand of her second daughter, Blandine von Bülow (now nineteen), was being sought by Count Biaggio Gravina (who was thirty-two). Son of a distinguished Sicilian family, he had a fine noble pedigree but his lack of money or livelihood was a source of concern and discussion over the next few days. At the same time, it was decided that the Wagners should offer a gesture of thanks to the aristocratic friends who had been so hospitable to them, in the form of "a musical reception." Rehearsals were held for that very special instrumental work now called the *Siegfried Idyll*. The first tryout, on March 16, was unhappy: "a horrible orchestra," noted Cosima. But she still took delight in the work and its memories.

The next day, Wagner went to the rooms of a local military band to rehearse the other two selections, both of them for just that kind of ensemble: Wagner's *Huldigungsmarsch* of 1864, and his *Kaisermarsch* of 1871. This time the rehearsal went very well: the music, and especially Wagner's conducting, made a great impression, while he himself was in merry spirits. When the guests came to the villa on the appointed day (March 18), the marches went well enough, but the *Idyll* was again badly played. To be sure, the performance may have been affected by the fact that, during the pause before it, Wagner had a "chest spasm," which was a serious cardiac seizure, one he did his best to disguise. When the guests left, Richard and Cosima wondered why they had undertaken such a rash venture. They were now more than ready to leave the Villa Gangi, which Wagner could no longer tolerate.[24]

In the wee hours of March 20, the family was seen off by their friends at the railroad station. With a stop at Catania, which did not impress Wagner, they proceeded to Acireale, where they were pleased by their lodging at the Hôtel des Bains and relaxed for a few days. Count Gravina arrived on March 23, and made a favorable personal impression as the Wagners got to know him. At Cosima's urging, on March 27, Wagner began taking notes for an essay, "On the Male and Female in Culture and Art."[25] Later that day, in the evening, the Wagner family and Gravina witnessed the elaborate display of respect accorded the aged and dying Garibaldi as he made a passage by train from Catania to Messina, a spectacle that all found deeply moving. The following day Wagner had a heart attack, his most serious to date, but not so grave that he did not recover quickly. Nevertheless, Cosima was greatly alarmed.

After a few days of rest, on April 1, they went by train to Catania where they were squired about and entertained by the Marchese di San Giuliano, who delighted Wagner by quoting a passage from *Tannhäuser*. A train ride to Giarre and Riposto the next day gave the Wagners their first clear view of Mount Etna. This experience was so satisfying that, on the following day (April 3), they made an excursion to Taormina where they were mightily impressed by the view. Cosima mentions cryptically that "R. is particularly delighted by the columns," but nothing otherwise is said about the famous Greco-Roman theater there. She does note that Richard, seeing a tiny island at the Taormina shore, expressed the wish that he had such a place where he could escape into isolation. And, at the end of the visit, Wagner took his son into the nearby public gardens, lecturing Siegfried on how unusually fortunate a boy he was, and what obligations this involved.

The issue of Blandine's marriage was meanwhile causing considerable tension, though no longer over the prospective bridegroom. Indeed, Count Gravina's father, Prince Ramacca, in the company of the Marchese di San Giuliano, called on April 8, and all was cordiality. Blandine's own feelings were well certified by now. But, as her actual father, Hans von Bülow was required to give his consent. His stubborn refusal to make a clear answer disturbed Cosima and made the irritable Richard explode in fury (April 7). Only the diplomatic instincts of the elder daughter, Daniela, eventually smoothed the way toward resolution. But all this was played out as the Wagners considered their next movements. They were already planning their "homeward journey" on April 5, but they did not leave Acireale until April 10, after a stay of twenty-one days. They moved on by train to Messina where, expecting to spend two days, they had to extend it to three. They had been "bumped" from the steamship cabin they were counting on for April 12, by no less than the former khedive of Egypt, so they had to make a new booking for the following day. In the interval, there were a few churches to visit. They sailed overnight to Naples, arriving on April 14. There, Count Gravina, who had accompanied them this far, took his departure, while Dr. Schrön was again on hand to greet them. They had time only for a quick carriage ride through town to the railroad station, where they took the overnight train to their final destination on this sojourn.

By the later years of his life, Wagner had become quite addicted to travel, and from 1880 onward, as we have seen, his range of possibilities only seemed to widen, and odd destinations once considered often lingered in his thinking. Thus, while in Palermo, Wagner spoke again of travel "through Spain, up the Nile, etc." on December 4, 1881. Two days later, he was again thinking "of a journey up the Nile." And on January 17, 1882, when "R. thinks of Spain," Cosima wrote to a prominent Wagner supporter in Barcelona "in order to be prepared for possible travel plans." But such ideas remained remote speculation, yielding to more immediate projects. On January 9, amid disillusionment with Palermo, the couple "think again of Venice." On January 25, they were already discussing reports of Venice as part of planning their next moves. Two days later, Cosima wrote "to Venice about the palazzo there recommended to us." Then, on March 5, Cosima reported that their "great hopes with regard to a furnished palazzo in Venice" were "now dashed."[26] These negotiations were, apparently, part of a longer-range projection, since hotel reservations had been made for immediate purposes, apparently at the Albergo Europa. After an overnight passage northward by train, the Wagner family arrived in the Lagoon City on April 15.

During the two weeks of this latest stay (Richard's fifth, his third with Cosima), the couple revisited favorite sites, and added some new ones. In their predictable stop at the Accademia degli Belle Arti, they devoted particular attention to that favorite painting, Titian's *Assumption*, for which Wagner could point up intensified meanings it now had for the two of them.[27] During this visit, too, Wagner made his first contacts with an organization that would later draw him into something of Venice's musical life: the municipal band, which played concerts in Piazza San Marco. Cosima takes notice only of a Friday concert they gave on April 21, reporting only that Wagner got the band to play for him Rossini's Overture to his opera *La gazza ladra* and was greatly pleased. There was actually much more to this encounter than just that, as will be seen in future chapters.[28]

On the other hand, an unpleasant ending to an old relationship was played out on April 29, their last day in Venice. Wagner had chanced to discover the address in Venice of his old friend Karl Ritter, with whom he had made his first visit to Venice and who now resided there. For whatever reasons, an estrangement had developed between them, and had become quite bitter. When Wagner went around to see him, he was denied entry, even though he was certain that Ritter was home at the time. The slight deeply upset him, and left a sad memory Wagner would recall later that year (September 21) when he and Cosima were back in Venice again.

Whatever their genuine pleasure in Venice, it was clear that they were there for a purpose: arranging for a subsequent, longer stay in Venice. That stay would, in fact, serve as the Wagners' vacation following the premiere of *Parsifal.* Two days after arrival, on April 17, Cosima was out palazzo hunting, without success. On the eighteenth, she and Richard both went to inspect two specific ones, the Palazzi Morosini and Loredan. On April 21, they were back at the Palazzo Loredan: presumably that known as "degli Ambasciatori," on the Grand Canal, by then an elaborate hotel. The next day Cosima was negotiating with its agent. The negotiations apparently broke down, and on their way out of town, on April 29, they turned their attention to the possibilities of the mezzanine apartments in the Palazzo Vendramin-Calergi. A new round of negotiations was undertaken thereafter in their absence from the city. Some complications were resolved by the following August 7, thanks to Count Gravina's direct intervention at Cosima's behest; the contract was formally signed on August 19.

On April 29, 1882, meanwhile, the departing Wagners were once again, as in October 1880, accompanied to the railroad station by a gondola flotilla of singers ("a sight which draws people onto all the bridges"). An overnight passage brought them to Munich and, after one night's stay there, they went on to Bayreuth on May 1. There they were soon joined by Count Gobineau, in his latest stay as a guest at Wahnfried. On May 22, with Humperdinck leading a choir in some music from *Parsifal,* the family celebrated what would be Wagner's last birthday anniversary, his sixty-ninth. These months, meanwhile, were devoted mainly to two projects. The more important of them was, of course, the premiere of *Parsifal,* which occurred on July 26, 1882. The work was repeated as part of the second full Bayreuth Festival, and the toil involved was again a great strain on Wagner. At one point, early in August, he had a severe but fleeting heart seizure while talking with the bass Emil Scaria (the Gurnemanz). Wagner pulled himself together as best he could and, in a highly personal gesture at the sixteenth and final performance, on August 29, he took the baton from Hermann Levi and conducted the end of Act III.

The other project was the wedding of Count Gravina and Blandine, performed first in civil ceremony on August 25, the anniversary of the Wagners' own marriage, and then in full church ceremony the following day. Her father, Hans von Bülow, had chosen to be present neither for the wedding nor for the opera premiere; in fact, he himself was married, for his second time, on July 19, three days after the premiere. Weary after all that these events had taken of their energies, Richard and Cosima were ready for recuperation in Venice. On September 14, 1882, they left Bayreuth—to which Wagner would return only in his coffin. Taking a train, they spent that night in Nuremberg, and the next day they were in Munich, to transfer for their final passage, overnight. The next day, September 16, they arrived in Venice.

That was to be, apparently, the one and only intended destination of this journey. That he would die there would make the triumph of Venice as Wagner's city of choice outside Germany, the "second Wagnerian city," decisive and definitive.

Chapter Three

From Residence to Mortality

The inevitable power of hindsight has made Wagner's last residence in Venice inseparable from his death. But when he went to Venice in the autumn of 1882 he clearly had no expectation or intention that he should die there. He was certainly in terrible health, something both he and Cosima knew well, even without understanding fully how bad it really was. It is also true that, on April 20, 1882, during their previous visit there, Cosima reported having made the observation (probably somewhat in jest) that *she* would like to die in Venice—to which young Siegfried responded that he would prefer to die back home in Bayreuth, which one day he would do. And it is further true that Wagner had, in his very first visit (in 1858), entertained some morbid thoughts about Venice. There was that same sense of decay and mortality in the Venetian ambience that others often perceived in it, complete with the special identification of the gondola's black color and canopy with funeral trappings. But he had quickly overcome that reaction and no longer associated Venice with mortality.

Despite his ill health and often cranky moods, Wagner did not see his career at an end. On the contrary, his last sojourn in Venice was filled with recurrent talk of future plans and activities. Again prompted by hindsight, commentators have often seen *Parsifal* as the logical crown and completion of his life's work, leaving him with nothing more to add. To be sure, there was no further creative project of major scale that he had set himself to fulfill. It had been his life's habit to draft his opera librettos over a long period of time, in advance of composing the music, and to have one or more such libretti in the desk drawer while he was composing music for a predecessor. Over the years, various operatic ideas had crossed his mind. As early as 1856 he had sketched a scenario for a "Buddhist" opera to be called *Die Sieger* (The Victors), but that never seemed to have been developed, and he had no explicit libretto drafted and waiting to be set beyond *Parsifal.*

For some years, in fact, Wagner had begun to think about a new direction for himself, beyond composing operas. Cosima begins notice of his indications of this in 1878, while Richard was well at work on *Parsifal:* ". . . we resolve to spend three months each year, from January to the middle of April, in Florence: 'I shall then write a symphony a year' "(April 5). Later that year (September 22): "He complains with indescribable humor that now, when he has to compose Kundry, nothing comes into his head but cheerful themes for symphonies . . . He says he will call his symphonies 'symphonic dialogues,' for he would not compose four movements in the old style; but theme and countertheme one must have, and allow these to speak to each other." (Whereupon he disparages the symphonic writing of Brahms.) On October 18, Cosima quotes Richard again as vowing to bypass the four-movement form. On February 4, 1879, he was back at this talk: "People will be amazed when I publish my symphonies, to see how simple they are, though they have already had examples of that in the marches and the *Idyll*." Later that year (March 31), he again professed, "I still want to write symphonies," and he repeated such assertions in subsequent months (May 29, June 12). The following year (August 14), he returned to this idea yet again: "I still want to complete *Parsifal*, then symphonies, then I will complete various bits of my work." On November 17, 1881, while they were in Palermo, Cosima notes his return to warning of the perils of symphonic finales and vowing, "I shall take good care to write only single-movement symphonies."

How much of this talk had been mere frivolity all along is difficult to decide. But since the recovery in 1877 of his youthful Symphony in C Major, Wagner had been reviewing it, even playing over parts of it in home music-making. It must have stimulated his thoughts of returning to this form whose finish he had considered accomplished by Beethoven. What he appeared now to contemplate was no longer the classical four-movement symphony at all, but the new idiom of the "symphonic poem" that was largely the creation of his friend and father-in-law, Franz Liszt. Indeed, Cosima reports that on December 17, 1882, while her father was staying with them at the Vendramin, Richard spoke in terms of a moderate "progressivism." After a discussion of Beethoven's *Eroica* Symphony, he said to Liszt:

> If we write more symphonies, Franz, then let us stop contrasting one theme with another, a method Beethoven has exhausted. We should just spin out a melodic line until it can be spun no farther; but on no account drama.

Just how much of this talk was still casual chatter is unclear, but the idea persisted. Cosima reported on January 10, 1883:

> He then tells me he has a number of themes and would like to write a symphony, but how will he find the tranquillity for it? (A few evenings ago, while in bed, he sang to me the theme of a "vigorous and warlike funeral march.")

Three days later she would note (January 13):

> And then later, when he is in his room, I hear him playing softly on the piano, the hovering forms draw close again; yesterday he said that his symphonies would be a melody spun out in a single movement, and today he frequently plays a melody of his own which has come into his mind, in the manner of an English folk song.

And, the following day (January 14):

> R. sits down at the piano and improvises lovely melodies which, as he tells us, are always piling up inside him. I tell him the fact that these blossoms are now sprouting within him is the reward for his collected outlook! "This is how we shall be," he says after playing. "Yes, this is how we shall sound," I reply to him.

A mere three days before his death he was rifling through old thematic scraps and notes, avowing he would never use them (February 10):

> In the gondola he tells me that he will still do his article about masculine and feminine, then write symphonies, but nothing more on the literary side, though he still intends to finish the biography.

What all this talk of symphonies really meant is difficult to determine. It is undeniably fascinating—if not a little frightening—to speculate on what Richard Wagner might have produced as a reborn symphonic composer. Even if such talk represented only passing fancies, it is clear that his capacity for inspiration and new musical ideas was hardly exhausted. And there was the other dimension to his projection of the future: his repeated assertions of his hope to revive his operas himself and perform the entire sequence of them at Bayreuth. He even linked his own future with dynastic vision, as Cosima documented on November 16:

> As we were leaving Saint Mark's today, R. said he would like to stage all his works in Bayreuth, then bring Siegfried to the point where he could assume control; that would mean living another 10 years, "for at the age of 23 a man already shows what he has in him."

As to his own longevity Wagner was a poor prophet, even if he was correct in envisioning his son's eventual fate. (But could he have predicted that Cosima would see to it that Siegfried would not take over control of the Bayreuth Festival until he was thirty-nine? Could he have anticipated that Cosima herself would in fact become his successor in running the festival?)

The point should be clear, however. Wagner in no way had any premonition or expectation of his own death during that last sojourn in the Lagoon City.[1]

Lasting five months, that final sojourn in Venice was his longest there with Cosima, exceeded in length only by the eight months of his own very first one (1858–59). For documentation of that first one, and on its brief successor (1861), we have Wagner's own words—often of a distinctly purplish hue and pseudo-poetical tone—as our guiding account. For all the subsequent sojourns, Wagner's journals, letters, and autobiography are replaced by the diaries of Cosima, with their meticulous chronicling—often sentimentalized, but systematically detailed and ever more voluminous. For this 1882–83 sojourn, however, valuable information can be added from little-used contemporary sources: one small book published quickly in 1883 by the opportunistic German writer Henriette Perl, the other published shortly after by an Italian Wagnerite, Giuseppe Norlenghi. (Those two books will be scrutinized in detail in separate chapters below, so as to examine their distinct perspectives and information.)[2] To those must be added the reports in the local Venetian newspapers. Some of the information in such local sources must naturally be incorporated into our account in this chapter. (They, too, have their own particular viewpoints, suggesting how Venice observed its remarkable guest; accordingly, they will also receive separate treatment, in chapter 5.) In this and the next chapter we will trace the Wagners' final visit to Venice through their own experience of it.

The Wagner family arrived in Venice on September 16, settling initially at the Albergo Europa. They moved two days latter into the Palazzo Vendramin-Calergi, at San Marcuola on the upper Grand Canal. This building ranks high among Venice's great Renaissance palaces. Its main bloc, facing the Canal through its magnificent facade, was built in the first decade of the sixteenth century, as designed for the Loredan family by the great architect Mauro Coducci and completed by the Lombardo family. (On its facade is carved a Loredan family motto of pretentious humility, the opening words of Psalm 113B [115], *Non nobis, non nobis Domine*, presupposing the further words, *sed nomini tuo da gloriam*: "Not unto us, not unto us, O Lord, but unto thy name give glory.") In 1581 it began its transfers through a series of owners, among them the wealthy Cretan-Greek family of the Calergi, under whom, in the early seventeenth century, an additional wing was designed and built by Vincenzo Scamozzi, to the right of the main bloc and set back from the Canal, behind a garden. That addition was demolished in 1658 but was then rebuilt later in the seventeenth century in its present form. In the eighteenth century the palazzo belonged to members of the Vendramin family. In 1845 it had been purchased by the Duchesse de Berry, widow to a pretender to the French throne, and then belonged to her sons, the Comte de Chambord and the Duca della Grazia, who renewed its collection of rich furnishings and added lots of Bourbon lilies to the decoration. In the twentieth century the palazzo was bounced among several new owners, but after World War II it was purchased by the municipality of Venice and, following restoration, it was opened in 1959 as Venice's winter gambling casino.[3]

By the 1880s, the newer wing of the palazzo had been made into apartments, and among other tenants at the time were a Count Bardi (related to another pretender to the French throne) and his wife, Adelgunde de Braganza. For a year's fee of 6,000 francs, the Wagners had leased an ample suite of fifteen ornately decorated rooms on the mezzanine floor. These included a large drawing room, plus an adjacent study for Wagner (which after a while he turned into an elaborate "blue grotto"), with windows overlooking the canal across the garden, while Cosima had a salon of her own that adjoined rooms for the children, bedrooms, and guestrooms. Into these facilities, on the afternoon of September 18,

Wagner and Cosima moved with the three girls (Daniela, Isolde, Eva) and Siegfried. Accompanying them was a large retinue. There was the pianist Rubinstein. One Sg.ra Corsara or Cordani, a Neapolitan (or Genoese?) holdover from the Palermo stay, was governess for the two younger Wagner girls. Heinrich von Stein (1857–87), a young philosophy student and writer, had been for some time now young Siegfried's tutor and a household regular. Two longtime servants from Bayreuth were the valet Georg Lang and the chambermaid Betty Bürkel, augmented by a cook and at least one other servant. The building itself had a porter, Pietro Falcieri (whom Wagner nicknamed "Garibaldi"). Specially engaged also were two gondoliers: the lesser one was named Antonio and the senior one was Luigi Trevisan, nicknamed Ganasseta. The staff was intended to serve not only the Wagner family itself but their frequent guests.

The weather had been stormy at the time of their arrival: two of the railroad bridges they crossed in the Veneto collapsed shortly after their passage, and there were terrible floods out in the rural areas. Wagner was apprehensive at first. He was constantly afflicted by dreams, often symbolic or frightening— which he regularly reported for Cosima's recording. He was worried about his health, especially his ever-more-recurrent heart spasms. At times, he would take refuge in doses of opium. After their first night in the palazzo, he even wondered if, failing to find peace in Venice, he should just return to Bayreuth. Further, he feared entrapment between King Ludwig and Giovannina Lucca over rights to *Parsifal*—the correspondence with Lucca was prolonged for weeks, to his annoyance. Richard and Cosima took gondola rides to the Piazzetta or strolled about the Rialto, but sometimes found it stressful to walk—long such a beloved recreation for him. When the whole family used a rare day of good weather (September 27) for a visit by vaporetto to the Lido beaches it was marred by a tragic case of a drowning accident there. But the old delight in Venice quickly returned to him. With no major artistic project before him, he turned more than ever to reading, and to his old penchant for writing essays. His genial report on the *Parsifal* production, which he wrote between October 22 and November 4, was published at the end of the year in the *Bayreuther Blätter* back at home. It contained some of his last printed reflections on the nature of lyric theater.

Along the way, he and Cosima revisited beloved monuments and works of art, he renewed his fondness for the Lavena café on the north side of the Piazza San Marco (and, alternatively, Florian's on the other side), and he patronized the Müntzer bookshop. At some point they renewed contact with their old friend, the pianist and teacher Angelo Tessarin. Cosima gives only two brief references to meetings with him, on November 1 and 5; later on (November 12), Wagner was irritated when Tessarin wrote asking for a monetary loan. The couple enjoyed watching a comet in the night skies at the end of October. After some postponements because of weather, on October 19 they made an excursion to the nearby island of Torcello, where his feeling of strain was capped by the latest heart spasm. Another such seizure had a disruptive effect on an event Cosima seems not to have appreciated: on November 5, she says, he was in his gondola with the girls on his way to the Piazza and when they "had heard strains of *Lohengrin*, he then tried to hurry, and that brought on the trouble!" He withdrew to Lavena to recover, and then invited Tessarin and the bandmaster to the Palazzo that evening to discuss the subject—for him ever important—of correct tempos.[4]

Meanwhile, comings and goings affected the household. Around October 6, Count Gravina and Blandine arrived in Venice for a stay on their own, which lasted to October 30. They joined the family in strolls and excursions—to Wagner's great pleasure, since he had become quite fond of "Biagino." Another visitor, meanwhile (October 14), was Dr. Heinrich Thode, a German art historian who was to marry Daniela three years later. On October 15, to Wagner's sorrow, the greatly esteemed tutor Stein left the family, having already been replaced by Ernst Hausburg, a Bayreuth copyist and coach who was to serve Siegfried until Carl Glasenapp (Wagner's eventual biographer) could take over the job. Wagner did not get along so well with Hausburg. Strains may have developed, too, with Rubinstein, who left on October 22. Three days later came news of an arrival that was not to happen: the sad death, twelve days before, of their dear friend Count Gobineau in Turin, on his way to join them in Venice. This was a devastating blow to Wagner, who brooded about it all day and ruefully observed at one point: "When one has at last encountered something, it slips like water through one's fingers." Gobineau's death continued to haunt him, and his thoughts even turned to Nietzsche.

Amid these arrivals, there was a different but special one: on November 7, Cosima reported the arrival of a proper grand piano for use at the Vendramin, one of Ibach manufacture. ("[It] pleases R. with its gentle tone, he writes to Herr I. that from now on he will write only soft music.") This was a timely step, for a little over a week later, on November 19, arrived the most important guest. This was Cosima's father, Franz Liszt, who had to be settled into the palazzo. There had been a bit of a muddle over where to lodge him: on November 15, there had been panic over a report that the Comte de Chambord, one of the family owners of the palazzo, might come to take up residence there, to the great disruption of arrangements. The Comte did not come, but instead came a kinsman, the Count Bardi, with his wife, Adelgunde de Braganza, and other relatives, who all filled the Palazzo wing to capacity. This required the Wagners to fit Liszt into their own apartments and share some of their space with him.[5]

With less than two year's difference in their ages, Wagner and Liszt were old friends who had shared so many ideas and perspectives, and had fought in so many causes together—Liszt, indeed, having been an early and generous champion of Wagner's works. But their personalities often grated on each other, and Wagner could not overcome a certain jealousy. The original jolt of Wagner's taking Liszt's daughter as paramour and then wife had been smoothed over, but frictions remained. Wagner had always had condescending opinions about many of Liszt's own compositions. Above all, he felt that when Cosima was with her father he (Wagner) was left out, and he resented what he considered the loss of her unvarnished attention to him—situations to which Cosima returns repeatedly in her diaries.

Nevertheless, Wagner recurrently urged Liszt to join the Wagner household and was often enraged when Liszt declined to do so. Now at the Vendramin, Liszt quickly recognized the isolation to which Wagner was committed: he tried to adjust to it, in denial of his own gregarious nature. So different were their personalities that their conversations were often at cross-purposes, and irritations were frequent, as when they could not even agree on how to spend an evening *en famille* together. Liszt found great pleasure in building a relationship with young Siegfried. But Liszt's restlessness was also shared by Daniela, with whom he had become particularly close, while she herself also chafed in Wagner's regime of seclusion. Wagner was furious at their efforts to have some social life of their own. Despite much disapproval, he at least arranged for Daniela to remove from the Vendramin and stay with Princess Marie Hatzfeldt-Trachtenberg, a close friend of Cosima's who resided at the Palazzo Malipiero.

Wagner had come to disapprove of Liszt's style of piano playing, and now he encountered the latter's astounding, quite advanced, and forward-looking late compositional style. Perhaps the prime case in point was that startling mood-picture *La lugubre gondola*, inspired by Liszt's viewing a characteristic Venetian funeral procession by gondola. (It was at first composed for violin and piano and then passed through two transformations as a piece for piano only.) Its morbid implications were to acquire prophetic application to Wagner himself, at least in retrospect—though some commentators have seen it as Liszt's clear premonition of Wagner's death and funeral procession. Prompted by such music, on November 28, Wagner expressed his concern to Cosima:

> —Late in the evening, when we are alone, R. talks about my father's latest compositions, which he finds completely meaningless, and he expresses his opinion sharply and in much detail. I ask him to talk to my father about them in the hope of preventing his going astray, but I do not think R. will do this. I go to bed with painful feelings, and I cannot stop thinking of the letter R. might perhaps write to my father—I compose it in my mind.

The next day (November 29), Wagner revived the subject:

> Today he [Richard] begins to talk about my father again, very blunt in his truthfulness; he describes his new works as "budding insanity" and finds it impossible to develop a taste for their dissonances ... [a passage obliterated]. ... He keeps talking about it to me, while I remain silent, sorry that there is nothing I can say in reply! . . .

At this very time of mounting tension over Liszt, Cosima was depressed to hear (through her father) the news that Hans von Bülow was seriously ill. The concatenation of emotions brought into play Wagner's mounting readiness to fall into rages. On the next morning (November 30), Richard and Cosima found themselves in a disagreement over Liszt's health and whether or not he was following doctor's instructions. Wagner lashed out at her for contradicting him. When she pleaded that she always tried to avoid opposing him he furiously denounced her pretense of virtue. Cosima reports her own willingness to accept reproach; she then relates that, when Richard later expressed regrets over what he had said, in their usual makeup kisses, for the first time, his lacked any warmth.

Fed by his constantly precarious health and his natural testiness, Wagner continued to have violent mood swings: he still found genuine delight in some things, but he could be sent into unexpected rages. Cosima noted on December 3: "Each time I visit him he is feeling either contentment or extreme irritation, the latter provoking him into expressions of a hatred for life."

On December 6, the newest arrivals were Adolf von Gross and his wife. Gross, a Bayreuth banker, had become one of the important administrators of Wagner's festival operation. He was at the moment a go-between for Wagner and King Ludwig in the prolonged negotiations over performance rights to *Parsifal* that endlessly vexed him. Above all, Richard and Cosima considered them good friends and enjoyed their company for the few days they stayed in Venice. Another welcome arrival was Joukowsky, who came on December 8, and was welcomed effusively.

Two days later, however, there was a significant local visitor: Count Giuseppe Contin de Castelseprio, president of the local Società Benedetto Marcello, which he had founded in 1877 as a Liceo or conservatory to further the study of music both past and present, under the name of one of Venice's most illustrious eighteenth-century composers. Wagner gave him one of his usual pedagogical lectures on tempo, but something more was brewing, as suggested by Wagner's visit to the count at the conservatory the next day (December 12). Two days after that, Wagner was angry at Liszt for being late to lunch, since the two were to go together that afternoon to the conservatory. When they were there, Wagner had more of his heart spasms, but Cosima was puzzled when Wagner said he would be returning to the Liceo on the morrow "since they have no conductor." Then it came out: Wagner was preparing another of his birthday/Christmas surprises for Cosima, a private performance of his youthful Symphony in C Major.

A student work, this had been composed when Wagner was nineteen, heavily under Beethoven's spell. Wagner himself humorously suggested (December 17) it could be placed between that composer's second and third symphonies. It had been privately performed twice in 1832, then publicly in Leipzig in 1833, and buried thereafter. Surviving only in parts that had been stored away, it was discovered in 1877 when a trunk Wagner had abandoned in Dresden was returned to him. Anton Seidl, then Wagner's assistant, had reconstructed the score (which would not be published until 1911), and Wagner had occasionally looked it over as a curiosity. He had already treated Cosima to other examples of his juvenalia: on Christmas day 1881 in Palermo, along with the almost-finished score of *Parsifal*, Wagner had given her the score of his C-major Overture titled *Polonia*, composed in 1836, lost, and returned to him in 1869. He thought of offering her the symphony in early December and, already on the tenth, he had written to Luigi Mancinelli to ask if the latter could organize in Bologna an orchestra of forty players and come with them to Venice for four days (December 23–26), to rehearse the work on the twenty-fourth and then perform it on the twenty-fifth. Mancinelli replied quickly that he and his players were already committed to a Christmas schedule in Bologna, but he suggested that Wagner turn to the Liceo Benedetto Marcello, and this Wagner had done, engaging an ensemble to be led by the distinguished violinist and teacher Raffaele Frontali. So now, for her, the full four-movement symphony would receive its first performance in fifty years.

There must have been some initial trials at the session of the fourteenth; that evening he spoke of rehearsal troubles and missing parts. Wagner decided that he needed the help of Seidl (who had reconstructed the score in the first place), but the young conductor was then busy touring with Angelo Neumann's company, so Wagner had summoned Humperdinck to assist. The first full rehearsal was the next day (December 15) and went well, to the mutual satisfaction of Wagner and the players. Another rehearsal on the sixteenth left Wagner even more excited: "he recalls the performance 50 years ago, after only one rehearsal, and says the present one will be much better." Wagner had taken the children to the rehearsal but Cosima herself was barred from attending these preparations, to her frustration. Still, the next day it was noticed how much good it did to Wagner's spirits that he was "back in his *métier*" of conducting. Nevertheless, that same day Wagner felt obliged to make profuse apologies to Liszt for some humiliating remarks he had made to him.

Exactly how emotionally combustible the atmosphere remained was pointed up in successive explosions on the eighteenth. That morning Humperdinck arrived and, as they were discussing some aspects of the symphony, Joukowsky unexpectedly entered the room to greet the new arrival. Enraged by the interruption, Wagner abruptly ordered Joukowsky out of the house. Realizing he had gone too far, Wagner quickly went to the artist's lodgings and knelt down on the floor to beg his forgiveness. The third rehearsal that afternoon went badly, and Wagner was further annoyed when some people attending left early, to dine with Liszt and Daniela. Wagner returned to the palazzo convinced the rehearsal was ruined. Then, when Liszt and Daniela were late in returning from their evening out, Wagner, feeling his authority over his stepdaughter had been totally compromised, viciously told her terrible news he had withheld from her until then: that Hans von Bülow had suffered a breakdown and had been taken to a mental institution. Already distracted by the illness of their daughter Eva, and now shocked by the situation of her ex-husband, Cosima was at her wits' end. The quarrel was not resolved that night. Two days later Cosima recalled hearing Wagner shouting from his bed: "I hate all pianists—they are my Antichrist!" perhaps with reference to Bülow, or perhaps to Liszt.

The next morning (December 19), the household remained in turmoil, but Wagner took the children again to the fourth rehearsal, which satisfied him. Before supper he made conciliatory gestures to Cosima but was rebuffed. Richard then fretted through the evening, and a passing remark from Cosima sparked new anger. They managed some mutual apologies after that, Richard claiming that the rehearsals had been exhausting for him; though Cosima remained in despair over what she had been put through. During the next day (December 20), however, Cosima was relieved by a better report of Bülow's condition: it was, after all, merely a concussion from a fall. Cordiality was restored. The fifth rehearsal that afternoon began badly, Cosima was told: Wagner was angry over the absence of two players, and only after addressing them in French did he restore quality to their work. The players were enthusiastic about him, she was told, understanding what he wanted and repeating his witticisms. He was, again, "very happy in his *métier*," professing irritation only at outsiders. Of these, he sneeringly singled out the Milan critic Filippo Filippi, whose Wagnerism he thought mere pretension, reacting accordingly.[6] But Wagner was taking pleasure in this early music of his—finding that in it, however much it was based on Mozart and Beethoven, "nothing is directly copied."

Conditions were calmer on the twenty-first, marked only by more sniping by Wagner at Liszt, who drew much of the ménage off to socializing elsewhere in the evening. On the twenty-second, however, Eva's health was better and Cosima now had the first chance allowed her to attend the final rehearsal, in the Sala Apollonea at the Fenice. In the course of the reading, Wagner had a heart spasm but, after conducting the first movement, he took a pause before leading the rest. Wrote Cosima:

> I sit in concealment far away from him and am touched to think that 50 years ago he performed this work for his mother, now for me. Then I take delight in the straightforward, courageous work, and I tell R., "That was written by someone who knew no fear."

The mood was fairly mellow on the twenty-third, and then excitement rose for the carefully planned event the next day, the actual concert itself, scheduled not for Christmas Day but for Christmas Eve. Selected guests and members of the press (such as Filippi) had been allowed at the rehearsals, but the official performance was before a rigorously restricted audience: Liszt and the children (lacking Blandine and Gravina, who were in Sicily); Humperdinck, Joukowsky, Hausburg, and the girls' governess; and Count Contin. Cosima's own account of the evening is a memorable document:

Toward 6 o'clock the tree is lit in the *sala*, and there is a very merry presentation of gifts in which our Italian servants join with great delight. My father, too, whom we imagined to be quite above such things, is with us heart and soul.[7] Around 7:30 we set off in three gondolas, with the moon shining and bells chiming, for La Fenice. Eva is allowed to come with us! The hall [the Sala di Ridotto or foyer, not the theater itself] festively lit; my father, the children, and I go in first, a friendly reception [from the invited guests]. Somewhat later R., received with cheers. The two first movements are played fairly quickly in succession, then there is a pause; R. comes to me and my father, talks to me very gaily. I send thanks to the orchestra players, which earns me an "*evviva*." At the end the players come to join us, and my health is toasted. Then R. murmurs in my father's ear, "Do you love your daughter?" My father looks startled. "Then sit down at the piano and play." My father does so at once, to everybody's cheering delight. Then in French R. relates the history of his symphony. Toward 11 o'clock we ride home, Venice transfigured in a blue light. The children enchanted with the evening, R. very content!

Italian sources add details that Cosima and other conventional accounts do not include. According to one journalist attending, at the end of the performance Wagner laid down the baton and sadly exclaimed, "I will never conduct again!" We are told that what Liszt played was *una sua nuova composizione*, but it is further reported that Wagner himself sat down at the piano and accompanied himself singing "Buona serra, miei signori!" from Rossini's *Il barbiere di Siviglia*! Finally, it was noted that, before he left the theater, Wagner donated his baton and music stand to the Liceo Benedetto Marcello—where these objects were preserved faithfully in glass thereafter.[8]

The family returned to the Palazzo Vendramin in a moonlit gondola ride. Before going to bed, Cosima reports, "R. badly wanted to read the [*Siegfried*] *Idyll*, but he gets tired all the same," finally retiring only "after admiring the most glorious of nights." Christmas Day itself was quiet and harmonious, but over the next two days Wagner was frustrated by the failure of his maneuvering on behalf of Humperdinck. In addition to using his help with the Fenice concert, Wagner had been trying to secure an appointment to the directorship of the Liceo Benedetto Marcello for his young protégé. Unfortunately, at least as Cosima tells it, this plan to put a German into such a post was forestalled by chauvinistic passions inflamed at the moment by the Oberdank affair.[9] Wagner was given formal notification of the appointment's failure by Count Contin on December 27. Wagner now felt guilty for having brought Humperdinck to Venice on ultimately false pretenses, and was particularly embarrassed to encounter him in the Piazza San Marco on a stroll there on December 30. But not all was gloom and tension. By December 28, Cosima reports, Wagner had begun writing an essay that capitalized on the raised spirits of the Fenice performance: a reflection on revisiting his youthful symphony, published as "Bericht über die Wiederaufführung eines Jugendwerkes," finished soon after and published immediately in the *Musikalischen Wochenblattes* of Leipzig in a New Year's issue dated to the end of

1882. Working on this "washes away his irritation," Cosima reported, and made him think happily about Venice, and aspects of the past.

By the end of December Wagner was more cranky than ever over the precious work space he had been forced to yield to Liszt when the latter had moved in with them. Troubled by a new heart spasm, the composer submitted to a family celebration on New Year's Day at the Palazzo Malipiero, residence of Cosima's friend, the Princess Hatzfeldt, in which Cosima coached the children through a festive show she had contrived, "The Miracle of the Rose" (*Rosenwunder*), her poetry fitted to music from her father's oratorio, *Die heiligen Elizabeth*, with young Siegfried playing a major role and Humperdinck accompanying—much to Liszt's delight. Though annoyed that not all the family (Liszt among them) would come along, Wagner and Cosima went to the theater to see Goldoni's *Le baruffe chiozzotte*, which they thoroughly enjoyed. The next day, Humperdinck took his departure from Venice, Wagner bidding him a warm farewell—in what was, in fact, to be their final parting.[10]

Wagner's shifting moods continued in the early days of the new year, with Liszt as the recurrent focus of his ire, in entries Cosima wearily recorded. On January 5 he was annoyed when "a number of society people" were invited to the Vendramin by Liszt to see a painting there. By the next day, he had cobbled his indignation into a literary analogy:

> . . . My father's manners and customs offend him, he says he is just like King Lear, his acquaintances the 100 knights, and his arrangements the Learisms. . . . During the night I hear him say, half-asleep, half-awake, "King Lear, horrible man." . . .

Cosima reported Richard's new anger at Liszt on January 9, framing a curious incident that evening. Sitting at the piano, Liszt played the slow movement from Beethoven's Seventh Symphony and the Scherzo from the Eighth: twice, Wagner came into the room dancing to the music, to general amusement. But, later on, Richard complained to Cosima that her father's tempo for the Seventh's Andante was all wrong, reflecting "a failure to appreciate the character of the piece." When, amid all this discontent, Cosima suggested they just pack up and return to Bayreuth and Wahnfried, "he cannot make up his mind to do so."

Ignored totally (and significantly?) by Cosima is an episode about which we know from the testimony of its subject himself, Luigi Mancinelli. The eminent Italian conductor was invited in early January by the Liceo Marcello to conduct two symphonic concerts in its facilities at the Teatro la Fenice. Desiring to win the composer's support for presenting some Wagner works, Mancinelli was allowed to call upon Wagner at the Vendramin. The conductor wished to present the Prelude to *Die Meistersinger*, and the combination of the Prelude and the finale to *Tristan*. Wagner was quite agreeable and sat down at the piano with Mancinelli to play, four hands, through these pieces, giving special instructions on how to make the connection between the *Tristan* Prelude and *Liebestod*—already a concert combination by then. Apparently, music by Liszt was also planned for the concert, but it is not clear whether Mancinelli also consulted with him.) In gratitude, Mancinelli invited Wagner to attend a concert rehearsal, which the composer is reported to have done, afterward saluting Mancinelli (in French), "You are the Garibaldi of orchestra conductors!" But it would seem that neither Wagner nor Liszt attended the actual concert, and Mancinelli changed his choice of Wagner's music after all.[11]

On the afternoon of January 13, Liszt finally took his leave of the Vendramin and set out for Budapest. There seems to have been little ceremony involved, beyond a reported last embrace on the palazzo's water-landing steps. Feelings were undoubtedly mixed: Wagner himself wondering—with some justice, as well as envy—whether Liszt's talent could have been used to better results. Cosima makes only the flattest reference to their parting, but it must have been a painful one for the two men. Certainly it marked a sad end to a personal relationship that had joined two of the greatest musical giants as well as longtime friends and collaborators. That same day, however, the Wagner family celebrated the birthday of their faithful Joukowsky. The evening before it was noted that the artist was to depart for Russia to attend a centennial celebration in honor of his own father, a distinguished man of letters. The Wagners sadly encouraged him to go, but in fact Joukowsky was to put aside the commitment and to choose, in prophetic loyalty, to remain in Venice with the Wagners.

Through January, meanwhile, despite occasional heart spasms, Wagner was given a series of massage treatments by Dr. Friedrich Keppler, a physician and surgeon based in Venice who had become the family doctor, and who was quite optimistic about the prospects for Richard's health. Wagner's delight in regular promenades through Venice was compromised by his debilitated condition.[12] His moods fluctuated, with episodes of deep disillusionment—over his Bayreuth projects, over Wahnfried, over promoting his operas—further fueled by his vexing negotiations of the moment with King Ludwig over plans for *Parsifal*. Nevertheless, he also had numerous episodes of good humor and even jesting. Above all, he found a new project on which to work—an essay upon whose title ("The Feminine in Human Life" or "The Eternal in the Feminine") he could not quite decide (January 26). And about this time he also wrote an introduction to a work by the former household favorite, Heinrich von Stein, that was about to be published. In the last days of January he was agitated over Angelo Neumann's proposal to bring his touring production of the *Ring* to Venice, which he strongly opposed.

Generally, however, the new month came on quietly. On February 4 the conductor Hermann Levi arrived. (We are told that Wagner impishly hid behind an entrance door intending to surprise him, but Levi entered so quickly that the trick did not come off, much to the composer's frustration.) Wagner and Levi quickly settled into extensive discussions of pending performance plans. But it was not all work for "the conductor" (as Cosima would identify him thereafter). As Levi later told his father:

. . . I went daily to him in the Palazzo Vendramin, arriving at 11 in the morning and leaving at 11 at night, had all meals with them, joined in the gondola outings, and every day we visited a different church. In short, I was intoxicated with sheer joy.

Levi also accompanied the Wagners on the evening of February 6, to join in witnessing the festivities that concluded Carnival. Wagner had had mixed feelings about the rowdy revelries of the masked participants over the days preceding. But he seemed to find a certain fascination in the closing events, as the family assumed a favorite perch in the restaurant called Cappello Nero, upstairs in the Procuratie Vecchie overlooking the crowded Piazza San Marco, where a platform was set up for dancing. Wagner went down to this platform briefly with the children, but his feelings about the whole thing were again rather mixed.[13] Cosima reports:

. . . at around 9 o'clock we set out to the Square for the Shrovetide celebrations. R. does this to please the children, who reward him with their gaiety. The impression is mixed; R. finds something touching about the procession carrying carnival to the grave, with its melody which he thinks to be an old one, but after going to the podium [the dance platform] with the children, he returns to me in the Cappello Nero looking sad. He says poor artisans were hopping around there without really understanding why. But the midnight bells and the extinguishing of the flames produce another fine effect.

Henriette Perl, the memoirist of Wagner in Venice, remembered seeing Wagner moving through the crowd with Daniela on his arm: "his step was elastic, even youthful, his head was held high." The momentary loss of Siegfried in the mob did not trouble him, either. On their return home, Wagner cheerfully greeted the beloved porter awaiting them with the formula, "Amico mio, il carnevale e andato" (My friend, the carnival is ended): the porter's return of the formula in a portentously deep voice was later remembered as virtually an omen.

Sleeping late after the long prior evening, on February 7, in the early afternoon, he and Cosima set out by gondola for the Municipal Cemetery Island of San Michele—supposedly because their gondolier Luigi told them that is where Venetians went on Ash Wednesday. But Wagner had apparently caught a chill or a cold, and the visit was cut short. Infections seemed rife in the household: not only was Wagner intermittently laid low during the next few days, but Levi came down with illness. (While the Jewish maestro was indisposed, the Wagners casually discussed their anti-Semitic tormenting of him, which was later perceived to have aggravated his condition.) For February 10, Wagner had contemplated taking Siegfried on an excursion to Verona or Bologna, but this idea was abandoned, perhaps because of his lingering indisposition. (The following day, after only a brief walk, Wagner was to return with serious heart pains.) February 10 was, however, the actual centennial date of Joukowsky's father's birth and, since the painter had forgone attending the commemoration of it in Russian, the Wagner family put on a celebration of their own for Joukowsky's sake. So warm was the feeling Wagner had for Joukowsky by now that, since five days before, Wagner had been talking about arranging with the landlord for a room to be provided in the Palazzo Vendramin for the artist to use as a studio.

February 12 began with the departure of Levi, still in bad health but obliged (and perhaps happy) to return to his duties in Munich.[14] Wagner seemed full of good cheer. At breakfast he gloated over his barber's compliments on his improving command of Italian—or at least his ability to make bad puns. At lunch, with Joukowsky on hand, Wagner was full of more bumptious humor. In the afternoon he took his daughter Eva out to his favorite café, Lavena on the San Marco Piazza, to treat her to chocolate. At suppertime there was discussion of a letter Liszt had written to a newspaper about "the Jewish problem." That evening, as Wagner read (in Friedrich E. C. de la Lamotte-Fouqué's *Undine*) and intermittently joked, Joukowsky drew two sketches of him—one in profile looking forward (which Cosima herself labeled "R. reading," the other full-face and looking down (labeled "R. playing")—for inclusion in Cosima's notebook.[15] At bedtime, he played thoughtfully over a passage from *Das Rheingold* and spoke loving words to Cosima, who recorded them dutifully (either before going to sleep or the following morning), in what was to be the final entry in her diary.

Tuesday, February 13, 1883, was a day of electrical storms and heavy rain, to almost melodramatic effect. On arising in the morning, Wagner observed casually to his valet, Georg Lang, "Today I must take care of myself." He took breakfast with Cosima, and it was supposedly then that the two engaged in a furious argument that plunged Wagner into emotional turmoil. But this supposition has been almost certainly disproved.[16] We do know that Wagner went on to spend the rest of the morning working on what he had said would be his final essay, now titled "On the Feminine in the Human" (*Über das Weibliche im Menschlichen*).

About 1:45 in the afternoon, arriving according to his regular custom, Joukowsky found a curious scene. Thirteen-year-old Siegfried Wagner had been practicing his piano lessons but his mother took over the keyboard. That Liszt's daughter was a superlative musician in her own right has often been overlooked in her submergence of herself into her husband's life. She sat entranced as she played a keyboard version made by her father of Schubert's song, *Lob der Tränen* (Praise of Tears). Siegfried recalled that it was the first time he had ever heard his mother play the piano. As they waited for Wagner to join them for lunch, Georg appeared to say that the master was not feeling well and that they should eat without him. Wagner apparently requested that a plate of soup be sent up to him so that he could go on working, and he instructed that a gondola should be scheduled for 4 o'clock to make a visit to the house of Alexander Wolkoff (Vassily Alekseevich Volkov), a Russian artist residing in Venice with whom Wagner had socialized.

Cosima went off herself to see him, and returned to say that her husband was suffering from more of his spasms and would best be left alone. So the company sat down for an otherwise agreeable lunch together. Cosima had, however, ordered the chambermaid Betty Bürkel to station herself outside Wagner's door to listen for anything alarming. She heard him moaning from time to time but then, when he began violent ringing of his bell, she rushed in to find him in agony at his writing desk. "My wife and the doctor!" he hoarsely commanded, and Betty rushed to summon Cosima who, in running fiercely to Wagner's room nearly shattered a half-open door on the way. Betty, meanwhile, sent the gondolier Luigi Trevisan (Ganasseta) to fetch Dr. Keppler; and Daniela sent word to cancel the scheduled gondola. Rushing to her husband, Cosima found him contorted in pain, and incoherent. With the help of Georg, she shifted him to a small couch in the adjacent dressing room and held him in her arms, trying to comfort him. (According to one account, the pocket watch Cosima had given him fell onto the carpet and he exclaimed, "Mein Uhr!"—his putative last words.[17])

Cosima tried rubbing his chest, often a relief for his heart pains. He seemed to relax and fall into a sleep, which Cosima thought an improvement. But when Dr. Keppler arrived about 3 o'clock, he saw it was too late, and he confirmed the impression by finding no further pulse. The body was pulled from Cosima's clutches and placed on a bed in an adjoining room (the one Liszt had used). Cosima flung herself upon the corpse, in a vigil she would keep on into the night, for twenty-five hours—her initial impulse apparently being to follow her beloved in death, Isolde-like. Joukowsky and the children were meanwhile waiting nearby, not aware of how serious the situation was, until Georg appeared, followed shortly by the doctor himself, to announce the terrible news.[18]

Not until the next day could Dr. Keppler and Joukowsky persuade Cosima to leave the corpse and lie down in a separate room, where, refusing nourishment, she would receive only her children. On the advice of Joukowsky and the Princess Hatzfeldt, Daniela took charge of immediate responsibilities, arranging to telegraph the news to Count Gravina and Blandine, to Liszt, to King Ludwig, and to Adolf Gross—the indispensable festival and family business manager. Gross and his wife Maria set out for Venice immediately, followed quickly by the conductor and devoted disciple Hans Richter. Matters were still chaotic on the fourteenth. Around 5 o'clock Dr. Keppler initiated the embalming, with the help of a Professor Hofmann of Berlin, and his observations of the body in this process seemed to him to confirming that Wagner's death came by massive heart attack.[19] All the while, Wagner's local friends, the painters Wolkoff and Ludwig Passini, had urged Daniela to have a death mask made by a local sculptor named Benvenuti. Cosima had forbidden this while she guarded the corpse herself, and at first Daniela firmly agreed. But Dr. Keppler finally persuaded Daniela that it should be done, and she stood by while Benvenuti, assisted by Passini, carried out this task (figs. 31–32).

On Thursday the fifteenth, Gross and his wife arrived: kneeling before Cosima, they accepted her charge to them of guardianship for her children. While Frau Gross attempted to comfort the family, her husband took over from

Daniela in managing the chaos, to deal with outside intrusions and to make all necessary arrangements. When the body had been prepared, a family viewing was arranged. With her daughter's help, Cosima had already cut off her long blond hair, which Richard had greatly admired, and now she placed it on the breast of the corpse, dressed in black and trimmings the family knew so well.

Through these days, Venice became a focus of worldwide attention. The death of Wagner, arguably the most famous (or infamous) composer in the world, was international news. Telegraph messages poured out of Venice to report the fact, while local Italian reports appeared instantly. Journalists rushed to Venice and besieged the Palazzo Vendramin. Letters and tributes poured in from all quarters. Shocked when he received the news in Budapest, Liszt wrote to Cosima to ask if he should join her in the passage back to Bayreuth. In consultation with Daniela, it was deemed best that he should wait to visit her in Bayreuth itself weeks hence.[20]

On the morning of Friday the sixteenth an elaborate bronze casket arrived from Vienna, and the body was placed in it. The cover had a little window over the face, which Cosima herself closed and locked. The local officials completed their legal certifications and seals, and the body was now ready for its final journey. King Ludwig had insisted that the corpse be brought back immediately to Germany, without any of the ceremonies or tributes that the city's authorities had hoped to offer. Daniela and Passini had made arrangements with the railroad to secure a special salon car for the transfer, and Gross had managed to get the railroad authorities to close the station to the public during the solemn passage.

Shortly after noon, the family luggage was loaded into a barge, including some furnishings now become mortuary relics, above all the sofa on which Wagner expired (fig. 33). At about 1 o'clock, the casket itself was carried out to the funerary gondola—Wagner's *lugubre gondola* after all!). The eight pallbearers included Hans Richter, Joukowsky, Dr. Keppler, Passini, and another painter friend, Franz Ruben, plus Count Contin and the violinist Frontali; the eighth not specified. In gondolas that followed were Cosima, clad totally in black, attended by Maria Gross and Cosima's son Siegfried; Passini and Daniela; and youngest daughters Eva and Isolde, attended by Joukowsky. The procession then formed for the short distance on the Grand Canal from the Palazzo Vendramin to the railway station, solemn and still under the bright Venetian sun. Cosima had ordered that there be no funerary music at any point, so that, aside from a tolling bell, the procession moved in silence. Disappointed that there was no opportunity for an immediate civic tribute or ceremony, hundreds of Venetians stood in silent homage in gondolas or on the embankments along the way.

At the empty station, the casket was loaded onto the funerary car that had brought the casket from Vienna, and in which the desolate Cosima sat alone in an enclosure of her own. In the separate salon car the family assembled, together with Richter, Joukowsky, and Dr. Keppler. The two cars left Venice after 2 o'clock, hauled by a local express train as far as Vicenza (where Dr. Keppler disembarked). It was then connected to a different locomotive as a train added onto the usual route that proceeded by way of Verona north through Innsbruck. There the retinue was joined by Hermann Levi, only so recently departed from Venice himself. The Italian, Austrian, and German authorities had agreed to exempt the train from any delays or inspections at frontiers. The following afternoon the train reached Munich, where a vast throng of mourners met it. It reached Bayreuth past midnight, the train standing under guard at the station through the night, while Cosima went directly to Wahnfried. Her fingers were so emaciated from her days without food that she nearly lost her wedding rings at the station, but, luckily, they were recovered by Joukowsky. On Sunday afternoon there was a final ceremonial of tribute (including some of Wagner's own music), a procession through the streets, and a burial service at Wahnfried, at the gravesite Wagner had himself prepared in a grove behind the house. Among the pallbearers then were Gross, Joukowsky, Richter, Levi, and Anton Seidl.

Richard Wagner's final return from Venice was now complete.

Chapter Four

Venice in Wagner's Eyes

What Venice came to mean to Richard Wagner is documented in more than the mere chronicle of his residences there. Fortunately, we have abundant testimony in his own words and thoughts. Wagner was, of course, a prolific writer as well as a composer. Though he often complained about the burden of his correspondence, he was an incorrigible writer of letters—one of the most prolific among cultural figures. He has also left us selective diaries, and his massive autobiography, *Mein Leben*, though that does not cover the last two decades of his life. Filling the gap, of course, are the voluminous diaries of his second wife, Cosima Liszt/von Bülow/Wagner.

As noted, despite the range of Wagner's travels during his career, and notwithstanding ideas about vacationing in other countries, the only land in which Wagner traveled for pleasure and relaxation was Italy, with Venice as the ever-increasing focus of that southward direction. In his own writings, it is only Venice among his Italian destinations that prompted extended comment, notably during the emotionally and creatively memorable stay of 1858–59. Even then, to be sure, Wagner's observations are rather generalized, poetic, and abstract, conveying his emotional reactions rather than discoursing on specific sites or treasures, which do not seem to have interested him much at the time. It is only in the latter four Italian sojourns, when Cosima was accompanying him, that we have far more pointed and specific expression of Wagner's reactions, in her relentless, outwardly idolatrous recording of "R.'s" words and thoughts. Out of such material it is not difficult to construct a full picture of how Wagner viewed Italy in general and Venice in particular.

To begin with, we must remember that the Italy Wagner visited over the course of thirty-one years (1852–83) was an Italy in very dramatic transition from fragmentation to unity, as was also the case with his own Germany. In a sense, his contacts with the peninsula spanned the whole process by which Italy became a nation.[1] At the outset, Italy was a "geographic expression" still striving to become an entity in modern terms. In 1852, the only truly "Italian" regime was that of Sardinia-Piedmont in the northwestern corner of the peninsula under the house of Savoy. In 1852, southern Italy and Sicily constituted the realm of the reactionary Italian Bourbon dynasty. The dramatic campaigns of Giuseppe Garibaldi (1807–82) shattered the Bourbon regime in 1860, leading to its union with the Kingdom of Sardinia and the technically premature proclamation of Kingdom of Italy under Victor Emmanuel II of Savoy. In 1852, a swath of central Italy constituted the Papal States under the Roman Catholic pontiff. After a long complex of diplomatic and military interactions between Sardinia-Piedmont's Prime Minister Camillo Cavour and French Emperor Napoleon III, Rome was claimed by the house of Savoy in 1870, to become capital of the unified nation. In 1852, most of northern Italy was controlled by the Austrian Hapsburg government. But, thanks to Cavour's manipulations, that control was effectively shattered in the plebiscite of 1860, which united Emilia-Romagna and Tuscany to Sardinia-Piedmont (with Florence as provisional national capital).

As for Venice, when Wagner first visited it in 1858, it was still (however precariously) an Austrian possession, a fact that worked to Wagner's advantage. Himself an ostentatious revolutionary in 1848, he had been a political exile for ten years, but was acceptable to a government of a kindred nationality but a separate legal system. Despite his 1848 credentials, he seems to have had no interest in the fact that Venice had undergone its own revolutionary upheaval, during the heroic rebellion in 1848–49 under Daniele Manin (1804–57), suppressed by the Austrian Army. (As recorded by Cosima, Wagner made only two references to Manin, one to the monument to him in the Campo named for him: October 18, 1880; the other, a vague allusion to a philosophical idea: November 3, 1880.) In 1866, as a final part of Cavour's program of eroding Hapsburg control, a plebiscite was held by which the population of Venice and the Veneto voted to unite that last portion of northern Italy to the emerging Italian Kingdom.

For Wagner, as for most nineteenth- and twentieth-century visitors, Venice appeared to have ceased development in 1797 when the old Republic was liquidated by Napoleon, leaving the city frozen in its past, without a living present. In his first visit in 1858–59, he was content merely to take note of his own compatibility with the Austrian rulers, as we have seen, while recognizing the chasm that yawned between them and their Italian subjects.[2] He was too preoccupied with his own problems in his brief 1861 visit to pay any attention to the situation of Venice (going to and coming from it by way of Austrian Trieste from and to Vienna). But it was a very different Venice that Wagner visited in subsequent years (1876, 1880, 1882, 1882–83).[3] Austrian rule had ended in 1866, ten years before the first of those sojourns. For all that Wagner noticed, however, such change might as well have never happened.[4]

Wagner's indifference to the life of this city, other than for the ways it affected him directly, was characteristic in general of his sojourns in Italy. At all times, he saw himself as an alien, however much he could accommodate or cultivate some details of local life. He seems genuinely to have liked the Italians as a people, although sometimes he could not resist making jibes at aspects of their alleged degeneration or inadequacies—suggesting a hint of Teutonic racialism in the background. Above all, he had little but contempt for Italy's musical life. From time to time, he might (reluctantly) allow himself to be drawn to some small corner of it, and he could (again reluctantly, or with qualifications) admire a small bit of it here or there, as at Naples. But he resisted any serious involvement in it, only in an exceptional case (in Bologna) connecting with a local performance of his own operas. He left their direct promotion to others—and for Italy that meant the redoubtable Giovannina Lucca. He suspected the capacity of Italian performers to deal with his music. Conductors Mariani, Mancinelli, and then Calascione were possible but scant exceptions. His unhappy experience with the *Idyll* players at Palermo certainly confirmed his suspicions, though he did seem to enjoy working with the augmented Liceo orchestra in Venice for his own last conducting effort. As to Italian audiences, Wagner was flatly opposed to the idea of Angelo Neumann bringing his touring production of the *Ring* to Venice when that possibility was first broached.[5]

During his residences in Venice, Wagner did his best to avoid local opera performances, always preferring the theater to the opera house. As for local music making there, save for the bands performing his music outdoors, and for the songs of gondoliers and laborers,[6] Wagner limited his contacts with Venetian musicians to some individual acquaintances during his 1858–59 stay, and to the players he engaged for his performers of the juvenile Symphony at the Fenice Theater in December 1882. In his self-absorption, Venice and Italy existed only for what they offered him, and for nothing beyond his own interests and perspectives. Ever less gregarious through his later years, Wagner liked to surround himself with his family and create a world of quasi-isolation and apartness—as Liszt discovered to his discomfort at the Vendramin.

In those terms, a part of Italy's meaning for Wagner was shaped by nostalgia. He habitually drew inspiration for his experiences in certain places. His voyage in the stormy North Sea off the coast of Norway (1839) grounded his conception of *Der fliegende Holländer*, though details are disputed. At least one encounter with old Nuremberg—in the summer of 1861, just before the quick visit to Venice and the Titian inspiration—was part of the genesis of *Die Meistersinger von Nürnberg*. But Italy accumulated a particular bundle of inspirational memories all its own, and ones that meant much to him. As we have observed,[7] scenic designs for two episodes in *Parsifal* were derived from his sightseeing in 1880: Klingsor's garden after the gardens of the Villa Rufolo at Ravello; the Grail Temple after the Cathedral of Siena. His recollections of other dramatic moments of creative inspiration are more dubious: such as the claim that his visit to La Spezia in 1853 generated the opening of *Das Rheingold*;[8] or that the end of the 1861 visit to Venice sparked ideas for *Die Meistersinger*.[9] Whether they were accurate or not,[10] these recollections demonstrate the more Wagner's delight in associating Italy, and Venice, with crucial moments of his career.

Venice unquestionably held genuine and vital associations for him, notably with his work there composing Act II of *Tristan*, and with the alleged inspiration he derived from a gondolier's song for the Shepherd's tune in its Act III.[11] It was clearly with the 1858–59 residence in mind that Wagner ventured some comparative remarks—including his rare thoughts on Florence—recorded by Cosima on March 9, 1880, while in Naples:

> . . . At lunch R. told us about the palaces in Venice, how fantastically beautiful they seemed to him, much more beautiful than "that boring Palazzo Pitti" in Florence; the conversation moves on to Venice, and he says that after a time it made him feel melancholy, and on one occasion he decided to go to Vicenza, arrived in Treviso, saw nothing there except dust and maltreated animals, and said to himself, "At least you don't have that in Venice."[12]

Still in Naples, he was waxing nostalgic again on June 12, 1880:

> . . . R. recalls Venice, the light he saw shining in his *palazzo* when he returned home of an evening in a gondola, its magical effect, "and yet my whole life was trouble and strife—not the sufferings and preoccupations of love, but the difficulty of being left in peace long enough to write my score."

During subsequent visits to Venice, and especially in the final sojourn, Wagner frequently returned to that most obvious focus of his nostalgia, the Palazzo Giustiniani, to revel in memories of his earlier life. On November 24, 1882, he took his family there "to show it to the children," as Cosima says. "It brings back memories of the dismal years, 'when I was standing still.' " Not all of his memories of the Giustiniani months were negative. Cosima reports that on November 27, 1881 (while they were in Palermo), she opined that a man could not be happy when solitary, to which Wagner responded: "What do you mean? The times of solitariness were my best—Lucerne, Venice."[13] By "best" here, of course, he may mean "most productive" rather than "most happy," though one can never be certain! Again in 1882 (October 2), after a stroll, Cosima reports: "In the Giardino Reale [between the Bacino and the Procuratie Nuove] he recalls that it was there that he first received the news of *Lohengrin*'s success in Vienna"—referring to its local premiere on August 19, 1858.

The massive documentation of Wagner's thoughts and remarks in Cosima's diaries reveals considerable fluctuation in attitudes. His propensity for saying what came into his mind, and Cosima's for recording it, resulted in many contradictory statements, some the product of momentary whims or grouchiness. He would frequently praise one place while he was in a different one, and he could entertain wildly divergent ideas about places (especially somewhere else) where he thought he would like to be. He regularly talked about relocating in the United States[14]—a prospect that staggers the imagination!

Simply within Italy itself, he vacillated widely as to his preferred location. To be sure, of the Italian cities Wagner visited, many seem to have excited him little. Bologna was, of course special for him because of the early interest there in performing his operas, but he apparently paid little attention to it otherwise. His brief visits to Milan and Florence evoked only limited interest or gratification. Rome, with its vast treasures and monuments from so many epochs, was notable for drawing very little response from him during his one substantial visit there, over a month in length. But, as he and Cosima admitted, his was very much a Lutheran reaction to a Catholic citadel. Of course, the first Italian city that attracted him was Genoa, as a result of his two early visits there (1853, 1868). Thereafter, however, Venice seems to have replaced Genoa in his priorities, though a twinge of the earlier choice occasionally could surface. Thus, as late as December 1, 1880, back at Wahnfried—after the Naples residence and their second visit to Venice together—Cosima had to defend herself against a curious accusation made by a Richard who was clearly fretting over the discomforts of the Bayreuth winter:

> . . . Over coffee R. had made me responsible for our having settled in Germany; he said he had wanted to stay in Genoa in 1868 [their first visit to Italy together]; once a decision had been made, it should be put into effect at once, but I had too rigid a sense of duty, and all the gods had been against my decision; we probably would have come to Bayreuth, but only for a short time, for the festival. . . .

And there was at least one other Italian city that could challenge Venice in Wagner's estimation: Naples. At one point (April 14, 1882), on their way between Sicily and Venice, they passed quickly through Naples—"as unique as ever!" Cosima exclaimed. She then caught her husband's impulsive judgment of Naples itself, "which R. declares to be the loveliest [city] of all." Yet, two days later (April 16, 1882), when they were in Venice, Cosima reports that they "delight in Venice," that a walk to San Marco "utterly enchants [Richard]; we are in no doubt that this is the loveliest place of all"—a remark that might refer to Venice in general or just to the San Marco area. Earlier, while they were in Venice in 1880, Cosima reports (October 30), "He is sad at having left Naples"— though the remark was apparently not intended as an unfavorable comparison with Venice, which they were leaving that day for the chilly north. In fact, as they departed among gondola serenaders, Cosima was moved to write: "Farewell, Venice!" On the other hand, disillusionment with winter quarters in Palermo (January 9, 1882) "makes us think again of Venice, which R. prefers to all other Italian towns." Indeed, Cosima's diaries regularly report Wagner's eagerness to reach Venice, or to his constant delight in the city while there, especially during the final visit.[15]

After a particularly satisfying contemplation of the Grand Canal from the Rialto Bridge during the final sojourn (October 11, 1882), Cosima observes: "he holds to his opinion that no other town can compare with Venice." In point of fact, Wagner was even then making comparisons with Venice, still sorting out his opinions of the three Italian cities in which he had resided the longest. Back in

1880, then in Bayreuth, he pontificated (November 19): "Naples is an intoxication, Venice a dream." But in the last visit he was more expansive. On November 7, 1882, amid delighting in Venetian sights, he "declares Venice to be the true Southern town, Palermo reminding him much more of our German towns; it is true that Naples has an African character, but Venice is Italian-Oriental." Lapses in the Venetian climate did, however, muddy the waters. On a gray day in November 1882 (the thirtieth), he was prompted to proclaim: "Palermo the finest climate, Venice the finest city."

At the end of the preceding month (October 31, 1882), they had been thinking of the future:

> . . . we talked about Wahnfried, Venice. I vote—and in the end R. agrees—against traveling and in favor of remaining as long as possible in Bayreuth and visiting Venice regularly.

A fortnight later (November 14), they were again thinking in the same line:

> R. also talks about our stay in Venice, the painful desertion of Wahnfried. We still do not know what our life is to be! We regret spending so little time in our lovely house, but the thought of the climate and much else besides makes R. shudder.

A few days further (November 18): "What Bayreuth could be if we were there! How gladly he would stay there if the town itself, and not only the weather, had somewhat more to offer!"

Some waning of enthusiasm, however, seems to have set in as the final sojourn progressed. Initially, Wagner had been very pleased with the Palazzo Vendramin: he took "pleasure in our lovely dwelling," reported Cosima on September 23. But, perhaps with the Venetian winter weather a reality around them and his health very uneven, Wagner had become disillusioned in the weeks before his death. In this spirit he brooded, and even came up with a startling suggestion for geographical revision (January 30, 1883):

> . . . he is in a subdued mood, as so often now in the hours of dusk; he regrets that our palace is so far from the [San Marco] Square, feels we have no luck with our arrangements (a statement he tries to take back at once, fearing that it will make me sad); he says this will probably be our last stay in Italy—in future we shall just make a long journey every year. He still thinks fondly of Naples (Villa d'Angri); recently he made the bold suggestion that Venice ought to be situated where Capri is—so that one could have the two of them combined! However, he says he will do anything which he can assume will please me.

The disaffection seems to have continued. On February 3, Cosima notes: "We [. . .] stroll up and down through the long Palazzo Vendramin, for which he no longer much cares." And, on February 5:

For the past two days he has been thinking of the Villa d'Angri, he would not be disinclined to rent it again, and in his mind he arranges our accommodations, saying he would like to live amid such striking surroundings. In bed he says to me "I have got the accommodations arranged."

Such shifts were, of course, typical of Wagner's mind and spirit—so soon impatient to be somewhere else. To be sure, there is no way of knowing where Wagner would have chosen to stay in subsequent sojourns: certainly in Italy, if not necessarily in Venice. Yet, we might well conclude that those darker perspectives during the last weeks of his life were an eleventh-hour aberration when set against the clear weight of prior opinions. For all his vacillations of judgment, it seems safe to say that Wagner generally had come to consider Venice as something like his favorite place on earth.

What made Venice special for Wagner can be perceived in several ways.[16] Always susceptible to historical stimuli, Wagner was fascinated by the city's past, even more than he had been with Palermo's Norman and Hohenstaufen associations. In his first visit to Venice, in 1858, he found on-the-spot illumination in reading Pierre Daru's *Histoire de la république de Venise*.[17] Early in the last Venetian residence, the Wagners ordered a new set of this work for Daniela, and Cosima undertook reading it with the children (October 19, 24, 1882). The very buildings themselves that surrounded their palazzo fired Wagner's imagination through their historical associations. Thus Cosima records later that month, on October 30:

> . . . In spite of the persistent rain R. is in good spirits. He gazes at the palaces opposite and exclaims, "What things like that have to tell about history and events!" And later he returns to the theme, admiring the building of these massive, elegant things in the middle of the sea.[18]

But the great lyric dramatist also saw another dimension of Venice's character. In 1858 he had already sensed the theatrical quality of the city and its life.[19] But he was even more fully aware of it in the final visit. Cosima reports his recovery from a heart spasm after hearing his music played in the piazza (November 5):

> . . . Not even this mood can prevent his enjoying the beauty of this place and drawing our attention to it. "This is a theater," he says, stopping in front of the twin columns [of the Piazzetta], and he indicates both stage and auditorium. ... He declares the place where the gondolas put in to be the loveliest urban spot anywhere.

The columns to which he was referring, of course, were those at the Bacino end of the Piazzetta (where the gondolas still "put in"), in their stage-like disposition. Yet, perhaps in a wider sense, and even unconsciously, Wagner was perceiving the inherent theatricality of Venice as a whole. To him it was veritably one grand stage set.

There were, to be sure frivolous attractions among the points of appeal. Wagner was drawn to one of the great stone lions set up in front of the Arsenale's portal—the ones pillaged from Athens or Piraeus by Doge Francesco Morosini in 1687. It enchanted Wagner upon his first discovery of it in the spring of 1882, when he initially likened it to his *Ring* characters Fafner and Fasolt, and then to Wotan (April 23). The following autumn he made at least two more inspections of "his lion," admiring it with his family (September 22) and then showing it off to the Gravinas (October 9). On his solitary walks, though, Wagner could relish just blending into the Venetian scene. Only a week before his death, Cosima records (February 6) her passing the Piazzetta with Daniela and Hermann Levi as the Carnival was drawing to a close:

> . . . on our way home I hear amid all the crush and noise "Psst!" and I know at once that it is R.; I tell my companions, who look around, and true enough, there he is sitting on the bench beside the Doge's Palace and in very good spirits; the air is splendid, and he has been happily watching two lovely boys of 5 and 7 playing with sand on the bench; he put some money in the sand pit for them. R. tells us this at lunch. . . .

In general, Venice appealed to Wagner, as to so many other visitors, for its visual richness. His primary response was to architecture. His appreciation of Venice as a great treasure-house of painting came to him only gradually: he was ready for that only by the time of his later Venetian experiences. Long a voracious reader, he was at first indifferent to art. During his first visit to Venice, in 1858–59 he put off any exploration of art and, in the end, he never admitted venturing into the Accademia di Belle Arti. In his second visit, in 1861, he was all but forced to go into it by Otto Wesendonck.[20] As has been seen,[21] Wagner credited his encounter with Titian's *Assunta* at that time for its profound inspirational effect. With Cosima he was to reaffirm his admiration for it during his last three visits to Venice (October 17, 1880; April 25, 1882; October 22, 1882).

Yet, by his own and explicit admission, Wagner began his Italian experiences as an uninformed and inadequate judge of art. He recalled that when he first visited Genoa in 1853, he was "without any guidance or capacity to hunt down Italian art treasures according to any systematic plan."[22] And, remembering his first visit to Milan in 1859 after leaving Venice, Wagner admitted defeat when he went to the Brera Galleries:

> there and then I realized that I would never be worth anything as a judge of paintings, for once the subject matter reveals itself to me clearly and agreeably, it settles my view and nothing else counts.[23]

Further on, while in Naples (March 18, 1880), Wagner reflected on museum visiting and was ready to shrug it all off:

More and more I find myself turning away from the plastic arts, from painting—it is like a curtain one pulls to conceal the seriousness of things.

For all that, however, Wagner continued to look. And he continued to comment. Whatever his limitations (admitted or otherwise), Wagner never hesitated to express opinions or reactions of the moment, about anything and everything. And Cosima was there to record his pontificating about painting at least as dutifully as she recorded his comments on everything else.

As his acquaintance with painting expanded, the creator of the "music of the future" proved to be hardly progressive in his artistic tastes. Of the Impressionist movement, he developed a low opinion, if an ill-informed one. The visit in Palermo from the painter Renoir (January 15, 1882)[24] prompted little respect:

> This artist, belonging to the Impressionists, who paint everything bright and in full sunlight, amuses R. with his excitement and his many grimaces as he works. . . .

Wagner took a dim view of the portrait sketch that resulted, but the visit led to further discussion:

> . . . This sitting brings us to landscape painting, and from there to a discussion which becomes so heated that, when R. says, "I have been hearing the same thing for twenty years," I leave the room. That produces a turn in the conversation which gradually restores us to the best of moods. Regarding portraits, R. declared, among other things: "What does that convey to me? The best thing a portrait artist can paint nowadays is a bloodhound!"

Wagner's even more arbitrary thinking on art, complete with a contrary position on portrait painting, is reflected in Cosima's reports of colloquies on September 29, 1882, at the Vendramin:

> . . . Then he amuses us with stories about the present-day painters called Impressionists, who paint "nocturne symphonies" in ten minutes![25] (At table recently R. said that for him portraiture was the main feature of painting, its true discovery. He said large historical compositions meant little to him. But tonight, expressing his preference for clean, not daubed, painting, he adds jokingly, "I am for Titian's *Tribute Money*.")

Cosima's entries for their travels in 1880 particularly repeat Wagner's preference for "Old Masters." Just what he comprehended under such a label is not always clear, though he did seem to draw the line at works beyond the fifteenth or mid-sixteenth century. Visiting the Capodimonte Museum in Naples with Cosima (April 24, 1880), he expressed shock at a different Titian painting, the portrait of Pope Paul III and his nephews (though actually for its subjects, whom he dubbed "beasts of prey!"). But he went on to take "pleasure in the old masters," singling out Ghirlandaio for praise, and especially Lucas van Leyden and

Albrecht Dürer, who left them "refreshed by German spirit, German humor, dili-gence, and art." That autumn in Venice, in two successive visits to the Accademia Gallery, Wagner "finds pleasure in the older pictures, which seem to him more accomplished" (October 26), and then (October 29) he singled out paintings of Carpaccio and Callot for particular praise. But he took a dim view of some of Michelangelo's paintings, particularly deriding the futility of portraying the Last Judgement (June 10, 1880). Much later (February 10, 1883), Wagner took on the entire Sistine Chapel

which R. calls a monstrosity; he says he would like to know if it was admired when it was first opened. I bring him M[ichel]a[ngelo]'s poem about this chapel, and it pleases him greatly.

Among "old masters," however, it was Raphael in particular who posed problems for Wagner. At first (March 7, 1878), he admired some of the great Italian's work:

. . . R. describes [Raphael's] *Sistine Madonna* as the most consummate work of art, pre-cisely on account of its fine restraint; the very fact that it contains so few figures makes R. feel that as a work of art it is more significant than Titian's *Ascension*, which all but transgresses its boundaries. The *Sistine Madonna* stands in the same relation to the *Ascension* as [Beethoven's] C minor Symphony (first movement) to the *Eroica*.

Nor was Wagner at all loath to make further musical analogies, as on September 4, 1879, while in Bayreuth:

. . . comparison between this melodic charm [of movements in Mozart's *Requiem*, "which R. greatly loves"] and the charm of Raphael's Madonnas; much about the *Sistine Madonna*; thoughts of R.'s next work about religion in relation to art; the beauty of Raphael free of desire.

But Raphael held associations that Wagner disliked. Thus, on June 27, 1880, while the Wagners were in Naples:

. . . In the evening we look through some folios; an engraving by Marcantonio [Raimondi] after Raphael (*Pietà*), which pleases me greatly, R. rejects entirely; classical beauty applied to this subject he considers reprehensible, and the reason for our decline. The head by Leonardo (sketch for the *Cena*) he finds too effeminate. . . .

The key to that objection to Raphael, as "the reason for our decline," has to do with Wagner's larger attitude toward the Renaissance in general, of which more in a moment.

Among Venetian painters, Wagner repeatedly enjoyed Bellini and Carpaccio, and of course preserved a special reverence for Titian. On the other hand, he displayed a strong antipathy toward Tintoretto. For example, recording their visit to the Scuola di San Rocco on October 7, 1880, Cosima notes that he scorned Tintoretto's great *Crucifixion*: "there is too much going on in the picture." Cosima herself seems to have had wider-ranging tastes and she sometimes endeavored to soften or bend her husband's views, with at least a modicum of success on occasion—even in the case of one of Tintoretto's paintings. On October 22, 1882, at his own suggestion, they went again to the Scuola di San Rocco, where Wagner "spent a long time looking at the *Crucifixion* and also *Christ before Pilate*." Then, the next day at the Accademia:

> . . . R. looks at many things with great calmness and concentration, among them the Carpaccios; he prefers the Saint John in Tintoretto's *Crucifixion* to the Saint John in [Titian's] *Assunta*, and in respect of his appreciation of this great work, I see to my joy that he is increasingly coming around to my feeling about it.

In all, Wagner appears to have approached painting with insecure and shifting reactions. When he first came to Venice he was no great habitué of art galleries, nor did he ever fully become one. Hampered in his later years by ill health and fatigue, Wagner was often content to let Cosima go without him to museums in the cities they visited. When he did go with her, it was often for the sake of pleasing her. Nevertheless, he learned to appreciate their gallery visits together, and the treasures of the Accademia in Venice became a joy they especially shared. While the emergence of Wagner's appreciation of painting progressed all through his visits to Venice, it was in that city that he was most fully tested, and it was that city that served most fully to draw out his reactions and thinking on art.

It might just be noted that, for all his conservative love of old masters and his suspicion of modern trends, Wagner came to enjoy socializing with painters. Indeed, whereas he isolated himself as much as he could from all but a few musicians and composers of his day, he apparently found the company of painters more congenial—and, of course, less competitive. Arnold Böcklin was among the painters he welcomed to Wahnfried. The closeness he (and his family) established with Paul Joukowsky is obviously the most striking case in point. But Wagner paid great attention to painters in Venice, whether or not he made commissions to them. It will be remembered that, during the last sojourn in the city, he particularly cultivated the Russian Vassily Alekseevich Volkov (or "Wolkoff": 1842–19??) and the two Germans Johann Ludwig Passini (1832–1903) and Franz Leo Ruben (1842–1920) then resident there. (The first two were to be instrumental in arranging for a death mask of Wagner to be made; while the last was the painter of some of the scenes from *Lohengrin* for King Ludwig at his castle of Hohenschwangau.)

Much more than painting, however, it was architecture that attracted Wagner's prime interest, and above all in Venice. The buildings of Venice—Venice the stage-set, we might say—entranced and absorbed him from his very

first stay there. Indeed, we may recall his own recollection in *Mein Leben*, already
quoted:

> It was very difficult for Ritter to induce me to interrupt my daily routine even to visit a
> gallery or a church, although whenever we had to walk through the city I was always
> delighted anew by the untold manifold architectural peculiarities and marvels.[26]

Wagner ever delighted in touring the city, whether on foot or by gondola. He
took two rides a day during his 1858–59 sojourn (the second often to the Lido
at sundown). With Cosima he made constant gondola trips during the later visits: they rarely used the vaporetti, and in 1882–83 had a pair of gondoliers at
their disposal at the Palazzo Vendramin.[27] He was forever inspecting buildings.
On one occasion (October 22, 1880), he made an interesting observation: "As
we glide along, R. remarks that here in Venice the gracefulness of the architecture takes the place of flowers"—a remark he supplemented with the conclusion, after a visit to the Papadopoli Gardens (November 12, 1882) that "one
feels no need for gardens in Venice."[28]

Among all the cities he visited, none other than Venice evoked from Wagner
so many explicit reactions to architecture, and far more than to painting.
Beyond the general impressions, he expressed extensive opinions on individual
buildings in Venice, especially its churches. Some he disliked. One was San
Zaccharia:

> . . . the church itself, the exterior [in early Venetian Renaissance style, by Mauro
> Coducci], which he finds too effeminate, as well as the [Gothic] interior, which does
> not appeal to him, leave him indifferent, but the Bellini painting fascinates him. . . .
> (September 30, 1882)

Another was Santa Maria Gloriosa dei Frari, which "makes no impression on
him" (October 8, 1882), though he greatly admired another Bellini *Madonna*
there. (He had a penchant for picking an outstanding painting in a building for
joint consideration with the building itself.) On the other hand, his favor fell on
a stylistic spectrum of examples. On November 9, 1882, it was the late-Gothic
Madonna dell'Orto (which, not noted, was the burial church of Tintoretto):
"The decorative church also surprises him greatly, and later he reproaches me for
not allowing him to look longer at the Cima [painting]!" Two weeks before
(October 7, 1882), they were delighted when, having become lost during a stroll,
they suddenly encountered that Renaissance gem, Santa Maria dei Miracoli, for
which Cosima evoked the now-standard analogy of "the jewel box." Despite his
reaction to Mauro Coducci's facade for San Zaccharia, he admired other works
of that architect, San Michele in Isola (October 19, 1882), and Santa Maria
Formosa (November 6). In the latter instance "both church and picture rouse his
interest, the former on account of its intimacy, the latter its magnificence." (The

painting in question, indicated only as being of a female martyr—"it could just as well be a queen of Palmyra as a martyr," he observed—must surely have been Palma Vecchio's grand altarpiece portraying Saint Barbara.)

Despite his unsympathetic response to the Frari—or, for that matter, to the interior of San Zaccharia—Wagner seems to have made no reaction to the other great example of Mendicant Gothic, SS. Giovanni e Paolo (Zanipolo), although he was impressed by the Verrocchio's grand equestrian statue of the *condottiere* Colleoni placed outside it (October 13, 1882). He also relished the Rialto Bridge, both for itself and as a vantage point on the Grand Canal (e.g., October 11, 1882).

But the building that excited and entranced him beyond all others was the matchless Ducal Basilica of San Marco. At one point (October 8, 1882) he ranked it among "his three churches ... the cathedrals of Siena and Pisa and Saint Mark's," his favorites among all he had seen. The family often used the Piazza as a meeting place, while they regularly visited the church itself. Cosima frequently records his unending delight in this remarkable edifice (e.g., October 12 and November 18, 1882). Perhaps especially since it became such an advantageous perch for people-watching, the church became so dear to him that during his final sojourn he would often sit at its entrance, if in a location not precisely identified. "We sit down between the pillars of the portal on Saint Mark's Square, R.'s favorite place," she reports on October 1, 1882. Feeling ill in the Piazza one day (November 8), he caught his breath sitting down "under the portal." So special was this favored spot that at one point (October 29, 1882) Wagner "says he would like to be painted there." There seems to have been serious exploration of this idea with one painter in their circle, but to no result:

> In St. Mark's Square he told me he had inquiries made of Herr Wolk. whether he would fulfill the wish I had expressed for a portrait of R. beneath the portal of St. M.'s, but Wolkoff has refused. (December 9, 1882)

Curiously, despite his admiration for San Marco and for Venice's past, Wagner was repelled by its Byzantine component. To be sure, during the earlier stay in 1882, he could speak of "the warm style of Byzantine churches," though mainly to wonder why it "could ever have been abandoned" in favor of the later neo-classical style he disliked (April 18). But early the next year (February 5, 1883), a week before his death, Richard and Cosima took it into their minds to seek out in San Marco what she calls "Zuccato's cupola, which we do not find." And with good reason. The reference was either to works by the later sixteenth-century mosaicist Arminio Zuccato in the church's sacristy (rarely accessible for viewing) or, more likely, the mosaics on the arch of the Apocalypse on the extended vault inside the west facade, carried out by Arminio and his brother Francesco in 1570–89 (considerably restored even by Wagner's time)—actually not in one of the cupolas. Failing in this quest, Cosima continues:

We look at the other mosaics, and R. observes how curious it is that people prefer the stiff, black fellows, on account of their age and authenticity, to the more recent mosaics, which are much pleasanter.

In other words, in this case Wagner was ready to prefer late-Renaissance mosaic art to the Veneto-Byzantine masterpieces of the twelfth and fifteenth centuries.

When, on October 19, 1882, the Wagners made an excursion to the lagoon island of Torcello, with its church full of magnificent Byzantine-derived mosaics of the (mostly) twelfth century, Cosima could only remark that she and her husband were "not greatly rewarded for the expenditure of time and energy." On November 16, 1882, while Richard was looking over some oriental textiles, Cosima observed offhandedly that "Byzantine things have no appeal for him." Nor post-Byzantine ones. The later Orthodox spirituality and décor of San Giorgio dei Greci, the sixteenth-century church of Venice's Greek community, earned only his contempt. Visited on October 11, 1882, it "strikes him as pompous, with its black Madonna and Saviour!" The next day he returned to it:

> In the morning R. talks to me again about the Greci church, saying that it does not give any warm feelings of Christianity but, rather, an impression of stiffness and pomp, like a relic of ancient Assyria!

As he familiarized himself with the painting and architecture of Venice, Wagner gradually revealed—or perhaps just formulated—a very definite, if somewhat muddled and inconsistent framework of artistic taste, one that also reflected some of his religious as well as aesthetic ideas. Its essence was simple: medieval style is good, Renaissance style is bad. It should be made clear that "medieval" for Wagner seems to have excluded Byzantine and Romanesque dimensions; the Gothic style probably seemed more congenial to him as a "northern" and even "Germanic" idiom. The most explicit expression of his viewpoint in Cosima's diaries is found in her report of one bit of Wagner's enjoyment, on November 5, 1882:

> Then, gazing at the Doge's Palace, he praises medieval architecture and says that with its passing all imagination, life, and invention were lost; the whole Renaissance leaves him cold.

Of course, there were often inconsistencies in Wagner's reactions, and we certainly find some in his ability to enjoy specific buildings, or paintings, of Renaissance provenance. But his concept of "Renaissance" style was apparently focused on its revival of Classical elements from Antiquity. Thus Cosima records (November 7, 1882):

> — Over coffee we talked about the Renaissance—whether the excavation of classical art had been an unmixed blessing, or had it not perhaps restricted the imagination, put

an end to naïveté? The arguments for and against are mentioned, R. says, "It shows that this art was not meant to be the last word."

That fixation on the noxious effects of the Classical revival upon art went back many years, and found echo just a week before he died (February 6, 1883) in the disgust he expressed as he looked out the window of the Cappello Nero café across to Sansovino's Procuratie Nuove, completed by Scamozzi and Longhena in the late sixteenth and early seventeenth century:

> . . . From the restaurant he gazed at the façade of the Procurator's Palace and said how boring, unimaginative, and uninventive he found it; in '58 he had told the painter Rahl the same thing, declaring what a different effect a Gothic cathedral had on him, compared with this imitative monotony.

Almost three years earlier, on June 27, 1880, in Naples, he put his ideas another way in reacting to a Raphael *Pietà*: "classical beauty applied to this subject he considers reprehensible, and the reason for our decline." The extension of his anticlassicizing, anti-Renaissance prejudices to painting are reflected in another, but more cryptic comment recorded by Cosima on November 11, 1882):

> I amuse R. with the information that Tintoretto had the Golden Calf borne by the 4 greatest painters, which fits in very well with R.'s conception of the Renaissance.

Absorbed as he was in the conflict of his "old masters" with "decline," Wagner seems to have taken little heed of Italian architecture or painting from the later sixteenth century or beyond. Of course, what we now understand as "Baroque" art has been defined for us largely in the century since Wagner's death. Much to which we would now attach that label must have seemed to Wagner simply an extension of the Renaissance as he conceived it, and a slide into degeneracy at that. One of the few Baroque monuments he did notice and react to was Longhena's great votive church of Santa Maria della Salute, which he saw as one more example of the blight of austere neoclassicism—to the extent that it could even make him think positively of Byzantine style (April 18, 1882):

> . . . Then S.M. Salute, whose cold interior utterly disgusts R.—He cannot understand how the warm style of Byzantine churches could ever have been abandoned in favor of this imitation classical whiteness.[29]

The simplistic concepts of the "medieval" as noble and the "Renaissance" as bad or corrupting or stifling have a familiar ring to them. That viewpoint was, of course, espoused by a number of aesthetes and artistic movements in the nineteenth-century epochs of the Gothic Revival and the Pre-Raphaelite movement. Wagner was certainly aware of one German group of painters known as the

Nazarenes, whose ideas distinctly anticipated and influenced the Pre-Raphaelites. Indeed, for one of them, Peter Cornelius (1783–1867: no relation to the composer), Wagner expressed explicit approval (November 4, 1878). By far the most important exponent of ideas in this vein, however, was John Ruskin (1819–1900), who argued most fully for them in his masterpiece, *The Stones of Venice* (1851–53).

It has gone largely unnoticed that Ruskin and Wagner actually were in Venice at the same time at one point. While Wagner was staying at the Hotel Europa on the Grand Canal with Cosima for their first visit to Venice together (September 20–27, 1876), Ruskin had just established himself at the hotel on the Zattere known as La Calcina, for the beginning of the ninth among his ten sojourns in Venice (September 8, 1876, to May 23, 1877). It is fascinating to speculate that they might have passed each other in the streets during the week when their respective stays overlapped. But there is absolutely no evidence that they ever met. Ruskin eventually learned about Wagner's music, and did not like it.[30] There is no indication, however, that Wagner knew anything about Ruskin. *The Stones of Venice* has never been translated into German. With only the poorest knowledge of English, Wagner is unlikely to have read anything of Ruskin's ideas about Venetian decline in relation to Renaissance degeneracy, ideas with many parallels to Wagner's own. Such similarities at least affirm Wagner's place—however coincidental and instinctive—well within one of those nineteenth-century intellectual currents that is usually bypassed by his biographers and commentators.[31]

Perusal of Wagner's aesthetic reflections inevitably reminds us how vacillating were his opinions and how frequent his self-contradictions, a result of his whimsical capacity for tossing off pontifications on the moment, which Cosima was all too eager to preserve. Beyond that point, such perusal offers us insights into Wagner's intellectual limitations. A musical genius with literary talents and philosophical pretensions, he was an active reader with a wide knowledge of literature, an important dimension of his interests. But his knowledge of art and architecture, for all his opinions, was thin. Beneath his strenuously opinionated posture of cosmopolitanism lay a profound cultural provincialism. Issues of Wagner's "dilettantism" have been discussed frequently. To consider Wagner's relationship with Venice offers important illumination to that side of him.

And that fact is itself based on another important reality. No other city seems to have meant so much to Wagner, historically, artistically, and nostalgically. As Cosima's relentless record documents, no other city elicited from him such extended expressions of his aesthetic and artistic reactions. For that reason alone, Venice—the "second Wagnerian city, after Bayreuth"—must be given its due in Wagner's history. His mind and his body may repose in and belong to Bayreuth, to be sure. But his heart and a part of his soul remained in Venice. It was more than a simple accident of timing that death caught up with him there.[32]

Part 2

Venice Absorbs Richard Wagner

Chapter Five

Watching

Against the plenitude of Venice-watching on the part of Wagner, there developed also a valuable and not widely known body of Wagner-watching on the part of the Venetians, notably as conveyed in the city's newspapers.

These were the afternoon journal *La Gazzetta [Uffiziale] di Venezia* (hereafter *LGdV*) and the morning paper *La Venezia* (hereafter *LV*). Their coverage of Wagner's stays in Venice was limited, especially at first. That reality reflected, among other things, the initial unfamiliarity of Wagner to most Italians, and their only gradual recognition of his stature as a cultural figure of major importance.

It was common for these two journals to give daily notices of *arrivati* (new arrivals) and *partenze* (departures) to and from Venice. Understandably, such notices would be limited, and restricted to travelers who were deemed of some standing or importance, at least as viewed by the Austrian regime in control of the city in the earliest epoch involved. Accordingly, Wagner's first visit to Venice, from August 17, 1858, to March 23, 1859, seems to have passed unnoticed by both journals, with references neither to his arrival nor departure.[1] While the various police and government authorities were interested in Wagner for his political reputation, only some of the local Austrian officials and musicians, a few visiting foreigners, and hardly any Italians, were aware of his musical achievements to that point.

Political notoriety was no longer an issue in 1861, at the time of his brief second visit to Venice, in the last years of Austrian rule there. But, so far as the local Italian public was concerned, he was still a personality of little interest. Not so with his wealthy patron, Otto Wesendonck of Düsseldorf, whose arrival from Verona and lodging at the Danieli on November 3, 1861, was noted the following day by *LGdV*, and whose departure for Vienna on November 12 was likewise recorded a day later by the same journal. But the coming and going of Wagner in this time period were not mentioned at all.

When Wagner and Cosima made their first visit to Venice together in September 1876 (ten years after the end of Austrian rule), they should have been recognizable as celebrities of some note. After all, they had just presided over the first production of *Der Ring des Nibelungen* at the new Festspielhaus in Bayreuth, a cultural event of international importance. Yet, neither the *LGdV* nor *LV* troubled themselves to mention the Wagner family among the *arrivati*. Someone must have tipped off their editors to what had been missed, however, for both newspapers caught up with these important visitors by the time they departed, on September 26. *LGdV* that evening managed the following notice—seemingly the first reference to Wagner in the Venice journals:

> *Partenza*—Riccardo Wagner with his family departed today from Venice on the 12:55 afternoon train routed to Bologna, where he will remain a few days before then going on to Sorrento. And this while the newspapers of Genoa were announcing his arrival in that city yesterday, and were certifying that he had taken up lodging at the Hotel d'Italie!

Less concerned with journalistic one-upmanship, *LV* reported the same basic first sentence of information about "Riccardo Wagner con la sua famiglia ed il suo seguito."

LV was caught unawares four years later when Wagner and his family made their next stop, on the way back from their stay in Naples. *LGdV*, on the other hand, was not only on the alert but was also able to display a belated assimilation of Wagner's importance by this time. On October 5, 1880, it published the following notice:

> Riccardo Wagner in Venice—Arrived yesterday at Venice the illustrious Riccardo Wagner with family and retinue [*seguito*] (15 people in all), and took rooms at the Albergo Reale Daniele. So far as we know, he will leave this evening
>   It is said that the purpose of his visit would be that of acquiring a palazzo on the Grand Canal; but we do not know if the most distinguished maestro has managed to secure it or not.[2]

Two days later, on October 7, *LGdV* recognized that the Wagners were remaining in Venice a little longer after all:

> Through a simple misunderstanding on the part of our informant, we announced the departure of Wagner from Venice, and that it was the illustrious maestro's intention to acquire here a palazzo on the Grand Canal. Instead, the distinguished maestro is still to be found among us, and it might not have been his intention to acquire a palazzo, but rather to take a lease on one, and this he has done, leasing for a period of time an apartment in the Palazzo Contarini delle Figure.

This much said, neither newspaper took any notice of the Wagner family's departure on October 30.

By the time of Wagner's fortnight stay in April 1882, his presence in Venice could hardly be treated cursorily. To be sure, neither of the two newspapers took notice of the Wagners' arrival on April 15. But attention was finally given them as the result of an unusual and striking instance of Wagner's plunge into the local musical life. Cosima's record of it (Friday, April 21) is quite terse:

... we go to St. Mark's Square; R. asks the military band for [Rossini's] *Gazza ladra* Overture, which is then played, and very prettily.

Understandably, the local newspapers made much more of this. The next day (April 22), the morning paper, *LV*, had the following notice (on its second page):

> Riccardo Wagner was strolling yesterday in the Piazza, while the municipal band was giving its concert.
>
> After this had played the duet from *Rigoletto*, the great maestro went into the [performing space] and, introducing himself to the eminent maestro Calascione, shaking his hand, he complimented him and his band-members for the lovely, precise, and effective musical performance that he had heard. He also expressed the wish to hear the Sinfonia to *Gazza Ladra* which was not on the program. Forthwith Calascione ordered the score to be brought and, before he had finished the concert, he had performed the Rossinian masterpiece, after which Riccardo Wagner renewed to Calascione and the band members his compliments and praises.
>
> This, coming from such a competent judge, gave Calascione and the players the most precious of satisfactions.

By the evening, however, *LGdV* had been able to expand on the episode more fully, and more proudly:

> Wagner and the Civic Band—Yesterday, during an intermission in the daily concert by the Municipal Band (*Banda Cittadina*) in the Piazza di San Marco, Riccardo Wagner, with one of his daughters on his arm, came forward to shake the hand of maestro Calascione, complimenting him for the fine performance and for the praiseworthy leadership that he observed in our Band. At the same time, the illustrious maestro indicated his desire to hear the Sinfonia to Rossini's *Gazza Ladra*, saying that he had not been able to come and hear it on Monday last, on which day it had figured in the program, and he requested this also on behalf of his own daughter, who so greatly liked that Sinfonia. Maestro Calascione, delighted that he could accommodate the great maestro, immediately ordered that the music be brought and had this Sinfonia performed in extension of the program, without omitting any of the pieces already set for the concert.[3]
>
> Afterward, Riccardo Wagner came forward once again to shake the hand of maestro Calascione.

Five days later, on April 27, amid some other reflections on the band and its work, *LGdV* noted that:

> ... following upon the praises addressed by maestro Wagner to our Band, maestro Calascione dispatched to the great German musician a letter that returned thanks also on the part of the entire Corps of the municipal band.

As we shall see below, there are two other accounts of this encounter of April 21 that differ on some details with the newspaper reports.[4]

Meanwhile, on April 22, *LGdV* also announced that on the morrow (Sunday afternoon) a military band, in the series of concerts called "Music in the Gardens" (*Musica ai Giardini*), would include in its program a Wagner arrangement, "Rimembranze nell'Opera *Lohengrin*." The performers were apparently not the same as Calascione's band, and whether the inclusion of this music was a conscious gesture toward Wagner's presence in the city is not clear. Neither journal paid any heed to that event otherwise, but Cosima herself did take ironic note of it:

> At 4 o'clock we go for a drive, wish to visit the Giardino Pubblico and hear something from *Lohengrin*, lose our way, however, and go on to the arsenal, a photograph of which attracted R.

At which point Wagner encountered the Arsenale lion that so excited him.[5]

Just how much the first encounter with Wagner meant for Calascione and his players, as well as for the Venetian public, is suggested by the next relevant notices by both newspapers. On Saturday evening April 29, *LGdV* published the following notice:

> Banda Cittadina—Tomorrow, Sunday, at the evening concert in the Piazza di S. Marco, the municipal band will perform a *pot-pourri* on Wagner's *Lohengrin*, an arrangement by maestro Jacopo Calascione, made expressly in homage to the great German maestro.

The next morning, *LV* published a virtually identical notice, though with a listing of other pieces on the program.[6] But any intended "homage" to Wagner went past him personally, since he and his family had departed Venice on the afternoon of the twenty-ninth, before either notice was published. Nevertheless, the event was enough to attract further attention from *LGdV* on May 1, the day after the concert. The report's writer—who clearly had some knowledge of the original opera, criticized some choices of material that Calascione did or did not work into his arrangement, but was generally positive about it. The bandmaster, the reporter stated, avoided making "just a patchwork and paste-up treatment" and had preserved "as much as would be possible of the work's character, with that splendor of harmony that is the chief gift of the great German maestro." The report noted that for "the ensemble that describes the daybreak [. . .] there were groupings of trumpets on the balconies of the Caffè Quadri's salon." The twenty-minute piece "is pleasing in every way and at its end there were ovations, and well-merited. [. . .]"[7]

Reading the two Venetian newspapers over the next few days, one might think that Venice's Wagner-consciousness had extended further beyond the composer's departure: both of them announced on May 4 that a military band would be including in its program a piece identified as the Waltz, *Les Americaines*, by

Wagner. But there is no such work by Richard Wagner, and the composer in question must surely have been the then widely admired Austrian bandmaster and composer Josef Franz Wagner (1856–1908).

With Wagner absent from the Venetian scene from April 29 to September 16, 1882, the two local papers had little to say about him in the interval.[8] *LGdV* did not list him and his tribe among the *arrivati* noted for September 16, the day of their latest and last arrival in Venice. But, four days later, on September 20, *LGdV* did catch up with the Wagners in a short notice on page 3:

> Riccardo Wagner—Come to Venice the day before yesterday is the illustrious Riccardo Wagner and his family. We believe that he has the intention of spending a long period of time at Venice.

There is nothing more in the papers about Wagner and his stay in Venice until November. That Wagner's isolation from Venice's musical community must have been minimal is suggested by an event given only passing reference by Cosima, in a passage already quoted, which sets the date as Sunday, November 5:

> . . . In the afternoon we arrange to meet in Saint Mark's Square, but I find him in Lavena's shop, having had a spasm. Riding in the gondola, he and the girls had heard strains of *Lohengrin*, he then tried to hurry, and that brought on the trouble! ... Hardly is the spasm over, however, when he beckons Tesarini and invites him and the music director to our house in the evening on account of the wrong tempi! But he then says to me, "I ought to forget who I am, make no sudden movements, and turn into a boring donkey!" . . . After supper (at which he eats almost nothing) he discusses the tempi with the musicians. . . .

From Cosima we thus have the suggestion that Wagner did not know about the concert in advance and had not planned in advance to attend it. For some reason local journalists were more than usually slow in catching up with the episode, for not until ten days later, on November 15, did *LGdV* give its account:

> Pot-pourri on "Lohengrin"—Some days past, in one of its evening concerts, the municipal band performed a *potpourri* prepared by maestro Calascione on *Lohengrin* by the illustrious maestro Wagner. The latter, who happened to be in the Piazza, sent personally to congratulate maestro Calascione and to invite him to his home. Indeed, in the evening maestro Calascione went there and received the most cordial reception and most lively congratulations and praises from the very mouth of the great musician. Maestro Wagner asked also of maestro Calascione where the band assembled to rehearse, since he wished to go, together with his wife, to assist at a rehearsal, to add to this *pot-pourri*, at a specified point, a ritornello—a ritornello that does not figure in the opera.
>
> We believe that, as to all this, the illustrious German master has been in contact also with Count G. cav. Contin, of Castelseprio, president of our Liceo Benedetto Marcello, of which the municipal Band is a dependent.

The *pot-pourri* would presumably be the same piece as that premiered the previous April 29, only hours after Wagner had left Venice. Did Calascione schedule it now because Wagner was back in town? Did he have those trumpets in the Piazza balconies again this time?—lacking any reference to such an effect, one suspects not. At any rate, we again have divergent reports of this incident to which we will return for comparison later.[9] As to Wagner's reported intention to participate in a band rehearsal and to contribute some new music to the arrangement, we hear no more. But the reference to contact with Count Contin may reflect, instead, the beginnings of negotiations toward the eventual Christmas Eve concert at the Fenice.[10]

Indeed, the composer's detachment is the more demonstrated by the Wagners' lack of any interest in, or reference to, a concert at the Liceo Benedetto Marcello, announced on November 7 as to be held on November 12, and then shifted a day later: a concert by conservatory musicians that would include a Fantasy on Themes from "Cola da Rienzi." On the other hand, *Lohengrin* itself was back in the news, for at this time the conductor Luigi Mancinelli was directing a new production of this opera at Bologna's Teatro Communale. There seems to have been little real idea about Wagner's attending, but the composer was not unmindful of the event, nor averse to cultivating his partisans. So it is that on November 18 *LGdV* reproduces a notice that had appeared the previous day in the Bolognese journal *La Gazzetta dell'Emilia*:

> The illustrious maestro Riccardo Wagner, [honorary] Bolognese citizen, happens now to be in Venice, from which he has written a courteous letter to Cav. Mancinelli to congratulate him for the fine performance of *Lohengrin* at our great theater and expressing his hope for a trip here to hear it.
>
> We would be very happy should this happen, and we think that at the Communale Wagner would find his music conscientiously and respectfully performed.

It may well have been on the foundation of this gesture to Mancinelli that Wagner would sound him out about providing musicians for the projected Christmas Eve concert. Nor would that be the end of Wagner's contact with Mancinelli, as we have seen, and on which more momentarily.[11]

Journalistic silence once again settled over Wagner, with no apparent notice taken by the newspapers of Liszt's arrival on November 19. It was not, indeed, until the Christmas Eve concert itself drew nigh that *LGdV* found a reason for giving the composer some attention—even if it mistook the location for the event it was adumbrating:

> A Family Celebration in Wagner's House—It is supposed to be a secret, but, on the contrary, everyone knows that, for the celebration of the anniversary—we know not if it is of the Nativity or of the birthday of his spouse—maestro R. Wagner will have

performed tomorrow in his own house, the Palazzo [Vendramin-]Calergi, a symphony of his, written during his youth. The performance, conducted naturally by the composer, has been entrusted to the orchestra of the Liceo e Società Benedetto Marcello.

No journalists were allowed to attend the performance on Christmas Eve: whether any from the local papers were among those admitted to the rehearsal on December 20 is not clear. But the writers for *LGdV* were trying to correct themselves on the matter of location when they published a pro forma notice on the event on Tuesday, December 26:

> A Family Celebration at the Liceo musicale Benedetto Marcello—Sunday evening at the Liceo and not in the Wagner house, as we had stated some days past, was held the family celebration—under aegis of music—that the German maestro wanted to prepare in honor of his spouse, giving a performance of a symphony of his written in his youth. No outsiders were invited there, they say, precisely to preserve for the celebration its family character.

The notice's failure to identify the Teatro La Fenice as the site of the concert is not, however, totally an error. As we have seen,[12] it took place not in the theater's main auditorium, but in one of its adjacent chambers, the grand Sala Apollinea, part of the rooms in the building in which the Liceo had been relocated in 1880. (Such unintended confusion will be encountered in our other accounts of the event.)[13]

Wagner's name arose a few days later in notices that clarify the report of a visit to Wagner at the Vendramin by the conductor Luigi Mancinelli, pegged to January 8, 1883, as already recounted.[14] Our only other report of this visit, and of Wagner's cordiality to the conductor, comes from the personal testimony of Mancinelli himself. There is no reason to believe that Mancinelli made it up, and the newspaper notices offer confirmation.

Specifically, a concert was planned for mid-January, one of many such events held as a benefit to raise money for one of the many floods that plagued the Veneto in these years—in this case, the floods that attended the Wagner's arrival in Venice the previous September. The first specific news of this benefit concert was published by *LV* on January 11:

> Concerto at the Liceo—It was settled the other evening: at Venice, the maestro Luigi Mancinelli, the eminent orchestra conductor, now director of the Bologna Conservatory.
>
> Under his direction have begun already at the Liceo B. Marcello the rehearsals for the grand orchestral Concert in honor of Wagner and Liszt, already announced.
>
> To be performed are two *sinfonie* [i.e., overtures] by Wagner, a piece by Liszt, the intermezzi for *Cleopatra* by Mancinelli himself, and a piece by Bizet.
>
> In short, it will a concert worthy of poem and story.

Two days later, on January 13, *LGdV* gave fuller notice of the program for the concert, now set for the fifteenth. It was noted that it had originally been planned to perform the complete score of Bizet's music for *L'Arlesienne*—though just how "complete" might be wondered—but that this idea had been abandoned, and only an intermezzo from it would be given. Wagner would be represented by only one overture, that to *Tannhäuser*. (It will be recalled that, according to Panizzardi, Mancinelli said he had discussed, and played through four-hand, the Prelude to *Die Meistersinger*, and the Prelude plus *Liebestod* from *Tristan und Isolde*. Whether this meant that Mancinelli wanted advice for his own general information, or that he planned to use these pieces in the concert but changed his mind, is not clear.) Liszt's contribution would be his symphonic poem, *Les Préludes*; the other pieces would be an intermezzo from Mancinelli's incidental music for Cossa's *Cleopatra*, and the concert overture to Alfieri's *Saul* by the Antonio Bazzini. On November 15 itself, *LV* gave its own notice of the program for the concert that evening, with the reminder that it was a benefit for the *inondati*. In the same issue, as an *appendice* (3), there was a full article on the concert, over the nom de plume of the paper's music critic, "Toni," to prepare the public for what was, after all, the event inaugurating the 1883 concert season in Venice.[15]

That afternoon, *LGdV* gave its last-minute reminder of the evening's concert, stressing that it was a benefit for the flood victims, and anticipating its quality with an almost nervous concern about public interest. The concert, it is pointed out

> . . . compresses exciting energy into a short space of time: Wagner, Liszt, Bizet, Bazzini, Mancinelli will hold the field, and with such champions the artistic joust certainly cannot fail to be interesting.
>
> Any recommendation of ours is pointless because our public would wish to attend this Concert, of truly exceptional, extraordinary, artistic merit.
>
> All those with refined and discerning taste; all those who hold the art in honor and like to make the acquaintance, among the most lovely demonstrations, of some of the best products of the different [stylistic] schools, will certainly not wish to ignore the Concert this evening, which, in addition, is under charitable auspices.

The following day, January 16, both newspapers printed reviews of the event. For *LV*, "Toni" waxed on long and enthusiastically about the orchestral playing, and likewise had praise for Mancinelli: apparently, in his first appearance as conductor in Venice, he had lived up to his reputation. *LGdV* was a bit more blunt on a crucial point: the concert had not been as well attended as hoped, perhaps because the benefit ticket prices had been too high. On the other hand:

> . . . The musical aspect went well, though it was not outstanding, but all the audience admired and applauded the magic baton of maestro Mancinelli.

This was clearly an important concert in its own right, deliberately planned as a cosmopolitan mix of Italian, French, and German music, under a conductor identified with introducing Italian audiences to international repertoire—notably to Wagner's works—and as offered to a city still somewhat backward in catching up with that repertoire. Whether the inclusion of music by Wagner and Liszt was at all motivated by the fact that both composers were residing in Venice at the time is not clear. What is clear is that neither composer attended the concert. Indeed, Liszt had departed Venice on the thirteenth, two days before it was held, and there is no hint that he had anything to do with it. As for Wagner, however, we have Panizzardi's report, based on Mancinelli's own information: that, as a result of their successful visit together on January 8, the conductor invited Wagner to attend a rehearsal for the concert. This he did, we are told, and at the end of it he congratulated Mancinelli with the accolade: "You are the Garibaldi of orchestra conductors!"[16] But there is no claim that Wagner sealed his enthusiasm by attending the concert. And, considering his total indifference to Italian musical life, a concert aimed to some extent at educating the Venetian audience should have held little interest for him; likewise the rehearsal, which he might have attended only as a show of atypical courtesy to Mancinelli.

Germane here, as elsewhere, is the point that Wagner had become increasingly reluctant to attend performances of his music by musicians he could not select and control. This attitude resulted not only from his hypersensitivity over performance style, especially as to tempo, but also from his reluctance to give seeming endorsement to objectionable renditions by the mere fact of his presence.

This entire episode is studiously ignored in Cosima's diary, where there is absolutely no reference to Mancinelli's visit or to Wagner attending a rehearsal, much less the concert itself. Since this silence was preserved by her epigone, Glasenapp, the episode is overlooked by Wagner biographers in general, who have not made use of Panizzardi. Cosima's silence here is a particularly noteworthy example of her passing over events that we know from other sources did occur. The fact, indeed, that she *never* makes any reference to Mancinelli *anywhere* in her diaries suggests some kind of animus, on which basis ignoring the conductor became household doctrine.[17]

In the weeks that followed the January 15 concert, Wagner's name again fades out of the Venetian newspapers. It appears in notices by *LV* (January 21, 24) and *LGdV* (January 24) reporting initial negotiations between the Teatro la Fenice and Angelo Neumann to have his traveling troupe present their *Ring* production there in April—a process to be considered below.[18] The *LV* account of the twenty-fourth particularly stressed the idea of the theater's directors, as communicated to Neumann,

that the Fenice, in homage to Wagner, who would still be residing in Venice, would be the first Italian theater in which the famous tetralogy would be performed.

We know that Wagner himself strongly opposed the project: he might well have obstructed it had he lived; or if it were to come to pass (as it did), he might well have left Venice to avoid it. But we at least can appreciate that, in this case, a Venetian musical institution was considering a musical enterprise involving Wagner's music in direct relation to his residence in the city.

Otherwise, the newspapers' silence on Wagner was not to be broken before the stunning event of February 13.

It is easy to perceive that the journalistic coverage of Wagner's residences in Venice was somewhat thin up to that point. This is much in contrast to our age of would-be interviewers or shameless paparazzi besieging celebrities, and of public hunger for news of their private lives. But ours is a relatively recent journalistic world. A century and a quarter ago, conventions of respecting personal privacy were generally understood and honored, unless blatant scandals were involved. And certainly the Wagners knew how to keep people away from them.

Also to be considered are the limitations to newspaper resources of the time, and especially in such a smaller and less prosperous Italian city as Venice. On this point, it must be recognized that the two Venetian newspapers were of very small physical scale: each number merely a single elephant-folio sheet folded to make four pages, each of those filled with text in some four columns. Cultural matters were prominent, but they faced a lot of competition. And, truth to tell, Venetian newspapers rarely had much space for, or concern over, "human-interest" features on people of whatever distinction who were visiting the city. Venetian journalists were certainly aware of Wagner's presence, above all in his last two visits. Nevertheless—whether because of a polite reticence, or lack of staff resources, or just a lack of extensive public interest, or all of the above—Wagner and his family and his music are given only sporadic treatment by the Venetian newspapers.

Until, that is, Wagner's death burst suddenly upon Venice and the world. At that moment, Wagner became a major subject for the city's journalists, and Venice became a brief focus of the whole world's artistic consciousness.

Chapter Six

Mourning

Wagner's death occurred too late on the afternoon of Tuesday, February 13 for either Venetian newspaper to give it attention, but from then on, and for the following days, even weeks, it became the commanding story for the Venetian press.

The reactions by each of the two newspapers might be divided into five stages classified as: (1) announcement (Wednesday, February 14); (2) obituary (Thursday, February 15); (3) tributes (Thursday–Friday, February 15–16); (4) departure (Friday–Saturday, February 16–17); and (5) aftermath oddments (Sunday, February 17 ff).

As the morning paper, *La Venezia* (*LV*) had the first word on the event, though the scramble of last-minute recasting of layout relegated it to page 2:

WAGNER—Deceased yesterday in our city was the musical genius of Germany.

The composer of *Lohengrin* was for some months among us with his wife and his delightful children, hoping that the mild air of our heaven might have served to restore him in health, delicate for some time. He lived reclusively in an apartment in the Palazzo Vendramin Calergi, receiving only a few friends.

The day before yesterday, Riccardo Wagner seemed to feel himself well—and he made an excursion around the Canalazzo by gondola. Yesterday likewise, around 3 p.m., he had arranged the same trip. But exactly at that hour, struck by a sudden illness, he needed to be put to bed.

Shortly after he expired!

In the city only toward evening did the fatal news spread—and made a profound impression on all, because the renowned maestro was revered by Venetians as the learned and amiable genius.

Last evening we went to the Palazzo Vendramin Calergi to have news.

—Riccardo Wagner is dead—there it was told—and his widow, kneeling before his corpse, crazed with grief, hardly believing that her beloved companion sleeps the eternal repose!

How many memories crowd upon our mind—the bold struggles that he sustained, the sublime victories that he achieved—the art that he created—the bitter enemies he had—the fanatical partisans that idolized him as a God—the crowned kings who knelt down before him!

No more—a corpse!

But from him rises a voice that will not die—and perhaps will become in time more powerful, more hearkened to, more beloved.

Of Riccardo Wagner we will speak another day. Today we place a flower, one more on his bier.

The musical world boasts two great masters—our Verdi, German Wagner—two masters, two schools.—Destiny has willed that Riccardo Wagner should die in Italy, the fatherland of Giuseppe Verdi. And Italy, for whom genius has no fatherland, also sheds a tear on the bier of the German master.

Riccardo Wagner had not yet reached seventy years. He was born, indeed, in Leipzig on 22 May 1813.

He anticipated death. When at the Liceo he conducted his youthful Symphony, putting down the baton, he exclaimed:

—I will conduct no more, I will write no more, *Parcifal* [*sic*] will be my final opera.

—Why, maestro?! he was asked.

—Because I will die.[1]

That evening, *La Gazzetta di Venezia* (*LGdV*) made a shorter announcement, and as far back as page 3:

Riccardo Wagner is dead

Yesterday at 3 p.m. Riccardo Wagner died unexpectedly. This news, so very unforeseen, united in the same grief all those who, identified variously with different schools, share greatly and profoundly in devotion to the art. Wagner had attained about 70 years. The illustrious maestro died in the famous Palazzo Vendramin, perhaps the most beautiful of so many that adorn our Grand Canal. His distracted wife lay her head upon that of her dear husband and could not believe his death. The entire family, by which Riccardo Wagner was adored, is crushed and broken under the weight of this misfortune.

In a more settled frame of mind, we will say something about the great star that has waned on the musical horizon.

For stage 2 on the following day (Thursday, February 15), the two newspapers had marshaled their full resources to print large-scale obituaries. That by *LV* was broadly retrospective, and from the start set Wagner and his art in the cross-currents of national tastes. One detects here the viewpoint of the journal's critic "Toni," already encountered, and here sketching out issues to which he would soon be returning more fully. The obituary begins:

WAGNER—The Germans adored him as a Messiah. The French hated him as an enemy. We Italians, so rich in musical art as not to be forced to envy the glory of others, appreciated him according to his rightful merit, without idolatry, without objections in terms of system. And therefore we may speak calmly of the dead Riccardo Wagner, in the same way that we applauded the living one.

The obituary then proceeds to review the composer's career, beginning with an emphasis on Wagner's bold, tenacious, and combative character and his long and uncompromising struggles with opponents and circumstances. It reviews the sequence of his operas, and his ambitious scheme to create his own performing venue, aided by the king of Bavaria. There is discussion of his musical style and dramatic objectives that set him in opposition to the art of Meyerbeer, Mozart, and Rossini, and caused controversy among Italians.

Wagner's music was called, in derision, the "music of the future" (*musica dell'avvenire*), and was put in opposition to our essentially melodic, clear, charming music. That's another issue that is not ours to discuss, much less to resolve. Certainly there will always be two schools, in the future as in the past, when there would arise partisans and enthusiasts for his powerful talents. And those who are impartial would say, as did our supreme master Rossini: There are only two kinds of music—beautiful and ugly.

And Wagner's music is beautiful, not only—as many insist—for profundity of doctrine but instead for boldness of conception, for novelty of expressions, for force and variety of colorism—and, above all, for the indissoluble union of the poetic ideal with the musical ideal, that makes the Wagnerian opera—*Lohengrin*, for example—comparable to a statue sculpted in porphyry: austere, incorruptible.

Wagner set to music the fabulous German legends and wrote the poetry for it. He selected his subjects from the realm that best suited his own sensibility—and he expressed it in such a way as no one could knowingly equal.

O Knight of the Holy Grail, sing the moving Wagnerian *adio* to the body of the maestro who created you!

Wagner—we said yesterday—anticipated his death. A few days before he said to a friend: They criticize my personality. But I am ill, very ill, and I would like to avoid everyone because noise annoys me.

The day before yesterday, signora Lucca was in Venice, she who, at the famous Bayreuth banquet, had placed a laurel crown on the brow of the maestro. Because he was ill, Wagner was not able to receive her. Yesterday she sent to prof. Frontali a telegram of condolence for the family members, saying that her nephew Ferrari was coming hither to represent her.

Telegrams of condolence from all Europe arrived yesterday at the Palazzo Vendramin Calergi. First that from the king of Bavaria, who asked that the corpse of the maestro should not be touched before one of his own representatives arrives. He will be here today—and today it will be decided what to do. It appears that the body will be transported immediately to Bayreuth, where the final rites will be held. Meanwhile friends of the family, among them the baron Fiers, consul of Germany, are seeing to all the most necessary concerns. The body was covered with flowers.

Wagner leaves his wife and five children, four girls and a boy. The widow is the signora Cosima Liszt, daughter of that abbé [i.e., Franz Liszt], divorced from Hans de [von] Bülow, another famous German musician, in order to marry Wagner.

As far as we learned yesterday, already dispatched to the railroad are a funeral car for transportation of the body to Germany, and a wagon-salon for the family.

What *LGdV* published later that same day (Thursday, February 15) was less an obituary, in the conventional terms of biography and critical assessment, and more its own attempt at an account of the composer's death supplemented by fuller data on funeral arrangements. It is actually the very first description of his death and its immediate aftermath to appear anywhere in print.

Riccardo Wagner—The news of the death of the illustrious musician has upset the artistic world. Yesterday, and today, telegrams arrive by the hundreds from all sides to the family, which lies prostrate under the weight of the unexpected misfortune. The day before yesterday, Wagner appeared to be slightly unwell, but for some hours in the morning he had set his mind to his routine. Around 3 p.m. he felt himself becoming worse: still, he ordered lunch to be served, but then he felt himself in a condition only to take some broth. Then he ordered his gondola to be made ready, hoping perhaps to find in the free air and in the poetic tranquility of our Grand Canal a little refreshment; but he was overtaken by illness before he could go down into the gondola. He was in his room, and wearing a red-colored garment; he rang the bell and asked for his wife. His Cosima rushed immediately and, seeing her husband very ill, sent for doctor Keppler, the family physician, unable to recognize death. The wife, accustomed already to such attacks, in the form of irregularity, to which Wagner happened frequently to be subject (it seems he died from cardiac failure), would not accept that he was dead. She clung to his neck hour after hour, with no way to pull her away. One can imagine the scene for the daughters and son, all extremely devoted to him.[2]

The news spread soon after, and then was a topic of discussion everywhere, with that sense of grief that is displayed in such circumstances, especially when men known to everybody are involved, as was this case.

Yesterday, in sign of mourning, our Liceo Benedetto Marcello was closed, the place where, some weeks ago, Wagner himself conducted a youthful symphony of his, specifically to celebrate the birthday of his wife. At the Liceo is still his music-stand and also, we believe, his baton.[3]

It is certainly not easy to obtain precise news of what is going on in that family, which has been struck so harshly by the misfortune, because it is, one might say, hermetically sealed off in its grief. The corpse of the illustrious maestro is laid out on his bed (the bed that his widow wishes to take off to Bavaria in order that she might continue to sleep in it)[4] and covered over with flowers from the family. In another room are the garlands sent by friends.

King Luigi [Ludwig] of Bavaria, as soon as he was informed about the loss of his friend, telegraphed that nothing be touched until a representative of his could arrive in Venice with instructions. It was for this reason that the widow did not at all want to allow the death mask to be made. The representative of the king of Bavaria has arrived, or is about to arrive. Also expected to come is the daughter who is at Palermo [i.e., Daniela Bülow-Gravina]; but, apparently wanting the family to set out as fast as possible, that daughter will not come here in course but will probably go on to Bavaria to see her father one last time.

And we could say *to re-see*, because, as we write, at 3 o'clock, the embalming should be taking place and then the body will be placed in a metal casket with a glass plate in the upper portion, specifically to allow viewing into it.

Initial thought was given here to a grandiose funeral appropriate to so illustrious a man; but then, the family made it known that it wished to leave as quickly as possible, together with the remains of its dear one. Arrangements were also made for a funeral car and a *salon* carriage; but since they wished to leave on a direct train, and, as the railroad regulations do not permit the transport of bodies on such trains, it was necessary to appeal to the Directory of the Fourth Section of the railroad from Upper Italy in Verona for a special permission. Partly for this reason and partly also because the casket from Vienna had not yet arrived, it will be necessary to delay the departure, which may be set for tonight or for tomorrow night.

Accordingly, all procedures will be limited to an escort of the most private type from the Palazzo Vendramin Calergi to the Railroad station, and the official funeral rites will take place in Bavaria: it is not yet known clearly whether at Munich or at Bayreuth.

We do know that the Commission of Monuments, on the proposal of Cav. Luciani, has expressed the wish that the Municipality arrange to put up a commemorative stone slab on the Palazzo Vendramin Calergi, where Riccardo Wagner died.

Comm. Astengo, Royal Delegate Extraordinary, has sensitively rendered the sentiments of the entire citizenry by sending to the illustrious man's widow the following:

Venice 14 February
Distinguished Signora,
The tremendous misfortune by which you, noble lady, were yesterday stricken, was on a scale as great for Germany as for all, for the art that has lost a genius, for the entire world.

Then Venice especially feels more keenly the bitterness of the unexpected loss of the great maestro, because, to the admiration offered to his innovative genius, it has added a reverent and cordial affection for the gracious guest who was accustomed for years to seek in this city tranquility, health, and new inspirations.

For these sentiments of the Venetian citizenry I hasten to make myself the intermediary to your illustrious ladyship, presenting with them the assurances of the most profound condolence.

Of Your Most Illustrious Ladyship
Most Devoted C. ASTENGO
R. Delegato straordinario
To the most noble signora
Cosima Wagner, née Liszt
The Royal Delegate has further decided that a Corona [a large metal funerary wreath] is to be placed on the catafalque, and is seeing to all the arrangements so that Venice might take part in a decorous and appropriate fashion in all the tributes that will be made to the illustrious maestro.

Stage 3 of the newspapers' treatment of Wagner's death followed on Friday February 16, as each journal dealt with the tributes being made to the deceased, thus leading up to the departure of the Wagner family with his body. The morning commencement belonged, of course, to *LV*:

WAGNER—From all parts of Europe come reports of the deep impressions stirred by the unforeseen death of Riccardo Wagner. We reproduce some telegrams:
Munich, the 14th—The news of the unforeseen death of Wagner has made a tremendous impression. King Luigi in utmost grief will be represented at the funeral rites. The body will be transported hither, where solemn tributes will be offered. It is said he will be buried in Bayreuth.
Vienna, the 14th—The news of the unforeseen death of Wagner stirred profound feelings in all circles. All the newspapers speak abundantly about it, producing obituary articles and lamenting the serious loss sustained by German art. Numerous public gatherings are in preparation. It has also been confirmed that the celebrated composer Abate Liszt will be present at the funeral ceremonies.
Berlin, the 15th—Munich has launched a subscription in order to erect a grandiose monument to Wagner.
All the Italian newspapers speak of Riccardo Wagner with high respect: so much animosity stands condemned before the bier of the great man. At Bologna in particular,

first of the Italian cities that honored Wagner in the theater, his death was deeply felt. Its mayor [*sindaco*] dispatched this telegram:

Signora Cosima Wagner.
Venezia.
Struck grievously by the news of the unforseen death of maestro Wagner, I hasten to convey my intense reactions to such a misfortune, expressing them together with sentiments of the most profound sympathy in the name of Bologna, which takes pride in numbering the illustrious Maestro among its honorary citizens.
Sindaco TACCONI

Milan was unfair toward the German reformer, but Torelli Viollier, quite candidly, writes in the *Corriere della Sera*:

Milan owes a debt to Wagner: Lohengrin was noisily condemned. A small minority of fanatical or self-interested auditors so disrupted the performance that impartial individuals were unable at leisure to rely on their first judgment, and Lohengrin was suppressed by reason of public decree! Milan, we believe, owes compensation to the memory of Wagner and therefore it ought to allow another of his operas to be given at La Scala with a performance worthy of the great German maestro. If La Scala should be a place for the highest aesthetic lessons, and not simply a place for pastimes, this suggestion of ours ought to be heard by those at the top level of direction there, as the pronouncement of a commanding obligation.

In the name of Venice, which takes pride in its guest Riccardo Wagner, the Comm. Astengo expressed to the signora Liszt-Wagner the condolences of the city with this most tender letter, in which the devastated widow may see represented the feeling of all Venetians:

(There follows the same text given the previous evening by *LGdV*, complete with the account, in the same words, of Astengo's dispatch of a *corona*.) *LV* then continues:

The directorship of the Liceo Marcello, has arranged everything late yesterday so that the tributes to Riccardo Wagner, before the body be returned to its homeland, should prove there to be as formal as possible. The Royal Delegate of the Municipality, Comm. Prefetto has joined with the Liceo. From all parts of Italy have arrived today dispatches requesting funeral news. The other evening from Milan came also maestro Angelo Tessarin, a friend of Wagner, and fervent apostle of the Wagnerian faith.

But—so it seems—the family, perhaps obeying a desire of King Luigi of Bavaria, has not, as late as last evening, given any acceptance to the tributes we have organized.

The other evening the sculptor Benvenuti made the death mask; yesterday the body was embalmed.

The body was then placed in a metal casket that has a glass lid.

Yesterday the Liceo Musicale remained closed as a sign of mourning

The Commission of Monuments proposes that a stone slab be placed on the Palazzo Vendramin Calergi, where Riccardo Wagner died. Excellent.

Here is the inscription mounted on the house in Leipzig (Brül, 88) where the maestro was born:

In diesem Hause/ward geboren/RICHARD WAGNER/an 22 mai 1813

Sig. G. Vizzotto designed and Boumassari lithographed the image of R. Wagner, taken from a recent photograph made in Munich. The portrait is the best possible likeness—the work praiseworthy. It will be a lovely souvenir of the illustrious maestro. It is on sale at the Gallo music shop for the price of one lira.

The Royal Academy of Santa Cecilia in Rome has sent to the widow of maestro Wagner a telegram thus composed:

> The president of the Royal Academy and Liceo of Santa Cecilia, in the name also of the academic corps, expresses the feelings of most profound sorrow for the total misfortune that has struck the art of music with the loss of the great stylistic leader, your spouse, whom the Academy has had the honor to include among its illustrious friends. MARCHETTI

> The body of Riccardo Wagner leaves Venice for Munich in Bavaria tomorrow at 2 p.m.

Not to be outdone by its counterpart, that afternoon (February 16) *LGdV* published an even larger catch-all article (occupying much of page 2) as its stage 3; indeed, since the journal went to press immediately following the departure of Wagner's funeral train, this article could open with elements of its stage 4:

> *Funerary tributes to Riccardo Wagner*—Today, at 2:10, the body of Riccardo Wagner left our city, accompanied by his family. The exterior casket (since there were three other internal ones) was in metal bronzed in three shades, with a crucifix, cherubs, foliage, lions' heads, in Renaissance style. The funeral car on the inside was decorated in black and silver. With the catafalque placed in the mortuary car, some 20 *coroné* were set in it, and then it was closed, and the municipal physician, dottor Gallina, affixed there the lead seals.

> At the station were the Royal Prefect comm. Mussi, Royal Commissioner comm. Astengo, Count Contin, president of the Liceo e Società Benedetto Marcello, with the entire faculty of professors, some of the principal musicians of Venice, many painters belonging to the Venetian artist circle, the municipal press, and representatives of Italian and foreign newspapers.

> As soon as it reached the station, the family entered the salon-carriage and lowered the curtains. Representing the family were the Russian painter Joukowski [Joukowsky] and Passini, plus the banker Gross. Likewise there was the banker Reitmeyer [*sic*] and others. In the vestibule the municipal fire brigade was lined up.

> Count Giuseppe Contin, turning to signor Gross, expressed in German how the Venetian art-world was in grief over such a misfortune befallen on art, and he begged him to become a kindly interpreter to the family of the feelings of profound condolence that all held in their hearts in this time of distress.

> Signor Gross replied that the widow was in such a state of agitation as would not allow her to respond, and that she might defer doing so to another time in writing.

> The representative of the king of Bavaria [i.e., Ludwig von Bürkel]—about whom there had been a mistaken announcement confused with the arrival of the banker signor Gross—is awaiting at the frontier.

> There was momentarily the idea to have a representative of our Municipality accompany the body of the illustrious deceased to the frontier, but he had not the courage to do this, seeing the family so greatly resistant to any intervention and so isolated. Venice

used its full strength to restrain the impulses of its own heart toward an illustrious guest, so very worthy of the most special tributes. But it managed to set a firm seal on its grief, scrupulously respecting the sentiments of the family, which, even from this, should be assured that Venice will always have the very highest reverence for the great musician, and the most lively affection for his family, so worthy of respect and of sympathy.

Signora Giovannina Lucca, who is proprietress of many of Wagner's operas for Italy, has neglected nothing to assert her high admiration and her devoted affection toward the illustrious deceased. Regrettably unable to come herself because of ill health, she has sent a representative in sig. Ferrari Giacomo and he saw to placing a splendid *corona* on the catafalque.

The same signora Lucca has ordered that at the time of the funerary conveyance her music shop should remain closed as a sign of mourning.

Also the publisher Ricorde [*sic*] sent telegrams in order to learn all possible circumstances of the illustrious maestro's death and in order to know if the funeral services had taken place here, or where.

Maestro Luigi Mancinelli, in the event that funeral services should be held here at Venice, wanted to be present at them and he even offered to conduct the *Requiem* by Berlioz or by Mozart.[6]

All the musical Institutes of Italy have sent telegrams, first among them being that of Bologna, from which also has telegraphed its mayor, since in the past it had conferred Bolognese citizenship upon Wagner. It is estimated that more than 300 telegrams have come to the family from all parts of the world.

Further on its page 2, and spilling onto page 3, *LGdV* attempted a belated substitute for the proper obituary it had failed to give on the day after Wagner's death:

Riccardo Wagner
Late afternoon on Tuesday [the thirteenth], in order to be in time to get it into the edition that is printed in the course of the night and that goes by the first morning post, we noted the sad news of the death of Riccardo Wagner, accompanying it with a few words. At the end we said that in a more settled frame of mind we would say something *about the great star that has waned on the musical horizon*; but, in better considered judgment, a preferable course seems to us to condense into a few formulations, digesting in a few words, just who was this most powerful musical genius, who had the forcefulness to fascinate the whole world with his most audacious innovations, with his lofty ideas.

There follows a substantial essay, seemingly at first of biographical character, appropriate to an obituary. But almost immediately it turns to critical evaluation, and in terms that seem to anticipate the strongly positive interpretations that the critic "Toni" would be setting forth on some of the same issues in reviewing the *Ring* production in April. But "Toni" was critic for *LV*, whereas this writer for *LGdV* sounds more like its critic who reviewed Calascione's *Lohengrin* fantasy or Mancinelli's Liceo concert on January 10, rather than the one who was to write on the *Ring* for this journal. These comments specifically deal with Italian reactions to Wagner's music. Briefly discussing Wagner's background, our writer posits Wagner's early disillusionment with the deteriorating musical and cultural life of his youth. Wagner thus plunged forward to revitalize it with a passion and energy that attracted both enthusiastic partisans and bitter enemies, who became locked in ferocious conflict: the animosity of Italian adversaries being exceeded only by that of French ones.

In rigorously strict terms, Wagner was not a true innovator. He followed the route, if not completely marked out, at least anticipated first by Rameau and then by Gluck, naturally bringing it to those proportions that the progress in musical science of newer times were allowing. It was essential for his grand vision that humanistic studies should attain a broader growth everywhere. It was essential for his grand vision that there should arise everywhere, and in great abundance, proper orchestral and choral Societies and to prepare taste for its major evolution and the means for directing it step by step to the desired loftiness of musical art. And in this laborious, fruitful movement he would have as collaborators the best living masters. With jealous zeal, cherishing likewise in their hearts the creed that for everyone stands for creative expression—in which Italy was and always will be foremost—they have recognized that drama ought to be served better, with fuller grounding, with clearer rationality, with loftier intentions. This, to sum up our opinion, is where Wagner's true merit resides.

So much has been written on this musical colossus over the course of so many years. In brief, so much has been discussed of his theories, his musical works, or of their philosophical-literary character, that it would be useless to pass in review what he has done and what he has said. Also, the cultural media are completely informed as to the artistic history of this illustrious man, who had given frequent evidence that he was a sincere admirer of many of our maestri, particularly Bellini—even though the latter might perhaps be the most negligent of all in the field of instrumentation, precisely that same field in which he, Wagner, reigned supreme.

Louis Blanc, in his *Storia dei dieci anni* [*Histoire de dix ans*] says that writing contemporaneous history is a sensitive and dangerous undertaking, and no less sensitive and dangerous for the contemporaneous historian is that of judging men of Wagner's stature. It is necessary that time should cast its calming pall over the men and the issues for a long spell of time. After some thinning in all the clouds of passion, it would be possible to secure a firm basis, a fixed point and not a misleading mirage.

We Italians are able to console ourselves and view without shame this catafalque that holds the great German musician. For, if we have sometimes opposed Wagner, it was simply because we were believing, and we still believe, that he could do harm to our musical school, even while we recognized the rightness of his ideas in ever so many matters. And also in these controversies, placing some restraint on that liveliness that is a part of our character, we have always held to moderation, never going beyond that courtesy to which all are entitled—and men of genius surely more than others. Certainly some other nations might not say as much, because they have been stained by their condemnations, not just in their newspapers, which have a lifetime of one day, but in the pages of works that are fated to endure.

As Venetians, then, we are obliged to offer an altogether special tribute to his memory, for the affection that he bore our city. That city was utterly delighted to offer hospitality, often and for long periods of time, to a man in whose name will be entered a most glorious page in the history of the art.

Following this article, at a little distance in the same number (still February 16), *LGdV* reproduced a message transmitted by Count Contin:

Ringraziamento.

With a deeply stirred soul, I fulfill the sad but honor-bringing assignment given me by the family of maestro Riccardo Wagner, that I make known publicly the fervent gratitude with which they are unexpectedly filled for the demonstrations of affection and esteem made to them by the governmental and municipal Authorities, by the press, and by every level of individuals and organizations, not only of Venice, but of all Italy, on the occasion of that great man's death, which the entire world mourns as a blow to art.

Ct. Giuseppe Contin

Only the following day, Saturday, February 17, could *LV* catch up with the funerary departure, in a parallel report:

WAGNER

By train at 2:18 yesterday afternoon, the body of Riccardo Wagner left Venice.

Only yesterday morning did the funeral casket of bronze arrive from Vienna, within which was placed the maestro's corpse. Even yesterday, before the afternoon, there was uncertainty that the shipment could take place because of the casket's delay.

But, at 1 p.m., the body was already at the station, and so all proceeded according to the desire of the family, which wanted to avoid any public ceremonial, as prepared by the Prefect, the Royal Delegate, or the Liceo Benedetto Marcello.

However, at the station at 2, many representatives were gathered: commend. Mussi, comm. Astengo, Ct. Contin, the other councilors, maestro Grazzini and the professors of the Liceo Benedetto Marcello, some journalists of Venice, and correspondents of Italian and foreign journalists.

On the catafalque were arrayed many *corone*: truly splendid was that of the Municipality and that of the Liceo Musicale. The bier was enclosed within a car in mourning decor and sealed; the Wagner family left in a salon-carriage.

Telegrams from Vienna to Italian journals stated that the Abbé Liszt had departed for Venice.

The news is imprecise. Liszt, Richter, and all the musical representatives of Germany and Austria-Hungary have left for Munich, where the funeral rites will take place.

Riccardo Wagner had finished writing his manuscript autobiography, which he gave to one of his daughters, charging her to publish it after his death.[7]

The distinguished Ct. Giuseppe Contin, president of the Liceo Musicale Benedetto Marcello, writes us thus, and we hasten to print it: [there follows exactly the same text by Contin that *LGdV* had printed the previous afternoon].

It is interesting to note that all these newspaper reports stress that the departure had been slightly delayed by late arrival of the casket from Vienna. More curious is the fact that neither newspaper, in all its details, paid any attention to the short and mutely solemn procession of funeral gondolas that bore the casket and the family members along the Grand Canal from the Palazzo Vendramin to the railroad station—amid the general display of popular respect and sympathy that was given particular note by Glasenapp.

Above all, whatever small details these newspaper accounts add to our established information on this episode, they reveal with fuller vividness the hasty scramble that followed Wagner's death. The family's reaction—further prompted by King Ludwig, the more so after Gross arrived to take charge—was simply the impatient desire to leave Venice as quickly and unceremoniously as possible. This haste clearly deflated Venetian leaders, who wanted to make elaborate gestures of mourning and respect, out of genuine sentiment but also out of a sense of civic honor. Already dawning was a glimmer of consciousness as to how much this mournful occasion could and should matter to Venice. World-class cultural figures rarely came to Venice to die, and already Venetians had a rudimentary awareness that Wagner's death among them associated them with something truly important. It was an opportunity not to be missed. The potential flamboyance of a Venetian civic send-off to Wagner's corpse was equally what Venetian leaders hungered to do and what the Wagners were anxious to avoid.[8]

That same afternoon (Saturday, February 17), *LGdV* began its stage 5 reports with the first supplemental details that would occupy the two newspapers for the following days and weeks:

Funeral Tributes to Riccardo Wagner.
— To round out the reports that we had given yesterday on the funeral tributes accorded Riccardo Wagner, in the most private fashion, we observe: that also yesterday our Liceo remained closed in sign of mourning, and that with the same intention the operation of the Municipal Band in the Piazza was suspended. Among the *corone* there was a particularly beautiful one, made up entirely of Alpine flowers, sent by the Mozarteum of Salzburg (Austria). To place it on the catafalque, the representative of the Mozarteum, the attorney dr. Oscar Berggruen, came directly from Vienna. Dr. F. Mamroth represented Vienna's *Deutsche Zeitung.*
—As to the arrival of the body at Bayreuth we do not yet have any news. It was supposed to arrive today, at 3:15 p.m., at Munich, where it was to make a stop of three hours and then go onward to arrive at 11 p.m. at Bayreuth. We know that a dispatch was sent to Munich but no reply has yet arrived.
—At about 6 o'clock, cav. Fiers, the German Consul, graciously informed us that the body of Wagner reached Munich, and that the illustrious maestro's widow has paused a little in the interest of some relief.

Over the next two days, *LV* printed its own supplemental reports, for a readership whose fascination with Wagner's death and departure had not abated. On Sunday, February 18, there were these tidbits:

Riccardo Wagner
Telegrams of various newspapers:
Berlin, the 15th. All the newspapers discourse in long articles upon the deceased: many are issued with black borders. The death of Wagner is regarded as a

public bereavement. A subscription has been launched in order to raise a monument.

Munich (Bavaria), the 16th. The entire realm is in mourning. Banners of mourning hang from theaters, museums, musical academies, as from many private buildings. The embalmed body will reach Bayreuth tomorrow morning, accompanied by Liszt,[9] Hans von Bülow,[10] Hans Richter, baron Hoffmann, indendant of the Imperial Opera at Vienna.

Numerous delegations from all parts of Germany and the realm arrive at Bayreuth. King Luigi will be at this station in order to greet the catafalque. The funeral ceremonies will be impressive. The Chorus of the Pilgrims from *Tannhäuser* and the great religious hymn from *Parsifal* will be performed.

On the following day (Monday, February 19), *LV* spiced its tidbits by raising anew the Italian response to Wagner's music:

Wagner and Verdi
Speaking of the death of the great German maestro, it seems fair to us to link the names of Wagner and Verdi. Misovulgo did the same in *Italia*, and he writes:
"I remember that, when I chanced one day to meet Verdi, there was discussion of the young, of their herding propensities, of the results they were promising. Our great maestro, with his customary common sense, spoke in these exact words: '. . . and the young should remember not to imitate either Wagner or me; we are two *vielles carcasses!*' Profound words, in truth! Through them Verdi answered, with his great authority, that reproach of the 'music of the future.' He who had surely testified, more exceptionally than unusual, to following the direction of the times, to profiting from what we have learned, was reckoning Wagner's *opus* as already a part of history, as a patrimony available for the benefit of anyone who wants to learn, joined with the classics and the old masters. Moreover, he was advising that one assimilate everything and imitate no one, neither himself nor Wagner; that one benefit rather from that which both have achieved for the art; that one not renounce the true, the beautiful, the good, in order to set out and follow this or that other *school* ... and above all not to deny one's own individuality."[11]

On that latter day, Monday, February 19, *LGdV* devoted space on its page 2 to its latest oddments, which it labeled as "Curiosities":

Curiosità—Signora Cosima Wagner, née Liszt, widow of the illustrious musical maestro whose loss the artistic world laments, chose to cut off her long hair, and had it placed on the catafalque that contained the body of her beloved spouse.—We make note of this deed alike for lovers of details and for collectors of curiosities.

A little further on, *LGdV* gives two reports from the Stefani news agency:]

Wagner's Body
Munich (Bavaria), the 17th—The body of Wagner arrived at the station at 2:30 p.m. It was awaited by an aide-de-camp of the King, bearing a laurel *corona*, and by numerous deputations. It will move on this evening for Bayreuth.

Wagner's Funeral Rites
Bayreuth, the 18th—The funeral ceremonies for Wagner took place with great display. Numerous deputations filed past the catafalque and deposited *corone*. In the cortège were the daughters of Wagner, the representatives of the King of Bavaria, deputations of artists, journalists, officials, an extensive crowd. Some speeches were made. Some songs were performed.

Venetians were still so stirred by Wagner's death—or at least so the city's press believed—that items continued to appear in the two local newspapers, a week following the death itself, and even after the obsequies for the composer had by then moved far away. On Tuesday, February 20, *LV* had something of at least local associations to contribute—and offering a last gesture to a genuine friend whom Wagner retained throughout his visits to Venice:

Wagner and Tessarin—Dr. Keppler has written to maestro cav. Angelo Tessarin this letter, that we are requested to publish:

Dearest M. Angelo Tessarin
Venice 16 February
Madam Cosima Wagner, immediately before the dispatch of the body of the great maestro, entrusted to me and to signor Shukowshi [*sic*] the agreeable assignment of going to seek her in the antechamber of the Palazzo Vendramin so as to conduct her, on behalf of signorina Daniela, to your daughter to press her hand and bid her farewell. And in just this way signora Cosima, through this gesture of courtesy (departing, only for you, from her rule of not wanting to deal with anybody), she meant to indicate to you her deep friendship for you always, and to soothe, if it would be possible, the sadness over the cruel departure of the illustrious deceased, who loved you out the most noble and deserved affection.—I take this opportunity, illustrious sig. maestro, to offer the expressions of my highest esteem and to proclaim myself
  your most devoted FEDERICO D. KEPPLER[12]

That evening (Tuesday, February 20), *LGdV* contributed what it could to continuing the momentum:

Funeral Tributes to Riccardo Wagner
—We see in the German newspapers, and also in many letters that have reached distinguished individuals of our city from Vienna and from Berlin, that all which Italy in general and Venice in particular did on the occasion of the death of the great musician found welcome echo in those two capitals. Thus, in these private letters as in the German periodicals, there are affectionate and sympathetic statements about Italy and about Venice in particular.
  We are delighted by this flow of sympathy also in the artistic realm; but we are privately of the opinion that we have not done anything more than our duty. To do justice to an illustrious man, and, what is more, a welcome guest, would be obligatory, absolutely obligatory, and we remain sorry that it was not granted us to display more

solemnly our so great respect toward his memory and our devoted affection toward his surviving family.

Portraits of Riccardo Wagner—On the occasion of the death of the great musician, a few portraits of him were made, as taken from his last photographs. Among those that have come within our view the most successful are: that from A. Edel, published by the *Gazzetta musicale* of Milan, and that published by the lithographic establishment of signora Adele Varola, widow Fraccaroli, by way of sig. Roman, in Venice.

The next morning (Wednesday, February 21), *LV* could find only a small bit of follow-up news from Germany:

For the family of Wagner—By telegraph from Munich, the 19th: it is said that King Luigi [Ludwig] has settled on signora Cosima Wagner an annual pension of 60,000 marks, [and] 20,000 for each of the great maestro's children. So thus do all the members of Wagner's family receive from the king an appropriate pension.

That evening *LGdV* had a further communiqué from Germany, but the virtually identical text was published, with additional material, the next morning (Thursday February 22) by *LV*, as follows:

Wagner—By telegraph from Munich dated the 19th:
    The state of signora Cosima Wagner has caused apprehensions. Hans Richter has remained with her at the villa. He reports that the last words of Wagner in Venice were: *My son should* ... and he was unable to continue further.[13] The dying man was referring to his son Siegfried who, lacking any musical aptitude, was destined to become an architect.[14]
    The *corona* placed by General Pappenheim on the catafalque in the name of the King bore the inscription: *Dem Unsterblichen* ("to the immortal one"). During the funeral, the band played the funeral march from *Siegfried* [*sic*], the chorus of pilgrims from *Tannhäuser*, and the religious chorale from *Parsifal*.
    At Milan a symphonic concert is being prepared in honor of the great maestro.—It will be directed by Franco Faccio[15]—and the program is as follows: *Lohengrin* Prelude; *Vascello fantasma* [= *Der fliegende Holländer*] Overture; *Tristano e Isotta* Prelude; *Tannhäuser* Overture; *Crepusculo degli dei* [= *Götterdämmerung*] Funeral March; *Parsifal* Prelude; *Cavalcata delle Valkiri* ["Ride of the Valkyries" from *Die Walküre*]—magnificent program, that embraces the entire Wagnerian output.
    Would it not be possible to organize something of this sort also at Venice—the city that felt the master's final breath?

That Venice might indeed make some such commemorative gesture, if in a totally different form, was revealed by *LGdV* the following afternoon (Friday, February 23):

Tributes to Wagner—We understand that [some] eminent citizens have the idea of asking the Municipality that the branch of the street which leads from the Rio Terrà della Maddalena to the Palazzo Vendramin should be named Via Wagner.

This would be an enduring tribute that Venice offers to the illustrious man, and that the municipal council will surely be glad to accept, thus supporting the public will.

And the following morning (Saturday, February 24), *LV* repeated this news, together with report of other tributes elsewhere and at home:

> Wagner—On March 13, the thirtieth day after the death of Riccardo Wagner, the Liceo Rossini of Bologna will offer a commemoration of the maestro. Enrico Panazacchi will speak, and the orchestra, directed by Luigi Mancinelli, will perform the Preludes of the most celebrated Wagnerian operas. If signorina Borghi Mamò and the tenor Tamagno should agree, it might also be planned to perform the first act of *Lohengrin.*
>
> We also understand that our Liceo Benedetto Marcello is considering a commemoration of Riccardo Wagner.
>
> It is suggested that the street of the Rio Terra della Maddalena as far as the Palazzo Vendramin, where the great maestro died, should be named Via Wagner. We concur in this proposal.

At this point, the daily attention to the mortal departure of Wagner wore out. The two newspapers fell silent on that matter, just as they were meanwhile picking up the thread of plans for the presentation of the *Ring* cycle at the Fenice by Angelo Neumann's touring company in April—which will be traced in subsequent chapters. Nevertheless, a few lingering crumbs could yet be added to the fading trail of the previous week, at least by *LV*. On March 11, it reported one curiosity:

> Wagner's gondola and carriage.—The wife of Riccardo Wagner (reports the German newspapers) has expressed the desire that the gondola, in which the maestro was accustomed to ride through the canals of Venice should be sent to Bayreuth. Further, she would like to have purchased by some friends of the maestro the railroad carriage that carried the body from Venice to Munich.
>
> It might work for the gondola, which could stand in a room;—but as for the carriage, what would the friends of the illustrious deceased want to do with it?![16]

Finally, on Tuesday, March 13, a landmark was noted:

> A month!—Today exactly a month ago at Venice Riccardo Wagner expired unexpectedly. Noting that other Italian cities—Rome, Turin, Bologna, Milan—have made or are going to make commemorations.

By now, however, the excitement over the ensuing *Ring* performances at the Fenice had quite taken over Venice's Wagner-consciousness, and the local newspapers put aside their attention to the recent episode of his death and final departure. Yet, the cessation was to be but an interlude. Venice could not, and would not forget Wagnerian associations with Venice, now reinforced so powerfully by the fact of his death there. Whether in tiny bits or in substantial material, the process of remembering Wagner would be a Venetian preoccupation for years to come.

Chapter Seven

Remembering

A German for the Germans

The patterns of Wagner memory in Venice began immediately, and assumed at once restricted yet substantial form.

Quite apart from the commemorative gestures and memorials to be discussed below, immediate efforts were made to capture the impressions, associations, and memories of Wagner in Venice that were given such sharp meaning by his death there. These efforts were embodied in two books, one published only two months after Wagner's death, the other in the year following (though written that summer).

There are strong differences between them. One was written in German. It was aimed at a German readership receptive to new ventures in Wagner idolatry. The other was written in Italian. It was intended to speed the promotion of Wagner's music in Italy by anchoring firmly the composer's ties to a piece of that land. The two books vary in their reliability, but each is an important source, containing details or insights that are not only plausible but sometimes quite valuable. Their contents have been drawn upon very unevenly in Wagner scholarship, but, as supplements to our mainstream knowledge, they deserve to be better known. They are testimonials to what Wagner and Venice had, by 1883, come to mean to each other. As such, they deserve not just absorption into the general pool of narrative information, but detailed individual expositions and analyses of their distinct character and perspectives. Consideration of the first book will be the subject of this chapter; examination of the other (by Giuseppe Norlenghi) will be the concern of the next chapter.

The first book, in order of publication, is the curious product of a curious personality. This was a bluestocking named Henriette Perl (December 14, 1845–May 10, 1915). Born in the Polish-Ukrainian city of Lwow or Lvov (known in German as Lemberg), she early acquired a multilingual and multicultural background. She was raised by relatives on her mother's side who were relocated in Italy, allowing her a fluent knowledge of Italian from a childhood spent in Naples, Palermo, Florence, and Venice. She trained to become an opera singer, but in 1861, not yet sixteen, she married a wealthy Austrian industrialist. For the next fifteen years she divided her time between Vienna and Prague, living a life of material comfort. But that life came to an end when her husband's family was caught up in the Austrian financial collapse.

From then on she took to earning her own living, translating and then writing romantic novels and travel books. The latter direction required her to take up a life of constant and wide-ranging travel, which included peregrinations around the United States. In 1878 she returned to Europe, eventually settling in Venice, to continue work as a writer. Along the way, she chose to adjust her name to "Henry Perl." The transfer of gender can generate confusion in matters of reference and citation, to say the least. It has been suggested that she may have been following the examples of "Georges Sand" and "George Eliot" in adopting a masculine nom de plume to give her writing easier entrée into a male-dominated literary world not always receptive to female intrusion. It was indeed easier at the time for a male author to achieve publication. Of course, the choice might also have been made to distinguish this book from her earlier writings, of a less "serious" nature. At any rate, she seems in this guise to have achieved some degree of financial independence, while in the process she was inspired to ambitious—not to say pretentious—efforts in entering the higher levels of society.

In this situation she found herself drawn to Wagner—whether out of genuine admiration for his music or simple, celebrity-hunting opportunism—at least during his final visit to Venice. As one of the foreign residents in Venice, she was active in its expatriate circles, and seems already to have been a friend of Dr. Friedrich Keppler, the German physician resident in Venice who became the Wagners' family doctor. Perl herself, despite apparent efforts, never managed to penetrate into the immediate circle around the composer—whose resistance to visitors and strangers was legendary. Though she gives a final hint that she may have visited the Palazzo Vendramin while Wagner was in residence, there is no sure evidence that she had much or any direct contact with him herself, beyond seeing him on public occasions. Once the Wagners were installed in the Palazzo Vendramin, whether through Keppler's help or her own persistence, she apparently managed to cultivate contacts with the family's servants and household staff. Through them she had palpable access to inside information on that household, which gives much of her reporting a weight that cannot be entirely ignored— despite her propensity for exaggeration, if not downright fabrication at times. In that sense, her account preserves immediate recollections that people in Venice had of Wagner's last residence there, along with actual facts about it.[1]

Just what literary plans Perl had been nourishing in advance of Wagner's death are not clear, but that event clearly crystallized what could have been an already-existing project. Here her friendly contacts with Dr. Keppler became crucial: beyond being a vital source of information, he might well have encouraged her or even suggested the project himself. Seeing her opportunity, she worked out her account, which ran a little over 150 printed pages, and rushed it to publication. She presumed a German readership, and it was in that language that she wrote. She gave the work to a publisher in Augsburg, the Royal Bavarian Court Press of Gebrüder Reichel. There it was quickly put into print in mid-April 1883,[2] less than two months after Wagner's death. That was a time when desire would be intense on the part of the composer's German admirers to have detailed word of his last months and days of life. Her Preface, dated in mid-April, places her as still in Venice at that point. It would seem, however, that this Wagner publication became her path back to a fully German identity, and it was in a small Bavarian town outside of Munich that she died, thirty-two years later, amid the early stages of World War I.

The full title of her little book is as follows: *Richard Wagner in Venedig. Mosaikbilder aus seinen letzten Lebenstagen. Mit einem Vorworte und unter Benuztung der Beobachtungen des Herrn Dr. Friedrich Keppler* (Richard Wagner in Venice. Mosaic-Images from his Last Days. With a Foreword and with Benefit of the Supervision of Hr. Dr. Friedrich Keppler). Two points emerge clearly from this combination of brief title and lengthy subtitle. One is Perl's acknowledgment of her dependence upon Dr. Keppler, even claiming his "supervision." By implication, she thereby asserted authoritative status through this association with a man so decisively close to the composer at the time of his death.

The other point is her use of the idea of her book as a "mosaic." This she develops in her *Vorwort*:

> To this little book we have given a subtitle, "Mosaic-images." We add that it does not pretend to be anything more than a collection of little stones and chips, some precious, others less so, laid out next to each other, which, taken together, offer to the numberless admirers of Richard Wagner an honest picture of the events, minor and major, that occurred in Venice in the final days of the great Master's life, so as to portray the related impressions and emotions they prompted in him.—In this work of ours we have not regarded even the smallest bit of stone as too trifling to be picked up along the way and incorporated into these "mosaic-images," so long as they seem to contribute to clarifying the lines in our picture. (91/3)

There follows a letter to Perl from Dr. Keppler, dated March 1883, which constitutes his oft-quoted "autopsy" report as to the causes of Wagner's death and the background of his health—so placed as to endorse the credibility of Perl's work through the doctor's prestige and authority.

The book proper is divided into fourteen chapters of varying length. Chapter 1 floridly establishes the glories of Venice as an appropriate setting for the final scene of the great composer's life. Purple prose flourishes further in the chapter 2, which imagines a moonlight passage by gondola through Venice, beginning as the Riva degli Schiavoni and thence along the Grand Canal, to the Palazzo Vendramin—perhaps with the assumption that most of her German readers would not be personally familiar with the topography and sights of the city, but in the process marking their specific associations with Wagner. Substance increases in chapter 3, which gives a history of the Palazzo Vendramin and ventures a description of it, outside and then inside, culminating in the anticipation of an eventual inscription that will record Wagner's stay there.

In chapter 4, Perl describes the actual arrival of Wagner and his family in Venice on September 16, 1883, and then, after the rapid loading of the Vendramin with their instruments and furnishings, the party's transfer to it on September 24. Even the garments that Richard and Cosima wore are reported. Likewise noted is Wagner's immediately jocund relationship with the palace's porter, Pietro Falcieri—younger brother of Giovanni Battista Falcieri, gondolier and confidant to Byron, in whose arms the poet died in Missolongi in 1824. Pietro was an aged but strapping, white-bearded man whom Wagner, using one of his favorite compliments for Italians, dubbed "Garibaldi." Perl describes the Wagners' selection of the various rooms for their purposes, and decisions about how the rooms should be decorated (lavishly, of course), culminating in his silk-bedecked and perfumed study; of which more will be said below. For all Wagner's love of the grand life, however, Perl stress his "democratic" personality and easy relations with the servants from the outset. The description ends with the first dinner enjoyed in the palace by the Wagner household—including the children Daniela, Eva, Isolde, and Siegfried, the governess Signora Corsani, Baron Stein, and Hr. Hausburg—before whom Wagner celebrated his German identity with Rhenish wine amid contrasts with the Italian atmosphere.

In chapter 5, Perl describes the Wagner household's daily life, once it was set-tled in the Vendramin. The degree of detail indeed supports the belief that the author drew information from the household's servants or the palace staff: data, therefore, of some reliability, much of it unique. As such, this chapter deserves quotation at length, even though (or, perhaps, especially because), some of its statements do not square with what we have otherwise understood.

And now began in the Wagner household that strict routine that one would expect to encounter only with a genius, and that would only be found where an iron self-discipline was joined with an insatiable creative impulse, which regards time as altogether pre-cious.—Richard Wagner was accustomed to arise from bed between five and six o'clock in the morning. The early hours of the morning were devoted to work. No one was allowed to disturb him then, and no one did.—In his black-satin garb he might be too cold: that soon happened, since the Venetian stone walls and stone floors (straw mats and carpets notwithstanding) released a coldness that, even when outside the summer vegetation was in full bloom and the sun was blazing, made warm garments a necessity indoors. Should he thus be too chilly, he wrapped himself in his large fur coat, which from his earliest days had found a proper location in a closet-set in his bedroom, whose entire furniture consisted of a large wardrobe.—Every day, in the early morning hours, he went there and took out the fur coat with his own hands [i.e., without a servant's help], an act to be considered incontestably democratic. For, Wagner generally retained, ineradicably in his blood, his old liberal thinking as regards the privilege of rank. It is a point of significance, how little he suffered himself to be served.

Georg Lang, the household servant, dealt with all practical matters, each more important than attention to his master. This fact clearly refutes the rather sybaritic reputation surrounding [Wagner], based upon his predilection for costly furnishings and garments, merely because he chose to discriminate between a good dish and one less good, and disdained neither a good glass of wine nor a genuine Havana cigar.

The early morning hours, until around about ten o'clock, Wagner spent alone with his work. During his Venetian residence, from his arrival there, he wrote exclusively essays in art criticism—although Italian newspapers claimed to be better informed on this question and asserted that Wagner in his last days (that is, during his residence here) had been working on a new musical work that he titled "The Penitent" [*Die Büsser*], and whose subject would be derived from the Indian legends of Brahma.—These same newspapers also claimed to know that major portions of this musical work were already completed.[3]

Contrariwise, there was another account that we were given by the German press, that the Master in his last days had developed a particular interest in Greek music, and that he was entertaining thoughts of pursuing the study of ancient Greek sources in Athens.—To bring back to life the long-lost music of the ancient Hellenes and to present it to our age would certainly have been an undertaking worthy of the genius of such a Master, save that Wagner contemplated neither the one nor the other of these projects, since he considered his life's work as completed.

The household personnel entered occasionally, though certainly in only exceptional circumstances, for the sake of small personal services to Wagner in his room.—He was accustomed to turn his back to the fully curtained window nearby and he whistled quietly to himself as he wrote. Sometimes also a glass of wine stood on the table before him, and even, when he was not feeling altogether well, a small glass of cognac.

The family took their breakfast separately. Around ten o'clock Frau Cosima went to her husband and apprised him of current matters.—Through her he learned the contents of letters just received, the important news of the day, and such other matters.—Then, as a rule, he took his hat and went down to the courtyard; arriving there, he looked repeatedly to the sky, made his way out onto the wide steps that led to the canal where he moved his hands, each extended separately, back and forth, as if he might thus test the air. This was a special peculiarity of Wagner. Frequently, too, when it rained (as was often the case in the autumn of the previous year [1882]), he asked the porter or his two gondoliers, who were usually lounging in the hall, about their opinions as to the possibilities of the expected weather.—Should sunshine be predicted by these meteorological experts, Wagner's thoughtful countenance immediately brightened, and with a "Bene, bene amico" he usually went straight through the cortile out the palazzo's rear door, which on the land side leads through a side alley to the Strada Nuova.

From there it is an altogether pleasant walk to the Piazza San Marco, while exercise seemed welcome to the Master; so from the beginning of his Venetian residence he frequently made this promenade in good weather.—With this he attended to small practical matters: he went to his banker (Wechselstube Reitmeyer), within the Procuratoria; frequently he also purchased trinkets for the children or for distant friends; he went to the barber, to have his still-youthfully flourishing hair cut; and repeatedly he made an excursion to Lavenna [*sic*], Venice's prime confectionery, where he had a hot chocolate and, on rainy or snowy days, a small glass of cognac, with which he ate some cake.

In the Haindl restaurant also, more than once, he would in petit-bourgeois fashion enjoy a serving of Emmenthaler cheese and a glass of cool beer, at a time when we could not fully relate his forenoon indulgence in Emmenthaler to Wagner's diagnosed gastric complaint.—Frau Cosima often accompanied her husband: then he reduced his itinerary to a visit to Lavenna, the confectioner, after which he passed back and forth through the Piazzetta (his favorite point) and directed his attention to the San Marco church.

Sometimes Wagner could be seen even with his entire family, though in that case it was mostly in the afternoon hours from four to six o'clock. Eventually, as autumn advanced further, they adjusted their early promenade to a later hour and it was often 12 o'clock or thereafter before they left the house.

The Piazza concerts, during the later months of the year, were played from one to three, and subsequently, when the days were longer, from two to four. Wagner sometimes found them boring and sometimes they gave him pleasure, according to his mood of the moment and the choice of the piece. The Overture to *Lohengrin*, as well as still other sections from this opera, played in a notably clipped tempo, once actually made him flee into Lavenna, where his face took on an almost menacing expression, even as he mingled with the other guests in the hardly very large shop. Hardly had he entered, he covered both his ears. This happened early on; later the ensemble seemed to have reached a better understanding of the tempo requirements of Wagnerian music.[4]—This issue is to be understood less as a lack of understanding on the part of Italian musicians than as a concession made to the taste of the Italian public, to which a musical composition is easily found too long. Since the *Lohengrin* Overture has come up, we might recall another episode from an earlier sojourn by Wagner in Venice.

In this case, it was during the winter of 1859 (before the outbreak of the Italian war[5]), which Wagner spent in Venice, where he resided in some rooms in the Palazzo Giustiniani. The Master was working at that time on his *Ring der Niblungen* [*sic*][6] and socialized with but two musicians; these were Tessarin, who presently lives in Milan and who (then perhaps the only musician in Italy who had some understanding of Wagner) had already by that time developed a boundless respect for Wagner, and Ludwig Stiassny [Stiatsny], the bandmaster of the Eleventh Infantry Regiment "Crownprince Albert of Saxony." . . .

What attracted Wagner to the latter was the precision with which the bandmaster knew how to perform his music; and it was indeed the *Tannhäuser* and *Lohengrin* Overtures that he chose to perform in the San Marco Piazza to honor the composer, resulting in Wagner's praise and their association. The Master even went so far as to direct, personally and frequently, the military band in the Chiesa dei Jesuiti, which had been converted by the Austrians into a barracks; from that the intelligent members themselves (mainly Bohemians) learned how to enter completely into the character of his music. . . .

All that pertains to the year 1859. In 1882 the occasionally quite uncomprehending character of performances by Italian bands angered or pained Wagner much more. Sometimes, though, they could even give him some satisfaction. Thus, for example, one day during the interval he approached the bandmaster [i.e., Calascione] and asked him to play something from the *Gazza ladra* [by Rossini]. That musician readily perceived that he was dealing with a distinguished foreigner, and was therefore especially courteous, although—as he subsequently related—he had absolutely no idea whom he had before him. Nevertheless, he responded with Italian civility that he regretted that he did not have the music for the requested piece just at hand, besides which he could not deviate from the program as announced. Wagner paid his respects and moved off in silence. Hardly had he turned his back, however, when one of the musicians informed the bandmaster as to the identity of the man who had spoken to him. No sooner had the leader heard who it was who had made the request than he sent a messenger after the orchestra parts for *Gazza ladra*, and, as the very next musical selection, it was played with *bravura* by the entire ensemble, eager to make a brave showing. Wagner, indeed, was exceptionally moved by this improvised little homage and at the conclusion of the piece expressed not only his thanks in cordial words but showered them with his heartiest praise. One horn player, however, was the recipient of the Master's particular recognition. (132–40/26–31)

Perl's accounts of the two different concerts in the Piazza (April 22 and November 5 in 1882) diverge on some details from other reports of the events, involving Wagner's early relationship with, and respect for, bandmaster Calascione. Her treatment of the one she discusses here, which we know happened on April 22, conflicts with the newspaper reports (though she hints that she had heard an account from Calascione herself); she quite ignores the one in November, which one would think she might have attended. These cases suggest that Perl sometimes had an incomplete grasp of incidents she describes. On the other hand, as we shall see in the next chapter, her report has some correspondence with that of Norlenghi.[7] Did they both have generally the same sources, perhaps among the band musicians?

Perl resumes discussion of the Wagners' daily routine in chapter 6.

> After this pre-midday promenade Wagner was accustomed at first to go home around one o'clock, to which hour the family had appointed the chief meal of the day. After the meal Wagner slept for about an hour.—The couple's two bedrooms gave out onto the garden and were more quiet than those facing the Canal, to which occasionally penetrated the voices of the gondoliers, bearing up their shouts to each other, and where could be heard the shrill whistle of the speeding little steamer [the vaporetto]. That was only recently come to the Canalazzo [Grand Canal], and was called "Tramway" by the local population, not without some cheekiness; but it was a horror to the gondoliers, as regards their business, and to all artistically sensitive people on aesthetic grounds.
>
> While the Master took his nap, Betty Bürkel, the trusted household servant, was, on the instructions of Frau Cosima Wagner, required to remain continually in the adjoining room, so as to be on hand in case the head of the house might want something.— Should the weather be favorable, the gondola was customarily ordered at half-past-four o'clock.
>
> Wagner had developed an enormous liking for going about Venice by water, to which nothing else was comparable, and, from the viewpoint of his poetic perspective, could be regarded also as the most pleasurable way of concluding a siesta.—For the most part, Wagner rode alone with Frau Cosima, but sometimes he also took one or another of his children.[8]—During the first half of October that previous year [1882], the weather was glorious—whereas in September it had been quite unpleasant. They did not restrict themselves merely to the Grand Canal and to the area opposite the Giudecca, but in addition entered into the labyrinth of the small canals which, for anyone who could really devote time to the beautiful fine points of Venice, are at least as interesting as the wide waterways, for all their surrounding artistic treasures.

In agreeable weather they chose to range out still more widely, past the Giardini Pubblici, on to the Lido seashore, to the islands of San Giorgio Maggiore, San Lazzaro, San Servolo, or even in the opposite direction, to Murano. These excursions, in which he inhaled the glorious, salty air, spiced by the warm beams of the autumn sun, did him indescribable good in his respiratory condition, which sometimes could be truly tortuous, and partly derived from his overwrought nerves, as had been the situation throughout all his lifetime, but as was subsequently revealed. . . . (141–43/31–32)

Here Perl digresses on Wagner's accumulating health problems, stressing the gastric and cardiac conditions, and then resumes:

More than once could Richard Wagner be encountered on his excursions in his rapidly gliding gondola, steered by two rudders; he sat leaning far back, with his feet spread widely apart, and usually in lively conversation with his family members. The youthful vitality of his character was shown by his gesticulations; he explained precisely to his loved ones the importance of this or that art work, while they all hung on his lips and listened to his every word as to pronouncements of an oracle.

As his closest intimates and those in his household testified, Wagner frequently asserted that he preferred a promenade by gondola to one in a carriage.—"No dust, no noise," was the motto with which he justified his preference. Back at home, for some hours thereafter Richard Wagner regularly experienced the benevolent effects of the sea air he had inhaled. It was thus a joy to observe him, revitalized, his hands on his back, striding back and forth in the room set aside for his special needs. No one, excepting Frau Cosima, had access to him during these hours. (143–44/32–33)

Perl goes on to describe the great closeness between Richard and Cosima, who understood his every need. In this respect, his life had been truly blessed. After his first marriage—unhappy, and childless—Perl asserts that Wagner had found ultimate harmony and closeness with Cosima. By the time of their stay in Venice, he could not be parted from her for a day. She had also become his private secretary.

When evening came, which always brought the family together, their spacious chambers shone with brilliant illumination.

So far as this matter was concerned, Richard Wagner might be reckoned among the fire-worshipers, and he subscribed to the adage, "Where there is light, there is joy."

The Italians—who, even in their refined patterns of life, showed their preference for a poverty of fire—could not escape astonishment that in the Wagner household, which hardly ever witnessed any social life beyond receiving a couple of intimate friends, shone evening after evening with the glitter of innumerable candles, such as in this country one would have burned only for a grand festive ball.

"It's one thing more that this great German gentleman has in common with Lord Byron," said the Vendramin's aged porter, steeped in the traditions of Venice, and in more than one instance our trustworthy authority.

"Even my brother, Byron's Fido [Faithful, i.e., trusty servant], never tired of telling what a great expenditure his master made for candle illumination." And, in fact, Byron's apartment on the Grand Canal virtually floated in a sea of light, and that was so even when he was altogether alone with his manuscripts of *Manfred, Parisina, Childe Harold, Don Juan,* all of which he polished, worked on, or edited during his long residence in Venice.

At seven o'clock at the outset, later in the winter at eight, following German custom, Wagner had supper, rather than the main meal, as has become conventional in this country. Having finished the meal the family gathered in the salon adjoining the smoking chamber; there they drank tea, whereupon by custom one of the daughters read aloud, while the others listened to the discourse.

Wagner himself always selected the reading; at times they read altogether cheerful, humorous things. And then resounded that joyous laughter of which we have already made mention in these pages, and that, to Richard Wagner—who was susceptible to jokes and humor as was no other man—came as a total surprise and always an overwhelming stimulus to merriment, since it sprang so heartily from his lips.[9]—Or else they read something quite serious or difficult, in which Wagner then, at tough passages, gave his family instructive explanations as to understanding them.

Once during the winter, when he was feeling quite well and was in consequence in a very cheerful humor, he declaimed something from his own works, in which he asserted his voice with such dramatic force that the members of the household, under the impression that he had suffered some calamity, rushed to him in alarm.

It was certainly true that, had Richard Wagner been born under the conditions of life and in the time of Shakespeare, he would have become a remarkable actor—which, indeed, Shakespeare had not been—and he would have interpreted his heroes better than anyone else.

These family evenings in the Wagner house were even enviable in their gaiety and attest most clearly to the unusual happiness that prevailed within these walls, where all those living under one roof were bound together by the inmost tenderness and the highest respect for one another. (146–49/34–35)

As the weather grew more chilly, Perl reports, Wagner became fearful that their rooms could not be properly heated, but his family assured him on that point, and they were proved correct. Nevertheless, his health remained a problem:

The Master, who felt an endless need for movement, and most especially after he had eaten (something that can now be explained), moved up and around virtually the whole time from the evening meal until about eleven o'clock, when he went to bed. The respiratory problems under which he labored as a consequence of his chronic afflictions make fully clear the significance of this movement to and fro; and that he often held his hands at his back finds its medical explanation in that, through this movement, he felt his chest was relieved.—For years his tailor was instructed to place on his jacket, directly over his back, a pair of pockets into which he could insert his hands, and his going about the streets in this manner was reckoned as Wagner's eccentricity, when on the contrary it is alone and exclusively to be ascribed to his need to breathe with less difficulty.—Like all people who suffer from conditions similar to those that had menaced the Master's life for a span of years, and on which the specialized medical journals of Italy cited below made notice,[10] Richard Wagner was often subject suddenly to fits of melancholia, as well as great irritability. On that point he frequently expressed himself to those around him: "People think me regularly ill-tempered, while I am really just ill." (149–50/36)

Not being fully aware of what the doctors had come to know, says Perl, Wagner's family members could enjoy their time with him without apprehension.

It is natural that, as soon as Richard Wagner's presence in Venice became known and the planned duration of his residence itself—from September to the end of April—was fixed, all those of importance who lived in Venice, or who considered themselves important, sought to join the great poet–composer and his family: especially those of the very numerously represented foreign colony, some of them coryphaios-types of the cultural world,[11] who lived a portion of the winter in Venice, such as Meissonier, Alma-Tadema, Pettenkofen, and others.—But, since he felt so content in his own circle of his numerous family and reckoned his time as so precious, Wagner's house remained closed to all, with the exception of a few outsiders, whom we will point out to the reader further on in this assemblage of information.

Accordingly, the Master generally spent the evenings in his own home, with the exception of a few occasions when he accepted an invitation from the Princess Hatzfeld [sic], with whom he had been friendly for years, and whose daughter, the Baronessa von Schleinitz, was, as everyone knows, regarded by the Master over a long span of years as the most ardent, artistically sensitive, and especially esteemed Wagner enthusiast.

Quite at the beginning of his residence, Richard Wagner gave thought to the matter of selecting a household physician for himself and his family.—One was readily at hand, for no one better in Venice could be selected for this than Dr. Friedrich Keppler, the foremost and most-sought-after German physician living here. As circumstances had it, Richard Wagner and Friedrich Keppler had already become acquainted with each other through the Princess Hatzfeld. As soon as he was settled in Venice, the Master made a point of asking Dr. Keppler to undertake, for the duration of his Venetian residence, the care of his own physical well-being and that of his family.

At the time, Dr. Keppler was involved in a journey of scientific nature in Germany and was, in fact, at Bad Soden, which Wagner himself had frequented in earlier years.

One might well imagine with what longing the Master, always more or less ill, anticipated Dr. Keppler's arrival. In the first half of the month of October the latter finally returned to Venice and from then on, every day and sometimes even more than once, he visited Wagner and his family, who soon treasured him as a friend and came to love him.

The presence of the Doctor, his confidence-inspiring, trusty, quintessentially German manner, always had the most favorable effect upon his patient, whose condition certainly benefited from that process that often makes the most effective medicine out of distraction and diversion from the thoughts of illness.

Nevertheless, Wagner loved to complain as much about his illnesses as over a hundred other pin-pricks of daily life that were never and nowhere lacking. —

In the presence of his family he never, or hardly ever, did anything that would make them at all anxious, whereas he could rely on the physician to be in this regard the most discreet and most accommodating personality.

So far in our narration we have not gone beyond the month of October, at which time Richard Wagner was as yet ostensibly a minor patient in his own home, whereas Frau Cosima herself suffered from illness a few times, before she adjusted to the climate, and even Wagner's children had this or that to complain of. (151–53/36–38)

Perl then reports that matters of health were set aside as new personalities came on the scene. She describes the happy welcoming of Count Gravina (who had been born in Venice) and his new bride, Blandine, whose presence bright-ened the Wagner household. At the same time, Wagner was able to become acquainted with Count Bardi who, with his wife had taken up winter residence in the adjacent *piano nobile* of the Palazzo Vendramin. Though their contacts were at first limited to courtesy calls, Bardi and Wagner were brought together more amicably as the latter became interested in the Count's work on experi-mental boats in the palazzo's *atrio* and on the Grand Canal. This new diversion gave Wagner much pleasure, but the advancing of colder or less clement weather curtailed or ended many of these outdoor pursuits, and Wagner poured more of his time into his morning labors, changing the hour of lunch from one o'clock to two and supper from seven to eight.

Perl reports the regular visits at this time of a little drapery jobber, who, hav-ing failed to please the composer at first, was eager to do better:

> This meant that he must completely redecorate the study, but, when someone tried to ask him how urgently, as to the "how" there was no response from him. Wagner's household circle gave him the label: Silence. Only, one morning the taciturn little old man was seen staggering around the courtyard as if transfigured; when asked what it was that had made him become so merry, he merely stammered: "He clapped me on the shoulder, he was satisfied"—not until much later would we come to understand the deeper sense of these words. (158–59/40–41)

Count Gravina and his bride departed after a sojourn of a little over twenty days. As their visit had brought the family much pleasure, their departure brought sadness, relieved by the prospect of a reunion the following year when they would all celebrate the composer's seventieth birthday.

The arrival of Liszt on November 19 is romanticized by Perl into an occasion of great mutual delight:

> When the two old gentlemen descended the stairs of the palazzo arm in arm, one could read in their expressions the joy that animated them, as well as the love they bore for each other. It was a moving expression of welcome, and except during work hours the two were constantly together. Frequently they could be seen sitting together before the broad window that let out to the Canal, always deep in intense conversation.
>
> A strong impression remains that they wished to spend so much time together and had much to discuss with each other, almost as if they had some presentiment that this would be the last occasion when they could speak together. Liszt enjoyed a fully good health and was wont to arise even earlier than Wagner.
>
> His manservant, a trusty man who accompanied him everywhere, named Achille Colonello and a Palermitan by birth, could tell all about it.—At the stroke of four o'clock Liszt every morning went to Achille's bed and reminded him that it would be time to begin the day.—Like Wagner, Liszt also appreciated these early hours as the most favorable ones for work.—Liszt's presence added a further attractiveness to the happy family circle in "Vendramin." (159–60/41–42)

Perl then introduces another close familiar, the painter Paul Joukowsky ("Schukowsky"). He had stayed with the Wagners in the palazzo for a while but then had moved to quarters of his own at San Trovaso, though he continued to spend the better part of every day with the Wagners. The arrival of Liszt prompted Joukowsky to paint a portrait of Liszt as an abbé, one that, despite the fact that portraiture was not his specialty, managed to capture the composer's spiritual side (fig. 20). That portrait joined in significance a painting the artist had made of the Wagner children at Bayreuth in 1881.

A full description of that painting becomes chapter 7 of Perl's book. It was based upon a *tableau vivant* of the Holy Family that Joukowsky designed for Christmas Eve 1880. In it, Daniela von Bülow was Mary, and Joukowsky's manservant Pepino was Joseph, while the twelve-year-old Siegfried played Jesus; Blandine and Isolde von Bülow and Eva Wagner were shown as angels—respectively playing lute, violin, and shawm. While the scene was posed, pianist Rubinstein played the opening chorale from *Die Meistersinger*. Wagner was utterly delighted by all this, and prompted Joukowsky to make an oil painting out of the scene. Perl's account matches well with that by Cosima herself.[12] But Perl devotes particular space to discussing this painting because, she says, it was at that time hardly known to the general public and accessible to her only through a photograph. Perl then describes in detail, first the setting (a Franconian landscape) that had been given to the scene, and then the treatment of the figures. She notes the special attention that Joukowsky gave to Pepino as Joseph and to the twelve-year-old Siegfried as Jesus, and finally she describes the way the four daughters were incorporated into the scene. The idealized character accorded these portraits, Perl says, represented Joukowsky's private tribute to the Wagner family, and reflected the same devotion with which he made his portrait of Liszt later in Venice.

Chapter 8 is devoted to an account of the events leading up to Christmas 1882, focused on the special performance of his youthful Symphony in C Major that Wagner arranged in honor of his wife. At the outset, and further on, Perl dates that concert to December 23. This was a confusion not only about the concert's actual date but also about the date of Cosima's birthday, and totally contradicts the testimony of Cosima herself, as followed by Glasenapp and recognized by all Wagner scholarship. Perl also follows the convention of the day in identifying the venue as the concert Hall of the Liceo Benedetto Marcello, which was the Sala Apollonea of the Fenice Theater complex.[13]

In describing the preparations for this event, Perl mentions the exclusion of anyone but family members from the rehearsals, and notes the illness that daughter Eva suffered at this time. In this period, too, Perl reports, the other daughters socialized at the home of Princess Hatzfeldt. Daniela herself developed a friendship of her own with a Signorina Passini, daughter of the water-colorist Passini. This Passini, together with his young friend Ruben, another painter, joined the small circle of friends at the Wagner household, as did one Signorina [Ada]

Pinelli, an old friend of Cosima. Still another key member of this circle was, of course, Dr. Keppler.

And a good thing, too, according to Perl, since Wagner's health was becoming a serious concern:

> The Master's illness then began to increase more and more: his entire capacity of resistance and his will of steel was required to preserve his understanding, pleasure, and interest in everything and everyone with which he was engaged.—In addition, the weather became burdensome; especially the fog that, in the Venetian wintertime, is a houseguest morning and night; it was hard on him, and his breathing difficulties always became intolerable on such days.—The household people relate that, on those frequent occasions when he went out of the house on foot, which happened at least once every day, he reached no further than the end of the little street that led out onto the Strada Nuova. After ten minutes, often even sooner, he returned almost breathless, his hands on his back, and bewailed his illness to anyone of the household who first came out to him.
>
> Moreover, when he thought himself alone, he sometimes wailed and groaned, so that people began to shake their heads suspiciously—all with the exception of his family, before whom he sought as much as possible to keep his sufferings concealed, and who were at pains to trace back his resulting irritability with others to no more than his basic physical condition. Still, notwithstanding all these hardly pleasant symptoms, Dr. Keppler, the physician attending him, believed for his part that Wagner's robust constitution would, after a few years of rest and an appropriate dietary regime, withstand the destructive forces that had been gnawing at him.—Unfortunately, the great Master had a low opinion of the doctor's prescriptions.—He should have avoided any excitation, but not only did he not avoid it, he explicitly sought it out.—His restlessly striving spirit knew no repose; if it was not one thing that kept him totally preoccupied, it was another.—He frequently experienced physical suffering, he was tormented by unbearable anguish. But, for all that, he quite believed he was a long distance from the evening of his life. He still believed he was destined for ninety years, and that even were he allowed to achieve them he would not have been able to complete what was left to him to do; so said he explicitly more than once himself.—The great legacy, that he left not only to his own nation but to the cultivated classes of all peoples, required so much more elucidation, which for the greatest part was still to be completed.—His great philosophical-critical work has therefore been left as a torso.
>
> How much, in the gray December days of the past year—and gray it was this time even for Italian skies—he would have discussed this matter with his friend Franz Liszt and the latter's daughter, Frau Cosima!
>
> But all this was impossible without excitement. It was not unusual for the Master, when he felt weak and exhausted, to have recourse to such nerve-stimulating beverages as might be found: tea, coffee, strong wine, and even spirits. These allowed him to assume his momentary well-being and put him in better condition to work than his consequently weakened physical strength and his partially injured constitution would have permitted him to do without such means of nerve stimulation.—Vainly the physician preached and warned; vainly the family implored.
>
> Wagner did not take such admonitions seriously; he derided physicians in general, who always forbade what they themselves most enjoyed. On the whole he wished all the recommendations to be considered as so much tomfoolery, by following which he

could not enjoy the slightest pleasure; there was, he believed, no urgency involved here.—Were he to feel ill, he shrugged it off as a mistake in diet, as catching a chill, still more often as the weather—which rarely pleased him, save when the sun shone bright and warm.

Beyond stimulating beverages, through which, like Voltaire, Wagner liked to heighten his nervous activity or to accelerate his digestion, there was also his special situation. To wit, he spent the greater part of the day, and even night, in rooms filled with quite overwhelming perfume odors, a situation to which we will return later, and which certainly bears some responsibility for the unexpected outcome, in that this further hastened even his steely constitution into a state of vulnerability. (172–75/48–50)[14]

This medical discourse finished, Perl is ready to report the concert, which she persists in setting on the evening of December 23, not Christmas Eve. Despite her recent illness, daughter Eva was able to join in the event, to everyone's great delight:

. . . The concert was scheduled for nine o'clock.—The Wagner family, with Liszt at the head, was represented in full, the hall was brilliantly illuminated, and closed to the public. Count Contin, Director of the Liceo Marcello, in whose Concert Hall the performance of Wagner's Youth Symphony took place, greeted the Master with a speech that, in carefully chosen words, emphasized the distinction that Richard Wagner was according the Institute with this gesture.—The orchestra shouted its approbation, Wagner expressed thanks and placed himself on the podium.

It was to be the last such time in his life, and the statement he made on that evening, when he put aside his conductor's baton, may be recognized as prophetic:

"I shall never conduct again!"—said he.

Why, Master? asked the few musicians who were near him and who alone had understood his statement.

"Because soon I shall die!"

This was not the only instance, during his Venetian residence, of his expressing a presentiment of death. Certainly these words were at odds with the prophecy of his ninety years, in which he also believed, or pretended to believe.—Such statements came from his lips, however, only when his illness raged so cruelly in his breast that it drove out all optimism.

The performance went brilliantly from the first, the Master was pleased, he thanked the musicians, and he departed the hall on the arm of Frau Cosima, who was both gratified and relieved.

The conductor's baton and the podium that the Master had used were immediately returned, and they remain in the Music Institute serving as a remembrance of Richard Wagner.

Notwithstanding the tragic and, unfortunately, all-too-prophetic statement that Wagner made at the conclusion of the performance, only a few minutes later he forced himself into a cheerfulness appropriate to the day.—Also, once come outside into the fresh air, he felt himself immediately much more well and at ease.—To be sure, it was raining in torrents that day; in such conditions, gondola transport proves extremely unpleasant, and, when Frau Cosima humorously questioned whether today it was his opinion that the gondola was preferable to the carriage, Wagner replied: "No, no, for rainy days the statement does not apply." (176–77/50–51)

This passage confronts us with some of the perplexities involved in evaluating Perl's little book. Setting aside her gaff on chronology, she shows herself very much the outsider as to the concert. She reveals little awareness of, or concern for, the actual details of what went on at the event, beyond dwelling on Wagner's doleful prophecy—for which her account is matched only by the exactly identical report by *LV* of February 14, perhaps her actual source. Her emphasis upon that pronouncement and its later implications relates to her commanding preoccupation with Wagner's problematical health. But she says (and perhaps knew) nothing about Wagner's ominous heart seizure during a rehearsal on December 22. Finally, her statement about torrential rain that night is quite at odds with Cosima's diary account of a rapturous ride home after the concert: perhaps Perl has invented this situation as an excuse for relating how Cosima—perhaps on another occasion— had teased Wagner about his preference for the gondola over the carriage.

Persisting in her shifting of dates, Perl goes on to describe the Wagner family's preparations for Christmas: the daughters decorated a Christmas tree in German fashion, and Wagner himself had gone in person to Lavena ("his favorite pastry-shop") to select the best goodies. But Perl moves quite beyond Cosima's terse reference to "preparations," in the process wandering off into a digression that involves a little excursion by Wagner of which Cosima made no mention:

> In the morning hours of December 24—the weather was, although overcast, extremely mild—Wagner had himself rowed to the great Pescheria behind the Rialto, so very much worth seeing in Venice on account of its variety of fish; there the spectacle of the fish and crustaceans set out with such good taste quite pleased him for a few moments.—It had become a practice of his gondolier [Luigi Trevisan] to convey his employer, as was frequently the case, where Wagner had conceded the choice or direction of the trip to this most trusted *cicerone*, who each time selected the most lovely points, or those appropriate to the day or season.—This understanding, however, so greatly delighted Wagner that, not infrequently after such a trip that had given him even greater than usual pleasure, he pressed a few lire into the hand of this man who was already a paid retainer in his personal service. (178/51)

These excursions frequently brought Wagner into the back alleys of Venice where he encountered some of the poorest of Venice's citizens and was wont to bestow generous little gifts of money to some of them. While this made him many friends among the poor, it was typical of his open affability and lack of pretension in dealing with all he encountered, according to Perl. He achieved considerable popularity, which was also extended, she claims, to the rest of his family, and especially to young Siegfried:

> . . . Thanks to Signorina Corsani, the charming, dark-eyed Genoese lady [their governess], who was assigned as their companion, the daughters spoke excellent Italian, whereas the Master never possessed any degree of facility in this language, and often mixed his Italian with French or, more often, German words.

The porter [Falcieri] of the "Vendramin," whom the Master most often addressed as "amico mio," also spoke some mangled German, hearing which always gave Wagner much amusement. The porter's grandson, handsomely picturesque, though named Bartoletto, was called by Wagner no less than "piccolo Vendramin," the memory of which the nine-year-old youth would retain all his life.

In this narrative, we have been concerned with all kinds of trivial details that, since they are so closely tied to so great a man as Wagner, are certainly not without significance. Thus it may here be noted that, for all his love of luxury—generally exaggerated—he actually maintained a household by no means that of a Grand Seigneur. To such belief one might easily be tempted when one hears of the quantity of rooms in which he lived, or thinks of the gaudy garments that he loved to see on his wife at home, or remembers the ostentatious outfitting that he ordered for his studio, and keeps in mind his own preference for expensive silk garments. But these irrefutable facts stand in opposition to his extremely small number of servants: he had merely four. They symbolize Wagner's domestic life as entirely bourgeois, by which terms the daughters fully accepted the requirement of carrying out at all times, with their own hands, the work that was hardly expected of young ladies with such cultivated upbringing. These four servants were responsible for thirty and more occupied rooms, for a numerous family, for scrupulously prepared meals, for an army of stoves to be fired, for a vast number of lighting devices to be kept in operation. Constraints like these are not only characteristic but—let us speak the truth—extraordinary for such a man as Wagner, since they impart to his domestic life a strenuously bourgeois quality, such as one would hardly expect for such a man as he. (180–82/52–53)

Perl's chapter 9 begins with resumed discussion of the Wagner household's Christmas celebration. That was done in full German style, with a spirit of gaiety and warm family intimacy that made Wagner feel young again, rendering what was to be his last Christmas a truly happy one. Meanwhile, she says, various newspapers carried all sorts of reports about Wagner's supposed plans: to go with his family and Liszt to Rome; to Sicily to visit Gravina; to the Ionian Isles and Greece. Wagner himself noticed little of this, thanks to Cosima's filtering of information. As the weather improved slightly, Wagner became deeply involved in his work. He did, however, anticipate the impending celebration of Carnevale, which in that year (1883) was being revived in the style of past times, through the work of Baron Girolamo Filiberto Cattanei and his associates. Wagner professed to be curious about its "scenic effects." There was concern about the impending departure of Liszt who, however, had agreed to stay with the family to celebrate the New Year.

At this point, Perl gives unusual details of two very different contacts. The first:

With Dr. Keppler Wagner frequently had extended conversations during this period, although this true disciple of Aesculapius, while he had himself already earned some laurels in the realm of poetry, was in musical and poetic matters an anti-Wagnerian in disposition; which Wagner understood, without resenting his physician and friend for this opposition. (184/55)[15]

The other contact of this moment (also involving Dr. Keppler) was the initial news conveyed to Wagner of Angelo Neumann's proposal to bring his traveling production of the *Ring* to Venice, to which Wagner reacted with furious and utter hostility.[16]

Which then brings Perl to New Year's Eve. Cosima's report was strikingly terse: "We have a New Year's Eve party and are all very merry, the children melt wax." Perl, however, ventures a more detailed, and quite colorful description:

> And now the last day of the year had arrived. On such a spirit as Richard Wagner, the particular enchantment that is involved in the final night of the year could not but have a special effect. The Master celebrated the change of year with raised glass amid his loved ones and felt better on this final Sylvester Night [i.e., Feast of St. Sylvester, December 31] than he had felt during the entire winter. No specter of gloomy presentiments, no specter of threatening peril, which he was facing at such a rapid pace. —
>
> The great hall of the Vendramin Palace was transformed into a flower garden, while outside mildly warm spring breezes wafted. Liszt's finger drew fiery melodies from the splendid piano, the young voices of Wagner's children sang choruses from *Parsifal*, Frau Cosima sat radiating happiness at the Master's side, encircled in brilliance and magnificence, as if she had just stepped out of the frame of a great painting by Paolo Veronese, her gown woven of gold brocade and deep red satin (Wagner's favorite combination). She seemed to generate the liveliest joy, endless happiness, exaltation.
>
> Where could dark forebodings be at that hour?
>
> Thanks to a wise dispensation, they were silent that night.—And when the family, with deeply felt kiss and handshake, separated from each other in the first hours of the new year, then Richard Wagner embraced his beloved wife with the passion of a young man and betook himself with his wife into his sanctuary.
>
> [*Here the author's own text ellipsis*]
>
> He conducted her, his so dearly beloved wife, into the chamber where no one other than he and she were allowed to enter, and the spirit of all the desire and love that he poured into his works overwhelmed him, as soon as he crossed the threshold of this seductive room. (185–87/55–56)

Perl's background as a writer of romantic novels seems here altogether to have gotten the better of her. It is in this embarrassingly purple vein that she ends the chapter with a description of Wagner's private room, his "blue grotto":

> . . . that was the chamber in whose outfitting the little old tapestry man outdid himself, the very same chamber in which, only a few weeks later, the Master would so unexpectedly give up the ghost. (190/58)[17]

At the beginning of chapter 10, Perl portrays the beginning of the new year as a happy time for the Wagner family, who were enjoying a distinct improvement in the weather and feeling very comfortable by now in their Venetian surroundings. But concern had been mounting over Wagner's health: Dr. Keppler attended him more frequently, and the composer began to take more seriously the recommendations about dressing appropriately for the weather and, above all, about following a strict diet. Very quickly, positive results were perceived and Wagner felt himself able to enjoy the Carnival as it was then beginning. At this point Perl breaks off to describe at length that particularly Venetian form of Shrovetide celebration. She presumably felt that her German readers, though familiar with their own *Fasching*, required some background on the Italian version of it. For us, her descriptions (here, and then further on) are of interest not only for the background but for a picture of its observance as it was undergoing a revival in her day—the more so since her view of it was that of a foreigner:

Fasching [Carnevale] is in Italy a thoroughly democratic institution, more than that, a socially leveling one. Elsewhere mainly only the young, the handsome, the wealthy, who, caught up in the vortex of carnival pleasure, join together in the wild round-dance. Not so in Italy, where, thanks to the milder skies, the greater part of Shrove Tuesday takes place in the open, and therein lies precisely the vast difference.—In closed rooms social standings are sharply defined, as against being under God's open sky, where there are no rules of dress, no admission cost, no extortionate prices for food and drink. —Likewise, one who has little or even no means at his disposal can participate here. Indeed, it costs practically nothing to dress oneself in some motley tatters of material, pleasantly disposed, and to cover the face with painted paper; this much even the lowliest, even the poorest, can do.

The qualities that are required for this riotous interaction lie, moreover, in the blood of the people themselves. Each one understands how to assume a pose, each is a *beau parler*, when it serves a purpose.—The Italians are nimble, easygoing, and lively, both women and men in general. Thus derives the tradition by which, at the time of Carnival, poor and rich, lovely and ugly, young and old, put on a disguise, tie a mask on the face, and rush out into the streets, in order to play their role in the universal comedy.—Old gray folks and youths, matrons and teenagers, bring with them an equal share of humor and spontaneity.—No one plays a bad joke on another. No ridicule, no laugh on the part of an onlooker, none of the restrictions always imposed on the part of public security authorities. Ordinary people are allowed to go on their way, in the knowledge that, thanks to a thousand years of experience, they would know how to keep within bounds.

But Venice, with its San Marco Piazza, which is always called, not without reason, a "roofless dance hall"; Venice with its labyrinth of little alleys and canals, with its secretive gondola, as if expressly created for masked disguisings; that Venice provides such a platform for masquerade whose equal one could not find anywhere else in the world. To all this is added, as has already been mentioned, the circumstance that in the past year the carnival impulse, which had gradually sunk in slumber, into decrepit sickness, has had new life breathed into it by the "Society of Venetian Celebrations," already referred to in this narrative, so that the old renown of Venice's world-famous Carnival might be restored to honor. And indeed, not for many years had the old city of the Doges seen so much masking activity within its walls as in the Fasching days it has shown this year.

In the center of the San Marco Piazza was erected, as in every year, the platform that is intended for the open-air dancing.—Bemasked crowds traveled back and forth on the Grand Canal in the little steamers known as *Tramway*. And also amid the diversity of the costuming the local folk demonstrated, in the masks that had long played so important a role, a very special skill. Many among these images were very much super-life-size forms, with monstrous perukes and especially well-designed caricature features.—One day, for example, "Lady Good-Humor" with "Prince Carnival," followed by a retinue of government dignitaries on down to the cooks, kitchen boys, and street scavengers, all appeared at midday on the railroad platform for Venice trains, and amid the hollering of a merrily excited crowd they made their solemn entry into the city.

One of the best-designed of these caricatures was that of the Minister of Agriculture, who stood on a plough buried halfway under carrots,—not to mention the fishermen of Chioggia, the negroes, the pages, the over-life-size *nobili* in medieval garb, who passed through the streets promenading arrogantly on the arms of equally gigantic comrades, and behind each a pair of richly garbed servants had to run, complaining of their hunger. Whoever sees these *Illustrissimi* with their retinue of starving servants, whoever hears them lament "Quanta fame, quanta fame" [So much hunger, so much hunger], will never forget it as long as he lives.

Richard Wagner, however, was enjoying himself in this motley throng that, as much under sunshine as in night's darkness, passed through the streets of Venice during this briefest and consequently most concentrated of Carnivals (which this year's was).—He certainly would state later on that he had entertained higher expectations, for which there could be no blaming such a master of scenic effects as Wagner surely was, quite apart from his other immortally great qualities. Nevertheless, that he enjoyed himself in the midst of this masked crowd, that he observed the wild crowd with interest, that he moved about a jolly man among jolly people, all that we can attest, since we have seen it with our own eyes.

His head thrown back, Wagner strode beside Frau Cosima with springy, youthful steps, through the wildest tumult, and his face always displayed the most unmistakable cheerfulness. It is really quite remarkable that Richard Wagner had, during the last four weeks of his life, actually felt much better than he did around the middle of his Venetian residence. That is attributable to the fact that in the South the season of rain and mists falls in the months of November and December, whereas during the month of January, although it was exceptionally cold (the temperature went down to two degrees), it was still sunny by day and starlit by night, a situation that, given the Wagners' great sensitivity to the weather, could not fail to have a significant effect upon his health. (192–96/59–62)

The vivid description of Wagner's rejuvenated aspect during Carnival, which she restates further on, is one of the few passages in Perl's book that is quoted with some frequency. It offers one of her most direct testimonies as an eyewitness. Accordingly, it is hardly to be overlooked, even if Cosima's day-by-day accounts of his physical condition present a less consistently rosy picture. Moreover, Perl's description of Wagner's delight in the Venetian Carnival must be set against the more restrained and far less consistently positive reports of the same event in Cosima's diary.[18]

Perl's chapter 11 begins with allusion to social evenings at the home of Princess Hatzfeldt, where her guests showered Wagner with expressions of their adoration. Their devout enthusiasm Perl compares favorably to what was once accorded the young Liszt. This prompts Perl further to observe that "Richard Wagner was a personality to whom no one could remain indifferent"—resulting in reactions that ran to extremes of admiration and hatred. In her scrambling of chronology, Perl next refers to Liszt's departure on January 13—which happened before launching of the Carnival festivities that she has just described. Mention of Liszt leads her then to note his involvement in family musicales, during which Wagner's youthful compositions were exhumed for presentation. That draws her back to renewed mention of the performance of the juvenile Symphony in C Major (which she still places at the Liceo Marcello, and on December 23). As her ramble is extended, Perl reports that Wagner offered in these days reminiscences of his youth. There follow considerations of such things as his hostility to Bismarck, and the evolution of his literary and musical style. They culminate in Wagner's difficulties with confronting in his old age the operatic music of his earlier years, as experienced in hearing it in Venetian band concerts—something we have already discussed.[19]

At last, Perl returns to her starting point:

> On January 13, Franz Liszt departed from Wagner; on the same palace stairs on which one had welcomed the other, they took leave of each other.—Once more they held each other in their arms, the two revered comrades-in-arms clasped breast to breast.— It was the last time that they would see one another. On the same date, one month later, would fall the day of Wagner's death. (201/64)[20]

Perl devotes the remainder of this section to Wagner's health in the last month or so of his life. At first it seemed to be improving:

> . . . His breathing difficulties occurred less frequently, although some people with whom he had close contact knew that on a few occasions during this final period, at intervals of about eight days, he suffered fainting spells. One such occurrence befell the Master at the confectioner Lavena, another time with his banker, Herr Reitmeier [*sic*]. Both times, as soon as the distress receded, he hastened to rejoin his gondola, which was awaiting him at the closest *riva*, and he instructed people that no one should make any mention of these situations to his family. (202/64–65)

These occurrences, which Wagner thought resulted from his exaggerated nervous state, failed to alarm him, says Perl. His confidence was communicated to his family and to those around him, while Dr. Keppler maintained his faith in Wagner's inherently robust constitution and his strong will. Wagner's intellectual strength was irrepressible, too, and was furthered as he regularly took his young son on his promenades. Siegfried's fascination with architectural monuments not only complemented that of his father but also boded well for the expectation that the boy was aiming at a career as an architect.

In chapter 12, Perl is ready to move us on to the long-anticipated climax. She begins, however, by completing a theme already introduced—one that, once again, stresses her own capacity as an eyewitness:

> The final days of Carnival came on and the wild merriment reached its pinnacle; Shrove Tuesday [*Faschingdienstag*] fell on February 6.—In the literal sense of the word,

the Piazza San Marco swam in a sea of light and offered a prospect of fairy-land beauty. Two bands of musicians played merrily and in very brisk tempo; there was jolly dancing on the platform. Innumerable masks and processions of maskers moved about with Italian vivacity and obligatory vocalizing under the Procuratoria, crowded into the cafés, and performed improvised comic pieces in the midst of the San Marco Piazza. Their harmless merriment, so inherently generated, challenged northern onlookers, who stood among them as if wanting to say: We are all too solemn to do this sort of thing, we live a life much too serious, we have meditated much too much, too much perused the pages of Kant, Schopenhauer, Darwin, and Heckel [i.e., Hegel]. These simple folks here do nothing like that, and who knows on which side true wisdom lies?!

Perhaps similar thoughts passed through the mind of the great Master in this last Shrove-night; in any case, his thoroughly artistic nature gained the upper hand, for he mingled in unaccustomed jollity with the surging crowds.—We have seen him with our own eyes, it was the last time, and his appearance has remained indelible in our recollection.

Wagner took his daughter Daniela by the arm and with her pushed through the midst of the most rowdy of the crowd of maskers. His step was springy, even youthful, his head held high. Anyone could see that this man, who regularly turned his back on general sociability, felt himself perfectly comfortable among this merry-making crowd, effectively participating in this Mardi Gras nonsense; that he, an unmasked man, imagined himself masked in the midst of this masquerading, childish mob. And in a certain sense, in that moment, he was just that, since he felt himself a participant in this wild charade.

Just like all the others, he would be on hand for the extinction of the Venetian Carnival.—It was just before midnight and Wagner took unmistakable pleasure in the traditional moment in which Mardi Gras and Lent, that is, indulgence and renunciation, joined hands fraternally; from the highest-level bacchanal to deepest penitence— a single brief step!

Midnight was tolled by the gigantic Campanile di San Marco, and ceremoniously those venerated bell-tongues took up the melodious rhythms they repeat each day. Wagner listened to them with head uplifted. Then, with the flickering lights suddenly extinguished as if by the command of some higher power, darkness surrounded the jolly mob and sacred hymns resounded all around in the air!

It was a theatrical touch, but Wagner knew how to appreciate it!

The image visibly pleased him, and we saw the Master enter the rooms of the "Al Bianco Cappello" restaurant in an elevated mood.[21]

It was perhaps the last evening of carefree cheerfulness in Wagner's life—no, not *perhaps*, it certainly *was*! An hour later, Wagner went home still fully caught up in the immediate impressions of these fresh experiences.

"Amico mio," he said to the aged porter who, because the Master was out of the house, had not yet gone to bed; "Amico mio, the Carnival is ended" [il Carnevale è andato!]. With that he clapped the old man on the shoulder. It was a scene that this servant, obviously favored by Wagner, never tired of telling, over and over, so deep was the impression that this made on the old man, especially with the Master's death ensuing so abruptly thereafter. (204–6/66–67)

This second part of Perl's description of Wagner and the Carnevale—complete with repetition of its rejuvenating effects on him—has become a particular contribution to the biographical literature on Wagner. Again, it carries her assertion of authority as an eyewitness. (One wonders: was Perl, by this time, already stalking Wagner and his family?) Her insistence that Wagner had a special capacity for appreciating the theatricality of the closing ceremony certainly makes sense.

Here in particular, moreover, we can contrast Perl's testimony with that of Cosima's, not so much to use one to discredit the other, but to observe two very different perspectives on the same episode. After reporting in her diary entry for February 6 that Wagner had happily spent some time that Shrove Tuesday morning sitting beside the Doge's Palace in fine weather, Cosima says that

> . . . at around 9 o'clock we set out to the Square for Shrovetide celebrations. R. does this to please the children, who reward him with their gaiety. The impression is mixed; R. finds something touching about the procession carrying carnival to the grave, with its melody which he thinks to be an old one, but after going to the podium with the children, he returns to me in the Cappello Nero looking sad. He says poor artisans were hopping around there without really understanding why. But the midnight bells and the extinguishing of the flames produce another fine effect. ... —We return home toward 1 o'clock. R. not entirely dissatisfied, but as I go to sleep, I hear him say, "I am like Othello, the long day's task is done." He asked me earlier whether I still care for him—he is so difficult![22]

That the accounts of Perl and Cosima are not irreconcilable was demonstrated long ago by Wagner's biographer, Glasenapp,[23] who drew on both and made a comfortable synthesis of the two, freely using Perl's details (and even verbiage) in particular.

A further contrast of accounts may be found for the very next day, February 7. Cosima reports tersely an excursion that was seemingly aborted:

> . . . Toward 1 o'clock we set out for [the cemetery island of] S. Michele, but R. is not feeling well, and we return home immediately. He feels uncomfortable at lunch—he probably caught a cold yesterday. . . .

For her part, however, Perl gives a very different account, one very much focused on the gondolier, Luigi Trevisan, from whom—probably as one of her important informants in general—she must have had this direct and quite contrasting account:

> On the day following [i.e., the carnival finale], on Ash Wednesday, Wagner felt disposed to make use of the lovely weather and to undertake a prolonged journey by water. As always, he again asked Luigi, his first gondolier, who would in such instances be his adviser: "Where do Venetians go today?"—and this well-informed guide replied: "To San Michele, illustrious Sir,"—whereupon he steered Wagner to Venice's splendid, recently built necropolis.—A magnificent view toward the Paduan and Vicenzan mountains makes this outing to the island that lies near Murano particularly rewarding. The weather was seductively beautiful, the Master left the gondola and, accompanied by the

brightest sunshine, made a stroll through the imposing necropolis of the Lagoon City, which he recognized for its treasured and admired merit. When he settled into the gondola in order to return home, Luigi asked his master whether the promenade had satisfied him.

"Absolutely"—responded Wagner, and added to it, "soon I, too, will take my rest in a similar place of repose!" —

Certainly on that morning his old, ravaging enemies had made themselves especially evident in the Master's breast and prompted him to this prophecy—sadly, to be fulfilled so soon thereafter. (206–7/67–68)

Perl's account of this episode is in conflict not only with Cosima's entry but also with the report by Norlenghi, who confirms Cosima in quite vivid details that were certainly obtained from Trevisan himself. It is possible that Perl (or Luigi himself) confused this incident of February 7, 1883, with an earlier and more successful excursion made to San Michele (Cemetery and church) that Cosima records for October 19, 1882.[24]

Perl proceeds from here to report on what was to be the last week of Wagner's life. She notes that the soprano Pauline Lucca had hoped to visit Wagner during a one-day stopover she was making in Venice, but that the composer's health did not allow it. A more significant visitor was the conductor Hermann Levi, whose arrival Perl places "between Friday and Saturday" (i.e., February 9/10), but which Cosima sets more authoritatively on the afternoon of Sunday February 4. Cosima's references thereafter to his stay in Venice are mostly concerned (beyond sneers at his Jewish identity) with the ill health Levi was suffering. Perl, on the other hand, makes much of the prolonged discussions that Wagner had with Levi, of such intensity that they stirred the composer to renewed agitation. This prompted Dr. Keppler's concern, but Wagner proposed to find relief in a little excursion with Siegfried, and the physician suggested either Verona or Bologna, conveniently within reach by train. This idea was approved, though it is never mentioned by Cosima. Scheduling it proved difficult. The idea was broached on Saturday the tenth, but the next day, the eleventh, it rained all day (as Cosima confirms). This, says Perl, put Wagner in a bad humor (which Cosima does not indicate); he spent "the greater part of the day" working in his study (which Cosima confirms if reduces).

Fretting over the weather, says Perl, Wagner finally decided to go out for a walk alone but returned after ten minutes clutching his chest and breathing with difficulty. His irritability continued through the day, but his mood improved in the afternoon and Dr. Keppler found him restored to good condition. In one of the discussions the two enjoyed so much, they renewed the idea of the excursion, expecting that improved weather would allow it within the next few days. Of all this Cosima says nothing; in fact, she reports Wagner spending time, and joking, with his barber; but Glasenapp accepted Perl's information, blending it in with Cosima's report.[25]

Perl gives an account of Wagner's activities on the next day—Monday, February 12, to be the last full day of his life. It is an account rather divergent from Cosima's. And here Perl explicitly states that a lot of her detail came to her directly and immediately from Dr. Keppler. She reports that in the morning Wagner arose feeling unusually well in health and spirits following a night of "restful sleep without interruption." (Cosima reports that he awoke once during the night and was annoyed at not being able to find his checkbook.) Since the rain had ended and a sunny day was in prospect, he particularly pleased Siegfried, Perl says, by proposing to go to his banker to secure the money needed for their projected little journey. For that purpose, says Perl, Wagner set out (presumably alone, at what time not specified) for San Marco. Usually, when he had errands to run in the city center, he would stop at Reitmeyer's bank, partly as a resting point should he have problems of breath or nerves. This time he went there for business—perhaps that was why he had been looking for his checkbook, as Cosima reported—and was feeling so well that he lingered for about a half-hour, chatting amiably with members of the bank staff.

Now, for her part, Cosima reports the departure that morning of Hermann Levi, still not quite well (of whom Perl says nothing here). Cosima notes that Wagner spent the morning working on his article, and adds that at lunch he entertained Joukowsky with "some very drastic jokes and anecdotes." She then states that Wagner went out in the afternoon with Eva (without Cosima herself, who was awaiting a visit from Princess Hatzfeldt) and "gave [Eva] some chocolate."[26]

But Cosima says nothing about what would have been Dr. Keppler's final house call, made according to Perl at the accustomed hour of 6 o'clock. In the process of reporting that visit, however, Perl is able to introduce herself. She reports that she met Dr. Keppler later that evening, when he told her of his visit and passed on to her a joke that Wagner had told him that day. From this episode, Perl concludes, among other things, that a jocular Wagner certainly felt well the day before his death.[27]

Perl is now ready to report the events of February 13 itself, in an account that is undeniably vivid in its detail. We must remember that Cosima has left us no report of her own, while Joukowsky's and Siegfried's recollections are brief and fragmentary.[28] Perl's account is, of course, secondhand, as is Ludwig von Bürkel's. Perl also pumps up her account by freely imagining thoughts she places into other people's heads. For all that, it remains undeniably the fullest and most immediate account, perhaps the closest we can get to an actual eyewitness description.

It was a dark and stormy day, she makes clear, allowing no thought of anyone venturing out, and forcing postponement of the planned excursion (to Verona). Wagner did, however, schedule his customary gondola ride for 4 o'clock that afternoon. "He had risen from bed at 6 o'clock and he set to work, presumably to distract himself without interruption for the entire morning." Here Perl seemingly contradicts the conventional picture of Wagner working that morning on his essay—a picture carried over from Cosima's explicit statement to that effect for the previous morning. Instead Perl states that he was occupied in plans for the revival of *Parsifal* the coming summer, whose every detail he was supervising directly. That had been, she says, the reason for Levi's visit, so that they could exchange ideas in person.

Perl says nothing about Cosima taking breakfast with her husband that morning—much less anything about any argument between them. Instead, as she would have it, all was business:

. . . On this very morning, Wagner made clear that, up to the 2 o'clock hour set for mealtime, he did not wish any further disturbance, a desire that even Frau Cosima always took very seriously, and in such a case she never entered her husband's room.— Nevertheless, she ordered Betty, household servant trusted over many years, to remain in an adjacent room, since the Master that morning had mentioned that he did not feel altogether well, and should he have need of something he would always prefer to receive it from the hands of this loyal servant. These instructions were neither something exceptional nor dictated by any particular anxiety, but were, on the contrary, a long-established practice, recognized as appropriate.

Thus, as on all other days during these hours when the Master wished to remain alone in his study, Betty Bürkel sat in the neighboring room, occupied with her needlework. The hours before midday passed one after the other without Wagner having expressed any sort of wish. Frau Cosima came more than once and received each time the same response: "The Master is working, he walks back and forth through the room following his custom, and he has not required anything."

Around 1 o'clock Wagner rang and asked the servant as she entered: "Is the gondola set for 4 o'clock?" The servant said it was so. "Good" and "in addition I want to eat in my room—some soup will do—I don't feel well."

This, too, was nothing exceptional: when Wagner was particularly immersed in his work or did not feel entirely well, it frequently happened that he partook of a tiny portion in his room and, in time for dessert, he joined his family.

A few minutes later the servant brought the requested soup.—For a while all remained quiet in the room; suddenly Betty Bürkel heard the sound of hasty movement back and forth, and thereupon a repeated and persistent coughing. Become attentive, she put her work aside and with silent steps approached the door. It would not have been long before she also heard groans of pain, which plunged her into great anxiety. For all that, she lacked the courage to disobey the Master's order and to go in without being summoned; but her apprehension would allow her to delay no further and she was on the verge of the decision to go to Frau Cosima when there came to her ear the soft cry, "Betty."

Frightened to death, the servant plunged immediately into the room, which, as already described, was divided by a curtain into two sections.—Behind this curtain, however, she saw the Master laid out on his sofa, half-covered by his furs and his feet propped on an adjacent armchair.

As the girl later reported, the Master's facial lines were frightfully distorted, while weakly and painfully the words escaped from his lips: "Call my wife and the doctor." These were his last words![29]

In frightful dismay, the terrified servant ran to Frau Cosima.—The latter in her turn rushed, stricken with dread, into the room of her husband, whose appearance forced upon her the great extent of his peril. "To the doctor—quickly to the doctor—call Dr. Keppler" was all that she could issue in the circumstances in which she was occupied with the suffering man, who lay insensible to all that was going on around him.

Within the Master's breast the pain strove and raged quite horribly, but he was incapable of giving expression to it other than in some pitiful groans and gasps. Frau Cosima, herself near to unconsciousness, held her husband's hands and attempted to provide relief with all the measures that, more than once before, had proved helpful in similar convulsive seizures. Though frightened to death, she had never perceived the full extent of the peril in which her most dearly beloved husband was now caught. She no longer attempted to revive him, especially when he suddenly became more quiet and his head sank on her shoulder.—The spasm appeared to have passed, his breathing was light, and Frau Cosima believed him to have settled into sleep.—She took this for a good sign: she tried not to breathe herself so as not to disturb her dear one, and with immovable eyes she looked only to the door, through which at any moment the doctor would enter and, as she firmly hoped, would bring aid.

The confusion in the house upon the report of the Master's sudden indisposition was so great that all quite lost their heads over it. Three messengers were dispatched one way or another to the doctor; the terrified children came to the door and dared not enter into the room where all was silent and their father was, as they believed, asleep.—A painful hour passed before someone was able to locate Dr. Keppler and the latter could be brought back to the palazzo.—With his entrance (this was the first time he had set foot in this phantasmagoric, tapestry-filled room), he found Richard Wagner still in the same position in which he lay fallen when Betty Bürkel rushed into the room upon his weak cry for help.—He had rested his head on the breast of his wife, who held him in both arms in a tender embrace.—The stricken man appeared to sleep; Frau Cosima, who had not ventured to speak so as not to awaken the sufferer, conveyed to the doctor, through a sign only, the understanding that her husband was sleeping after the attack.

The physician gave not a moment's credit to this illusion and had immediately recognized that he was not dealing with a sleeper. He approached Wagner, examined pulse, heart, and head, and confirmed the horrible reality.

Richard Wagner had ceased to be.

Death must already have occurred quickly, without the unfortunate wife having even suspected the awful truth.

Himself deeply stricken by this unexpected disaster, Dr. Keppler spoke not a word, but raised the corpse in his strong arms and set it on the magnificent lounging bed, of which a description has already been given.—As soon as the deceased lay peacefully on the bed where he loved to rest, the physician found the right words to communicate the lamentable fact to the unfortunate wife, who had not yet fully understood the horrible reality.

No sooner had Frau Cosima heard pronounced the words "He is dead!" than, emitting a heartrending shriek, she flung herself on the corpse of her husband and, embracing it, collapsed as one insensible.

All of the doctor's efforts to pull the unfortunate wife from the dead man's neck remained futile, and, even when she returned to consciousness, she was impervious to all consolation. To Dr. Keppler now fell the dismal obligation of communicating to the children, who had been awaiting at the door in deathly anguish, the cruel misfortune that had befallen them with such pitiless force.

Who could dare to describe the dreadful lamentation, the heartrending grief, that this unexpected news of tragedy elicited from these young spirits who, conditioned by the radiance of good fortune, had idolized their father! (215–22/72–75)

Perl here pauses to suggest the mental framework of the Wagner youngsters, who had seen him age but could not conceive of his dying: a genius of such lofty status had to be immortal. The news of his death left them stupefied. They could only think, instead, of their mother. She had been inseparable from Wagner, deeply apprehensive over his health during their travels. They would have recalled now, Perl imagines, an occasion when they had been at a transfer station four years before. Counting over ninety railroad carriages in one long train, they had jokingly told their mother that such was to be the number of their father's years.

. . . and now—now all that came to naught, all that turned to mockery.—The great, the unique, the idolized man, and above all their father, who yesterday had moved happily among them, was dead, dead,—dead!

"And our mother?" they asked repeatedly of the physician and thus summoned him to recollection of the strong obligation that he now owed to the unfortunate widow. Thereupon the children joined with him and sought, in concert with him, to remove from their father's corpse the wife who, as if frozen in grief, was resisting any consolation. —

A supremely dramatic vision:—This chamber that belied the situation—glistening and bristling with gold brocade and with shimmering, smooth silk—mocking in its colors of the rainbow, sparkling in artificial beams of unwavering sunshine. And in the midst of all this, on his bed of life's pleasures and joys he alone could imagine, was He, the great deceased. Bent over him, disheveled in grief, cursing her own life and enduring only for the sake of her, and of her children's wishes, was the widow, the wife, who but a few hours before, hanging upon his neck, had received and returned his life-warming kisses, with no thought of their separation! —

The children circled about, so greatly blessed in spirit, so like their parents, and crushed by grief, overpowered for the first time by the frightening perception of endless emptiness! —

What a tableau, unforgettable to anyone who had seen it! And outside, the crowd of the curious was growing minute by minute. The report of the Master's sudden, serious illness had spread like wildfire through Venice. Already the wire-service report was flying out into the wide world and announced the likely passing of the meteor that throughout the decade had enthralled the whole world's cultivated people. Already the interested and the curious were making a pilgrimage to the palazzo's portals; they questioned, they besieged, and had to be content with a shoulder-shrug, with a raised glance, from the household servants.

"Richard Wagner has become very ill and the physician is now at his bedside." Up to 3:30 pm on the afternoon of February 13, no one in Venice knew more. Finally, Dr. Keppler descended the stairs in the cortile. —

"The physician, the physician!"—was heard from all sides and everyone drew near to him, awaiting his statement.

"Richard Wagner has died one hour ago as a result of heart failure," said the doctor, profoundly moved and with bared head, to the tensely expectant crowd; whereupon he immediately hastened away, for there were many sad duties he was required to fulfill in the next thirty-six hours.—The helpless family, borne down by grief, he had meanwhile passed on to the care and keeping of their best friend, the painter Paul Schukowsky [Jukowsky], so beloved by the Master.

"Richard Wagner dead, dead"—whispered everyone in confusion, and outward rolled the speedy waves that always become the bearers of evil news,—outward into the broad stream of public life, where it resounds stormily with all its inherent, elemental force, so that the ground on which it falls moans and groans. One hour later the sad news had spread over the entire city; in the coffeehouses, on the street corners, people cried out: "Riccardo Wagner il famoso tedesco, Riccardo Wagner il gran Maëstro del Vendramin è morto!" (Richard Wagner, the famous German, Richard Wagner the great Master of the Vendramin, is dead!) As to that, however, an indescribable and, from an Italian standpoint, inexplicable excitement was generated, that confirmed still further the power of Genius.

Since the death of Garibaldi [June 2, 1882], no news had made such an impact upon the general population as did the sudden death of the great Master; and here his greatness was little more than suspected, not recognized.

The rain fell in torrents, from a distance the thunder rumbled, as in summertime, and for an instant the lightning illuminated the angry firmament.—The wire service labored without ceasing and carried to all points of the compass the heart-breaking intelligence of the demise of one of the mightiest spirits of all time.

And we [Perl herself] also were, at that time, at the telegraph office that was besieged by people from all regions. We had the opportunity to speak with Luigi, the Master's gondolier, who was at the point of sending dispatches of the Wagner family to Munich and Berlin.—Luigi's emotions hardly allowed him to speak; in his haste and confusion he had taken Wagner's umbrella and showed it to us with the words: "And to think, that he had carried it yesterday, the good, gallant, special man, who never had a nasty word for us, even when he was so miserable.—Here, here, look at his name"—and he showed us the ivory handle with the initials R.W. "And now he had to die, *per bacco* [by Jove], how many would leave the world in his place!—*Poveretto, Poveretto!*"—and the man gave himself over without restraint to his naive but genuine grief.

Since his sending of the dispatches required a good bit of time—five thousand dispatches with reference to Wagner's decease were sent during the night of February 13–14, and on the following day from Venice to the most distant destinations[30]—Luigi turned to us once more. "Even his little cat"—continued the loyal servant in his need for communication—"he first acquired it two months ago, and he came just at the right time to save it from drowning, it would not touch anything today, the animal knew what he had lost, he was continually following the Maëstro close behind." (223–28/76–79)[31]

Coming at last to her chapter 13, Perl launches next into a purple-prose description of what she calls "the final act of the sorrowful tragedy," noting in the process the worldwide grief over Wagner's death:

He himself, the King of musical art, yet lay pale and motionless on the precious pillows of his grandiose bed; near him, overcome by grief, her thick, long, blond hair let loose—as he had loved it—his wife.

Her eyes fixed immovably on him, her breath warming his death-chilled countenance and his hands—with her hair, that had been so dear to him, soaking up the tears flowing so bitterly, insensible and inaccessible to any impact of the outside world, and insensible to any word, even that came from the lips of her children—thus she lay beside the benumbed corpse of that man who, for her, had been no man but a god!

And through the entire long night she remained by his side, alone with him, without speaking, without taking a drop of refreshment,—always whispering softly to him what her love, the immensely profound feeling which she felt for him, could inspire in her in the hour of their separation.

Not alone should he spend his first night in the realm of death—not alone—she would watch over him, to gaze on his beloved countenance, as long as no one could remove his mortal body, as long as she could have access to his countenance. The others would fulfill their sad obligations, of which she was not capable.

She knew only one obligation, to remain by him whom in life she had loved so indescribably and so unalterably, whose great, deep heart she had possessed so fully and totally!

Each passing hour strengthened her resolve, she held vigil the whole long night with him, she relinquished him not for a minute with the coming of day, she took nothing for herself, she said nothing, she ignored the children whom she forgot she genuinely loved. —

For twenty-six full hours she would not be torn from his body, and who knows whether she would have ever left her dead husband had she not been laid low by a physical breakdown that rendered her unconscious—an exhaustion that allowed Dr. Keppler and the children to pull her arms from the deceased and administer some drops of strengthening wine.

Nevertheless, when her consciousness eventually returned and she was able to grasp anew the bitterness of her destiny, she spoke again for the first time and with the following words:

"It is shameful that I still live, were I to have died Richard would have immediately killed himself!"

That was the kind of marital devotion that united these two extraordinary people. Frau Cosima's grief was quite striking, and fully worthy of this man to whom it was tendered.

With him, with the great man whom she had been so happy to call her very own through the years, with him also was extinguished the light of her life, the sunshine withdrawn from her existence.

And while the grieving lady, brooding in her heavy sorrow, forgot time, place, and the draconian necessity of the final separation from her beloved deceased, in the broad palazzo hall friends and admirers hastily ran up and down to prepare everything for a grand ceremony worthy of him who lay there mute and cold.

The magnificent sarcophagus, meanwhile, was ordered from Vienna.

Dr. Keppler was entrusted with the embalming; he expected the ambassador of the king of Bavaria at any hour.

The deputation of the city of Venice was sent to the palazzo in order to transmit to the widow of the great composer and poet, in the name of the city, a message of condolence that attempted to express the sympathy with which it shared her sorrow, and at the same time communicated that the city had proposed a funeral ceremony worthy of the great deceased.

Frau Cosima conveyed through her true friend and admirer Paul Schukowsky her heartfelt thanks for these fine gestures, she explained at the same time that she had decided to transport her dead husband with total restraint.

Funeral "crowns" [wreaths] of the most splendid kind were delivered to the palazzo, of which the most exceptional was the commemorative wreath of the king of Bavaria and a black-gold one from the king of Italy; also a rich wreath from the Circolo Artistico, with the inscription "Venezia a Riccardo Wagner."

Countless floral gifts from other societies and private parties arrived, among them wreaths from the Princess Hatzfeldt and her daughter. The aforementioned lady and Hans Richter of Vienna were the only outsiders who were allowed to see the Master in death.

Princess Hatzfeldt, herself in advanced years, and an ardent admirer of Wagner, upon the sudden news of his death, which was brought to her on Tuesday, February 13, just as she was about to sit down to table, was taken with a serious fainting spell. Notwithstanding, however, she hastened, as soon as she had recovered consciousness, to her dead friend at the Palazzo Vendramin.

According to the wish of King Ludwig II of Bavaria, the corpse of Richard Wagner was not to be touched before the arrival of his ambassador.

Herr Gross, the banker, one of the co-founders of the Bayreuth Theater, was therefore chosen to carry out the wishes of his king with regard to the arrangements for his dead friend.—But the unhappy wife's state was so despairing that she was in no condition to receive anyone, not even the king's ambassador.

Fräulein Daniela von Bülow, Paul von Schukowsky, and Dr. Keppler received Herr Gross, even as they were receiving the numberless messages of condolence and dispatches and were preparing the necessary arrangements for the funeral and departure.

Special correspondents and reporters from all regions were meanwhile arriving in Venice and had settled themselves in the spacious halls of the princely Palazzo Vendramin, hastily putting on paper all that they saw and heard.

Up to his very death, however, nobody entered, nor had anybody even seen, the rooms as they were at the time when the Master resided there. From hour to hour the family expected the arrival of the son-in-law, Graf Gravina, from Palermo, and Franz Liszt from Pest.—Both, however, were unfortunately not in a position to reach Venice immediately.

In the interim, Richard Wagner's death mask was made by the locally very important sculptor Benvenuti. Dr. Keppler, however, with the help of his assistants transferred to the next room the corpse which, until the arrival of King Ludwig's ambassador, had been untouched. There they carried out its embalming, following the Wickersheim method—a highly respected procedure.

After the embalming was completed and the Master lay in his expensive coffin clad in his black silk frock coat with the black velvet beret on his head, he looked truly handsome.[32] Frau Cosima knelt in silent despair at the foot of the bier.—This was on Thursday, February 15 in the later evening hours—she had just cut off her precious long blond hair, which Richard Wagner had loved so very much, and had laid this on his breast in a red silk cushion,—she herself, up until that time, had not taken either food or drink, which certainly put her in a critically serious condition.

And now the inevitable moment could no longer be deferred.—The departure would take place on Thursday night. Outside the railroad station, in readiness for the past twenty-four hours, stood the carriage that was to carry the great departed homeward over the Alps. But many things still remained to be done and therefore the departure was settled for Friday the sixteenth at two o'clock in the afternoon. (228–35/79–82)

Finally, chapter 14 carries the story and Perl's book to its conclusion:

The last night at the Palazzo Vendramin would remain something unforgettable for all who shared the experience; the entire family waited together at the open sarcophagus of the irreplaceable man and they all did not weary of looking at him over and over, in the very brief time still allowed them, to imprint on their minds the features of the departed.

The children cast shy, anxious glances at their mother and dared not, even with a single word, disturb that lady who sat there, a picture of despair, bereft of her hair ornaments, as if all life had been drained out of her.

And he, who had been everything to her, who had shared with her even the smallest anxiety, he looked out indifferently and softly slept "the long sleep of the weary," unmoved by all her sorrow and grief!

On Friday the sun gleamed and glittered already at early morning and the sky was as if scrubbed clean.

In the courtyard of the Palazzo Vendramin an agitated activity prevailed, the household staff rushed about in deep mourning; the representatives of both the Italian and the foreign press attentively observed every incident and vainly sought to arrange entry for themselves into the death chamber.

Among the musicians we particularly noted were Hans Richter from Vienna, Tessarin from Milan, the director of the Conservatory, Count Contin of Castelseprio, and Professor Frontali. We heard the last-mentioned direct a request to Schukowsky, that he might see the Master one last time and kiss his hand. (Frontali had dealt extensively with the Master in connection with the recently held performance here of Wagner's "Youth Symphony.") We thereupon observed how Paul Schukowsky withdrew and then, after scarcely a few moments, returned to express his regrets to Frontali that his wish, so understandable to him, could not be granted.

Also the representatives of the Municipality appeared, in order to propose anew, in the name of the city of Venice, an escort guard worthy of the great deceased; but Frau Cosima declined this gesture of tribute, as she had the first time, and again with thanks, confining her requests to the closing of the railroad station and the cessation of any kind of funeral music, which she anxiously discouraged in view of her indescribable misery.

Quite unwillingly did the Municipality follow the unshakable wishes of Frau Cosima and renounced, although regretfully, their elaborate plans and testimonial of sympathy, through which they had intended to honor the memory of Richard Wagner.

The palazzo was surrounded by security guards on the street front, because of the crowding of members of the public.

Dr. Keppler was at the palazzo by early morning, in order, in concert with messrs. Paul Schukowsky, Gross, Passini, and Ruben, to help make the many necessary arrangements for the transportation of the body and the departure of the family.

Around twelve o'clock began the dispatch of the chests and trunks, which were brought to the railroad station on specialized gondolas, since the family had decided to take immediately to Bayreuth all the property they had brought with them.

Several pieces of furniture that had served the special needs of the Master and now were treated as precious relics, were next brought down; these were: a red damask sofa, upon which lay a particular fur with which Richard Wagner had been covered during the last hours of his life; further, the armchair on which the dying man rested his feet, and finally the wastepaper basket from his study.—These objects required a gondola all of their own and had to be brought along in a passenger carriage, in order that they might travel to the North at the same time as the family.

A few minutes later was brought down also the bed in which the Master had rested during these last months of his life and which henceforth would remain the resting place of his widow.—In addition to the bed, one could also see, however, a large, wooden rack, as wide as it was long—this was the frame for that costly lounging ottoman that had formed the central point of Richard Wagner's study.

In the midst of all this, telegraph messengers were observed arriving every minute with dispatches, for from the outside world during these three days came messages of condolence, and indeed by the second day after Wagner's death their total ran up to three hundred and eighteen telegrams.

Amid these preparations, as the hour of 1:30 in the afternoon approached, the sun beamed and the water shimmered in alluring green. The few people standing in the inner court [cortile] of the palazzo, participants connected in one way or another to the proceedings, began to form a lane. As the hand of the clock indicated, there could be only minutes remaining before the great moment in which the deceased would be brought down through the halls and entrusted to the sparkling waves.

The last ceremony within the magnificent building, whose honor in part had been to shelter the lofty genius through so many months, commenced.

The footfalls were audible and eight men, among them Hans Richter, Paul Schukowsky, Dr. Keppler, Passini, Ruben, Contin, and Frontali, advanced down the wide stairs with the heavy, splendid bronze sarcophagus, decorated with four lion heads, and brought it down.

In reverential silence the men strode with their illustrious burden through the solemn ranks and carefully bore the deceased to the gondola.—After them came the servants of the house with countless wreaths and floral offerings, with which the sarcophagus was decorated and a second gondola was quite filled. —

A solemn pause ensued, each person had the anxious feeling that he must endure a sight that would wrench his heart, since the friends who became the deceased's escort of honor were already returned to the chamber of desolation, in order to collect the widow and children for this last mournful journey through the city that had become so beloved to them and in which they would endure such a mournful event!

After a brief interval Frau Cosima appeared on Dr. Keppler's arm, leading by the hand the young Siegfried, the Master's only son.—Their closely contained, maturing, otherwise quite upright aspects seemed altogether shattered.—Passini with Wagner's daughter Daniela, followed them, Hr. Schukowsky and Ruben led the two other daughters, Isolde and Evchen. —

In solemn silence the bereaved moved through the respectful space made by the obviously quite emotional crowd, in consideration of the mourners' grief. Silently they entered into the black-bedecked gondola, silently in the lifeless vessel they glided through the long watery planes of the Grand Canal, their eyes directed steadily toward the little boat that floated before them and that carried the sarcophagus, richly decorated with laurels and palms, in which rested the dear departed.

The sun shone brilliantly on the day of February 16, it sparkled wantonly in the green-and-blue flow of water, thoroughly warmed by the sun; sadly the trees, agitated by the wind in the garden of the Palazzo Vendramin, bent their branches, as if to offer their farewell salute to the great dead man.—From the distance sounded the bells of one of the towers of this city so rich in campanili, it was the only music that the widow's ear, become so sensitive and intolerant, was unable to exclude.—A fearfully sad tolling, with which her tears began anew to flow uncontrollably and her heart almost stopped in its anguish.

How often had she taken this route at his side—how often did she make rapturous exclamations over this magical city!—Yes, not only did the sun shine warmly then, but she perceived its warming rays, she rejoiced in them and was made happy by that, since she still was by his side! —

Today he was taken from her—the magnificence of the day was an insult, the glorious buildings of the unique city were distortions!

And finally they arrived at the place from which they would take the blustering steam train to the solid earth [i.e., the *terraferma*], through valleys and meadows, over hills and mountains to their German homeland, to the soil of their fatherland, in order to restore the sovereign of two artistic realms to the earth that proudly would take him as its own.

In accordance with the widow's wish, the railroad station was closed off, and the only ones present were a few administrative officials who did not lose the opportunity to take part in this final gesture of respect to the great poet–composer. —

The magnificent funerary carriage, decorated in black, which the "Concordia" Undertakers Society of Vienna had sent to Venice, stood ready for the reception of the corpse. To this was adjoined the salon carriage in which the family, accompanied by their friends who would give the mourners an escort part of the way, took their place. Both carriages were attached to the express train departing around two o'clock. The funeral transport would then pursue its path, by means of a prearranged special train, first by way of Vicenza, then through Verona, Ala, Kufstein, and Munich, on to Bayreuth, the Master's final resting place.

After the bereaved had taken their places with their companions in the two [*sic*] salon-carriages,[33] the curtains on the windows were carefully closed, the final bell strokes sounded and thereupon began the progress that carried the dead Richard Wagner from the Lagoon City on homeward over the Alps.

A feeling of unending anxiety bore down upon our soul,—only now did we feel the painful, irreparable loss in its full scope, which we and, with us, the world now suffered.

"Yet, his works are immortal!" —

We and the numberless host of his admirers have said it to ourselves. And yet, we are unable to pull our mind back from the powerful happenings of these last days, to find any comfort for our heart!

Involuntarily our steps turn back to the palazzo halls where the great deceased dwelt, and we request permission once again to be allowed to pass through the chambers in which each and every thing brings back reminders of him, of the last days of his earthly pilgrimage.—Quite absorbed in his image, we walk through the long apartments in which still prevails the fragrance of roses—the Master's favorite perfume. With the feeling of deepest melancholy, we tarry in his room, now stripped of its magnificence, in which Richard Wagner had labored up until the last moment of his earthly presence. —

Betty Bürkel, the loyal maidservant of the Wagner household, was the only one who yet stayed behind, and was busily engaged in packing the many possessions still remaining: that same maidservant who had been destined by fate to receive the last words of the dying man, the same one who peered into his blurred eyes when he was looking all round for help.

As Dr. Keppler assured us, the Master's death-struggle had been an extremely difficult one, especially aggravated by the fact that he was entirely deprived of speech.

"Redemption to the redeemer!"

These judiciously grand words from the sublime *Parsifal* poem the Vienna Wagner Society wrote as inscription on the wreath that it had placed on the coffin of Richard

Wagner, and are also those that comforted us amid our thoughts of his death agonies. And as we departed the celebrated building in a mood of reverent grieving, the place and its recollections awoke within us as we boarded the gondola that would take us homeward along the Grand Canal. Already the numberless stars twinkled in the arch of the heavens, and we must involuntarily think of that autumn night on which we, our breast swelling with happy expectation, mounted the stairs of that magnificent building that had been destined to shelter the great Master and also, sadly, to entomb him in its walls.

Yet, only the earthly shell of Richard Wagner has been taken to his grave, he himself, however, will live on and will give confirmation the truth that he himself—intoxicated by his own Genius, drunk with the exultation of an enthusiastic crowd—spoke in Zurich to the great Russian musician Serov: "We are the gods of this earth!"

And not only in his immortal works will the regenerator of German artistic criticism live on, but also in the remembrance of anyone who has had the good fortune to associate with him, to explore the full treasure of his intellectual profundity.

From now on, however, the facade of the Palazzo Vendramin in Venice will be decorated with a marble panel as a permanent marker, a visible testimony to the remembrance of Richard Wagner's residence and death!—A pilgrimage site for the pilgrims of sacred art from all countries! (235–46/83–88)

Perl's account of the aftermath of Wagner's death obviously drew her into a good deal of fanciful, even fictionalized writing. How could she know the thoughts and feelings she attributes to Cosima and the others? Yet, her apparent sources among the servants must have provided her with so much of what she uniquely describes. Nowhere else do we learn fascinating little details: the story of the little cat Wagner had adopted; the Countess Hatzfeldt's receipt of the news of Wagner's death; Cosima's ostentatious pronouncement on what her husband would have done had she been the one to die.[34] Especially in Perl's portrayal, Cosima's behavior in general can easily strike us as a theatrical show. Yet, there is no doubting Cosima's devotion to Richard, for all the tensions between them. In an era that loved melodramatic display, Perl's picture of Cosima's grief does not seem really incredible—no less than her vignette of the poor gondolier's grief. And where else do we learn the important little atmospheric fact that it was raining heavily on February 13?

Perl goes well beyond the newspaper accounts in her detailed picture of the tumult that marked the three days following Wagner's death. One can be sure that Perl herself was in the palazzo confines—perhaps thanks to her connection with Dr. Keppler—and was an eyewitness to what she describes. She is not the only eyewitness to Frontali's vain request,[35] but her picture is a touching one. Above all, she reports most fully the removal for shipping of the Wagner family possessions, and the harvesting of relics from the death room: not only the sofa, but the armchair with its fur, and the great bed and the ottoman frame. (Were these furnishings ones the Wagners bought themselves during their stay, or were they part of the palazzo's own inventory? If one believes the Italian newspaper report about Cosima's wish to purchase the gondola and the funeral carriage,[36] one might conclude that she made the distinction between taking what she owned and buying what she did not.) Perl alone tells us that Betty Bürkel remained behind to arrange transfer of remaining possessions.

Following her little slip over the number of salon-carriages, Perl tapers off her account as the funeral train leaves Venice; even though Dr. Keppler, who rode in it as far as Vicenza, could have reported on that much of the trip. Of the obsequies in Germany, and at Bayreuth, she did not trouble herself to learn or report. Instead, however, she gives us a highly personal bit of final eyewitness testimony, something remarkably vivid. Amid her lofty grieving for the departed German genius, she tells of returning to the Vendramin, to which she gained admittance (from Betty herself?) in order to brood her way through the empty rooms and their lingering associations. And in the midst of that, she seems to suggest that she might, have, after all, visited the palazzo in the previous autumn. (Of course, had she met the Master at the time, she surely would have told us about it! Might she have been scouting the servants while the boss was away?)

For all her professions of German cultural pride and ardent adoration for Wagner, we are still left with some question about Perl's motivations. Her interest in the composer—opportunistic or otherwise, and probably in play from an early point in his stay in Venice—was fundamentally journalistic. Wagner was a world-class celebrity. Then, in the weeks following his death, there was a sudden market for the latest news about the Master's final days. Perl does not seem to have had more than passing knowledge of his operas, and she shows little interest in musical matters themselves. Her real concern is with biographical anecdotes and observations that can make up her "mosaic." Given the idolatrous German audience she was addressing, she has nothing critical to say about the "genius" she is so eager to glorify. In her portrayal, hardly any warts are on display. Everything possible is done to present Wagner as a warm and human individual, with particular stress put on the blissful happiness and mutual affection rampant within the composer's family circle. The constant preoccupation she displays with Wagner's health, even allowing its anticipatory ties to his death, obviously resulted from her friendship with Dr. Keppler, the family physician. To that connection was added, as has repeatedly been noted, some degree of access, whether through Keppler or on her own, to at least a few members of the household staff. Indeed, one may often presume that, when any of them were featured in some narrative, those servants themselves were her source. Certainly her account of every episode involving Dr. Keppler's presence would have been derived from his own reports to her.

Perl's dependency upon Keppler as a source might be viewed in another way, however, serving actually to invert what we understand about her book. It has been suggested[37] that Keppler may have been a source, or the only source, for the description of the family scene in the hours after Wagner's death, as published in the *LGdV* on February 15, or its like. It has been suggested further that

Keppler was discreetly but firmly reprimanded for breaching family privacy in so doing.[38] This opened an eventual rift between the doctor and the family circle, generating the latter's conclusion that Keppler was "an acknowledged charlatan" whose treatment was actually responsible for Wagner's death. Accordingly, Keppler retaliated by freely providing Perl with information for her book.

Indeed, one might carry this picture of things one step further. Could it be that Dr. Keppler's determination to defend and vindicate himself from insinuations of "malpractice" in Wagner's case have itself become one of the reasons, if not the central reason, for Perl's writing the book in the first place? Was she his tool, rather than he her resource? Obviously, she had her own literary aspirations and opportunistic goals in undertaking the book on her own, but hers and the doctor's agendas could well have become complementary in generating the project. It is worth remembering that *only* in the preface to that book did Keppler publish his pseudo-autopsy report after Wagner's embalming; while the recurrent excursuses on Wagner's illnesses and Keppler's treatment run through the book on a more than coincidentally massive scale. Seen thus from the doctor's perspective, Perl's book might well be viewed as a work of polemic on his behalf.

Those are questions that can never be definitively resolved. And, if Perl's motivations must be scrutinized critically, so too must be the credibility of whatever she reports. Still, her account can by no means be dismissed out of hand. We have noted some instances of clear or apparent inaccuracy, particularly at odds with newspaper reports of the moment. (One must wonder sometimes how much she read the local Venetian journals, if at all!) And there are often statements made for which one would wish corroboration. Nevertheless, in the final judgment, Perl's little book deserves not only what limited acceptance it has already achieved but still more serious attention and respect in the literature on Wagner. For all her stylistic quirks, her little "mosaic" stands as both a crucial source and an interesting, even charming period piece in its own right.

Chapter Eight

Remembering

An Italian For the Italians

If the year 1883 provided the chance to exploit the fresh news of Wagner's death for a German public, it also offered the opportunity to promote Wagner and his music to an Italian public.

Henriette Perl hastened her little book into print within weeks of Wagner's death, quite single-mindedly, to retail what immediate information she had about the great composer's final months, for feeding to a German public that was altogether familiar with him and his music. Our other writer of the year 1883, however, had a double purpose. He did wish to document information about, and to preserve recollections of, Wagner's final Venetian visit. But he also recognized the opportunity provided by the newsworthy death of the composer to promote Wagner's music to an Italian public little familiar with it, or even hostile to it. For him, however much he admired Wagner the man, it was Wagner the musician that was his ultimate concern, whereas for Perl it was only Wagner the cultural celebrity who interested her. Perl in her way was a high-class gossipmonger, whereas our Italian writer was a musician, deeply involved in the Italian musical world of his day.

It is difficult to find much information now on Giuseppe Norlenghi. Clearly one of those Italians who had become enthusiastic Wagner champions during the cultural factionalism of the moment, he is virtually forgotten today.[1] But he was one of the first Italian writers to produce a substantial book in Italian, and for Italian readers, that combined a biographical sketch of Wagner with proselytizing for his music. This is his *Wagner a Venezia*, a volume of 224 pages that appeared early in 1884.[2]

The book was completed within six months of Wagner's death: its preface is dated August 1883, in Venice. At the beginning of his preface, Norlenghi notes the distinguished composers who, before Wagner, had ended their days in Venice: the native Benedetto Marcello of the eighteenth century, and two other foreigners who died there, the Neapolitan Domenico Cimarosa (1749–1801), and the German expatriate Johann Adolf Hasse (1699–1783), who expired a century before Wagner did (though on December 16).

Norlenghi begins his justification immediately:

It seems to me something extremely interesting, especially for the friends of Wagner (and by friends I mean the admirers of the man who was someone distinguished, and of the artist who was a genius), to collect some details of the last phase of his life, which was spent and ended here. These I had from individuals who actually, for one reason or another, were in contact with him and whom I regarded as worthy of absolute faith, and these I have set down faithfully, soberly, and without pretentious or irreverent amplification. (vii–viii)

He pursues his emphasis on the inseparability of the man from the artist.

. . . Accordingly, perhaps for the future historian these few particulars, these small anecdotes, that—for someone who does not just look superficially—somehow illuminate quite well the true character and the artistic faith of Wagner, will not be devoid of usefulness. (viii)

Norlenghi admits that the subject of Wagner's artistic struggles and achievements is a vast one, with a large literature amid which he is a novice and a modest amateur. But he has plunged honestly and frankly into artistic controversies:

When the occasion arises to speak of Italian art, I have written frankly and loyally what I think as to the genuine dangers that are menacing it, and I have attempted to depict quickly the wretched situation in which, to its damage, it flounders. (ix–x)

Here Norlenghi acknowledges yet a third goal of his book: not only to document and to champion Wagner, but to deliver a critique on the state of music in the Italy of the moment. He will address this topic, he indicates, because art is not for an isolated elite but is the patrimony of all, giving him the right and obligation to express himself on it. He ends, however, by returning to his partisan goal, with an aspiration now made rather poignant by the neglect his book has suffered:

I hope, however, that the friends of Wagner will not find totally unacceptable this little work of mine, which has, if nothing else, the merit of precision in the reports concerning the last days of the precious life that all lament, and that they will be willing to accept it with sympathy at least for its respectful intent.
And it is to them that I entrust it and dedicate it. (x–xi)

Norlenghi divided his book into five chapters, preceded by an introduction. The latter he begins by describing his closest personal encounter with his subject.

The first time I saw Richard Wagner was at the end of a day in October of 1882, under the canopy of one of those little steamers that make the passage from the Lido to Venice.
With me was a young friend of mine, an Armenian magistrate who had become a refugee to Venice from the massacres that afflicted Egypt in that year [June 1882].

Sadness was the dominant note on that day, for all the people who are usually so merry when they return at that hour from the sea to the city. We had witnessed an appalling scene on the terrace of the bathing resort.

A noble young Polish girl, defying the stormy day and the particularly powerful wind, had chosen to venture into the sea. Although she was accompanied by a bathing attendant, there came a terrible moment in which a wave tore her from the powerful arms of her strong guardian. She was drowned! Her father, her sister, her fiancé, powerless to save her, had witnessed her struggle from the beach, emitting desperate screams. Then, all but insane, they had fallen on their knees with a pleading look to heaven.

My companion was immersed in that kind of sad listlessness that is a reaction to severe agitations of the spirit, when, suddenly indicating with his eyes, he said: "You see that gentleman; that is Wagner." I felt a shock at that name, and, turning my head in the direction indicated, I saw an old gentleman in a large, plain, wide-brimmed hat, and a gray overcoat. Next to him was standing a lady with luxurious and completely white hair, with a face of an unusual pallor, and of a perfectly oval shape.

I confess that, despite my admiration for the author of *Lohengrin*, what impressed me at that moment was the lady, who I then realized was Wagner's wife, the lady Cosima Liszt, daughter of the famous pianist. I had never before seen a woman's image more individual. On her face could be perceived clearly the outlines of a great original beauty; and, in the eyes that almost never left Wagner, a boundless affection, an almost maternal one for the illustrious companion of her life.

With them were two fair and rosy youngsters, two true children of Arminius [i.e., Germans],[3] and a pale, delicate, graceful boy; Sigfrido, the last child of Wagner.

Through a curious association of ideas—governed then by the profound impression experienced at the Lido—in looking steadily at the great musician, whose features I could not make out clearly because of the faint light, I was reminded of the scene in his *Vascello Fantasma* [Phantom Vessel, i.e., *Der fliegende Holländer*]. It was when the sweet Senta, frantic over her abandonment by her lover—who, believing himself betrayed as always, had disappeared into his fatal vessel—threw herself into the sea to meet him in death. So my mind was filled with those passionate, tormenting notes when the steamer halted, and all arose to disembark, I was able to draw near to Wagner and observe him a little better. Rather slight in body, of an awkward and feeble behavior—his face individual and quite expressive, his brow high and broad, his two little eyes full of radiance and charm—Richard Wagner gave me the impression at that moment of a man still full of energy, whose youthfulness of spirit is in constant struggle with a weak and broken body. I saw him on further occasions during the winter and that initial impression I reconfirmed for myself.

Yet, on that day I would never have thought that, scarcely four months later, I would be going to the railroad station to give my last reverent salute to his corpse as it was on its way to Bavaria. (1–4)[4]

Of Norlenghi's five chapters, the first four seek to fulfill one of his two intentions in writing the book: that is, to introduce the life and works of Wagner to an Italian readership still little familiar with either; and, in the process, to speak out on Italian musical life in general. In that sense, those first four chapters are part of the history of Wagner reception in Italy, and will be considered as such below.[5] Nevertheless, the first chapter itself is worth dealing with here, since its biographical concentration does make reference to Wagner's general associations with Italy.

Norlenghi strongly believed the life and the works of Wagner should not be considered apart from each other. He stresses that point by titling this first chapter explicitly "L'uomo e l'artista," working from the truism that "the man and the artist" are inseparable. The chapter gives a concise sketch of Wagner's life and career, mingling biographical data with references to the composer's emerging operatic output. Along the way, Norlenghi makes rather murky reference to the series of concerts Wagner gave at the Théâtre Italien in Paris in January and February 1960, concerts that "divided the public and musicians into two camps, one that extolled him to the point of excess, the other that sought furiously and by all means to destroy him." From here Norlenghi jumps, in a chronological lurch, to events of two years before:

> In this same year [actually 1858] he visited Italy and at Venice he wrote *Tristano ed Isolda*, an opera that, they say, under the influence of the lovely Italian sky, he had composed with maximum fluency. And, what is something curious, it is perhaps the only one of his musical creations that, amid great beauties, would involve intricacies and obscurities. (18)

Norlenghi does not avoid reference to Wagner's tumultuous personal life, or, in general terms, his involvements with women, in the midst of his stormy artistic career. The scandal of the *Tannhäuser* production in Paris, the genesis of the concept of "the music of the future," the composer's rescue by Ludwig II, the completion of the *Ring* and the plans for the Bayreuth theater, are all surveyed. Cosima Liszt—"a lady of the highest sensibilities, truly worthy of him" (30)—is introduced in discreet brevity along with their children. Other Wagner works are mentioned, culminating in *Parsifal*. Likewise the building of "Wanfried" [*sic*], the idyllic new family home, where one might have expected the great composer to find ultimate personal and artistic peace.

> But such was not his destiny ...
> In his final years he was many times in Italy, where he loved its warm and fragrant climate and the sweet songs of the people.
> Naples and Palermo, and finally Venice, welcomed him; he adored the sea, as vast as his own intellect.
> And in Italy, at Venice, he would die ... (33)

Norlenghi closes with a tribute to Wagner's devotion, despite endless controversy, to the high ideals of art.

From here our author continues his proselytizing and sermonizing in his next three chapters—"La missione e l'ideale di Wagner," "Il musicista ed il pubblico," and "Wagner e l'arte italiana"—which he considered integral to the overall plan of his book, but which, as stated, will more logically (for our purposes) be scrutinized below. And so we shift to the last of Norlenghi's five chapters, which, at eighty-one pages, also happens to be the longest single segment, by itself over one-third of the book's total length. It finally brings us to the intention he affirmed at the outset, to report information about Wagner's final stay in Venice, the intention that he expected would give his book its ultimate value.

He titles the chapter "In Palazzo Vendramin-Calergi" and, appropriately, he begins it with an introduction to that building itself: "the most splendid of the splendid edifices that are on Venice's Grand Canal." In this introduction (142–47). Norlenghi fixes its location, reviews its history and sequence of owners, and gives a description of its appearance.

> In this splendid palazzo Riccardo Wagner, with his beloved family, spent the final months of his life. Into this palazzo he entered, gay and smiling, on 18 September 1882. On 16 February of the following year his venerated corpse left it. (147)

Norlenghi then surveys Wagner's visits to Venice before 1882. At the outset, he makes a total chronological and topographical hash out of the first one, extending his earlier confusion:

> Wagner had been in Venice many times before. In 1860, a refugee from his homeland, he stayed there for some time. He lodged then in the Piazza S. Marco, in the Albergo of the same name, he wrote here the greater part of his *Tristano ed Isolda*, and from the windows of that Albergo that gave out over the piazza, he assisted with the performance of his overture to *Tannhäuser*, magnificently played by an Austrian band, for which he himself had written the score. (148)

Now, Wagner's first visit to Venice was in 1858–59, not 1860. For only one night after his arrival did he stay at the Hotel Danieli, near but hardly over the Piazza San Marco. He promptly found continuing lodgings in the Palazzo Giustiniani on the Grand Canal. He did frequent the Albergo San Marco to take his supper there, but he did not lodge in it. We know that Wagner was impressed by the performance of his music, including the *Tannhäuser* Overture, given by the Austrian band, and the composer himself did report that he listened to them playing these pieces from the Albergo San Marco. Wagner also tells us he visited the band at its rehearsal.[6] But there is no evidence whatsoever that Wagner himself arranged that piece for these performances. Concerning at least that early phase of Wagner's Venetian associations—of which he was clearly not a witness himself—Norlenghi displays disappointingly sloppy knowledge.

Our author says nothing about the brief visit in the autumn of 1861. He also passes quickly over the "few days" of Wagner's next stay in Venice, in September 1876, with his family. The sojourn following, in October 1880, he misdates cursorily to 1879, and he next assigns to "the spring of 1881" the stay in April 1882. He must have been unable to understand that Wagner made *two* visits to the city in 1882, not just one. Norlenghi then reports, from his own observation, a curiosity nowhere else recorded:

. . . He resided then in the sumptuous Albergo d'Europa, located in the most splendid position, at the beginning of the Canalazzo [Grand Canal]. I have visited the apartment that he occupied on those different occasions (he always wanted that one) and that is on the *secondo piano* of that Hotel. A splendid parlor, from the windows of which the eye scans over the entire magnificent Bacino di S. Marco as far as the Lido; nearby a small room as a study, then, up a little internal stairway, a cheerful bed chamber: all constituted his lodging. It is the same apartment lived in by Verdi, the same lived in previously by Meyerbeer; a curious coincidence. It is a hotel full of artistic memories, this magnificent Hotel d'Europa, and the register-book of travelers for that hotel is precious, because in it are names like that of Riccardo Wagner, whose signature, entered by the Master, is written in large characters by his own hand. (148–49)

For all Norlenghi's muddling of chronology, this passage is interesting because it helps clarify our information about the hotels where the Wagners lodged in their four visits to Venice as a family. Norlenghi suggests that they "always" (*sempre*) stayed at the Hotel Europa. That is well-established for the 1876 stay, as attested by Cosima (September 19),[7] and for the second 1882 stay there is a backhanded reference by Cosima (September 17).[8] On the other hand, the lodging in 1880 was apparently at the Hotel Danieli, as suggested by Cosima (October 4),[9] Norlenghi notwithstanding. That leaves the visit in April 1882, on which neither Cosima nor Glasenapp give any information. One might, therefore, take Norlenghi's word on that count, and presume they stayed at the Europa then, as well.

Norlenghi now leaps back to the earliest of these family stays:

One evening in 1876 when Wagner was in Venice at this hotel, a band of *pittori* (the name that is given to wandering singers, I don't know why) went under the windows of the Europa to serenade the master.

Wagner was most flattered by it, and with his usual generosity he sent them 100 lire as a gift. When the *pittori* returned the next evening, Wagner sent them for it another 50. But they were so dissatisfied that, in their indiscretion—apparently matching their regular singing out of tune—they waited until he should go out, and they surrounded him at the end of the Calle del Ridotto, perhaps to demand still more money, the rascals! Wagner was very upset by this disgusting scene, whose motive he perhaps did not understand, and he returned immediately to the hotel pale and agitated. (149–50)

This was not the first time that Wagner had encountered street singers in Venice, and it would not be the last.[10] But Norlenghi completes his gleanings from the Europa:

The chambermaid who had always served then, and who is still in service at the house, could only extol to me the politeness and affability of Wagner, of his lady, and of his very polite children.

This is a general chorus of all those who, in whatever capacity, were in contact with him. When he was not subject to the attacks of the illness that tormented him, and that would lead him to the grave, he was a man of goodness and of admirable charm. All those in Venice who came anywhere near him, especially his subordinates, remained devoted to him in an extraordinary way.

Then in 1882 he was again in Venice in the spring, as always at the Europa, and in the same apartment. (150–51)

This brings Norlenghi to his account of the Piazza concert of April 1882:

> One day in April of that year, the twenty-first around two, the good Calascione, maestro of the civic band, was beating time to his players—who with their concerts delight the pigeons and the children who alone populated [the Piazza] S. Marco at that hour—when a piazza waiter who was followed by an elderly gentleman with a gentle girl on his arm, asked to speak to him. Calascione approached them, and they asked, in the name of the person whom he guided, the favor of having the band play the overture of *Gazza ladra*. Calascione replied that this piece was not on the program, therefore this would not be possible. The elderly gentleman and his group went away. But to a certain one of the players it leapt to mind that this gentleman could be Wagner, whose arrival the journals had announced, and then naturally they hastened to find the way to honor this request.
>
> Some men who were strolling in the piazza were sought, and they were told that the overture would be played. They were ordered immediately to find the score in the archive, and in fact a half-hour later the brilliant overture by Rossini was performed beyond the program.
>
> As was proper for him, Wagner was unusually grateful to Calascione for this kindness, and approached him, and thanked him, extending his hand and calling to him "Bravo Kappelmeister." But when Calascione wanted to offer a compliment to the greatest composer in the world (those are his words), and spoke the name of Wagner, the latter interrupted him brusquely and walked away from him.
>
> The overture to *Gazza Ladra* seemed most greatly pleasing to one of his daughters who, with him that day, displayed great enjoyment of the performance, and it seems that Wagner had requested it in response to her wish. (151–52)

Here we have essentially the same account of this incident as we showed Perl giving, in our previous chapter. It is an account, as noted, that diverges in important ways from the report in the local newspapers at the time. The divergences suggest that, at the least, Perl and Norlenghi had somewhat the same source(s) or informant(s) for their accounts, and that it was not the newspapers.[11]

Norlenghi next turns to the general picture of the Wagner stay at the Vendramin, beginning with a touch of eyewitness testimony, and thereby introduces someone who was clearly a principal source for him.

> The last time that Wagner arrived in Venice, and unfortunately in the extremity of his health, was Friday September 15, 1882. "The accursed Friday," Luigi, his faithful gondolier, the *suo amico*, said to me with tears in his eyes: "Look, sir, these things always end up badly here." (153)

Norlenghi continues with a direct report: after three days at the Europa Hotel, while the Palazzo Vendramin was made ready, Wagner and his family moved into an apartment there of thirty rooms.

Wagner came to Venice to restore his ravaged health, and to refresh his spirit. He had spent the summer around Palermo at the Villa d'Angri [*sic*]; and he intended to stay in Venice through the winter and part of the spring, up to May. (153)

More muddling. Norlenghi seems to place the residence in Palermo immediately before this arrival in Venice in autumn 1882: in fact, the Palermo stay was during the winter of 1881–82, at the Hôtel des Palmes and then the Villa Porazzi/Gangi. The Villa Angri is not near Palermo but near Naples, and the sojourn there was in January–August 1880. Of course, the travels that began in Palermo in late 1881 did end with a stop in Venice in April 1882, and that fact may have helped to confuse Norlenghi. Clearly, however, his information on Wagner before September 1882 (save perhaps on some things in Venice) was seriously inadequate or defective.

Norlenghi catalogues the Wagner household at the Vendramin. Of the family, besides Cosima, he begins with Wagner's step-daughter, Daniela von Bülow. Norlenghi makes a point of noting that she "bore the name of her grandmother, the Countess d'Agoult, the celebrated writer (Daniel Stern)"—that is, in a feminine form, and as added to the surname of her father, Cosima's first husband. Then there were Wagner's own three children, Isolde and Eva, "most charming young girls," and "the little" Siegfried. Of the household staff, there was Siegfried's tutor, "a young, very cultivated German" (i.e., Stein), "a lively Neapolitan lady as companion for the young ladies" (i.e., the governess Sg.ra. Corsani), George (Lang) "Wagner's faithful manservant," and "an aged chambermaid Betty [Bürkel]," to which Norlenghi adds "a groom (*staffiere*) and other persons of basic functions." Thereby he implies a somewhat larger group of servants than did Perl, in her ode to the simplicity of Wagner's household.[12] Of course, his last statement may refer to, or include, the palazzo functionaries, the porter Pietro Falcieri (called "Garibaldi" by Wagner), and the gondolier Luigi Trevisan (nicknamed "Ganasseta").

Norlenghi also takes note of the early, brief visit of Wagner's other step-daughter, Blandine von Bülow, wife of Count Gravina. Then Norlenghi draws further on putative local sources:

> Regular visitors to the Lido certainly have memories of that most agreeable family, which, during all of September, boarded the vaporetto as a foursome: those lovely young girls; that very interesting elderly man, that lady with the white hair. Even for those who knew not who they might be, they caught the eye, so much was their distinctiveness and the sympathy they inspired, whose joyful, calm faces, full of affability, would only a few months later, be disfigured by sorrow, by grief. (154)

A charming picture: though neither Perl nor Cosima herself confirm that the family took vaporetto rides "every day" (*ogni giorno*) in September.

On to the family routine:

Life in the Wagner house was serene and well-ordered. Like all German families, who very much liked, and with good reason, their own privacy, and who found the greatest pleasures in private life, so also the Wagner family lived in a kind of sweet isolation. Few were those privileged to be admitted to the Palazzo Vendramin, many fewer the times Wagner went out at evening.

Wagner despised not good company but the festivities, the parties, etc., generally everything of that artificial and decadent life which come to be called pretentiously "society life." His more concentrated pleasures he found in the closeness of his loved ones.

He arose briskly at 6, took a bath, he dressed in one of his famous dressing-gowns with the little beret and the slippers of the same color (of these ensembles he had three particularly rich and luxurious kinds, one black, one white, and one red) and he made a little stroll through the great rooms of the apartment, he took a saucer of coffee with the children who at that hour had their breakfast, and he returned to his chamber.

At 9 breakfast was brought, which he had together with his wife. He then went into his study, and no one was allowed to disturb him, under any pretext.

Precisely at midday came the barber to shave him—Wagner held firmly to punctuality—and after about an hour he went out by gondola, either alone or with his wife, or with one of his children.

Usually he then visited some artistic monument of the city, but more particularly the churches, for which he had the greatest affection—"I am the worst kind of Lutheran," he sometimes said jokingly to the boatman Luigi, "but I greatly love your churches." (Wagner, it is known, was a Protestant.)

Then he made a brief stop in the Piazza: he frequently went into Lavena's, the fashionable bar, he had a glass of cognac or a hot chocolate, he made a short walk, and returned.

At 2 sharp a bell signaled the lunch hour, and all the family came together.

Wagner maintained a good table: he ate little, but he wanted choice dishes; almost every day they prepared a partridge; and many fruits that he liked very much. He took coffee in the parlor, with the family, then he retired to his study.

At 5 he went out again, and returned *in città*, as he called the center, San Marco. At seven he returned home, a half-hour after supper, then he moved with the family into the parlor; they took tea, a gaming table was set up, and they remained there conversing and gaming. At 11 all went to bed.

This was the usual life in the Palazzo Vendramin. Wagner usually stayed in his study from 10 to 12, and from 2 to 4:30. He was composing an opera on the Indian mythological subject *I penitenti*. What treasures of sounds would have been achieved with that Indian setting, so rich in colors and of warm sounds, had not grim Fate cut short so unexpectedly his precious days. (155–58)[13]

Norlenghi's picture of Wagner's routine may be compared with that given by Perl's, which is more detailed but also divergent on some points. It is particularly interesting that Norlenghi says nothing about the devotion of many family evenings to reading literature, as described in their different ways by both Perl and Cosima. On the other hand, Norlenghi has taken far too seriously the rumors about Wagner's supposed new operatic project.

We are next told of those few fortunates who were allowed to visit the house. The Russian painter "Jouchowsky" was the most regular one, but also came the painters Passini and Ruben, as well as the "distinguished Russian gentleman," Wolkoff. On the distaff side, the daughters were regular visitors to the home of Princess "Hasztfeldt," while Cosima had a close friendship with the Sgra. Pinelli, "a very spirited lady of Berlin, although she went by an Italian name," who wintered in Venice.

Then, some odd observations:

> Wagner was very rarely at the pianoforte. He had two of them, excellent and gorgeous, brought from Bayreuth, but through the entire winter he played the piano three or four times.
> Who usually played more was the lady Daniela, an accomplished pianist, a born musician. (158–59)

The assertion of Wagner's abstinence from the piano is curious. Perl makes several references to his playing, while Cosima's diary repeatedly speaks of his sitting down to play, if not at length, at least in small installments. Here again, Norlenghi seems to have lacked sufficient "inside" sources.

Next, a more personal portrait:

> Usually Wagner was in an excellent mood. When his illness did not torture him—for then he was insufferable, even with the solicitude of his family, for which he had a veritable adoration—he was of a good temper, of an expansiveness, and of a happiness quite childish. He greatly delighted in those who surrounded him.
> Those who never had observed him, who never knew anything of his life, persist, parrot-like, in speaking ill of the man—even when (such grace!) they would grant his artistic genius—to portray him as sulky, arrogant, disagreeable. They would need to talk with all those here in Venice who had been near him, from Count Contin, the Liceo president, to the boatman Luigi, from the violinist Frontali to the least of the domestics, in order to understand how much he was refined in manner, affable, kind, good, charming.
> They would understand how much regret, how much reverent affection this illustrious man has left behind here, he who so many like to portray as a kind of cannibal, a savage.
> He was beloved by his gondolier Luigi in a most remarkable way. A fine type, that Ganasseta (Luigi Trevisan). A strong, lean, sunburned, man of sixty years, he gave the appearance of forty, full of good humor, but at the same time with devout fondness for his employers, and one of those characteristic types of gondoliers of a disappearing sort, of those types that Byron liked so much.
> Of a fully proven loyalty, [Ganasseta] had acquired the boundless confidence of the great artist. Wagner called him "suo amico, suo carissimo amico" [his friend, his dearest friend], and when he came to the Piazza and went to his usual tobacconist to buy some cigars, the first one was always for "caro Luigi."
> It is necessary to heed such eloquent words of affection when one finds this good boatman speaking about Wagner; it is necessary to see for oneself his eyes bathed in tears when he recalls the kindness of his dear employer, when he describes the tormenting particulars of his death.
> In his arms Wagner breathed his last breath. (159–61)

That final statement anticipates a curious fiction about Wagner's dying moments that we will encounter again below, and reflect upon then.[14]

Norlenghi continues with some Luigi-derived recollections:

> Outside the house everyone more or less plays a role; it is within the family, it is in intimate contacts with friends, with dependents, that a kind of touchstone is passed over the true character, over the true temper of a man.
>
> Well then, Riccardo Wagner—the man who one evening, I believe in Berlin, refused contemptuously (and he had had his own good reasons) the high honor that the German Emperor intended to give him by inviting him to his box—more than a few times, when he disembarked from the gondola, he passed his hand across Luigi's brow in order to feel if he was very sweaty, often regretting, despite the gondolier's normal protests, having made him tire himself so much. And this great labor was mostly to drive the gondola from the Palazzo Vendramin to San Marco, twenty minutes en route; and almost always, beyond the pay and his further allowances, he rewarded the boatmen for their brief effort with laudatory and opulent tips.
>
> "I will never find such good employers," Ganasseta always said when speaking of Wagner and of his family.
>
> And the eloquence of these facts renders any comments unnecessary. (161–62)

Next comes a picture of Wagner's favorite haunt:

> The Lavena bar is the fashionable meeting place in winter. When the streetlamps begin to light up at [Piazza di] San Marco, when business is finished, when visits are ended, all make their stroll in the piazza, awaiting the dinner hour. It is into this elegant hideaway that the *belle mondane* of Venice, and the real *demi mondaines*, and the elegant folk, and the idlers, and all those who want to see or to be seen, are like a procession into it, where they come to take the tonic beverages that stimulate the appetite. Almost every day at 5 to 6, Wagner made his little stop at Lavena, and remained there a half-hour, often conversing with the manager of the shop, with whom he was very friendly. He went in alone or with his wife, or with one of his daughters, then he was rejoined by the rest of the family and on most occasions the first room—in which there is a bench and which is narrow like a corridor—was fully occupied by the fascinating family.[15]
>
> Wagner usually took some tea or a glass of cognac, in the rear room, and at Lavena is still preserved the little table on which he was served, and the chair that the great man used every day.
>
> When he left, he took the arm of his wife, who was taller than he, and he made five or six circuits around the piazza, stopping before the shop windows, and always humming in a low voice; and whoever was near him could often hear him hinting at broad melodies, full of elegant runs, always his own, so very typical of him. (162–63)

Norlenghi moves on to his version of an incident also reported by Perl, regarding Wagner's renewed dealings with bandmaster Calascione:

> However, the illness that had entrapped his life, and that would carry him off from the world and to glory, allowed him no respite.

Several times even on the street unexpected assaults struck his heart.

It was a day in November [specifically, Sunday, November 5], and Calascione, the maestro of the band had given respectful notice to the master that on that day would be performed in the piazza, in his honor, a composition on *Lohengrin*.[16]

Wagner promised to attend and stepped from his gondola at the Piazzetta around 5. He had scarcely taken a few steps when he recognized that the band in the piazza was already playing *Lohengrin*. He might have too much quickened his steps to arrive in time, or it would have been the effect of the nasty, humid wintry day: it happened that after a few minutes he felt himself faint, and, in a most painful state, he went accompanied into Lavena, sturdily supported by Cav. Tessarin, who was with him.*[17]

But he improved pretty quickly; and he asked Tessarin to thank Calascione and to invite him to his house for the next day.

The next day [*sic*] Calascione went to the Palazzo Vendramin. Wagner received him very cordially, praised him for his composition, and expressed satisfaction with the tempi taken by Calascione in his interpretation. He made only one observation, that he had taken too strict a tempo in the sublime peroration of the duet between Elsa and Ortrud, and specifically its *stretta* was too rushed.

By way of justifying himself, Calascione said that he had taken that tempo as he had understood it the year before when *Lohengrin* was performed at the Fenice. And he went on to speak of the sacred fire (*fuoco sacro*: perhaps our "inspiration" or "interpretational initiative") that sometimes he elicited.

Wagner shot back: "That fire, that fire! That water! all these people boast of this *sacro fuoco*, and on that pretext they interpret the music contrary to the composer's intentions. That fire! It is the composer who determines the *fuoco* should happen when the situation requires it, when the dramatic moment calls for it!"

Wagner had a genuine hatred for those orchestra conductors who, either to make a big show of their so-called *sacro fuoco*, or to find a guaranteed but vulgar effect, interpret the music of others recklessly: they compress and expand the tempi at their whim, and without any regard for the composer's intentions. And he was right, the more so because Wagner had such scrupulous respect for the requirements of the drama, and his music was created with the sole purpose of illustrating and of greatly enhancing the dramatic situation, but always of making it logical.

He was not an artist willing to sacrifice the logical requirements of the situation for ovations that were virtually dependent upon effects more coarse than aesthetic; nor, on the other hand, did he need them—certainly not he.

On that account he was most strict on this issue of tempo, and he always spoke of it when he discoursed on music, as of a matter of the very highest significance. (164–67)

Wagner's constant preoccupation with correctness of tempo is well attested by others, especially Cosima, but Norlenghi's vignette with Calascione is particularly vivid. (We might assume that Norlenghi had a direct account from the bandmaster himself.) Our author's report of the Piazza concert and Wagner's involvement parallels Perl's, though it avoids her misunderstanding of the composer's fainting fit and his retreat to Lavena's as an impatient shunning of Calascione's performance.[18] Cosima generally confirms Norlenghi's picture, though she puts Wagner's invitation for that evening, not the next day, and apparently for Tessarin as well as Calascione; though, on the other hand, her report of the occasion is quite terse.[19]

Now an important new visitor is introduced by Norlenghi:

> In the early days of December [specifically November 19], the Abbè Liszt came to
> Venice to visit Wagner and the family of his daughter. The romantic and mystic artist,
> who fired so many imaginations, who was adored by so many women, the author of
> those *Hungarian Rhapsodies*, so brilliant and impassioned, the creator of those *Preludes*
> so full of idealism, the great and celebrated pianist now transformed into the old abbè,
> but always worldly, always enthusiastic for art, came to Venice. His goal primarily was to
> keep company with Wagner, his son-in-law, and to try to divert him as much as possible,
> since his spirit was so particularly depressed in these last months, so full of unhappy
> forebodings, and with ever more frequent attacks of his illness. He went to take up res-
> idence with Wagner. The Palazzo Vendramin was altogether full: how much art, how
> many artists in that cultural enclosure! (167–68)

At this point, Norlenghi devotes several pages to sketching the life and career
of Franz Liszt, perhaps on the assumption that his Italian readers were not really
familiar with that great musician and romantic personality, much less with Liszt's
championing of Wagner's music. Liszt's impact on the Wagners' Venetian residence is then considered.

> Liszt suddenly became, in the Palazzo Vendramin, the veritable organizer of amuse-
> ments, of practices, of little entertainments. It was Liszt who received and presented
> guests, who introduced his protégés to Wagner, and put his lively and spirited stamp
> on the simple, almost monotonous life that was led in the Palazzo Vendramin. It was
> Liszt who persuaded Wagner, always with the goal of distracting him, to go one
> evening in December, to the Hatzfeldt home, for a little performance that was organ-
> ized there.
>   For this artistic celebration there had already been a good many rehearsals, and
> among those taking part in it were Madame Pinelli and Miss Daniela Bülow. Liszt reg-
> ularly wanted to participate in the rehearsals, asserting his right as being the grandfather
> of one of the performers, Miss Daniela!
>   The performance took place the evening of December 10.
>   Here is the exact program:

> **DIE GESCHWISTER [THE SIBLINGS]**
> A PLAY IN ONE ACT
> BY GOETHE
> CHARACTERS

> | | |
> |---|---|
> | *Wilhelm* | Ada Pinelli |
> | *Marianne* (his sister) | Daniela Bülow |
> | *Fabrice* | Adolphe Fiers |
> | *Postman* | Franz Ruben |
> | *A Child* | Isidoro |

> *Palazzo Malipiero 10 Dec. 1882*

> The performance was beyond reproach, and in the most powerful scene, between
> Wilhelm and Marianne, Wagner was not able to withhold his tears.
>   Wagner greatly enjoyed himself and, addressing himself to Sgra. Pinelli, who had
> taken the part of Wilhelm, and delivering the most extravagant praises, he said: "You

remind me in such a moment of Agnese Schebest (a celebrated artist, wife of David Strauss) in her greatest moments."

And that was no small praise.

To commemorate the birthday of the Princess, also given was a scene of declamation with music by Liszt, drawn from his *Santa Elisabetta*. One part, of the Minstrel, was taken by little Sigfrido; the piano was assigned to Sgr. Humferding, a pupil of Liszt. Then there was dancing, and a supper closed this most successful celebration.

Before the departure of Liszt from Venice (he stayed about a month), there was another musicale at the Hatzfeldt house directed by Liszt himself.

One can picture how Liszt was celebrated, surrounded, almost covered with compliments and compliments. With his good-natured humor, Wagner said "everyone rushes over to my father-in-law, and they virtually abandon me."

I believe it was in that same evening, there being many people present there, he said jokingly "All painters to Venice, every painter," perhaps with the same caustic humor with which Goldoni once made a character in one of his plays say "all bills to Verona, every bill." (171–74)

Norlenghi's account of the festivities *chez Hatzfeldt* on (Sunday) December 10 is confirmed by Cosima's diary entry for that date,[20] though with nowhere near the detail he supplies. Such detail presumes the report of some eyewitness, one guesses, but some of it is problematic. The reference to a Liszt pupil named "Humferding," not readily identifiable as such, suggests a misspelling for Humperdinck. But Humperdinck never studied with Liszt, and did not arrive in Venice until December 19—indeed, Norlenghi's failure to mention his stay at the Palazzo Vendramin is itself a curious omission. Could he have played at the subsequent musicale of which Norlenghi speaks? But Cosima mentions no other such event that Wagner attended at the Hatzfeldt residence. The Princess's soirees were regularly held on Thursday evenings, and Cosima notes one or another of the daughters going their with Liszt (e.g., December 21), but without Richard, or Humperdinck.[21] One has the impression that, however his information was derived, Norlenghi has confused some things here.

Norlenghi continues with two anecdotes, one charming, the other ridiculous:

An oddity. Wagner observed an absolute rigor when he was occupied composing in his study. His isolation was strict. No one was allowed to enter, under any pretext, if not summoned. Oh, perhaps there would be someone exceptional, or rather an *exceptionelle*, for such was a charming, all-white little kitten that Wagner greatly loved, and that always played with him, with its bold and clever postures. Wagner held her on his knees even when he was writing.[22]

Yet another such oddity, in the way that Wagner had of composing music, was this. He had his valet provide him with a very large quantity of silk cockades in different colors—white, turquoise, blue, red, etc., etc. Two servant-women were constantly employed to this requirement.

Then he placed them in his study, on the pianoforte, on furniture, on the wall, even affixing them with their pins, and with these he arranged various designs that he went on changing, little by little.

Perhaps by this measure he settled the initial design upon his melodies, while from the harmony of colors perhaps he derived then the sublime harmony of their sounds. Naturally these are all conjectures that I scarcely dare to note. Yet the authenticity of this task of Wagner's, one that he repeated two or three times a week and to which he assigned so much importance, is undeniable. (174–76)

Norlenghi returns to stories of Wagner's relationships and opinions:

Wagner adored his Sigfrido, and he took the greatest pleasure in the little boy's quick understanding and in his musical inclination. One day, when he was in a very good humor, he said "Caro Luigi, today I want to make you appreciate the musical ability of my son; let's go into the parlor." Ganasseta did not understand anything when Wagner set himself at the pianoforte and began to improvise and to play. The little Sigfrido followed the music that his father was making, whistling, but with a precision, with a secure intonation, to be marveled at.

Wagner was beaming, Madam Cosima, who was also there, wept with joy, and all three—the good Luigi understanding that he was the entire public, as I might say, not self-interested—enthusiastically applauded the little artist.

With this in mind, I remember an incident on the day following a benefit concert given at the Liceo, in which none other than the distinguished Luigi Mancinelli, come for that purpose from Bologna, had masterfully conducted the Overture to *Tannhäuser* and the intermezzi from the *Arlescienne* [*sic*] of Bizet. By coincidence in the Mercerie passages, I found myself near the young Wagner, who was with members of his family. It rained torrentially that day and the young boy was going on ahead, banging his umbrella, even in people's faces, concentrating entirely on whistling one of the brilliant intermezzi of Bizet, with the greatest exactitude. And probably he had only heard it the evening before, at the Liceo, where he had been in attendance with his tutor (Wagner had been expected to attend the concert, but he managed to beg off) since it is probable that he would not have heard that music in his father's house. It is said, however, that he has a still greater inclination to drawing, and that he may be destined for a career in architecture. (176–77)

The foregoing is a unique and interesting reference to the concert of January 15, conducted by Mancinelli, which Wagner avoided and Cosima ignored.[23] This seems to be the only report, however that Siegfried did attend it.

At this point, Norlenghi digresses, even retrogresses. As he had already done earlier in his book, he describes again Wagner's contempt for "star" singers who cared only for their own virtuosity, at the expense of a composer's intentions, for which they had no understanding or respect. And he stresses anew the example that Wagner himself set, sacrificing quick success for long-term artistic achievement. But, Norlenghi insists, there are exceptions to so many irresponsible singers, to be found among the fine German artists committed to Wagner's cause. This leads our author into recollections, both musical and sentimental, of the Neumann company's appearance in Venice. Those comments will, accordingly, be considered in an appropriate place below.[24]

The digression ended, Norlenghi returns to his anecdotage:

As I have said other times, Wagner was of a boundless generosity. Money was for him only a means for securing the greatest satisfactions and for doing good. There was no one who presented himself at the Palazzo Vendramin begging help and assistance, for whatever reason, who would leave Wagner without generous benevolence, and there was no pauper whom he encountered on the street who was left with empty hands.

One winter day he was sitting outside Lavena. In front of that shop's window—so full of toys, of tasty bonbons, of elegant little things—a poor child in tatters, with bare feet and scarcely dressed, stood looking intently with eyes staring in wonder and desire. She scarcely felt the intense cold, perhaps immersed in the thought of the bliss that she supposed all these delicacies would provide. Poor child, they were not destined for her, these lovely things. Wagner saw her, and signaled her to approach.

The little girl, confused, trembling, with no idea what that old gentleman wanted of her, perhaps fearing his reproaches (since the poor are naturally apprehensive), went to him.

Wagner stroked her gently, spoke to her some words in German—which for her were like a cabalistic language—but gave her a delicious pastry, and a silver coin to take to her mother. The wonder, the pleasure, the gratitude, would hardly allow her to murmur a thanks. Then she went away beaming, with her little treasure in hand. What more happiness for her that day?

Despite his considerable income—only because the copyrights for his operas secured him a very substantial annual income—Wagner naturally was in the habit of not paying much attention to money (a habit of all men of genius); so that he would sometimes deny himself making some acquisition (which likewise would apply to genius).

One such time, he happened to see a splendid antique bedspread. Wagner had a great passion for antique objects; and for bedspreads he then had a particular weakness—certain splendid flower-decorated coverings always lay on his bed, and he always brought them with him in his travels. Wagner greatly admired the delicate design and the artistic effort in this covering, but when, upon his asking the price, the shopkeeper responded that he could not sell if for less than 3,000 lire, Wagner replied that perhaps it was too expensive for him, and then he muttered so that he could be heard, "Verfluchtes Geld, verfluchtes Geld." ... [Accursed money, accursed money]. (183–86)

Norlenghi is now ready to address one of the major events of the Venetian residence.

At Christmas fell the [birthday] anniversary of sgra. Cosima. Wagner, who adored his wife, was accustomed to celebrate this day with great solemnity. And he already had planned to perform, on that evening in honor of his spouse, a youthful symphony of his, when certain favorable circumstances, which I am going to relate, made it possible, because, beyond a family celebration, this occurrence ought to survive as a splendid highlight in the history of the Liceo Musicale di Venezia, *Benedetto Marcello.*

The Liceo Benedetto Marcello was established in 1877 through the initiative of Conte Giuseppe Contin (however modest, the most illustrious musician and most ardent music lover), of attorney Ugo Errera (likewise a most distinguished musician), of Sig. Cesare Trombini (eminent orchestra conductor), and of other determined citizens. It is an institution that does honor to Venice, and that has all the support of the total citizenry that would deserve it. It is the city's sole musical institution that has a comparatively flourishing life. Its winter concerts, where some fine music is well performed, and whose public is by far the most refined that Venice could have, are like a delightful oasis in the artistic-musical desert of Venice. Oh, where is the artistic Venice of a time when its four Scuole (of the Mendicanti, of the Pietà, of the Ospedaletto, of the Incurabili) compelled the admiration of the musical world, where Jommelli, Hasse, Porpora, Scarlatti were summoned as music teachers within them;[25] when Benedetto Marcello created his sublime Psalms, and taught music in Venice, and married the lovely Rosanna Scalfi, after having trained her divine voice;[26] when, given the beginnings of lyric theater there, the most celebrated composers wrote for its honest and famous theaters?[27] But those were good times for art, which certainly did not hinder (as is held in the general foolish prejudice) the development of free and civilized life, and of business; those good times in which music came to be taken seriously, and holy and reverent was its faith; those glorious times … and yet so very distant.

The Liceo Marcello is, in any case, an institution that has come to promote the magnificent traditions of Venice, if only for the purpose of preserving some part of them.

At its concerts the public becomes educated to the taste for good music, and the associates who support it—among whose names shines most brightly that gracious one of the queen of Italy [Margherita], a most cultivated patroness of music—do good work.

The Liceo concerts were, after all, undoubtedly the best preparations for the magnificent and enthusiastic triumphs of *Lohengrin* and the *Anello del Nibelunge* [*sic*] in Venice, and this is indeed a fine achievement.

Wagner wished to make the personal acquaintance of Contin, and he requested Raffaele Frontali, friendly and able professor of violin, with whom he had become acquainted through the Princess Haztfeld [*sic*], to introduce him.

Contin and Professor Frontali betook themselves to the Wagner home one day in December. They were received with the utmost friendliness by the great artist, who went to meet them in the antechamber and led them into the parlor, where were madam Cosima and the Princess Haztfeld; next the two ladies departed, and then began an extremely interesting artistic conversation in with Wagner took the leading place, with his usual vivacity. Wagner immediately addressed his favorite subject, the interpretation of music on the part of orchestral directors and of singers.

He gave many praises to the artistic perception of Italians in general, but he deplored that, perhaps through their Mediterranean character, they allow themselves to drag the music too much, and to draw out the tempi more than is necessary.[28]

And to explain his concept more plainly, he sat himself at the pianoforte and played the heavenly prelude to the first act of *Lohengrin*, making evident how he intended it should be interpreted. I remember how, some days later, when he [Contin] related to me the details of that visit to the supreme Maestro, he said to me, in effect: "I don't know if Wagner may be a pianist in the true sense of the word, but I certainly have never heard the piano played with greater expression than his."[29]

The day after, Wagner wanted to repay the visit to Contin and, knowing that he spent virtually all day at the Liceo, to whose good operation he dedicated all his time, he went to find him at the Liceo itself.[30] He was received with such consideration as could be imagined, by President Contin, by Academic Counselor Errera, and by some others of the rectors. Wagner enquired earnestly as to the circumstances of the Liceo, its artistic direction, the teachers, the graduates; he was struck with great admiration for the beauty of the premises, and, going into the most elegant concert hall, he said, "Ah, what a lovely hall, if I might have it in order to perform my symphony at Christmas, I would be most happy," and he asked if they were able to allow its rental. Contin naturally replied that the Liceo would be greatly honored to offer its facilities to the great artist, and, going on to speak of the orchestra for the performance, Contin pointed out to him that, in order to have a full orchestra, beyond that of the Liceo, he must have recourse also to outside personnel.

Wagner expressed the desire to hear the Liceo's orchestra, consisting of the teaching faculty and the alumni, and Contin asked it to assemble on the fourteenth, to be placed at Wagner's disposition. Indeed on that day around 5, all were ready—with what apprehension can be imagined—and Wagner himself directed them in the overture to the Magic Flute of Mozart, played by the orchestra at first sight, with great dash [*slancio*], so much that Wagner was fully satisfied with it. At this rehearsal performance the Abate Liszt also was present.[31]

Admiring the elegant facility, pleased in general with the orchestra, Wagner decided then to perform with it, in that hall, his youthful symphony in honor of his wife, and he entrusted to Frontali all the financial dealings with the orchestra players; and immediately on the following days they began the rehearsals. (186–92)

Of these rehearsals, Norlenghi now gives us the unusually detailed description of an eyewitness.

One cannot imagine something more interesting than these rehearsals, which took place on the fifteenth, sixteenth, eighteenth, nineteenth, twentieth, and twenty-first of December. Access was forbidden to all, because the matter was totally private. From a nearby room, whose doorway opened onto the orchestra platform, I and some few others, were able to attend some of these rehearsals. One day, though, an indiscreet fellow imprudently made himself visible to Wagner, putting his head too far out, and the gracious indiscretion of Contin, who had given us the permission as members of the Liceo and as admirers of Wagner, of necessity came to an end.

Present in the hall were usually only Wagner (who conducted), the distinguished maestro Carlo Rossi (who was like his lieutenant, to convey to the players some wish of the Maestro), and now one or the other of Wagner's daughters.

· The wife, in whose honor the festivities had been organized, only attended the general rehearsal on the twenty-second, because she wanted to maintain its surprise.

When Wagner conducted he appeared rejuvenated by thirty years. The performers were electrified under his magical baton, which recalled him as the famous director of the orchestra of London, and of Petersburg, when Wagner conducted his music there, inspiring enthusiasm. One of the players said to me: "We were working miracles those days, we achieved twice what even we believed possible for us, as if against our will, without our knowledge." And those who spoke those words to me were always expert.

Wagner was of a man of charm, of splendid generosity. One day, for example, when some players through a misunderstanding were late, Wagner was extremely angry with them. "I do not wish to delay, it is necessary to be precise in appointments, I am not a man who ought to be kept waiting," he said to the culprits, who then understood their fault. But then at the end of the rehearsal he said "My dear friends, let us forget everything"; he was adorable.

Although he did not speak Italian comfortably, he found certain obvious, flexible words with which to make himself understood. "Piano, pianissimo, pianississimo," he said at times, and likewise "forte, fortississimo" when he needed, creating new superlatives, but which matched perfectly his idea, and were most effective.

One time, to give the idea of an expressive accent, he said "sighing, sighing, like the Bridge of Sighs" [*sospiroso, sospiroso, come il ponte dei sospiri*]. He called the trumpet player Cavazza "the Garibaldi of the trumpet" for his strength, and oboist Callistani "la prima donna" for his sweetness of tone, which these experts knew how to obtain from their instruments.

The Symphony, in Beethoven style, was in four movements, the first in C major, in common time [*tempo ordinario*], and many times, to make a unified start, he sang the first measures with the words: "Let's go, friends [*Andiamo amici*], like this:

| - - - mi | so - o - ol - mi | mi mi - - |
| - - - An | dia a a mo'a| mi ci - - |[32]

It was, in short, a burst of spirit, of charm, and the totality of artistic concepts and advice filled with precision and nobility, in the course of these most fascinating rehearsals, remained forever an indelible memory for those who took part in them. In the hall for two of them was the critic Filippi, specifically come to Venice to pay respects to the supreme Maestro.[33]

The day of the final rehearsal, when he was about to begin, Wagner was stricken by one of the customary attacks of his illness, which were unfortunately becoming every more frequent.

He was carried out into a nearby room and assisted with all his remedies, and he recovered so quickly that I believe that not even sgra. Cosima, who was in the hall, had suspected anything. He conducted the rehearsal as usual but after he had finished he said to Frontali, "I will never conduct again," perhaps with gloomy foreboding.[34] (192–96)

Norlenghi's assumption about Cosima's awareness of his attack is contradicted by her own testimony:

. . . around 4 o'clock we go to the rehearsal, which I am allowed to attend, hidden from sight! First we stroll in Saint Mark's Square, then enter the Teatro La Fenice. It is very cold! R. has a spasm, but he conducts the first movement, then, after quite a long pause, the others. I sit in concealment far away from him. . . . (December 22, 1882)[35]

Though our author attended at least some of the rehearsals—held in the Liceo's concert hall (the Sala Apollonea of the Fenice Theater)—he was apparently not present for the *prova generale* on the evening of December 22. He was certainly not present personally at the actual performance. At least he avoids Perl's erroneous dating of it to December 23.[36]

The evening before Sunday the twenty-fifth, Christmas Eve, the festivities took place. Wagner arrived at the Liceo after having celebrated the holiday in the Palazzo Vendramin, in whose hall was set up a splendid "christmas tree" under which all the family and all the servants had found their gift. Then Wagner climbed into his gondola with all the family and Liszt, and the magnificent hall of the Liceo [*sic*], all mirrors and gilding, splendidly illuminated, welcomed all these happy people. Of outsiders there were only the Count Contin and sig. Jouckowsky [*sic*], personally invited by Wagner, and sgr. Bassani, the conductor, invited I believe by Liszt. The festivities were in honor of his wife and for his family, and Wagner wanted no one else.

Wagner's Symphony was performed, under his own stupendous direction—that evening he had a splendid and sumptuous baton. Then Wagner asked Liszt to take over the piano and Liszt improvised and played as only Liszt knows how to improvise and play.

Then Wagner offered an ample and splendid refreshment for all the orchestra and the family and the few invited guests. The ladies were in sumptuous and elegant *toilettes* and Wagner's daughters radiant in loveliness and grace. Count Contin spoke eloquent words for the occasion, to which Wagner replied in French with great animation, thanking all for their cooperation in this celebration made in honor of his beloved wife, and thanking in particular Contin (whom he said he found congenial from first encounter). Clapping him amiably on his shoulder, he added "that we would agree on this I thought immediately when I saw him," and finally he embraced him and kissed him.

At this point shouts and applause broke out, and the celebration ended most amiably when Wagner went to the pianoforte and played the motive, "Buona sera, miei signori" from the *Barbiere* [*di Siviglia*, by Rossini]. It was the artistic and witty dismissal for all those who had taken part in this artistic and family celebration, which would remain in their memory as one of their dearest recollections. The symphony by Wagner is unpublished, and Wagner composed it at age twenty.

This joyful celebration, this artistic homage to his wife, cost Wagner around 2,000 lire. Whims and gratifications from a great artist and a great gentleman. The baton that Wagner used to conduct at the rehearsals is kept at the Liceo, which retains it as a sacred relic. To have Wagner conduct its orchestra at the Liceo will be an enduring artistic glory for the Institute that bears the name of the great Venetian musician Benedetto Marcello. (196–99)

Norlenghi next adds some unique vignettes as to the kinds of cultural interchange that Wagner could enjoy, and that Cosima has otherwise documented so copiously.

Wagner was a man of a vividness and a clarity of expression, particularly when he was setting forth his artistic principles or when he was narrating the stories of his dramas, truly wonderful. One evening in the spring of '81, sgr. Ruben reported to me, in the Hasztfeld [*sic*] house were gathered a few guests, invited to honor Wagner who was in Venice at that time.

"We were seated around a table, all concentrating on the rendition of the magic fire scene in Walküre, which the pianist Joseph Rubinstein was playing. Wagner, who was in the midst of us, step by step as the pianist proceeded with the music, declaimed for us the part of Brunhilde [*sic*] and described to us the dramatic situation. It was an extraordinary thing. We were all held there under the spell of his voice and of his narrative, which was of a clarity and a flexibility [*plasticità*] to make them absolutely hang upon his lips. It was one of the most powerful artistic thrills that I have ever experienced," added Sig. Ruben, a distinguished and most intelligent young artist, a person who certainly not to be suspected of exaggeration or pretenses.[37]

And this same Ruben, discoursing on Wagner's genuine, not pretended affability, and charm, told me about one day encountering Wagner out with his family on the street, and specifically on the bridge of Canareggio, which, then being under repair, was without railings: embracing him, Wagner jokingly drew him toward the water, threatening to throw him in "if he would not be good." (199–201)

From here Norlenghi jumps to the next important event of Wagner's last sojourn in Venice, with details that complement in interesting ways the parallel account by Perl.[38]

In the month of January 1883 Venice was in full revelry, because, Carnevale being short that year, the public and customary festivities began more quickly than usual. Some strong-willed youngsters had organized a comic fair, with a range of raffles, meant to generate aid for the families devastated by the floods that had brought squalor and misery to various sections of the Veneto in the autumn of the previous year.[39]

Some kiosks had been set up in the piazza and within them the members of the committee were selling little paper balls in which the fortunate would sometimes find something with a number stamped on it, a number that entitled one to an article that, if sometimes practical, was usually just a joke.

It was, after all, a matter of benevolence, and these stands were besieged by a merry and charitable crowd, who competed with each other in presenting their money for such a pious purpose as this.

The Wagner girls found a world of enjoyment there, and made frequent rounds with their brother and with their governess, from one stand to another, acquiring numbers, or rather pieces of paper, and unrolling them one after another mournfully, because most times they contained nothing. And Wagner himself went once to the last stand by the Orologio—at least, so I have been assured—to make a purchase, or better, to convey his obol for the flood victims.

Likewise the usual platform was set up in the piazza. This platform came to be like a little hall within the grand one that is the Piazza San Marco itself, although certainly nothing aesthetic, and in the Piazza San Marco it might seem, on the whole, most considerably discordant. Nevertheless, splendidly illuminated in the evening, with a crowd of maskers in every style who were dancing enthusiastically on it, it proves quite pleasing to the eye, and is a means for bringing greater animation to the piazza. Therefore, it is set up almost every year, and, now that the famous Carnevale di Venezia is reduced to a rowdy merrymaking and nothing else, the spectacle of the platform, and the eccentric dances that weave about on it, constitute one of the strong points of the program of all the committees that organize the festivities.

Wagner was greatly delighted by this feast of light and colors constituted by the Piazza San Marco when so extraordinarily illuminated, by the whole crowd of maskers. Also by that crowd of people among whom are seen so many very beautiful faces of ordinary women who recall the most superb examples of Giorgione and of Tiziano, women who then disappear for all the remainder of the year. And it is natural, if one may say, it is always a new spectacle for even the Venetians who see it each year; so much more should it astonish Wagner who found himself at Venice in Carnevale for the first time [sic]. Therefore, against all his usual custom, he came into the piazza two or three times during this season. On Tuesday [February 6], the final evening of Carnevale, the piazza was particularly lively, the cafés crowded with lovely ladies who vainly awaited some lively masker, the platform full of impassioned and indefatigable dancers. Light, crowds, uproar, that was the sum-total of the Piazza San Marco on that evening.

Wagner likewise wanted to be in the piazza with his family on that special evening, and he rented an apartment in the hotel of the *Cappello Nero*, whose windows opened onto the piazza.

There he went, 'round about 9 o'clock with all the family, and they remained there past midnight, admiring the festivities in the piazza and cheerfully passing those hours.

Wagner was in a most happy mood all evening. Then he and his company went down from the hotel, and they walked up to the Bacino Orseolo, adjacent to the piazza, to meet their gondola, which was there awaiting them. Just as Wagner was about to step into it a band of boys from among the ordinary folk, who, each with a little lantern in hand, and singing at the top of his lungs the traditional "El va, El va, El va" (= *Il Carnevale se ne va, è finito*) [If Carnival goes, it's over], were performing the funeral rites for the dying Carnevale. Wagner removed his hat and, shaking it, he also began himself to sing with the chorus *el va, el va, el va*, laughing with great delight in so typical a scene. (201–5)

Immediately we have another vignette that contrasts with the reports of Cosima and Perl.

The day after, Wednesday the Quaresima [Ash Wednesday], around two, Wagner summoned Luigi [Trevisan], and dear Luigi said, "Today all folks go out to enjoy themselves and to stroll on the Zattere;*[40] for our part we will go to San Michele." San Michele is the place where the dead repose. What a curious idea; what sad foreboding troubled Wagner that day?

They entered the gondola, Wagner with his wife. Luigi, at the poop, pushed the prow of the boat toward the sad little island. When they were about to arrive, an attack of his illness struck Wagner, but one more severe than the usual. It was a terrible moment, he seemed dead. What anguish for that poor lady, alone there in a boat in the midst of the lagoon. Luigi did not lose heart. With a few vigorous strokes he landed at San Michele. They took Wagner, who was unconscious, Luigi on one side and sgra. Cosima on the other, and they moved him into the little cemetery church.

With that he recovered. Perhaps the cool air of the journey—to take refuge from which at first he was enclosed in the gondola, gasping under its canopy [*felze*]—made him well; perhaps he had already overcome the crisis, since in fact a few moments after being carried outside the gondola he felt better: his frightened and cognizant eyes met the anxious ones of his still troubled wife, and his hand squeezed strongly the calloused and honest ones of the faithful Luigi. He returned home, but Wagner's serenity of spirit no longer revived in him from that day.

Such attacks, likewise frequent, henceforth prostrated him; he understood his end to be approaching.

However, he dissimulated and sought to calm his family. Death with its black wings was ready to call at the Palazzo Vendramin—was already eyeing its victim. (205–7)

Norlenghi's grim and foreboding account of this episode is in strong opposition to Perl's picture of the event as a fully cheerful excursion.[41] Falling in between those is Cosima's more offhanded reference: "Toward 1 o'clock we set out for S. Michele, but R. is not feeling well, and we return home immediately. He feels uncomfortable at lunch—he probably caught a cold yesterday" (February 7, 1883). The obvious disparities may result from the differing degree of household source information available to Perl (considerable) and Norlenghi (little). On this specific episode they would presumably each have relied on

gondolier Luigi; either he gave them different information or the diverse under-
standings produced the divergent pictures.

But Norlenghi, who rarely has much to say about life within the Vendramin,
gives a very strange little domestic picture:

> For two or three days [after S. Michele] Wagner remained at home under care, and one
> day when the family was gathered gloomily at lunch—since Wagner when ill rested in his
> room—he suddenly came into the dining room and, humming a tune, he put his hands
> over his wife's eyes, telling her to guess who did it. What a merry surprise for the family!
> But these were the last flashings of that spirit which refused to break down; they were the
> last flickerings of that brilliant flame that was to be extinguished forever. (207–8)

A further chance for Norlenghi to build up forebodings for The End, this
account finds no confirmation in Cosima's diary. In no way does she show us
Wagner confined and under treatment "for two or three days" after the trip to
S. Michele. In fact, she reports that on the next day (February 9) she and
Richard took a gondola ride to the Bacino and strolled around the area toward
S. Moisè. It is true that, for the day after that (February 10), Cosima reports
some wild swings of moods:

> . . . R. is not feeling well and he is very depressed; as we are finishing breakfast he says
> he hates himself because he is such a nuisance to me!—I rehearse Fidi in a speech for
> lunch, R. thinks it too long, goes to his room, and writes a verse. We come to lunch late,
> since he had a spasm. But he is in good spirits, tells us various things from the *Fl. Blätter*;
> then mention is made of his 100th birthday, which we will surely live to see and hope
> to celebrate! R. Leaves the table for a moment, then returns, the champagne is poured
> out, Fidi rises to his feet—but he has forgotten it all! I prompt him from a distance, but
> it is of little help. Then the telegram is brought to R. according to his instructions, he
> reads the merry saying, and the effect is quite splendid—a mood of great hilarity makes
> its triumphant entrance!" (February 10, 1883)

That entry is the closest thing to the jollity that Norlenghi describes, but still far
from his account; and there is nothing else Cosima reports for February 9–12
that could at all correspond to his report. Where did he get this tale?

Norlenghi immediately adds another curious anecdote, intended to continue
his morbid momentum:

> All gone was the Wagner of the previous months, when at Lavena one evening Frontali
> [the Liceo violin teacher] came in to pay his respects and, when sgra. Cosima hap-
> pened by at that moment, he introduced Frontali to her with the words *c'est le violon*,
> *c'est le violon* [it's the violin], leaving his genial and expert friend in some puzzlement
> that Wagner would have wanted to call him "the violin" through *antonomasia* [name
> replacement]. Quite vanished was the Wagner who was almost always happy, with
> refined facetiousness always ready on his lips; he had aged by many years in those days.
> (208)

There is no indication of date for this retrospective incident. But it may correspond to an encounter that Cosima reports for November 19, already referred to: "In the afternoon we [she and Richard] meet in Saint Mark's Square (at Lavena's where he makes arrangements about quartets with a violinist; the latter asks him about Brahms and Dvořák! ...).″ The muddle over names Norlenghi describes might account for Cosima's failure to specify his identity precisely.

Frontali returns immediately in a more directly connected account:

> On Sunday [February 11] he went out a little, on Monday again. On that day he encountered Frontali in the Merceria and, embracing him with, he said in a joking tone "Come tomorrow to meet me, I will have some mournful things to tell you"— those words, spoken the day before his death, were to become prophetic. ...
>
> It was a sad day, that Monday: it rained and Venice was more melancholy than usual; the persistent, gloomy winter showers had recently ended, and it was around sunset, sad sunset, when Wagner, leaning on the arm of the younger of his daughters, set out toward the Piazzetta, at whose channel his gondola awaited. He was exhausted; he climbed into the gondola and, while his daughter went in under the *felze*, he remained outside, resting there, and he contemplated at length the lagoon which, at that hour, on that gray, discolored, sad day, inspired in the soul sadness, anguish.
>
> He remained leaning against the canopy for some time. He was unable to take his eyes off that pale and disconsolate lagoon. Perhaps he foresaw that he would see it no more; and the gondola all the while went on slowly toward the Palazzo Vendramin.
>
> At evening things were happy. He mingled with his family longer than usual, and, further, he told some anecdotes with unaccustomed spirit—he had not for some time been in such a fine humor. (208–10)

By this time Norlenghi has shed any disguise in his determination to move the reader melodramatically on to the climactic event. On the whole, there is little in Cosima's account of those last two days that corresponds directly with these stories.[42]

Having already said virtually nothing about Liszt's stay with the Wagners, Norlenghi is no more interested in the visit by the ailing Hermann Levi in those last days, and rushes on now to his culminating episode:

> The morning of Tuesday, the fatal February 13, he awakened at the customary hour and dressed himself.
>
> He occupied the morning as was his custom, then about two he proceeded to summon Luigi.
>
> He was in a little room near his bedchamber that opened to the garden when Luigi came to receive his instructions.
>
> "Dear Luigi," he said, "today at four you will have ready the gondola that we require for making an excursion" (he was going to see some old paintings) "and you will also summon a man who is able to row, to accompany Sigfredo in a *sandalo*."*[43] Luigi very discerningly pointed out that it would be better for Antonio, the usual [prow-gondolier], to be accompanying the boy, as a more reliable man and someone of the household, and he might be the one charged to follow after the gondola, instead of a boatman

from outside. "Ah, very good, dear Luigi, you are right, you are right my dear Luigi," and so saying Wagner moved toward the nearby bedchamber. In that room was the chambermaid who, believing Wagner at the meal table, because the luncheon bell had already sounded, was there to tidy up things. Hardly gone in, Wagner felt his strength failing and let himself fall onto a little armchair near the bed, groaning desperately.

The stunned chambermaid ran to the dining room to inform Sgra. Cosima, while Luigi rushed to Wagner to aid him. "Wife … wife … doctor … wife …" were the only words that he was able to speak, then nothing, and he fell back with his head vacant, while sgra. Cosima was terrified but, not yet suspecting the terrible truth, was already kneeling beside him.

Luigi rushed out of the palazzo and ran to summon Dr. Keppler, who lived at a great distance. Keppler, a German physician who had dwelt for some time in Venice and who was then treating Wagner, was engaged at the moment in operating on a lady in the hospital which he had founded.

Seeing Luigi, when he had broken in on him almost violently, with his eyes bulging, Keppler, without changing his garb, without even washing his hands, ran to the Palazzo Vendramin. Unfortunately, it was all futile.

He found the wife still kneeling by Wagner and the children terrified and weeping in the room. Sig. Jouckowsky [sic] was trying to comfort them, and they still did not suspect the tremendous truth.

They were made to withdraw but, when Keppler, five minutes later, came to deal with them and invited them to offer their final prayer beside their father's corpse, there was a scene of the utmost anguish which is impossible to describe.

He attempted to have sgra. Cosima withdraw, but she could not. She herself, aided by Luigi and Keppler, carried Wagner to his bed, then she covered him anew and lay down beside him. She stayed there the whole night. (210–13)

This account of Wagner's death does not conflict seriously with the much more detailed description by Perl, save on the matter of Luigi Trevisan's involvement. Norlenghi is the only reporter who credits him with being present at the moment of Wagner's collapse, who makes him *the* messenger to Dr. Keppler, and who has him join both the doctor and the widow in placing Wagner's body onto the bed. But at least Norlenghi does not repeat the earlier assertion that Wagner died in Luigi's arms! Perl, who obviously had information directly from members of the household staff, and particularly from the chambermaid mentioned (Betty Bürkel), says nothing about the gondolier's involvement, beyond his receiving instructions for scheduling the gondola. (Perl has three messengers sent out to find the doctor; and she has Keppler alone lift Wagner onto the bed, saying nothing about the presence of the valet, Georg Lang.) It would be difficult to reject her testimony on the point, even on the issue of silence. Norlenghi, on the other hand, clearly relied much more exclusively upon Luigi's own statements. It is not far-fetched to think that, in the weeks and months following Wagner's death, the old gondolier began to embroider his actual role when he spoke to others about it.[44]

Two particular sources of our author's information are again put on the scene as Norlenghi describes the immediate aftermath of the composer's death.

While the fatal news was being spread around the dismayed city, Frontali was the first who carried it to the center. Around four I found him in the piazza, he was devastated, pale as a dead man. He spoke to me—and his emotion choked his voice—the terrible truth.

"I went to the Palazzo Vendramin where yesterday Wagner had invited me and I found him dead"—he could hardly say it: "I will never forget that moment."

The illness that drew Wagner to his grave was a *dilation of the heart*. He also had other severe disorders, particularly of the stomach. In the final stages he suffered so much that Keppler was obliged to give him frequent injections of morphine.[45]

It was a terrible night, that of February 13 to 14, in the Palazzo Vendramin. They had not been able to pull sgra. Cosima from the room where Wagner lay; Luigi stood guard at the threshold while sgina. Daniela, with disheveled hair, dressed in white, roamed about forlornly through the rooms and now and again asked Luigi in anguish for news of her mother. The children were agitated, broken by grief; all the domestics were dismayed.

The sad dawn of Wednesday found the forsaken lady still close to the corpse of her Riccardo.

The lamentable tale, the magnificent creation of Wagner, had become the sad but sublime reality. The new Isolda did not wish to be separated from the corpse of her Tristano.[46]

Meanwhile in the city nothing was spoken of other than the baleful event.

Telegrams arrived, from outside, from all the world, asking news and details.

All the newspapers of Venice, regardless of political or artistic allegiance, came out in large columns edged in black, full of expressions of grief and of biographical details on the illustrious deceased. Likewise the more important newspapers of Italy.

The most contradictory news reports circulated as to what arrangements the family would make for the transportation of the body. I remember that we crowded around Frontali and Contin to have news, about which not even they were certain, while the family, still devastated by the terrible blow, hesitated to take decisions.

On Thursday, Keppler, assisted by another physician, sgr. Pesenti, performed the embalming of the corpse and, after many urgings by close intimates to the reluctant family, the very skilled sculptor Benvenuti made the [death] mask of Wagner. The family, however, set the condition that this mask would remain with them, and this final precious memory of the illustrious man, very well accomplished, is preserved by the family. Wagner's close friends, however, and with them naturally all the admirers of the great deceased, hope that the family would not wish to deprive them of this relic and will permit its reproduction. And it is not to be doubted that the illustrious family will understand the seriousness and the sanctity of this reverent desire.

Count Contin, the Liceo orchestra, the artistic societies, the whole city was meanwhile preparing to pay solemn homage to Riccardo Wagner.

But the family asked that its grief be respected and, entrusting Contin with giving its thanks to the population, it requested that everything should proceed without ostentation. And he agreed to submit to this wish.

A crystal coffin was sent from Vienna, in which Wagner's corpse was placed so that it could he transported to Bayreuth. From Bavaria representatives of the King and friends arrived.

On Friday, the sixteenth, at two in the afternoon, the corpse was transported to the [railroad] station in a special vessel. In another gondola, rowed by Luigi, stood the grieving family. Under the station's canopy Wagner's admirers stood dejected, quiet, deeply moved, awaiting the moment for giving their last salute.

The external coffin, a most refined piece of work, was of metal, with *putti*, foliage, lions' heads, all in bronze hue and in Renaissance style.

It was placed in a carriage decorated internally in black and silver. Then on the coffin were placed magnificent funeral *corone*, among which was a splendid one from the city with the inscription:

VENEZIA A RICCARDO WAGNER—FEBRUARY 1883

and other handsome ones from the Liceo Marcello, from the Circolo Artistico, from other societies, from sgra. Giovannina Lucca the publisher of Wagner's operas in Italy: twenty-two in all.

At the station were Count Contin for the Liceo, the painter Nono for the Circolo Artistico, comm. Mussi, the City Prefect, comm. Astengo, Commissioner for the King at Venice. Then artists, musicians, gentlemen of the forestry settlement, friends, admirers.

As soon as the family arrived at the station, they took their places in a reserved carriage in the train. There were no speeches, but emotion was on the face of everyone. Count Contin alone spoke in German some few words for the occasion to sgri. Jouckowsky [*sic*] and Gross, who represented the family, which lowered the curtains and closed the shutters of the car; immersed in their grief, they wished to avoid all the displays by that sad public.

It was 2:09; a whistle was heard, then a bell, and the train began to move. It was a tormenting, unforgettable moment. We all had our eyes bathed in tears when, with hat in hand, we saluted for the last time the body of that great man. He was thus speedily, with gloomy—despairing—escort, being conveyed toward Germany, which awaited anxiously and reverently its great patriot, its musician, the artist who had honored and brightened his century.

There, to Wanfrüd [*sic*], was the corpse borne, there it was laid to rest, there Wagner finally found peace, eternal peace.

On the Palazzo Vendramin, which has by now become a place of pilgrimage for anyone who admires what is beautiful, what is great, what is sublime. On those walls that had witnessed the passing of a genius will stand a stone panel voted by the city to commemorate the great and sad event.

On the house where Wagner was born in Leipzig can be read in a marble inscription:

IN THIS HOUSE
WAS BORN
RICHARD WAGNER
ON 22 MAY 1813

The same eloquent inscription is followed in the new panel. For Wagner the name and the event suffice for what one wishes to record. Anything more would diminish the extraordinary eloquence of that name and that event.

The gracious family did not forget Venice and Italy. If proof were needed of that, amid the recent terrible disaster of Casamicciola, which brought desolation and death where there had previously been joy and paradise,[47] one of the first significant donations, which came with marvelous flush of charity from friendly and loyal Germany to alleviate the losses of the poor survivors, was that *of the family of maestro Riccardo Wagner* dispatched to the [relief] committee of Venice.[48]

And the city that bore witness to his mourning surely views with gratitude this sensitive thought.

Nor will Venice and Italy forget to pay heed, from time to time, to the fact that on its soil Riccardo Wagner passed his final days, that under its lovely sky expired the stormy soul, the towering spirit, that brightened with such vivid light his century, whose aspirations he understood, to which he left as a legacy, a glorious legacy, his austere, grandiose, immortal art. (213–22)

As with Perl's little book, so also with Norlenghi's, we are dealing with the effusions of an admirer. Where Perl was making her appeal, somewhat opportunistically, to a German readership already devoted to Wagner and his music, Norlenghi was addressing his fellow Italians as an apostle to them on behalf of an art and artist not yet fully recognized by them, but to which he felt deeply committed. Both writers were witnesses to Wagner's final stay in Venice, if neither was in any way close to him. Norlenghi lacked the greater access to household informants who allowed Perl much greater detail on life within the Palazzo Vendramin. On the other hand, Norlenghi had important contacts in the musical world of Venice and was able himself to witness a little of Wagner's involvement in it.

In reading each book, we obviously must discount some of the rose-tinted, dewy-eyed perspectives they convey. We need not forget the reality of so much harshness and so much meanness of spirit in Wagner's character, not to mention in Cosima's as well. Nevertheless, the anecdotes and observations of Perl and Norlenghi, whatever their biases or sympathetic intentions, give us glimpses of Wagner as a human being that are plausible and, at times, even endearing.

Part 3

The "Ring" Comes to Venice

Chapter Nine

Italy, Venice, and "Wagnerism"

It would be, and has been, a terrible mistake to assume that the connections between Wagner and Venice ended with the composer's death in February 1883.

Such personal connections were, in fact, part of a large and complex picture, of which one element developed immediately upon the composer's death: the process by which the operas and the aesthetics of Richard Wagner were received on the Italian musical scene in general. And that process of reception was itself a part of the still-larger picture of cultural upheaval in the years during and after the unification of Italy. At the risk of oversimplification, we might say that even that larger cultural struggle was a microcosm of the conflict that was inherent to nationalism—as to whether a nation was to remain mired in its own separatist provincialism or to join a larger cosmopolitanism. Such conflict was the more heightened in those nations newly become independent.

Much of the generation that grew to maturity in the aftermath of Italy's unification became disillusioned with the new nation's emerging complacency and bourgeois blandness. Opera, which was firmly established as Italy's cultural medium par excellence, both at home and abroad, became one of the principal battlegrounds on which young rebels found they could struggle with what they considered stale traditionalism.[1] The emerging oeuvre of Giuseppe Verdi seemed to represent the perpetuation of a lyric theater that essentially extended the bel canto idiom of the first half of the nineteenth century. Musicians and journalists began to talk of finding a new direction, a reform of Italian operatic writing, and as early as the 1850s the early published ideas of Wagner were picked up and advanced as a plausible basis for such reform. Wagner's ideas, and in turn his music, soon made him a symbol of radicalism and reform—eventually, the prophet of "the music of the future" (*la musica dell'avvenire*) for Italian intellectuals in general. This was especially true among the rebellious circles of young bohemian musicians, the so-called *scapiliati* (the disheveled ones). Many of them became enthusiastic partisans of "Wagnerism" (*wagnerismo*), if sometimes for their own purposes rather than out of uncritical commitment or personal Wagnerian propensities.

The printed scores of Wagner's earlier operas began to circulate in Italy and to stimulate debate after mid-century. The year 1868 was one of particular landmarks. In that year, Giovannina Lucca (1814–94), owner with her husband of a

publishing house in Bologna, seized the opportunity to secure the rights of publication and of licensing for Wagner's operas in Italy. She and her house began
earnest promotion of these works.[2] Meanwhile, one of the leaders of the *scapiliati*
circles, the composer, writer, and critic Arrigo Boïto (1842–1918) had become
identified as a standard-bearer of the reform movement associated with
Wagnerism. At a banquet in November 1863 in honor of his kindred spirit,
Franco Faccio, Boïto made his infamous speech in which he called for cleansing
the altars of Italian art as if from the stains of a brothel. That remark gave particular offense to Giuseppe Verdi, who considered himself to be its target. Boïto's
assimilation of Wagnerian stylistic elements was demonstrated climactically in the
original version of his own first opera, *Mefistofele*, which received its premiere in
Milan on March 5, 1868. This opera provoked a storm of reaction and criticism,
as much for its supposed "Wagnerism" as for its unwieldy length. In fact, Boïto
was never a slavish Wagnerite, holding reservations about Wagner's influence and
models that grew with the years. He had already, by 1868, prophesied that the
days of Wagner's influence were passing, and his own compositional identification with Wagnerian style was actually quite limited—symptomatic of the fact that
Italian radicals often used the slogans of "Wagnerism" as weapons of convenience
in the pursuit of their own quite explicitly Italian program.

The actual arrival of Wagner's operas in Italian opera houses was only to come
in the 1870s. The initial breakthrough was the famous Italian premiere of
Lohengrin, the first of any of Wagner's operas to be given in Italy, and the one
that became by far his most popular with Italian audiences. Its performance on
November 1, 1871, was, not surprisingly, given in Bologna, base of the Lucca
publishing enterprise. Conducted by Angelo Mariani, it was presented not in the
original German but in an Italian translation credited to one S. de Castrone,
Marchese della Rajata. There were apparently artistic problems in the performances of this production. It may have been those, as much as stylistic incompatibility, that prompted the acerbic reactions of Verdi, who attended a
performance on November 19. But the production was received generally with
approval and even enthusiasm by its audiences, for whom it was, at worst, an
exotic curiosity.[3] It so moved Boïto that, perhaps with the further encouragement of Giovannina Lucca, he wrote a letter of gratitude to Wagner himself. The
latter's response, *Ein Brief an einen italienischen Freund*, perhaps also encouraged
by Lucca, was a promotionally astute expression of the hope that one day the
glories of Italian and German genius could be brought into productive union.
Boïto translated this essay for wide dissemination throughout Italy, and he continued to lend assistance to the circulation of Wagner's operas in the peninsula
by making performable Italian translations, even as his own sympathy for the
German master's idiom waned.[4]

The Wagnerian penetration of Italy depended heavily at first upon *Lohengrin*.
Scarcely a month after its Bologna debut, it was given in Florence. On March 20,
1873, under Franco Faccio—now shifting from composing to conducting, and

as a champion equally of Wagner and Verdi—*Lohengrin* became a storm center in the more volatile musical citadel of Milan. Nevertheless, it went on quickly to regional productions in Trieste (1876), Turin (1877), Rome (1878), Genoa (1880), and Naples (1881). Meanwhile, the Luccas pursued their momentum in Bologna by promoting the first Italian production of *Tannhäuser* on November 7, 1872, once again using an Italian translation by Castrone. The reception was less positive, presaging the *Lohengrin* debacle in Milan the following March, but *Tannhäuser* began its own round in turn with productions in Trieste (1878), Rome (1886), Turin (1888), Naples (1889), and Milan (1895).

In all of this Venice was a late contender. Its Teatro La Fenice actually made its belated entry into the lists by pulling off a coup of sorts—the first production in Italy of *Rienzi*, given under local conductor Carlo Ercole Bosoni on March 15, 1874, using a translation by Boïto. That version did not reach Bologna until two years later, and Rome four years after that. On the other hand, *Lohengrin* arrived at the Fenice only when Emilio Usiglio conducted it on December 31 1881, and January 2, 1882, again using the Castrone Italian translation. *Tannhäuser* was not to arrive until still later, on January 21, 1887, in the Castrone translation. *Die Meistersinger von Nürnberg*, which was first produced in Milan (December 1889) in A. Zanardini's translation, and then in Turin (December 1892), did not reach Venice until December 26, 1899. For *Tristan und Isolde*, first given in Boïto's translation in Bologna (1888), Venice had to wait until February of 1909. And *Parsifal* came to Venice only in 1914—even then, given only in a concert presentation, in view of the prevailing Bayreuth monopoly on staged performances.[5]

To put all that in some perspective, however, we might note that the Fenice did not present any opera by Mozart until 1914—and then his early German singspiel parody, *Bastien und Bastienne*, 147 years after its composition and as translated into Italian. The first mature Mozart opera was staged at the Fenice only in 1934, and then as part of an international festival, under the visiting Clemens Kraus: *Così fan tutte*, a mere 144 years after its composition.[6]

As these data suggest, Venice was not one of the foremost musical centers in Italy in the later nineteenth century and even beyond. To be sure, the Fenice Theater was still a house of some importance. It was the site of numerous premieres of new Italian operas—though between Verdi's *Simon Boccanegra* (1857) and Leoncavallo's *La Bohème* (1897) few operas of major or enduring substance were launched there. Even through the twentieth century the serious pickings were comparatively slender: Stravinsky's *The Rake's Progress*, 1951; Britten's *The Turn of the Screw*, 1954; Prokofiev's *The Flaming Angel*, 1955. The Fenice had Venice's only serious and enduring operatic company, despite changes in management and periods of closure. Of the great number of opera houses that had flourished in the Republic's musical heyday in the seventeenth and eighteenth centuries, very few survived credibly into or through the nineteenth. There were the old Teatro San Benedetto, become the Teatro Rossini, the older Teatro San Giovanni Crisostomo, become the Teatro Malibran, and the Teatro San

Salvatore, become in turn the Teatro Apollo and the Teatro Goldoni. None of these gave uninterrupted offerings or presented works of substance or durability. The old church institutions had lost their past musical establishments. Such a musical community as Venice had for much of the nineteenth century was a shifting circle of performers and teachers. Their tastes were narrowly traditional and set a tone of extreme conservatism for the city's musical life, discouraging interest in European developments at large.

There was no lasting institution of musical instruction until 1876 when the Liceo Benedetto Marcello was founded. It began its instructional program in 1877, at first installed in the *piano nobile* of the fifteenth-century Palazzo Da Ponte in the San Maurizio district. In 1880 it was transferred to the San Fantin district, and settled in the complex of the Teatro La Fenice, utilizing its subsidiary hall and rooms, the Sale Apollonee. By the end of the century, it had begun renting space in the sixteenth-century Palazzo Pisani in the San Stefano region and in 1897 it was formally transferred there, where it remains to this day.[7] Aside from its student ensembles, Venice had no permanent concert orchestra through the nineteenth century, nor any securely established chamber ensembles, beyond what ephemeral salon patronage allowed. The only regular public performances of instrumental music were provided by that quintessentially Italian institution, the Municipal Band. This was, as we have seen, a quite excellent group of musicians, eventually authorized at fifty-six to sixty players, and led in succession by two really fine musicians, Nicolò Coccon (1826–1903) and Jacopo Calascione (1841–1907). Its function was understood as essentially one of popular entertainment, rather than serious art, even though it could serve the latter cause to some extent, by default.[8]

In music, then, as in other respects, Venice was in the nineteenth century a backwater. Napoleon's destruction of the decaying Venetian Republic in 1797 was followed by a half-century of oppressive foreign domination that made the city a fringe holding of the Austrian Empire. Union in 1866 with the emerging Italian nation brought hopes of revival both culturally and economically. There were signs of reawakening with the revival of the art and prosperity of the traditional Venetian glass industry, released from past Austrian restriction. Venice would become an important center of the Art Nouveau movement. On the other hand, it was caught up in the distractions of the continuing irredentist movement focused on recovery of Trieste. There were also social and political tensions, particularly attending the progress of the socialist movements. The economy of the city itself and its Veneto hinterland was generally in decay, only eventually generating schemes for industrial and commercial revival. Hopes for a newly flourishing Venice could not be realized quickly. In cultural life, Milan, Florence, and Rome had taken precedence, leaving Venice behind as a comparatively provincial city, especially in musical terms.[9]

Still proud in its richness of monuments and art, and already for centuries past an attraction to travelers, Venice was emerging first and foremost as a tourist attraction. Visitors were drawn in increasing numbers, at first artists and writers, but ever more loungers and vacationers, from the upper classes on down into the bourgeoisie. The city was slow to adjust to the growing traffic, but by the later decades of the nineteenth century it had developed extensive facilities to accommodate the tides of tourism.[10]

It was thus on Venice's culturally somewhat marginal scene that suddenly occurred one of the important steps in the Italian reception of Wagner. It was to become the city where Wagner operas would first be presented by a fully German cast, and in the original language, not a translation. Moreover, the step involved none of the previously seen operas, with their familiar medieval or Christian subjects, but those monumental evocations of Nordic mythology— nothing less than the entire cycle of *Der Ring des Nibelungen*. To be sure, the Venetian public had been sensitized to Wagner as one of the greatest artistic personalities of the day thanks simply to his highly publicized residences in Venice and especially to the dramatic climax of his death there. This may or may not have won new converts to his art itself. Indeed such Wagner performances as were already heard in the city had apparently hardened some elements in the Venetian audience against the composer's idiom.[11] Nevertheless, Wagner was a cultural fact, a Mt. Everest to be confronted rather than denied or ignored. Thus, when only two months after Wagner's death in Venice, the city was offered this new Wagnerian extravaganza, its public was galvanized and its cultural landscape thrown into a convulsion.

The Venetian reaction to this event was, of course, only a small part of the larger saga of the Italian reception of Wagner's operas, a prolonged and complex story. To follow that reaction in comparative isolation risks offering only a kind of distorted exaggeration. Nevertheless, to do so does present a microcosm, a case study that can contribute fuller understanding of both the public and critical mentalities that permeated the macrocosm of the Italian Wagner reception in general.

Our focus on Venice and its reactions also allows us a more detailed look than might elsewhere be found as to the operations of the organization that brought this earthquake to the city's musical life. Thus, we must for the moment turn our focus away from Venice alone, in order to introduce that organization, and the individuals involved in it.

Chapter Ten

The "Wandering Wagnerians"

Angelo Neumann (1838–1910) was born an Austrian Jew, one of a number of that religious background who braved Wagner's anti-Semitism to serve the Master with fervent devotion.[1] Trained as a singer, he took baritone roles in various Central European opera houses from 1859 to 1876. In 1862 he joined Vienna's Hofoper company, just when Wagner was first introducing his music to that city. Neumann became an immediate convert, and was able to sing the role of the Herald in *Lohengrin* at a performance the composer attended. Neumann's enthusiasm for Wagner's music was brought to a new pitch when he participated in Vienna productions of *Tannhäuser* and *Lohengrin* in 1875 that the composer himself directed. The thirty-seven-year-old singer took part in the casts and was overwhelmed with Wagner's skill as a director. The experience was so inspiring that Neumann decided to become a stage director himself.

Taking a position with the Leipzig opera, Neumann overcame numerous obstacles to launch his career there in the summer of 1876 with a staging of *Lohengrin*. That August, however, he attended the second of the three cycles in Wagner's own staging of the complete *Ring des Nibelungen* at his new Festspielhaus in Bayreuth. Neumann was overwhelmed by this experience, and he conceived the idea of mounting the production in his own house in Leipzig. At first Wagner refused, hoping as he did to repeat the cycle's production at Bayreuth the following year. Since that plan failed, Neumann was able, partly with Liszt's help, to negotiate performance rights for Leipzig. When he appeared at Wahnfried, the Wagner Bayreuth residence, to negotiate in person, Cosima—never one to miss quoting her husband's anti-Semitic remarks—described Neumann as the director "from Leipzig and Israel," adding that, in securing a favorable financial deal with the money-hungry composer, Neumann showed himself "just what such gentlemen always are" (January 21, 1878). Neumann's own recollections, by contrast were of a cordial and mutually happy agreement.

As Cosima said, "we need money," and so Wagner was willing to entrust to Neumann the first full-scale production of the complete *Ring* outside of Bayreuth. The results (1878) were highly successful and pleased Wagner, who professed satisfaction that his art had flourished in his own native city. It was in the preparation of this *Ring* mounting, too, that Neumann accepted as conductor, on Wagner's recommendation, the gifted young Anton Seidl (1850–98). Trained in part by Hans Richter, Seidl had become a Wagner protégé, living in Wagner's home and assisting with preparation of the Bayreuth *Ring* in 1876. Seidl became chief conductor at Leipzig in 1879, and with his help Neumann continued to develop productions of Wagner's operas, so that by 1882 he had staged all of them—save, of course, *Parsifal.*

Neumann's production of three cycles of Wagner's *Ring* in Berlin in May 1881, with the cantankerous composer in attendance, was climaxed by an incident of public discourtesy on Wagner's part. This was apparently the result of a sudden flash of the composer's cardiac afflictions, but the misunderstanding brought a temporary breach between them. Matters were mended,[2] however, for each man needed the other.

During negotiations for the Berlin *Ring* over the winter of 1880–81, Neumann had also been considering possibilities of taking his production to London, and even beyond. As he found Wagner favorably disposed to all his dealings, Neumann included in a letter of January 8, 1881, a report on his progress and the broaching of an even bolder idea. Neumann wrote to Wagner:

> . . . To be the herald, abroad and beyond the oceans, of that new musical world your genius has revealed to us all, that sublime mission stirs me to such a degree that I have abandoned all other plans for the future. I am confident of accomplishing triumphantly my great task, as long as you, our Reformer, will stand unhesitatingly at my side. Then I know that whatever I accomplish under your banner will be truly achieved.

Neumann then laid out his proposals for a contract with Wagner that would allow him exclusive production rights to the *Ring* above all, but to two other operas (*Tannhäuser* and *Lohengrin*), for presentation in Berlin, London, Paris, St. Petersburg, and even "America" (the United States), during a period between January 1, 1882, and December 31, 1883. In exchange, Neumann promised Wagner payment of 10 percent of all gross receipts. Whatever doubts the composer might have had about this proposal, he pronounced himself fully agreeable, as he promptly replied in a letter of January 10, addressed to "Dearest Friend and Benefactor" (*Geehrtester Freund und Gönner*):

> To all your plans and propositions I can make no objection, since I perceive clearly that you are the right man for the undertakings. . . . As regards America, you know well that I myself have up until now been strongly caught up in the plan by which I would personally go there to reap a fortune (having none now!). I certainly suppose that going in person would constitute no small factor, but the dread of the excessive strains to me personally made me hesitate: so gladly can I let you serve in my stead, since you could carry out my wishes in these matters if only on a modest scale.
> . . . You have done me great services, and have secured for me revenues for which I had given up hope.[3]

With his post at Leipzig nearing termination, Neumann spent much of the autumn of 1881 negotiating with the disputatious and ever-fretful composer over the character of their grand new scheme: the organization of a new company, to be called the Richard Wagner Theater (or "The Wandering Wagner Theater"—*Das Wandernden Wagner-Theater*). Its purpose was to take Wagner's operas on the road, as a complete production unit. Wagner had his doubts, not the least on matters of finance, as well as on fine points of exclusivity in performing rights. Nevertheless, in view of the funding secured by Neumann himself, Wagner could not but agree. With Seidl as his partner, Neumann had now become the chief apostle of Wagner's operas, promising to be a reliable source of income as well as a disseminator of Wagner's art.[4] In a remark to King Ludwig II, Wagner called Neumann his "Foreign Minister" (*Ministerium des Auswärtigen*).[5]

Neumann failed after all to bring a new production of *Lohengrin* to Paris, so he presented it instead in Leipzig in February 1882, following a triumphant *Tristan und Isolde* there. These productions allowed him to hone his newly developing company, built around many of the leading Wagner singers of the day, Bayreuth veterans among them. Proposing to hire a full chorus and full orchestra, he now projected a tour (itinerary not yet fully settled) to run from September 1 1882, to May 31 1883, which would involve performing a total of thirty-six cycles of the complete *Ring*, these to be the tetralogy's first presentation in each city. Wagner, who had been amazed that a company could produce a fine *Tristan* without his personal involvement in the rehearsals, was ready to muffle his doubts that his complex cycle could work under these conditions.

Never easy to deal with, and always ready to hector and dictate, Wagner could not but respect Neumann's undertaking, though Cosima lets us know that anti-Semitic sneers were always at the ready on the home scene. Perhaps it was as a covert one that, early in all these negotiations (September 14, 1881), Cosima cites Wagner's calling Neumann "an Assyrian inscription restored to life." (The day before, Cosima has her husband describing Neumann as "a rose exuding earnestness.") More directly, Wagner expresses backhanded sympathy for the way Neumann is confronting all his challenges "with Semitic earnestness" (*mit semitischen Ernst*; January 26, 1883). And, while praising Neumann for bringing the complete *Ring* to wider audiences, he observes, "How curious that it should have to be a Jew!" (October 17, 1882).[6]

Testing their undertaking in London, the Wandering Wagnerians gave four complete *Ring* cycles there (May–June 1882), the first performances of this colossal work heard in England. Returning to Leipzig in that summer, Neumann concluded his service there with a veritable fireworks display—a comprehensive run of all the Wagner operas from *Rienzi* through *Götterdämmerung*. Amid all that, he had what would be his last personal meetings with Wagner, while attending the premiere performances of *Parsifal*. Wagner had wanted this final opera to be performed only at Bayreuth, though he sometimes vacillated over the idea that he might grant even that to Neumann. During performance intermissions, Neumann discussed unhappily with other attenders (including the Viennese critic Eduard Hanslick) premonitions that Wagner's lifework was now done and that his death might be near.

The full launching of the "Wagner Tour" began in Breslau in early September 1882, where the practice was established of complementing the *Ring* performances with a concert of Wagner excerpts. Stopping at Posen to give "a monster Wagner Concert," the troupe proceeded to Königsberg for a full cycle and concert there. Wagner was kept in touch from the outset, responding to news with advice on future plans and with regular demands for his royalty payments. It was while the company was in Königsberg that Neumann received a cheery telegram from Wagner announcing the family's departure for the Palazzo Vendramin on Venice's Grand Canal. The tour next stopped in Danzig and Hanover to give the cycle-and-concert combination. Theater facilities in both cities were so inadequate that an outdoor circus tent had to be used to accommodate shifting sets and properties. Giving only concerts in Magdeburg and Hamburg, the company arrived at the beginning of October in Bremen, to encounter serious difficulties in securing a proper theater on affordable terms. Clearly, the tour was still somewhat improvisatory in nature: details and bookings had to be arranged along the way, sometimes at the eleventh hour. But the successful performance of the *Ring* in Bremen brought Neumann an offer to take over management of its theater, an offer on which he deferred decision.

After a full cycle given in Barmen, only the concert was presented in Elberfeld, Cologne, and Frankfurt-am-Main. In Leipzig, a complete cycle and (October 18) the concert represented a joyous homecoming to what had been the company's point of origin. Three days later, the company began its *Ring* cycle in Berlin, while its concert the evening before was so highly acclaimed that Neumann was persuaded to repeat it. His singers also participated in a performance (a benefit for recent flood victims) of Beethoven's *Fidelio*, a work that the troupe had apparently prepared as a backup option. While in Berlin, as he pondered the Bremen appointment, Neumann was pummeled with advice to settle there artistically instead of in Berlin—where, in fact, Wagner himself had been projecting ideas of another theater, to be built to his purposes, with a company built around Neumann's. But the Bremen officials pressed their case, and Neumann accepted the job there. Also in Berlin, the troublesome pair of star singers, Heinrich and Therese Vogl left the company, to the relief of everyone but Neumann himself, who still respected their artistry.

While other stops were being planned, the performers went to Dresden in mid-December to give a concert and two performances of *Die Walküre* only. After spending the Christmas holiday in Berlin, the singers and orchestra gave concerts in Cassel, Detmold, and Krefeld, while the rest of the company proceeded to Amsterdam to prepare for the Wandering Wagnerites' initial venture outside of Germany on this tour. For the first half of January 1883, they performed the full cycle and a series of concerts there. Negotiations for further bookings were slow and so the troupe used Amsterdam as their base in the middle of January, from which they carried concerts to the Hague, Rotterdam, and Leyden. It was during this interlude that Neumann received a curious letter from Wagner (dated January 13),[7] in which the composer reaffirmed his ideal of creating a new Bayreuth-style theater for his works in Berlin, if that could be achieved. He advised Neumann strongly against wasting his time in Bremen, even suggesting a return to Leipzig as preferable to that. Above all, he expanded his earlier scheme for Neumann to take his company on a major tour in America. Wagner had stated in the past his idea of going there in person, to make heaps of money; but, given his own poor health, the composer admitted, it would be best for Neumann to go in his place.[8] Quoting this letter in his memoirs, Neumann expressed regrets that the Berlin scheme never came to pass.

Completion of arrangements allowed Neumann's crew to perform a series of cycles plus concerts at the Théâtre Royale de la Monnaie in Brussels, to what Neumann considered the most enthusiastic reception of his entire tour.[9] Following concerts in Ghent and Antwerp, the singers and orchestra returned to German territory, while leaving the chorus and technical personnel behind in Brussels, given a lapse in securing commitments for theaters in which to perform their operas. Concert performances arranged for Darmstadt, Karlsruhe, and points beyond would not suffice to cover expenses, while renewed budget problems were already serious.

It was amid this intermittent uncertainty in the latter weeks of January 1883 that the possibilities of taking the tour into Italy were considered. Neumann himself noted:

> At the very opening of our successful career I had received many invitations to go to Italy with the Richard Wagner Theater. But the Master, who was then still with us, had very earnestly warned us against Venice and Italy; and the offers had not been sufficiently tempting for me to insist.[10]

The prospect at least of Venice itself, however, seems to have come up, perhaps through the initiative of Count Giuseppe Contin, founder/director of Venice's music conservatory and a local friend of the composer—the latter, of course, himself in Venice at the time. But Wagner was altogether opposed to such a prospect. According to Cosima (January 30), Richard was greatly upset by news that Neumann and Co. would indeed bring their *Ring* to Venice, and promptly "sent a telegram of disapproval." She then adds (January 31) that the next day Neumann sent a cable from Brussels stating that no appearance in Venice was planned. This picture seems quite at odds, however, with what had already been understood and arranged in Venice itself.

For, on Sunday, January 21, the journal *La Venezia* announced that a proposal had been made by Angelo Neumann to the Fenice Theater to present the complete *Nibelungi* [*sic*] tetralogy, with all the necessary forces, and that this proposal was under consideration. Three days later, on January 24, the same journal reported that the Società Proprieteria of the Fenice had unanimously accepted Neumann's plan:

> [The management] also expresses the desire—and it will be communicated to Neumann—that the Fenice, in homage to Wagner, who would still in April be residing in Venice, would be the first Italian theater in which the famous tetralogy would be performed.

On the same day (January 21), the other journal, *La Gazzetta di Venezia* [*LGdV*] reported likewise, but with less certainty about Venice's priority of status. The acceptance, it was reported, was framed in the desire to stress

> the opportunity that, among the cities of Italy, sig. Neumann chose for his artistic tour among us, Venice should have the first place.
> It was not then known if this desire could be fulfilled, because it was not known what commitments signor Neumann might already have contracted, and also because of some speculation as to the route still to be agreed upon.

Given these publicly announced negotiations, it is strange that the Wagners would not have heard about them, or at least reacted to them, before January 30—if, that is, we can trust Cosima's relentless reporting. Alternatively, in denying such plans, was Neumann engaged in some devious dealing? Given his consistent honesty and integrity, such behavior would have been uncharacteristic. Still, the inconsistencies remain. An assumption that Wagner would still be present in Venice when the performances were presented might have struck Neumann as a wonderful promotional device in his consideration of that city as a venue, and indeed as the first venue in Italy. On that count, he might then have had to pursue his idea with caution, discretion, and even a veil of deception. But the picture is not at all clear. Perhaps the best conclusions are that Neumann seriously took up the possibilities of Venice, even while the Venetians themselves were not quite certain of the prospect; and, then, that Neumann suspended or abandoned the idea in view of Wagner's objections.

While Seidl took the singers and orchestra off for further concerts in Mannheim, Heidelberg, Baden-Baden, and Freiberg, Neumann was indeed negotiating new theatrical engagements—mainly in Germany. He passed through Stuttgart to join the rest of his company in Aix, where the next cycle performances were to be mounted on February 14. It was there, that morning, that Neumann was shattered by the sudden news of Wagner's death in Venice the day before. Amid grief and dismay, it was agreed that the performance of *Das Rheingold* should proceed that evening, with memorial tributes added. As he returned to his hotel just before the performance, however, Neumann was jolted further to find a letter from Wagner awaiting him. At first elated to think this proved the composer was actually still alive, Neumann realized that the letter's date of February 11, two days before the reported death, did not alter the grim fact after all.

Wagner's last letter to Neumann was full of advice and suggestions, including reactions to ideas for further touring destinations (especially in Central Europe), and ending with yet one more request for money due to him. But Wagner was clearly still in doubt about the matter of the tour's moving southward:

> Are you really contemplating Venice? I fear that would be an unlucky notion; for of all the Italian cities Venice certainly is the least progressive; yet I myself should not advise you to try any of the others. There's only one topic in this town just now—"Revenge for Oberdank!"
> Germans mix well with Slavs, but never with Romans or Latins; Belgium is a good hybrid, half and half Flemish, etc. . . .[11]

Clearly, the idea of going to Venice was still in the wind in early February after all. But, on that terrible day of February 14, Neumann had more immediate concerns. At the end of that evening's *Rheingold*, he read to the audience from the stage the concluding felicitations of Wagner's last letter, and then, as Seidl began conducting the Funeral March from *Götterdämmerung*, the entire audience stood in silent homage.

Seidl and Neumann broke away from the company to attend Wagner's funeral rites in Bayreuth, which Neumann found quite unworthy of the composer's deserts. The two men then rejoined the troupe's cycle of performances in Düsseldorf. The disciplining of another obstreperous singer (Franz Krückl) occupied Neumann as the company moved on to concerts in Wiesbaden and Mainz, followed by the full cycle in Darmstadt, before returning to Karlsruhe— where money problems again arose. Only there, at last, did Neumann confront the idea of Italy and make his decision:

> . . . Now [after the Master's death], however, came Signor Avoni as fully accredited agent to me in Karlsruhe. There the negotiations for the Teatro Fenice in Venice and the Teatro Comunale in Bologna gradually took on firmer lines. I thus finally decided to take up both these cities.[12]

This statement does not seem to square fully with the announcements in the Venetian newspapers some three weeks or more earlier. But those announcements, and Wagner's renewed expression of objections in his last letter, suggest that Neumann had kept Venice in mind all that time, and felt able to make a positive decision only when Avoni came to deal with him, after February 14.

In Strassburg, braving anti-German sentiment by the local French population, the company staged the tetralogy just before Easter; and then, in Basel. While the concert team gave a performance in Zurich, Neumann rushed to Stuttgart to cobble up preparations for the cycle's performance there. That accomplished, the staging crews began their move, while the orchestra and singers gave a concert in Munich that served to conclude the German part of the Wagner Tour's itinerary. The next destination of the Richard Wagner Theater was now Venice.[13]

Questions linger at this juncture. Would Neumann indeed have decided to go to Italy—and especially to Venice—had Wagner not died at this time? Had he not, and had Neumann gone ahead with such plans, would Wagner have accepted any involvement in them? or tried to head them off? or simply left Venice in protest?

Though such questions will never have definitive answers, there are clues to consider, even if derived from a source inconsistent in reliability. This is the account of Wagner's final stay in Venice, as written by "Henry"/Henriette Perl, a work already analyzed above. Alluding to extensive conversations that Wagner is supposed to have had with his physician, Dr. Keppler, Perl seems to set the following incident to just before or around New Year's Day 1883:

> One day the rumor came to Wagner's ears that Angelo Neumann was involved in a scheme to bring for presentation in Italy his "Ring of the Nibelungen," beginning in Venice. The mere idea that this project might come to realization filled the Master with the most furious rage. Right now [as Perl writes in March 1883] this bold scheme has come to pass: the name of Angelo Neumann is in bold display on posters ringed in black mourning border, which announce on every street corner in Venice the "Ring of the Nibelungen" for the coming days; the house (the Teatro La Fenice) is totally sold out for the entire cycle. Were Wagner still alive he would have endeavored, at all costs, to frustrate Hr. Angelo Neumann's scheme to make Italy familiar with his Tetralogy. For, more than once, the Master had stated to Dr. Keppler and others at times, when the rumor of this undertaking came to his ears: "As long as I live, this performance will never take place."[14]

Perl—whose book was published in mid-April 1883, was clearly writing this just at the time the Neumann cycle was directly impending in Venice. She shows little understanding of the considerable background to Neumann's company and his arrangements with Wagner. But Perl's familiarity with Keppler is no more to be overlooked than the doctor's closeness to Wagner. So this report may actually contain a good bit of truth as to Wagner's adamant opposition to Neumann's plans for Venice—if not for all Italy.

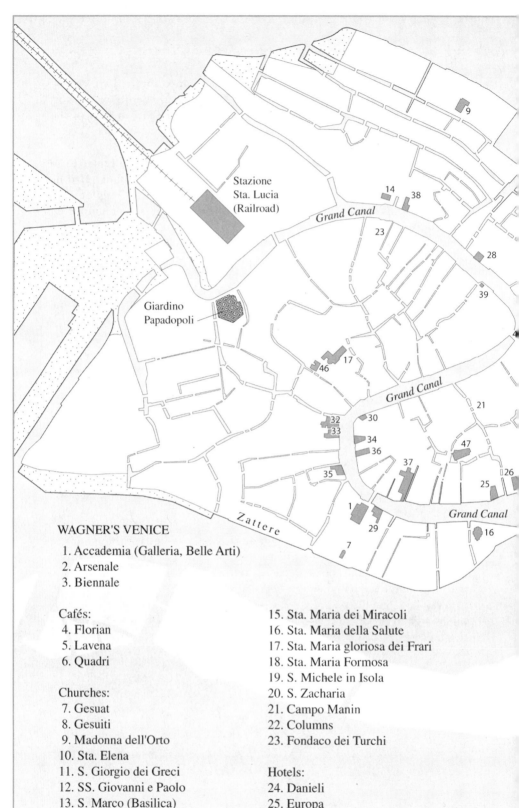

WAGNER'S VENICE

1. Accademia (Galleria, Belle Arti)
2. Arsenale
3. Biennale

Cafés:
4. Florian
5. Lavena
6. Quadri

Churches:
7. Gesuat
8. Gesuiti
9. Madonna dell'Orto
10. Sta. Elena
11. S. Giorgio dei Greci
12. SS. Giovanni e Paolo
13. S. Marco (Basilica)
14. S. Marcuola

15. Sta. Maria dei Miracoli
16. Sta. Maria della Salute
17. Sta. Maria gloriosa dei Frari
18. Sta. Maria Formosa
19. S. Michele in Isola
20. S. Zacharia
21. Campo Manin
22. Columns
23. Fondaco dei Turchi

Hotels:
24. Danieli
25. Europa
26. Giustiniani

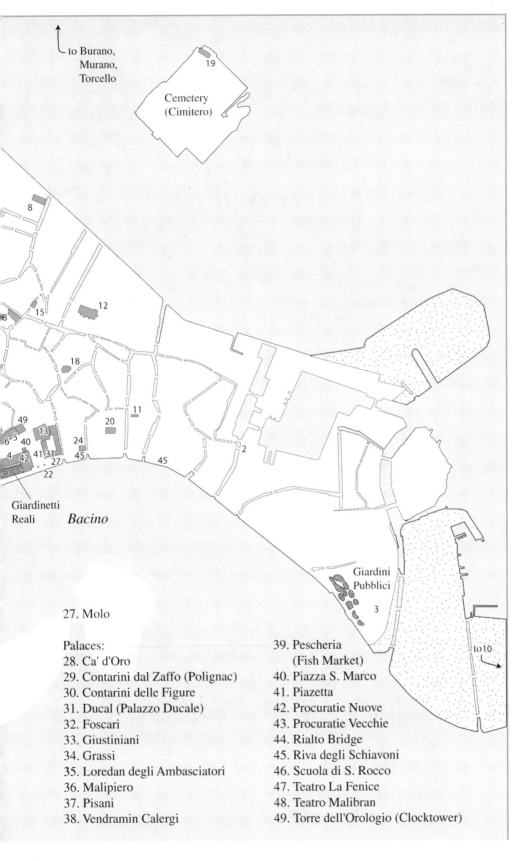

to Burano,
Murano,
Torcello

Cemetery
(Cimitero)

19

8

12

15

8

18

11

49

20

13

6 5 40

24

4 42 41 31

45

27

45

45

2

22

Giardinetti
Reali

Bacino

Giardini
Pubblici

3

to 10

27. Molo

Palaces:
28. Ca' d'Oro
29. Contarini dal Zaffo (Polignac)
30. Contarini delle Figure
31. Ducal (Palazzo Ducale)
32. Foscari
33. Giustiniani
34. Grassi
35. Loredan degli Ambasciatori
36. Malipiero
37. Pisani
38. Vendramin Calergi

39. Pescheria
    (Fish Market)
40. Piazza S. Marco
41. Piazetta
42. Procuratie Nuove
43. Procuratie Vecchie
44. Rialto Bridge
45. Riva degli Schiavoni
46. Scuola di S. Rocco
47. Teatro La Fenice
48. Teatro Malibran
49. Torre dell'Orologio (Clocktower)

Chapter Eleven

Today the Fenice,
Tomorrow All Italy

A month after Wagner's death, the Venetian newspapers began to alert public attention to the coming of the *Ring* to the Fenice. On Thursday, March 15, *La Venezia* (*LV*) took notice of the fact that the theater had been closed during Carnival, and expressed ironic hopes that the public's deprivation would soon be relieved. The next day, *La Gazzetta di Venezia* (*LGdV*) reported that an emissary from Angelo Neumann was in Venice to negotiate all the necessary arrangements with the Fenice management. Neumann himself, it was noted, was still in Stuttgart, and he and his company would not arrive in Venice until the middle of the next month. As a result, the performances could not occur much before April 20–25, although possibly a little before; the schedule depended upon arranging speedy transportation from the railroad. Also involved was negotiation for the workers who would be required to sustain the venture.

On Sunday, March 18, *LGdV*, followed the next day by *LV*, transmitted Neumann's own formal announcement that the company's performances would take place around the middle of April (specifics still unsettled). Both journals repeated the observation that this was to be the tetralogy's first presentation anywhere in Italy, while the *LGdV* went on more fully to identify the four parts of the work, and promised further details to follow.

Catering to the possibilities of its readers' heightened Wagner-consciousness, the *LGdV* on Thursday, March 22, informed them that the Court Theater of Munich was to present performances of Wagner's operas, in chronological order, running from March 25 to April 13. That series would allow the public the exceptional opportunity to follow, in only fifteen days, the evolution of the composer's style—though, to be sure, lacking not only *Parsifal* (reserved for Bayreuth) but also the *Nibelungen* "trilogy" (i.e., the three full operas plus *Rheingold* as prologue). The report noted that ticket sales were well under way, and that performances would likely be sold out in a few days.

On Saturday, March 24, *LV* was the first to give details for the Neumann's Venice presentations. It specified the performance dates (April 14, 15, 17, 18), identified members of the cast and staff, and provided information on ticket prices and railroad facilities. The next day, the same journal reported the arrangements for Neumann's next stop in Bologna. It was generously mentioned that Bologna had, in fact, done more than Venice ever had to honor Wagner. On the practical side, it was reported that editions of the Wagner libretti were in preparation: "To have the translation of the four libretti would be, it seems to us, indispensable for the public."

Racing the competition, *LGdV* on Tuesday, March 27, picked up Neumann's announcement of details in its turn, giving the dates and titles for the four parts of *L'Anello del Nibelunge* [*sic*]. The extended and multifaceted notice also included detailed information on the various ticket rates. (Series subscription for four evenings: box chairs, 75 lire; floor and stalls, 15 lire, benches, 30 lire. Individual evenings: box chairs, 25 lire, floor and stalls, 5 lire; benches, 10 lire; topmost gallery, 1.50 lire, numbered close seating, 3 lire.) Likewise, news of purchase locations, and assurance of extended validity for railroad tickets.

What is interesting in this March 27 notice, however, is a listing of the Richard Wagner Theater personnel. First, there is a catalogue of artistic roster:

> Women: Hedwig Reicher-Kindermann, singer of the Imperial Court Theater of Berlin; Auguste Ihlè, singer of the Municipal Theater of Frankfurt am Main; Katharine Klafsky, Auguste Kraus, Anna Stürmer, Orlanda Riegler, Therese Milár, Elisabeth Lindemann, Elise Freitag, Georgine Hellwig, Rosa Bleiter, Bertha Hinrichsen, Elise Telle, [all] singers of the Municipal Theater of Leipzig.
>
> Men: Anton Schott, singer of the Royal Court Theater of Hanover; Georg Unger, singer of the Bayreuth Theater; Julius Liban [*sic*], singer of the Imperial Court Theater of Berlin; Dr. Franz Krükl [*sic*], singer of the Municipal Theater of Hamburg; Josef Chandon, singer of the Municipal Theater of Breslau; Robert Biberti, Hans Tomasczek, August Ulbrich, Adolf Wallnöfer [*sic*], Friedrich Caliga, Franz Pischek, [all] singers of the Municipal Theater of Leipzig.
>
> Orchestra director, Anton Seidl; Substitute director, Paul Geissler.
>
> 70 orchestra players; 40 choristers and 40 supernumeraries (stage extras); scenic director, R. Müller; scenographer, M. F. Lütkemayer; stage manager, M. A. Schick; manager for fire and vapor effects, A. Grethe.
>
> The wardrobe, weapons, and properties were produced according to original designs of Prof. Doepler of Berlin, the weapons and the properties deriving from the renowned workshop of M. Goersch and H. Schneider, purveyors to the Imperial Court Theater of Berlin.

This listing (plus the cast bills to follow) includes plentiful data on the composition of Neumann's troupe, serving to supplement what he himself provides. Such data should also be placed against his own amusing description of the transportation problems that such a traveling organization involved. Writing of his operations in Germany earlier in the tour, he observes:

> As time was an object, our trips were generally by special train. Hitherto the largest wandering theatrical troupe had been that of Meiningen; but they had only a third as

many persons and appliances as we—to say nothing of their having no orchestra, with its instruments, etc. Our special train carried one hundred and thirty-four people, five freight cars full of sets, properties, costumes, and the instruments for an orchestra of sixty. From Breslau to Königsberg cost us 6,600 marks, and from Posen on an added 300; for there we were made to take a guard for the freight, for which I had to pay in spite of all my protests.

My petition to the Ministry of Railroads for reduced rates elicited the reply that such rates could only be made to managers of circuses and menageries. So if I had only added a few elephants, lions and tight-rope walkers to my staff I might have had the benefit of this reduction! From the rates we got for the special trains of the Richard Wagner Theater in Germany, however, I am still somewhat in doubt as to whether the Railroad Ministry took the Richard Wagner Opera Company for something greater or less than a circus. In Italy this question had a different response, as we shall see.[1]

Neumann was to note subsequently that, having been launched from Stuttgart at midnight on April 9, the transfer of all the scenic apparatus to Venice was further complicated by having then to move it all from the railroad station by boat to the Fenice Theater, involving "unusual difficulties."

The composition and mobility of Neumann's company were dealt with yet again by *LGdV* in a long background article published on Tuesday, April 10:

> The personnel of this traveling company consists of the following: the artists [i.e., singers] of the Teatro Riccardo Wagner are 34; the orchestra players from 60 to 70, with two directors; the chorus consists of 30 voices. There are then 1 stage director, 1 scenic manager, 1 stage manager, 1 foreman with a crew of 16 workers, 1 lighting director, 1 set director, a few scenic painters, a treasurer, and, finally, 1 travel manager, who precedes the company and organizes the journeys that are normally undertaken on special trains together with all the apparatus, such as sets, flies, properties, weapons, wardrobe, etc. Add up the amounts and you have a total of 140 to 150 persons.
>
> To give an idea of the routine and the promptness in the operations of this mobile theater—to characterize it as such—we would point to this fact, that having closed their performances at Bretislava [*sic*] with *Crepuscolo degli Dei*, the following morning, at 9 o'clock, performers and material departed for Königsberg where, on the evening two days after their departure from Bretislavia [*sic*], they went onstage with *Rheingold*. That journey cost about 2,000 marks; but the situation is such that the more the traveling company spends to make the schedule efficient, the more they profit, because the enormous ordinary daily expenses are all-consuming.

Over the late days of March and the early ones of April, the newspapers recurrently posted information about access to tickets and special arrangements to accommodate the expected strains on transportation and the traffic in visitors to Venice during the days of the Neumann performances. *LV* in particular (March 10) also devoted attention to work undertaken at Fenice to prepare the stage for the coming performers, and to organize the management offices "because subscribers have already begun to deluge them in grand number." In addition, it was noted that, "as a precaution against the dangers of fire," the stage facilities "have been sprayed with an incombustible substance."

In the days before the opening date, the two journals continued the drumbeat of preparatory announcements. *LGdV* (in its multipurpose article of April 10) announced the availability of libretti, at the former Gallo music shop in the Orologio Merceria, urging their value. *LV* noted (the next day) that the Italian libretto translations, using Zanardini's rhymed version, could be had at the Casa Lucca, outlet of the Lucca publishing house. In likewise staggered fashion, *LGdV* (April 12) and *LV* (April 13), it was announced that an exhibition of thirty-four photographic portraits of the lead singers in Neumann's company were on display outside the Fenice. *LV* on Thursday, April 12, announced that "the numerous artists, singers, players, stage personnel" of the company would begin to arrive that day. The next day, it assured its readers that the production was being readied for the next evening's opening.

In its April 13 notice, *LV* added two interesting tidbits. One was the reported reaction by a Roman newspaper to an apprehensive communication sent to it from Berlin by "the distinguished [Italian] pianist signor Pirani":[2]

> Pirani is concerned about *L'Anello del Nibelungo* at the Fenice, and he writes: "Be on alert! this is a critical [*decisivo*] moment for Italian art." How so? Why? Has Pirani such a low opinion of our art?! Or perhaps the Italian operas that are performed in Germany are a menace to German art?

But the second item was the announcement that, on that same day (April 13, the day before the opening), Giovann[in]a Lucca, proprietor of Wagner's works in Italy, would arrive. Italian observers appreciated little of what that meant, but Neumann himself soon found out.

Looking back later, he recalled:

> At our first appearance in Venice she had introduced herself as the owner of the copyrights for Wagner's works in Italy, on the strength of an early contract with the Master for which she had paid ten thousand francs, and which had long since lapsed. She had then declared that she should forbid our production of the *Nibelungen* in Venice and Bologna—and by law, if necessary! Yet I noticed directly that she seemed keener about money than about the law, and asked her how much she wanted.
>
> Mme. Lucca was a tall stately woman with imposing features and a great deal of manner. She had been charmingly cordial, and it was indeed on the occasion of a dinner she gave in our honor that all this transpired. She assured me in her magnificent way that the matter could be arranged quite amicably if I paid her a certain indemnity for each city. Venice was rated at two thousand francs, Bologna at one thousand two hundred, Rome and Turin at two thousand, and Trieste (which she, in her kindly generous way, added to the map, and called an Italian town) at one thousand francs.
>
> As I did not care to keep my "Nibelungen hordes" idle while I awaited the result of a long and tedious process at law, there was nothing to do but to pay her demands.[3]

Nor was that the end of Neumann's problems with Mme. Lucca, as he would soon discover.

Meanwhile, as the *Ring* performances drew nigh, the two journals were constrained to prepare their readers in some way for what lay ahead. The first such venture was undertaken on Monday, April 9, by *LV*, whose music critic, following prevailing fashion of the day, wrote under a nom de plume as "Toni." Concerned not only to preview the tetralogy itself, he wanted to address as well the broader issue of Italian reactions to Wagner up to that time. Under the heading of "Artistic Conversations" (*Chiacchiere Artistiche*), he begins by quoting a Milanese critic:

> "Do certain great artists have no choice but to die when the broad public withholds due reverence to the works of their genius? Whoever has, time after time, observed the Milanese audience in the Conservatory hall—inattentive, hissing, stirring in their chairs, at the interpretation of some Wagnerian page—and who was then present at the Teatro Carcano last evening, would have to answer Yes! More than a thousand persons were there for some three hours, sincerely enjoying themselves, with no need to indulge in any *posturing*, and maintaining such eager attention that, setting aside La Scala, one would by now not expect to find bettered in Milan."

Thus wrote the distinguished Gramola in the *Corrier della Sera* of April 5. At the Carcano Wagner was commemorated with the performance of some sections from his more acclaimed operas—among them, two items from the *Niebelungi*, the *Cavalcata* [Flight] of the Valkiri and the funeral march from *Götterdämmerung*. And only the other day the Milanese public passed as the most anti-Wagnerian one in Italy; indeed, its most famous hisses were those directed at *Lohengrin* by the La Scala spectators. One must say that the world goes forward, even despite anyone who wants it unchanging.

But beware of exaggerations. He is mistaken who insists that we Italians are guilty of repudiating the treasures of our art in the name of Wagnerism. He is mistaken who would wish, in homage to those treasures of ours, that we flee from the music of Wagner as if fleeing from a plague-carrier.

It is a fact, however, that the passionate controversies stirred up around Wagner—and by the man's own agitation and provocation pursued with the fervor of an apostle— have quieted down. There are fewer of us who, at the blink of an eye, cry out for the crucifixion of Wagner without knowing him. That is, there are fewer of us who are ignorant, because by now no one at all of good faith can fail to accept, for example, the melodiousness, the clarity, the theatricality of *Lohengrin*, that once was absolutely denied. Biagi,[4] who stands in musical art as a reactionary, no great celebrator of Wagner in Florence, has sung the praise of *Lohengrin*.

But between *Lohengrin* and the *Nibelungen*—so it was thought—extended the same difference as between *Lohengrin* and an early period opera of our Verdi. The well-informed found in *Lohengrin* new forms, but could not recognize the new school. On the other hand, in the *Nibelungen* that new school—the new melodrama (or, better, the new *music drama*, for which Wagner has fought all his life)—emerges fully into the light. Is it a manifestation artistically perfect? Does it suit the Italian public's taste? Questions still to be resolved. Meanwhile, what matters is that one should go to the performances without preconceived ideas, without animosities, without grudges—neither intentionally enthusiastic nor intentionally hostile. And this will surely prove true at the Fenice on next Saturday, Sunday, Tuesday, and Wednesday—the facts that I adduced at the outset make me certain of it.

The plot of the *Nibelungi*—I would not even attempt to summarize it, for that would take up too much of the space that our journal can allow to matters of art—is altogether fantastical. It is an old myth, a legend that goes back to eras prior to the Middle Ages, which Wagner has recreated in his musical poem. This represents the struggle between Siegfried—a divine hero, descendant of Wotan, father of light—with the dragon, the monster in which darkness is personified. *The Ring* from which the tetralogy takes its title, is the powerful talisman with which one can become master of the gold of the Rhine—I repeat, we are in absolute legend, in absolute fable, whatever one wishes to call it. Spectators who want to follow the action's development—which otherwise appears in sufficient clarity as unfolded in four evenings—will be aided either by the translation of the poem made by Zanardini[5] or by a type of theatrical program explanatory of the tetralogy scene by scene.

Volumes of metaphysics have been written on Wagner's *Nibelungen*. The Germans are not satisfied with Wagner the poet, Wagner the musician, Wagner the creator of a new artistic school—they want also the philosopher. In contemplating the truly vast concept of the *Nibelungen*, they will uncover the poet's lofty thought, which portrayed in the tetralogy the slow fading of the ancient world, of the society in which idols were material things, in order to give place to the Christian world, in which God is spirituality.[6] And the favored audience of initiates who attended in 1876 the performances at Bayreuth was deeply aware also of the philosophical importance of the work.

I strongly doubt that the thousand spectators of the Fenice, on the final night of *Götterdämmerung*, will be thinking of the triumph of the Christian world over the pagan world, after the struggle born in *Rheingold*, developed in *Walküre* and in *Siegfried*, and concluded with the death on the funeral pyre of Siegfried himself. They will be thinking, however, about the musical effects of the tetralogy—because it is essentially on those that the curiosity of our public is founded.

Speaking musically—at least to the extent that the more authoritative critics have said of it—*Der Ring des Nibelungen* is a challenge—a rebellion, as our revered Florimo has written. Wagner himself, when he related the historical and psychological origin of his work, asserted that he "had sketched and carried out a dramatic plan of such vast proportions that, considering only the requirements of my subject and of my ecstatic idea, I had renounced all hopes of seeing such a project ever performed." A good many years passed, however. No less critical, too, was the Wagnerian enthusiasm of the King of Bavaria, because he would create [*sic*] the Bayreuth theater, destined for the performance of the *Nibelungen*.

I have before my eyes several newspapers—from Berlin, Strassburg, Stuttgart—which are all concerned with the *Nibelungen*, and with the vocal and orchestral performances of the company directed by signor Angelo Neumann, the same one we will see at the Fenice. I am not going to report a single item from such newspapers because—such are the humors of a cultivated public!—I will not be accused of wanting to agitate, or show favor to, such predictable disposition toward *posturing* as I have condemned at the outset.

I will say only that, as to the originality and on the novelty of the artistic conception, as to the creation by means of the *Nibelungi* of a new aesthetic—all parties are in agreement. It has nothing, altogether nothing to do with the musical forms hitherto used and also abused on the stage. If our public wants to encounter, to enjoy, and to applaud arias, romanzas, duets, terzets, ensembles in the tetralogy, it will suffer a great delusion. On the stage the drama evolves in melopoeic form, and the flow of the dialogue is

maintained rigorously as in spoken drama. The orchestra, which has maximum importance in the work (so much so that a Strasburg journal calls *Der Ring des Nibelungen* a
tremendous symphonic painting), illustrates the stage drama, taking the part of the
chorus—says a critic—as in the tragedies of Aeschylus and Sophocles. It weeps, laughs,
curses, blesses, sobs, shudders, loves—and in it is profusely lavished, with prodigal
frenzy, the melody that flows continuously (as Panzacchi[7] finds) is extended with a variety and potency that on more than one occasion reaches the miraculous.

Right now in Italy there will be a good many commemorations made of Wagner—the
orchestras of Milan, of Bologna, of Naples have performed the *Cavalcata delle Valkiri*,
with which the second day of the tetralogy concludes [*sic*]. Everywhere this piece has
stirred up a storm of applause—and a Neapolitan colleague, signor Pagliara[8] (fiery as
Neapolitans are)—writes that "the *Cavalcata* is perhaps the most amazing piece yet created, if is regarded as an impetuously descriptive outpouring from the orchestra."
Quite the same judgments have been made by Milanese colleagues whether
Wagnerphiles or Wagnerphobes—those who have become apostles of Wagner, those
who up until yesterday were his tenacious opponents.

Here I make a firm final point: I certainly do not believe that I have by any means
underrepresented the colossal Wagnerian work with which, as I have said, poets, musicians, and philosophers have become engaged. I am satisfied to be stimulating, as
much as the requirements of the journal allow, the public's interest in the performances of the tetralogy, which—whatever be the judgment delivered on Richard Wagner
and his school—constitute a true and impressive artistic event.

Less ambitious at first than its competitor, *LGdV* published on the following
day (April 10) the article already quoted, giving background on the organization and operation of Neumann's company.[9] But only three days after that, on
Friday, April 13, did this journal publish an article that corresponded to the
essay by "Toni" for *LV* of April 9. The unidentified *LGdV* writer writes in somewhat parallel terms, if more impersonally, foreswearing anything but some cursory ideas about the tetralogy's general nature. He then proceeds:

The plot is drawn, it is said, from the Germanic and Scandinavian mythical world: that
is, and put crudely, a fable accompanied by lightning, by thunder, by rainbow, by light,
by darkness, by water, by land, etc., etc.

This fable revolves around the struggle between the gods of the northern mythic
heaven, the gods who dwell on the surfaces of the earth, or giants, and those who
always, properly understood, rule mythically in the abysses of the earth. All aspire to
domination of the world and struggle with each other to that end. The object of this
struggle is the gold concealed at the bottom of the Rhine, which comes into the possession of Alberich, the Nibelung, by whom is made the fatal ring.

We in no way undertake to hold forth on the philosophical intentions and on the concepts of various types—always, however, based upon the eternal struggle of the passions—that have suggested such a subject to Wagner, because we would risk
disagreement with many analysts. The quintessential point is this: that Wagner had conceived this thing called a poem but that is actually a fable, because the character of his
cloudy, transcendental, extravagant genius drew him, more than anyone else, to deal
with topics inherently fantastic and exceptional, with which he could wander at his

whim into the realm of abstrusities. Also underlying this idea for the work might be (or rather is) a healthy philosophical concept. But that would merely serve as his means, whereas his end lies in his goal of generating a new art. And Wagner, who quite understood himself, knew how to maintain his freedom from exactly that element of his subject's abstruseness, which for him might have justified the abstruseness of form.

Only the more so, therefore, can we just send our presumed readers back to the poem that they can find in the libretti, in which they will discover a little of everything, but always in the sphere of the supernatural or of the fantastical.

The German company is now with us, and at the Fenice work proceeds speedily to prepare the staging.

The anticipation is naturally great, since the genius of the German master was, after all, extraordinary. Also, since there is no ready certainty of being able to rehear such a work, especially in its entirety, any person even of moderate artistic culture really ought now to hear this *Tetralogy*, a work that cost its author a good twenty-two years of preparation and toil, which is about twice the time spent by Dante in writing the *Divine Comedy*!

It is therefore necessary that the public arm itself with patience and persistence. The great patrons of Wagner in 1876 departed the theater weary, thoughtful, dismayed. The great uproar, the prolonged darkness, the continuous mental tension, strained them to the utmost. As for those not conversant with this type of new art, imagine with what disposition they will be departing the theater!

It is, however, necessary to listen, and to listen respectfully and with great attention, to ponder and to study its every phase. For how much could a single hearing of such difficult music reveal, and through such phantasmagory of setting, of lights, of shadow, of clouds, of thunders, of lightning? This *Tetralogy* is the most grandiose and most perfected opera bequeathed to our artistic heritage by that illustrious man who was Riccardo Wagner, deceased not long ago in this very Venice that was so congenial to him, and that held him in high esteem, great deference, and profound respect, however much the great majority of the population had not the slightest understanding of the artistic ideas for which he was exalted in high renown, thanks to the most powerful support.

As the day of the opening arrived, the two newspapers settled down to specifics. On Saturday, April 14, *LV* printed an excited reminder that the first opera of the cycle would be performed that evening. It gave a brief digest of its plot. Noting that the orchestral preparations in particular were being completed, the article concluded:

> As for the music—we have said the other day: the novelty, the originality of the Wagnerian artistic conception is absolute. One must go to the theater disposed to hear a score that one has not encountered in anything else. Will it please? will it displease? We will speak of it tomorrow.

For its part, *LGdV* on the same day gave fuller attention to information about the production itself, explaining: "We publish this in full because, whatever be the outcome of this artistic event, it will take its place in the artistic history of Venice." It then gave a formal announcement of the evening's presentation of *Das Rheingold* (l'Oro del Reno), with Neumann's cast listed:

Wotan	⎫	Hans Tomasczek
Donner	⎬ Dei	August Ulrich [*sic*]
Froh	⎪	Adolf Wallnöfer [*sic*]
Loge	⎭	Friedrich Caliga
Alberich	⎫ Niebelungi	Dott. Franz Krückl
Mime	⎭	Julius Lieban
Fasolt Gigante		Josef Chandon
Fafner Gigante		Robert Biberti
Fricka	⎫	Elisabeth Lindemann
Freia	⎬ Dei	Elisa [*sic*] Freitag
Erda	⎭	Rosa Bleiter
Woglinde	⎫	Terese [*sic*] Milàr
Wellgunde	⎬ figlie del Reno	Auguste Kraus
Flosshilde	⎭	Orlanda Riegler

Also listed were the company's staff, from conductor Seidl on through the stage personnel. The setting for each of the scenes was given, though the fourth was overlooked. And it was noted that there would be a twenty-minute intermission between the second and third scenes—a practice that Wagner did not envision, and one that is certainly not allowed in performances of our time. Possibly Neumann offered this as a sop to novice audiences (Venetian only? others?) who would not be prepared to sit for some three hours without interruption. On the other hand, it was finally observed that:

> The beginning of each act will be announced with two fanfare signals: with the first the public is invited to take its seats; with the second is announced the beginning of the act.

This statement suggests that conventions observed on a grander scale at Bayreuth today have a long background.

The cast listings that *LGdV* would indeed give for all four of the opera performances are of some historical interest, especially as a demonstration of the ways in which Neumann used his singers in the various roles. And that point touches on one amusing incident which marked the performance of *Das Rheingold*. As Neumann relates it:

> . . . Just before the appearance of Erda, [Hedwig Reicher-] Kindermann, who was not singing that night, came to beg, "Herr Director, let me do the Erda this evening—please—*please!*" She had not sung this role in Leipzig and Berlin or London, and not on our tour, though once in Bayreuth in 1876, but never since that time. I refused, saying she had quite enough to do with the Brunhilda in all three of the coming performances. But she insisted and pleaded—finally saying, "Just for this one night! You must remember this is our first night in Italy! Let me sing Erda just this once—I shan't ask for any pay!"
>
> Still doubtful as to the strain, in view of her coming performances, I finally gave way, and there was just only time to throw the long gray veil over her evening dress and to beg the singer of that night to resign in her favor, for at that moment came Erda's cue!

As she rose from her cleft in the rocks, imagine the surprise of all the artists on the stage—the gods and giants in Valhalla—when those mighty tones rang forth from out the cavern. Even Seidl was nonplussed for an instant, for no one had had the least inkling of it.

At the close of her song the enthusiasm of the audience was not to be restrained—they sprang from their seats and leaned over the rails of the boxes, calling loudly for a repetition of the scene. Once,—yes, even twice,—we encored that scene (think of it: the Erda scene), and the frenzied Italians would not be satisfied till Seidl tapped impatiently for the continuance of the performance.

This I should truly call the most remarkable triumph of her remarkable career—for the applause was spontaneously given, not to the world-renowned Hedwig Reicher-Kindermann, but, as it was supposed, to a simple unknown Rosa Bleiter.

The following morning the Italian papers came out with glowing headlines on the glories of our Bayreuth production, mentioning Rosa Bleiter at great length as the greatest operatic star of the future. Now, however, appeared Rosa Bleiter herself at my office, complaining that Reicher-Kindermann had ruined her reputation by setting a standard she could never live up to. But I soothed her, and said that in the future when Kindermann sang that role, she would do so under her own name.[10]

Both the Venetian newspapers reported the opening production on the morrow. Each took notice of Seidl's deft gestures, made alike to national consciousness and to current events. With his German orchestra he opened the proceedings by playing the Italian anthem, the *Marcia reale d'ordinanza*. That he followed with *Heil dir im Siegerkranz*, the German version of the tune that began as the British anthem ("God Save the King") and which, as the anthem of the German Empire under Prussia was also the anthem of Bavaria. The latter's appropriateness was defined by the fact that, the day before, an Italian prince of the house of Savoy, the Grand Duke of Genoa, had married a Bavarian princess. The audience, it was noted, responded warmly to these gestures.

As for the opera itself, *LV* did note that there had been concern among the participants about the performance, since there had been no rehearsal. The anxiety of the perfectionistic Giovann[in]a Lucca was particularly mentioned. But the journal limited itself to the briefest notice of the evening's success, setting this pattern for the subsequent performances, so as to reserve extended and cumulative criticism for later publication. For its part, *LGdV* gave an extended review immediately, as it would do for the successive evenings. These reactions will be considered en bloc below, in our next chapter.

But *LGdV* noted that the principal singers were accorded three curtain calls. And it concluded this April 15 review of *Das Rheingold* by listing the cast data for the performance of *Die Walküre* that evening (for some reason, capitalizing the names of only two leading singers):

Siegmund	ANTON SCHOTT
Hunding	Robert Biberti
Wotan	Dottor Franz Krückl
Fricka	Elisabeth Lindemann

Sieglinde	Katharine Klafsky
Brunhilde, Valkire	REICHER-KINDERMANN
Gerhilde	Elise Freitag
Ortlinde	Anna Stürmer
Waltraute	Georgine Hellwig
Schwertleite	Rosa Bleiter
Helmwige	Therese Milàr
Siegrune	Berta Hinrichsen
Girmgerde	Elise Telle
Rossweisse	Orlanda Riegler

Having noted that the audience for *Das Rheingold* the evening before had been "not crowded," the *LGdV* writer observed that the public for *Die Walküre* was indeed "crowded":

> The boxes were almost totally occupied; on the orchestra floor the section for standees was filled, and that of the reserved seats was likewise, for the most part.

The opera's reception was enthusiastic, the audience obtaining an encore of the *Cavalcata* (or "Ride of the Valkyries"). And the pattern established by the newspapers on April 15 obtained the next day, Monday, April 16: *LV* made only cursory comments and reserved full discussion for later; while *LGdV* had more to say and ended with the listing of the cast for *Siegfried* to come on the next day's evening:

Siegfried	Georg Unger
Mime	Julius Lieban
Il viandante (Votan)	Hans Tomasczek
Alberich	Franz Pischek
Fafner	Josef Chandon
Brunhilde	REICHER-KINDERMAN [*sic*]
La voce dell'ucello del bosco	Auguste Kraus

Monday, April 16, was itself a day of repose for the company and Neumann used it to deal with at least a part of what must have been his unfolding plans for activity in Italy after the Bologna engagement. An official of the German embassy in Rome arrived bearing an invitation to present the entire *Ring* in the Italian capital, with the idea of adding this to the festivities honoring the newly married Savoy Duke and Wittelsbach Princess. Neumann had grave doubts that the Roman musical world would have the interest or resources to sustain such a visit, but guarantees were given that the visit would be underwritten by the German ambassador and the city of Rome, while a rebate by 75 percent was granted to the company on the expenses for transportation by special train in all of Italy. On that basis, Neumann gladly signed a contract with the Teatro Apollo in Rome.

On Tuesday, April 17, with the performance of *Siegfried* to come that evening but no performance from the previous evening on which to comment, the two newspapers tried to keep up the Wagnerian fever with reminders and incidental notices. *LGdV* mentioned the fact that the Civic Band concert in the Piazza di San Marco that day would include a potpourri of music from Wagner's *Lohengrin*. On the other hand, while offering its listing of that evening's *Siegfried* cast, *LV* undertook a survey of reviews published elsewhere on Venice's *Ring* performances to that point: a consensus of approval was noted, but the Venetian writer took occasion to mock other reviewers for their factual mistakes:

> . . . One of them saw signor Neumann conduct the orchestra, one affirmed that signor Lieban (the really wonderful Mime) is a tenor [which, in fact, he was!], while someone even heard a chorus of great effect, sung by the dwarfs. A chorus of the Nibelungs?!— O shade of Riccardo Wagner, pardon him who insults your school!

The notice further reported reactions of various commentators to the simple fact that the *Ring* had arrived in Italy: some seeing it as a mark of cultural progress for the nation, others seeing it as merely a point of curiosity.

In a "P.S." added to this notice, however, the writer for *LV* cited—with humor but also with some indignation—a snide comment made in a Bolognese journal. Bologna, after all, had special status among Italian cities in its lively relationship with Wagner and his music, far more so than Venice. So there was bound to be some irritation that the Lagoon City, rather than Bologna, was to have the honor of hosting the first *Ring* in Italy. According to *LV*, some such irritation must surely have inspired the Bolognese journal named *Don Chisciotte* (or "Don Quixote") to write

> that the Venetian public, which has ears only for gondoliers' songs, was not worthy of being the first in Italy to judge Wagner's *Nibelungi*. This assertion by the Bolognese journal is a stupidity—but a stupidity as big as its Asinelli Tower.
>
> We believe that few other audiences have given, as did ours at the Fenice, evidence of intelligence, of discernment, of politeness toward the performances of *Rheingold* and *Walküre*. On Sunday, several hundred people stood crowded together for four and a half hours in the pit like pickled herrings in a barrel—and there was not a single moment of restlessness to disturb the musical performance.

Don Chisciotte is trying to describe an audience of which it is totally ignorant.

On Wednesday, April 18, both journals gave short reviews of the previous evening's *Siegfried*, citing high points. *LGdV* noted that "The audience was very numerous, almost full, and its behavior yesterday was also most worthy of praise [. . .]," adding that Seidl received a special ovation. Both journals also gave the cast listing for that evening's performance of the final *Ring* opera, *Götterdämmerung*.

Siegfried	Georg Unger
Günther	Hans Tomasczek
Hagen	Robert Biberti
Alberich	Franz Pischek
Brunhilde	REICHER-KINDERMANN
Gutrune	Auguste Krauss [sic]
Woglinde	Therese Milàr [sic]
Wellgunde	Katharine Klafsky
Flosshilde	Orlanda Riegler
I Norma	Anna Stürmer
II Norma	Berta Hinrischen [sic]
III Norma	Katharine Liebermann

Both papers omitted mention of the singer in the role of Waltraute. *LGdV* also apologized should any of the names have not been given correctly, observing that the works were unfamiliar and the roles were switched regularly between operas.

The cast announcement precipitated a small but potent protest. Neumann recollected the performances candidly from his viewpoint. Delighted by the excited response to *Rheingold*, he also noted that *Walküre* was "enthusiastically received" (*begeistert aufgenommenen*). But the *Siegfried* performance on the seventeenth "turned out less favorably." The reason, he frankly admitted, was

the indisposition of our Siegfried, Georg Unger, who had one of his periodic attacks of singing off-key. These Italians have such correct and sensitive ears that they made it rather unpleasant at times for the singer. But Kindermann's magnificent impersonation of Brunhilda roused them to such a pitch that, before the final act, we hoped that they had forgotten their first unfortunate impression. Yet here we were mistaken. . . . [Despite all the other fine performers they appreciated,] Georg Unger they could not and would not tolerate, those keen Italians![11]

At this point, on the morning of April 18, Teutonic diplomacy was reasserted. The German consul presented himself before Neumann, joined by a delegation of students, who announced that, should Unger sing that evening, or appear in any other event, they would make a disruption that would halt the performance. Neumann sent them away with a rejection of their demand for altering the cast, since he had no singer able to replace Unger—who, he thought, could still bring off his role of Siegfried. Neumann recognized, however, that any demonstration against Unger might come only when he was alone on the stage, whereas the popularity of the other singers would forestall a demonstration that would include them. Since Siegfried appears alone only at the beginning of Act I of *Götterdämmerung*, he connived with Reicher-Kindermann for her to come onstage ahead of time, to be with him as a shield from the outset. After some objections, Unger came around, and the strategy worked:

. . . Scarcely had Brunhilda [Kindermann] appeared, when a storm of jubilation broke out all through the house and Unger's entrance was quite unnoticed. Not even the slightest hiss mingled with the acclamations of their favorite. And, as Unger was in very good voice that night, he got through his performance quite successfully.[12]

And, indeed, the two Venetian journals reported cordial reactions to the opera. Enthusiastic ovations were especially accorded Reicher-Kindermann and Seidl, with a curtain call even required of Neumann himself.

Neumann still had one last round of work to see to. The recurrent pattern of augmenting the full *Ring* cycle with an evening concert of Wagner excerpts was to be supplemented by a unique prologue, one precisely fitted to the Venetian setting: a memorial concert at the site of Wagner's death barely over two months before, at the Palazzo Vendramin-Calergi. The local newspapers announced both events, *LGdV* on April 17 and 18, *LV* on April 18 and 19—in the former instance characterizing it as "a pious intention that does honor to those distinguished artists."[13] *LGdV* was able to describe the memorial tribute immediately on the evening of the nineteenth, *LV* following the next day. They noted that the assemblage began at three o'clock in the afternoon, as upward of 400 gondolas gathered about, and the balconies of the surrounding houses were crowded with people. Seidl and his orchestra arrived at 4 o'clock in a bloc of linked barges. But Neumann himself left us the most colorful description:

. . . that afternoon on the Grand Canal, before the house where Richard Wagner lived and died, the members of the Master's Opera Company arranged a stately tribute to his memory that was worthy indeed of the name they bore. The municipality of Venice had placed at our disposal their great gondolas of state—and in these Anton Seidl and all his orchestra took their places. The artists [i.e., singers] followed in six smaller gondolas, linked together in well-known Venetian fashion, and all about us darted the slender boats conducting us in state to the Palazzo Vendramin. Here they hovered about—flower-decked and beauty-laden! All the nobility of Venice was on the Grand Canal, and as many strangers as could find a boat. All deeply impressed, they floated a silent throng, celebrating with us the apotheosis of our hero.

Arrived at the Palazzo Vendramin, I joined our group of artists on the balcony, while Anton Seidl below with his orchestra began the first great strains of the Funeral March from *Götterdämmerung*. Reverently, we uncovered our heads as the music floated up from the water, and all about us the crowds mutely followed our example—crowds in boats and on the quays, even on the roofs of the adjacent houses. In utter silence they listened to this mighty masterpiece, that came like a message from the gods—wafted across the waters in all the matchless glitter of that warm Italian sunshine, and mingling with the scent of gardens and the throb of spring in the air among those verdant islands.

After a suitable pause came the *Tannhäuser* Overture, which called forth thunders of applause though the first had been received in fitting silence. With this we closed our pageant, and to the inspiring strains of the *Marcia reale* the whole flotilla wandered slowly homeward down the Grand Canal, or threading in and out among the smaller ones.[14]

Then came the climax. At 9 o'clock that evening (Thursday, April 19) the singers and the orchestra, under Seidl, presented their farewell concert at the hall of the Liceo Benedetto Marcello—that is, the Sala Apollinea of La Fenice. There had been the appropriate newspaper announcements. In its notice the day before, *LGdV*, communicating information directly supplied by Neumann, had listed the Wagner excerpts to be presented: the Overture to *Tannhäuser*; the Trio from *Götterdämmerung*; the Prelude and Liebestod from *Tristan und Isolde* (Augusta Ihlè as soloist); the duet of Elsa and Ortrud from *Lohengrin*; the Prelude to *Parsifal*; the septet from *Tannhäuser*. In their announcements, both journals took specific notice of the point that the repertoire was presented with the permission of Giovannina Lucca, perhaps reflecting Neumann's care in maintaining his truce with lady! The newspaper reviews the following day indicated the extra (non-Wagnerian) numbers added as encores: tenor Lieban sang two songs by Schumann, while Auguste Kraus sang an aria from *Don Giovanni*.

Neumann himself recalled this event with almost rapturous satisfaction:

> That night at the Richard Wagner concert, Herr [Adolf von] Gross from Bayreuth and the scene painter Joukowski [*sic*], who had planned the *Parsifal* decorations, were our guests. Among the many memorable evenings of our tour this concert, after our recent stately memorial service, made the most indelible impression on my mind. It was a mild evening in April, full of the mysterious magic of Venice; a night of perfume and the shimmer of moonlight among the gardens. The great casements in the music hall stood wide, and past and present mingled in indistinguishable harmony as the music stole gently out over the silent waters. One could imagine no more perfect setting for the duet between Elsa and Ortrud. Auguste Kraus (later to be Seidl's wife) as Elsa with her fresh young beauty and her glorious voice; and Kindermann as Ortrud—singing as no other could ever match her. That was our farewell to Venice.[15]

In their reviews of the next day, the two Venetian journals give added perspective, and on one count actually contest Neumann's recollections. *LGdV*, observing that the audience was the largest crowd ever seen in the Liceo hall, asserted that the heat was suffocating—not quite Neumann's balmy April air. There was, of course, praise for the singers, but above all for the magnificent orchestra, which had clearly taken both the public and the critics in Venice by storm. This journal went on at some length on the matter, stressing a point of connection:

> Of this concert there will remain undoubtedly the dearest memory from every viewpoint, because, through it, the German orchestra has understood how to honor the memory of Wagner, who shortly before his death had himself conducted an orchestra in this very same hall.

The writer then went on at length to discuss the "Teatro Wagner" orchestra: explaining how it followed Wagner's concepts of orchestral structure; and extolling its homogenous, disciplined, and totally integrated playing, as well as its attentiveness to the conductor:

> . . . More than a choice collection of distinguished professionals, this orchestra seems like a confraternity, an association of brothers devoted to the contemplation and the worship of art in general, but of Wagner in particular.
>
> Amid these moonbeams, and with the distressing prospect facing our orchestral players because of the controversy now hanging over the theaters, it is inappropriate to make criticisms or comparisons, so we limit ourselves therefore to saying—look and learn.

But *LV* put the final touch to it, noting:

> . . . Today the Neumann Company leaves Venice, fully satisfied with the brilliant result it has had, a result the brave artists richly deserved.

And Neumann's troupe did indeed depart that next day (April 20) for Bologna where, the evening after that, they launched their *Ring* cycle at the Teatro Comunale with *Rheingold*. Neumann reports an amusing story about the alarm registered by a grandee of the Bologna musical establishment upon seeing all the steam on the stage during the rehearsal that afternoon. Reassured that this was in fact a carefully planned part of the show, the gentleman was lavish in his praises for the vaporous effects once he had seen the performance. *Die Walküre* followed on the twenty-second.

The next evening, marking their stage "intermission," they were to give their concert. There was to be a novelty this time, however, for it had been planned and announced that Seidl would take turns at the podium with the distinguished Luigi Mancinelli, celebrated as one of the leading conductors of his day.[16] At the rehearsal that afternoon, however, Mancinelli's difficulties in adjusting to Wagner's music, and the singers' difficulties in adjusting to his direction, combined, according to Neumann, to dictate the unhappy decision to cancel the concert. Then, following *Siegfried* on April 25, Neumann was faced with another alarm as the company prepared for its *Götterdämmerung* on the next evening. On the morning of the performance, the erratic Georg Unger announced his latest indisposition. The anxious Neumann therefore sent in, as substitute Siegfried, the young Adolf Wallnöffer, who had studied the role as a "cover" but had to go on with no orchestral rehearsal. He was altogether successful, crowning a performance in which Reicher-Kindermann was herself given, as Neumann recalled, "an ovation such as I have never since witnessed."

The progress of the Bologna performances was followed with some care by the Venice newspapers, alert to any comparisons with the company's visit to their own city, and not without some competitive spirit. The Venetian journals, however, did not feel compelled to have any representatives of their own on the scene, content to be dependent upon their Bolognese colleagues. Both journals cited reports of the cordial reception given *Rheingold* on the twenty-first—"a success equal to that achieved in Venice," reported *LV* (April 23). This newspaper went on the next day to cite another Bolognese account of that performance:

> The public of Bologna has not betrayed its reputation for intelligence. The first part of the *Anello del Nibelungo* had a splendid and unexpected success last evening. I say "unexpected" because the public, forewarned by the result that the tetralogy had had in Venice, had come to the theater with the expectation of being bored by *Rheingold*, which is certainly the least accessible and least interesting of the Wagnerian cycle.

LV then passed on reports of the particularly enthusiastic reception the following evening of *Die Walküre*, marked by a repetition of the Cavalcata, by new acclaim for Reicher-Kindermann, and by wild ovations at the end.

In its turn, meanwhile, *LGdV*, on April 23, transmitted its own report of the previous evening's *Walküre*, noting that this work had given much more pleasure than the previous opera, with more crowded attendance and more lively applause. The report then returned to a familiar source for some reactions to *Rheingold*:

> It is amusing, symptomatic, and, at the same time, witty, how much *Don Chisciotte* writes. After having said that *the public has no obligation to understand*, the writer adds: *Do you think you understood the first part of the Nibelunge the other evening? I myself would not swear I did: nevertheless, I clapped my hands.*
>
> And he wrote more beyond:
>
> "But here, in the Tetralogy, we are not only outside of the Italian operatic traditions, but beyond whatever ones we have known until now. The dramatic element in the musical poem is entirely lost; the musical sentence is entirely lost; the musical sentence is submerged in the infinite melody, song is made skeletonic to the point where it is no more than a dialogue.
>
> "From the convention of *Trovatore* or of *Poliuto* we have moved swiftly to another convention, not a happier one as I believe—artistical, but certainly not cheerful. Now take a public—that is to say, a crowd—assembled in a hall kept dark to listen for four hours to music thus conceived, and tell me if you can trust the enthusiasm and the ovations of that public! But what do you want it to do! There are some poses that you just have to put up with; the kind of person who pretends to be bored by a morning program at the local singing club [Società del Quartetto] has to pretend to be entertained by the prologue of the *Nibelunge*, and as followed through only one evening.
>
> And after all that, such a person is lucky!"

The uncomfortable humor of *Don Chisciotte* must have appealed to the Venetian journalists precisely because it paralleled the analytical unease of Venetian critics themselves, those still wrestling with their reactions, as we shall observe in the next chapter.

LGdV took one further notice of the Neumann company's reception in Bologna, though only on April 29, five days after the concluding *Götterdämmerung*. Its perspective was somewhat less glowing than what Neumann himself was to cherish:

A little more, a little less, the success that the *Tetralogy* had at Bologna was equal to that at Venice, with the difference that there *Götterdämmerung* pleased less than at Venice.

La Gazzetta dell'Emilia says, speaking of the *Crepuscolo degli Dei*: "As to the success of the opera, in itself it was equal to that which greeted it in Venice, and in its first presentation at Bayreuth.

"Most lively applause for the Prologue and for the Funeral March; at the end of the former and the latter a curtain call for the singers, a courtesy curtain call, cool, feeble, and, as one might say, without conviction."

And, after that, summing up its assessment, this newspaper says:

"The *Tetralogia* in its entirety is not a theatrical work: it constitutes a work of polemic; it is the expression of the excess of a new form of art, in opposition to the excesses of the old school.

"We do not salute—nor has our Bolognese public saluted—the bold banner of revolt that the great master has unfurled. But we have not thereby lost our perception and our awareness of the true expressive form of art, buried within the exaggerations of an ensemble of artistic criteria that are praiseworthy, embodied in their practice and possible applications.

"An intelligent habitué of the Comunale encapsulated very well the public's overall impression, with a series of responses—monotonous, if you will, but quite true. To a friend who had asked him: 'What part of the *Tetralogy* pleased you most?' the habitué responded: *Seigfried.* And next? *Seigfried.* And then? *Seigfried.* And yet after that? *Seigfried.*

"In truth, the second [full-length] day [i.e., *Siegfried*] is all of the *Tetralogy* that will survive on the stage."

Meanwhile, the Richard Wagner Theater was moving onward. In his ever-cheerful memoirs, Neumann observes that the sets and properties for each opera had been loaded on their train after each performance. Immediately at the end of the final opera, its materials and the orchestra's instruments could be packed aboard with carefully organized efficiency, so that the company was ready for departure promptly on the morning of the following day, April 25:

> It was a bright spring morning as we left the walls of Bologna behind us, sped on our way by hosts of new friends (the mayor, the German Consul, etc.) who had come to see us off. Many "Arrivedercis" they shouted, while handkerchiefs, flags, and banners waved in the sunlight. Their wish that we might return was never fulfilled; yet I must say that after an interval of over twenty years I look back with grateful pleasure to those days in Bologna—that stately old Italian town, the Nuremberg, one might say, of Italy. The place, too, where *Lohengrin* found its first early recognition on that side of the Alps.[17]

Stopping to give a concert in Florence that evening, the company arrived in Rome on April 27. On the following day, before the *Rheingold* performance scheduled for that evening, Neumann put down a threatened strike by the orchestra members (who sought a 30 percent pay increase) by threatening in return to dissolve the company on the spot. The performance went on after all, and *Walküre* was given the following evening (the twenty-ninth). In that performance, Seidl was obliged by protocol to interrupt one of the finest passages in its Act I in order to play the Italian royal anthem when the king and queen arrived at that point. *Siegfried* was performed on May 1, the concert on the second, and *Götterdämmerung* on the third. Neumann reports that the Roman audience's response was highly enthusiastic. At the concert, the *Tannhäuser* Overture had to be repeated; and, upon the queen's request, Lieban added some Schubert songs as command encores. In urgent discussion, the company was pressed to revise its route and to go further south to Naples. But Neumann had by this time negotiated an engagement in Turin as his next stop: despite Neapolitan offers to indemnify the Torinese authorities for a delay, the director remained firm to his commitments. Neumann did bow to one bit of public pressure, however, and presented a repeat performance of *Walküre* in Rome on May 5. On the following day they set out on their special train to Turin.

In that city's Teatro Reggio they presented their full cycle (April 8, 9, 11, 12), with the concert (April 10) midway between the operas. The grand duke of Genoa and his Bavarian bride attended the concert as focuses of the festivities. And Neumann pulled an atmospheric stunt, having the entire orchestra section of the theater turned into an elaborate garden—like a magical grove of Armida, he said—through which was filtered the music played from the stage. Turin marked, however, the first of eventually two serious cast losses. There Katharina Klafsky—the brilliant new soprano whose career Neumann had helped to launch in Leipzig and then in his touring company—contracted typhus and had to be left behind. (She was later to resume her career in Bremen and rocket into her full but short-lived success).

From an early point, Trieste had been projected as the next stop on the Wagner Theater's itinerary, but a slight alteration of schedule was now considered: an offer from Milan was too good to be ignored, and Neumann was able to arrange postponement of the engagement in Trieste so as to fit in the stop in the great Lombard city. It was at this point that the formidable shadow of Giovannina Lucca fell upon the unsuspecting Neumann. She had come to Turin to attend (i.e., monitor) the company's performances there. It was on the last night of that cycle that she struck anew:

> When all arrangements had been made, and our contract then signed with Milan, and then permission had been settled to postpone performances for Trieste by about a week, Mme. Lucca surprised me one night in the midst of the second act of *Götterdämmerung* with the announcement that she should forbid our Milan performances. Nothing I could say or do seemed calculated to move her. She declared she had only given her permission for the first specified cities, thinking we should fail in our undertaking; but now that she realized how tremendously successful we had been, she wished to reserve the proprietary rights for herself. She, personally, would present the *Ring* in Milan the next year.
>
> I tried to show her the utter absurdity of attempting such a work with only foreign [i.e., non-German] artists; and then to make her see how deeply she was injuring the sacred cause of Art. But, clinging to her point, she announced her firm determination

to give the *Nibelungen* herself in Milan, no matter what the cost. So nothing was left but to wire frantically in all directions . . . readjusting arrangements with Trieste, inasmuch as . . . the performances had to be canceled in Milan, where Frau Lucca, on the basis of her prior rights for Italy, had abruptly forbidden our Milan presentations.[18]

Packing up that night, the company set out in their train the next day (April 13). Their intended route thence to Trieste necessarily took them by way of Milan, where their train was stopped and they were confronted by the Count Francesco Dal Verme, owner of the theater that had engaged Neumann for the now-forbidden *Ring* performances. Backed by local authorities, the count ordered the confiscation of the company's materials—sets, properties, instruments—until his contract was fulfilled after all. Only a clever bit of purse-snatching by the quick-thinking Reicher-Kindermann rescued the company's treasury from confiscation as well. With the help of the German consul, Neumann was able to prove to the count that Mme. Lucca's 1868 contract with Wagner did predate (and accordingly trump) his own of 1882, so that the lady was within her legal rights in banning the *Ring* in Milan, rendering Neumann merely a helpless victim. The count stood down from his demands and a compromise was arranged by which Neumann's company would present at the Teatro Dal Verme a performance of Beethoven's *Fidelio* on May 15 and the standard Wagner concert on the next evening.

The audience response to the *Fidelio* performance was rated by Neumann as "one of the most thrilling memories of our tour." Most of the numbers were applauded wildly and encores were called for. In dealing with the choice of overtures, Seidl and Neumann had used the "Leonore" No. 1 as the curtain-raiser (instead of the E-flat "Fidelio" one), and that was repeated at audience insistence. The practice of playing "Leonore" No. 3 during the break in Act II, well-established long before Mahler's alleged precedent-setting, was honored here. The audience wanted a repeat of that. They demanded it, Neumann said, "with a spirit that one rarely sees even in Germany." It was granted, but Neumann had to deny a second replaying of it to spare the weary orchestra. Likewise, to spare the badly strained Reicher-Kindermann, he forbade her repeating Leonore's great Act I monologue, which had been accorded a tumultuous ovation.

The wonderful keenness and musical sensibility of the Italians was shown again in these Milan audiences. They never hesitated either to praise or to blame; and their ears were so acute that at the least false note of one of the horns, for instance, some one or another enthusiast would rise in his seat and, pointing to the unfortunate offender, would hiss loudly.

I think we all left the theater that night in rather an exalted mood—Auguste Kraus [Marcelline], Anton Schott [Florestan], Dr. Krückl [Pizzaro], Lieban [Jaquino], and above all Seidl with his orchestra and Reicher-Kindermann—each came to me in turn to say how fortunate they felt themselves to have taken part in such a glorious performance.[19]

The next day (May 16), before the Wagner orchestral concert, Neumann faced a now-familiar threat:

> . . . And again Frau Lucca appeared at my office, like Banquo's ghost, to announce that she must protest against our playing the *Tannhäuser* Overture, which had always been our opening number.

This time Neumann was determined to stand up to her. He refused to change his plans. Taking refuge in predictions that the performance would be bad and badly received, she stormed out.

> That night, just as Seidl raised his baton for the opening of the Overture, Frau Lucca stalked majestically into her box. I am not sure whether she recognized the first few bars, but a gentleman who accompanied her soon leaned over and whispered something in her ear, at which she turned suddenly and scowled into my box, which was near! Although the success of this number had hitherto been most unqualified, I confess I looked forward to its reception here in Milan with some uneasiness. But the audience broke out at its close into rapturous applause, and Seidl had to give his men the signal for an encore. Then Frau Lucca rose abruptly from her seat and frowningly withdrew to the gloom of the background.[20]

Indeed, Neumann recalls, the audience wanted the Overture played a third time, but had to be denied. Nevertheless, his firm behavior this time had won a certain respect from the lady, even if she persisted in her scheming:

> Our triumphant success naturally did not modify Frau Lucca's mood, as she wanted the field to herself for the Wagner tour she contemplated next year. Yet, in spite of all this, we parted with most friendly professions. She told me that I was the first man who had ever opposed a direct prohibition she had made. Then she asked me if I would come should she send for me the following year to direct the tour she had planned, with an Italian orchestra and singers from La Scala. To this I answered that neither I nor any other man could ever carry out such a project. Frau was quite angry at this answer, though I could see that it had made some impression. I later learned that this clever and energetic lady had made the most determined efforts to carry out her plan. She even applied to many artists of the Richard Wagner Theater (and thus, to German singers) to help her out—Katharina Klafsky, Anton Seidl, Adolf Wallnöffer, Julius Lieban, and others—asking them to learn the roles in Italian and join her troupe. Yet, as was naturally to be expected, such an enterprise never materialized.[21]

With their still-laden special train now released, Neumann and his company left Milan and proceeded to Trieste (May 17)—with this entry into Austrian territory thereby passing out of Italy. The performances in Trieste of the *Ring* (May 18–21) were highlighted by the second casualty among Neumann's leading singers. Hedwig Reicher-Kindermann had contracted an illness during the tour's stay in Amsterdam and had shown signs of strain at points along the way. In Trieste she caught a severe chill, which prevented her from singing in *Walküre* and *Siegfried*. Against all advice, she insisted upon portraying Brünnhilde in *Götterdämmerung*, in what was to be her last performance. Totally exhausted, she was put under medical care. The company went on to Budapest where it presented the full *Ring* (May 23–27) plus a repeat of *Walküre* (May 28) and another *Fidelio* (May 29), with Amalia Materna—who had created Brünnhilde at Bayreuth in 1876—taking Reicher-Kindermann's roles. Budapest was to have been the tour's final stop, but an added engagement had been contracted as early as the company's time in Venice. On they went to that extra conclusion, in Graz, where they launched their closing *Ring* cycle on June 1. That very night Neumann received a telegram announcing Reicher-Kindermann's death and imminent burial. Filled with genuine grief for such a personal and artistic loss, Neumann rushed by train to Trieste, to attend the meager obsequies, and then he hastened back to Graz as the tour concluded there with *Siegfried* on June 4 and *Götterdämmerung* on June 5, 1883.

Accomplished over nine months, the epochal tour of the Richard Wagner Theater was ended and the company disbanded, at least for the moment. Neumann devoted himself for the next few years to directing the theater of Bremen, with Seidl (who married Auguste Kraus there). Then, from 1885 onward, he settled at the German Opera Theater of Prague. He pressed the cause of Wagner in both posts, as he insists. During these years, he received strong solicitations to bring his traveling Wagner productions back on tour again, to such places as London, Copenhagen, Stockholm, Christiania [*sic*], and Paris, as well as several cities in Italy. But all of the company's sets and materials had been put in storage, and no proposal promised returns sufficient to defray the costs and justify the efforts required to resuscitate them.

Not, that is, until proposals from the Imperial Opera of St. Petersburg, Russia, moved Neumann to reactivate the company. Of course, personnel changes were inevitable. Many singers from the original roster were no longer available or viable, so a partly new cast had to be created. And Anton Seidl, convinced that Wagner had deputed him to become his apostle in America, had taken up the post of principal conductor of the Metropolitan Opera in New York in 1885. To replace him, however, Neumann had his distinguished and able conductor at Prague, Karl Muck. New scenic staff was also assembled. But a Russian chorus and orchestra were to be employed—the former proving to be excellent, the latter requiring some German reinforcements. When all was put together, the company gave four *Ring* cycles and two Wagner concerts between March 11 and April 2, 1889, all with great success—the first performances of the tetralogy in Russia, an event of enormous impact on Russian musicians. After precarious negotiations, it was arranged that the company should go on to Moscow, where it gave a complete *Ring* (April 6–7, 9–10), a concert (April 8), and a repeat of *Walküre* (April 11). Though the reception was good, Neumann remembered, it was not as enthusiastic as that in St. Petersburg. One of those attending the complete Moscow cycle was the dour and hostile Leo Tolstoy.

Neumann left Moscow on April 13, 1889, and with that the peregrinations of his Wandering Wagnerians came to a definitive end.[22] He resisted requests for a return to Russia, and watched as others attempted it in vain. For the rest of his years, he settled down to his labors in Prague, dying in 1910. Meanwhile, a year before Neumann's tour to Russia, Giovannina Lucca finally resolved her years of bitter rivalry with the Ricordi publishing firm of Milan by selling to them her company—and, with it, her Wagner rights.

Through all of this, as Neumann's Richard Wagner Theater moved further and further away from Venice, that city's journalists paid its movements ever more sporadic and scanty notice. But the company's impact had by then been made in the Lagoons. The first confrontation of Italian public and critical opinion with Wagner's great tetralogy and the full effects of his art were to be worked out in Venice only in the aftermath of the company's efforts there. It is to those reactions that we must next turn.

Chapter Twelve

Venetian Assessments

Though the twentieth century was to reap the often-bitter harvest of modern nationalism, the nineteenth century saw its full flowering, long seeded in Europe's volatile soil. In our time, it may be easy to underestimate how much nationalism and national consciousness affected nineteenth-century cultural life. Indeed, during the latter half of the twentieth century, musical styles have tended to become globalized, to a considerable extent either blurring or eliminating any sense of "national" traits, especially in European musical life. But, a century before that, it was difficult for Europeans not to think of their cultural activity as separate from their national identity.

Understandably, this mentality was particularly strong for peoples who had achieved recognized and firmly established nation-state status only during the course of that century. Of many examples, Germany and Italy stand out—each newly unified, but each with strong collective cultural traditions of long background and active reassertiveness. Accordingly, the promotion and reception of Richard Wagner's music in Italy was necessarily deeply colored by nationalistic sensitivities and by intensified consciousness of differences between musical styles and expression that reflected supposed national identities.

Such sensitivities and consciousness can be recognized—on the part of the German performers on the one side, and of the audience and critics on the other—in the reactions to the Richard Wagner Theater's appearance in Venice.

Consider, as prologue, the glowing account that Angelo Neumann himself gave of his company's opening night of the *Ring* at Venice's Teatro la Fenice, with *Das Rheingold*:

> On the fourteenth [of April] opened our memorable first production of the "Nibelungen Ring" in Italy. Those Italians are such thorough artists that the greatest innovations are understood and appreciated at their first hearing. How keenly the Master would have enjoyed seeing his beloved Venetians, with whom he had always felt himself so thoroughly at home, glorying in that first scene of the Rhine maidens with an enthusiasm we had never witnessed, even in our own native Germany. And we must consider that this public had never been in any way educated up to this much-criticized work, heretofore considered so obscure.
> Enthusiasm mounted to a frenzy from scene to scene. . . .[1]

Neumann's sentimental speculation on how Wagner himself would have reacted to the Venetian audience's enthusiasm hardly squares with the composer's own cynicism about that public, as Neumann well knew. And the impresario's portrayal of Venetian enthusiasm for *Rheingold* surely reflected the glow of his nostalgia, as well as a certain stereotype of Italian musicality.

Moreover, the highly positive picture Neumann gives of the Venetian reception accorded to the *Ring* operas is leavened by the reactions of local Italian critics. It is true, of course, that major-city newspapers around the peninsula sent critics or correspondents to the Fenice to report the Italian premieres. Himself a Venetian, Giovanni Salvioli wrote as correspondent for *Archivio musicale* in Naples. Under the pseudonym "Sordello," Dino Mantovani wrote for publication in Rome. Among other critics were those whose reviews were published without their names in *Il teatro illustrato* and in *Il mondo artistico*, both of Milan, and in Florence's *La Nazione*. General discussions were also provided by Francesco d'Arcais for *Nuova antologia di scienze, lettere ed arti*, published in Rome and Florence. Detailed consideration of all their reports would, of course, provide a comprehensive, if somewhat repetitive, picture of the general Italian reception of Wagner at this juncture.[2]

Our focus here, however, is Venice's relationship to Wagner. Perforce, we are thus limited exclusively to Venice's critics, in order specifically to capture a sense of that city's reaction to this momentous episode in its cultural history. (There were, to be sure, reports sent by Venetian commentators to newspapers elsewhere, such as Milan; but, for convenience's sake, we will deal only with what was published in Venice itself.) As already encountered, these critics are, of course, the anonymous writer for the afternoon paper, *La Gazzetta di Venezia* (*LGdV*), and for the morning paper, *La Venezia* (*LV*), a writer at first anonymous but soon identified as "Toni."

The two represent a simultaneously contrasting and complementary pairing. Both appear to have had some familiarity with Wagner's output, and both were readily familiar with some of the critical literature on the composer, both pro and con, both Italian and international. But the anonymous *LGdV* writer was clearly conservative, an Italian traditionalist, and basically unsympathetic to Wagner's music and aesthetics. He (as one assumes his gender) had some stylistic illusions, writing in a somewhat pretentious and fussy style and always using the first-person plural "we" rather than the singular, more personal address. He seems to presume some education on the part of his readers, quoting passages from French writers in the original rather than in Italian translation. By contrast, "Toni" writes in a somewhat more direct style, if with often wild mannerisms of sentence structure and punctuation. Once he is published over his own name, he always uses the first-person singular "I." More to the point, while honoring his national tradition, he is more open-minded and cosmopolitan in taste: not a rabid Wagnerite, to be sure, but displaying an understanding and sympathetic reaction to that composer's music as something with its own definite value and beauty. Taken together, then, and representing one of the citadels of Italian operatic tradition, these two writers provide in microcosm something of the opposing (even mixed) responses made by Italian sensibilities in Italy's first encounter with Wagner at his most challenging, in his *Ring*.[3]

Each of our two critics adopted parallel approaches to treating the *Ring* performances: to give only preliminary reports of the first three nights while reserving a full estimation until the cycle was completed. The preliminary notices by "Toni" were indeed quite brief, with his comprehensive survey then very extended, whereas the *LGdV* writer had more to say along the way and was not so expansive at the end.

As we have noted, both critics were at pains to stress the behavior of the Venetian audience at the performances. Part of this attention was to emphasize that the Venetian public was taking Wagner seriously. By noting misconduct that the audiences avoided, our critics were perhaps implying how such audiences often *did* behave under other circumstances. Nevertheless, reporting on April 15 after the first evening, *LGdV*'s writer was full of pride for his fellow citizens:

> We say it promptly, if only for fear of forgetting it: never have we seen in a theater an audience so docile, so patient, so calm, and which held so firmly in this docility, patience, and calmness to the end, even though the largest part of it exercised herculean willpower to sustain attention. It was as if a vow had been made, binding not simply through its own love of art, but as a commitment of conscience. No ogling the boxes, no whispering with neighbors; they remained still, attentive, as if absorbed in contemplation, fearing that any sort of distraction would cause the missing of a detail whose importance might later affect a comprehensive judgment.

Writing on the next day, following the performance of *Walküre*, the same critic reiterated:

> . . . the audience was extraordinarily attentive, conscientiously open-minded, remarkably patient, indeed really quite long-suffering, as if it comprised a jury at an assize court.

Going on, however, to assert that "only two or three pieces" in the score gave pleasure, this critic perhaps projects his own negativity by asserting that

> the remainder did not please an audience that is impartial, open-minded, true. This is the Venetian audience—calm, intelligent, dispassionate—that judges with great responsibility, as does perhaps no other audience in Italy, certainly foremost among them. Altogether the opposite has been written outside Venice: that everything pleased it [the Venetian public]; that they were carried to seventh heaven by every page of the score. Nothing could be further from the truth. The audience was fair, decorous, admirable. It heard everything and—we state it—it was bored without making complaint. Whenever there was any occasion for doing so, it applauded warmly and effusively, forgetting the oddities, the confusions, the excesses, the redundancies. . . .

The writer for *LV* (unidentified at this point, but presumably "Toni") began his April 15 report on *Rheingold* with a parallel observation that the audience listened "with devout attention, and there was not a single moment of discontent." But, trying to go beyond mere civic self-congratulation in the documentation of public reactions, he observed:

> The discussions among the audience were impassioned. We heard one person condemn the music for too much simplicity, and another person condemn it for too much complexity. All agreed, however—and we with them—as to the harshness of the subject for our taste.

The next day, he wrote:

> At the end of *Rheingold* yesterday it was a subject of lively discussions within groups of citizens. We have heard of Germans praising the open-mindedness and the intelligence of our public, which wished to listen—to listen devoutly—to the product of the new art before judging it. It would not let itself be transported into enthusiasm, which would have been absurd at a first hearing of music so different from the usual. It was an audience that applauded the clear and more effective bits without letting one of them pass unobserved. Among Venetians, amid the very diverse opinions—one finding the opera sublime, another finding it musical nonsense—this stood out: it was impossible to grasp all of the power of the concept. But it could be recognized, it could be comprehended, that the concept was born of a great mind—stubborn, strong, knowledgeably rebellious against whatsoever obstacle of customs, tastes, traditions. On the excellence of performance, all agreed.

Both critics returned to audience reactions as a vehicle for expressing their own impressions along the way. Thus, in his report on the *Rheingold* performance, *LGdV*'s writer, after describing high points in the work, moved easily from what he thought the audience thought to what he himself plainly thought:

> When the performance was over, however, nearly everyone looked each other in the face and, though recognizing in *Rheingold* a musical work of grand, strange power, declared that they had put their shirts into a sweat in order to understand something that they had little comprehended. In fact, that poverty, if not to say absolute lack, of song from the voices, that continuous dialoging without any ensemble piece, properly said, without a chorus, indeed, without anything that served to break the monotony— sweet, refined, at some points even voluptuous, if you will, but always monotony—does not suit Italian taste. . . .
>
> Maestro Wagner has chosen to concede nothing to the audience: a song or a hint of song seems about to happen, but suddenly it changes, it evaporates, it becomes lost in a sea of various chords, of extravagant passages. Florimo[4] had put it well, calling this Wagner's indefinite melody, because it has neither rhythm nor regularity nor contour; and we say this not as restricted to the voices, but extending also to the orchestra.

Deferring any further discussion of the music itself, the *LGdV* critic commented on the performance. Among the singers, he noted favorably Lieban as Mime, Caliga as Loge, Biberti as Fafner, and Riegler as Fricka. To these he added "Bleitner" as Erda, not only misspelling her name, but falling into the trap of her last-minute replacement by Reicher-Kindermann, as told in the previous chapter.[5] He then, however, passed on to one subject on which he was to agree fervently with "Toni":

> The orchestra, lovingly directed by maestro Anton Seidl, is stupendous, even if not sufficiently numerous for the work it is required to perform. For example, the violins lack that smoothness which cannot be had without a great number of the best players. What is achieved is really fine. For example, there are seven horns: in Italy we are grateful if, in an even more numerous orchestra, four of them are at hand.
>
> The contrabasses, all four-string rather than three, are few. Four contrabasses, however good, are insufficient for such an ensemble. In Italy there is never a performance of importance without eight, or at least six contrabasses. Timpani magnificent and all the instruments of the best. Their ensemble is well integrated. Acceleration is perfect and if at any moment some slip in intonations was heard—as, for instance, with the horns at the beginning of the Prologue—it was something fleeting.

Quick praise was added for the stage machinery—"carefully programmed so that the performance was mounted in a few hours"—plus other features: "Wardrobe and decor most praiseworthy and sets not beautiful but of some effectiveness."

When he reported on April 16 about the performance of *La Walkiria* the night before, the *LGdV* critic renewed his praise for the orchestra—"a paradisiac beauty, altogether worthy of that extraordinary genius in the realm of harmony who was Riccardo Wagner ..."—with only passing reference to the singers and staging. For the rest, he again cast audience response in terms of his own outlook:

> . . . With so much foundation we persist in the opinion that [Wagner's] genre does not at all agree with our own taste, and not merely because the Italian audience does not want to be attentive, to be profoundly attentive, even when attending the theater. Our audience proved that yesterday itself, comprehending with wonderful and rapid perception the first act of *Valkiria* and all features of the instrumentation, phrase by phrase, thought by thought. But this is because we absolutely do not think otherwise. Woe betide if, in pursuit of fashion, we do not continue to understand as in the past, even as we assimilate advances in [musical] science, taking them on as powerful supplements to that taste of ours which the whole world has proclaimed the best.
>
> ... As they continue to see, hear, relish things that disagree with the eye, the hearing, the palette, our senses adapt, even unintentionally, to assimilate it [the work] into its own framework. We admire and even imitate Wagner in the science of harmony; but enough!

As he moved on to April 18, reporting the performance of *Siegfried* the previous evening, our *LGdV* critic tossed off a few quick judgments. This opera, he thought, was of surpassing descriptive power, but its wonderful moments were set against long stretches of declamation that became boring—"in the second act the first part could be omitted." He praised the performance, especially noting Reicher-Kindermann and Lieban for their excellence. There was even, we are told, a special ovation for Seidl. But, once more, it was the orchestra that captivated our critic:

> . . . a performance like that of yesterday could not fail to make a great impression. The chief objections are overcome with an ease that surprises, that enchants, and that leaves a deep impression, if also a sense of sadness, since you cannot help posing this question: *When ever will I hear a collection of artists of this type? When ever will I hear an ensemble so integrated, so delightful, so heavenly?*

With the performance of *Götterdämmerung* on April 18, both critics were free to undertake retrospective and comprehensive judgments. The writer for *LGdV* wasted no time, and on April 19, he set to work in an extended article titled *Appendice*, but spreading over pages 1–2 of the journal. He began with comments on the final opera itself, and on the audience's reactions to it as he perceived them:

> The first act, that is, the prologue and first act, seem rather infelicitous, because they belong to the worst of their type—that is, to the tiresome. We find the second act better, and the third act better than the second. In the last one we find, among other things, the scene of Siegfried's death, which is truly marvelous in inspiration and realization. And then there is the Funeral March, of which a repeat was demanded by a loud clamor, a march that is something truly great in concept and in its martial character, most appropriate to the Bayard[6] of the German-Scandinavian legend, rendered immortal by Wagner. The crowded and stubbornly impartial audience, as usual, followed yesterday's performance with extraordinary intensity, and gave perhaps yet less evident signs of impatience than it had shown at some scant moments during the preceding evenings, when the boredom—produced by those endless dialogues, declamations, spiced by nervous, disorderly, raving outcries—made it somewhat restless. There was, however, no whispering in stall, in box, or on bench.

Our critic for *LGdV* goes on to report the audience's acclamations on this final night of the tetralogy for two particular artists. Reicher-Kindermann (who, he says, recalled the vocal character of the famous Teresa Stolz[7]) received an abundance of flowers, while "the most illustrious maestro Anton Seidl, who is a musician of the first rank," was given "a gigantic laurel wreath." The writer then takes this as a cue to criticize the vocal demands of Wagnerian style, using as his main example Reicher-Kindermann

> who was the brightest ray of light in this evening, and who is a true ornament of the German lyric theater. It was a pity, a real pity, that this distinguished artist could only be heard in that thankless role [Brünnhilde], in which [. . .] there are unbecoming

cries of passion, resembling the sounds of raving, while instead, in her situation, she should have been in the soft rush of so sweet a passion as love. And, as for voices, we would like appropriate experts to explain what miserable torture has been inflicted upon Wagner singers in this *Tetralogia*. We are not talking about the tenor, who is so totally throttled to the extent that no celebrated singer of ours would undertake that part [Siegfried]. Rather, we restrict ourselves to Brunhilde, who is a true victim, requiring nothing less than the bronze, fiery, strong, ringing voice of *Reicher-Kindermann* to survive it. Not infrequently do we hear this or that Italian master accused of mistreating voices! But such people—who, we assume, are hardly qualified judges—might take the trouble to consider *Unger, Reicher-Kindermann*, and the other principal singers of the Company, and they will discover the truth.

The *LGdV* critic then stands back from the entire *Ring* cycle:

> Drawing a balance sheet on the music of the *Tetralogia*, we would say that, excepting five or six pieces that are in the usual forms, all the rest consists of monologues, of declamations, of dialogues, of preludes, of fragments of descriptive music. Those five or six pieces would occupy a half-hour's time; conversely, even with the entire *Tetralogia* reduced by such serious deletions, it still takes up about eighteen hours. We repeat, eighteen hours!!

The writer notes that, in publicizing the coming of the *Ring* to Venice, pains had been taken to remind the public that any judgments should take into account the handicaps of a traveling company with limited preparation time, and of a work whose own composer had never expected could reach a wide audience. Our critic then renews his praise for the patience, fine behavior, and intelligence of the Venetian audience, withholding (as he had) its full judgment until the entire cycle was completed. Now, therefore, was the time to express his judgments, however limited by the space available to him.

To begin with, the *LGdV* critic opines that the "mythic drama" of the *scuola del Wagner* allows great play for the mind, but gives little place to the heart, which, with rare exceptions, "in Wagner's philosophical music is an organ of no use to the spectators and serves exclusively for the circulation of the blood!" From here he launches into the balance of his comments, focused almost entirely on comparing Wagnerian style to Italian style, very much to the disfavor of the former. Thus, as for the *Ring*,

> . . . viewed in its totality . . . the result is very discouraging for art—as we conceive of it in Italy, thanks be to God. One might, on the other hand, declare this a comforting result, in the sense that our art is shown as so superior in displaying less preoccupation with science, while it is so much richer in inspiration and is brightened by that sacred fire which is the primary feature of genius.

The writer concedes that it is good for Italy to have the opportunity to encounter this work, admittedly marvelous in many ways, by the composer who

has been such a pioneer in the advancement of the art of music and of performing organizations "so that they might serve as the foundation and the guidance for a new musical direction in the world." The opportunity was even more
apt, coming as it did precisely in the wake of Wagner's recent death in their very
city. But our critic is confident that Italian musical life may learn from the
German school without slipping into servile imitation or losing its own artistic
conscience. He therefore anticipates that the Neumann company will receive a
welcome throughout Italy equal to what it has enjoyed in Venice. "The public
should take care, however, not to lower its own taste, because even wine that
tastes moldy can become welcome to the palate with habit."

Once again, our critic praises the Venetian audience, though distinguishing
between its "serious and impartial" majority of participants and

> those insignificant portions that, out of fashion, or habit, or so as to appear intelligent,
> or in an unwholesome passion for originality, not only place Wagner's music in the sev-
> enth heaven, but speak ill of our [Italian] masters, who—whether they like it or not, it
> is really true—have stood and still reign supreme in the whole world's art. And that is
> not just our opinion, but has the agreement—polite, however, sincere—of foreign
> experts distinguished in musical studies.

But, laments our critic, "this unhealthy phenomenon"—that is, a cult of Italian
Wagnerism in taste and compositional emulation—has indeed come into being.
Even though much has already been said to refute so misguided a direction, our
writer believes some judgments should be reiterated, and he begins by quoting
Francesco Florimo on the Wagnerites' "aversion to melody":[8]

> They do not understand what scope and power melody could have. Enamored of
> progress, they think they have composed an imperishable work when they have man-
> aged to put together a sequence of chords, for the most part dissonant, which, aimed
> at deafening the audience, have originated in their own distraction. Today, to be a com-
> poser requires both genius and art; one cannot be separated from the other. Art serves
> to develop thought, to give rhythm to the melody, and to enable both elements to
> express the sense of the word—so to say, to furnish with well-organized orchestration
> the idea that itself should be totally supreme. Yet, all that, however cultivated and even
> classical, will never succeed in creating a single phrase of inspired song. *Genius reveals
> itself by way of art, but art will never succeed in creating genius.*

LGdV's critic next quotes a passage from an earlier Venetian critic, Antonio
Sartini,[9] which had been published in a Venetian magazine, *La Scena*, on January 22,
1876, at the time of the first *Ring* production in Bayreuth:

> Melody is no more. Dissonances, notes, disjunct phrases, breaks made in continuity, all
> follow one another, pile up on themselves, and exhaust themselves as they penetrate
> the eyes [*sic*] of the hearer, who does not, and cannot, understand anything.
> Mathematics, this sterile truth, has been imposed upon the sweetest of the arts; science

and philosophy have been made to dance in justification of absurd principles, and the specific consequence of all this is that the idea goes nowhere and dies, the audience is bored, and, after one has been compelled to rack his brain to figure out some distant and imaginary semblance of an idea, it still has gone nowhere.

Our critic then turns, with full agreement, to the first of two French commentators, the Marquis Achille de Lauzières, quoting him in the original French:

> It would henceforth be quite childish not to recognize that art has undergone a kind of transformation, especially in consequence of the great importance assumed by instrumentation, so that it would be absurd, even dangerous, for contemporary composers not to accept this transformation.
>
> It no longer suffices today to have received from nature a felicitous musical disposition, to have a ready imagination, to have likewise what is called enthusiasm, insight, inspiration. One needs science, acquired by long and serious studies, to come to the aid of the artist, so that the work that he begets wins full approval and has a long life.
>
> To be born a musician is fine, but this is not enough; patient, assiduous, stubborn toil must be paired with natural gifts. The modern school has quite understood this, and we its students must become practiced in harmony before producing any works.

Finally, our *LGdV* critic turns to his other French commentator, Henri Cahen, for a "spirited assessment of the Wagnerian School," again given in French:

> *Active.* Always polished instrumentation, sometimes some lovely orchestral effects.
>
> *Passive.* Denial of melody, cancellation of rhythm; constant revolt against the laws of harmony; lack of charm, debasement or, at least, subjection of the human voice, which remains ever the first and most beautiful of instruments, despite the efforts of the moderns and of the anatomical theories of today's professors of voice.

There are many other French critics of Wagner, notes *LGdV*'s writer, citing one:

> Berlioz, for example, the great Berlioz, writing of Wagner, ventured to say that *the audience applauds him when the misery ends,* that is to say, that the audience is grateful and pleased only when his music stops!!

The *LGdV* writer acknowledges Wagner's long struggles and controversial career, devoting his life to creating a quintessentially German school of music, "taking for its model his country's speculative, transcendental, abstruse philosophy." With great self-sacrifice he pursued his course, even when it seemed wrongheaded.

> . . . And still another idea got into his head: that of abolishing the *sung opera* by substituting for it the *declaimed drama.* He wished to free the art from conventionalism, so as to approach reality. It is ridiculous, he said to himself, that one is aroused, one loves, one dies, while singing. Therefore, let there be war upon song, so as to make place for dialogues, for declamations, for musical *speech.* But musical speech is melody, which is the

primary and more noble part of the divine art of sound. On the contrary, he, Wagner, with an extraordinary talent, wished to entrust the primary role in musical speech to harmony, imagining thereby he could better reach his goal. He would not have agreed that, in reversing the roles, what had seemed gain on one side was loss on the other. He came to this result: that is, that a man who suffers, or is about to die, does not emit more melodious, touching, sweet sounds, but mutters some word, while the violin, the oboe, the English horn, takes his place in order to set forth the situation, under a muddle of harmonies, chords, dissonances. No more the protagonist, father, husband, and lover who, when dying, says farewell to his loved ones in a manner affecting, touching, heart-rending, a manner that until now has seemed to be the function of the musical language. The protagonist, without any such ceremony, would whisper it in their ear: the instruments will know what is the best way to say it to relatives; and the double basses, the violas, and the violoncellos, with a bit of trombone and even horn, will be the chorus!

The better to match the truth, according to Wagner, the principal course of art must follow this road! . . . One ought to go to the theater to learn science, philosophy, and even philology. Philology indeed, since that results logically in learning if the interpretation—or, better, the signification—that is given to the text musically and by the orchestra is really what is called for in the particular instance. No more could one possibly be a master of music who was not a profound philosopher, philologian, and scientist. Otherwise we would just have so many illiterates!

In the realm of art we have reached the point that, whereas in spoken drama one frequently dies or makes love with vocal inflections that quite resemble song, in lyric theater it is required that one makes love or that one dies while declaiming, or speaking, or screaming desperately! . . .

With this new art, theaters would become Athenaeums, Institutes of Science, or—what is easier—nursing homes!

After having looked so much askance at Wagner's new school of German style, *LGdV*'s critic comes to a surprisingly positive conclusion, by taking up the ideal given by the recent lecturer at Venice's Ateneo

> . . . that we expect from a wedding of the schools, German and Italian, that the art [of music] may be drawn to more lofty and noble heights. Our more illustrious masters have already perceived this need. Verdi, Boïto, Ponchielli, and a few others have given very happy demonstrations of that fusion, nevertheless preserving for their works that predominantly Italian imprint which is the secret of our superiority, the true reason for our glory.

Our critic could not have known how soon this prediction was to be fulfilled.[10]

Extensive as the foregoing *LGdV* critique might have seemed, it was dwarfed quickly by the outpouring from "Toni" for *LV*.

On the days following each performance of the first three operas, the reviews for *LV* (presumably by "Toni," but unsigned) were particularly cursory, primarily devoted to reporting on the audience reactions, as already cited. On April 19, following the performance of *Götterdämmerung*, another brief notice was given on that event itself, along with notice of the concerts of tribute on the Grand Canal and in the Marcello Liceo the next day. As to the opera, *LV* noted the enthusiastic reception, especially for its high point, with special praise accorded Reicher-Kindermann and Seidl; it also reported the special curtain call for Neumann himself. Paralleling the critic for *LGdV*, *LV*'s notice ended: "So now, when will we be able to hear *l'Anello del Nibelungi* again?"

Immediately following this, *LV* presented its *Appendice*, entitled "Artistic Chatter" (*Chiacchiere Artistiche*), which, as signed explicitly by "Toni," initiated his journal's promised overview of the tetralogy. Far exceeding the scope allowed by the other newspaper, this venture took the form of a series of four essays in five parts (the first two joined on the nineteenth) that appeared on successive days, each devoted to a distinct topic of discussion.

Alluding indirectly to alarm sounded by the pianist Pirani, "Toni" opened his Part I by addressing the issue that was to dominate his entire essay for *LGdV* that afternoon. He would do so, he promised,

> . . . without the conceit of critics who believe they have the holy mission of rescuing the endangered destiny of our national art.
>
> Is, then, this blessed national art so insecure on its foundations that a crusade should be proclaimed against *l'Anello del Nibelungo*, that terrible enemy? But if—as the opponents of the Wagnerian school say and write—the enemy is an artistic absurdity, a stupidity, a degradation of taste, of what are we to fear? The ugly in art has never murdered the beautiful. Rather, in the way art survives, the ugly, the absurd, the paradoxical—by way of confrontation—serve to reaffirm the beautiful as yet more attractive, more welcome, more tasteful.
>
> You, then, who believe—and your good faith is praiseworthy, respectable—that, in writing against the school of Wagner, you are restoring the national art to more secure foundation, your reasoning is defective. On the contrary, you should applaud the tour of the Neumann Company in Italy: since, in carrying around the peninsula the absurdities of the Wagnerian school, it does great service to the Italian school in demonstrating—by way of confrontation—[Italian] superiority, or really its invincibility.
>
> But things do not work this way.
>
> For the public, an impartial judgment would say that eclecticism is a compelling obligation.

The artist, says "Toni," of necessity belongs to a stylistic school, supporting it utterly and convinced of its superiority.

> . . . Yet the public has faith only in the beautiful—which is not the property of a system, but must be discovered in the most diverse ideas, in the most varied forms, the greatest contrasts. That I am familiar with Raphael does not wipe out Rubens, and Rubens does not wipe out Raphael—they both remain great, whatever the differences in the way painting is to be understood. And, closer to us and in another art, Zola the realist, preeminently objective, does not wipe out Dichens [*sic*], preeminently idealistic and subjective. "What Italian school and German school!" exclaimed Papa Rossini: "there are only two kinds of music, the beautiful and the ugly."
>
> Away, then, with illogical fears. The beauty of the Italian musical school will continue to be revered, beloved, immortal, for all the *Anelli del Nibelungo* that may be born in

Germany and may be performed in Italy. And the beauties of Rossini, Bellini, Verdi continue among the moderns, while they will never wipe out the beauties of Wagner. Are there, then, any beauties for us in the *Nibelungi*? and how many of them are attractive? how many influential on taste? There lies the true, the only discussion.

"Toni" then launches directly into his Part II. He notes the unprecedented public discussion of Wagner that the Neumann Company's performances have prompted. Open-minded observers want to make a fair judgment of the German composer's rightful place in musical history, without the "fetishism" (*feticismo*) displayed by anti-Wagnerians. "Toni" addresses one of these fetishes: that young singers attempting to sing Wagner would be ridiculed.

> A beginner? But who would be so special, so daring an artist as to initiate an artistic career with *Rheingold*, with *Walküre*, with *Siegfried*, and with *Götterdämmerung*? These are the products of prolonged, thoughtful meditations; of a will of steel that breaks but does not submit; of a genius that seeks to look beyond the known world, that wants to create a new one; of a series of thorough, demanding, most patient preparations.
> Riccardo Wagner was raised to lofty status in the musical world with *Lohengrin*. With the knight of the Holy Graal he has given to modern art an idiom powerfully supported, revered, studied. He has shaped a new style. Criticism is chained to Rossini, the wizard of sensuality, enchanting tone-painter, the ultimate Ariosto of music; to Bellini, delicate and sentimental, the poet of tenderness and of charm; to Meyerbeer, grandiloquent, proud in his expansive forms, gigantesque, odd but grandiose; to Verdi, imaginative, facile, impetuous, the popular idol for having revealed, with wonderful clarity of textures, the people's own love for fantasy. Such criticism, I say, tied to these geniuses of modern art, found Wagner heavy, austere, shunning all triviality, pure as a Greek statue or as a bejeweled creation of Benvenuto Cellini.

"Toni" then notes the individual operas (*Fliegende Holländer, Tannhäuser, Lohengrin, Die Meistersinger*) in which Wagner began to exhibit his new style, a style that brought him much criticism and ridicule. Only with the Bologna performance of *Lohengrin*, however, could the Italian realize how much Wagner had influenced such French composers as Ambroise Thomas and Charles Gounod, especially in the latter's *Faust*. But the true fulfillment of Wagner's development came with *Tristano e Isotta*, the *Nibelungen*, and *Parsifal*, in ways revealing "a severity, an integrity of character, a firmness of reasoning exclusively German."

> When Rossini wrote those divine pages of *Mosè* that contain the scene of darkness and the return of the light, he said: "This I write for myself." Then, composing the duet for tenor and baritone, he exclaimed, with his delicate irony: "And this for you, public— sovereign!"
> "This for you, sovereign public!" Wagner would never have said that. And so, with formidable spear in hand like his Wotan, he went forth into the battlefield of criticism: a ruthless, ferocious opponent to those who did not conceive of art as he did. The polemics became as ferocious as a brawl with jack-knives. There was no invective from which one side or the other would be restrained. Now that we have heard in the

Nibelungen the Wagnerian manner of conceiving drama, on stage and in the orchestra, it is understandable why, in the polemical frenzy, Wagner would go so far as to write that [Mozart's] *Don Giovanni* was "musique de table," that Rossini's orchestra was a "gigantic guitar," that the music of the *Ugonotti* [Meyerbeer's *Les Huguenots*] was a "monstrous counterfeit of drama."

The remaining combatants were giving tit-for-tat [*rendevano pan per focaccia*]. Rossini, setting a Wagnerian piece upside down on his desk, sneered "Actually, it is just the same both ways!"

But I have entered into the criticism of Wagner's system before exploring it. ...

And so on the morrow, April 20, "Toni" took up the matter of *il sistema wagneriana* with Part III of his *Conversations*. First, he addressed the question of its origins:

How was it born? Did Wagner conceive it, or had it a different genesis? Some critics have drawn into the controversy Gluk [*sic*], who had written in the famous preface to *Alceste*: "I restrict the music to its true function of serving the poetry, without interrupting the action or chilling it with superfluous ornaments. I did not wish to disrupt the dialogue with display passages, with sharp divisions between an aria and its recitative." They also bring in Liszt who, when in German journals he wrote analyses of the Wagnerian system, stated that the master of the future "was bringing the Glukian principles to fulfillment in his operas, through the power of inspiration and of erudition." Therefore, say the critics—on the dictum *nil sub sole novi* [nothing new under the sun]—Wagner is Gluk's offspring; credit for the idea belongs to Gluk. I would note that Cristophoro Gluk died on 15 November 1787, twenty-six years before Wagner was born.

If any readers who have just attended the Wagner operas have also heard any of Gluck's music, suggests "Toni," they surely recognize the great difference between them:

... while wanting music to serve the poetry without interrupting the action, Gluk employed song and observed the forms of song, as did all the masters who had written for the theater, from the day on which lyric drama became an artistic commodity. Wagner quite to the contrary: since he cast from himself, like some despised garment, all the contrivances [*artificii*] used until then to express melodramatically any kind of situation. And the difference is not one of form or style: it is of substance.

What, then, is the character of Wagnerian style?

To prepare the public for the performances of the *tetralogia*, it was stated, printed, and likewise repeated in Venice that the Wagner of the *Nibelungi* was abstruse, difficult, complicated, incomprehensible. On the contrary, in my opinion, the four operas we have heard at the Fenice have nothing of these negative qualities. I went to the theater in the belief that I would not understand one iota. When the performance ended, I was left with the conviction that the wedding march in *Lohengrin* is more abstruse, difficult, complicated, than the entire tetralogia. (I exclude from consideration of the music the difficulty in keeping up with the murky subject matter and the German dialogue.)

Always giving my opinion, I say that precisely the opposite is the outcome: that it is actually the excessive, obstinate, continuous, inexorable simplicity of the system that generates the sense of fatigue, of oppressiveness, that I and the audience have experienced when leaving the theater after four-and-a-half hours of *Walküre*, after four-and-a-quarter hours of *Götterdämmerung*.

Duets, trios, quartets, etc., the ensembles, the finales, the chorus—all represent so many complexities [*complicazioni*] in music. They allow the melodrama to be varied in its effects. They allow—as a painter would say—the musician's palette to be enriched so that he can be lavish with chiaroscuri in his images, and to adjust the tones, so as to strengthen the effects of particular parts to give the totality more force.

Now, Wagner renounces—and it is an essential renunciation, at the heart of his system—all such contrivances. He says: my characters *will speak* as in tragedy, and the orchestra will unfold, will explain, will illustrate, will paint, will sculpt the passions, the situations, the phrases, the words, the settings. The music will only be the medium for a more powerful representation, and almost "conceptual exposition" for the ideas, the characters, and the action that the poet offers to the audience. But, while remaining in melodrama, the action will be set forth in fullest possible conformity with truth, with reality.

To illustrate the point, "Toni" tots up the small quantity of "complexities" in the *Ring* scores: limited male chorus in *Götterdämmerung*, an even scantier female one in *Walküre*; duets only for Brünnhilde and Siegfried in the end of *Siegfried* beginning of *Götterdämmerung*, or for Siegfried and Gunther in the latter; trios only for the Rhine Maidens, in *Rheingold* and *Götterdämmerung*, or for Brünnhilde, Gunther, and Hagen in the latter:

. . . In fifteen hours of music [as "Toni" calculates the full cycle's length], perhaps a half-hour of vocal complexities, precisely the opposite of how much there is in all other familiar scores.

What, then, in place of "complexities?"

The principal concept of the system is the indissoluble union of the poetic idea with the musical idea, so that music and poetry might be conveyed within the same thought in the artist's brain. Music and poetry therefore have equal importance, neither should one be sacrificed so as to give greater prominence to the other. The orchestra is the greatest factor of dramatic effect. It is not only the cloth on which the characters embroider their dialogues, but it unfolds the action in all its facets, in all it occurrences, even in its more minute details. In each act, we have in the orchestra a symphonic poem that describes the setting and the situations, introduces the personalities, shows their secret thoughts, and reveals them to the spectators, even if the personalities do not speak. Bring to the tetralogia as listener a blind man who has been given no advance notice about its type of music and about the actions portrayed, and he will understand immediately when one is among the waves, in the forge, in the forest, amid the fire: because the orchestra reproduces the murmur of the water, the noise of the forge, the solitude of the forest, the crackling of the flames; because the orchestra makes the point of the leaves' rustling, the birds' twittering, the file's scraping—and, as contrived by Wagner's knowing hand, this is brought off with a miraculous clarity. Also, when he wishes to describe the character and the sentiment of a personality or to delineate a complex situation, then he rises to even greater heights. He makes us experience for ourselves the profound joy experienced by Brunilde [*sic*] when she is awakened and once again beholds light: the relief that the spirit feels when the sun breaks through the darkness of the night; Mime's alarm when Wothan leaves the Nibelungen cavern and the sky flashes lightening; the terror of the struggle between Siegfried and Fafner; the grief that follows the death of Siegfried; the fire of passion, the impulsiveness [*slancio*] with which Siglinda and Sigmondo, or Brunilde and Sigfredo, fall into each others' arms.

It is true: in the Wagnerian system there is less concern for the human voice than for the voices that can be drawn from the instrumental body. Melodic song is replaced for the most part by poetic lyricism [*melopea*], and melody, as if banished from the stage, is placed in the orchestra. Therefore, the great part of the public has difficulty in accepting an innovation that runs altogether contrary to the practices common in lyric theater until now. But to me that seems a result more of the system's application than of the system itself. In the second act of [Verdi's] *Rigoletto* we have the duet between the jester and Sparafucile that, up to a certain point, might be regarded as composed according to the same artistic principle as that from which derives all the music of the *Nibelungi*. But in that passage the dialogue is enclosed within a melody measured after the old system. The artistic doctrine is the same, while the application is different.

I have endeavored to show that the inherent merits of the Wagnerian doctrine are: the perfect fusion of the music with the poetry; the prodigious clarity of the dramatic situations; the perfect painting of the setting in which the action is initiated. But it must be added that inherent defects of the doctrine are prolixity and monotony: the former resulting from the rejection of all the set-piece contrivances [*artificii*] that serve to diversify the vocal effects; the latter from the duration of the scenes, become necessary since, by the doctrine's very nature, they are dialogues played out in the same manner as in spoken tragedies. . . .

But, I repeat, the accusations made against the tetralogia—of being obscure, difficult, indecipherable—are false. I realize that those who went to the theater without knowing a word of German, without having familiarized themselves with the subject matter, and in all probability without following the performance with the Italian libretto—that such people have understood nothing. They have guaranteed that they would not understand and would be mortally bored, because the Wagnerian system is so much better appreciated when the tragedy being performed is understood. On the other hand, someone who speaks German, who has first absorbed the subject into his being and blood, will have experienced the fatigue that results from the drama's abstruseness, from the prolixity of the action, and from the crushing monotony of certain segments. But, of indecipherable music, obscure in its effects, he will have found little.

In his succeeding Part IV, published by *LV* on April 21 (this time on page 1), "Toni" moves on to consider how Wagner put his ideas into actual practice in the *Ring*.

The Wagnerian doctrine does not run counter to the immortal laws of beauty. Rather, it agrees with those very laws so much better than other doctrines that it approaches the perfectibility of musical drama. It is a basic fact that truth or reality in a musical drama can never actually happen because in real life no one functions while singing. It is a basic fact that the arts, in order to represent acts and ideas, utilize their own means: painting, of colors; sculpture, of marble; music, of sounds. But, the less there is of contrivance [*artificiosità*] in representing the action or the idea, the more there is of actuality, of truth in artistic conception. Naturalism in literature has its counterpart in the Wagnerian system in music.

The difficulty, says "Toni," is that Wagner applied his theories

. . . to a poem that is idealized, hazy, murky, abstruse, steeped in metaphysics—a poem from which, nevertheless, the German critics draw lofty ethical and historical reflections. We are certainly not Germans . . . in art we prefer passion, human passion, to the idealized and the abstractions of mythology. In art, we put the heart in first place, then the mind. We are more excitable, and we are more of the opinion that art elevates one to the high spheres. It would be possible to cite many thousand examples of melodramatic situations that are warm and effective and that have become popular, even though set in music without a scrap of originality, of refinement, of gravity.[11]

By contrast with "the northern peoples," says "Toni," the southern ones have "humanized" the old gods, divested them of mystery and recognized them as trivial or ridiculous.

The northern peoples, on the contrary, still perceive—as Pluto of [Offenbach's] *Orphée aux enfers* might say—the fragrance of mythology. The Germans are still enamored of Walhalla, the gods, the giants, the walkiries, of ancient Scandinavian myth. They preserve, perceive, love the traditions of their old and destroyed Olympus. They extol Wagner when on the stage he restores to life the heroes of the Middle Ages. They talked it up with greater fervor, and were even more laudatory, when he translated a poem of Scandinavian mythology into musical terms in the *Ring des Nibelungen*. They see in the poem the symbolic struggle between wealth and love, between the pagan world and the Christian world—the victory of love over wealth, of Christianity over paganism.[12] The subject, for them supremely idealized, takes on in music new emphases, new forms, new aspects, a new language. The musical tones convey so perfectly the love of the Walkiria, the crafty nature of Wothan, the slyness of Loge, the coarse grandeur of the giants. They give—if I might be allowed the expression—such clear snapshots of the physiognomy of the Nibelung rascals Alberic and Hagen, the heroes Sigmundo and Sigfredo, the good Gunther, the timorous and scornful Mime, the sweetly sinful Siglinde, that the more intelligent or more educated [Germans] go into raptures and proclaim the *Anello del Nibelungo* a national symphonic poem, saying even *Here is our Dante! our Shakespeare!*

For Italians, however, "Toni" says such idealized and mythic subject matter is only likely to invite condemnation or ridicule.

Nevertheless—such is the power of genius!—Wagner had the thousands upon thousands of spectators at the Fenice fastened to their seats through fifteen hours of beauty. Not even one of his fiercest opponents rose and reached for the door before the illustrious Seidl had put down his imperious baton. Not a single voice was raised in complaint against some ill-tuned singing of Sigfredo [i.e., Georg Unger!], of the Walkürie, of the daughters of the Rhine. Not one of those murmurs so likely in such a close, dense, uncomfortable crowd of people who, when bored, might disrupt the extended performance.

It has been reported that the success of the *Nibelungen* was a success of curiosity and nothing else. No! Curiosity was replaced by interest, and, at many points, by enthusiasm. And it was natural that this should have happened in Venice, where the audience is—as it should be—most intelligent, eclectic, discriminating.

Let us agree: to the inherent prolixity of the system is joined the poetic prolixity of Wagner. To set forth a dramatic situation that others would unfold in one quarter of an hour, he expends on it three [quarters]. Thus, the duration of certain scenes—duration that contributes a great part of the monotony to the totality—is overwhelming, distressing. Let us agree: in his desire that the orchestra express all details of the drama, at times it slips into the absurd, so ill-defined are the outlines of the situation or of the sentiment whose musical sculpting is intended. But: when the scene stays within the limits of the possible; when the music of the *Nibelungi* manages in its own ways to convey precisely the dramatic situation—anyone, then, who does not experience profound, unforgettable sensation should abandon hope of ever understanding serious manifestations of the art. He will never experience, as should be experienced, a symphony of Beethoven, the conspiracy scene of [Rossini's] *Guglielmo Tell*, the great finale of [Meyerbeer's] *Le Prophète*, the final scene of *Don Giovanni*, the incantation of *Der Freischütz*, the duet between Philip and the Inquisitor in [Verdi's] *Don Carlos*, the finale of [Bellini's] *Norma*. He will have cast out hearing from among his senses, and there will remain to him only what they vulgarly call "a little amusement." But his entire being [his *io*] will be unreceptive, weakened, disturbed; all the fibers of his body, all his spirit, will be unresponsive to an artistic event.

That Riccardo Wagner may be the orchestra's god; that he may know how to obtain, from the more difficult instrumental combinations, the most simple, brilliant, clear effects; that he may be master of sublime harmony, able to draw from his orchestral mass sounds never before imagined or thought possible—these all acknowledge, Wagnerites or Wagnerphobes. There is no need to become lost in examples. On the other hand, the Wagnerphobes insist that Wagner does not speak to the heart. I say that he does so speak, when the drama requires it: in the finale of *Walküre*, in the last act of *Götterdämmerung*; when Siglinda and Sigmundo, or when Brunilde and Siegfried show their love; when Brunilde sings *Greetings O Sun, greetings O light!* and exchanges a kiss with Siegfried; when Brunilde weeps over the corpse of her beloved. The lyricism in these situations is outstandingly melodic, but not coarse (since many confuse vulgarity with melodic facility); to it he weds a harmony of sounds in the orchestra so new, enchanting, electrifying that through the ears it grants

… a sweetness to the heart,
That he who does not experience it cannot understand
—and I do not venture to explain it.

Yet, in the *Anello del Nibelungo* there are not only major scenes of passion: there are also great symphonic paintings that describe other tragic situations and, especially, settings in which the tragedy comes to pass.

Aware that he has rambled, "Toni" jumps the next day, April 22, into his penultimate essay (Part V, though mislabeled as "IV"), which attempts to clarify

Wagnerian theory in operation. He begins by proposing a dichotomy between Rossini and Wagner:

> *Rossini*: Music is creative invention [*creatrice*] and not representational [*imitatrice*] art. It imitates only reality that itself generates sound. It should inspire laughter, tears, sadness, terror; it should not imitate laughter, tears, sighing, rage. Music is *ethical* atmosphere that fills the place where the action takes place; it therefore aspires to a goal more elevated, more expansive, more abstract than the words of the drama.
>
> *Wagner*: Music is essentially creative invention, but that does not prevent it from also being representational. Additionally, like painting and sculpture, the closer it comes the better it reproduces or imitates the truth; therefore it does not only imitate what normally produces sound, but, by means of sound, presents the likeness of the passions, of the sentiments that are being revealed in the drama. It *actually* laughs, weeps, rages, is dejected, is melancholy. So much the better, therefore, does it inspire in the hearer joy, sadness, melancholy, terror. The music is not merely the *ethical* atmosphere that occupies the place where the action itself takes place. Action and music thus constitute a robust, firm, untouchable totality—a statue sculpted from a bloc of granite.
>
> To see the two theories in application, let us take a complex dramatic situation: certain characters who would be differently affected by the same happening. We consider, that is, a conflict of emotions: in the old system, duets, trios, ensembles, finales.
>
> In such pieces the different passions motivating the characters ought to be—according to the Wagnerian doctrine—fully expressed, sculpted within the music. According to Rossinian doctrine, on the other hand, it would suffice that the musician should convey to the spectator the overall character of the action.[13]

"Toni" mentions some classic cases of traditionally rooted Italian composers (Rossini, Donizetti, Verdi) creating set-piece ensembles in which dramatic verity and musical inspiration were sublimely fused into coherent entities, while still allowing diverse expressions, even simultaneously. But such examples resulted "from the genius of the master rather than from the musical system." There were even many cases where the words were fitted to already-written music.

> In the *Anello del Nibelungo* we have instead a good many pieces in which—although, and even because, the characters sing one at a time and the orchestra sets forth or illustrates the dramatic situation—the different emotions of the characters, within the framework of the same piece, achieve musical expression of their diverse and even opposing personalities.
>
> Some examples: I indicate the pieces that have impressed me in particular.
>
> In the second act of *Rheingold* the giants, before releasing Freia to the gods, pile up in front of the goddess as much gold as would suffice to conceal her; and that requires all that the gods took from the Nibelung. The giants rejoice; Wothan is enraged, because he must yield the gold acquired through such cunning and effort; Fricka implores Wothan to agree, in order to recover her daughter [actually, her sister]. A complicated situation: but the music conveys clearly the tinkling of the heaped-up gold, the rage of Wothan, the anxiety of Fricka, the greed of the giants. And, when Freia is returned to the gods, a great hymn of joy rises from the orchestra.

In the first act of *Walkiria*, Sigmundo, welcomed into Hunding's house, tells him and his wife Siglinda his own history. Siglinda, who felt a deep sympathy for Sigmundo as soon as he entered the house, is deeply moved by the account of his misfortunes, and sympathy is changed into love, into that love to be expressed in the subsequent duet with such force of expression. Hunding, on the other hand, recognizes Sigmundo from the account as his enemy and plans to kill him. A complicated situation: but, while Sigmundo speaks and the others listen in silence, the music expresses precisely the narrator's experiences, Siglinda's love, Hunding's fury; and we are quickly given the feeling that such love and hatred will surely be fatal to those characters.

In the second act of *Siegfried*, that character has killed the dragon (Fafner) who guarded the cave of gold. Alberico and Mime are eager to possess that treasure but lack the courage to face the dragon's ragings in order to defeat it. Once that monster is a corpse, they come together from separate directions at the mouth of the cavern in order to enter it. Once there, the strong, bold Alberico becomes embroiled with the feeble and timid Mime: they insult each other, come to blows, one wanting to kill the other so as to become sole master of the field, until Siegfried returns and they flee. The situation seems simple; but it is not, considering the differing personalities of the two who compete for possession of the gold; the music expresses precisely the bold rage of Alberico and the abrupt anger of Mime, usually so crafty, but cowardly.

In the second act of *Götterdämmerung* is the most complicated scene of the tetralogy. The five characters are augmented by the chorus of Gunther's soldiers. Brunilde believes herself abandoned by her beloved Siegfried, who wishes to marry Gutruna because he has imbibed a magic potion that makes him forget the first woman and love the second. Siegfried, who does not remember the past, denies the betrayal. Gunther, who loves Brunilde, is distressed; Hagen, who has contrived that situation through his schemes, rejoices; and the warriors, at first merry over the wedding of the man to whose support they were pledged, are left in amazement, agitated, frightened. Here we do not have a finale with the usual elements [i.e., as in standard Italian opera]: a melodic statement of the soprano (Brunilde), the refrain of the motive on the part of the others, the final resolution with the chorus. Rather, the dialogue goes forward as in all dialogues: even the choral phrases are spoken; but the expression of the diverse sentiments is perfect, a framing of marvelous totality and effectiveness in its projection of all the characters. Thus, the German critics did not err in declaring that this scene, wherein the Wagnerian method is applied to a dramatic situation of such intricacy and difficulty, constitutes a masterpiece of musical drama.

I have pointed out four scenes in the tetralogy, one for each of the days of the cycle. But I could multiply the examples, omitting them so as not to bore the readers who, if they attended the performances, may transfer the analyses to other parts of the *Anello* to which they could be referred.

The descriptive power of physical phenomena: this diverges from the merits that even those more hostile to the Wagnerian system acknowledge to the *Nibelungen*. My distinguished colleague of the *Gazzetta*, with whom I do not agree in analytical judgment and general view of the work, did draw from his vocabulary warm words of admiration for the two acts of *Siegfried* that contain descriptions of the laboring at the forge and the forest onto which Fafner's cave opens. Join to those two acts the first part of the initial act of *Rheingold*, when we hear and see in the music the bottom of the Rhine; the *cavalcata delle walchirie*, through which we *see* orchestrally the horses mounting the scene; a storm, often and of differing character, but always presented so well in copying nature. And all this as achieved, not by means of crude or disconnected sounds, but in the unity of the orchestral and vocal painting, created in the brain cells of the master, like Minerva in the brain of Jove.

Now "Toni" is ready for "Part VI and last" on April 23, intended as a summation, and to be the longest of the essays. He begins by recalling Wagner's fear that the scope of his ambitious work might have precluded hope of ever seeing it performed. Such skepticism, our critic suggests, might even explain why the composer "may in some scenes have lost the measure of time" and even why he had "written vocal parts so taxing, so burdensome." So, how did it work out in the Neumann production?

The performance of the tetralogy that we heard at the Fenice was a model of perfection in orchestral terms; on the stage, only in some moments outstanding in vocal terms but mediocre for the rest; likewise mediocre was the scenic machinery.

Reading the libretto, I asked myself how certain tremendous difficulties of performance could ever be overcome: the daughters of the Rhine swimming in the middle of the river, the circle of fire surrounding Brunilde, the combat with the dragon, etc. In practice, I have observed that, with a little good will, for better or worse—and rather worse than better—it is a matter of aiming at intended effects, at least by way of approximation. The Neumann company's scenery, its stage mechanism, its (by now already aged) costumes, ought to have a drastic overhauling. But the audience was wise in not being fussy—in closing an eye (and even two) to some shabbiness of the scenic apparatus. The music should suffice, and it did suffice to mitigate all that.

No words are sufficient to praise the orchestra. Among the sticklers for precision may be reckoned the violins, the violas, the cellos, the contrabasses, the brass instruments one by one. You are not surprised by the absence of a bass drum, by the ceremonial trombones, by the four-string violone. I am concerned with the results: for I would not dream of giving lessons in orchestral organization. And the results, for the orchestra directed by sgr. Antonio Seidl—the young friend of Riccardo Wagner—are truly prodigious. The mathematical precision does not exclude sentiment and brilliance [*slancio*]. The individual merit of the players does not exclude—rather, it reinforces—the blending of the tones; individual instruments have disappeared. And it is from the union of the various tone colors that derives the truly orchestral color, something of the indefinable and of the indefinite: murmur, lament, laughter, pattering, roar, calm, storm—everything Wagner wants, Seidl understands and inspires in his players. Thanks to this solidarity of ensemble, the emergence of one featured instrument becomes the more prominent when it happens: few times have I *felt* such a unison of violins as what accompanied the reawakening of Brunilde, or a horn's blast like that which announced Siegfried.

As to vocal performance: superior and mediocre. Best among the women were Reicher, Bleiter, and Kraus; of the men, Schott and Lieban; Reicher and Schott *cantanti di forza*, Kraus and Lieban *di forza* and *di grazia*. The singer [Klavsky] who, after having been so forceful in the role of Siglinda, at the Marcello made me realize what a treasure of sentiment and delicacy she would be in the role of Elsa (*Lohengrin*). The singer [Lieban] who, having projected into the theater's air the piercing notes of Mime, sang at the Marcello the *Ungeduld* of Schubert, employing mezza voce with enchanting grace.

I leave the mediocre ones to their fate. I trust that—obliged by respect for music that I need hear no more than once, and at my choice of time—I will never again listen without protest to bad singing comparable to that of the Walkirie in the Cavalcata, or of sgr. Unger in the role of Siegfried.

It has been represented to me that the Wagner of the *Ring des Nibelungen* is abstruse, contorted, incomprehensible. And I have found him so simple, even so inexorable in his simplicity as to become, precisely for that reason, monotonous and diffuse in many pieces.

Those who, following Wagner, venture to write music of the future [*musica dell'avvenire*] actually offend present taste with their comparatively noxious dissonances, banging the timpani amid orchestral din. Well, I have found Wagner serene, calm, shunning any dissonance that does not produce harmony or any noise that aims merely at making an uproar. Some disciples insult their master.

I have been told that one must beware of this immigration into Italy of Wagnerian music, because it constitutes a powerful menace to Italian art. Even the pianist Pirani, an otherwise able and agreeable person, has written from Berlin to the *Riforma* and Crispi's journal[14] a few days before the immigration had reached Venice: "Be on alert! this is a crucial [*decisivo*] moment for national art." But I have too much enthusiasm for beauty, in whatever place I find it, to refuse to recognize it in the Wagnerian school just because it differs from that of our national school. On the contrary, I also believe that manifestations of the art, however divergent—even opposite in origins, in aims, in results—are entitled to the respect of public and critics; for, in this world there is some room for everything.

"Toni" then repeats some of his earlier assertions about the Wagnerian or "futuristic" ideals: that the theories must be distinguished from their application; that this system is hardly antithetical to traditional principles of beauty, and is less radical than many think; that, even if "at least for now, not easily digestible by the masses, it deserves to have, among those with intelligence, cultivation, and good taste, some passionate admirers and enthusiastic partisans." He then redraws his balance sheet for Wagnerian style:

> . . . Inherent virtues of the doctrine: the fusion in one total integration of poetry with music and of music with poetry; the all-but-realistic projection of the characters and of the dramatic situations; atmospheric painting. Inherent defects of the doctrine: the diffuseness produced by the length of the dialogues that go forward in developing an incident as in a tragedy (so much so that some have likened the *Anello del Nibelungo* to the tragedies of Sophocles and Aeschylus, with the difference, I would say, that in the Greek tragedy the chorus appears at particular times to illuminate the action while in Wagnerian opera the orchestra never ceases its illustrative function and rather is itself an integral part of the tragedy); the monotony resulting from the abandonment of the set-piece forms [*artificii*] that serve to make the vocal effects more varied.
>
> But as for the system's application:— A more human drama is captured—more lively, passionate, and universally comprehensible—than that which comes from Scandinavian mythology. Rather, the goal is to amplify the poetry by musical setting so that the audience would be interested not only in that setting but also in the poem. Brought to the scene is a greater expansion of melody, because Wagnerian doctrine does not in any way reject melody, the way it does reject vulgarity. In such application, the system's inherent defects can be corrected to the point of enhancing its merits even more.

There remains the question of influence on the taste of composers and public.
And here it is certain that the masterpieces of the Italian school are not at risk when confronted by this colossal score of the German school. It is a matter of two beautiful women. The one—thickly painted in vivacity, boldness, elegant coquetry—steals kisses and caresses. The other—severe in the purity of her contours, haughty, dignified in bearing, in her actions, in her attire—compels admiration, respect, and reverence. The first more easily bestows her favors and is intoxicated with herself. The other is slower to grant the delights of her austere beauty; yet, should she make you hers, you feel the joys of a love less intoxicating but more chaste and tenacious.

So, let us be careful. With the *Anello de Nibelungo* the call has been made to sound the trumpet blast of revolution. It is the voice that was raised already by Marcello in sacred music; by Gluk, Weber, Rossini, and Verdi in the lyric theater; by Beethoven in the symphony. It does not belong to one nation, to one school, to one individual, but to that great benefactress of humanity—ART.
Toni

Thus, then, did our two critics respond to the challenge of Wagner and his *Ring*. If diffuse, dated, hardly authoritative as analyses by now, their essays are worth making accessible at last in such fullness, as windows into what it was like for Italians to begin coming to terms with so significant a foreign cultural phenomenon at a time of tenuous transition in their own musical life. Again, it is difficult for us today to realize what difficulty faced Italians of a century-and-a-quarter past in confronting so complex an idiom as that of Wagner, so vastly different in so many ways from that to which their culture had conditioned them.

When one comes down to basics, of course, both of our critics understand their task quite simply as the explication of the "new" Wagnerian style vis-à-vis the familiar Italian traditions. For the critic of *LGdV*, that is a relatively simple matter: while many things can be admired in Wagner's tetralogy, as it stands, it ultimately falls short of the principles of Italian taste and traditions—which are regarded as unquestionably superior (because, of course, they are "ours"). By contrast, "Toni" is more open-minded and positive, asserting that the "new" Wagnerian style and the traditional Italian style are different, but not necessarily competitive, and that Italians can still cherish the latter even while also understanding and appreciating the former. Each writer makes comments that still have validity today, though obviously "Toni" is so much more extensive in his explication—in essays that can still be read with some profit by someone today seeking introduction to Wagner's musical language.

Yet, especially within "Toni's" extended commentary, one is struck by the total absence of a subject now deemed central to understanding Wagner's operas, and especially those of the *Ring*: the matter of the *Leitmotiven*. Each writer appreciates just how important the orchestra is to Wagnerian style. But neither of them recognizes the body of musical tags and motives Wagner weaves into his scores, and develops, with a significance that has long seemed to represent the key to understanding the progress of dramatic action and characterization. Absence of this element is particularly striking in the case of "Toni," who, in his explanation of the orchestral role, understands very well its vivid pictorial and descriptive qualities but seems little conscious of thematic recurrence as a compositional and dramatic device.

Identification of recurrent motives and their use in composition, explicitly with regard to Wagner, goes back as early as 1860. Wagner himself was cautious about discussing leitmotifs in his work, fearing that preoccupation with them would lead to oversimplification in understanding his works. He never used the now-familiar term for them, but referred only to "musical symbols." But he did sanction reluctantly the first systematic guide to the recurrent themes in the *Ring* cycle. That was written by his enthusiastic partisan, Hans von Wolzogen, and published in 1876 in conjunction with the first Bayreuth performance of the whole tetralogy. There continued to be lively discussion of Wagner's idiom of leitmotifs in the following years, so it would have been possible for our critics to have been acquainted with this matter. But virtually all of the published discussions were still in German, and one has the sense that neither of our critics was conversant with that tongue.[15]

Accordingly, even the extensive and perceptive analyses by "Toni" would appear gravely inadequate from the standpoint of the present-day understanding of Wagner. On the other hand, the fact that our two critics are unaware of, or pay no attention to, the matter of the leitmotifs may be of interest in itself, in showing the different perspectives of those first approaching Wagner's music when it was still new and controversial. Is that difference merely a shortcoming on their part, or does it suggest that perhaps, after more than a century, we ourselves have become disproportionately fixated on Wagner's use of leitmotifs as the key to understanding his operas?

As we have this rare chance to encounter in bulk the first reactions of one set of Italian professional critics to Wagner's tetralogy, one more question naturally comes to mind: did they look at any of the scores?

They were certainly acquainted with at least some (if not all) of Wagner's operas, and knew a good bit of the critical and polemic literature of the day. Neither of them, however, had apparently previously heard the four *Ring* operas, at least in full. How did they prepare for their encounters with them, and particularly with the Neumann performances? Certainly by reading the libretti in advance—if in Italian translations. The scores themselves were theoretically available: the four *Ring* operas had been published in full orchestral scores in Mainz in the successive years of 1873–76; one assumes they might well have been available in Italy through the Lucca agency. But in all of their preliminary articles, their reviews, and their analyses, our two critics give the impression that—beyond hearsay and libretto study—everything they learned of Wagner's actual music came essentially from hearing it, from experiencing it in the theater or concert hall, rather than from studying the printed page. In this respect, we may contrast them with the eminent Viennese critic of the day, Eduard Hanslick (1825–1904), who would do exhaustive research before many of his review assignments, usually taking pains to look in advance at the appropriate scores. His reputation as Wagner's implacable enemy has been grossly exaggerated, and his perceptive, penetrating, sometimes positive, but often caustic comments on the *Ring* at the first Bayreuth Festival in 1876 make interesting reading as a foil to what our two Venetian critics would write.[16]

Now, consideration of how the two critics of *LV* and *LGdV* treated the *Ring* production of April 1883 does not yet exhaust the Venetian response of that year to the Neumann Company's visit. It is, in fact, altogether apt to examine at this point parts of Giuseppe Norlenghi's memoir of Wagner in Venice. We have already examined the bulk of that little book in chapter 8, but it included sections whose discussion have been deferred until now.[17]

As has been seen, Norlenghi devoted most of his book to biographical and anecdotal reporting, predominantly as related to Wagner's final residence in Venice, through his death there. But Norlenghi's broad purpose was to introduce Wagner, his life, and his music to an Italian public still only dimly aware of or sympathetic to such things. In the introduction to the book, Norlenghi made clear that he expected to go beyond biographical matters and to plunge honestly and frankly into artistic controversies:

> When the occasion has arisen to speak of Italian art, I have written, frankly and loyally, that which I do think as to the genuine dangers that are menacing it, and I have attempted to depict quickly the wretched situation in which, to its damage, it flounders. (ix–x)

Norlenghi states from the outset that he writes as a modest amateur and an humble admirer. But he was clearly a committed Wagnerian, writing with proselytizing goals. Though clearly knowledgeable musically, he was writing not as a critic in professional terms, but as an advocate. In that respect, he is obviously different from the two Venetian critics already discussed. Yet, focused on the Venetian scene, Norlenghi is responding not only to Wagner's death but to the then-recent appearance of Neumann's *Ring* production just thereafter. He clearly makes reference to that landmark event in Italy's confrontation with Wagner's music, and he could assume it was still likely to be fresh in the minds of many of his readers. Indeed, Norlenghi does not hesitate to make his own assessment of the Neumann productions, and even of the Venetian critics who reviewed it. To that extent, his extended comments deserve bracketing with those of our Venetian critics, especially "Toni." At the same time, however, they provide a broader picture of the Italian pro-Wagner context within which our two critics were reacting.

As we have seen, in his first chapter ("L'uomo e l'artista"), Norlenghi combined a biographical sketch with a tracing of Wagner's initial operatic output, stressing the idea that the composer's life and works were part of an indivisible unity. That led him naturally in his second chapter, "La missione e l'ideale di

Wagner" ("The Mission and Ideals of Wagner"), to take up Wagner's artistic goals.

Norlenghi first attempts to clarify just how Wagner's "revolution" and "reform" in opera should be understood—initially as deriving from his admiration for ancient Greek theater, but truly intelligible only in the broad history of the operatic form. Of that Norlenghi attempts to give an overview. He traces it quickly from Monteverdi (noting some of his operatic work in Venice) through Peri, Lully, Alessandro Scarlatti, Hasse, Jomelli, Bertoni, and Pergolesi: for all its high points, the form's confining features carrying within them the seeds of oncoming "decadence." In what would become (as we have already seen) the conventional litany, Gluck is singled out as the exemplar in reforming opera, with such contemporaries as Mozart, Cimarosa, and Paisiello assisting in making the connection between *classicismo* and *romanticismo*. Opera entered a new epoch with Rossini, his work rounded out by "the most-sweet Bellini, by "the dramatist" Donizetti, and by "the powerful colorist" Verdi, with the German Weber and the internationalist Spontini making their contributions.

> But the decadence advanced at a brisk pace, however concealed under a splendid appearance of vitality.
> And the reason for it was evident. The same forces that brought about the death of "classic" opera in the 1700s, were killing remodernized opera. Conventionalism, virtuosity, and the lack of lofty artistic intent, prevailed anew, and were so much the more dangerous as they were the more brilliantly and openly made evident. (52)

While Rossini's valedictory *Guglielmo Tell* had hinted at what might come, it was left to Wagner, working through his series of masterpieces, to bring opera to its new levels of beauty, dramatic power, and lofty artistic idealism.

> In the highest regions of thought, national boundaries disappear, humanity remains. Homer, Dante, Shakespeare, Goethe were creative for the whole of humanity, and they were the great beacons of human thought.
> Thus Wagner; and, beside Homer, Dante, Shakespeare, and Dante, grateful humanity will one day place Wagner on the Olympus of the immortals. (58)

In his third chapter, "Il musicista ed il pubblico" (The Musician and His Public), Norlenghi addresses himself at length to defining the stylistic characteristics of Wagner's art. As his prime case study, he turns to *I maestri cantori di Norimberga* (*Die Meistersinger von Nürnberg*) as "the most complete, the most original" of Wagner's operas. He surveys its plot and characters, observing that the setting is a lively new urban world of craftsmen and artists, opposed to the dying social order of feudalism, but also struggling to replace decadent older art with new and vital creativity. The focus of the combat was, Norlenghi asserts, the *tabulatura*, the code of rules by which the comically ominous Beckmesser operates, as opponent to the wise Hans Sachs and to the boldly innovative Walther von

Stolzing. It was that stifling *tabulatura* that the truly creative spirits of music struggled against—Palestrina, Pergolesi, J. S. Bach, Rossini, Schubert, Bellini, Donizetti, Mozart, Verdi, and, above all, Beethoven.

Norlenghi identifies the accusations Wagner faced from a new crop of ignorant critics and mediocre singers—indeed, he makes a snide pun against the title of his exemplary Wagner opera, calling the self-occupied vocalists who resented Wagner the self-appointed "Master Singers" (in capital initials but without italics). Their accusations charged Wagner with unwillingness to accommodate singers in traditional terms, and with a fatal lack of melody. Wagner's struggles against such reactionary bitterness were thus perfectly represented in *Die Meistersinger*, a struggle to go beyond captious critics and convince the public. He was one of those figures, like Monteverdi, Lully, and Gluck, who was destined to come upon the artistic scene with the courage to set lyric drama on its true course. This was a course in which music was not a distraction from drama but was to reenforce the drama, to illuminate the characters, and to clarify the meanings. Relentlessly conventional character types and voice-range associations generated obligatory musical forms and functions with stifling inertia.

> . . . Inspiration, truth, expression, drama, all that was in second place, while in the first, the solo, the ensemble, the finale. The orchestra accompanied and did no more, and was unable to indulge its whims save in the overture. And the public, long habituated to these forms, wanted opera in its turn always the same way. Woe to the reformer, woe to the innovator, who would not have had the strength and the power to make his own mark in that way.
>
> And composers always were obliged to find new variations on that format, in order to interest the public that was greedy for novelty and for music longed for and exciting. They racked their brains to create new melodies, ingeniously contrapuntal ensembles, finales developed along grandiose lines. It was a desperate course for one who achieved the first goal, to excite that decayed, perverted, and sensually overrefined taste; it was a last-ditch struggle for one who has come up with the tidbit more spicy, more cleverly seasoned, to suit that decayed, sick taste.
>
> And so it is in Italy, and everywhere. And currently it finds its vogue in France particularly in that historical *grand opera*, a semi-choreographic spectacle, of grandiose but often baroque proportions.
>
> On the contrary, how much simplicity, how much poetry, how much expression, and at the same time how much true drama is there in the Wagnerian concept. (86–88)

To show just how successfully Wagner has replaced the old conventions with revitalized creations, Norlenghi surveys the individual operas and points out some of their characters, stressing the musical function.

> The music follows the drama; and, I would say, it does not interrupt at certain points, so as to allow time for the audience to offer a little applause, so as to allow opportunity for the performer to take a quick bow; it moves forward, just as the drama moves

forward, always in conjunction with it, always subordinate to its requirements, but, precisely for that reason, always full of expression, of truth, of charm. (90)

Wagner thus uses the overture, not as entertainment, but as preparation for moods and characters in the drama to come.

And in this regard, hardly ever found in his musical drama, from one segment to another, is tonic resolution that would constitute a stopping-point; rather, the segments are always connected to each other, up to the end of the scene in which the drama has halted. (90–91)

This quality has helped delay immediate popularity for Wagner's operas, but it demonstrates his courage in rejecting chances for quick acclaim,

. . . out of respect, out of integrity, out of homage to art. *Ars severa* [the strict art] has certainly never had a priest more devout than Wagner.
  For those accustomed to this new form of musical drama (and the process of introduction to it is itself something interesting), how many rewards, how many full satisfactions are obtained! It is a delicious voyage into pure, ethereal, voluptuous, lofty regions, it is a voyage into a country of sweet illusions, it is oblivion, it is happiness.— Oh how superior is this music of Wagner to all that made with the sole aim of amusement. (91)

Norlenghi once more contests the accusation that Wagner's music is not melodic. He compares Wagner's melodic achievements with those of other composers, including Gounod, Meyerbeer, Weber, and Rossini. As for the French, Norlenghi pays particular tribute to the greater originality and picturesqueness of "the genial music of *Carmen* of that Bizet, so immaturely enraptured with art, with glory." He compares *Lohengrin* to Gounod's *Faust* and, while granting respect to Gounod's lyric gifts in his operas and songs, Norlenghi must rate that composer's *Faust* as much beneath Goethe's grand poetic conception, even while indebted to Wagnerian style.

This pronouncement leads him to a recollection of a contact that Norlenghi had with the conductor of Angelo Neumann's *Ring* production in Venice the previous April.

I remember that, one evening in discussing this issue with the distinguished Anton Seidl when he was in Venice to conducting the Tetralogy, I expressed to him a certain surprise that Wagner had not been enticed by that colossal, radiant poem of Wolfgango Goethe, and had not prepared himself to set it to music, for which he was certainly not lacking the means and the powers. But Seidl answered me (in a language four-fifths German and the rest Italian), that, if four evenings were required for the *Anello del Nibelunge*, for *Faust* perhaps not even ten would suffice.
  Indeed that is true; and too great was Wagner's artistic conscience for him to think of reducing Goethe's *Faust* to a single little stage opera. (95)

This recollection prompts Norlenghi to reflect on Wagner's harsh treatment in Paris with the *Tannhäuser* fiasco there in 1861. But, if the French were too conservative to recognize his genius, there were more receptive ears elsewhere.

> . . . Bravo our Italy, a hospitable and artistic land, despite a few frogs croaking at the sun, bravo our Italy, that has given such a splendid, such an intelligent reception to the new art. Bravo Italy, under whose lovely sky Giuseppe Verdi, accepting the new ideas, has given us in his *Aida* something shining with color, with passion, with idealism. And, for all that, remaining himself: Verdi, original, holding high his great individuality, waving gloriously the Italian artistic banner. (97–98)

Norlenghi addresses anew, and more intensively, the question of Wagner as a gifted melodist. He stresses what Wagner has added to his most illustrious predecessors:

> Wagner represents a virtually total innovation. He joins the freshness of Mozart to the sweetness of Bellini, to the richness and magnificence in development of Beethoven. His melody is of an amplitude, of a magnificence, of a distinctiveness totally his own. (99)

As reinforced and interwoven by the orchestra, Wagner's melody serves the words, and conveys a range of emotions, moods, or images. It is part of a lofty art, and Norlenghi warns that it is an art not to be judged on quick encounter, but one that requires the same patient absorption and assimilation as are needed for the appreciation of paintings, sculptures, and other art works. He goes on to discuss the composer's distinctive use of harmony and tonality, and of various compositional techniques, culminating in "the extraordinary, Beethoven-like orchestral power of Wagner." He then confronts the accusation that this power provokes:

> It is said, "Wagner is a marvelous orchestrator, but he is so poor in imagination; he might end up being an eminent symphonist, but he lacks theatricality!" (111)

To counter that latest reactionary canard, Norlenghi quickly surveys the lively dissemination of his successive operas, culminating in his housing of his "new musical language" in his own theater at Bayreuth. Viewing the spread of Wagner performances internationally, Norlenghi understandably begins with the recent tour by Angelo Neumann's production—of which he seems to have had a low opinion.

> In Italy the Tetralogy—mutilated at many points, even essential ones, sung in a language that few know, within a performance (save for that by the orchestra and in some of the main roles) quite impossible, with a hasty and mediocre stage setting—engrossed and totally absorbed the attention of a diffident and badly disposed public, and made a triumphal progress, from Venice to Rome, from Bologna to Trieste, leaving in everyone

the desire to hear again this significant masterpiece. Wagner lacks theatricality? And how is it that his operas stir enthusiasm in all Europe; that England (which one loves to call anti-artistic while on the contrary it is particularly devoted to the art of music, and passionate about culture) hailed Wagner as a god; that free America wanted Wagner to create the grand inaugural march for its great festival of labor at Philadelphia,[18] and wanted from Wagner himself the written story of his life? It is true that in France they wanted none of it from *Tannhäuser* onward, but are not the French famous for their exclusiveness? So much the worse for them if they don't want it. Then too, the world is not Paris, even if Paris is France. *Rienzi, Tannhäuser, Vascello Fantasma, Lohengrin* in particular—are they not very popular by now in Italy? did they not always have an enthusiastic reception? (113–14)

The case of Milan, Norlenghi admits, is special. It rejected *Lohengrin* just as it did Boïto's *Mefistofele* ("one of the more beautiful operas that the younger Italian school has given us in recent years"). Just as Milan gave the gifted Boïto's opera a second and more favorable hearing,[19] so too, Norlenghi is confident, it will do for *Lohengrin,*

> . . . just as it doubtless would have heard the Tetralogy with religious respect, if special circumstances, or exaggerated fears, had not blocked its performance.[20] (115)

In the end, Norlenghi concludes, the false "Master Singers" and their rule book (*tabulatura*) have resisted in vain. Just as the Nurembergers came around to acclaiming Walter von Stolzing, so the musical public has learned enthusiasm for Wagner's "new revelation": *Die Meistersinger* is a microcosm of Wagner's own artistic triumph. And the opponents of innovation who have been deploring him will come to include Wagner himself among the hallowed masters to be set in opposition to subsequent innovators.

In his fourth chapter, "Wagner e l'arte italiana," Norlenghi makes a final assault upon anti-Wagnerism by focusing on the objections his own Italian countrymen have been raising, above all the idea that "Wagner is a danger to Italian art." According to them

> . . . It is his fault if inspired composers do not emerge in Italy; woe betide if the music of Wagner, if the *Anello del Nibelunge* becomes the fashion in Italy; Italy and Italian art will be ruined. (119)

Norlenghi specifically cites the Italian pianist in Berlin

> who perceived the need to save the motherland and telegraphed to a journal in Rome. "If *L'Anello del Nibelunge* comes to be given in Italy, watch out for Italian art, it stands in the greatest danger." (120)[21]

Norlenghi even cites Verdi's assurance: "the music of the future does not frighten me" (119). Italians who have just been impressed by Wagner's *Ring* are

hardly unpatriotic for being so. Norlenghi rails at those who think Italian musical art is in a feeble state. At the same time, he traduces those who try to isolate
Italian taste, enslaving it to an artificial chauvinism defined solely by great Italian
masters (Palestrina, Pergolesi, Marcello, Scarlatti)—those same critics who
argue that Italians alone have created a sublime idiom of harmony and melody,
those who worship Rossini, Bellini, Donizetti, and Verdi only to exclude the
"threat" of a Wagner.

He likewise mocks those *italianissimi* (super-Italians) who are really pseudo-
Italians—who really care little for Italian art, and mimic a cosmopolitan attraction to works of bad taste (e.g., the operettas of Offenbach and Suppé). For
them, Wagner is simply a fashionable *sensation* whom they do not understand,
while simultaneously failing to understand their own tradition, and not encour-
aging the best of Italian creativity. He rails at those who profess enthusiasm for
Wagner without understanding him, at those who, claiming an Italian love for
melody and expressiveness, cannot recognize it in Wagner. They are the ones
who are excited only by the cheap displays of vocal idols, whereas the true possibilities of the human voice are realized only in great music. ("Singers are made
for music, not music for the singers"—an epigram that could generate lively
debate even now!). Norlenghi's point is, Wagner is not for the superficial
listener.

The recent Neumann tour of the *Ring* production had allowed only single
hearings of the work, and that raises for Norlenghi the question of how Italians
can assess so complex a work. How and where are repeated hearings to be
had?—abroad or at home? Can local musicians and theaters accommodate it?
And what about critics who give their judgments after just one hearing?—as had
just been the case in Venice. He cites Wagner expert Filippo Filippi as to the
number of hearings and the degree of intensive study required to make sound
judgments—"But, or course, these are absurd scruples for such infallible ones.
Ah, the blessed pride of certain people" (132).

Many of those hasty judgments have simply been made so as to poison the
public against Wagner, says Norlenghi. They plant anxieties about a Wagnerian
inroad into Italy, about the corruption that Wagner's music will bring to Italian
music, about supposed incompatibilities between Italian and German tastes and
repertoires. But Italian audiences are capable of confronting and appreciating
the works of great German composers (Weber, Wagner).

Norlenghi adds an extra-Wagnerian sermon. He wishes that critics and journalists might apply themselves more constructively to advancing Italian musical
tastes and interests. The government might recognize better that the access to
painting, sculpture, and other arts could be facilitated. More fundamentally,
music conservatories should be reformed and music education more liberalized.
Now constrained by false economizing, theaters should be open more regularly,
so that singers and players will not leave the country but will have full employment. The quality of repertoires should be improved, and critics should become

more responsible and should contribute to the elevation of Italian art. That should be the goal of cultural patriotism, not simply the salvation of Italian art from Wagner. Italian musical life is in an artistic depression, but it is not to be rescued by the *wagnerofobi*, who prefer a cultural *protezionismo* to the promotion of creative thought.

> Oh the fine respect, the fine faith, that *these saviors* have, after all, in Italian art, if they represent it as an impoverished, dying art, abandoned by all, for which the terrible name alone of Wagner would suffice to make it gasp its final breath!
>
> Ah no, fortunately. While they are afraid, Italian art is not yet at that point, and laughs at their anxieties.
>
> Is not Giuseppe Verdi in Italy? Are there not then Boïto, and Ponchielli, and so many willing and able to hold the banner high?
>
> Is there not perhaps still a band of young talents ready to assemble?
>
> Italian art is still full of vitality, despite the wretched, mean, miserable surroundings that they have made for it, poor art.
>
> To what heights, to what boldness might it yet reach if in Italy it were desired and attempted to rouse the public from apathy, from indifference, regarding all that it thinks is art!
>
> Let there be less soul searching, less intellect, less rhetoric, and more enlightened love for art; fewer appeals to sensation, fewer saviors from the coffee shops, and more sincerity; more breadth of ideas, and, above, all fewer shabby economies—and then Italian art will revive as magnificent and bold, for which it certainly does not lack the powers.
>
> In Italy, everything invites one to high artistic pleasures: the blue sky, dazzling nature, the sweet language that *is* music. And once art was everything.
>
> Wake up, Italy, from that guilty sluggishness, from that demoralizing indifference, and return to that worship of music, the most perfect of the arts—not to a superficial or shallow worship, but to one sincere, lofty, and reverent. And then Italian art will rise again to the heights of its glorious traditions. Then, too, it will be impossible for anyone to oppose Wagner with exclusionist and restrictive arguments—Wagner, such a genius who, as the illustrious Filippi has written, dominates our century, and from whose influence no one among contemporary composers has been able to escape.
>
> Such is the wish of good men. (138–40)

And so Norlenghi ends his fourth chapter, and his set of preachments. His little book is a fascinating work but its three chapters of pro-Wagnerian propaganda are particularly interesting as expressions of what earnest Italian *wagnerismo* was like when the *Ring* came to Venice.[22] His ideas even have some familiar reverberations today. Let it suffice here to note again how the figure of Verdi fits into Norlenghi's perspective. He is, it would seem, far less cautious about Verdi than the two Venetian newspaper critics. All three of them remind us that in 1883, however they admired or were fascinated by Verdi, Italians regarded him not as in the simple continuer of the Rossini–Donizetti–Bellini line of the comfortable bel canto, but as their "modern" composer: connected to the past and not opposed to it, but still someone new. For Norlenghi, Verdi's identification with new ideas in music and lyric theater is very much a Good Thing. Thus, for Norlenghi the existence of Verdi as an Italian representative of "progressivism" confirms that admiration for Wagner's "progressivism" by Italians is hardly unpatriotic.

Angelo Neumann could have had no idea of the cultural hornet's nest he was helping to stir up when he went to Venice.

Part 4

Wagner and Venice Amalgamate

Chapter Thirteen

Memory and Commemoration

If Wagner had not died in Venice, he would have registered in the city's annals as one of many notable visitors, but little more. His death there, however, quite transformed the connection of composer and city.

Over the years, even centuries, Venice has been the residence (transient or permanent) for multitudes of people, distinguished or otherwise. It is curious, however, that few foreign visitors or residents of truly great fame have died there. The poets Robert Browning (1899) and Ezra Pound (1972) are among the scant examples—the latter buried in Venice (in a much-visited grave in the Municipal Cemetery of San Michele), the former not. To them, some admirers would add the name of the eccentric Anglo-Catholic writer, Frederick Rolfe, self-styled "Baron Corvo," who died in poverty in Venice (1913) and is stowed in a *colombaia* in the San Michele Cemetery. The flamboyant American patroness of art, Peggy Guggenheim (1979), arranged for her ashes to be interred in the garden of her famous museum on the Grand Canal. Among composers, Wagner is exceptional.[1] He stands out even more uniquely in the degree to which Venice took him posthumously to its bosom. A few plaques for the others, but enduring memory and potent memorials for Wagner.[2]

There are, of course, several layers to this prolonged story. Wagner the composer remained controversial in Venice and all Italy, used as a symbol still by Italian avant-gardists.[3] But his very death became woven into the imagery of Venice itself as a symbol of decay and decadence.[4] At the same time, especially beyond Venice itself, Wagner's death became the subject for remarkably lively development in fiction. That is a story in itself, which is to be addressed in a separate study. Our concern here, however, is specifically how Venice itself treated Wagner's memory.

In the years immediately following Wagner's death, the picture is slow to develop.[5] Full performances of Wagner's operas materialized only haltingly throughout Italy. In Venice itself, before Neumann's *Ring* cycle in 1883, there had been local presentations only of *Rienzi* (1874: the Italian premiere, sung in Italian) and *Lohengrin* (1882: likewise in Italian). Subsequently, *Tannhäuser* was given in 1887, and not again until 1900, nor thereafter until 1914—in all cases, in Italian. *Lohengrin*, overwhelmingly the most familiar of the Wagner operas in Italy, was revived in 1889, and again in 1898, 1906, 1911, and 1912—in all cases in Italian. 1899 saw productions of *Die Walküre* alone (revived in 1909) and *Die Meistersinger* (its first time in Venice), both in Italian. *Tristan* was not mounted until 1909, likewise in Italian. *Das Rheingold* and *Götterdämmerung* individually were presented in 1912 and 1913, while *Parsifal* could appear only as one of five productions mounted in Italy (in Italian) once the opera had been wrenched from the Bayreuth. (Venice would not see the complete *Ring* again until 1957, and then again in 1968, both times German by then; but not until 1961 would *Der fliegende Holländer* reach the Venetian stage; likewise in German.)[6]

But there are other musical indicators of Venice's attention to Wagner. Central among these are the outdoor band concerts that were a regular feature of Venetian cultural life—as elsewhere in Italian cities and towns. These were given around the calendar, several times a week, usually in the evenings in warm weather, moved to afternoons in colder seasons; usually in the Piazza San Marco, though sometimes on the Riva degli Schiavoni, in the Giardini Pubblici, or in other locations. The core group was the Banda Cittadina, or Municipal Band, maintained out of civic funds. As time passed, other local bands were added, those named for Bellini and Manin, plus the band of the Istituto Coletti. There could also be the military bands of one or more locally stationed army regiments. By the early years of the new century, there were as many as five bands operating at the same time. But their frequencies of performance varied, and the Banda Cittadina was the anchor and mainstay.

The repertoires of these bands stressed light and entertaining pieces, but could venture into more "serious" territory. Using special band arrangements, they balanced composers of established popularity against current ones who had caught public attention, primarily the latest Italian opera masters. These band concerts were thus an important medium not only of entertainment but of educating their audiences, however cautiously, and helping to popularize some new music. Their repertoires are therefore both an index to public tastes of the day and a clue to the progress of the latest music.

The key figure in all this for Venice was Jacopo Calascione, Sicilian-born director of the Banda Cittadina.[7] He will be remembered as the bandmaster who had some personal contacts with Wagner himself and had even been given praise and advice, on two occasions in 1882. At least by then, Calascione had developed an interest in Wagner's music, as witness a *Grand pot-pourri* of music from *Lohengrin* that Calascione arranged and gave a spectacular first performance in the Piazza on April 30, 1882.[8] He soon prepared a band adaptation of the Overture to *Rienzi*. Over the years, he included these in his concert programs, at first cautiously, but gradually adding the *Tannhäuser* Overture—or, alternatively, a *Gran pezzo concertato* on that opera.

The first anniversary of Wagner's death drew some recognition in Venice. The Benedetto Marcello Liceo held a commemorative event, which was recorded on February 13, 1884, by *La Gazzetta di Venezia* (*LGdV*). But it is not clear that Calascione undertook anything special. For some time our band leader seems to have paid no attention to the anniversaries of Wagner's death, even though his commitment to Wagner's music was becoming more concentrated. Then, on Friday February 13, 1891, Calascione devoted his afternoon Piazza concert to an all-Wagner program: several pieces from *Tannhäuser*; the *Rienzi* Overture; two items from *Lohengrin*, including Calascione's *Gran pezzo concertato* from that opera; and the Funeral March from *Götterdämmerung*. This last piece, played for the first time, was repeated by audience demand. The entire concert—apparently Calascione's first all-Wagner program—was announced as one of two offerings "in commemorazione di Riccardo Wagner." The other was a chamber-scale concert of Wagner's music that evening at the Liceo Benedetto Marcello, built around a lecture on the composer and his ideas.[9]

February 13, 1891, was a landmark in Calascione's commitment to Wagner. From this point on, an anniversary concert to commemorate Wagner's death became an established tradition. Between those annual events, Calascione also gradually expanded his Wagner repertoire, and his programming of it. The momentum, thus established, assumed new relevance with the tenth anniversary in 1893. On February 13 of that year Calascione offered his "Commorazione Wagneriana," containing seven of his arrangements, by now firmly anchored around the *Götterdämmerung* march.[10] Wagner pieces appeared with increased regularity in Calascione's concerts through 1893. Moreover, at least two other concerts given in Venice that year included Wagner works: the Marcello Conservatory Orchestra included the *Parsifal* "Good Friday Music" (March 5); and, in the second concert by the newly formed Società Filarmonica di Giuseppe Verdi (May 14), the *Siegfried Idyll* was played. Venice seems to have developed a more Wagner-friendly atmosphere, with the tenth anniversary as perhaps a specific stimulus to its emergence. To be sure, there was opposition. At the time of the bandmaster's death, a memorial article noted that "Wagner was his idol" and added: "This idolatry sometimes even cost him [Calascione] some ridicule, certainly undeserved."[11]

Calascione was apparently undeterred by any such hostility, continuing to expand his attention to Wagner, amid the leadership he was displaying generally in the introduction of newer generations of composers, foreign and domestic. With his Wagner repertoire still growing, Calascione could include among the six items for his anniversary concert on February 13, 1901, new versions of music from *Lohengrin*, *Tristan*, and *Parsifal*, as well as the "Magic Fire Music" and the "Ride of the Valkyries" (*Cavalcata*) from *Die Walküre*, with the *Götterdämmerung* Funeral March now established as the indispensable memorial gesture.

Calascione's advancing Wagner agenda was furthered by the emergence of the famous art exposition, the Biennale, held in Venice every spring and summer in odd-numbered years—events that specifically attracted visitors from around the world to augment the regular audience of locals and tourists. Calascione's band concerts (both in the Piazza and at the Exposition grounds in the Giardini Pubblici) became regular components of the *Esposizioni*, several afternoons or evenings each week. Many of these concerts were devoted to music of a single composer, and there would be at least one all-Wagner program each year. Nevertheless, the annual February 13 Wagner concert in the Piazza, clearly offered for the local audience, was Calascione's distinctive contribution to Venice's musical life and to the memorialization of Wagner in that city.

Though he was clearly the founder of the event, he was soon joined by an important collaborator. The Princesse Edmond de Polignac (1865–1943)— born Winnaretta Singer, and wealthy heiress to her father, the inventor of the Singer sewing machine—was one of the great cultural patrons during the first half of the twentieth century.[12] She and her husband were passionate admirers of Wagner's music, and were even friends of his family. In 1900 they had bought a palazzo on the Grand Canal with plans to make it a part-time residence, among the many other wealthy expatriates of Venice's international community. When the Prince died shortly thereafter (August 1901), she decided to create a memorial in his honor—and thereby, perhaps, to make her splashy entry into Venice's cultural and social whirl. By the beginning of 1902 she offered to create an endowment, involving a considerable sum for the time, and named for her late husband. This would guarantee "a perpetual realization" of the annual commemoration of Wagner's death each February 13 by the Banda Cittadina. It was stipulated that the band would play selections from Wagner's operas, and specifically the Funeral March from *Götterdämmerung*. Finally, thanks to the Princesse's contacts in Venice's high society, she had arranged that the concert's venue would be transferred from the Piazza to no less than the Palazzo Vendramin, the very building where Wagner had died. This proposal was submitted to Venice's city council and accepted.[13]

The arrangement was probably timed deliberately to accommodate the immediately impending February 13. And its prospect provoked a new Wagner-consciousness. On the very anniversary day itself, *LGdV* devoted a long article on the festivities to come that day, using the nineteenth anniversary of Wagner's demise to take stock—for Venetians and others who might have needed reminding—of how deeply Wagner's associations with Venice had taken root. The city was the site of the great Bayreuth master's last days and death, after which the greatness of his life and work achieved ever more triumphant recognition. Of that final connection Venice had cherished the memory, promptly mounting a commemorative marker on the Vendramin's land-gate wall in his honor.[14] Further, we are informed, a bust of the composer had been set up in the lobby of the Teatro La Fenice and it was adorned with a laurel crown each year on the anniversary of his death. Fired by such evidence of the Wagner–Venice link, *LGdV*'s writer took pleasure in the certitude, as guaranteed by the Princesse's benevolence, that such a celebration would be revived to mark the twentieth anniversary of Wagner's death in the following year.

For this 1902 concert itself we have accounts not only from the local newspapers but also from the Princesse herself.[15] It was held in the cortile of the Palazzo Vendramin, with a large crowd also attending beyond, along the Grand Canal. The *Götterdämmerung* March was the prime item on the program, which also included pieces from *Tristan*, *Parsifal*, and *Die Meistersinger*. Calascione and his musicians were highly praised. The Princesse herself graciously noted later in her memoirs that "the Banda Municipale played the Funeral March very creditably." The invited guests were given a buffet by the owner of the Palazzo Vendramin and Wagner's erstwhile landlord, the Duca della Grazia, whom the Princesse grilled for his recollections of what Liszt and Wagner had been like as his tenants.

Calascione renewed his regular promotion of Wagner's music through 1902, finding further company. As a fund-raising event on behalf of the rebuilding of San Marco's Campanile—which had collapsed spectacularly just weeks before, in July—the orchestra of the Società Verdi held an evening concert. Its main attraction was the celebrated tenor Francesco Tamagno, who sampled his signature role in Verdi's *Otello*. But the program also found space for Wolfram's song from *Tannhäuser* (sung by a certain Giuseppe Kaschmann), as well as the Prelude to *Meistersinger*

Calascione again had special moment in the Wagner spotlight. On October 9, 1902, *LGdV* reported that, on the previous evening, the Banda Cittadina's concert in the Piazza was attended by no less than Siegfried Wagner, "figlio dell'immortale maestro." Then thirty-three, Siegfried had already begun what was to be his own extensive career as a composer of operas. Unlike others of his family, he cherished lively affection for Italy and its monuments, visiting the country a number of times in his mature years. On this particular trip, Siegfried was accompanied by his brother-in-law Henry Thode, the art historian who was married to Daniela. The band concert's program included the Overture to *Tannhäuser*. At the end, Siegfried went among the players to praise them and Calascione for their performance. Twenty years earlier, when Siegfried himself was not yet thirteen, his father had done the same thing, and one guesses that the younger Wagner must not only have remembered that gesture but deliberately emulated it. Nor might the parallel have been lost on the bandmaster himself.

That the Wagner–Venice connection had become firmly institutionalized as a matter of civic pride can be seen in the attention to the twentieth anniversary of the composer's death. Indeed, the attention was twofold. First, on the date itself, February 13, 1903, the annual band concert was presented in the cortile of the Palazzo Vendramin, with the Duca della Grazia's guests listening from his apartments, and enjoying a reception thereafter.[16] The second event followed a fortnight later (February 26). Under its conductor, Rodolfo Ferrari—described as an "entusiasta studioso di Riccardo Wagner"—the Società Filarmonica di M. S. Giuseppe Verdi presented an ample program of excerpts from six Wagner operas. On the day before, *LGdV* went to the effort of printing a full-column list-ing of the program's contents, with detailed notes designed to explain each selection in its dramatic context. A capacity audience attended, we are told, attentive and enthusiastic through the full two hours. In its review of the concert the following day, *LGdV* called it a landmark event of enduring memory. The writer went on rhapsodically to praise Wagner's music as making all other music seem inferior. Whatever the hyperbole, the suggestion seems clear that Venice's audiences had by now taken Wagner's music, as well as his memory, to their bos-oms within the two decades since his death.

Before 1903 was over, Calascione had one more landmark moment, and again in collaboration with his "partner," the Princesse de Polignac. Siegfried Wagner was back in Venice and on the evening of Friday, October 2, Calascione offered a concert by the Banda Cittadina in the Piazza to honor both Siegfried and the Princesse. It was an all-Wagner program, of course, and at its end both the younger Wagner and the Princesse again circulated among the musicians to con-gratulate them.

Calascione's programming policies were progressing to the point at which he was performing about as much Wagner as Verdi. And the annual anniversary commemorations continued. For February 13, 1904, the performance was held once more in the Vendramin cortile. The Duca della Grazia again played host to "a select segment of notables of the local and foreign aristocracy"—though the patroness, the Princesse de Polignac herself, was not able to attend. The program mixed familiar Wagner arrangements with more examples of Calascione's ever-developing new ones. Such was his confidence in this reper-toire that he felt free to give several all-Wagner programs through each season, beyond the anniversary ones, and to sprinkle Wagner selections in his concerts generally during the ensuing years.

The year 1907, to end so tragically, began grandly. The usual anniversary con-cert was postponed to February 15, because of a conflicting schedule commit-ment the band had on the thirteenth. By this time the concert was held in the portico of the Fondaco dei Turchi, opposite the Palazzo Vendramin, rather than in that building itself, a locale that had been held in reserve in case of inclement weather but was now the planned location. The Princesse was still the patroness, but the Duca della Grazia was no longer there as host. More to the point, the new location would provide access and space for a larger audience. The pro-gram offered six of the band's by-now standard Wagner repertoire, beginning with the requisite Funeral March from *Götterdämmerung*. In announcing the con-cert that day, the newer journal *Il Gazzettino* (*IG*) printed a substantial article that offered its readers Italian translations of two of Wagner's letters to Mathilde Wesendonck at the beginning of the composer's sojourn in Venice in 1858—let-ters describing his first reactions to the city.[17] "To Venice the master returned several times and in February 1883 he died here," the article writer concluded.

The Banda Cittadina was not alone in playing Wagner in concerts over subsequent weeks, especially as the year 1907 brought Venice's Seventh Biennale (April 28 to November 17). Concerts were given abundantly by the five bands then active, in numerous settings—the Piazza San Marco, the Campo Manin, the Riva Degli Schiavoni, as well as the Exposition site itself. Of the concerts not held at the Exposition, one might estimate that at least one-quarter of them included at least one Wagner selection. It was Calascione, however, who commanded the scene. He conducted the Exposition's opening concert, including one composition of his own and one by Wagner. The regular Exposition concerts thereafter, three to five evenings a week, were given almost entirely by the Banda Cittadina, and hardly one of them was without at least one Wagner piece. Many of the concerts were devoted to a single composer, but only one of them was entirely of Wagner's music (while Verdi rated two), and for the five mixed-program concerts in a more formal series in July and August a Wagner selection appeared in only three. As if to make up for a seeming neglect of Wagner, in some nineteen concerts, which Calascione and his band gave either at the Exposition or the Piazza between September 1 and October 1, only one lacked a Wagner selection.

The Banda Cittadina apparently went on vacation for most of October, and other bands offered concerts in the interim, playing Wagner sometimes but not often. Without connection to the concerts, but presumably for the art fanciers in town, *LGdV* on October 22 transmitted a story derived from the French journal, *Ménestrel*, about how Renoir was able to make a portrait of Wagner at Palermo (February 1882).[18] Six days later, *LGdV* printed a supplementary article, correcting any suggestion that this event—presumably the making of a portrait while Wagner was in Italy—was unique, describing an early instance in 1880, by the Baron de Pury.[19]

On the date of that second article, October 28, 1887, the Banda Cittadina was to give its Piazza concert that evening, the first appearance since its vacation. Its program was fairly typical for the day—pieces by Berlioz, Rossini, Verdi, Schubert, and Boïto, though no Wagner. In the midst of leading pieces from *Rigoletto*, Calascione suddenly collapsed, dying instantly of a heart attack. A robust man who had never known bad health, the burly Sicilian was dead at sixty-six.

The shock was enormous, both immediately in the Piazza and throughout the city over the next few days. The newspapers heaped tributes upon him, while messages of condolence and memorial wreaths poured in. An elaborate funeral was given for him on October 31. Lorenzo Perosi's *Requiem* was conducted by the director of the Società Verdi. Members from four of the local bands were in the funeral procession. Three eulogies were delivered, by the *sindaco*, or mayor, Filippo Grimani, the president of the conservatory council, and by Calascione's assistant, disciple, and now acting director of the Banda Cittadina, Giuseppe Marasco, also professor of clarinet at the Liceo. After the funeral, Calascione's body was taken to the Municipal Cemetery on the San Michele Island for burial.

Despite the international reputation his laudators claimed for him, virtually all of the expressions of sympathy and tribute came from Italy and Italians. Notably absent was any message from the Princesse de Polignac; more significantly, nothing from Siegfried Wagner, or anyone else in Bayreuth. The Wagner connection was ignored in the funeral eulogies, though not in the journalistic treatments of Calascione's death, however meagerly. *LGdV* noted that Calascione had been proud of the personal praise given to him by Wagner and Boïto. *IG* went even further, as we have noted, stating that "Wagner was his idol," even at the cost of "some ridicule, certainly undeserved." This journal further took occasion, on the day before Calascione's funeral, to make a muddled conflation of the two separate contacts of the bandmaster with Wagner in 1882. At the end of the story, the writer has Wagner "congratulating and praising Calascione," calling him "my dear colleague."

> That affectionate phrase remained carved on the heart of Calascione, who sometimes loved to remember it with warm satisfaction.[20]

If nothing else, this garbled account does indicate that Calascione's personal connection with the great Wagner was firmly established and remembered in Venice.

For almost a quarter-century, Calascione had brought Wagner's music incrementally before the Venetian public, through his arrangements and performances. His sudden death left uncertain how much of that championship would be carried on, and, more generally, what new leadership the Banda Cittadina would have. Marasco was the logical acting deputy, though the band's concerts were suspended until November 10. When they resumed on that date, in what was reported as an *omaggio* to the deceased director, the program was a conventional one (with no Wagner). *IG* reviewed it with the observation that Marasco "proved himself a brave disciple of the lamented maestro." The concerts played during the subsequent weeks under Marasco continued the memorial tributes, but gave no evidence that he intended to take up the cause of Wagner his predecessor had championed.

Of course, the firm establishment of the annual anniversary commemorations was not to be denied, especially with the Princesse de Polignac's irresistible backing. Moreover, February 13, 1908, was the twenty-fifth anniversary of Wagner's death. Accordingly, Marasco conducted this annual event, at the Fondaco dei Turchi, so successfully that it was repeated in the Piazza the following day "by public request." Two days later, however, the picture changed. On February 15, it was announced that Marasco had been bypassed and that the band's new director would be Carmelo Preite,[21] who took over from Marasco exactly two months later. Like Marasco, Preite made clear that he would not follow fully in Calascione's footsteps as a committed Wagner advocate. Still, Preite did program Wagner pieces occasionally, and he fully accepted the obligation of presenting the annual anniversary concerts, which continued each February 13 at least up to 1914. The Princesse de Polignac—who was a recurrent resident in her palazzo, where she ran a salon that rivaled her Paris counterpart—continued to attend.

The year 1908 also saw more evidence of Venice's Wagner-consciousness. The twenty-fifth anniversary commemoration of Wagner's death was planned to include also a special lecture, "Sul pensiero artistico e sociale di Wagner" by a Professor Guido Podresca. This was actually delayed, not to be delivered until June 28, reviews of it appearing in the two papers the next day. That Venetian readers were presumed to have continuing interest in things Wagnerian is illustrated at random by *LGdV*'s printing, with no particular connections (and perhaps mainly as space-fillers), of: (a) a collection of Wagner anecdotes (March 19);[22] (b) a report from a French journal about a French commentator's thoughts on the influence of Wagner on French music (April 9); (c) and anecdotes about "Wagner's Last Hours" (June 23).[23]

Stirrings far greater, however, were in the making by autumn of 1908. The first inkling came in the last days of September, when both newspapers reported that a monument to Wagner was to be installed in the Giardini Pubblici. This would be a bust of the composer, carved in marble by the German sculptor Fritz Schaper of Berlin.[24] There was a little confusion over a statement that it was the result of a public subscription, but it was soon made clear that this was a gift of a wealthy Berliner, Adolph Thiem, a great Wagner admirer. Announcements were also made of the events designed to surround the dedication of the monument: its unveiling, with the participation of the Banda Cittadina; a luncheon in honor of Thiem; and a lecture by a Wagner scholar and editor, Gualtiero Petrucci.

The ceremonies proceeded as planned on October 8, 1908, and were reported the next day in the two newspapers, each including sketches of the monument. The weather was ideal for the dedication at 10:00 o'clock. The journals were careful to list the dignitaries attending: local officials and notables, including leaders of musical organizations; the Princesse de Polignac was identified, and reference was made—to "molti personaggi della colonia tedesca"—a likely hint of what must have been an important force behind the gift. The unveiling was carried out while the Banda Cittadina under maestro Preite played the "gran marcia del corteggio" from *Tannhäuser*, heard by the audience "con religioso silenzio."

Both newspapers included drawings of the monument as well as verbal descriptions. The likeness was pronounced as excellent. Wagner's thoughtful gaze out to the Lido was noted, and it was commented that surmounting inscription of the composer's name on the pedestal was placed an allegorical carving. This shows a pelican, piercing its breast with its beak, embodying an age-old Christian tradition that alludes to Christ's sacrifice for human redemption. As *IG* explained it, this is a creature "that nourishes its children with its blood, symbolizing the maestro's life, sacrificed entirely for the achievement of the artistic ideal that was his constant and unwavering guide."

Following the unveiling, there were speeches.[25] First place was assigned to the donor himself, Adolph Thiem. He affirmed that he had long dreamed of asking Venice to allow him to create a monument to Wagner in this city. He was furthered in that goal by the publication of Wagner's letters to Mathilde Wesendonck [e.g., in 1904]:

> These letters offer us a quite moving vision of the state of his soul and are the clear proof that Venice itself, with the splendor of its wonders, with its air saturated in poetry, gave wings to his creative power and transformed the drama of *Tristan und Isolde*, already born in the Villa Wesendonck at Zurich, into harmonies never before imagined.

Thiem traces Wagner's creative pursuit of that great project to the composer's exile in Venice—mistakenly identifying his "refuge" there as the Palazzo Vendramin! Wagner triumphed over sufferings and suicidal impulses to realize his artistic potential in *Tristan*, Thiem asserts. Thus Wagner, while still in Venice, managed to press on, to renew his old plan for the mighty *Ring* cycle. Thiem then traces Wagner's continuing struggles, personal and artistic, culminating in the creation of his "temple of art" in Bayreuth and of *Parsifal*. Thiem next speaks of the importance to Wagner of his wife Cosima, mother of his only son, Siegfried, and continues:

> Riccardo Wagner always returned to Venice, which had become to him a second homeland. Here in Venice in 1883 this colossal genius expired. The mournful news stirred in the entire world the most profound grief and the keenest sympathy for the inconsolable family. It will never be forgotten how Venice honored its great fellow-citizen in his death. He had been a king in the realm of artistic thought: as a king he was conveyed from Venice to his homeland.

In offering this monument, Thiem says, he and Schaper wish only that it will "recall to the citizens of Venice the features of Wagner, as they had seen him every day, and as he had become to them." He expresses regret that neither Wagner's widow nor his son could attend this ceremony, nor even Schaper himself. The sculptor was unfortunately ill, while Siegfried had been called away urgently elsewhere. But, Thiem insists, Siegfried had been able to inspect the monument before its shipment here and had spent a moment of profound contemplation at its feet. Addressing the civic representatives, Thiem concludes: "I deliver this monument to the custody of the City of Venice, so dear to the heart of Riccardo Wagner."

Following appropriate applause "for his most gracious sentiments regarding Venice," the city magistrate Arturo Chiggiato took the podium as representative of the mayor. With warm thanks he accepted this gift of "the image of the supreme artist [placed] in this Venice that preserves marks and eternal memories of his life and of his work." Chiggiato recalls how Venice had played such a role in Wagner's career, beginning with the composer's "refuge" in Venice when he turned the magic of gondolier songs into the sublime music of *Tristan*. "His 'dreaming Venice'—the chimeric city, as he called it—then welcomed him at the peak of glory." For his final visit, Wagner enjoyed his close family circle, particularly in the revival of his youthful symphony. With some hyperbole, Chiggiato goes on:

> Venice, first among Italian cities, welcomed and applauded his wondrous conceptions, even when they had to await for so many years that admission to citizenship that Art holds in every country.
> Finally, of course, Venice was the scene of Wagner's death: . . . the Grand Canal was the magic highway by which the glorious body was conveyed to its final repose; from the Grand Canal, inspiration for sublime song, comforter of sublime sorrows, that reigning spirit soared to immortality.
> . . . In this Italian land, whose beauty and arts he loved and honored, rightly is raised, as an imperishable sign of homage, the monument that Venice will preserve with pride and admiration.

After the applause for these words, the Banda Cittadina played its other selection, "The Entry of the Gods into Valhalla," from *Das Rheingold*. Then, as the public was released to inspect the new monument, a select group adjourned to the Grand Hôtel des Bains on the Lido for a festive luncheon at noon, in honor of Hr. Thiem. Among the participants noted were the mayor and maestro Preite—though not explicitly the Princesse. Amid the details, it was reported that the printed menu featured on its cover a view of the Grand Canal that included the Palazzo Vendramin, plus a portrait of Wagner.

As the final event, at 3:00 p.m., the Liceo Benedetto Marcello offered a special lecture to mark the occasion.[26] There were again notables whose presence was to be noted. The lecturer, Professor Gualtiero Petrucci, opened and closed his address with recognition of Venice's importance in Wagner's life, but was largely devoted to analyses of Wagner's style and works. He did suggest that a certain *latinità* could be found in Wagner's spirit. And he took note of Bologna as in fact "the first among the Italian cities to welcome the works of the great master." At the end, said the reporters, "The orator raised again a hymn to Venice, as guardian of its traditions and promoter of the most noble initiatives for the cultivation and development of art." It remained only to record the various telegrams sent and received in order to seal the occasion.

The new flurry of attention to Wagner that this donated monument involved—with its clear demonstration of involvement by the local foreign community as well as by the foreign donors—soon had an evident riposte. The following year, 1909, was the year for the latest Biennale, the eighth. This was set to open on Saturday, April 24. A few days before that, there were successive announcements—by *LGdV* on the twenty-first and by *IG* on the twenty-second—of a special event to be part of the opening ceremonies on the twenty-fourth. The event involved the inauguration of another monument at the Giardini Pubblici, a monument about which virtually nothing had been said previously. This was to be a bronze bust of Giuseppe Verdi, created by the cav. Gerolamo Bortotti.[27] The unveiling was, however, to be a simple affair. *LGdV* made that clear: "It will not be an official ceremony, though in the afternoon there will follow, in the precinct of the Exposition, as the first concert [of the Exposition], an entire program of the great Italian master."

And so the monument was unveiled, as both journals note, "senza speciali cerimonie." There were speeches, but entirely focused on the opening of the Exhibition itself.[28] The presence of various visitors, notables, and artists was reported, though there was no mention of Bortotti himself, who apparently was not in attendance for the occasion at all. The announced concert program was performed—with no member of the Società Filarmonica Giuseppe Verdi in sight—by the Banda Cittadina under Preite: excerpts from Verdi's *Nabucco, Rigoletto, La forza del destino, I Lombardi, Aïda,* and *I vespri siciliani.* It was a program that Preite and his band would repeat two days later. In between, though, at a concert program for the twenty-sixth, Wagner's *Tannhäuser* Overture found its place.

Both newspapers described the Verdi bust as an excellent likeness of "the able and modest artist." It was mentioned that the composer is shown holding in his hand a page of music, with the notes of the famous chorus "Va pensiero sull'ali dorate" from *Nabucco.* The pedestal, a separate work by one Galvan, is decorated with a bronze lyre adorned with a classical wreath. Above this is a plate on which are inscribed in gold the words "A Giuseppe Verdi—Venezia."

That inscription subtly conveys a point stated plainly by *IG* (April 25): that it was "decretato dal Consiglio Comunale"—a work commissioned by Venice's own city council. In other words, it was not the gift of some donor or some cultural agency, but a publicly financed work. The rather backhanded treatment of its dedication as a sideshow to the Exposition opening is odd, but suggests that the monument to Verdi might have been rushed into being out of civic embarrassment, in an attempt to balance the attention paid to Wagner with honor to a native son, at least on the part of some nationalists.

Such an impression is the more obvious when one views the pair of monuments as they may still be seen today. They stand beside the Bacino, near the main entrance to the Giardini Pubblici, and its Garibaldi monument, at what has been called the Montagnola. The busts are placed on either side of a little park enclave, effectively an ensemble. Yet, there is an ironic quality to the ensemble. Each composer looks out, straight ahead, neither seeming to notice the other. These two giants of opera, rivals in their day, are frozen for all time in mutual disregard.[29]

Whatever cultural tussle the successive monuments to Wagner and Verdi may have represented, there was to be one more gesture made, returning the balance in favor of Wagner. (After all, Wagner died in Venice, while Verdi did not!)

To be sure, it was business as usual on Sunday, February 13, 1910, when the annual Wagner concert was given by the Banda Cittadina in the ground-floor *atrio* of the Fondaco dei Turchi. As before, tribute was paid to the Princesse de Polignac and her generous sponsorship of these events. The program was full of familiar repertoire, though by this time Preite had transferred the requisite *Götterdämmerung* Funeral March from the opening to the conclusion. *LGdV* reported the next day that, despite cold weather, wind, and the moisture resulting from excessive high tides, there was a substantial and enthusiastic audience in attendance.[30]

As always, tidbits about some new Wagner publication or oddment continued to appear in the newspapers here and there. But the autumn of 1910 brought the striking news of the year. On Thursday, September 29, *LGdV* trumpeted in a headline: "An Inscription by G. D'Annunzio for Riccardo Wagner at the Palazzo Vendramin Calergi." The article that followed begins by recalling Wagner's associations with the great Renaissance palazzo—but repeating the mistaken one about part of *Tristan* being composed there. The site of his death has by this time become a focus of pilgrimage for admirers of Wagner, it is claimed. "To commemorate the renowned maestro, nothing is omitted," asserts the writer, who recalls the annual memorial concert, sponsored by the Princesse de Polignac and held now at the Fondaco dei Turchi, opposite the Vendramin. "The performances of Wagner are frequent in Venice, by the band (if not, unfortunately, in the theater or by orchestra!), more than in any other Italian city." The writer also recalls the gift to the city of the bust of Wagner installed in the Giardini Pubblici two years before.

Now, the writer reports, "a committee of ladies, of artists, and of writers of every country" has decided to prepare a sculpted portrait of Wagner for mounting "in the cortile of the maestro's domicile." The project, planned for some time, was furthered definitively by Gabriele D'Annunzio during his residence in Paris. *LGdV*'s writer detects some Gallic snobbism in the planning in Paris of "an autumn intellectual festivity in the lagoons in the name of Riccardo Wagner," through the agency of Italy's leading poet—who has himself written that "the soul of Venice is autumnal." Nevertheless, despite the undeniable veneer of aristocratic game playing, D'Annunzio was indeed involved. Denied the presidency of the committee, he had been persuaded to devise the inscription to be added to the marble sculpture that itself has been created by the Venetian sculptor Guido [*sic*] Cadorin, then resident in Paris.[31] Our writer notes that, in connection with the presentation of this new monument, "un concerto sinfonico vocale" is planned; the ceremonies have been planned for the end of autumn, but might have to be postponed to next year. We are next given the text of D'Annunzio's contrived inscription, whose sense might be translated thus: "In this palazzo the spirits heard the last breath of Riccardo Wagner become eternal, like the tide that laps the marble stones."[32] To which would be added the dates of Wagner's death, and the date of the commemoration.[33] The writer finally notes D'Annunzio's identification of himself with Wagner's death through his famous novel, *Il fuoco*.[34]

The following day, September 30, *LGdV* added more information and some clarifications. The plan for the monument had been hatched the previous autumn—(amid the Verdi commemoration, one wonders?)—by several Viennese, including [Rudolf] Winterberg and [L.] Guttmann. The committee that pursued the plan was formed, however, in Paris, under the auspices of two musical organizations, "Ut Mineur" and "Les Amis de la Musique," with mess. [P. A.] Cheramy and [F.] Custot as respective presidents. The committee also included the Contessa Seilern, Baronessa [Mme. Louis] Stern, [Max] Rikov [or Rikoff], and the German singer Schabber-Zolder. They were partnered in Venice by the Contessa A. Morosini, Contessa [Elsa] Albrizzi, and Duchessa Canevaro. *LGdV* now gave the sculptor's name correctly, as *Ettore* Cadorin. It also clarified the sculpture's planned location: not in the Vendramin cortile, but "on the garden wall of the Palazzo Vendramin, overlooking the Grand Canal under a green bough."[35] The dedication would be in October after all. Two further notes were added. The king of Bulgaria, having seen the sculpture during a passage through Paris, had subscribed to make an important financial contribution—because of which, in fact, he had been advanced ahead of D'Annunzio to be honorary president of the committee. And Siegfried Wagner had expressed "flattering words for Italy and for those who had joined to give substantive form to the memory of and the homage to his immortal progenitor."

On October 3, *IG* caught up with all this, giving the same information as the foregoing. Both newspapers, on October 25 and 26, announced the actual date of the ceremonies, and their specifics. *IG* added to such data a description of the sculpture—actually a low-relief profile portrait of the composer:

> The plaque, of which we may give the design is—as we have already said—a distinguished work in form of a concave medallion, rendering in three-quarter [profile] the characteristic features of Wagner, in most excellent likeness: high forehead, aquiline eye and nose, a chin jutting out as with an ancient captain of enterprise, the hair that appeared to flutter in the winds of the melody surrounding that head like some halo.
>
>   From one side and the other arose two rich boughs: one of oak, symbol of that genial force that fought a great battle for art and for humanity; the other of laurel as emblem of poetic inspiration.

At 2:30 on the fine autumn afternoon of Wednesday, October 26, 1910, the festivities began. The invited guests, having arrived by gondola or launch, gathered at the portico of the Fondaco dei Turchi, opposite the Vendramin and the new monument. The two newspaper reports stressed the international, multilingual nature of the gathering, including members of the foreign (at least German) press. Identified among the notables were the leaders of the Venetian municipality, as well as leaders of the donating committee, and members of Venice's resident foreign colony. Also mentioned, besides the director of the

Liceo Marcello and a representative of the Ricordi music publishers, were composer Wolf-Ferrari (recently resigned as director of the Liceo), and cav. Vincenzo Cadorin. The last of these was himself the creator of the Wagner plaque in the Lavena Café, but was also father of the sculptor Ettore Cadorin; Vincenzo presumably represented the sculptor himself, who is not specified as being present. (No mention is made of the Princesse de Polignac, apparently not in attendance on this occasion.)

Stationed also at the Fondaco, the Banda Cittadina under maestro Preite played the *Meistersinger* Overture. The sculpture was then unveiled, following which Max Rikoff, speaking for the International Committee, delivered a short speech in French (summarized in Italian in the newspaper accounts). Rikoff expressed the hope that the new monument would recall Wagner to memory for all those who passed it by on the Canal. Its message was for all people. Genius, he affirmed, knows no distinctions of school, or national origins, or frontier separations. True art transcends nationality and brings to earth a reflection of heaven. Homer, Plato, Virgil, Dante, Shakespeare, Newton, Molière, Pasteur, Mozart, Beethoven—all rise above mere national origin. So with Wagner: Germany claims him as its son, but he belongs to all humanity. It is in that spirit, Rikoff asserted, that a group of his admirers, representing "all nations" have carried out this project. "In his name I submit that the beauty of art is a type of religion, and of that beauty Riccardo Wagner was one of the most committed and greatest of its apostles."

When Rikoff finished and was applauded, it was the turn of the Sindaco (mayor), Conte Filippo Grimani. He briefly recollected the memorials for Wagner already achieved in Venice: the plaque at the entrance to the Palazzo Vendramin, voted by the Commune just after his death; the bust of Wagner by Schaper donated by Adolf Thiem and mounted "in the verdant precinct of the Public Gardens"; and the annual concert commemorating his death, as sponsored by the Princesse de Polignac, by which "the Municipal Band has this section of the Grand Canal resound with the performance of some of the most impressive creations of the distinguished master." Now, says Grimani, we have the International Committee's new tribute, in the form of Cadorin's sculpture.

> Venice, which welcomed Riccardo Wagner when he had reached the apogee of his glory, which was to him an inspirer of sublime melodies, which felt with deep emotion his final breath, could only rejoice at this new homage paid to so much grand memory in being made to assume custody of the marble memorial committed to it.
>
> Such an obligation I have the honor to assume in the name of the Commune, while I express warm thanks to the International Committee for their noble initiative, which honors simultaneously the Maestro, whose genius has left a blazing imprint of inextinguishable light, and Venice, which preserves everlasting traces and memories of him."

Following the applause, Preite led the Banda Cittadina in the *Götterdämmerung* Funeral March and the "Entry of the Gods into Valhalla" from *Das Rheingold*.

The *LGdV* account reports the high praise given to the band and its leader, "greatly admired in particular by the foreigners." Both the committee and the local notables expressed their praises to "Cadorin" (presumably Vincenzo, for transmission to Ettore). It was noted that to the new sculpture were attached two wreaths, one from the Liceo Marcello, the other from the Parisian Amis de Musique. "At 3:15 the last gondolas of the participants passed on speedily into the glory of the sun that kindled glitterings of silver on the water."

The sculpture, inscription and all, may still be seen as installed, on the brick wall overlooking the Grand Canal, to the left of the facade of the palazzo, though perhaps upstaged now by the entrance into the Vendramin's water portal as Venice's winter Casinò.[36] Taken together with the plaque on the Campiello Vendramin entrance to the palazzo, and with Vincenzo Cadorin's plaque in Lavena's, the installation of the Schaper bust in the Giardini Pubblici and of Ettore Cadorin's plaque on the canal wall of the Palazzo Vendramin completed the constellation of monuments to Wagner that Venice either created or welcomed.

Can any other *forestiero* lay claim to so many monuments in Venice? Together with the anniversary concerts to commemorate his death, Wagner thus received attention on a scale that Venice has accorded no other foreigner—or, for that matter, hardly any of its native sons.

Chapter Fourteen

Surviving Significance

Between 1901 and 1915, a confluence of motivations had instilled in Venetian consciousness a powerful awareness of a bond between the city and the great German master. The Italian Calascione and the French Princesse de Polignac each made their contributions out of intense admiration for Wagner's music, and even personal connections of their own with the composer and his family. The Italian D'Annunzio had his own agenda of glory by association. Members (especially Germans) of Venice's international and expatriate community apparently saw Wagner as a symbol that gave it leverage in promoting its own significance in the city's cultural life. And Venice's civic leaders had come to recognize Wagner, through his life and death there, as an ineradicable part of their city's memory: indeed, a useful addition to its total mythology.

But then came World War I, which brought considerable disruption to Venice, in all aspects of its life.[1] After an initial attempt at neutrality, Italy entered the war in May 1915 on the side of the Allies, set against the Central Powers, which included the German and Austrian Empires. At the expense of the latter, Italy had hopes of territorial gains, and soon found itself caught in brutally bruising confrontations with German and Austrian forces in the Alpine regions. Close to the explosive northern frontier, Venice was the first city in Italy to suffer attack. On May 24, 1915, within days of Italy's entry into the war, Austrian air assaults and bombings began, and there were recurrent bombardments thereafter. D'Annunzio moved to Venice that July, making the city his base for swaggering air operations against the Austrians, and subsequently for his quixotic seizure of Fiume (1919–21).

The war transformed all aspects of Venice's life. Much of the international community was dispersed, tourism was wiped out, and normal cultural life virtually collapsed. The city's monuments were swathed protectively and many art treasures were removed elsewhere for safekeeping, though bombardments inflicted physical damage on the northern part of the city, causing much anguish. Venice's hotels and spare buildings were gradually turned into hospitals for wounded soldiers, especially after the disastrous Austro-German breakthrough at Caporetto in October 1917. Gloom and stagnation enveloped the city.

Under such circumstances, it might well be expected that the connections between Wagner and Venice would slip into oblivion. In point of fact, that did not happen.

By the end of World War I, of course, Italian artistic life had moved a long way from the culture wars of Wagner's last years. Italy had shed its struggles over nationalistic exclusivity and had become part of the larger, more cosmopolitan world of European artistic life. Italy had its own new generations of artists, writers, and musicians, caught up in movements of experimentalism and radicalism. Such composers as Catalani, Puccini, and Giordano, among others, had shown that Wagnerian dramatic ideals and musical techniques could indeed be made compatible with, and be assimilated into, new phases of Italian lyric theater. Italian audiences were less and less likely to view Wagner's music as a suspicious and dangerous intrusion from the outside. Especially so when one of Italy's leading musicians, Arturo Toscanini, had himself become a passionate champion of Wagner. His example was soon followed by the likes of Victor de Sabata and Vittorio Gui, among others.

For the Lagoon City itself, moreover, there was one institution that demonstrated that the Wagner–Venice connection should not be lost and would not be: the band concert commemorating the anniversary of Wagner's death.

Among the many cultural casualties of the war years had been the concerts, and even the very existence, of the Banda Cittadina. Its members had been drained away by manpower needs, and its revival would have to start almost from scratch. It was taken for granted that Carmelo Preite would resume his leadership. On January 14, 1919, *Il Gazzettino* (*IG*) reproduced a message from the municipal governments that indicated the problems and prospects involved:

> The civic Band Corps that is now being reconstituted, following the Council's resolution of 15 December past, is not able to resume its concerts immediately because many band members are still in active military service, because many of those on leading parts are missing, and because the necessary numerical proportions among the instrumental groups are still lacking.
>
> For all that, the appropriate attention can be devoted in such a way that—with the Band Corps reconstituted even in reduced proportions, and allowing for a short period of rehearsals needed for the consolidation of a sufficient repertoire—the band will be able to resume its concerts in the early days of February.

That hope proved too optimistic, and temporary resources had to fill the gap. *IG* noted on February 1 that a band concert would be given in the Piazza the next day—by the U.S. Marine Band! February 13, 1919, passed with no reference to the Wagner anniversary, much less to any concert. Indeed, the recreated Banda Cittadina made its first appearance only on Sunday afternoon, March 2, and specifically in a memorial tribute to a composer very much other than Wagner. This was Arrigo Boïto, who had died in Milan the previous June, but who—having been born in Padua and having spent his childhood in Venice—could be claimed in particular as a local son. The announcement of the event by *IG* made clear that the band was still struggling.

> . . . The distinguished maestro Preite has been able to strengthen the Band temporarily with some military personnel here by permission, for which he obtained an authorization from the military High Command.

Gradually, the band worked into some regular functions. On March 7, it played some patriotic music as part of a public rally in the Piazza over the disputed territorial issues in Dalmatia. And on March 16, the band began what would now be the regular Sunday concerts in the Piazza. Thereafter, Preite confirmed anew that he was no committed Wagnerian, and only very sparingly would the German master's music begin to appear as normal selections in the programs. Of course, the question of rebuilding the band with sufficient numbers of qualified players might also have affected his hesitation to program much Wagner. But another factor could have been the absence from the scene of the Princesse de Polignac. Her endowment of the anniversary concerts had apparently not survived the war, and she now concentrated her patronage on commissioning new music, while consistently basing herself in Paris.

As for Preite, however, Wagnerian traditions caught up with him, and vice versa, in due course. The year 1923 marked the fortieth anniversary of Wagner's death. Preite did lead a Piazza concert on the hallowed date of February 13, but there was no Wagnerian music at all in its program, and no outward notice was taken of the Wagnerian associations of the date. Nevertheless, the anniversary was not to be forgotten after all. Five days later, on Sunday, February 18, 1923, Preite led an all-Wagner concert specifically designated as a fortieth-anniversary commemoration. It was like old times again, with a program of familiar excerpts from *Tannhäuser, Parsifal,* and *Die Meistersinger,* as well as the "Rhine Journey" and the Funeral March from *Götterdämmerung.*

Only a few days later, on February 21, did *IG* get around to making any substantial comment on the concert, but with some colorful reflections, as much on the setting as on the music:

> The concert of Wagnerian music performed this past Sunday in the Piazza San Marco by the municipal band was heard by an audience of several thousand people with all the respect that the artistic works deserved, indeed with that feeling of religious devotion that our people, of their diverse classes, feel and display for any true and genuine artistic presentation.
>
> Unfortunately, there have been noticed some troublesome intrusions by other sounds; turns of fish wheels, shouts, trumpetings. But perhaps it would be extreme to demand in the piazza that absolute silence which cannot be had in enclosed theaters, where the disturbance of whispering, of chattering in the stalls, of jolting coughs, is endless.

Even the church bells wanted to make their voices heard. But the bells of San Marco did not give notes out of tune: though quite a number otherwise had been so.

The audience showed itself enthusiastic about the entire concert and displayed the proper sentiment with spontaneous and warm applause despite the chilly air. Notwithstanding the low temperature, no one would imagine an enclosed hall for the concert: the Venetians knowing well, through the disputes of other ages, the difficulty, even the impossibility, of such a concert comprehending all the people in a different atmosphere.

What hall offers the advantages to be found at San Marco, so wonderful in the framing of the Procuratie, with a setting of an ever-enchanting beauty? Advantages of capacity, of acoustics, of freedom, that it is useless to explain because everyone knows all about it.

The Piazza seems designed for the band and that for the Piazza. Who—what good Venetian—can conceive of the Piazza without its band?

We have such a hall, we have a band such as that of maestro Preite, against which none might stand as equal. Who could even entertain the desire for changing anything?

Without giving or expecting any response, we turn to this past Sunday's concert, which has had such an outcome—although a concert of music not all of it easily absorbed and not by everyone—that an audience of thousands of citizens have devoted themselves to it. The concert was given as an anniversary commemoration for Riccardo Wagner, who, as is well known, died forty years ago in the Palazzo Vendramin Calergi. Such was the beauty of the performance that we have heard a round of voices calling for a repetition.

And this concert was indeed repeated, on the following Sunday, February 25, with reminders given of its memorial significance.

The article writer can be forgiven for devoting his piece less to the Wagnerian anniversary and Wagner's music, and more to a burst of civic pride over the Piazza itself as a musical venue. Certainly anyone who has heard a musical event in the Piazza—beyond, of course, the banal café band performances—will appreciate what made our writer so proud.[2]

By the time of the 1923 revival of the memorial concert, Preite had apparently assembled and trained a sufficient number of qualified players to be more confident in his programming. Thereafter, Wagner selections—all still, one assumes, in Calascione's transcriptions—became regular, indeed frequent, components of the Banda Cittadina's concerts. Calascione's spirit had clearly triumphed!

It is beyond our scope here to trace in detail the further contributions of the band to sustaining the memory of Wagner in Venice. Rather, we might bring our survey to a close with consideration of two very different episodes that cast contrasting light on the continuing consciousness of the Wagner–Venice connection.

The first episode occurred the year following the fiftieth anniversary of Wagner's death in Venice.[3]

For all of Italy, the years immediately after World War I were ones of social turmoil and political instability, leading to the establishment in late 1923 of Benito

Mussolini's Fascist dictatorship. Only after a decade of power had established Mussolini as a swaggering and supposedly model example of the confident dictator did the Italian leader agree to meet with his seeming counterpart, Adolf Hitler. The latter had just attained the German chancellorship in January 1933, and was yet working to establish his Nazi dictatorship. Mussolini could still command considerable international respect: diplomats, both German and otherwise, even looked to him to be a mediating and moderating force in the face of Hitler's potential recklessness. While Hitler was convinced that he and Mussolini shared ideological principles that would make them logical allies, immediate tensions existed between them, especially over Hitler's apparent goal of annexing Austria. There were logical reasons they should meet, and this was arranged for June 1934, with Venice fixed as the setting.

It was not an auspicious encounter for either. Mussolini was clearly the dominant personality of the two, and put all his pomp on display, while Hitler appeared shabby and eccentric, a nervous novice. Mussolini relied too much on his own incomplete command of German as he tried to talk directly with Hitler, while the latter's racist ramblings became more than Mussolini could understand or abide. When they parted, there was little sense of closeness established: Hitler, to be sure, expressed great admiration for Mussolini, but evoked little respect and much contempt from Mussolini. Within weeks of their meeting Mussolini was to be shocked by Hitler's bloody purge of his former associates and then to be outraged by Hitler's role in the Nazi putsch in Austria, including the brutal murder of Austrian Chancellor Dollfuss, the Duce's friend and ally. The Venice meeting by no means foreshadowed the process of gradual reversal of status, by which Mussolini would become the weaker partner in the Axis alliance, eventually in humiliating dependency on Hitler.

If only a passing moment in the events that led to World War II,[4] that first meeting of Mussolini and Hitler in Venice in 1934 deserves attention here for what its program shows—and does not show. Hitler arrived in his personal aircraft at 10:00 in the morning, on Thursday, June 14, 1934, at an airport at San Nicolò di Lido. Mussolini greeted him personally, and immediately found ways to upstage his guest. Hitler was taken by launch for a stop at his lodgings at the Grand Hotel des Bains on the Lido. At 11:30 he went by launch to the Piazzale Roma, from which he was driven by limousine up the Brenta Riviera to the specific site Mussolini had chosen for the conference, and where the Duce himself was already lodged. This was the massive Villa Pisani, a veritably regal eighteenth-century pile that had been used variously by Napoleon, the Hapsburgs, and the Savoy monarchs of Italy. Mussolini showed Hitler briefly around the extensive grounds before lunch. The first formal discussions were held in the afternoon, after the Führer was given a sightseeing tour by launch down the Grand Canal and around some islands.[5] That evening, a concert was held in the courtyard of the Palazzo Ducale.

The next morning, June 15, Hitler was taken on a tour of the current Biennale, then in full swing. Accompanying him were Vittorio Cerruti, the

Italian ambassador to Berlin, with his wife, Elisabetta, and also Count Giuseppe Volpi. The latter was Venice's most enterprising citizen: financial and industrial wizard, he was the creator of the industrial complex of Marghera on the mainland, designed to revive the Venetian economy. He had been Mussolini's finance minister (1925–28), and, as the Biennale's president since 1930, he had committed himself to revitalizing it. Volpi was no champion of the radical art then in fashion. He hardly disagreed with the strong disgust expressed by Hitler, whose utterly reactionary tastes found pleasure only in the banal, retrograde display at the German pavilion.

Meanwhile, Mussolini had become disillusioned with the Villa Pisani, inadequately prepared for its functions, while a heat wave and a plague of gigantic mosquitos prompted him to shift locale. The two met again at a wretched lunch at the Lido's golf club, following which the two men held an awkward but critical conference on the golf course. Following that, the two proceeded to the Piazza San Marco for a scheduled rally. A clumsy parade and display gave Hitler a poor impression of Fascist Italy's military and naval might. And, while he did have a chance to admire Mussolini's crowd-pleasing oratory, he was unhappy with the Duce's misleading simplifications of agreements made on the Austrian situation. That evening, it was Hitler's turn to play the host, at a banquet in Mussolini's honor at the Grand Hotel. Il Duce was so bored and disenchanted by this point that he walked out of the affair early. Hitler was left the next morning (June 16) with one more sightseeing engagement, a tour of the Basilica of San Marco, in the company again of Ambassador Cerruti. Taken by launch to the Lido airfield, Hitler then flew back to Berlin.

It must surely be noted by now that something was missing in that entire episode: Richard Wagner. As is well-known, Adolf Hitler was a passionate admirer of the music and the person of Wagner, whom he had made his ultimate idol and model.[6] An early friend of the Wagner family—Siegfried, his wife Winifred, and their children—Hitler became virtually a member of their household, as well as a regular attender, patron, and eventually manipulator, of the Bayreuth Festivals.[7] The previous February had marked the fiftieth anniversary of Wagner's death in the Lagoon City. Yet, virtually *no* attention seems to have been paid, in this 1934 visit, to the poignant Wagner connection with Venice, on the part of Hitler himself or his hosts.

Ernst ("Putzi") Hanfstaengel, who was the Nazi Party's foreign press secretary and "unofficial court jester," as well as an enthusiastic amateur pianist, claimed in his memoirs that it was he who brought the two dictators together. He was one of those in Hitler's circle who hoped Mussolini could serve as a moderating influence on Hitler. Encouraged by his friendship with Ambassador Cerruti and his wife, Hanfstaengel tells us, he made a visit to Rome in February 1934, during which he had two interviews with Mussolini. In the second one he proposed to Mussolini that the Duce should have a personal meeting with the Führer, using the following argument:

Your Excellency, it seems to me essential that you and Herr Hitler should meet. You are both admirers of Wagner and that will give a common starting point. Think what it would mean if you invited him to the Palazzo Vendramin in Venice where Richard Wagner died. He would gain the benefit of your long experience and obtain much-needed insight into the problems of Europe as seen from outside Germany.

Hanfstaengel says he won Mussolini's agreement, and he promptly set to work wooing Hitler to the idea.[8]

However much Hanfstaengel was behind the plan, the Wagner association apparently was never made a matter of concern as the meeting came to pass. It was actually arranged by Vice Chancellor Franz von Papen, in conjunctions with others around Hitler.[9] The cultural associations of Venice seem not to have been an issue at all. Given the preoccupation with the Austrian question, the selection of Italy's most northeastern city of importance might have seemed geographically appropriate. It was certainly clear that Mussolini had no intention of giving the meeting particularly exalted prominence by holding it in his capital, Rome.[10] At any rate, no apparent attempt was made to play to Hitler's Wagnerism in the itinerary.[11] There was no laying any wreath at the Vendramin—which, as it happens, was owned at the time by Count Volpi! One wonders, as he rode by it on his cruise down the Grand Canal, did Hitler even recognize the Vendramin, much less understand any of its possible significance for him?

The implications of this episode might easily be exaggerated. The memories of Wagner's connection to Venice *did* survive in the city, on through the twentieth century. Even if regular commemorations may have slacked off or been eroded by time, the memories were there, close to the surface of consciousness, ready to be drawn upon anew. After World War II, the Italian practice of performing Wagner's operas in Italian translations—even Siegfried Wagner himself had conducted a complete *Ring* in Bologna in 1930–31—yielded to the original language, and Italian audiences in general were made more comfortable and familiar with the composer's German identity. General publications devoted to Venetian cultural life still gave attention to Wagner's place in it.[12]

Above all, anniversaries of Wagner's death continued to inspire activity. For example, in February 1953, the Benedetto Marcello Conservatory of Venice mounted an exhibition, in *celebrazione del 7 anniversario della morte di Riccardo Wagner*, held in their headquarters, the Palazzo Pisani, and titled *Mostra Riccardo Wagner nel Mondo*. Containing musical autographs, documents, iconography, and mementos, the exhibition had been organized by the Bayreuth Festival under the auspices of the German Foreign Ministry and had been presented the January preceding, but was reorganized in Venice, enriched by some of the conservatory's own holdings, and timed to open on the sacred date of February 13.

It was, however, the hundredth anniversary of Wagner's death that showed how much memory could be stirred up. While Wagner celebrations were held widely around Italy, Venice itself was massively awash in Wagneriana in February

1983. The centerpiece of it all was another exhibition, *Wagner e Venezia*, which opened on February 13 to run until July 31, and was situated at the Palazzo Vendramin-Calergi itself. Filled with its own rich collection of textual and visual materials, it was able to take advantage of its location by opening for display the very room in the palazzo in which Wagner died. *IG* followed in detail the preparations for this exhibition, and its writer (February 11, 6) expressed the hope that something of this display might be made permanent—which, in the fullness of time, actually did come to pass.

That was, however, not the only exhibition of the moment. The Fenice Theater ran a *mostra* of its own, titled *Wagner, Caricatura e Fotografia*. It contained a wide range of display, in diverse media and in varying spirit, including material on loan from Bayreuth. *IG* described it (February 12, 3) it as "a kind of *identikit* that reflects Wagner's years of greatest celebrity." Meanwhile, *IG* reported (February 9, 15) the showing of films that dealt with Wagner.[13] The next day it identified two of them: Tony Palmer's massive biographical film *Wagner*, with Richard Burton and Vanessa Redgrave, in a prerelease showing; and Hans-Jürgen Syberberg's complex cinematic adaptation of *Parsifal.*

At the Fenice Theater, two presentations were timed to the anniversary. One was a local production of *Parsifal*, opening on February 11, and later praised by *IG* (February 13, p. 17) as better than what Bayreuth did with this opera. But the Fenice also presented at the time a concert conducted by Peter Maag, with Katia Ricciarelli as soloist. Its program included the *Siegfried Idyll*, the "Youth" Symphony, the *Wesendonck Lieder*, and the Prelude and *Liebestod* from *Tristan*. In connection with the opening of the Fenice's *Parsifal* production, *IG* offered articles on Wagner's multifaceted musical personality and on the difficulties of singing Wagner, plus an 1886 poem on Wagner by Mallarmé, given in the original French as well as in Italian translation.[14]

Most striking of all was a cranky article published by *IG* on February 13 (7), under the title "Between suggestion and myth, the leit-motiv of death: That gondola which so impressed Wagner. ..." Its author, Giuseppe Campolieti, takes as his starting point the reactions of Wagner to the gondola with its funeral associations and "the romantic myth" of "Death in Venice," and matches it with the "Death of Venice" in 1797 and its own implications. Thus, he sees great irony in the busy commemoration in 1983 of Wagner's death, a century before, at the same time that Venice is caught up in its fatuous recreation of Carnival, backed by the policies of the Fenice Theater through its projection of "Liebestod forever!" He pillories these alleged absurdities:

> . . . the "real" Carnival, behind the grotesque grin of its mask, bears its inescapable funereal figure.
> But then, how is it done, to plunge into this ambiguous, perilous Venetian game and emerge unscathed? We return one more time to the "science" of the Teatro Fenice, which, having adopted the mythical bird of recurrent resurrection [i.e., the phoenix],

is able to say for itself, for Venice (and for its friends): "semper eadem" [always the same way].

That the Wagner–Venice connection has continued to remain alive and potent in Venetian memory, down to this moment, is not to be denied. We may mention another, more recent exhibition, a photographic display titled *Itinerari Veneziani di Richard Wagner: Immagine d'epoca e foto di Mario Vidor*, held in the Piazza San Marco in 1995, its contents also published.[15]

Surely the most enduring symbol, however, is the organization, the Associazione Richard Wagner di Venezia (ARWV), founded on February 13, 1992, under the leadership of the distinguished academic, Professor Giuseppe Pugliese. Its broad purpose is to sponsor conferences and cultural events relating to Wagner studies. With the cooperation of the Municipality of Venice, the ARWV undertook a continuing function of great significance. On February 13, 1995, the municipality gave to the organization the room in the Palazzo Vendramin Calergi's mezzanine where Wagner died. This room (whose restoration to its condition in 1883 has been undertaken) is now accessible to visitors by appointment. Such a function was expanded with the creation of the Centro Europeo Studi e Ricerche Richard Wagner, which in December 2003 received donation of the vast Josef Lienhart Collection of Wagner research materials, now on display in adjacent rooms in the Vendramin mezzanine and accessible upon request.[16]

Thus, in the room where Wagner expired on that terrible day of February 13, 1883, there beats the heart of his still-living memory in Venice.

Epilogue

The Seal of Fiction

There is yet more to the story of Wagner and Venice.

The confirmation of the indissoluble connection between the two is provided by still another dimension, that of fictionalization.

Perhaps more than any other composer, Wagner has inspired a large literature of fictional treatment, through a string of novels written during more than a century since his death. Their motivations were diverse, but generally included admiration for the Master. They varied in their scope, but all worked their way up to Wagner's last residence in Venice and his death there, if not focusing on that altogether. The opportunity to portray Wagner's personality while also evoking the highly charged Venetian scene was simply irresistible.

The work of fiction that might first come to mind is not about Wagner's death at all, but was clearly inspired by it, and authored by a writer deeply influenced by Wagner's music and aesthetics: this is, of course, the famous novella, *Der Tod in Venedig* (1911) by Thomas Mann (1875–1955), which uses the Venetian scene for the demise of the character that was something of the author's self-projection. But it was preceded by another highly personalized self-projection, by another major writer: the novel *Il fuoco* (1900) by Gabriele D'Annunzio (1863–1938), in which Wagner's presence and death in Venice is the charged backdrop to the author's fictionalization of his affair with the actress Eleonora Duse. And, on the other side of Mann, yet another major writer, Franz Werfel (1890–1945), produced his *Verdi: Der Roman der Oper* (1924), in which a highly imaginary portrayal of the Italian composer is likewise played out against the backdrop of Wagner's final stay in Venice.

Understandably, German writers, working for a German public, contributed the ensuing efforts, under the shadow (though not always under the sway) of the Nazi regime, from its origins to its demise. The Swiss-German writer Gustav Renker (1889–1967), as a digression within his novelistic output, produced *Finale in Venedig. Ein Richard Wagner Roman* (1933), with Wagner as the hero against a young counter-hero of the writer's invention. More than half of the book depicts the interaction of the two in Venice, through Wagner's death, presented with often very fine imagination. On the other hand, Zdenko von Kraft (1886–1966) was virtually a professional Wagnerian as a prolific writer. During 1919–20, he published a trilogy of novels that gave fictionalized presentation of selected episodes in the Master's life through the first Bayreuth Festival, which he republished in a single volume as *Welt und Wahn* (1940). He then wrote a more ample fictionalization of the remaining years of the composer's life, published as *Abend in Bayreuth. Roman* (1943), chapters 54–94 comprehending the earlier visits to Italy, through the end in Venice, treated in very imaginative detail.

The culmination of that phase of fictionalization was a remarkable novel, referred to in these pages: *Carneval der Einsamen: Richard Wagners Tod in Venedig* (1947), by Eduard Joachim von Reichel (1892–1954) who wrote under the penname of Joachim von Kürenberg. It is an extraordinarily multifaceted confection focused on Wagner and on those around him but including a dazzling cast of supplemental characters (such as D'Annunzio, Duse, Verdi, Boïto, and Oscar Wilde).

At a much greater remove from the world of Wagner veneration are three more recent publications. The left-wing East German writer Egon Günther (b. 1927) has produced a vast and wildly surreal fantasy, *Palazzo Vendramin: Richard Wagners letzte Liebe. Roman* (1993), in which Wagner's postmortem wanderings are intermingled with the adventures of a figure based on Judith Gautier-Mendès, one of Wagner's historical inamoratas. The last fictionalization, *Carrie Pringle* (2001), a play by Graham Billing (1936–2001), takes its theme from the now-discredited fable of the errant Flower Maiden.

All the writers mentioned were well-versed in the sources for Wagner's life and death, and could dramatize and embellish it with generally secure foundation. It is, of course, their capacity for bringing their episodes to life, often with remarkable vivacity, that points up how captivating the Wagner–Venice connection truly is. And through these fictionalizations we can achieve that much more deep a feeling for that connection. In effect, they set a final, definitive seal upon it.

Detailed exposition and analysis of these fictionalizations is not possible in the present volume, and therefore will be undertaken in a projected successor publication.

Fig. 1. Palazzi Giustiniani (photo by author, 1989)

Fig. 2. Richard Wagner, Feb.-Mar. 1860 (photo portrait, Petit and Trinquart, Paris)

Fig. 3. Cosima and Richard Wagner, May 9, 1872 (photo portrait, Fritz Luckhardt, Munich)

Fig. 4. Cosima and Richard Wagner, Feb. 1, 1874 (photo, Adolph von Gross, Munich)

Fig. 5. Cosima, Siegfried, and Richard Wagner, Feb. 1, 1874 (photo, Adolph von Gross, Munich)

Fig. 6. Cosima Wagner's children costumed as Wagner opera characters, May 22, 1875: *upper left to right*, Eva von Bülow as Eva; Isolde von Bülow/Wagner as Isolde; Blandine von Bülow as Elisabeth; *lower left to right*, Siegfried Wagner as Siegfried; Daniella von Bülow as Senta (photo, Adolph von Gross, Munich)

Fig. 7. "The Holy Family": *upper left to right*, Blandine, Eva, Isolde as Angels, Joukowsky as Joseph; *lower left to right*, Siegfried as boy Jesus, Daniela as Mary (painting, Paul Joukowsky, 1880–81)

Fig. 8. Siegfried and Richard Wagner, June 1, 1880 (photo portrait, P. Biondi e Figlio, Naples)

Fig. 9. Richard Wagner, July 10, 1880 (lithograph, Alfred de Bovet, 1895, after painting: Edmond Jean de Pury, Naples)

Fig. 10. The Wagner family at Wahnfried, Aug. 23, 1881: *upper left to right*, Blandine, Heinrich von Stein, Cosima, Richard, Joukowsky; *lower left to right*, dog, Isolde, Blandine (standing), dog Mark, Eva, Siegfried (photo, Adolph von Gross, Bayreuth)

Fig. 11. Richard Wagner, Jan. 15, 1882 (painting, Auguste Renoir, Palermo)

Fig. 12. Richard Wagner, 1882 (portrait: Paul Joukowsky, Palermo; oil on canvas, 15.5 x 12.5 cm.; private collection)

Fig. 13. Richard Wagner, May 1, 1882 (photo portrait, Joseph Albert, Munich)

Fig. 14. Palazzo Vendramin-Calergi, façade from SW (photo by author, 1981)

Fig. 15. Palazzo Vendramin-Calergi, façade and garden from S (photo by author, 1992)

Fig. 16. Richard and Cosima Wagner at land entrance to Palazzo Vendramin, winter 1882–83 (painting, anonymous)

Fig. 17. Land entrance to Palazzo Vendramin (Casino Municipale), 1978 (photo by author)

Fig. 18. Luigi Mancinelli, inscribed in Venice, April 1882? (photo Venice)

Fig. 19. Franz Liszt (photo portrait, Vianelli, Venice, 1880)

Fig. 20. Franz Liszt (painting, Paul Joukowsky, Venice, autumn 1882)

Fig. 21. Paul Joukowsky (photo)

Fig. 22. Hermann Levi (photo)

LUIGI TREVISAN detto GANASSETA
Gondoliere di R. Wagner.

Fig. 23. Luigi Trevisan, "Ganasseta" (drawing, Giacomo Favretto)

Fig. 24. Luigi Trevisan on his gondola (photo)

Fig. 25. Giuseppe Contin di Castelseprio (photo)

Fig. 26. Raffaele Frontali (photo)

Fig. 27. Richard Wagner rehearsing *Tristan* (engraving: Gustave Gaul, 1886, after photograph by J. Löwy, Vienna, 1875)

Fig. 28. Baton and music stand used by Wagner, concert of December 24, 1883, with beret (photo)

Fig. 29. "R. playing," Feb. 12, 1883 (drawing, Paul Joukowsky)

Fig. 30. "R. reading, 12 Feb. 1883" (drawing, Paul Joukowsky)

Fig. 31–32. Death mask of Richard Wagner, Feb. 14, 1883 (Benvenuti, with Ludwig Passini)

Fig. 33. The sofa on which Wagner died on Feb. 13, 1883 (photo, Bayreuth)

Fig. 34. Richard Wagner's casket, in re-opened grave, Wahnfried, Oct. 7, 2002 (photo, Bayreuth)

Fig. 35. The Assumption ("Assunta") of the Virgin Mary (painting, Titian, 1518)

Fig. 36. The Flower Maidens in *Parsifal*, Bayreuth, 1882: Carrie Pringle left in middle line (photo)

For der fährt nach großem Ziel,
Fern am Steuer ruhig sehen.
Unbekümmert ob ein Kiel
... und Tadel heimlich sprechen ...

... 1883   ... Neumann

Fig. 37. Angelo Neumann, ca. 1883 (photo card, with inscription from time of the Venice performances of the *Ring*)

Fig. 38. Anton Seidl, ca. 1890 (photo portrait, New York)

Fig. 39. Hedwig Reicher-Kindermann as Brünnhilde (photo portrait)

Fig. 40. Georg Unger as Siegfried (photo portrait)

Fig. 41. Plaque in honor of Wagner, in the Café Lavena: "Riccardo Wagner frequented this place, thinking and writing: 1878–1883" (wood carving, Vincenzo Cadorin; photo by the author, 1984)

Fig. 42. Plaque commemorating Wagner's death, Grand Canal wall of the Palazzo Vendramin (marble by Ettore Cadorin, verse by Gabriele D'Annunzio, 1910; photo by Christopher N. Barker, 1996)

Fig. 43. Wagner and Verdi busts, Giardini Pubblici, Venice (photo by the author, 1984)

Fig. 44. Wagner bust (marble, Fritz Schaper, 1908; photo by the author, 2006)

Fig. 45. Verdi bust (marble, Gerolamo Bortotti, 1909; photo by the author, 2006)

Fig. 46. Siegfried and Cosima Wagner (photo, Kester, Munich, 1923)

Part 5

Addenda

Addendum I

Wagner and Titian's Assumption (to chapters 2–4)

This massive painting, now spectacularly hung above the high altar of the Franciscan church of Santa Maria Gloriosa dei Frari,[1] was displayed from 1816 to 1919 in the Accademia degli Belli Arti, where Wagner saw it.

In his treatment of the 1861 episode, Gregor-Dellin suggests that "Titian's Virgin bears a significant facial resemblance to Mathilde, with her small round chin and rosebud mouth, and one of the figures left behind on earth is reaching after her ascending figure with a conspicuously outstretched arm."[2] Against such a perception, we have Wagner's own later comments, as quoted by Cosima Wagner in her diaries, on December 8, 1880:

> The *Assumption* was mentioned again at lunch, and R. said that in the facial expression the pain of a woman in childbirth is mixed with the ecstasy of love, and this is why the closeness of the apostles and the disciples and all these false relationships are so disturbing

—a reaction that Wagner then immediately regretted.

That later reaction reflects curiously on a crucial fact about Wagner's 1861 meeting with the Wesendoncks in Venice. He discovered at that time that Mathilde was pregnant—and, of course, by her husband. In a subsequent letter that Wagner wrote in late December 1861, while he was briefly back in Paris, he obliquely acknowledged this fact and accordingly wrote an effective, if rhetorically coated, ending to their emotional ties, as foreshadowed by the recent unhappy time in Venice.[3] Nevertheless, in that letter, as well as in a prior one he wrote to her from Paris on December 21,[4] Wagner speaks repeatedly of his preoccupation with "my Nürnberg mastersingers," and he even relates this project to his recent Venice journey. In describing his trip back to Vienna from Venice, he remembers the journey's length and painfulness, and his enforced distractions, in relation to his chronic vision problems resulting from astigmatism:

> . . . Unfortunately my visual functions are growing ever duller; nothing rivets my gaze, and each locality, with all that appertains thereto—were it the greatest masterpieces in the world—distracts me not, remains indifferent to me; my eye I have for nothing but

distinguishing of day from night, now, light from gloom . . . I see no pictures more, save inner ones and they clamour for nothing but sound. But no impassioned vision would consent to lighten me on that grey journey; the world itself appeared a toyshop; and that took me back to Nürnberg, where I had passed a day last summer and there are plenty of pretty things to see. At once it resounded to me as an overture to the Mastersingers of Nüremberg.

Continuing, Wagner reports the eagerness and productivity with which he plunged into the new project when he was back in Vienna.

Following so closely upon the previous month's visit to Venice, these epistolary comments perhaps offer a more accurate recollection of the painting's links to the gestation of *Die Meistersinger* than what he wrote in his memoirs nearly two decades later. Clearly, the departure from Venice was genuinely related to his renewed commitment to this opera, and was even involved with his conception of its overture. In the letter to Mathilde, Wagner makes no reference to finding inspiration in Titian's painting. On the contrary, his admission of visual difficulty in viewing works of art might refute emphatically his later assertion that the painting was so explicit a trigger to his creative imagination.

Among recent attempts to explain Wagner's problematical linking of Titian's painting to the genesis of *Die Meistersinger* there is one by the composer's great-granddaughter, Nike Wagner. She suggests that Wagner was struck by the great painter's scale of perspective, elevating the Virgin to a lofty plane from which she can observe the world below—a perspective that corresponded to Jean Paul's idea of humor as an "inversion of the exalted." That would imply the "bird's eye (or God's eye) view" through which he could look down upon the antics of his Nürembergers.[5] On the other hand, Peter Wapnewski[6] has extended probing observations he had made in 1978, proposing that the Virgin Mary had become for Wagner a symbol of transcendent love, earthly renunciation, and transfiguration through self-denial. Those are, of course, themes that permeate so much of Wagner's dramatic thought. The encounter with Titian's painting, at a time when Wagner was struggling over renunciation of Mathilde, would thus, argues Wapnewski, have prompted the composer to connect this concept to Hans Sachs and to that character's transcendent renunciation of Eva.

Cosima and Wagner himself seem to have worked out an alternative perception of their own in this line. On September 4, 1879, amid a discussion of art back in Bayreuth, Cosima ventured to "compare Titian's *Assumption of the Virgin* . . . with Isolde's transfiguration." And in a later echo, near the end of his life (Cosima, October 22, 1882), Wagner himself added another twist to this perception of the painting:

> R. denies that the *Assunta* is the Mother of God; it is Isolde, he says, in the apotheosis of love, whereas in the *Sistine Madonna*, "this wonderful inspiration," one sees, for all the consummate beauty, her utter unapproachability: "Good Lord, to have any ideas about her!"

The latest interpretation, by Joachim Köhler,[7] concludes that Wagner first saw it as an image of transfiguration through sexuality and childbearing, then fitted it to his concept of a new heroine in Eva of *Die Meistersinger*, still later to be realized most fully in *Parsifal*'s Kundry.[8]

This painting continued to be an absorbing focus of attention for Wagner, particularly as his perceptions were augmented by Cosima's. She seems to have admired this painting even before she saw it in person: on August 15, 1869, she records showing a reproduction of it to her children on the occasion of the Feast of the Assumption. Her first direct encounter with the painting, in her first stay in Venice in 1876, was overwhelming—"as if I were hearing a Beethoven symphony for the first time" (September 23).[9] It is tempting to wonder if her reactions came to influence Wagner's own "recollection" of how much the painting inspired him in November 1861. It was, after all, during their 1880 stay in Italy that he dictated to Cosima the 1861–64 section of *Mein Leben*, in which he made the assertion that the painting had prompted his conception of *Die Meistersinger* and its Overture. In that process, could Cosima have nudged him into making the assertion?

At any rate, the painting acquired considerable shared meaning for the two. During their 1880 sojourn in Venice, Cosima recorded that she took here daughter Daniela to the Accademia "to pay our respects to [Titian's] *Assumption*" (October 12); while, five days later, Richard made his own pilgrimage to the painting, though he came away from it with theological misgivings (October 17). Then, in their penultimate visit to Venice in the spring of 1882, Richard and Cosima again responded to the power of this painting. In her account (April 25), Cosima begins with a renewal of her placement of the painting with another supreme masterpiece:

> . . . we rest in front of [Titian's] *Assunta*, and it makes a glorious impression. When I say that it is a totality, rather like the 9th Symphony [of Beethoven], R. says, "Oh, we have nothing so perfect in music—that is all experimentation."—The glowing head of the Virgin Mary recalls to him his idea of the sexual urge: this unique and mighty force, now freed of all desire, the Will enraptured and redeemed. He is unable to do justice to God, the "bat," though he feels it is finely painted. However, he is captivated by the apostles. What blissful moments do we spend there! Every time he regards the head he gives an exclamation of delight. . . .

Finally, it was in conversation with Cosima in Venice the following autumn (October 22, 1882), that Wagner returned to the idea of Titian's Madonna as Isolde, quoted above.

By this time, through the years with Cosima, Wagner seems to have allowed Titian's Madonna to be drawn away from any associations with Mathilde Wesendonck, and into broader imagery.

In sum, like an idée fixe, Titian's painting had become a recurring subject for associative variation and revised perception, down to the end of Wagner's life.

Addendum 2

A Scandal Debunked: Carrie Pringle (to chapter 3)

An elaborate structure of speculative interpretation has grown up around the person of soprano Carrie Pringle (1859–1930), of British background though born in Austria and trained in Europe.

Some incontrovertible facts are known. During the years 1878–83 she intermittently pursued vocal studies in Milan. Apparently at Hermann Levi's suggestion, she auditioned for Wagner in August 1881. She sang as one of the Flower Maidens in the premiere production of *Parsifal* (fig. 36). She twice sent telegrams to the Wagners: one on May 22, 1882, to congratulate Richard on his sixty-ninth birthday; and then in February 1883 to express condolences to the family on his death. She was not engaged for the revival of *Parsifal* at Bayreuth in 1883, presumably on the basis of vocal inadequacies.

Beyond these facts, there are undocumented (or undocumentable) assertions, revolving around the central assumption that she had been caught up in an amorous affair with Wagner. From such an assumption evolved a story that Cosima, in a jealous rage, arranged an "accident" for Pringle, by which she was made to fall through a trapdoor on the Bayreuth stage and thus injured during rehearsals for the 1882 premiere of *Parsifal*. But the most significant assertions are: (1) that an arrangement was pending for her to visit Wagner at the Vendramin in February 1883; (2) that this prospect prompted a furious argument between Richard and Cosima on the morning of the thirteenth; (3) and that Dr. Keppler had something to do with all this, or at least recognized the argument as a decisive factor in Wagner's collapse that day.[1]

The beginnings of all this tangle are apparently a statement by daughter Isolde von Bülow-Beidler that there had been "an extremely violent scene between my parents" on the morning of February 13. The statement may have been stimulated by the bitter arguments and disaffection that flared up between Isolde and her mother in 1913, prompting her to cobble up stories about Pringle's having an affair with Wagner; Isolde's own son seems to have fed the rumors with a report about Cosima arranging an injurious accident for Pringle.

Out of the rumor-mills that flourished at Bayreuth in the 1930s came a report embodied in the strange diaries of an odd hanger-on there, one Benedikt Lochmüller, who accepted uncritically all the stories he was told and delighted in recording them. The actual diary in question seems to have disappeared but was transcribed by Herbert Conrad. Among gossipy entries for March 1933 is one dated the fourteenth:

> The last woman Wagner loved was a certain Pringle (pronounced Pringel); she was of English extraction, came from England. She came to Bayreuth in 1882, the year of Parsifal; for the first time; she was a chorus member, in Parsifal evidently a solo Flowermaiden; she is said to have been from a good family; a serious, well-bred person; she is said to have been very beautiful. It is said that Levi introduced her to Bayreuth. But Wagner apparently knew her before 1882 and therefore before her appearance in Bayreuth. She was then—in 1882—Richard Wagner's lover. And, moreover, in Bayreuth, at the time of the festival. But the liaison continued after the Festival. When Wagner left Bayreuth for Venice Miss Pringle turned up in Venice too—her telegram from Milan has survived—there too she was Wagner's lover. Cosima, who was very angry at this, reproached Wagner for it in February 1883, reproaches that wore him down and from which he died suddenly on 13 Feb. 1883. Cosima collapsed completely from her guilty conscience at his death, she considered herself to blame for his premature death.[2]

This kind of gossip was drawn into the serious Wagner literature only in 1962, in an article by the French scholar Jean Mistler, who records his picking up of the Bayreuth rumors:

> Thirty years ago, persons worthy of trust repeated to me something that Wagner's daughter, Isolde, had told them: on the morning of the 13th a telegram arrived at the Palazzo Vendramin from Miss Carrie Pringle, the Flowermaiden from *Parsifal* whom we have already mentioned. Travelling through Italy, the young Englishwoman asked the Master when she could visit him. Her telegram came to Cosima's attention and a violent scene is said to have ensued.[3]

Mistler's essay did not win much immediate attention, and the ideas he was advancing were developed only in 1978 by Herbert Conrad.[4] The latter's argument was given further, veritably definitive, and even more widely circulated exposition by Curt von Westernhagen, in his biography of the composer but especially in his article "Wagner's Last Day." In that Westernhagen reviewed Wagner's contacts with Carrie Pringle: he rejected the accusation that Cosima was responsible for any accident causing injury to Pringle, but he accepted the plausibly of the quarrel between Richard and Cosima on the morning of February 13.

While a few Wagner biographers passed over or frankly discounted the February 13 episode, Westernhagen's case seemed so effectively argued that his conclusions were taken as authoritative and accepted by a number of others.[5]

Since then, however, Stewart Spencer, in the 2004 volume of *Wagner*, the journal of the Wagner Society of London that he edited, has published his article subtitled "Wagner and Carrie Pringle."[6] In that article he scrutinizes all the sources, literature, and issues involved in the Pringle controversies. Wielding a scholarly razor worthy of Ockham, Spencer has brought us back to the limited facts of the matter. Thereby he has so deflated all the speculation and sensationalism that the Wagner–Pringle "romance," and associated assumptions or assertions, will be quite difficult to take seriously hereafter.

That said, we note the stubborn persistence of the discredited story of Pringle's "role" in Wagner's last day, which is still taken as fact in the most recent popular biography of the composer by Stephen Johnson.[7]

Life After Wagner (to chapter 2)

It is interesting to note that a number of those who had been close to Wagner at one time or another would not long outlive him. **Friedrich Nietzsche** did not die until 1900, but he had already, by 1883, been slipping into the pathetic insanity that would destroy him. Once Wagner's devoted disciple and helper, **Hans von Bülow**, Cosima's first husband and father of Daniela and Blandine, despite a brilliant career as conductor and pianist, slipped into his own deepened mental instability in the years after Wagner's death, finally dying in a Cairo hotel in 1894. A differently poignant loss was Nietzsche's sometime friend, a beloved member of the Wagner household as Siegfried's tutor, and a writer and thinker whom Richard greatly admired: **Heinrich von Stein**, who on June 30, 1887, died at the cruelly premature age of thirty, only four years after Wagner.

Still closer to Wagner's death, of course, was the passing of **Franz Liszt** on July 31, 1886. Liszt had finally settled in Bayreuth and was staying in a small house across the alley from Wahnfried when he died. There had been a still-unexplained breach between him and Cosima in the interim, and her treatment of him at the time of his death was notably cold, even cruel.[1] He was buried, not on the Wahnfried grounds but, as would be his grandson Siegfried Wagner and the conductor Hans Richter, in the Bayreuth Municipal Cemetery—though set off by himself in a curious little pseudo-medieval mausoleum.

Only weeks before Liszt's death, deposed **King Ludwig II** of Bavaria died on June 13, 1886, by drowning in Lake Starnberg, under circumstances that are still controversial and much debated. Mentally troubled but convinced that serving the cause of Wagner and his music was one of the great missions of his life, Ludwig had sometimes felt betrayed or manipulated by the composer, while he himself often caused Wagner vexation. But there is no doubt that Ludwig's lavish generosity to Wagner was one of the things that brought the king to difficulty, discredit, and disaster.

The most tragic, and proximate, of all these deaths, however, was that of the Russian-born **Josef (Joseph) Rubinstein** (1847–84), the amanuensis, copyist, arranger, and promoter of Wagner's music, dear to Wagner for his playing of Bach and Beethoven at family evenings, or even during rehearsal duties. Wagner often treated him like a trained seal, primed to perform on the command of an instant. A prickly individual who got along badly with most of the Wagner family

(Cosima called him "Malvolio") and even with the tolerant Joukowsky, he was a bundle of internal torments, despite his genuine gifts. A veritable caricature of the "self-hating Jew," he came from a wealthy Jewish family. His father had to be persuaded periodically (even by Wagner himself) to support him. Perhaps oversensitized by the anti-Semitism all around him, he had already felt at odds with his Jewish identity when, in 1872, he read Wagner's *Judentum in Musik*. In the great composer's hostility to Judaism, Rubinstein saw exactly the guidance he needed in dealing with his own "Jewish deficiencies." His devotion to Wagner personally commended himself to the composer as much as his musical talents. Yet even Wagner could find him trying: just two days before his death, in an anti-Semitic exchange with Cosima, Richard, irritated with visiting conductor Hermann Levi, opined of Jews "that one should really have nothing to do with Israelites—either it causes them emotional disturbance, or it finds expression in arrogance, as with J. Rub" (February 11, 1883).

Rubinstein was associated with the Wagner household for long periods of time, at Bayreuth, and in Naples. Having taken up residence himself in Palermo, he was instrumental in drawing the Wagners there and was a frequent presence during their stay. He apparently made his residence in Venice during the first five weeks of Wagner's final stay there, and was a frequent visitor at the Palazzo Vendramin. But he departed on October 22 and was not in Venice at the time of the master's death.

In 1884, some nineteen months after the composer's demise, Rubinstein traveled in utter despair to Lucerne, where he had first met Wagner (April 21, 1872). There, at age thirty-seven, Rubinstein committed suicide (September 15). As a form of consolation, he was buried in Bayreuth, if in its Jewish cemetery.[2]

Siegfried Wagner, the composer's son, had strong memories of the pianist at the time of the Naples residence:

> The unhappy Joseph Rubinstein, busy preparing the vocal score of *Parsifal*, was among the less appealing personalities in our circle of friends. He showed clearly to my mother and to us children that he was there only by our father's wish and that the family was really a useless, burdensome appendage. My mother put up with this calmly, since she had understood his good and significant qualities; for us children, on the other hand, he was becoming so repugnant that there was need for judicious maternal admonitions that we refrain from openly offensive expression. I characterized him as "unhappy." That he certainly was. Often he admitted to my father that he suffered on account of his race: that, Kundry-like, he yearned for redemption. That he believed he might find through my father and his art. Shortly after February 13, 1883, bereft of his benevolent protector, reduced to desperation, he took his own life. The sense of aversion that we children had felt toward him was understandably transformed into pity, when we later were able to gain insight into his gloomy soul.[3]

Richard Fricke, one of Wagner's deputies in the preparation of the 1876 *Ring* at Bayreuth, also recalled at least one episode of Rubinstein's chronic mental disturbance.[4]

Of course, many in Wagner's circle—**Hermann Levi** (1839–1900), **Hans Richter** (1843–1916), **Adolf von Gross** (1845–1931), **Anton Seidl** (1850–98), **Engelbert Humperdinck** (1854–1921), and even **Paul Joukowsky** (Pavel Zhukowski) (1845–1912) himself—were still to have years of life and career ahead of them in 1883. Likewise **Mathilde Wesendonck**, who lived until 1902. The most striking case of all, however, was certainly that of Cosima Wagner— whose own life after her husband's death has been only sparingly studied for its own sake.[5]

After Wagner's burial, this talented and tough woman at first secluded herself on the upper floor of Wahnfried, in prolonged mourning for the man to whom she had so utterly devoted herself. Anxieties about the direction of the Bayreuth Festival under the indispensable but stumbling management of Gross and others prompted her to come out of isolation. By 1886 she had assumed full direction herself, determined to fulfill her understanding of Wagner's intentions, and committed to creating a true cult of Wagner and Wagnerism. Under her sharp eye and iron hand, the festival productions and allied activities gradually established an enviable artistic standard, and only the decline of her health forced her in 1906 to yield control to her son, Siegfried. Thereafter, Cosima withdrew again into seclusion, in a residence adjacent to Wahnfried, where she died, not quite ninety-three years old, on April 1, 1930—with cruel irony, only weeks before her son. She was laid to rest beside Richard in the Wahnfried grave, forty-seven years (slightly over half her lifetime!) after his burial. (It should be recalled that Cosima was thirty-two and Richard was fifty-seven when they married in 1870, with a twenty-five-year disparity in their ages; and that she was forty-five when he died at age sixty-nine in 1883.) In the years after 1883 she did travel a good deal, mainly for reasons of health, and even to Italy, with at least one trip to Palermo (when her son-in-law Count Gravina died). But apparently she never returned to Venice—dare we suspect, for obvious reasons?

Of the children (see figs. 6, 7, 10), the youngest, Wagner's son **Siegfried** (1869–1930), nicknamed "Fidi," has already been mentioned. Wagner first thought he should become an architect, in view of the boy's early interest in that subject, as particularly fired by his Italian experiences. But that interest waned and, in his twenties, he shifted definitively to music. Following studies with Humperdinck and Richter he emerged as an able if not distinguished conductor (making his debut in the Bayreuth pit in 1896) and a prolific composer in his own right (producing all of eighteen operas). His quirkish personality and his covert homosexuality—or, more properly, bisexuality—created some tensions as he assumed his father's mantle, but he asserted himself, took over the Bayreuth Festival from his mother, and was able to run it for a quarter-century.[6] Upon his death, much to the anger of his sisters, control passed to his widow, Winifred (née Williams, 1897–1980), of mixed British/Danish parentage and the adopted daughter of an old Wagner friend and collaborator, Karl Klindworth. It was under Winifred that the Wagner family and the Bayreuth establishment were drawn into lively association with Adolf Hitler and his regime, leaving a shadow of contamination that has never been completely dispelled in the eyes of many—including some of the composer's great-grandchildren.[7] After World War II, the festival was allowed to resume under the direction of Siegfried's sons (and the composer's grandsons), Wieland (1917–66) and Wolfgang (b. 1919) Wagner. The latter yielded control only in April 2008, to his two daughters, Richard's great-granddaughters.[8]

Of the daughters, all but one lived into the dark world of World War II. Daniela, Isolde, and Eva worked with their mother and then their brother on both administration and production at the festival, through Siegfried's lifetime; the first and last of them became particularly embittered by Winifred Wagner's arbitrary regime thereafter. **Daniela von Bülow** (1860–1940), nicknamed "Loulou" or "Lusch," in 1886 married the German art historian and philosopher, Dr. **Henry Thode**, who first appeared on the scene in a visit to the Wagners in Venice in October 1882. The marriage proved childless and unhappy, ending in divorce in 1914 after his steamy affair with Isadora Duncan. As Cosima's health declined, Daniela was increasingly drawn (together with Eva) into caring for her mother. Grudgingly given responsibility for a Bayreuth production in 1933, she finally became completely estranged from family and festival and settled for her remaining years in the earlier family home at Villa Tribschen near Lucerne.

Blandine von Bülow (1863–1941), known as "Boni," as we have seen, married Count **Biago Gravina** (1850–97). She was pregnant with the first of their three children at the time Wagner died and was unable to attend his funeral. In growing torment over his family and financial situation, Gravina committed suicide. Blandine never remarried but attended to her children and remained apart from the Bayreuth world for the rest of her long life. **Isolde von Bülow** (1865–1919), "Loldi," in 1900 married a musician named **Franz Beidler** (1872–1930), who had joined the musical staff at Bayreuth four years before and occasionally conducted performances. They had a son but were pushed out of the Bayreuth world by Siegfried, who disliked Beidler and dismissed him. Isolde had been born while her mother was still officially married to Hans von Bülow and was hence legally his daughter. For some years Cosima herself furthered the pretense, only gradually admitting Isolde's true paternity. In 1913, anxious to lay claim to her familial rights, Isolde went to court to have herself officially recognized as Wagner's daughter. She lost the case and became definitively estranged from both her mother and her brother. Ravaged by tuberculosis and effectively abandoned by her adulterous husband, she died six years later. In a grotesque epilogue, her body was exhumed and reburied with Beidler after his death (1930), only to be joined by his second wife after her death (1975).[9]

Eva Wagner (1867–1942) figured significantly in transmitting the Wagner heritage. For one thing, she took it upon herself to go through her mother's diaries and to excise passages deemed to be embarrassing to the family. Further, with her mother's encouragement, she was attracted to **Houston Stewart Chamberlain** (1855–1927), who had been become an ardent Wagnerian, welcomed by Wagner himself in Bayreuth in 1882. Thereafter, he became a devoted associate of Cosima in creating a Wagner "cult," in 1896 publishing an early biography of the composer, among a number of writings on his music. Chamberlain was also a rabid anti-Semite, and his treatises won the admiration of Adolph Hitler; Chamberlain thus became the future dictator's eventual conduit into the Bayreuth circle. In 1908, after the dissolution of Chamberlain's first marriage, he and Eva were wed, and he became even more firmly entrenched in the Bayreuth establishment, to his death.[10] Meanwhile, Eva shared with Daniela the ·care of their aged mother and then, equally disillusioned with the regime of Winifred Wagner at Bayreuth, joined her sister at Villa Tribschen. In the middle of World War II, Eva was the last of the Wagner children to die.

Addendum 4

Verdi on Wagner's Death and His Music (to chapter 6)

It is worth recalling that Verdi's reaction to Wagner's death was altogether of a piece with the comments quoted by *La Venezia* (*LV*) on February 19, 1883 (see above, p. 100). When he heard the news on February 14, he wrote to Giulio Ricordi:

> Sad. Sad. Sad!
> Wagner is dead!
> When I read the news yesterday I may truly say that I was crushed! Let us not discuss it. It is a great individual who has disappeared! A name that leaves a powerful imprint on the history of art!

Having written this, he changed the word *potente* in the final phrase to *potentissima*, so as to read "a most powerful imprint."[1]

It was just slightly over a month later (March 24) that Verdi wrote another letter to Ricordi, in which he reacted to some foolish statements by the baritone Victor Maurel about what Verdi's projected *Otello* would offer, including "some great lessons for young musicians of the future." Verdi observed:

> It has never been and never will be my intention to give lessons to anyone. Without regard to schools, I admire everything that pleases me, I do as I feel, and I let everybody do as he pleases."[2]

Such benign and sage moderation repeats the sense of the quotation that *LV* published, as noted. But both assertions contrast with the more frankly partisan tone of an earlier letter, one Verdi wrote to Giulio Ricordi on April 20, 1878, in which he drew very sharp lines between German and Italian styles, lines he believed should be preserved. "We are all working, without meaning to, for the downfall of our theater," he begins, pointing out the new penchant in Italy for founding organizations that promulgate instrumental music on German principles:

... why in the name of all that's holy must we do German art if we are living in Italy? Twelve or fifteen years ago I was elected president of a concert society ... I refused, and I asked: "Why not form a society for vocal music? That's alive in Italy—the rest is an art for Germans." Perhaps that sounded foolish then as it does now; but a society for vocal music, which would let us hear Palestrina, the best of his contemporaries, Marcello and such people, would have preserved for us our love of song, as it is expressed in opera. Now everything is supposed to be based on orchestration, on harmony. The alpha and omega is Beethoven's Ninth Symphony, marvelous in the first three movements, very badly set in the last. No one will ever approach the sublimity of the first movement, but it will be an easy task to write as badly for voices as is done in the last movement. And supported by the authority of Beethoven they will all shout: "That's the way to do it. ..."

Never mind! Let them go on as they have begun. It may even be better so; but a "better" that undoubtedly means the end of opera. Art belongs to all nations—nobody believes that more firmly than I. But it is practised by individuals; and since the Germans have other artistic methods than we have, their art is basically different from ours. We cannot compose like the Germans, or at least we ought not to; nor they like us. Let the Germans assimilate our artistic substance, as Haydn and Mozart did in their time; yet they remained predominantly symphonic musicians. And it is perfectly proper for Rossini to have taken over certain formal elements from Mozart; he is still a melodist for all that. But if we let fashion, love of innovation, and an alleged scientific spirit tempt us to surrender the native quality of our own art, the free natural certainty of our work and perception, our bright golden light, they we are simply being stupid and senseless.[3]

A kind of supplement to all this came in 1892. On April 7 of that year, Hans von Bülow wrote from Hamburg an overwrought letter to Verdi. Twenty years before von Bülow had written an article critical of Verdi and, now that he had recognized Verdi's great late works in the interval, he apologized profusely, proclaimed his love for Verdi and his music, and ended with the exclamation: "Viva VERDI, the Wagner of our dear allies!" Having received the letter, Verdi wrote in reply from Genoa on April 14, 1893, assuring von Bülow that "There is no shadow of sin in you, nor is there any need for repentance and absolution." Verdi expressed gratitude for the generous compliments of so distinguished a musician:

However that be, this letter of yours, unexpected, written by a musician of your distinction, and of your importance in the artistic world, has given me great pleasure. And that not for my personal vanity but because I perceive that the truly superior artists make judgments without prejudices as to schools, nationalities, time.

If the artists of North and South have diverse inclinations, it is good they are diverse. Everyone should maintain the *particular characteristics of his nation*, as the great Wagner has said.

Happy you who are still the sons of Bach! ... And we? ... Yet we, sons of Palestrina, at one time had a great school ... and ours! Now it is delegitimized, and threatens ruin! If only we could go back to the beginning![4]

It is a simple fact that Verdi and Wagner never met in person, nor even had any indirect dealings. The story of Verdi's contacts with Wagner's music, and how his reactions to it may be interpreted, are a complicated subject and continue to prompt study.[5]

Addendum 5

Wagner's "Blue Grotto" in Venice and His "Luxury" Addictions (to chapter 7)

Biographers of Wagner have long taken for granted the fact that the composer liked to create for himself a private sanctuary in his living quarters. But detailed descriptions of these arrangements are scanty in our sources, and are rarely scrutinized together.

It is clear from his account in *Mein Leben* that Wagner established a plush setting in his apartment at the Palazzo Giustiniani during his Venetian stay of 1858–59. The first testimony from another hand as to Wagner's special kind of luxurious "nesting" deals with his settlement in the Vienna suburb of Penzing in 1863, using his profits from conducting in Russia. In 1906 one Ludwig Karpath transcribed the reminiscences of Bertha Goldwag, the designer and purveyor who decorated Wagner's apartment. In her recollections we can perceive the model clearly established:

> . . . Except for a single room, there were no difficulties, as all the rooms were furnished in the usual way, albeit elegantly. Only a single room, as I say, about the size of a closet, was decorated with extravagant splendour in keeping with Wagner's most detailed instructions. The walls were lined in silk, with relievo garlands all the way round. From the ceiling hung a wonderful lamp with a gentle beam. The whole of the floor was covered in heavy and exceptionally soft rugs in which your feet literally sank. The furnishings of this boudoir—as I should like to call this room—consisted of a small sofa, a number of armchairs and a small table. All the seats had expensive covers and cushions, which he generally used to support his elbows. . . . No one was allowed to enter this room. Wagner always remained there alone and always during the morning. *Without my having to ask him*, he once said that he felt particularly at ease in such a room, as the wonderful colours inspired him to work.

Berta Goldwag went on to recall that "Wagner always needed plenty of warmth to feel comfortable," requiring lots of lining and padding, as well as color and flair. "Of course, the Master went in for a certain luxury, I made him lots of clothes and dressing gowns. . . ." When Wagner moved on to Munich and settled there, Goldwag was summoned to serve him again:

> I travelled twice to Munich *in order to furnish Wagner's rooms there along the lines that were already familiar to me*. Here, too, I decorated a closet just as I earlier described it and to this end remained in Wagner's house for some considerable time.

Required to obtain "silk shirts, dressing gowns, covers, and so on," Goldwag had to sneak them through Austrian customs as intended "for a countess in Berlin." When Wagner moved yet again, to Switzerland, Goldwag "*saw to the furnishings for a third time*" at Tribschen.[1]

There is, of course, ample testimony from others simply as to Wagner's love for the best in clothing, and especially silks, and as to his requirement of silk undergarments because of his skin sensitivities (especially his inability to tolerate cotton next to his skin), resulting from his erysipelas.

As for his private sanctuary, Wagner's practices seemed to vary over the years. In his ultimate mansion in Bayreuth, called Wahnfried, he spent much time in its commodious and lavish first-floor drawing room, but for his creative work he shut himself "in a simply decorated room on the upper floor, the walls hung with grey satin, its only ornament a portrait of Cosima by Lenbach."[2] It seems as if it was when Wagner dwelt for periods of time abroad, particularly in Italy, that he required the fuller insulation of enfolding luxury.

We have a hint of how Wagner used a favorite method to establish some degree of self-isolation, during his stay at the Hôtel des Palmes in Palermo in early winter 1881–82. Ernest Newman reports a lingering effect of Wagner's longtime use of extra-strong perfumes on his garments and in his living quarters. Guy de Maupassant, the first of many who in subsequent years visited the Wagner apartment, was astounded to discover the powerful odor of rose perfume in a wardrobe, and he was told that this survived from Wagner's storage there of his well-infused clothing. According to Newman, the persistence of such strong odors was recorded thereafter well into the twentieth century, prompting him to wonder if clever hotel managers might not have renewed such fragrances over the years, so as to play upon the gullibility of visitors.[3]

Nevertheless, the ultimate embodiment of Wagner's requirement of a luxurious sanctuary was achieved in what he devised for himself in 1882–83 at the Palazzo Vendramin, and called his "blue grotto."

Despite frequent references in the literature, only rarely are contemporary descriptions explored. There are, in fact, very few of them, and the most detailed is the one given by Henriette/Henry Perl. She precedes her description, early in her book, with an initial defense of Wagner's often-criticized love of luxury in general, and particularly in his working chamber.

> As soon as Wagner entered into his study, the real world, along with the gray garments of his daily miseries, fell away from him. The aspect of the happy, joyous splendor of

color, the rustling and crinkling of the silks, the perfect designs of expensive laces, the rose-charged air of the Persian garden, all that he had to see, to feel: it had become a requirement for him, toward his artistic and ethical means.—This atmosphere, and none other, exerted upon him a purely miraculous magic, which he required in order to produce something purely miraculous. (127–28/24)

The description itself Perl chose to interpolate into her highly charged account of Wagner's last New Year's Eve. Having told us of Wagner drawing Cosima amorously into his private chamber, Perl goes on to give us this feverishly colored picture of that chamber:

The brightest blaze of light dazzled the entrants, although one could not see whence derived this light, against which only Sun and Moon might compete in brightness. As if conjured up by invisible forces, this magical light overflowed the chamber, in which fantastic and fantasy-inspiring splendor competed with artistically rich prodigality.— The first impression was so utterly surprising that it did not really allow one to be certain of the exact origin of this effect.

All of this served to transport the senses, and with them the soul, into a dreamlike magical state.—That strange light, as bright as day and at the same time so voluptuously muted, the walls covered with pale-rose-red and water-green satin, overlaid with expensive white laces, and these further intertwined with heavy, wide, red, gold-streaked strips of satin!

Everywhere the eye beheld large, luxurious, artificially wrought satin roses; the floor itself, which a thick, multicolored Arabian carpet covered, was sprinkled with such roses. These artificial flowers, however, exuded the quite expensive rose perfume and circulated through the chamber such an atmosphere of nervous excitation which could not fail to have ill effects for the health of any continuing occupant.

The entire central part of this hall-sized chamber, however, was occupied by a bed of such colossal dimensions as to be quite amazing. This bed, built in old-fashioned style, was elevated barely a foot high off the ground and was covered with heavy satin in the color of frozen tea, or more properly "iced tea." Six pillows of correspondingly commanding size, of the same color and the same material, surrounded this oversize ottoman after oriental custom. The heavy red decorated satins, the gold-brocade quilts spread all around in extravagant abundance, made this furnishing into a true showpiece of exaggerated splendor.

Of expensive Rhine-green satin also were the chairs, which were decorated with big red satin roses that, in their turn, were augmented further with a binding interwoven in gold.

A magnificent piano was, in corresponding fashion, enveloped in glistening silk and fully covered with roses.

The windows were veiled by sixfold curtains, starting with the darkest blue, moving above that into lighter-shaded blue, red, and green colors, so that the light from outside was almost entirely blocked.

Even day, with its changing whims and with its shifting effects of light, must not disturb the inspiring harmony of this artificially created Eden!

Here, in this enchanted chamber, which owed its origin to a profoundly intense need for poetry, it always seemed to be bright day, or always bright night; here was the scent of roses without cessation, while all the dust and cloud of everyday life dispersed totally before this fantastic luxury borrowed from the fairy-tale world.

When he entered this chamber, Wagner may have experienced things comparable to what affects the smoker of hashish as soon as narcotic vapors go to work on him.

He considered himself far removed from the world, the weight of the years dwindled, the anxieties and torments of life gave way, as soon as the multicolored but harmonious chaos of luxury and glitter flashed upon him; the bewildering perfumes embraced him and buried all the impressions of the daily world beneath their spicy breath.

About a quarter of this hall was marked off by a heavy satin curtain, which displayed likewise Wagner's beloved color compilation of pale rose, green, blue, and bright red.

A decoration after [Austrian painter Hans] Markart!—which presented to the viewer the impression of a stage set, to the extent that even here the eye was presented with a sea of wild waves of silk, gossamer, and brocade, fantastically brought together. In the background glitters a rich mass of expensive garments, of which the master himself frequently made use, as the mood came over him. A favorite costume among these was a gown, made according to old German style out of gold brocade, interwoven with silver threads.—This expensive garment Wagner also wore in that last Sylvester Night [i.e., New Year's Eve] of his life, and in addition the familiar black-velvet beret, which adorned so appropriately the creative brow with its headful of rich white hair. (187–90/56–58)[4]

For all the hypercharged prose, this is a remarkable description, and the only one of its kind. (Note, by the way, Perl's other allusion in passing to the sacred room's aspect during the postmortem scene: 224/76.) Hers is also the report of a virtual eyewitness, it would seem. Perl explicitly says that on February 16, 1883, following the departure by train of Wagner's corpse, she went back to the Palazzo Vendramin and was allowed to walk through the newly vacated rooms

in which still prevails the fragrance of roses—the Master's favorite perfume . . . we tarry in his room, now stripped of its magnificence, in which Richard Wagner had labored up until the last moment of his earthly presence (243–44/87).

What Perl did not see (or smell) for herself she could have absorbed at close second hand from Dr. Keppler—who actually had seen the room in his turn at the time of Wagner's death—as well as from any household servants she came to know.

Against Perl's testimony we can draw upon a few passages in Cosima Wagner's diaries. First, as to fancy costume, we have a report from October 12, 1879, well before the final Venice residence: ". . . in the evening he appears in his new velvet jacket and long waistcoat as 'Louis XIV,' and again expresses his disgust with present-day fashions." Then, in Venice on October 17, 1882, describing a discussion with Richard about household expenditures—whose total surprises him!—she interpolates parenthetically a kind of illustration:

(A delivery for Dan[iela] from Milan contained among other things a green velvet jacket, called Rembrandt, which he put on and in which he looked exactly like Figaro.)

Another passage is from January 24, 1883, only weeks before Wagner's death:

We are diverted from [our] dismal thoughts by my remarking how pretty his room (blue grotto) is, and this leads us to his desire for colors, for perfumes, the latter having to be very strong, since he takes snuff. "Taking snuff is really my soul," he says very drolly. At the start, he describes how gently glowing colors influence his mood, but later in the conversation he denies any connection and says very emphatically, "These are my weaknesses."

No latter-day scholar has made more of this subject than Joachim Köhler, who has eagerly sought anything that might put Wagner in a bad light. Köhler has thus ventured this description of his own, in discussing Wagner's situation at the Vendramin:

. . . The furniture was in the style of Louis XVI, but Wagner added his own personal touch with the fabrics and perfumes he had brought with him. In one room, the scent of beeswax candles was mixed with the attar of roses rising from satin flowers, and a chiaroscuro light entered through five blue curtains whose different shades, from the deepest cobalt to a delicate forget-me-not, allowed the level of brightness to be effortlessly controlled. Wagner called this room his "Blue Grotto."

There was also a secret rose cabinet in Venice, and when Joukowsky entered it unobserved, he was reminded of "Klingsor's magic garden thought up by Wagner when high on hashish." There were pale pink satin wall hangings everywhere, all of them decorated with bunches of fragrant roses, and, lit by candles in an altar chandelier, there was also a grand piano entirely covered in champagne-coloured silk as Wagner could not bear the gondola-black of the wood. A polar bear rug and an image of the Madonna added a touch of contrast.

Hidden behind red silk curtains was a cupboard containing Wagner's most hallowed possessions: fur-lined brocade and silk coats ranging in colour "from pitch-black to violet and bottle-green, and from crimson and orange to pure white," which he wore depending on his mood. He called them "Brabant," "Corwall" and "Franconia," no doubt allusions to the scenes where his operas are set. According to Cosima, a green velvet jacket called "Rembrandt" made him look like Figaro, and even his dyed silver hair shimmered with a green light.[5]

For those paragraphs Köhler cites only two sources. One is the pair of passages in Cosima's diary. The other is *not* Perl, to whom he never makes reference, although it is clear that his description is heavily based on hers, even down to some minute specifics and phraseology. Instead, Köhler gives as his second source Joachim von Kürenberg's novel, *Carnival of the Lonely: Richard Wagner's Death in Venice.*[6] "Although Kürenberg was a novelist, he spoke to many eyewitnesses, all of whose accounts are entirely trustworthy." Now, Joachim von Kürenberg was the pen name of Eduard Joachim von Reichel (1892–1954). Reichel/Kürenberg did spend some time in Venice, coming to know it well. By his time, however, the "eyewitnesses" of Wagner's stay there would long have vacated the scene: Kürenberg's novel was published in 1947!

Köhler gives no page reference(s) in his citation of Kürenberg, but the latter devoted a number of passages in his novel to Wagner's "Holy-of-Holies"

(*Allerheiligste*) and luxurious tastes, upon which Köhler surely drew. It is revealing to examine these Kürenberg passages in full, to recognize just how much he did.

The earliest of these come in a chapter (10) titled "The Mysterious Room" (*Das gehiemnisvolle Zimmer*). It is set at the beginning of October, when Wagner found himself confined indoors by bad health and deteriorating autumn weather:

> Thus would Wagner make himself quite invisible to his closest circle; he lives now only in his study, where he also sleeps and often takes his meals. Besides Frau Cosima and the servant Lang, no one dares enter the secret chamber. In the palazzo it is known that this room has been hung by Lechner [the decorator] with costly fabrics and fitted with likewise selected furnishings, that there stands his Erard (piano) on which Wagner is accustomed to compose, and next to it his worktable. Hardly one of the daughters knew more.
>
> They sit with their mother in the adjoining room, with their manual tasks and listen anxiously for coughs and any noise that penetrates to them from the Holy of Holies. When Frau Cosima hears footsteps, she knows that he has some pains. Hearing movements back and forth is thus for her the evidence that he has lain down, upon which he is accustomed to put his hands under his head so as to achieve freer breathing. (65)

A little further on, Kürenberg describes how Wagner would follow a daily schedule: after his rising, he would regularly begin his "morning labor":

> . . . For this morning productivity he takes out a brocaded or silk coat from the built-in cabinet. He chooses the color according to his humor: from jet-black through violet and ice-green, crimson and orange, to pure white. In Venice he favors coats that are lined with expensive furs, since, as he asserts, the thick stone walls block out any sunbeams and the marble floors radiate infernal coldness.
>
> Should anyone succeed in surprising the watchful ladies and in opening the door to the secret chamber, he would discover first of all the back of the stooped man in a sulfur-colored silk fur coat, over whose collar hang his short, uncombed, gray hair-strands; further, he would find on the writing table a glass of cognac and perceive that the drinker is whistling softly to himself. What must astonish the visitor most, however, is the bewildering odor in this study. It derives from wax candles and from satin roses, that are saturated with rose-oil, which Frau Cosima imports directly from Bulgaria in large flasks. These paper-roses are fastened with thread onto the chairs, table legs, and walls, even on the legs of the piano, which has needlework in champagne-colored silk. Such roses also lie on the precious tapestries on the floor. Much space is taken up by an irregular bed, which stands in the middle of the room and is decorated with a polar-bear skin and innumerable pillows. Quite noteworthy is the window decoration: here hang five curtains, one upon another: from deep cobalt-blue to the lightest blue. In fact, these have been disposed according to the Master's taste so that the room receives no daylight at all—then dozens of honey-candles burn—or, however, it is only illuminated faintly by a kind of twilight *à l'heure bleu* through the lightest curtain. (66–67)

The next important segment of the novel that Köhler would surely have exploited comes in a chapter (24) entitled "Klingsor's Magic Garden" (*Klingsors*

Zaubergarten). This chapter introduces into the author's large and lively cast of historical characters the artist Joukowsky. His long association with Wagner is recalled, including his involvement in Wagner's adapting of the Villa Rufolo garden at Ravello and the Cathedral of Siena as models for *Parsifal* settings. Having become the household *cicerone* for matters artistic, Joukowsky is shown conducting an informal seminar on painters, Venetian and otherwise, at an afternoon "tea hour" gathering of the family circle in mid-December. Cosima is restless, and Wagner smells something burning, though the thought is laughed off by the others.

But Frau Cosima is not to be dissuaded from her suspicion. She opens the door to Wagner's study; in barely an instant she cries out: "Fire!—It's burning!—Water, quick, water!—It's really ablaze!"

Joukowsky and Stein are promptly in position. The girls and Siegfried haul water, which, with united energies, is poured on the burning window curtain; it had caught fire from a candle.

Wagner, who avoids all unpleasantries, has escaped into an adjacent room and has sat down behind a folding screen.

Amid this episode Joukowsky acquires access to the Holy of Holies. He now understands that this room should be entered by no stranger and always remains closed. Joukowsky has the sense of being in a stage set for Klingsor's Magic Garden as thought up by Wagner in a haze of hashish. Everywhere satin roses drunk with rose-oil, light rose-red silk tapestries, altar lamps with candles, the polar-bearskin fur carpet and the piano covered in silk, since Wagner cannot tolerate the black enamel paint color. In the further part of the room—behind the bed—hang silk curtains in mixed colors: reseda-green, lavender-dyed, and scarlet-red. Behind this curtain stands the wardrobe for the Wagnerian luxury coats, each of which had its name, such as Brabant, Cornwall, or Franconia.

Once the fire is extinguished, the multihued blue window curtains are speedily drawn and the curiosity-seekers are moved away by Frau Cosima. She is visibly upset over this profanation of the sacred place.

Frau Cosima attempts to restore the flow of interrupted conversation, but without success. No more for today! And that does it for these tea hours in the Palazzo Vendramin.

But Wagner has other plans for Joukowsky, and he ends by calling for a glass of cognac.

These are not the only passages in Kürenberg's novel that dwell upon Wagner's luxurious living at the Vendramin.[7] But they are the prime ones to put beside those of Perl and Köhler. Examining them together clarifies the sequence. Perl's texts are the obvious foundation for everything. Kürenberg was heavily indebted to Perl: in his quite substantial bibliography, so unusual for a novel, Perl is very much present. But many aspects of Kürenberg's descriptions are simply the elaborations of his own fertile imagination. As can be seen, Köhler in his turn drew upon both Cosima (fully cited) and Perl (not cited). But Köhler, while he has even added a few touches of his own, has been willing to take Kürenberg's vivid fictions and credit them as facts, even adapting some of them almost word for word.[8]

To sum up, lest the reader be a bit confused by this point: Cosima offers the carefully restricted personal testimony; Perl offers secondhand testimony reliably acquired; Kürenberg offers well-founded imagination; Köhler offers unclarified collage under the guise of fact.

Köhler has given other attention to Wagner's passion for perfumes and soft luxury garments—partly drawing on the recollections of Bertha Goldwag. Köhler's purpose is to attribute these tastes to a covert and infantile effeminacy on Wagner's part, and to further the allegations made as to the composer's supposedly long-standing delight in private cross-dressing.[9]

As to Wagner's luxury garments, by the way, it might be noted that Norlenghi (155)—who is cited by neither Köhler nor Kürenberg—speaks of Wagner having three such gowns, each in a different color (black, white, and red), though without any "names." Norlenghi also writes (175–76) of Wagner's requirement for an endless supply of silk cockades in different colors, which the composer placed around his study in constant rearrangement.

On different indulgences, notice how deftly Perl gave an inverted hint about the possibility of Wagner's using hashish. There are suggestions that he did resort at times to some dosages of opium as a painkiller. Meanwhile, his intense devotion to snuff has been noted above and is attested elsewhere.[10]

Addendum 6

What Made Wagner Laugh?
(to chapter 7)

Among the things that become clear as one reads more and more about Wagner is the fact that, despite his well-established irascibility, he did have a strong sense of humor, and he enjoyed joking, even clowning. He was famous for punning, and he could stoop to childish pranks at time.[1] Two of our sources under consideration provide previously overlooked testimonies to Wagner's humorous side.

With no particular reference to anything else, perhaps just as a way of filling otherwise unassigned space, on March 19, 1890, *La Gazzetta di Venezia* (*LGdV*) printed the following short article, in its category of *Riviste e Giornali*, which sampled material published elsewhere.

L'UMORISMO DI WAGNER

What would the admirers of Wagner have said, on a day in 1876 at Bayreuth, upon seeing the maestro dance a fine capriol in the middle of a concert hall to express the joy given him by the hearing of some good music? Wagner was sixty-two years old, but he had not yet forgotten the youthful gymnastic prowess for which he was celebrated among his friends. Still, the Bayreuth public certainly did not remember such prowess, and would be greatly amazed. Nevertheless, to dance a capriol or to walk around on his hands would seem the maestro's most common way to express strong enthusiasm.

One evening, after having heard a sonata by Listz [*sic*] on the piano, at the final chord he left the seat upon which he had been seated and crawled on his hands and feet toward the master saying: "Fritz, my friend, I must come to you on four legs!"[2]

Wagner also believed in showing that way how very humorous he was. But he was still more humorous on the day when, encountering on the building stairs one of his all-too-numerous unknown admirers, he was asked by the man in which palazzo lived Riccardo Wagner, he replied casually: "On the second floor," and he continued to go down while the other man went on up. Animals were one of the great maestro's passions. He loved dogs most particularly and during the years he spent in Dresden he wanted to train a parrot [*pappagallo* in Italian] named *Papa*. When the luncheon bell sounded, signora Wagner addressed the parrot with these words: "*Papa*, call your master!" And *Papa* shrieked: "Riccardo! Libertà! Santo Spirito Cavaliere!" They were the Italian words taken from the libretto, for *Cola da Rienzi* and *Libertà* further bore witness of the master's revolutionary sympathies. *Papa* was also endowed with another talent.

He knew how to imitate the sound of a door when it opened, and Wagner enjoyed it every time when one of his guests turned around upon hearing the parrot's voice, to see who had come into the room.

Since Wagner loved to laugh, he provided the newspapers, the critics, the books with so much material for caricatures and mockery.

One time—recalls the *Daily Telegraph*—he was able to make the emperor laugh by refusing a summons to his box, stubborn as a baby, despite the repeated requests of the gracious sovereign. Then, when he finally agreed, the emperor said to him, perhaps to impose penance on him: "Dear Wagner, I am very pleased with myself for not knowing how to play the flute as did my great-grandfather [i.e., Frederick the Great of Prussia]. I am pleased about that because you might want to put me against my will in your orchestra!"[3]

The ineffable: even he wanted to be humorous.

The second illustration is to be found in Perl's *Richard Wagner in Venedig* (212–15/70–72). To her account of the events of the day before Wagner died, we might prefix the observation of Cosima herself, that at lunch that day Wagner entertained Joukowsky with "some very drastic jokes and anecdotes." Matching her report in much greater detail, however, Perl recounts a conversation she (Perl) had with Dr. Friedrich Keppler, her important source, when she met him the evening before Wagner died.

. . . That very same evening [February 12, 1883], we [Perl] had occasion to see the physician. And conversation turned to the poet-composer and his manner of telling a story.

"Today," the physician asserted, "Wagner was in unusually high spirits, he felt better than ever, and he related several humorous tales, one of which gave me very special amusement. It goes this way: During the Franco-Prussian war some *bon vivants* of the financial world in Berlin arranged a fine dinner. During dessert discussion arose about, among other things, the bravery of the German soldiers, etc. One word led to another and the conclusion was, it is a pity that there are also Jews among them, though they have hardly any pretense of personal courage, much less military bravery. One of the businessmen in attendance felt offended by this assertion and opined: 'Well now, I am willing to dispute the evil reputation of my co-religionists and to enter into a wager of twenty thousand thalers, that I am capable of finding a Jewish soldier who will seize a French battle flag and bring it home victoriously.'—'And I bet the same amount,' interjected a Christian businessman, 'that a Jew will never seize a battle flag in war.' —

" 'So, we shall see.' The argument ended, and the wager was settled before witnesses.

"Herr von X, the Jewish banker, quickly found a soldier of the Mosaic persuasion who seemed particularly fitted for his purpose, and promised him 20,000 shiny thalers in the event that he should succeed in seizing a French battle flag and could provide the evidence that he really had seized it.

"It was not long before the Jewish warrior returned to German soil with the requisite victory trophy.

"Doubts of all sorts were voiced, but, one and all, they were mollified by the testimony of the colonel of his regiment and by all the remaining verifications that certify the authenticity of the fact in such situations.

"So then, it really was true, that the seeming impossibility had come to pass; a Jew had managed to seize an enemy battle flag and bring it home in triumph!

"The Jewish businessman rejoiced and gave to his colleague who had lost the wager, and to his associates, a dinner that, for the refinement of its servings and likewise for the excellence and superabundance of wine, excelled even that dinner which had first occasioned the wager. Following the repast, the valiant warrior, who had been seated at the table, as befitting his merits, was to receive payment of the stipulated reward. The great moment approached. His wealthy patron took the warrior aside—the two had already partaken copiously of the wine—and, as soon as he saw that he was alone with him, he said to his brother in Judaism: 'Listen, friend, the money is now yours for sure, here it is before you; but tell me frankly, how did you manage to seize the banner? For, the story that you have honestly told me still is not clear to me.'

" 'How did I manage it?—that is extremely simple,' he responded to the question without evasion. 'I looked and looked for a long time, until I found a French ensign-bearer who was a Jew like me; I took him aside and said to him: Friend, I know a scheme by which you can earn ten thousand thalers cash—what you have to do is pass on to me your regimental banner. I was naturally sorry about the ten thousand thalers that I had to give up to him, save that I calculated that the remaining ten thousand would be better than nothing. The Frenchman was no fool and accepted the deal, which was mutually profitable.' His patron laughed, said nothing, and paid up."

This is the amusing little story that Wagner told Keppler on Monday February 12, 1883, and which we heard from the doctor's mouth that very same evening.

The anecdote is typical. On the one hand, it shows how readily Wagner made simple jokes about Judaism—although in his heart he nourished no hostility toward the Jewish element, as demonstrated certainly by his many statements of admiration for the Jews. On the other hand, the anecdote displays a man who, able to tell such a story with humor, must certainly have felt himself completely well, which was thus the reality of the situation on the eve of Wagner's death. (212–15/70–72)

Perl's effort to dispel any suggestion of anti-Semitism on Wagner's part in telling this joke is awkward at best. If the joke is not frankly anti-Semitic, it is certainly an indicator about the deep-seated stereotypes about Jews that were taken for granted among Wagner's contemporaries. In reporting the joke, Perl may have revealed more than she intended.

Addendum 7

*Diagnoses and Autopsies
(to chapters 3, 7)*

By far, the most extensive discussions and portrayals of Wagner's health in his
last months of life are given by Henriette Perl, as have been presented above in
the exposition of her book.[1] And, also as observed, such concentration on her
part was allowed—if not effectively required—by the close association she
claimed with Wagner's physician, Dr. Friedrich Keppler. Also, in that context, it
is Perl and Perl alone who has transmitted to us what is often described as
Keppler's "autopsy" report—indeed, she presents it as a kind of entrance poster
at the very beginning of her book, and as the substance of a sanctioning letter
to her from Keppler himself.

In point of fact, the text in question is not a formal or official autopsy in the
clinical sense. It is, instead, Keppler's personal report on Wagner's health and
causes of death, based on observations he made during the course of his
embalming of Wagner's body on February 15, and presumably summarizing
notes he had made both at that time and earlier. It has been quoted often over
the years.[2] It follows here, in English translation of the full text as Perl transmitted it:[3]

Richard Wagner suffered from a very advanced enlargement of the heart, notably of
the right ventricle, with consequent fatty degeneration of the cardiac tissue. In addition, he suffered from a fairly extensive enlargement of the stomach and from an
inguinal hernia on the right side. The latter was exceptionally difficult to hold in place
and had also been aggravated over a long period by the wearing of a highly unsuitable
truss, so my very first advice to him consisted in prescribing a suitable truss.

The ailments from which Richard Wagner suffered during the final months of his life
were primarily disorders originating in the stomach and intestines, especially a high
degree of meteorism [abdominal distention by gas]. Accompanying this, though only
secondarily, in consequence both of direct mechanical constriction of the thoracic cavity induced by a massive generation of gases in the stomach and intestines, and also of
a reflex action by the gastric on the cardiac nerves, were painful disturbances in the
action of the heart which ultimately, by rupturing the right ventricle, led to disaster. It
goes without saying that the countless mental excitements to which Wagner was daily
exposed by his peculiar outlook and disposition, by his sharply defined attitude toward

a whole series of burning issues in the realms of art, science, and politics, and by his notable social standing, did much to precipitate his unfortunate demise.

The actual attack that so abruptly terminated the master's life *must* [the doctor's own italics] have been similarly occasioned, but it is not for me to engage in conjecture on the subject.

The medical treatment that I had prescribed for Wagner consisted in massaging the abdomen and applying a suitable truss. I avoided medicinal treatment as far as possible because Wagner was in a bad habit of taking numerous strong medicines prescribed for him by various physicians whom he had consulted in the past, often in large doses and all at once.

Dr. Keppler understood his patient well personally as well as medically. Particularly interesting, therefore, is his veiled but firm reference to "mental excitements" as an immediate cause of the fatal heart attack. That has been suspected by such scholars as Westernhagen and Gregor-Dellin as the doctor's tactful allusion to the alleged argument between Richard and Cosima that morning. Such suspicion, however, unfortunately depends upon the fanciful (and now-discredited) stories surrounding Wagner and Carrie Pringle, discussed in addendum 2 above.

One aspect of Keppler's observations was his discovery of how very much damage must have been done to Wagner's heart by what we would now identify as excessive cholesterol intake. Though Cosima was fanatically concerned about his sleeping (she regularly began each day's entry by reporting how he had managed the previous night), she has surprisingly little to say in her diary about food, beyond recurrent references to Richard's love for beer. But occasionally she could admit, in the last years, that he made mistakes in his diet and would slip into error (e.g., lobster). Apparently Wagner had a particular passion for large quantities of bread and butter with his coffee, which must have aggravated his digestion. His physicians in Bayreuth contributed to the difficulties by misdiagnosis of his problems and by recommending copious intake of red meat and champagne—much to Wagner's delight! It seems clear now that Wagner suffered from angina pectoris, not yet understood in his day, and that his heart was asphyxiated as a result of thoracic compression and reduced arterial capacity.[4]

Despite her clear alliance with and dependance upon Keppler, Perl give hints of some controversy over the doctor's handling of Wagner's health and information he gave as to the nature of the composer's death. Thus, in a note of her own, indicated by an asterisk (*) in the text, Perl slips in an alternative perspective of Italian derivation:

From various Italian journals in a range of medical specialization, Professor G. Barbiglia has published the following notes concerning the illness and the true cause of the death of the great composer.

Dr. Barbiglia states: the illness of which Richard Wagner was the victim had displayed its initial symptoms a good many years earlier. They had already appeared in 1878 (also a year in which Wagner had resided in Italy), as happened often the first signs of an amiloidean degeneration of the three large organs digestively crucial to the abdominal area, that is, the liver, the spleen, and the kidneys. Such degeneration was revealed with certainty both by the physical effects recognized from clinical examination, and by the chemical analysis of his urine, and at the time an ominous prognosis was outlined, communicated with all possible delicacy to family members and to the friends of Richard Wagner. Meanwhile, the progress of the amiloidean degeneration, in such fashion as would affect the heart and, ultimately, the brain, appeared to be inevitable.

Already in the following year, in late autumn of 1879, also aware of an irregularity in his heartbeat, he began to complain of temporary conditions of dizziness and giddiness, of difficult breathing, and of shortness of breath, and of suffering, although at extended intervals, sudden fainting spells. The full extent of the danger in which Wagner had been living uncertainly seemed thus clear to the doctors' eyes, while, on the other hand, it was henceforth indisputable also that the Master's cardiac tissue was damaged by the destructive process of the amiloidean degeneration. Consequently, there resulted from it a notably diminished capacity of resistance by the heart to all mechanical and physical phenomena of pathological character, which had the additional effect of accelerating the beating of the pulse.[5]

Perl never makes clear if she is quoting this analysis to challenge or discredit Dr. Keppler's report. Not available to her (at least for publication) is any further evidence from him. We may, however, actually have some earlier perspectives by Keppler on Wagner's health, if problematically transmitted.

A novel published in 1947 may seem a dubious source for Wagner's medical reports, but perhaps not when the novel is Joachim von Kürenberg's *Carneval der Einsamen*, which has already been cited in addendum 5. Though a work of fertile fantasy, it is also based upon very through research. In one testimony to such research, the bibliography that concludes the novel, Kürenberg has no less than three entries (p. 301) that cite manuscript (privately owned) or obscurely published notices on Wagner's death, including a diary. In the specific chapter (20) in the novel in which Dr. Keppler is introduced and explored as a character, Kürenberg quotes from two texts that would presumably date from early to mid-December 1882. The first (132) is presented as an entry in the doctor's own journal:

> The Patient has become frail and retrogressive, his powers of resistance almost ruined. Physical excitation must under all circumstances be avoided, mental work remain limited to a few hours, and social engagements above all not even considered.

The next (132–33) is identified as from a letter Keppler wrote to Cosima:

> Herr Richard Wagner of Bayreuth has been under my treatment for eight weeks. His case involves a widely advanced expansion of the heart with consecutive, fatty degeneration of the heart muscles. Also confirmed is the following: on the right side, internal strip-hernia, deteriorating along a badly situated truss. Herr Wagner currently suffers at the beginning of winter especially from stomach and intestinal troubles, above all from high-level meteorism. Additionally, in direct secondary line, mechanical

contractions of the chest cavity as a result of severe accumulation of gas in the stomach and bowels, as also by reflex of the stomach and heart nerves. From this the patient derives painful interruption in his heart action, which, through a rupture of the heart chambers, could bring about a catastrophe.

Following his usual format, Kürenberg gives no explicit source citations for these passages, but we are left to assume that, in his generally strict fashion, he derived them to one or another degree of directness from his bibliographical references.[6] Their absolute authenticity has yet to be established. (Cosima nowhere indicates reception of any such letter.) Comparing the passages with Keppler's well-known "autopsy" report, as just quoted, we can see that Kürenberg's texts are quite consistent with it. They might be seen on the one hand as Keppler's actual anticipation of the fatality to come, which his "autopsy" report was even crafted to confirm. On the other hand, they could have been confected ex post facto, either by the doctor himself or by Kürenberg, to suggest remarkably prophetic diagnoses of the patient who had been under extended and close observation.

However skeptically we accept them, these two passages are worth keeping in mind as possible supplements to our information on the perception of Wagner's health in the last months of his life.

Addendum 8

Four Short Accounts of Wagner's Death (to chapters 7, 8)

From over the course of days, months, and years, came some seven distinct reports of Wagner's death, varying in length, all of which must be considered primary sources. In chronological order, they may be reckoned as follows:

1. Report printed by *La Gazzetta di Venezia* (*LGdV*) (February 15, 1883)[1]
2. Ludwig von Bürkel's letter to King Ludwig (February 20, 1883)[2]
3. Joukowsky's letter to Liszt (February 20, 1883)
4. Joukowsky's letter to Malwida von Meysenbug (February 22, 1883)
5. Literary account by Perl (published April 1883)[3]
6. Literary account by Norlenghi (finished August 1883, published early 1884)[4]
7. Joukowsky's reminiscence (diary?)
8. Siegfried Wagner's recollection (published 1923)

Of these eight, four (numbers 1, 2, 5, 6) are fully quoted at proper places throughout this book, as indicated. It seems appropriate to append here the other, generally shorter, accounts (numbers 3, 4, 7, 8). As will be seen, each makes some contribution of pieces to the mosaic of Wagner's last hours.

Three of them (two being letters) come from the hand of the Wagner family's cherished friend, the painter Paul Joukowsky. The first of these three was written in French to Franz Liszt, on the same day as Bürkel's to Ludwig. Liszt had not yet been able to leave Budapest and attend the funeral at Wahnfried, and efforts still needed to be made to inform Cosima's father of the background situation.

Wahnfried [Bayreuth], 20 Feb. 1883
Dear and honored Master!
  I will attempt to give you a short report of the past week, beyond assuring you, up to some point, as to the state of health of Madame your daughter. She lives, that is the main thing; she sleeps a little, she takes a little milk and some white wine every day, but she has eaten nothing for 8 days. She sees absolutely no one except her children, with whom she is calm and serene and sweet. I believe that she is resigned to living. At any

rate this is more than we had been able to hope for the past week. She has sustained our terrible and long voyage better than we had been able to suppose. One dreaded the musical displays, funeral marches, etc. Despite all the preparations, our prayers have been followed completely and we have proceeded with our dear coffin and our dear sufferer through crowds absolutely silent.

Dear Master, I do not know if you have been able to receive precise reports as to Wagner's end. I know well that, if I were good for anything, I should have given you something some time ago; but I was as someone paralyzed. It is only today that I was able to free my heart from its numbness. On February 13 Wagner arose and said to his valet, *heute muss ich mich in Acht nehmen* [today I must proceed carefully]. Nevertheless, he took coffee with his wife and set to work on his new essay, *Das Männlich und das Weibliche* [The Male and the Female]. Up to meal-time he remained in his room. At two o'clock he sent us word that he had been having his usual cramps, and that we should go to table without awaiting him. As always, we were cheerful. In the midst of the meal Betty came to tell Frau Wagner that he was asking her to come immediately. The children and I awaited their parents in the salon until four o'clock. Doctor Keppler had already come at three, which had been altogether reassuring. But at four o'clock we began to be anxious, for we were all supposed to leave with Wagner in order to go see Walkoff's [*sic*] house. All of a sudden we heard despairing cries and the servants told us the truth.—He had died in the arms of his wife, he had fallen asleep without pain; for it had been a heart attack, in the wake of the stress caused by his customary cramps. When the doctor came it had been too late. Madame Wagner remained beside him the entire first day and the following night. At two o'clock, on Wednesday, the doctor was able to remove her into a separate room. I am quite unable to give you a report on the days passed in Venice, when we were divided between our own grief and our extreme concern about losing Madame your daughter as well. We left Venice on Friday at two o'clock. Gross accompanied us here from Venice; Levi and Porges had joined us at Innsbruck, M. de Bürkel arrived at Koufstein on behalf of the King. Saturday, at eleven o'clock, we arrived at Bayreuth. Sunday he was buried at the base of the garden at Wahnfried. At Bayreuth, we had found virtually all his friends. We had followed the coffin as far as the entrance to Wahnfried. There we other close friends had borne it to the tomb with the children. The minister spoke the prayers and then everyone, save for the children, left Wahnfried, and the coffin was placed in the ground by the mother and the children.

We now hope that calm will settle in the hearts so immensely aggrieved. The children, who are admirable and are examples to us all, kiss your hands.

I do the same and am your devoted

P. Joukowsky.[5]

Among other things, that letter is apparently the source for the report of Wagner's morning words to his valet.)

Two days later, on February 22, Joukowsky wrote to another family friend, Malwida von Meysenbug:

[His death] was as glorious as his life. We were all waiting for him to appear at table, for he had sent word to us to begin lunch without him. In the meantime he had sent for the doctor on account of his usual spasms; then at about 2:30 he sent Betty to fetch Frau Wagner. The doctor came at 3:00, which made us all feel easier; but around 4:00, since nobody had come out of his room, we became worried; then suddenly Georg appeared and told us simply that it was *all over*. He died at around 3 o'clock in the arms of his wife, without suffering, falling asleep with an expression on his face of such nobility and peace that the memory of it will never leave me. She was alone with him the whole of the first day and night, but then the doctor managed to persuade her to go into another room. Since then I have not seen her, and I shall never see her again; nobody will, except for the children and Gross and his wife, since he is their legal guardian. She will live in the upper rooms of the house, existing only for his memory and for the children; everything else in life has ceased to exist for her. So write only to the children, for she will never read a letter again. Since her dearest wish, to die with him, was not fulfilled, she means at least to be dead to all others and to lead the only life fitting for her, that of a nun who will be a constant source of divine consolation to her children. That is great, and in complete accord with all else in her life. . . .[6]

(The foregoing is apparently the only reference to the "noble and peaceful" look on the dead composer's face.)

Finally, in a later collection of reminiscences, Joukowsky wrote one more parallel account that can be used to supplement those preceeding:

On February 13 I went, as usual, to the Palazzo Vendramin, around 1:15 p.m. There I found Mme. Cosima who was playing to her son Siegfried the *Lob der Tränen* by Schubert. It was the first and only time that I had seen the illustrious lady seated at the piano.

There was conversation until about 2; then the servant Georg came to report that, since the Maestro did not feel well, we should have lunch without him. Before sitting down to table Cosima went into her husband's study. She returned immediately, saying, "My husband is having one of his usual attacks, but one rather mild. I have left him because he indicated to me his wish to remain alone."

Thus reassured, we took our places at table as always.

Suddenly, we heard the bell sound twice, with great vehemence. At about the same time, the chambermaid Betty arrived, extremely pale, telling Cosima to come out immediately. She jumped to her feet and ran quickly. Meanwhile, Betty dispatched Ganasseta for the doctor. We remained there, deeply disturbed, waiting silently. Around 3 Dr. Keppler was heard to arrive. A little after that came the gondola that was meant to bring the Maestro to the painter Wolkoff. As Daniela was about to go out to inform the painter that he would not be able to go to him and to advise the doctor to stop in with us before departing, the servant Georg came in and, turning with sobbing to Daniela, he said: "Oh, gracious signorina (*gnädiges Fräulein*), the kind master (*gnädige Herr*) is dead." In no time I supported her on my arm, while the whole house was filled with cries and wailing.

A few moments later Doctor Keppler entered saying that there was nothing more to be done. Then, turning to the children he announced: "Your father is dead!"[7]

Our final, and very much later account was given by Siegfried Wagner in a passage from his "Recollections" (*Erinnerungen*) that is often quoted or referred to. Siegfried, of course, was not yet sixteen when his father died. Produced forty years after that event, his recollections are distant in time and fragmented in character. Nevertheless, they include some valuable small details.

In these recollections, Siegfried speaks of incidents during the family's visits to Italy, as already quoted. As to the final stay in Venice, he notes: "The happiest event [of the last Venice residence] was the performance of my father's early symphony for the birthday of my mother. It was the third time I was able to see him conduct" (32–33). But the most important memory is the following:

> Of the last day in my father's life, an incident involving my mother remains distinct in my recollection. Although she was a mistress of piano playing—her music teacher Séghers had said of Liszt's two daughters: "Blandine will be an excellent musician, Cosima a great artist"—I had never heard her play; her activity on behalf of my father was so all-absorbing that she had to neglect the piano altogether. It was on that February 13, I was sitting in the salon and was practicing at the piano. My mother entered. She went right to the grand piano and she began to play. To my question as to what she was playing, she answered, with a transfigured look: "Schubert's *Lob der Tränen*." A few minutes later the chambermaid brought the report that my father was fatally stricken. Never will I forget how my mother rushed out through the door. A power of the most vehement anguish displayed itself; with it she flung herself so violently against the half-open door-wing that this was almost shattered. When in later years, during rehearsals for the Festival, I saw her demonstrate such roles as Kundry, Isolde, Sieglinde, or Brünnhilde, I was often forced to remember those moments in Venice; her demonstration was of antique grandeur, such as I have seen again on the stage only once: at the portrayal of Othello by the then already seventy-seven-year-old Salvini.[8]

As can be seen, Joukowsky anticipated Siegfried's report of Cosima's unique piano playing, but only Siegfried speaks of the violence she did to the door on her way to her dying husband.

Addendum 9

Wagner's Last Words
(to chapter 8)

Without a single, definitive, eye- (and ear-)witness account of the death scene, we are dependent upon those that are technically secondhand ones on this issue. Perl, who presumably had the reasonably close testimony of Betty Bürkel reports that Wagner said, *to her*, "Call my wife and the doctor". (*Rufen Sie meine Frau und den Doctor*), and Perl makes the specific assertion that those were his last words. Next closest in timing would be Ludwig von Bürkel's letter, which says nothing of the composer's last words. Norlenghi reports explicitly that Wagner's last utterance was "Fraù ... fraù ... dottor ... fraù." His source is not stipulated, but one presumes it was Luigi Trevisan, whom Norlenghi places on the scene as a witness. (And, as can be seen in the next addendum, that stated proximity became firmly established tradition.)

But another tradition has developed: to wit, that in the last instants of life, Wagner noticed that his pocket watch, a treasured gift from his wife, had slipped out of his pocket as he struggled for breath. Supposedly he gasped "My watch" (*Meine Uhr*)—those, accordingly, being his last words. The source for this statement was presumably Georg Lang, Wagner's valet, who apparently was also in and around the death chamber, and who is even said to have assisted in the placement of Wagner on the bed. That these "last words" are lacking in the account by Perl (and Norlenghi) is not decisive, since Perl apparently obtained her information from Betty Bürkel, who had left the room directly on hearing Wagner's first "last words," and would not have been present to hear this putative second set. Perl makes no mention at all of Georg Lang's presence in the room; in fact, she rarely ever speaks of him. Was he one important member of the household staff that Perl had no contact with or access to? Glasenapp, who was close to the Wagner family and could gather sound information, found no problems in accepting both of these "last words."[1]

Yet another account emerged, however. As already noted, the Venetian newspaper *La Gazzetta di Venezia* (*LGdV*) included in a collection of odds and ends in the aftermath of Wagner's death, published on February 22, 1883, the assertion of still one more final utterance by the Master. The conductor and family friend

Hans Richter is said to have stated that Wagner spoke the unfinished sentence, "My son should ..." (*Mio figlo deve ...*, in *LGdV*'s notice). Richter's own source is not mentioned.[2] This utterance has been picked up by a few accounts, most strangely by the early French biography of the composer by Adolphe Jullien (1886), who gives the statement as "*Siegfried soll.* ..." In that form, it is even more clearly identified as a prescription for young Siegfried, and presumably as to his intended career in architecture. Jullien cites no source, and confuses matters further with his setting of the fatal scene:

> . . . he [Wagner] was about to step into his gondola, some discussion arose, and he gave way to a fit of anger: suddenly he started up from his seat, choking, and cried, "I feel very badly!": He fell fainting.[3]

Could all this have come somehow from accounts given by Luigi Trevisan?

We are left, then, with three sets of "last words" from Wagner—a number respectfully noncompetitive with the seven accorded Christ! We have the "wife/doctor" outcry apparently attested by Betty Bürkel. We have "My watch," possibly from Georg Lang. We have the advice for Siegfried, uncertainly attested and possibly from gondolier Trevisan. Either or both of the first two have gained wide acceptance, but the third enjoys limited credence.

Addendum 10

Luigi Trevisan (to chapter 8)

Throughout the accounts of Wagner's residence in the Palazzo Vendramin, the figure of Wagner's chief gondolier, "Ganasseta" or Luigi Trevisan (figs. 23, 24), recurrently appears. Ultimately, he plays a role as a source of information for Henriette Perl and, even more, for Giuseppe Norlenghi, as their reports make clear. It has already been hinted that Luigi well may have exaggerated or embroidered his reports, especially as to the episode of Wagner's death. He convinced Norlenghi that he was present when Wagner was stricken by his seizure, making himself a crucial participant, virtually in place of Georg Lang. Perl tells us there were three messengers sent to find Dr. Keppler: Luigi makes himself the only one, and the successful one. Luigi also makes himself one of the guards outside the death chamber in the aftermath.

That he was involved in errands to the telegraph office, as portrayed by Perl, seems quite plausible, and we can accept the moving picture of his grief and reminiscences at the time, and as further described by Norlenghi. That his emotions were sincere need not be doubted, and they receive touching confirmation in a parallel vignette preserved in the pages of Panizzardi.[1] That author cites an account by the Milanese music critic Dino Mantovani, who wrote under the penname of "Sordello," and who published in his journal, the *Gazzetta musicale di Milano*, on March 11, 1883, his own account of the departure of Wagner's body from Venice. He reports that, when leaving the railroad station after the train's departure, he encountered *il buon Ganasseta*, "his manly and loyal face furrowed with tears." Luigi's outpourings of grief were reported by Mantovani in the speaker's original Venetian dialect, and might be rendered as something like this:

Look here, sir, he [Wagner] showered me with coins, with gifts, and with caresses. When we drove him in the gondola he gave me a ten-lire note, and packages of cigars and snuff, and you should see how he treated me at the palazzo. The night of his concert he gave me a hundred and fifty francs as a gift, he gave so much because he was pleased and very happy. And now, were he still alive, bless him, I would say that I would serve him all my life for free. And he deserved that much, poor man, good as an angel even with all that suffering from the sickness that tormented him!

There we have a documentation of Luigi Trevisan's heartfelt devotion to Wagner, and of his grief for him in the immediate aftermath of the great man's death. But Luigi soon learned that his association with Wagner made him a person of importance in his own right. On March 27, 1883, some six week after Wagner's death, *La Gazzetta di Venezia* (*LGdV*) was busy reporting preparations for the Neumann touring company's presentation of the *Ring* in Venice, and it added the following aside:

> The Viennese Academic Wagner Association, through the agency of the distinguished signor Teodoro Reitmeyer [*sic*], noted banker in our city, conveyed to the gondolier who was in the service of Riccardo Wagner a gift of 100 (one hundred) lire, accompanying such a sum with the following testimonial of affection toward our citizenry: *To the able gondolier Luigi Trevisan—worthy son of beautiful Venice—offered in token of esteem for the affection and loyalty he displayed to the immortal German maestro Riccardo Wagner.—L'Associazione Accademica viennese 'Wagner'—Easter 1883.*

It would have been difficult for the good Ganasseta not to have had his head turned by this attention and such a gesture. He had become a celebrity! Perl's book, already enriched by his testimony, was published the following month in Germany. Norlenghi was still writing his account, not completed until that August. Would not Trevisan have been tempted to enlarge upon his recollections by then, as he was interviewed by Norlenghi? How much would a stimulated imagination have compromised an honest heart?

The Luigi legend (among others) persisted for yet one more appearance, as late as 1908. On June 23 of that year, *LGdV* published an article adapted from a French journal. This article has apparently never been noted before and deserves to be presented here in full.

THE LAST HOURS OF WAGNER

In connection with the twenty-fifth anniversary of the death of Wagner, the *Revue musicale* of Lyons has printed an unpublished account of the last days of the wizard of Bayreuth.

Wagner seemed near to recovering from an indisposition that had provoked some anxiety. Surrounded by the care of his wife, of his daughters, of his father-in-law Listz [*sic*], of [the latter's] granddaughter Daniela de Bulow, he had resumed the composition of his Buddhistic drama, "The Victors" [*sic*].

Every evening at sunset, those who frequent the Piazza San Marco saw him arrive, enclosed in an ample cloak and with his characteristic beret of black velvet. Accompanied by his family, he came to sit at the Lavena Café and conversed, throwing bird seeds to the pigeons. The prolonged daily gondola rides, the ardor displayed in directing the final concert at Christmas, had reassured his family.

On Tuesday February 13, Wagner rose at his accustomed hour and, dressed in the rich scarlet-silk robe of a Venetian senator, with a beret of the same color, he proceeded through the vast halls of the Palazzo Vendramin, worked, spent some time with the family, and around one he received his faithful gondolier Canasseta [*sic*] to settle with him the ride for the day.

These daily conversations greatly delighted the maestro, happy—he said—to make some progress in the Venetian dialect and thus to understand better the thousands of fables, the little tales, the affectionate jests of the sons of the lagoon.

That morning, Wagner was in a particularly jocular vein: he laughed heartily at the jokes of his gondolier, while he heard the ringing of the luncheon bell at two. Precisely always, the maestro rose to rejoin his family promptly, moving through the bed chamber. At this instant Canasseta saw him unexpectedly put his hand to his heart and fall down on a couch. The poor gondolier rushed anxiously to him, gathered in his arms the maestro whose eyes were already dimmed, as he stammered: "Frau! ... Doctor! ... Frau! ... Doctor! ... They were his last words.

Assisted by the faithful old Betty, Canasseta placed Wagner on the bed, enveloped in his scarlet silks. In rushed Cosima Wagner, Listz [*sic*], Siegfrid, the three young daughters, the doctor: the whole house was turned upside down; all were overwhelmed by terror.

All aid was useless, gone was all hope: Wagner was stricken by a dilation of the heart.

If nothing else, this quaint retrospection tells us something about the durability of what must have been the self-serving reports of Luigi Trevisan. (It is amusing, to be sure, that this article cannot spell his nickname correctly; but then, the famous Liszt fares no better!) Assuming that Luigi was the source for the general story, we might thereby infer confirmation for the speculation that he was the source for the report of Wagner's last words (see the previous addendum). Beyond that, this article is the only period comparison of Wagner's rich scarlet apparel to the state robes of a Venetian senator that I have encountered.

Addendum 11

Angelo Neumann and Wagner's Anti-Semitism (to chapter 10)

The issue of Wagner's anti-Semitism is a complex one involving much discussion, of course. Its involvement with the case of his devoted disciple, Angelo Neumann, is only one instance that provokes reflection.

To King Ludwig II of Bavaria Wagner wrote in a letter of December 30, 1880:

> . . . I shall continue and speak of another man who is, however, merely something of a curiosity. He is the opera director of the Leipzig Municipal Theatre, Angelo Neumann, a man of Jewish extraction, and strangely energetic and extremely devoted to me, in a way which—oddly enough!—I find even today is true of the Jews whom I know. He was the first person to put on a complete performance of the "Ring of the Nibelung" in Leipzig, which he did with lasting success; proud of his achievements, he now intends to win the highest renown for himself. . . . Angelo Neumann is now planning to give four performances of the complete cycle next May in Berlin's large Victoria Theatre. . . . But Angelo is now growing even bolder, and he has asked my permission to visit Petersburg, London and the whole of North America with his army of Nibelungs, and for this purpose—in order to avoid all competition—he has requested exclusive worldwide performing rights for three years. He will pay me one tenth of the gross receipts, and thereby seek to spare me my own trip to America, which I had considered as being necessary. It is quite likely that something will come of this. . . .[1]

It was to Angelo Neumann himself, however, that Wagner made one of his controversial statements, in letter to him of February 23, 1881. In it, the composer emphatically denied any connection with a rabid anti-Semitic movement then raging in Berlin.[2] Wagner's denial seems to have been, however, largely a tactical maneuver in a ticklish situation.[3] But note Wagner's observations in another letter to King Ludwig, of November 22, 1881, in which he explains his dilemma in dealing with his Jewish devotees:

> —I have had to exercise the most extreme patience, and if it is a question of being humane towards the Jews, I for one can confidently lay claim to praise. But I simply cannot get rid of them: the director Angelo Neumann sees it as his calling in life to ensure that I am recognized throughout the world. . . .* If I have friendly and sympathetic

dealings with many of these people, it is only because I consider the Jewish race the born enemy of pure humanity and all that is noble in man: there is no doubt but that we Germans especially will be destroyed by them and I may well be the last remaining German who, as an artist, has known how to hold his ground in the face of a Judaism which is now all-powerful.

To which Wagner appended the following footnote (*), as marked:

Because of their dealings in paintings, jewelry and furniture, the Jews have an instinct for what is genuine and what can be turned to lasting value, an instinct which the German has lost so completely as to give the Jews what is genuine in exchange for all that is not.[4]

On Wagner's attitudes toward and expressions about Jews and Judaism, there is an almost endless and never-resolvable discussion.[5]

Addendum 12

Wagner and America
(to chapter 10)

Wagner had entertained schemes for going to the United States recurrently through his career. He first considered them as early as 1848, and again in 1854, hoping to escape his creditors. During his first stay in Venice, he wrote in a letter of March 1859, to his wife Minna, of his enthusiastic interest in a scheme for him to pursue money-raising in the America.[1]

In later years Cosima's diaries are filled with Wagner's chronic ideas about betaking himself to America, where he seriously imagined he could make a fortune. Despair over the financial setbacks of the first Bayreuth Festival particularly stimulated those ideas. While in London in 1877, he contemplated an elaborate offer from the Hungarian-American impresario Bernard Ullmann. In a letter of May 13, he proposed "to accept Ullmann's American offer, put my property in Bayreuth up for sale, set sail across the ocean with my entire family, and never again return to Germany."[2] (Cf. Cosima on that date). There was more talk of it intermittently in 1879 (e.g., November 17, December 17 and 14). The impulse was renewed in early 1880, just after the Wagners had settled into the Villa Angri in Posilipo. Cosima reports on February 1, 1880, that Wagner, amid a new depression, proposed to settle in America, in Minnesota (!), where he would build a school and new home, and to which he would transfer performances of *Parsifal.* America, Wagner had decided, was the new Hellas.

With this in mind, and seeking help in making arrangements, he wrote to Dr. Newell Sill Jenkins—an American dentist settled in Dresden, a highly cultivated man who had treated both Cosima and Richard himself (e.g., September 21, 1877), and had become a good friend.[3] Jenkins wrote to contacts back home, including the eminent critic John Sullivan Dwight, but was assured the project was impossible. Jenkins (grandfather, by the way, of the latter-day conductor and musicologist of the same name) then personally visited the Wagners at the Villa Angri on April 1 and strove to disabuse the composer of his illusions and delusions about the United States (cf. Cosima for that date). But Wagner still considered the idea of a conducting tour in America. By autumn he was projecting that it would run from September 1881 to April 1882, and would range as far as

California. All along, however, concerns about risks to his health, identity, and creativity challenged these schemes. And then financial tensions eased: on January 12, 1881, Cosima records his abandonment of the idea, in view of his passing on the assignment to Neumann as a surrogate, quipping: "*Ich-Neumann* will be going." Cosima quickly caught the point: " 'Your alter ego,' I cry, and we laugh heartily over R.'s notion."[4]

Nevertheless, America held repeated fascination for Wagner. His frequent references to it are recorded over the years in Cosima's diaries. While the Wagners were staying in Heidelberg in 1877, she reports (July 15) their brief meeting with General and, by then, ex-President Grant—with whom they shared no common language for conversation! At least one event in particular caught his attention, as an exception to his minimal concern with the politics of the moment (especially across the Atlantic). This was the shooting of President James A. Garfield by a crazed assassin July 2, 1881. On September 2 of that year, Cosima records Wagner's detailed attention to reports of improvement in the wounded president's condition; and then she notes on September 20 Wagner's solemn reaction to the news of Garfield's death the previous day. Earlier on, Cosima had mentioned (November 2, 1878) Wagner's reference to his *Grosser Festmarsch* (or *American Centennial March*) being played in Munich in the presence of Ulysses S. Grant, who was then on his post-presidential world tour.

Addendum 13

The Wandering Wagnerians Beyond Neumann (to chapter 11)

It might be worth noting the careers of some of Neumann's troupe, especially after he dissolved it.

Katharina/Katalin KLAFSKY (Sieglinde, Wellgunde), was born in Hungary in 1855. A part of Neumann's Leipzig company (1876–82), she left his touring in Turin due to illness, as mentioned; but she resumed her singing in Bremen and Vienna, settling in Hamburg, where she sang a wide range of roles with great success. (She was one of the Neumann singers invited in vain by Giovannina Lucca to sing their roles in Italian for her planned productions.) She was at her peak when sudden death carried her off two days after her forty-first birthday, in 1896.

Auguste KRAUS (Wellgunde, Waldvogel, Gutrune) was born in Vienna in 1853 and made her debut at the Hofoper there. Her association with the roles of Wellgunde and the Forest Bird began when she sang them in the Vienna premiere of the *Ring* (1879). Two years later she joined Neumann's Leipzig company; she was naturally brought into his touring troupe, and thereafter followed him to Bremen. She had known the conductor Anton Seidl since their days together in Leipzig, and in 1884 the two married. In that same year she made her debut at the Metropolitan Opera as Elisabeth in *Tannhäuser*. In 1885, Seidl became conductor of that company, and the couple settled permanently in the country, becoming American citizens. In his Wagner productions (1885–88) at the Metropolitan (many of them American premieres), she sang the roles of Sieglinde, Forest Bird, and Gutrune in the *Ring*, as well as of Elsa (in *Lohengrin*) and Eva (in *Die Meistersinger*). When Seidl died unexpectedly in 1998, she retired, but she outlived him by almost four decades, until her death in Kingston, New York, in 1939 at age eighty-six.

Julius LIEBAN (1857–1940) was a distinguished German tenor, acclaimed in both opera and art song. He was recruited early by Neumann as the latter built his ongoing ensemble, and Lieban's brilliant portrayal of the dwarf Mime in *Rheingold* and *Siegfried* became one of the anchors of the traveling Wagner Theater company. Lieban was the son of a Jewish cantor, and was thus one more of those paradoxical Semitic Wagnerites. When Wagner saw him in Neumann's Berlin *Ring* in the spring of 1881, Cosima recorded a typically backhanded compliment: "Mime 'a Jewish dwarf,' R. says, but excellent" (May 3, 1881). Julius had three brothers, all of whom became singers. As late as 1907, he and his youngest brother, Adalbert, participated in a Berlin recording of Johann Strauss the Younger's operetta, *Die Fledermaus*—though abridged, its first extended appearance on discs.

Anton SCHOTT (Siegmund) was born in 1846 and made his debut at age twenty-four. He was already enjoying a wide-ranging career when he was recruited by Neumann for the touring company. (He was another of the singers approached by Giovannina Lucca for her projected company.) Thereafter, he went on a tour of the United States. with the Damrosch Opera Company (1884–85), also singing Tannhäuser and Siegmund at the Metropolitan Opera. He was among the Neumann singers who rejoined the troupe for its visit to Russia in 1889. His subsequent career included a return to the Metropolitan Opera to sing Siegfried (1894).

Anton SEIDL (1850–98) was destined to be Neumann's podium counterpart in the mission of spreading the Wagner gospel. In his native Pest, Seidl was a student of Hans Richter, and then the twenty-two-year-old musician joined Richter amid the beginnings of the Festspielhaus at Bayreuth. Totally captivated by the composer and his music, Seidl was taken into the Wagner household and for six years he served as amanuensis and factotum, absorbing all he could of Wagnerian aesthetics. For the 1876 production of the *Ring*, he was coach, staging assistant, and backup to Richter. Bearing the most glowing endorsements as the perfect Wagnerian, respected by Wagner himself with rare warmth and consistency,[1] Seidl was sent by the composer to serve as conductor for Neumann at Leipzig; he also conducted the Berlin cycles. When Seidl was on his way back to Bayreuth to help with work on *Parsifal* in the summer of 1881, Cosima in her diary entertained gossip about a supposed "relationship" between him and Reicher-Kindermann (August 23, 25). Seidl became a cornerstone of Neumann's touring company, developing its modest orchestra into an ensemble of superlative accomplishment. Seidl followed Neumann to Bremen, and in February 1884 he married soprano **Auguste Kraus**.

The couple then moved the following year to New York, where Seidl became principal conductor of the Metropolitan Opera (1885–91) and then conductor of the New York Philharmonic (1891–98). It was in the latter capacity that he conducted the first performance of Dvořák's "New World" Symphony (December 16, 1893). He also conducted other local ensembles tirelessly, especially in Brooklyn, developing a strong affinity for Tchaikovsky and even for some American composers—cellist/composer Victor Herbert was a particular protégé. But Wagner was Seidl's great specialty, and he is credited with building a cultivated American audience for that composer's music, while also setting new standards for orchestral performances of the highest quality. In 1897, he conducted in London and at Bayreuth, but, already an American citizen, he had become deeply attached to his new homeland; he was planning new projects in New York when he died suddenly in 1898 at age forty-eight, deeply mourned by all.[2]

Georg UNGER (1837–87) made his operatic debut only at age thirty, but attracted such attention that he was accepted by Wagner to create the roles of Siegfried at the first Bayreuth Ring in 1876 (fig. 40). He sang in Wagner concerts in London the following year. Though taken as the model of the early *Heldentenor*, he eventually disappointed Wagner, not least for the singer's frequent cancellation of appearances. He then sang for Neumann in Leipzig, but he was already facing intermittent vocal difficulties when engaged as Siegfried for the tour. His career effectively ended in that venture, and he died at fifty.

Addendum 14

Norlenghi on Neumann's Musicians (to chapter 12; also 8)

As we have seen (pp. 235–38), Norlenghi had dismissed backhandedly the Neumann production of the *Ring* in Venice. But, quite apart from his three chapters devoted to discussing Wagner's ideas and works, Norlenghi returns later to that production in the course of his long final chapter, on Wagner's last residence in the city. At that point, Norlenghi could draw upon positive memories, for at least three of the performers involved.

In a digression in praise of Wagner's high musical standards, Norlenghi had noted the composer's contempt for the irresponsible behavior of *le dive*, the pampered super-singers who misrepresent a composer's intentions in seeking their own glory.[1] It was difficult, Norlenghi says, for Wagner to find proper interpreters of his music, when he was anxious to place artistic integrity before cheap success.

> And I have spoken of some splendid exceptions, because in German artistry the most celebrated singers have understood all this, and have placed all their powers at the service of Wagner, and of his lofty art.
>
> Now, setting aside famous and beloved names that come to my mind, and not wanting to speak only of singers that we Italians have been able to hear, I believe that those who have attended the Tetralogy will not forget the names of Edwige Kindermann [fig. 39], the ideal Brunhilde, of Anton Seidl, the illustrious orchestra conductor, of the lovely signora Krauss [*sic*], the sweetest Sieglinde, of the highly talented Lieban, Mime—even while leaving aside all the others, in all fairness, hardly inferior.
>
> Poor Edwige Kirdemann [*sic*]. Lovely, young, an artist to the core; art had to kill her.[2]
>
> Poor butterfly fluttering around the lofty flame, its sublime radiance had drawn her into its fiery spiral ... and, like the fair butterfly, it had to be consumed. This heroine of art: when in Venice they made a point of her badly deteriorated health, when they advised rest, she answered sweetly "art wants me"; for her it was "my life." And the gracious lady who, ill, exhausted, dragged herself with difficulty about her splendid rooms in the Grand-Hotel by day, was in the evening, on the stage of the Fenice, the gallant, powerful Brunehilde, and her feeble, hoarse voice, by evening full of true sacred fire, was clear and ringing.
>
> Poor Edwige Kindermann, she went on ... and Bologna, Rome, Turin, Trieste, they acclaimed her with delirious raptures ... they were her funeral elegy, those raptures.

The emotions, both potent and delightful, that sweetly stir our mind, our heart, those unforgettable, sublime emotions—she felt them before and more strongly than we did, and they killed her. They were the final and bleeding shreds of her poor life that she was giving us, with her poetry-filled singing. To us who were unperceiving, to art, she gave those final breaths. ... Poor daughter of the Gods; behind the lofty Brunehilde stood a suffering martyr. ...

And she kept going on ... and she returned still more ill, but always into the breach. Then at Trieste—her high mission fulfilled, when repose smiled upon her, and the strengthening tranquility of her family smiled upon her still further, and perhaps she was thinking again of life—a final collapse killed her in a hotel room, without the comforts of her dear ones, without being able to give her last kiss to her sweet Francesco, to the lovely little boy who was awaiting his mamma.

There in lovely Trieste, there in the poetic cemetery of St. Anna, between the blue Adriatic and the green hills, there beneath that sublime workmanship of bold nature, rests her body. ...

There, at that verdant soil where they sheltered her, thoughts return sadly to the sweet moments through which they once wandered in lofty and fanciful worlds. ...

A flower for the grave of the gracious lady, of the great artist.

More fortunate than she: Seidl, the brilliant musician, the youth full of life, and the fair and lovely signora Krauss, blooming in freshness and in health, have tied Hymen's sweet knot. A toast to you, gracious and lucky couple. If these lines may fall before your eyes, and if you have not forgotten the merry evenings at the Bauer [Hotel] in Venice, and if, among the many and diverse acquaintances you have made in Italy, you recall that of the writer of this book, accept his most sincere greetings, his simple and merry predictions of a happiness without ending. (179–82)

Addendum 15

Norlenghi's Further Thoughts on Wagner (to chapter 12)

In April 1885, Norlenghi participated in a gathering in Rome dedicated to Wagner and his work, and featuring a Wagnerian concert organized by Giovanni Sgambati. The address Norlenghi gave was published the following year in a short forty-page quarto volume under the title *Ricordo Wagneriano: Parole lette per la commemorazione di Riccardo Wagner alla Associazione Artistica Internazionale di Roma*.[1] In many ways, that address represents a digest of some of the ideas he had already presented in his *Wagner in Italia*.

After commenting rhetorically on the passing of Wagner, Norlenghi addresses the stereotype that Wagner was an enemy of Italian music—the very Wagner who was inspired so much by the Italian scene, including Venice, where he worked on *Tristan*. It must now be recognized that, with his new and commanding school of music, Wagner is the savior of opera—an idiom, after all, so dear to Italians. The assumption that the school of Wagner is in opposition to that Italian school, ultimately represented by Rossini, requires scrutiny.

That Italy has been the mother of opera as an art form is reaffirmed as Norlenghi traces its evolution from Poliziano, Peri, and Monteverdi, through Lulli (Florence-born, remember!), to (Alessandro) Scarlatti. The age of Hasse and Pergolesi placed emphasis upon the singer, setting the scene for the reforms of Gluck. The evolution through Classicism to Romanticism was carried forward by Mozart, Cimarosa, and Paisiello, and crowned by the trail-blazing work of Rossini, joined by "the very sweet Bellini, and the dramatic Donizetti, and Verdi the powerful colorist" (26). To these could be added the cosmopolitan Spontini and the German Weber. Nevertheless, a renewed decadence set in, again descending to concentration on mere virtuosity and cheap effect. To this came Wagner as a reformer, seeking to renew the lofty tradition of Monteverdi, while drawing upon the resources added by Palestrina, Bach, and Beethoven, in recreating the "modern *dramma musicale*." Rather than advancing "a form contrary to national traditions," as critics have judged superficially, Wagner's work actually "descends in direct line from the classic Italian opera, and we may justly consider Wagner as one of our own" (29–30).

Wagner, says Norlenghi, despised the vulgarity that tainted the earlier work of Rossini, a vulgarity brought to new depths by Meyerbeer, and against which Wagner was "the musical Luther." It was rather the mature late style of *Guillaume Tell* that prompted Wagner's admiration for Rossini, who was thus the muse to *Rienzi*, and whom Wagner treated with such respect in their famous meeting in Paris. As for Gluck, so also for Spontini, Wagner had great admiration. Those who carp incessantly about "Italian art" forget that Wagner particularly delighted in Bellini's music, along with the earlier works of such other Italians as Palestrina, Allegri, and Marcello. Though bombarded with defamations of Wagner, the Italian public has come to recognize the truth, finding in the lyricism of *Lohengrin* and *Tannhäuser* no hostility to Italian art. "The *music of the future* is by now in Italy, no less than in Germany, the music of the present" (34).

Paying final compliments to his Roman hosts, Norlenghi comments on the ensuing concert program that Sgambati has prepared for them. He reviews the plot of *Der fliegende Holländer*, sets the scene for Wolfram's song to the Evening Star in *Tannhäuser*, and finally considers the *Siegfried Idyll*. He lingers over that serene, intimate, and lucid music, "of an inspiration more fresh, more spontaneous, than anything ever issuing from Wagner's pen": a work, Norlenghi claims, that had "never been performed in Italy" (38–39).[2] Paraphrasing the old royal salute, Norlenghi is ready to end with *Wagner è morto, viva Wagner*, convinced that "Wagner does not die, Wagner is immortal" (40).

Notes

Chapter One

1. Carl Friedrich Glasenapp (1847–1915), an early admirer of Wagner, and author of the first "authorized" biography of the composer (2 vols., 1876–77; 6 vols., 1905–11), reports a remark that Wagner made to his friend and artistic aide, Joukowsky: "It is incredible—and you must not laugh—that I have had built for me a house [Wahnfried] in a place where it is possible to live only one month out of the year!" (quoted by M. Panizzardi [see next note], vol. 1, 154, n. 1).

2. Though Wagner's visits to Italy are treated in all the standard biographies of the composer, studies specifically focused on this particular aspect are rare. The most recent overall one is the essay by Carlo de Incontrera, "I viaggi di Wagner in Italia." One of its few predecessors is Karl Ipser's *Richard Wagner in Italien*, but that is a simple narrative work with little comment or analysis, though its period illustrations are valuable.

The earliest work of this type, however dated (and written before Cosima Wagner's diaries were accessible), remains the most comprehensive. This is by Mario Panizzardi: *Wagner in Italia*, in two volumes. Volume 1, *Note biografiche*, was published in 1914 and deals with the virtually complete span of Wagner's stays and experiences in Italy; it, too, contains some rare period photographs and illustrations. Volume 2, *Pagine di storia musicale*, published in 1923, deals with the performances of Wagner's operas. Born in 1863, Panizzardi was a critic and journalist who greatly admired Wagner and his music. Prior to the two-volume work just cited, he published a collection entitled *Wagneriana* (Genoa, 1907).

The only recent study, *Richard Wagner und Italien: Vom Zaubergarten zur Lagune*, by Paul Gerhardt Dippel, is at once brief but very broad, discussing not only Wagner's own visits to Italy but also the various meanings and symbolisms the land had for Wagner, and his uses of these in his operas. On a more cursory scale, however, there is now the section on Wagner's involvement with Venice in John Julius Norwich's new book, *Paradise of Cities: Venice in the 19th Century*, 171–91.

3. Richard Wagner, *Mein Leben*, 2 vols. (Munich: F. Bruckmann, 1911), vol. 2, 572–77; English trans., Andrew Gray, *My Life* (New York: Dodd, Mead, 1911), 583–89; or Wagner, *Mein Leben: Erste authentische Veröffentlichung*, ed. M. Gregor-Dellin, 561–66, or corrected edition (1976), 494–99; trans. Gray, *My Life*, 482–87. Cf. Panizzardi, *Wagner in Italia*, vol. 1, 3–6; Ipser, *Richard Wagner in Italien*, 21–24; Incontrera, "Viaggi," 9–11; also, Newman, *The Life of Richard Wagner*, vol. 2: *1848–1860*, 286–88; Gregor-Dellin, *Richard Wagner*, 353–55, abbreviated trans., Brownjohn, 240–41 (eliminating mention of Italy itself in this journey!); Watson,

Richard Wagner, 127. Many other current biographies of Wagner ignore this brief episode. See also Dippel, *Wagner und Italien*, 41.

4. Westernhagen, *Wagner*, 2nd ed., 183, or trans. Whittall, *Wagner: A Biography*, 181.

5. Wagner, *Mein Leben* (1911), vol. 2, 590–93 or (1963), 579–80 and (1976), 511–12; *My Life* (1911), 602–4 or (1983), 498–500. Cf. Panizzardi, *Wagner in Italia*, vol. 1, 11–18, and 243–56 (the latter quoting Wagner's letter to his wife, Minna, and attempting at length to identify the hotel where Wagner stayed); Ipser, *Richard Wagner in Italien*, 27–32; Incontrera, "Viaggi," 11–12; Newman, *Life*, vol. 2, 388–91; Gregor-Dellin, *Richard Wagner*, 374–76, trans. Brownjohn, 248–49; Westernhagen, *Wagner*, 183–84, trans. Whittall, 181–83; Gutman, *Richard Wagner*, 149; Watson, *Richard Wagner*, 132–33; Dippel, *Wagner und Italien*, 41–44. It should be noted, however, that Wagner's account of this episode in his later autobiography has in recent years been dismissed as self-mythologizing fantasy: see Deathridge and Dahlhaus, *The New Grove Wagner*, 39–40. On the other hand, a more open-minded attitude is expressed by Warren Darcy, *Wagner's "Das Rheingold"* (Oxford: Oxford University Press, 1993), 62–64.

On the broader issue of the character of *Mein Leben*, and its reliability as a source, see the trenchant assessment of Stewart Spencer, in *The Wagner Compendium: A Guide to Wagner's Life and Music*, ed. Barry Millington (London and New York: Thames and Hudson and Schirmer, 1992), 182–86.

6. *Correspondence of Wagner and Liszt*, trans. Francis Hueffer, rev'd. ed. by William Ashton Ellis (New York: Scribner's, 1897), vol. 2, 243–44.

7. Generally on the 1858–59 stay in Venice, see Wagner, *Mein Leben* (1911), vol. 2, 677–91, or (1963), 664–78 and (1976), 586–98; *My Life* (1911), 689–704 or (1983), 572–84. Cf. Panizzardi, *Wagner in Italia*, vol. 1, 26–44 and 259–64 (with a rich gallery of photographs); Ipser, *Wagner in Italien*, 43–74; Incontrera, "Viaggi," 12–19; Newman, *Life*, vol. 2, 558–84; Gregor-Dellin, *Richard Wagner*, 442–50, trans. Brownjohn (much reduced), 288–91; Westernhagen, *Wagner*, 248–57, trans. Whittal, 250–59; Gutman, *Richard Wagner*, 182ff, 190ff; Watson, *Richard Wagner*, 183; Dippel, *Wagner und Italien*, 49–60; more superficially, Norwich, *Paradise of Cities*, 174–82. More broadly, see the old study by Lippert, *Richard Wagners Verbannung und Rückkehr*, or trans., England, *Wagner in Exile*, espec. 94–134/91–125.

This sojourn is treated only glancingly by Köhler, *Der Letzte der Titanen*, 538–39, or trans. Spencer, *Richard Wagner: The Last of the Titans*, 418–19, as part of a provocative treatment of Wagner that is only marginally biographical and more concerned with his emotional, psychological, and intellectual evolution.

8. Destined to die in Venice, Wagner took as his first impression of Venice an all too appropriately funereal one: the gondola (including the black canopy or *felse* no longer used for the tourists now). The gondola as a symbol of death was an image that struck many other visitors upon first catching sight of this austere, almost phantasmagoric, and uniquely Venetian boat. Note that the introduction into Venetian canals of the now-familiar *vaporetti* or water-ferries, originally steam-powered, did not begin until 1881, so that gondolas were, in 1858, still the normal means of water transport around the city. The increase in the number of bridges and in pedestrian strands was yet in progress at the time, so that movement around Venice then required more use of water transport than it does now.

9. *My Life*, 572–73, using Andrew Gray's translation; text, ed. Gregor-Dellin (1963), 664–65 or (1976), 586; partial Italian translation by Incontrera, "Viaggi," 13. The Gray translation is also quoted by John Julius Norwich in his anthology, *A Traveller's Companion to Venice* (New York: Interlink Books, 2002), 228–29.

10. *My Life*, trans. Gray, 573; text, ed. Gregor-Dellin (1963), 665 or (1976), 587–87. A larger portion of the Gray translation is quoted by Norwich, *Traveller's Companion*, 165.

11. Using the version in *Selected Letters of Richard Wagner*, trans. and ed. Spencer and Millington, 418; text in *Richard Wagner an Minna Wagner* [ed. Hans von Wolzogen], vol. 1, 303; also trans. Ellis, *Richard Wagner to Minna Wagner*, vol. 1, 365–66. On his financial dealings with his landlord, Wagner much later recalled to his then wife, Cosima, one comical episode, which she reported in her diaries (see below, p. 328, n. 5) on November 16, 1882, and regarding a building *commissionaire* named Zuski or Suski or Susky: "... when R.'s rent was due at the Palazzo Giustiniani, he had no money with which to pay it; he asked Suski to borrow it for him with interest; the latter soon brought it to him and told him he had got it from the landlord himself, who lent out money on interest!" Wagner's failure to record this amusing incident in *Mein Leben* or other writings may or may not discredit this later recollection recounted to Cosima.

12. Trans. Ellis, *Richard Wagner to Mathilde Wesendonk*, 35–36; text, ed. Golther, 37–38; or Sternfeld, ed., *Tagebuchblätter und Briefe an Mathilde Wesendonk*, 70–71. Incontrera, "Viaggi," 13, quotes passages from this, in Italian.

13. Trans. Ellis, *Richard Wagner to Mathilde*, 36–37; text ed. Golther, 39; ed. Sternfeld, 72; a small portion of this in Italian translation by Incontrera, "Viaggi," 14.

14. Trans. Ellis, *Richard Wagner to Mathilde*, 41–42; text, ed. Golther, 44; ed. Sternfeld, 78.

15. Trans. Ellis, *Richard Wagner to Minna*, vol. 1, 370; text, ed. Wolzogen, vol. 1, 306.

16. Trans. Ellis, *Richard Wagner to Minna*, vol. 1, 374–78; text, ed. Wolzogen, vol. 1, 310–13; also ed. Kersting, *Richard Wagner Briefe*, 368–71. Portions of the Ellis translation are quoted by Norwich, *Traveller's Companion*, 131–33, 166.

On the preceding day, September 27, Wagner had written a letter to Liszt, contesting misunderstandings about his choice of Venice, and including some parallel observations: "... As an Austrian city, Venice exists for me only in so far as it does not belong to the German Confederacy, and as I may consequently live there in security. This has proved to be true. Unfortunately I could not prevent my landlord from trumpeting about my stay here, which in consequence was made public sooner than I desired. The police which, once more, asked for my passport, has, however, returned it to me with the remark that there is nothing against my undisturbed stay at Venice ...

"You will be pleased to hear that Venice has not disappointed my expectations. The melancholy silence of the Grand Canal, on the banks of which I live in a stately palace with large rooms, is sympathetic to me. Amusement and an agreeable diversion of the mind is afforded by a daily walk in the square of St. Mark, a trip in a gondola to the islands, walks there, etc. I will turn to the art treasures later on. The entirely new and interesting character of the surroundings is very pleasant to me. I am waiting for my grand piano, and hope to resume my work without interruption next month. My only thought is of completing *Tristan*, nothing else...." (*Correspondence of Wagner and Liszt*, vol. 2, 249–50).

17. Trans. Ellis, *Richard Wagner to Mathilde*, 44–45; text, ed. Golther, 46–48; ed. Sternfeld, 80–81; complete translation by Incontrera, "Viaggi," 15–16, but misdated to September 30.

18. Trans. Ellis, *Richard Wagner to Mathilde*, 87–90; text, ed. Golther, 91–95; ed. Sternfeld, 127–32.

19. *Correspondence of Wagner and Liszt*, vol. 2, 255–56.

20. In a letter written to Liszt on November 21, Wagner describes himself as "literally run after by foreign princes" and speaks of one "D." who is clearly Dolgoruki. Wagner also speaks of "a Venetian music-teacher, who has been made an enthusiast for German music by you and me. This amused me very much" (*Correspondence of Wagner and Liszt*, vol. 2, 262–63).

Angelo Tessarin was a figure who turns up repeatedly during Wagner's stays in Venice, as will be seen. There are problems of precision with his name. In his autobiography, Wagner called him "Tessarin" but elsewhere identified him as "Tessarini." In her diary references, Cosima spoke of him as "Tesarini." In their notes to her *Tagebücher*, editors Gregor-Dellin and Mack have named him "Luigi Tesarini," while an Italian publication of *Mein Leben* has tried to identify him with the composer Francesco Tessarin (1820–89). Perl, Norlenghi, and the Venetian newspapers all confirm "Angelo Tessarin" as the correct form. See Incontrera, "Viaggi," 51, n. 18.

Tessarin was a native Venetian, born on August 16, 1834. He emerged early as a successful pianist, not only performing locally but publishing a good many piano pieces of his own. He also composed vocal works, among which was *Inno Saloto*, for chorus and orchestra, presented April 6, 1875, at the Fenice to honor a visit by Hapsburg Emperor Franz Josef to King Vittorio Emanuele. Other such pieces included *Marinesca* for tenor, choir, and orchestra or band; and *Serenata* for chorus and orchestra. Tessarin relocated to Milan in his later years, and died in Marseilles on February 20, 1909.

Between their first acquaintance in 1858–59 and their reunion in 1876, Tessarin and Wagner may have kept in some kind of contact. On April 4, 1873, Cosima reports of the receipt of a letter from Tessarin giving an account of the production of *Lohengrin* in Milan. (". . . he says the hissers—there were about 50 of them—were paid by Ricordi," that is, the Italian publishing house rivaling Wagner's agents, the Lucca firm.)

21. Trans. Ellis, *Richard Wagner to Minna*, vol. 1, 383–85; text, ed. Wolzogen, vol. 1, 316–19. Some parallel perspectives on Wagner and these Austrian musicians are offered in Henriette Perl's book, *Wagner in Venedig*: see, pp. 109–110, Wagner's mention of "Stumme von Portici" refers to Auber's opera *La Muette de Portici* ("The Mute Girl of Portici").

22. *My Life*, in the Gray translation, 576–78; text, ed. Gregor-Dellin (1963), 668–71 or (1976), 589–92; portions translated by Incontrera, "Viaggi," 16–17; portions of the Gray translation given by Norwich, *Traveller's Companion*, 133–34, 229–30.

The imagery that inspired the September 3 letter to Mathilde, the October 28 letter to Minna, and his account in *Mein Leben* seems to have sunk deeply into Wagner's memory. A dozen years later, when he wrote his short book *Beethoven* (Leipzig, 1870), he quite directly paralleled his earlier verbiage to illustrate the effects of time and space on music: "During a sleepless night I once stepped out on the balcony of my window, above the great canal at Venice: dreamlike the weird city of Lagoons lay spread out in the shade before me. From the soundless silence arose the strong hoarse note of a Gondolier awakened on his barge; at varied intervals he called into the darkness till, from furthest distance, a like call answered along the nocturnal canal. I knew the ancient melancholy melodious strain, to which Tasso's familiar verses were set in his time, but which assuredly is as old as the canals of Venice and their population. After solemn pauses the far-reaching dialogue grew livelier, and at length appeared to merge into unison, till, far and near, the sounds again softly sank to silence.

"What could the Venice of daytime, radiant with sunshine and motley with crowds, say of itself, which that resounding night-dream did not bring home at once, and infinitely deeper? (Trans. Edward Dannreuther, 3rd edition, London: William Reeves, 1903, pp. 22–23.) Much is made of this passage by Maurice Barrès, *La mort de Venise* (Saint-Cyr-sur-Loire: Christian Pirot, 1990), 77–84; and by Raymond Furness, *Wagner and Literature* (New York, St. Martin's Press, 1982), 48–49.

23. *Correspondence of Wagner and Liszt*, vol. 2, 255.

24. Köhler, *Der Letzte der Titanen*, 539–51, trans. Spencer, 419–29, places great emphasis on the impact that reading Schopenhauer had at this time, and especially on its influence on the creation of *Tristan und Isolde*, Wagner's work in progress in Venice. The emphasis of Schopenhauer's influence on it has now been extended back to the initial conception of the libretto itself, as well as the music, by Eric Chafe, *The Tragic and the Ecstatic: The Musical Revolution of Wagner's "Tristan and Isolde"* (Oxford: Oxford University Press, 2005).

25. Pierre Antoine Bruno, Comte Daru (1767–1829), was a Napoleonic general who produced in his last years the pioneering *Histoire de la république de Venise*, published in nine volumes (Paris, 1817–21). This was the first comprehensive historical study based upon research in the Venetian archives, by then opened under the Austrian regime. It consolidated negative interpretations of the Republic as having slipped into failure and decadence in its last years, and as therefore richly deserving Napoleon's suppression. Quickly translated into Italian, the work prompted a number of patriotic responses from Italian writers, but Wagner most likely would have read the French original. Considering Daru's prejudices, it is interesting that his history led Wagner to a more positive perception of earlier Venetian government and society.

26. *My Life*, in the Gray translation, 579; text, ed. Gregor-Dellin (1963), 672 or (1976), 592–93.

27. Trans. Ellis, *Richard Wagner to Mathilde*, 99–100; text, ed. Golther, 100–101; ed. Sternfeld, 138.

28. For Wagner's later recollection of the aborted Vicenza/Treviso excursion, p. 63.

29. Trans. Ellis, *Richard Wagner to Minna*, vol. 2, 444–45; text, ed. Wolzogen, vol. 2, 43–44. For all Wagner's talk about reuniting with Minna and relocating with her, they would never live together again; nor would Minna ever visit Venice.

30. Trans. Ellis, *Richard Wagner to Minna*, vol. 2, 455; text, ed. Wolzogen, vol. 2, 52. Wagner was (to Minna's dismay) seriously considering an invitation for a five-month engagement in New York: an arrangement that never came to pass, but that launched his recurrent idea of going to the United States to make his fortune. See addendum 12, pp. 313–14.

31. The documents of Crespi's efforts, and other texts, are included in the appropriate chapter of Lippert's *Richard Wagners Verbannung*, 99–105, 118–30 (plus appropriate notes, 230–35), trans. England, 96–100, 111–21 (notes, 198–201). It might be observed that this Maximilian, Viceroy of Lombardy-Veneto during the brief period of 1857–59, was the hapless Hapsburg Archduke who was a few years later to become the "Emperor of Mexico" and who died there before a rebel firing squad in June 1867. One wonders if, in that year, Wagner took any notice of the sad event, or gave any thought to the tragic Archduke who had granted him so gracious a favor.

Wagner never made any retrospective reference to the execution in the later part of *Mein Leben*, written well after Maximilian's demise.

32. Trans. Ellis, *Richard Wagner to Mathilde*, 111–12; text, ed. Golther, 115–17; ed. Sternfeld, 153–55.

33. *My Life*, in the Gray translation, 585; text, ed. Gregor-Dellin (1963), 678–79 or (1976), 598–99. The opera was apparently *Il duca di Scilla* by Enrico Petrella (1813–77), which Wagner saw two nights after its premiere on March 24. The ballet was a five-act extravaganza, *Cleopatra*, by one G. Rota. Cf. Panizzardi, *Wagner in Italia*, vol. 1, 52–53; Incontrera, "Viaggi," 19–20.

Chapter Two

1. Wagner further reports that, upon his return to Vienna, he presented to his young disciple, the composer Peter Cornelius, "a model of a gondola I had bought for him in Venice and which I accompanied with a little canzona in nonsensical Italian." *My Life*, in the Gray translation, 667–68; text, ed. Gregor-Dellin (1963), 773–74 or (1976), 683–84. Cf. Panizzardi, *Wagner in Italia*, vol. 1, 57–61 and 281 (with the canzona text); Ipser, *Richard Wagner in Italien*, 77–80; Incontrera, "Viaggi," 20–21; Newman, *Life of Richard Wagner*, vol. 3, 151–53; Westernhagen, *Wagner*, 294–95, trans. Whittall, 299–300; Gutman, *Richard Wagner*, 205–6; Watson, *Richard Wagner*, 183; Dippel, *Richard Wagner und Italien*, 66–67; Norwich, *Paradise of Cities*, 182–84.

2. See addendum 1.

3. Ipser, *Richard Wagner in Italien*, 83–85; Incontrera, "Viaggi," 21–22; Newman, *Life of Richard Wagner*, vol. 4, 161 (curiously terse); Westernhagen, 380–81, trans. Whittall, 404–5; Watson, *Richard Wagner*, 238. This visit was ignored, or overlooked, by Panizzardi.

4. Beyond inevitable treatments of her in biographies and studies of Richard Wagner, Cosima Liszt/Bülow/Wagner has herself inspired a popular literature of her own. The first and still the most extensive biography is that of Du Moulin-Eckart, *Cosima Wagner*, trans. Phillips, followed by his own vol. 2, subtitled *Die Herrin von Bayreuth* [no English translation]. That is a somewhat romanticized and idolatrous treatment, and it was followed more concisely in German by Millenkovich-Morild, *Cosima Wagner: Ein Lebensbild*. An earlier biography, *Cosima Wagner-Liszt: Der Weg zum Wagner-Mythos*, was left unfinished by Franz Wilhelm Beidler, Cosima's grandson. He was the son of conductor Franz Beidler and Cosima's daughter Isolde, whose fight with the family over her claim of Wagner's parentage led to the exclusion of her and her children from the Bayreuth circle. Beidler was a staunch anti-Nazi intellectual and sharp critic of the Bayreuth establishment. Together with some of his other relevant *Ausgewählte Schriften*, the biography has been published by Dieter Borchmeyer (Bielefeld: Pendragon, 1997).

In English, meanwhile (and usually ending treatment at 1883), see also: Marek, *Cosima Wagner*; Sokoloff, *Cosima Wagner*; Geoffrey Skelton (also translator of her diaries), *Richard and Cosima Wagner*. Her relationship with Wagner has been most recently surveyed by Jonathan Carr in his well-founded popular book, *The Wagner Clan*, 1–8, 17–54. The most provocative treatment of Cosima, however, is the caustically negative picture of her as a manipulative, controlling, and even malevolent force in Wagner's life, developed through the later part of Köhler, *Der Letzte der Titanen*, but especially 676–733, or trans. Spencer, 528–75.

5. For this sojourn, we can now draw upon Cosima Wagner's *Tagebücher*, 2 vols., ed. Gregor-Dellin and Mack, vol. 1, 1002–19; trans. Skelton, vol. 1, 922–37. Hereafter, Cosima's diaries are referred to simply by entry date, allowing convenient access alike to the German or English versions. As we shall have ample occasion to observe, Cosima's diaries were written with self-serving motives, reflecting her own biases and agendas, and her entries are often notable for omissions or oversimplification. Nevertheless, as used with critical care, the diaries still remain an essential and fascinating source.

In general on this residence, see: Panizzardi, *Wagner in Italia*, vol. 1, 73–105; Ipser, *Richard Wagner in Italien*, 93–95; Incontrera, "Viagii," 22–26; Newman, *Life*, vol. 4, 541ff (concentrating on the break with Nietzsche); Gregor-Dellin, *Richard Wagner*, 728–31, trans. Brownjohn, 439–41; Westernhagen, *Wagner*, 477–83, trans. Whittall, 506–12; Gutman, *Richard Wagner*, 352, 359–60; Dippel, *Wagner und Italien*, 70–74; Norwich, *Paradise of Cities*, 184.

6. See addendum 1.

7. Cf. the general citations in n. 5 for the encounter. The most recent monograph of relevance is Georges Liébert, *Nietzsche et musique* (Paris: Presses Universitaires de France, 1995), trans. David Pellauer and Graham Parkes, *Nietzsche and Music* (Chicago: University of Chicago Press, 2004), which thoroughly probes Nietzsche's relationship with Wagner and his music, and includes the most up-to-date bibliography. Beyond other general works on the philosopher's life, note: Dietrich Fischer-Dieskau, *Wagner und Nietzsche* (Stuttgart: Deutsche Verlags-Anstalt, 1974), trans. Joachim Neugroschel, *Wagner and Nietzsche* (New York: Seabury, 1976), 152–55; and Köhler, *Friedrich Nietzsche und Cosima Wagner*, trans. Taylor, 117, 123–32. Köhler has returned to the relationship in his *Der Letzte der Titanen*, 647–75, trans. Spencer, 505–28. See also Dieter Borchmeyer's essay, "Wagner and Nietzsche," in Müller and Wapnewski, *Wagner Handbook*, 327–42; and, most recently, Bryan Magee's *The Tristan Chord: Wagner and Philosophy* (New York: Holt, 2000), 282–341. See also Frederick Rutan Love, *Young Nietzsche and the Wagnerian Experience* (Chapel Hill: University of North Carolina Press, 1963); Roger Hollinrake, *Nietzsche, Wagner, and the Philosophy of Pessimism* (London: George Allen and Unwin, 1982).

8. Already at midpoint in the stay, Cosima could find time for self-indulgently bittersweet reactions: "A week gone by, how rich, how great, how happy, and how poor, how trivial, how desolate! Poor, small, desolate in everything that concerns our own affairs, but how indescribably rich the strange impressions!" (November 19, 1876).

On the previous day Cosima had noted that, plagued by awareness of the Bayreuth debts, Richard "becomes bitter looking at art treasures, and I, too, regard them with the deepest melancholy."

As for reactions to St. Peter's: Wagner and Cosima were viewing the late-Renaissance/Baroque church we know today, whereas Luther would have seen the Old St. Peter's, dating back to Constantine the Great, and by Luther's day badly antiquated, already in the process of replacement. Cosima must have been using St. Peter's simply as a symbol of the general degeneracy of the papacy that Luther perceived on his own visit to Rome in 1510–11.

Wagner's son Siegfried gives a tart vignette of the stay in Rome, in his *Erinnerungen*, 8 (also trans. Spencer, in his anthology, *Wagner Remembered*, 271): "During this journey my father was in the best of moods throughout this [1876] journey. Only in

Rome did he slip into a bad humor. He was harassed by tactless people, and the sight of so many priests irritated him, . . ." and, Siegfried notes, his father was deeply concerned all this time over the Bayreuth deficit.

On the contacts Wagner made during the 1876 stay in Rome, see Jung, *Rezeption*, 95–96, or, in Italian translation (of its Part 1 only) as her essay "La fortuna di Wagner in Italia," in *Wagner in Italia*, ed. Rostirolla, 57–225, 126.

9. On this episode, see Jung, *Rezeption*, 38–39, or "La fortuna," 77–78. See also Panizzardi, *Wagner in Italia*, vol. 2, 291–93.

10. On the sojourn of 1880 in general, we have Cosima's diaries, of course, as well as the later and diversely personal comments of Siegfried Wagner, *Erinnerungen*, 9–16. See also: Panizzardi, *Wagner in Italia*, vol. 1, 109–50; vol. 2, 199–204 (specifically on the visit to Ravello); Incontrera, "Viaggi," 28–37; Newman, *Life*, vol. 4, 622–29; Gregor-Dellin, *Richard Wagner*, 787–92, trans. Brownjohn, 480–84 (compressed, eliminating account of the Florimo encounter); Westernhagen, *Wagner*, 519–33, trans. Whittall, 550–64; Watson, *Richard Wagner*, 300–303; Dippel, *Wagner und Italien*, 75–87; Norwich, *Paradise of Cities*, 184–86.

11. Wagner still relished long walks alone, while he also might venture into Naples on his own, sometimes with mixed reactions to the local scene resulting. Thus, Cosima on March 17: ". . . In the afternoon he takes the streetcar into town, tells me on his return, 'I must not go out without you, I get too sad, I see everything too closely, awful impressions; today an old man who made one wonder what a life of misery and vice he had led, and then all those stupid faces in the car, the men with their moustaches, the women with their hair over their foreheads, which makes even the prettiest look so vulgar.' "

Cosima goes on to note that, while "he was collecting these impressions," *she* was back at the villa pondering what it would be like "to die during love's embrace" instead of living on in "a betrayal of this sublime death wish," since life's "highest yearning points to death." Which contemplations might we judge the sublime, which the ridiculous?

12. Giovannina Lucca, née Strazza (1814–94), was a far stronger personality than her somewhat shallow husband, Francesco (1802–72). She had regular dealings with Wagner, including her several visits to him in Bayreuth, and there are frequent references to her throughout Cosima's diaries. Her forceful activity only increased after her husband's death. Though she frequently vexed him, Wagner clearly respected her aggressive efforts on his behalf. Cosima quotes him (May 23, 1872) as saying of her: "Nature originally intended to make a man, until it realized that in Italy the men were not much use, and quickly corrected itself." During the final stay in Venice, Cosima records (November 1, 1882) gossip about her as passed on by "our good friend" (apparently Angelo Tessarin): "how every month she falls in love with some young opera composer." The difficulties she was to give Wagner's apostle, Angelo Neumann, will be sketched in chapters 9–10. On her, see Panizzardi, *Wagner in Italia*, vol. 2, 128–31.

13. The production of *Lohengrin* in 1880 was the second of that opera in Rome. Luigi Mancinelli, who was becoming a leading champion of Wagner's music in Italy, was supposed to have conducted the earlier production, in 1878, but he was stricken suddenly by typhoid during rehearsals and was replaced by the composer–conductor Amilcare Ponchielli. Mancinelli was, however, able to conduct this 1880 production. In gratitude for his efforts, Wagner sent him a photograph of himself, autographed and with a con-

gratulatory inscription. On these early Rome productions, see Jung, *Rezeption*, 96–97 or "La fortuna," 128–29; Panizzardi, *Wagner in Italia*, vol. 1, 117–21; vol. 2, 69–73.

Luigi Mancinelli (1848–1921) was one of the most distinguished Italian musicians of the late nineteenth and early twentieth centuries. Though he began as a composer, and returned to that function regularly, his energies were increasingly directed toward conducting. In that capacity, he achieved his greatest fame as the most important maestro of his generation in Italy. He conducted widely around Europe, with a particular focus on Bologna, where he founded its Società del Quartetto (or Concert Society) and regularly directed concerts and opera. He also taught at Bologna's Music Conservatory (1881–86). Giovannina Lucca came to regard him as the leading Wagner conductor of the day in Italy.

Despite reservations about his "eccentricities," Wagner was willing, as we shall see, to have Mancinelli conduct the revival of the Symphony in C Major on Christmas Eve 1882 and undertook the task himself only when Mancinelli was found unavailable. (See p. 50; also, on Wagner's further dealings with Mancinelli, pp. 53–54, 84, 87 and 336–37, n. 11; 345, n. 17; as well as Jung, *Rezeption*, 42–44, or "La fortuna," 80–82.) Mancinelli continued winning high praise from some observers—such as the younger conductor, Felix Weingartner, who thought that Mancinelli could teach German conductors a thing or two about Wagner. There is regrettably little substantive literature on Mancinelli. Giacomo Orefice's *Luigi Mancinelli* ("L'Italia Musicale Moderna" series, Rome: Ausonia, 1921) is simply a survey of this musician's compositions; L. Silvestri's *Luigi Mancinelli: Direttore e compositore* (Milan, 1966) is unfortunately unavailable to me. See figure 18.

14. Panizzardi, *Wagner in Italia*, vol. 1, 125–26; vol. 2, 166–68, drawing upon Florimo's own account; cf. Incontrera, "Viaggi," 31. The complete absence of this episode in Cosima's diary is puzzling and problematical.

Francesco Florimo (1800–1888) was one of the more interesting personalities of nineteenth-century Italian musical life, with a rich and diverse career as librarian, teacher, composer, historian, and critic. A fellow student of Bellini at the Naples Conservatory, Florimo became one of that composer's most devoted friends and champions. Florimo composed memorial music for Bellini, was responsible for having the latter's remains brought back to his native Catania, and wrote an important (if not always reliable) biography of him. Florimo went on to become a major figure in the musical life of Naples and at its conservatory. A passionate musical nationalist, he became a personal friend of Verdi and an ardent opponent of Wagner's musical influence in Italy. His concerns came to a head after attending the Bayreuth production of the *Ring* in 1876, which prompted his publication of a vituperative pamphlet, *Riccardo Wagner e i wagneristi*. After Wagner's visit and astute courting of him, Florimo produced an expanded version of the book, in which the treatment of Wagner was considerably more gentle. That edition was published in 1883, just after Wagner's death and the Neumann tour. Active to the end of his days, Florimo remained a grand old man of Italian cultural conservatism, not to say reactionism.

15. Panizzardi, *Wagner in Italia*, vol. 1, 126; vol. 2, 183–87, where the letter's full text is reproduced in the original French. Cf. Newman, *Life*, vol. 4, 626. Though the letter is dated April 22, Cosima reports the dictation of it on the following day.

16. Panizzardi, *Wagner in Italia*, vol. 1, 143–44, relates that the Wagners were surprised to encounter in Perugia the conductor Luigi Mancinelli, who was there to direct performances of Ponchielli's *La gioconda* and Verdi's *Messa da Requiem*. Wagner promptly invited him to have dinner with them at their hotel. The source for this

report was the personal testimony to Panizzardi of Mancinelli himself. Here again we have an event completely absent in Cosima's daily chronicle. In point of fact, it seems that Cosima never mentions Mancinelli anywhere in her *Tagebücher*. For so relentless a name-dropper as Cosima the omission suggests some kind of animosity. See above, n. 13 and the other locations it cites. At any rate, such omissions remind us again that one must always reserve some caution in using Cosima's diaries as a definitive source.

17. Siegfried's interest in architecture had already emerged as early as the family travels in 1876: "After the first Festival of 1876—artistically so brilliant if financially unfortunate in outcome—we made a journey by way of Verona, Venice, Bologna to Rome and Naples. At that time was awakened in me a passion for architecture. Like one possessed I ran from church to church, from palace to palace, and my first efforts at reproducing these impressions with pencil on paper were initially quite clumsy, but gradually became altogether acceptable, so that my parents observed with smiles, but also with delight, this really surprising talent as it evolved" (S. Wagner, *Erinnerungen*, 8; also trans. Spencer, *Wagner Remembered*, 272).

Siegfried also writes elsewhere (e.g., p. 16) of the delight he took in these Italian explorations. Samples of Siegfried's youthful drawings, in his early sketchbook, are included in Kraft's *Der Sohn*, see 23–24; also Pachl, *Siegfried Wagner*, 54–57.

18. Joseph Arthur Comte de Gobineau (1816–82), was a French diplomat, traveler, and versatile writer. His books included his *Histoire des Perses* (1869), a series of exotic tales, *Nouvelles asiatiques* (1876), an extended poem, *Amadis* (1876), and a set of imaginary Renaissance dialogues (1877). By far his most important effort was his four-volume treatise, *Essai sur l'inégalité des races humaines* (1853–55), setting forth his theories of natural inequalities among the races. Though this was not the first of his writings that Wagner read, the composer came to study it carefully: he was excited by some of it, but disagreed strongly with other aspects, and in their personal encounters they could argue violently. But Gobineau became a close friend of the Wagners, visiting them at Bayreuth, in May 1881 and in May 1882. As we shall see (p. 47), Gobineau's death in the autumn of 1882 was a harsh blow to Wagner. Meanwhile, Gobineau's racial ideas had wide influence, affecting the likes of Nietzsche, and becoming central to the thought of the later Bayreuth ideologue, Stewart Houston Chamberlain. For a sketch of the Gobineau-Wagner connection, see Rose, *Wagner: Race and Revolution*, 135–41.

19. On this in general: Panizzardi, *Wagner in Italia*, vol. 1, 153–71; Incontrera, "Viaggi," 38–42; Ipser, *Richard Wagner in Italia*, 149–52; Newman, *Life*, vol. 4, 664–69; Gregor-Dellin, 799–800, 817–18, trans. Brownjohn, 488–89, 503–4 (eliminating the attempted contact with Ritter); Westernhagen, *Wagner*, 543–47, trans. Whittall, 575–79; Gutman, *Richard Wagner*, 414–18; Watson, *Richard Wagner*, 308, 309; Dippel, *Wagner und Italien*, 88–91.

20. It is interesting that, for all their culturally and historically motivated sight-seeing, Richard and Cosima seem (from her accounts) to have paid little attention to what should have been an important shrine, the gathering of the tombs of the Norman and Hohenstaufen rulers in Palermo's Cathedral.

21. In a letter of March 1, 1882, addressed to King Ludwig, Wagner commented: ". . . As to music, Sicily is the most impoverished part of Italy, and operatic activity is very little cultivated here; but it just happens that some members of the upper classes have attended performances of my works, for example in Munich in past years: among these a young Marchese Guccia made himself known to me and through him we have come to know almost all of Palermo's higher aristocracy—indeed, become friendly

with a part of them. Here I found an old-fashioned patriarchal life, the most simplistic relationship between masters and dependents, the latter of whom come almost entirely from just the population of aristocratic properties. Each one of these princely families possesses a palace of venerable and magnificent splendor, a grandiose country seat in the neighborhood of the city, with incomparably beautiful gardens—often open to the public—as well as broad holdings in the territory beyond. Within this aristocracy I have a friend of exceptionally warm devotion in the Count Almerita-Tasca who, already married for nineteen years, reckons as his posterity some twenty-one grand-children, has princes and marchese as brothers-in-law. The ardor of these naïvely illus-trious fellows now matters little since, for all that, my nature inclines to privacy, and in the end I leave it only to our growing daughters to take part in these pleasures pre-pared for us. . . ." (text in Strobel, *König Ludwig II und Richard Wagner*, vol. 3, 235).

22. The basic study of all this is in Schuh, *Renoir und Wagner*, which gives a German translation of the artist's extensive and highly detailed recollection of the episode, with analysis of the four portraits, plus related material, all fully reproduced. Renoir's letter recollection may be had in English translation, in the collection *Wagner Remembered*, ed. Spencer, 264–68; a more abbreviated version is to be found in Barth, Mack, and Voss, eds., *Wagner: A Documentary Study*, 240–41.

In 1867, Renoir had made a pencil sketch of Wagner, based upon a photograph. The location of that sketch is now uncertain. Joukowsky's rough oil sketch is repro-duced in figure 12.

23. The Hôtel des Palmes to this day preserves memories and markers of Wagner's stay. For an apparent memento of that sojourn, see addendum 5.

24. It is not clear how Wagner obtained the parts and materials needed for these works to be performed. Did he carry them with him in his voluminous luggage, or had he planned the event long enough to have the material sent to him from a home source? We do read in Cosima's report of Christmas Eve 1882 that there was a copy of the work at hand for perusal—a particularly sentimental choice for ending the evening that had held the birthday concert at La Fenice. May we wonder if Cosima carried the manuscript with her on travel as an inseparable treasure? If so, she might have had it with her on the 1881–82 trip.

The choice, too, of the *Siegfried Idyll* for the Palermo concert is interesting. Written for small chamber ensemble, this work combines some German cradle-songs with themes from the opera *Siegfried*. It had been composed in 1870 at Tribschen as a Christmas/birthday present for Cosima: it was first called "Symphonic Birthday Greeting," and was long known to them as the "staircase music" (from where the musicians who premiered it played from), the *Tribschen Idyll*, or simply at the *Idyll*. (Cosima's first reaction is recorded in her entry for December 25, 1870.) Wagner professed it his favorite composition and was greatly pleased when Liszt praised it as well, but it was regarded as a "private" work, with understandably deep meaning for Cosima—who called it her "sweet secret" (December 25, 1872), and guarded the manuscript carefully. Once, she reports (August 5, 1871), she lent it to the visiting Friedrich Nietzsche for his perusal, and there was an unhappy domestic flap over his careless failure to return it to her directly. (A sampling of Cosima's attitudes toward the piece is offered by Sabor, *Real Wagner*, 196.)

After its first playing for Cosima and the family, it was repeated in subsequent years in domestic musicales involving guest musicians, and Wagner would sometimes play parts of it for her on the piano. Hans Richter (who had learned the trumpet just to play in that first "staircase" performance at Tribschen) made at least one special arrangement of it. Apparently for violin and piano four hands, it was played brand-new by Richter (on violin), Richard, and Cosima on January 15, 1971. Either the same adaptation or a separate one was then played for the Wagners by some musician guests on January 30 of that year. The composer himself even thought about tinkering with the work, to Cosima's horror. On January 14, 1874 she writes: "He tells me he has been thinking of doing the *Idyll* for a large orchestra, but it would not come out so well; I tell him I should be appalled to see this work handed over to the general public." The climactic family enjoyment of it came (appropriately) on Christmas day of 1878, when Wagner had members of the Meiningen Court Orchestra appear for a family concert including the *Idyll* in its original scoring.

When, under financial pressures, Wagner allowed its public performance and then its publication (1878), Cosima was deeply and repeatedly pained. The score was her personal possession (she sometimes slept with it under her pillow), and only with great reluctance and anguish did she yield it up (e.g., August 20, October 4, November 19, November 30, December 10, all 1877), insisting in the long negotiations involved that she would "sacrifice" it only in return for complete clearing of their debts. At the end of 1877 (December 1877) Wagner received with satisfaction a four-hand piano arrangement he had made of it, and this was played repeatedly in the Wagner household thereafter, as a kind of welcome consolation for its public release. But Wagner himself seems to have shared Cosima's regrets, according to her report of December 12, 1878: ". . . Regarding the *Idyll* he says: 'I ought not to have published it. Everything one publishes is cast before swine, but now and again a blind hen comes along and finds the pearl.' . . . When we are upstairs, R. says of the *Idyll*, 'It is the only work of mine which comes straight from my life; I could write a program for it down to the last *t*.' " The performance at Porrazzi was probably only the second time Wagner conducted it in public, the first being at a concert of his works at Meiningen on March 10, 1877. The reason for its inclusion in the 1882 reception is not stated, but perhaps it suggested that the Wagners were granting their Sicilian friends a special degree of intimacy through this highly personal work (even in a terrible performance!).

This event would appear to be Wagner's only involvement with local Sicilian musicians. While incorrectly putting Wagner's arrival at the Villa Gangi on March 4, Panizzardi, *Wagner in Italia*, vol. 1, 158–63, records an incident that would have occurred at some time during the stay: "Having learned that in the Gangi house existed an old *spinetta* that had been played on by Vincenzo Bellini, he wished to see it and on it he played the chorus of the Druids from the first act of *Norma*." This story must have come to Panizzardi from a descendant of the Gangi family. There is no mention whatsoever of the incident in Cosima's diary chronicle, an omission which does not disprove it, though her silence does raise some doubts.

25. These notes were entered in what is known as Wagner's "Brown Book," a bound volume that the composer used as an intermittent repository for ideas and jottings as they came to him in the years after he had finished *Mein Leben*. The whole has been published as *Das Braune Buch*, ed. Bergfeld, trans. Bird; the sketch referred to being, respectively, on 244–45 and 204. Earlier jottings, from the residences in Naples and Palermo, are also included, respectively, on 237–44 and 198–203.

26. This message was conveyed, Cosima notes (March 5, 1882), by a letter from Dr. Friedrich Keppler, the German doctor prominent in Venice's foreign community, who would later become the Wagners' family physician during their final stay in the city. They had apparently been put into contact with them by Princess Hatzfeldt, and

it is interesting to discover that they already had dealings with him many months before he became their medical attendant.

27. See addendum 1.

28. See pp. 81–82, 109–110, 146. Also, Barker, "A Forgotten Early Champion of Wagner," espec. 8–9.

Chapter Three

1. Writers on Wagner have sometimes suggested, quietly or even openly, that the composer went to Venice in the autumn of 1882 clearly expecting he would die there. Most recently, for example, Carr, *Wagner Clan*, 54. To be sure, the declining state of Wagner's health was evident. To us it is strikingly visible in one of his last photo portraits, taken in May 1882, amid preparations for the *Parsifal* premiere: see figure 13.

For general accounts of this visit (up to the day of Wagner's death), see: Panizzardi, *Wagner in Italia*, vol. 1, 175–225; Ipser, *Richard Wagner in Italien*, 179–206; Incontrera, "Viaggi," 43–47; Newman, *Life*, vol. 4, 697–710; 510–21; Gregor-Dellin, *Richard Wagner*, 827–39, trans. Brownjohn, 510–21; Westernhagen, *Wagner*, 555–60, trans. Whittall, 586–92; Gutman, *Richard Wagner*, 446ff; Watson, *Richard Wagner*, 312–14; Skelton, *Richard and Cosima Wagner*, 297–305; Dippel, *Wagner und Italien*, 93–100; Norwich, *Paradise of Cities*, 186–90. Attention may also be paid to the account of the composer's first biographer, Carl Friedrich Glasenapp, in his *Das Leben Richard Wagners*, vol. 6, 679–755; Glasenapp was to have served as Siegfried Wagner's tutor, and, though he was not himself present in Venice at the time, he had access to direct information from the Wagner household—above all, to the contents of Cosima's diaries.

2. The short book by Henriette ("Henry" Perl, *Richard Wagner in Venedig*) will be explored thoroughly in chapter 7. Giuseppe Norlenghi's *Wagner a Venezia* will receive detailed examination in chapter 8.

3. See Massimo Gemin and Filippo Pedrocco, *Ca' Vendramin Calergi* (Milan: Berenice, 1990). Norlenghi, *Wagner a Venezia*, 143–47, includes an admiring description; Panizzardi, *Wagner in Italia*, vol. 1, 175ff, supplements a description with exterior and interior photographs that preserve something of appearances from the time of the Wagners' residence. There are very general treatments of this monument in large-scale volumes concentrating on extensive and even lavish illustrations: Lauritzen and Zielcke, *Palaces of Venice*, 147–50; Alvise Zorzi and Paolo Marton, *Venetian Palaces* (New York: Rizzoli, 1990 = Italian edition, *I Palazzi Veneziani*, Udine: Magnus, 1989), 238–46; and Giuseppe Mazzariol, Atilia Dorigato, and Gianluigi Trivellato, *Venetian Palazzi* (Cologne/Cittadella: Evergreen/Taschen, 1998), 53–64, wherein it is bizarrely stated (55) the mezzanine suite of apartments "was the home of Richard Wagner for some years (where he composed his *Parsifal*)"! Meanwhile, Italian commentators would invent the further idea that he had composed *Tristan* there!

4. The bandmaster was Jacopo Calascione, and the *Lohengrin* arrangement was Wagner's own, made for him. For the more extensive information in this episode in our diverse sources, see pp. 81–82 (Venetian journals), p. 110 (Perl), and p. 151 (Norlenghi); also Barker, "Forgotten Early Champion," 11–14.

5. On this residence, see Walker, *Franz Liszt*, vol. 3, 424–29.

6. Filippo Filippi (1830–87), the prominent critic in Milan, was one of Wagner's earliest advocates and enthusiasts in Italy: see Panizzardi, *Wagner in Italia*, vol. 2, 119–25; Jung, *Rezeption*, 433–35.

7. Glasenapp, *Das Leben*, vol. 6, 745, and Panizzardi, *Wagner in Italia*, vol. 1, 210, report that at lunch that day Liszt received from Joukowsky a painting of St. Francis of Assisi, "under which Wagner had written some verses that would, unfortunately, be his last." Joukowsky's gift of a painting to Liszt may have some relation to a recent connection between them. Prior to his arrival in Venice, Joukowsky had visited Liszt in Weimar. There, in late September and early October Joukowsky painted a portrait of Liszt, which the latter wanted as a gift to the piano-maker Vincent Risch of Toronto, Ontario, Canada, as thanks for a very fine instrument that Risch had made and sent to Liszt. The portrait, showing the composer three-quarter-length and seated in a large chair, was almost harshly realistic in portraying the aged composer. But it greatly impressed many admirers, among them the Grand Duke of Weimar. Accordingly, Liszt asked Joukowsky to make a copy for the Grand Duke. This Joukowsky did, but only in Venice, where Liszt apparently allowed further sittings. This "Grand Duke's copy" was smaller, showing Liszt full-face in bust only, and without the chair; and the elaborate frame was one that Joukowsky personally selected in Venice. It is this painting that is noted by Perl: see p. 115 and figure 20.

The inital painting was sent to Risch, who displayed it with great success in the showrooms of the Mason & Risch piano firm, which occasionally loaned it to the Royal Toronto Conservatory of Music. After the firm's dissolution, the painting disappeared from view and its whereabouts are now unknown. But the "Duke's Copy," by whatever process, also came into the hands of Risch and at the time of the Mason & Risch dissolution auction was acquired by a private owner in Ontario who still owns it. This painting, now in bad condition, was traced and discovered in 1993 by the Liszt scholar Alan Walker: it is reproduced, through the kind courtesy of Dr. Walker, as our figure 20. He has told the story of these paintings in his article "Joukowsky's Portraits of Liszt," *The Hungarian Quarterly* 34 (Summer 1993), 142–47; more briefly, his *Franz Liszt*, III, 423–24 and n. 17.

8. These details are provided by Panizzardi, *Wagner in Italia*, vol. 1, 211–12; but for more basic information and sources, see p. 117 (Perl), and pp. 158–59 (Norlenghi); also the comments of Siegfried Wagner, p. 305, on which cf. Pachl, *Siegfried Wagner*, 62. See also the commemorative volume, ed. Verardo, *Il Conservatorio di Musica Benedetto Marcello di Venezia*, 41–44, 50–52. Included among its references is the text of a notice of December 28 in *Gazzetta Musicale di Milano*, reporting on Wagner's Christmas Eve concert and announcing the January benefit concert to come in January: presumably a dispatch from Filippo Filippi. The baton and music stand are shown in figure 28.

9. Guglielmo Oberdan, also known as Wilhelm Oberdank (1858–82) was a leader of an Italian irredentist movement to claim for Italy the city of Trieste, then under Austrian control. He organized a conspiracy to assassinate the Emperor Franz Josef during a visit to the city in August 1882, but the plot was foiled at the eleventh hour and Oberdan[k] was arrested. After imprisonment and trial, he was sentenced to death by hanging and his execution had just occurred, on December 20, 1882, making him for many Italians a martyred patriot.

10. This is reported by Glasenapp, *Das Leben*, vol. 6, 749, followed by Panizzardi, *Wagner in Italia*, vol. 1, 216, who state that an elaborate farewell luncheon was offered

Humperdinck by the Wagners. Of all that Cosima makes no mention in her entry for January 2, or any other date.

11. The report of this event, by Panizzardi, *Wagner in Italia*, vol. 1, 216–17, was based entirely upon the testimony of Mancinelli himself, as personally conveyed to the writer. The concert in Venice is confirmed otherwise: see Verardo, *Il Conservatorio di Musica Benedetto Marcello di Venezia*, 44–48 (with documents). We know that the program, on January 15, 1883, included the following works: the Overture to Alfieri's *Saul* by Antonio Bazzini; the *Intermezzi sinfonici* (five of them, mixing those from the now-familiar Suites) from Bizet's *L'Arlésienne*; the *Intermezzi sinfonici* Mancinelli himself composed for Cossa's drama *Cleopatra*; Liszt's *Les Préludes*; and Wagner's *Tannhäuser* Overture.

Wagner's involvement, in helping Mancinelli and in attending a rehearsal, seems at odds with our composer's otherwise careful avoidance of involvement in Venice's musical life. The fact that such an episode is ignored both by Cosima and (following her) by Glasenapp raises again the possibility of selective blind spots in the Wagner household's "management" of its history. In point of fact, Cosima does seem to make an oblique reference to what must have been the event in question. In her entry for January 17, she writes: ". . . At the recent concert in which the *T* Overture was played, the program compared it—as a mark of praise—to the *Guillaume Tell* Overture; this produces from R. the remark that everything the Italians, Rossini in particular, provide in the way of ensembles, choruses, etc., is terribly vulgar, but is not so with the French, and he agrees with me when I say that the French are more civilized. . . ." The *Tagebücher* editors take the designation "*T*" to mean *Tannhäuser*, which would make the allusion fit the Mancinelli concert. That Cosima should otherwise ignore it at least suggests how indifferent Wagner would have been to attending such an event. For more on this, see pp. 85–87 and p. 154. See also Jung, *Rezeption*, 42–44.

Verardo, *Il Conservatorio di Musica Benedetto Marcello*, 48, reports an invitation made by the Liceo to Wagner to attend a concert on February 8, apparently ignored by the composer, as by most writers on him.

12. "He returns home much delighted with the sight of the lively lanes, and observes that it is better for him to go out without me, however silly that sounds, but he is ashamed of his attacks when he is with me, the need to walk so slowly" (Cosima, January 30).

13. For full comparisons of the accounts we have for Wagner and the Carnival, see pp. 120–25; 160–61; 349–50, n. 18. Levi's report is quoted in Sabor, *Real Wagner*, 287. Notice Levi's further comments, quoted in the next note, which anticipates the picture of Wagner's robust bearing during Carnival that would be so strongly rendered by Perl.

14. On February 15, two days after Wagner's death, Levi wrote a letter to his father, looking back on in grief on his last contacts with the composer: ". . . It was my good fortune to see him 24 hours before his death . . . he was in a most cheerful mood [during Carneval], as we strolled in the procession of masked revellers on the Piazza as late as midnight. He led the way with his daughter Isolde, striding with the liveliness of a young man . . . it was a glorious night, and at 1 o'clock we drove home. The following day the Meister complained that he was not feeling well and did not appear at the dinner table, but the day after . . . he was quite well again. . . . On Monday midday I left Venice, the Meister accompanied me to the stairs, kissed me

several times—I was much moved—and 24 hours later!!!" (unpublished letter, as translated in Sabor's *Real Wagner*, 288).

15. The profile sketch was inscribed by Joukowsky: "R. playing," the full-face one "R. reading. 12 Febr. 1883." Cosima herself, however, makes no reference to the sketches in her diary entry for the date, her last one. See figures 29–30.

In a note that she added to Cosima's diary after February 13, Daniela von Bülow recalled: "When there was talk of the studio which he [Wagner] wished to acquire in the Palazzo Vendramin for Joukowsky, he replied to Mama, who wanted him to sit for his portrait, that he no longer wished to be painted, he was satisfied with the one photograph showing him three-quarter face, and he wanted to hear no more talk of pictures."

16. See addendum 2.

17. On Wagner's "last words," see addendum 9.

18. Reporting the details of Wagner's death is complicated by the curious number of divergences in our various accounts. This chapter's narrative represents a working digest of what is generally agreed upon in the standard literature. But here and in the chapters that follow will be seen many inconsistencies or downright contradictions to be confronted, if not reconciled.

Not surprisingly, Cosima never made an entry for February 13, and discontinued the diary for good. With its cessation, the closest we can get to an "inside" account of the fatal day and its immediate aftermath is to be found in two letters, both written on February 20, 1883, in immediate proximity to the event. One of these was written by Joukowsky to Franz Liszt and quoted in addendum 8 (together with two other recollections by Joukowsky). The other was written by Ludwig Bürkel to his master, King Ludwig II, which is placed at the head of this book as a prologue. (There are also the recollections of Adolf Gross, who hastened to Venice to assist the Wagner family, reproduced in Du Moulin Eckart, *Cosima Wagner*, 1000–1002, trans. Phillips, vol. 2, 890–91: but these only treat the days following the death, and not the fatal day itself.) Next come the detailed accounts of "Henry Perl" and Norlenghi. All of these sources will be discussed and compared in chapters 7 and 8. Quite immediate, of course, are the Venetian newspaper reports, which will be examined in chapter 6. In due course, many of these sources were drawn upon by Glasenapp, *Das Leben*, vol. 6, 772–85, and then later by Panizzardi, *Wagner in Italia*, vol. 1, 229–37, among the earliest secondary treatments. Siegfried Wagner's recollections of his father's final day, in his *Erinnerungen* (1923), are quoted in addendum 8, which also surveys all of the shorter sources.

Among the more standard biographical accounts, see: Newman, *Life*, vol. 4, 711–16; Gregor-Dellin, *Richard Wagner*, 840–43, trans. Brownjohn, 521; Westernhagen, *Wagner*, 560–62, trans. Whittall, 592–94; Skelton, *Richard and Cosima*, 305–6; Incontrera, "Viaggi," 47; Norwich, *Paradise of Cities*, 190–91. The scattered account by Köhler, *Der Letzte der Titanen*, 792ff, 806–9, trans. Spencer, 622ff, 634–36, is colored by deep hostility toward Cosima.

19. Keppler's so-called autopsy report is presented and discussed in addendum 7.

The latest comments on all of this may be found in Köhler, *Der Letzte der Titanen*, 795–97, trans. Spencer, 624–26; and in Spencer's own article, " 'Er starb' " (cited on p. 377, n. 2), 64–65. There is a full discussion of Wagner's health, illnesses, and medical treatments by two physicians, Thiery and Seidel, in their article titled " 'Ich behage mir nicht,' " 491–502, trans. Spencer, 3–22. An important conclusion of their study (21–22) is that Keppler's report should be treated with critical caution, due to its transmission through Perl. As will be observed in the lengthy quotations from her book in chapter 7, Perl herself gives repeated comments on Wagner's health problems, undoubtedly derived in large part from Keppler. Indeed, as will be discussed on pp. 138–39, Perl may have written her book in part at the prompting of Keppler, as a vehicle for defending himself against accusations of malpractice in treating Wagner.

20. Liszt gave expression to his feelings about Wagner's death in two more compositions of the period. Soon after hearing the news, Liszt wrote a short piano piece entitled *R.W.—Venezia*, a brief study in anguished disjunction that clearly reflected Liszt's own deep grief and sense of loss. Then, after he had attempted to join the reclusive Cosima at Bayreuth, Liszt participated in a concert in Weimar on May 22, 1883, a memorial tribute to what would have been Wagner's seventieth birthday. As part of the concert, Liszt conducted the orchestra in the Prelude and Good Friday Music from *Parsifal*. Preparation for this event must have focused his attention on that opera's music, and reminded him that Wagner himself had pointed out a resemblance between a principal theme in the opera and the music for Liszt's own earlier cantata, *Excelsior!* Just before the concert, therefore, Liszt composed a more personal tribute, a piano piece called *Am Grabe Richard Wagners* (At the Grave of Richard Wagner), in which reminiscences of their two compositions are commingled. Often over the past years, Liszt had regularly created piano paraphrases and transcriptions of the music by other composers of the day that he admired, arrangements that he could play in public as generous and unselfish promotion of their talents. He had done so frequently with Wagner's music. In this final gesture, this great-hearted man paid his last homage to the colleague and son-in-law whom, for all his flaws, he held in profound respect. (There are also alternate versions Liszt has left us of this piece, for organ, and for string quartet with harp.) On all of this, see Walker, *Franz Liszt*, vol. 3, 429–33.

Chapter Four

1. For general background, see: Bolton King, *A History of Italian Unity, Being a Political History of Italy from 1814 to 1871*, 2 vols. (New York: Scribner's, 1899); G. F. H. Berkeley, *Italy in the Making, 1815 to 1846* (Cambridge: Cambridge University Press, 1932); Denis Mack Smith, *Italy: A Modern History* (Ann Arbor: University of Michigan Press, 1959, revised ed., 1969); Spenser M. Di Scala, *Italy: From Revolution to Republic, 1700 to the Present* (Boulder, Colo. and Oxford: Westview Press, 1995).

On Venice itself, there are two important publications in Italian: Giovanni Distefano and Giannantonio Paladini, *Storia di Venezia, 1797–1997* (Venice: Supernova-Grafiche Biesse, 1997); and *Storia di Venezia: L'ottocento e il novecento*, vol. 3. *Il novecento*, ed. Mario Isnenghi (Rome: Istituto della Enciclopedia Italiana, 2002). In English, there are also two new treatments of the post-Republic city. An extensive and wide-ranging survey of its cultural life, with rich bibliographical annotations, is given by Plant, *Venice, Fragile City*. More coherent, and aimed at a general audience is Norwich's *Paradise of Cities*, which develops its treatment mainly through the experiences and involvements of over a dozen cultural figures (including Wagner). Something of the same approach, if on a smaller scale, was attempted in another good popularized evocation of the period, by Christopher Hibbert, in his *Venice*,

255–311. More substantial is John Pemble's *Venice Rediscovered* (Oxford: Oxford University Press, 1995); also Julian Halsby's *Venice, The Artist's Vision: A Guide to British and American Painters* (London: B. T. Batsford, 1990).

The specific subject of Venice under Hapsburg rule, falling into three distinct periods, has yet to be covered in a comprehensive synthesis, at least not since the rather technical study by Augostino Sandonà, *Il Regno Lombardo Veneto 1814–1859, la costituzione e l'aministrazione. Studi di storia e di diritto; con la scorta degli atti ufficiali dei dicasteri centrali di Vienna* (Milan: L. F. Cogliati, 1912). For very specific segments, there are: R. John Rath, *The Provisional Austrian Regime in Lombardy-Venetia, 1814–1815* (Austin, Tex. and London: University of Texas Press, 1969); Paul Ginsborg, *Daniele Manin and the Venetian Revolution of 1848–49* (Cambridge: Cambridge University Press, 1979); Andreas Gottsmann, *Venetien 1859–1866: Österreichische Verwaltung und nationale Opposition* (Vienna: Österreichisches Akademie der Wissenschaften, 2005). Rich cultural material is presented in the various subject essays by various specialists in the massive exhibition catalogue, *Il Veneto e l'Austria: Vita e cultura artistica nelle città veneta 1814–1866* (Milan: Electa, 1989).

2. See pp. 12, 14, 15–16.

3. See pp. 24ff.

4. On one small matter Wagner apparently accepted the need for changes in Venice (though linking the point to a typical anti-Semitic aside). Of a conversation on January 30, 1883, Cosima reports: "At lunch Jouk. argues heatedly against *vaporetti*; R. replied that he could not feel such concern about them, since they have a place in our modern world, in which the Jew Guggenheim is also one of Venice's benefactors; and if one wished to preserve Venice in its old state, one would also have to put the old families back in the palaces!"

5. See pp. 119–20, 180, 183.

6. See pp. 8, 16.

7. See pp. 29, 32–33.

8. See pp. 4–5.

9. See addendum 1.

10. See Gregor-Dellin, *Richard Wagner*, 248–49 (on 1853), and 308–10 (on 1861); also Newman, *Life*, vol. 2, 151–53 (on 1861).

11. See p. 16.

12. See p. 18.

13. A natural phenomenon prompted another recollection, when the family took note of a comet visible in the Venetian sky that autumn. On October 24, 1882, Cosima reported "A discussion of the comet, which the children have seen, brings us to a similar appearance in 1858, seen here then by R., and the conjectures surrounding it." On the 1858 comet, see p. 16.

14. See addendum 12. It may be remembered that Wagner did have one highly profitable dealing with Americans: earning $5,000—crucial in 1876 for his Bayreuth funding—as the fee for his potboiler, the *American Centennial March*, commissioned for the Philadelphia celebration of the one-hundredth anniversary of American independence: see pp. 237; 370, n.18.

15. November 20, 1880: "The [Bayreuth] heavens press down on us, heavy and leaden-gray; R., all but exasperated, talks of Venice." October 9, 1880: "his delight in the city is unbounded, whether going by boat or on foot." September 25, 1881: His delight in Venice and our dwelling [the Vendramin] grows daily." October 24, 1882: "In the afternoon R. and I walk to the Rialto; the wide path from our house to the

Church of S. Felice pleases him enormously, and he resolves to take frequent walks along it. We then ride to the Piazzetta; in the moonlit haze the whole place looks glorious, and our homeward journey through the narrow canals gives us a dreamlike joy." November 9, 1882: "In the afternoon we ride to St. M.'s Sq. The view to the right from our palazzo delights R.; later he points out to me the Salute, looking in the mist 'like a ghostly dream,' also S. Giorgio [Maggiore], everything, and a walk through the arcades gives him much pleasure." December 28, 1882: "Around lunchtime we stroll on the Piazzetta in the most glorious sunshine. R. is in a particularly good mood . . . Venice pleases him. . . . "

16. One way comes in the stimulating suggestion made to me by my colleague Professor Marion Miller: that Wagner may have become fond of Venice partly because it reminded him of a small artisan's community, comparable to old Nuremberg, thereby fitting his vision of the ideal city as a small sphere. Some such reminders would certainly have come from his regular walks through Venice's lanes and *calli*, lined as they were with the shops of artisans (including shoemakers). This line of thought points up the need to study more fully Wagner's political ideas—especially his ambivalences and doubts about the course that Germany was following during his later years—in relation to his cultural ones. Of course this topic gives added point to Wagner's recollection that it was in Venice in 1861 that he found his inspiration for beginning *Die Meistersinger*, his idealized portrait of the artisan community of Nuremberg. See also Gualtiero Petrucci, "L'origine dei Maestri Cantori," *Nuova Antologia* 217 (January 16, 1908): 293–300. Wagner's favoring a nostalgically fantasized neomedieval world of artist-craftsmen parallels what was promulgated by so many Pre-Raphaelites and supporters of the Gothic Revival. (On Wagner and these themes, see pp. 74–75 and n. 31 below.)

At the same time, Wagner's own vision of medieval Germanism was itself inconsistent and varied throughout his life. Note his earlier essay, dating from 1880, titled "Kunst und Klima," published in Wagner's *Gesammelte Schriften und Dichtungen*, 4th ed., vol. 4 (Leipzig, 1907), 207–21; trans. William Ashton Ellis, *Richard Wagner's Prose Works*, vol. 1 (London, 1895), 249–65. In that muddled effusion, Wagner projects a negative conception of medieval civilization in general, as a religion-dominated order not derived from Nature (by comparison with the order of Classical Hellenism), but a desolation of culture and the spirit. On the other hand, Wagner constantly denounced the Renaissance as a movement, as Cosima regularly records in her diaries, sometimes with clear national implications. On January 11, 1874, she reports that he "curses the Renaissance, which undermined the German character."

At any rate, in the light of Wagner's comments of November 7, 1882, quoted just above, it would seem that, as of that moment, he saw Venice as a city least comparable among his favorites to any German counterparts, medievally idealized or otherwise.

17. See p. 17.

18. Cf. his reflections on the church of San Marco on October 12, 1882: "[we] go into the church, visit the vestry, which pleases R. very much—particularly the inlaid work. As we leave the church he says, 'The Crusaders certainly trod this floor before us.'"

Or, in the prior visit, on April 23, 1882, after trying to explain to Siegfried the dissolution of the monasteries: "R. replies to him earnestly, telling him what a pitiless power these magnificent buildings served, what symbols of arrogance they had become, though built for a completely different purpose. It is true, he continues, that the power which is attempting to take their place is not promoting the cause of sublimity, either, and so the situation is serious, and we are probably experiencing the last days of a pleasant illusion. 'But we should strive to preserve, to see history as a great teacher, and not to begin again from the beginning, tearing everything down,' he says, having been much moved in S. Marco by the thought of how much work had been done on this noble building over many centuries."

19. See pp. 10, 12.

20. See pp. 22–23.

21. See addendum 1.

22. *Mein Leben*, ed. Gregor-Dellin (1976), 511; trans. Gray, 498. For some general comments about Wagner's attitudes toward Italian painters, see Dippel, *Wagner und Italien*, 45–48.

23. *Mein Leben*, ed. Gregor-Dellin (1976), 598; trans. Gray, 584. But Wagner went on to remember that he could make some progress: "I gained a deeper insight into the effect produced by the purely artistic significance of a painting when I stood before Da Vinci's *Last Supper* and had the same experience as everyone else. The original work has deteriorated so badly that the paint is almost entirely ruined, yet after one has examined more closely the copies reconstructing the original, which are placed permanently alongside it, and then turns again from the copies to the ruin of the original, everyone experiences, as I did, that one's eye has become visionary, and one suddenly perceives with the greatest clarity what it is that cannot be copied."

24. See pp. 36–37; 332, n. 22.

25. Here Wagner could have been thinking of Whistler, who often used musical terms ("nocturne," "symphony," "etude") as fanciful titles for his paintings, especially portraits. During his own stay in Venice itself, from September 1879 to November 1880, Whistler produced an enormous output of remarkable pastels and engravings on scenes in the city. But then, there seems little likelihood that Wagner could ever have seen any of these.

26. *Mein Leben*, ed. Gregor-Dellin (1976), 591–92; trans. Gray, 577–78. See p. 16.

27. On the Wagners' relationship with their gondoliers, see below, p. 348, n. 8.

28. It might be remembered that Wagner was well aware of the Giardini Pubblici (Public Gardens) at the expanded east end of Venice, to which he regularly went for refreshing strolls during his first residence in Venice, in 1858–59. See pp. 9, 11, 15.

29. The best he could otherwise say for the Salute came in his pointing it out to Cosima on a gondola ride, "looking in the mist 'like a ghostly dream' " (November 9, 1882).

30. In his massive biography, *John Ruskin* (combined edition, New Haven, CT: Yale University Press, 2002), 718, Tim Hilton records Ruskin's attendance at a performance (on June 29, 1880) in the first run of *Die Meistersinger* (or, in fact, of any Wagner opera) in England. His reaction was distinctly negative. At the intermission, he arose, stretched, and confessed: "Oh, that someone would sing 'Annie Laurie' to me!" The next day, on June 30, he wrote to his friend, Georgina Burne-Jones, and was far more emphatic in describing his reactions: "Of all the *bête*, clumsy, blundering, boggling, baboon-blooded stuff I ever saw on a human stage, that thing last night beat—as far as the story and acting went; and of all the affected, sapless, soulless, beginningless, endless, topless, bottomless, topsyturviest, tongs- and boniest doggerel of sounds I

ever endured the deadliness of, that eternity of nothing was the deadliest—as far as the sound went. I never was so relieved, so far as I can remember, in my life, by the stopping of any sound—not excepting railroad whistles—as I was by the cessation of the cobbler's bellowing; even the serenader's caricatured twangle was a rest after it. As for the great 'Lied,' I never made out where it began, or where it ended—except by the fellow's coming off the horse block" (*The Complete Works of John Ruskin*, ed. E. T. Look and Alexander Wedderburn, vol. 37: *Letters of John Ruskin*, vol. 2: *1870–1889* [London and New York: George Allen/Longmans, Green and Co., 1909], 402. Quoted in the Introduction to *Wagnerism in European Culture and Politics*, ed David C. Large and William Weber [Ithaca, NY: Cornell University Press, 1984], 20–21; and partially quoted by Sabor, *Real Wagner*, 296.)

A year later, in a letter to J. A. Fuller Maitland (May 1, 1883), Ruskin remarked: "It wasn't *you* who took me to the *Meister Singers!* so you may put your conscience at ease about that. But I'll have it out with somebody else, some day [. . .]" In an explanation the recipient gave of this letter, he reported: ". . . In the previous year [1882] I had been one of a party which was made up in order to introduce Mr. Ruskin to Wagner's *Meistersinger*, as it was felt that although the music might be too modern in style for him to appreciate, yet the story might be expected to appeal to him. The expedition was a complete failure, and he was unspeakably bored; hence the allusion. . . ." (ibid., 450–51).

To be sure, Ruskin did go the following evening, with Mrs. Burne-Jones, to attend Mozart's *Don Giovanni*, with Adelina Patti in the cast. This he enjoyed enormously, as he reported in a letter of July 2 to another friend. But the soundness of his musical judgment should be rated carefully. Consider his assessment of another great musical master, in a letter written the previous year: ". . . how did you get to understand Beethoven? He always sounds to me like the upsetting of a bag of nails, with here and there an also dropped hammer" (to Dr. John Brown, February 6, 1881, ibid., 340).

31. The striking convergence of Wagner's ideas with Ruskin's thinking has never been adequately raised or seriously pursued, not even in studies where one would expect to find it considered: for example, in Aberback's *The Ideas of Richard Wagner*, where the matter is altogether ignored (in both editions). The only attention to the issue I have thus far encountered is in Paul Robinson's pungent discussion of *Die Meistersinger* in the fifth chapter of his enormously stimulating book, *Opera and Ideas: From Mozart to Strauss* (New York: Harper and Row, 1985), espec. 224, 225, 228, and 235.

32. On another "Wagner city," and its role earlier in the composer's career, see Chris Walton's *Richard Wagner's Zurich: The Muse of Place* (Rochester, NY: Camden House, 2007).

Chapter Five

1. It would seem, to be sure, that most of these arrival/departure notices stressed those made by boat, whereas Wagner's passages in 1858/59 were made by train. Despite Wagner's assertion that his landlord saw to it that his presence in Venice received some attention by local papers (see p. 10), I have been unable to find any, at least in the two daily journals.

2. For some reason, *LGdV* felt obliged to make one of those corrections that actually produces a mistake where there had been none. On October 9 it asserted that Wagner had arrived on October 5, whereas the earlier notation of October 4 had been correct.

3. Following standard practice, on the day of the concert itself *LV* had listed the contents of the program, and they illustrate the kind of fare to which Calascione and his public were accustomed. The concert was scheduled to last from three to five o'clock, and would contain seven items: 1. March, *Defilè*, by Calascione; 2. Prelude and Introductory Chorus, from *Lucrezia Borgia*, by Donizetti; 3. Mazurka, *Giulia*, by Carisi; 4. Duet of Finale II, from *Rigoletto*, by Verdi; 5. Polka, *Nanà*, by Errea; 6. Terzetto finale from *Faust*, by Gounod; 7. Galopp, *Devadacy*, by Dall'Argine.

4. See pp. 109–10 (Perl), p. 146 (Norlenghi). This concert, and further newspaper reactions to it are discussed in more detail in Barker, "A Forgotten Early Champion," 8–14.

5. See p. 67.

6. The six other items were: a piece by a certain Grandi, and another by one Mattiazzi; the Overture to Auber's *Les diamants de la couronne*; the finale from Donizetti's *Belisario*; a cavatina from Bellini's *La sonnambula*; and a Galopp by Strauss identified as *Il fuoco della gioventù* (and apparently the *Jugendfeuer*, Op. 90, of Johann Strauss, the Elder).

Sorting out the arrangements from *Lohengrin* is difficult. *LV* in this April 30 notice stated that the concert that evening would offer the first performance of Calascione's "homage" *pot-pourrì*. On the other hand, *LV* had already noted on Wednesday, April 12, that the Municipal Band would play that evening a piece identified as *Reminiscenze di Lohengrin*. Was this a different, earlier arrangement by Calascione himself? perhaps a preliminary score on which he based the *pot-pourrì*? Could it have any relation to the *Rimembranze* piece played by the military band in its concert in the Giardini Pubblici that the Wagners missed on April 23?

7. The full text of this notice is in Barker, "Forgotten Early Champion," 10–11. One wonders if the writer of this item had heard the Bologna performance of *Lohengrin*. As will be seen below, he was more favorable to Wagner's music than the critic who would write so unsympathetically for *LGdV* about the *Ring* production in Venice a year later.

8. It is to be noted here that the second folio volume for the year 1882 of *LV*, covering the months of July–December, was repeatedly unavailable to me in my applications at the two Venetian libraries used. I am thus lacking this journal's coverage for the first three-and-a-half months of Wagner's stay in the city—admittedly, a regrettable gap, though probably not a grave or crucial one.

9. See p. 109 (Perl), p. 151 (Norlenghi). On this episode, see also Barker, "Forgotten Early Champion," 12–14.

10. See p. 49.

11. See nn. 13 and 16 to chapter 2; also p. 50; 53–54; 330–31, n. 13; 336–37, no. 11; 345, n. 17.

12. See pp. 51–52, and p. 115 and 158.

13. See p. 117 (Perl), and 158–59 (Norlenghi).

14. See pp. 53–54.

15. It was not unusual for Italian journalists of the day to write under pithy pennames, and the Venetian "Toni," apparently *LV*'s regular music commentator, was a case in point. This article by "Toni" is an interesting foreshadowing of what we will

find this critic (and his counterpart for *LGdV*) doing on a larger scale three months hence for the grand production of Wagner's *Ring* at the Fenice: that is, providing the Venetian readers and concertgoers with an introduction to, and background on, music not likely to be familiar to the local audience. To be sure, the paragraph on the *Tannhäuser* Overture was a modest one; and still shorter was the one on *Les Preludes*, mostly devoted rather to Liszt's generous support to other composers, and on his works in general.

But there was a long paragraph on Antonio Bazzini (1818–97), virtuoso violinist, pedagogue, and composer, who had been an important champion of early Romantic music in Italy, especially Mendelssohn's. He was one of the dozen other composers whom Verdi and his committee selected to contribute a movement (in his case, the *Dies irae*) to the cooperative *Messa per Rossini* planned to mark the first anniversary (1869) of the latter's death, but abandoned. Bazzini's operatic work was limited, but his orchestral and especially his chamber compositions made him an important figure in the circles of musicians attempting a revival of instrumental writing in nineteenth-century Italy, so heavily overshadowed by the preoccupation with opera. Ironically, during his time as composition professor and then director at the Milan Conservatory, Bazzini's students included Catalani, Puccini, and Mascagni, representatives of exactly that ongoing preoccupation. His path and Wagner's seem never to have crossed, and it is likely that the latter knew little or nothing of him.

"Toni" also devoted a paragraph to the tragic life of Bizet, discussing also his music for *Carmen*, now an international sensation; and there was a concluding paragraph on Mancinelli.

16. Panizzardi, *Wagner in Italia*, vol. 1, 216. The name of Garibaldi was held in the greatest awe. As we can observe here and elsewhere, Wagner found it a useful nickname to bestow on Italians he wanted to flatter or charm.

17. There are possible reasons for some such animus against Mancinelli. After the death of Angelo Mariani (June 1873), Mancinelli, while still trying to juggle careers as composer and conductor, came to be regarded by Giovannina Lucca as the next candidate for the champion of Wagner's music in Italy. Tensions between Lucca and the Wagners may well have then prejudiced Cosima against the conductor. Subsequently, Mancinelli's treatments of Wagner's operas when he conducted them in the later years of the nineteenth century brought him mounting disrespect. He would make arbitrary cuts and textual adjustments, to suit Italian tastes, and followed local practices by employing Italian translations of the texts, at least at first. Eventual perception of his stylistic incompatibility with the composer's style led to his marginalization on the international scene as a Wagner conductor. Of course, any negative opinions Cosima might have derived from all that would have followed Wagner's death and would not have been reflected in the diaries at the time she was writing them.

18. See pp. 182–83, 186ff.

Chapter Six

1. Depending on its accuracy, this report (derived from stories about the Christmas Eve concert) might suggest one of the rare moments of gloomy fatalism Wagner reliably documented for this stay in Venice. For his predominant optimism, see the beginning of chapter 3.

2. Excluding only the first sentence, this entire paragraph, and only that, has been reproduced in the original Italian by Spencer, " 'Er starb,' " 66. (This is the only published use of which I know of any of these Venetian newspaper accounts.) Printed only two days after Wagner's death, the details of this scene can only have come from someone in the Wagner household, who was solicited by, or communicated with, *LGdV*'s reporter. Spencer suggests that this someone may have been Dr. Keppler, which would be plausible; and Spencer also sees this as involved with a subsequent misunderstanding and dispute: see addendum 2.

3. For these objects, see figure 28. *Il Conservatorio di Musica Benedetto Marcello*, 48, reports the responses of Contin and the Liceo upon the news of Wagner's death (including a facsimile of the letter of condolence he sent to Cosima on the fifteenth), and the idea of a commemorative concert, which was abandoned in view of Cosima's determination to keep observances to a minimum.

4. This odd statement is confirmed by Perl: see pp. 134–35.

5. At this point, by means of an asterisk, the editors of *LGdV* connected a large footnote with fuller details on those objects of tribute so common at important European funerals of the day, the "coronas" or imitation floral wreaths: "Among these *corone* there were some especially beautiful, for example that of the Municipality of Venice, metallic, 1 meter and 35 centimeters in diameter, velveted in black and gold with a white band inscribed on top: *Venezia a Riccardo Wagner—febbraio 1883*;—that of the Liceo, in fabric of black and silver velvet, laurel and oak with myrtle among them, band of black silk inscribed on top: *Liceo e Società Musicale Benedetto Marcello—febbraio 1883*;—that of the Circolo Artistico Veneziano, with a diameter of more than a meter, in velvet and silver with grape-clusters of wisteria, lilies, and white *caudenti*, and accompanied with little batches of lily-of-the-valley; white mohair [*moïrè*] band with inscription: *Circolo Artistico Veneziano—febbraio 1883*;—that in metal, in black and glittering silver, over a meter in diameter, with the inscription on a costly sash: *Al sommo genio dell'arte Riccardo Wagner.—In segno di eterna ammirazione devotamente offre Giovannina Lucca* [To the lofty genius of the art of Richard Wagner— Giovannina Lucca devotedly offers in token of eternal admiration], etc., etc." All these *corone* were produced in the workshop of signor Giulio Frollo.

The aspect of the external bronze casket itself may be seen in figure 34, as photographed when the Bayreuth tomb was opened for cleaning.

6. This is the only reference to Mancinelli's gracious proposal to offer such musical homage to Wagner, one more detail in the curiously skewed relationship between the two.

7. This strange statement must be some misunderstanding by the reporters; it has no basis in fact or existing documentation.

8. These perspectives are very vividly conveyed by Perl, in her account quoted on p. 134.

9. Here and elsewhere, Venetian reporters had the mistaken understanding that Liszt would be involved in the Bayreuth reception and funeral rites, which was not the case: see p. 58.

10. Likewise a mistake: Bülow, in bad health, was devastated by the news of Wagner's death, and could not have attended the funeral. He did, however, make a gracious gesture to Cosima. Hearing of her total surrender to grief, he sent the famous telegram: "Soeur, il faut vivre" (Sister, one must live).

11. For further consideration of Verdi's reactions to Wagner's music and to his death, see addendum 4.

12. Curiously, at the time of the first concert commemoration of Wagner's death, the *LGdV*, on February 15, 1891, reprinted from that *LV* publication the text of this letter written by Keppler to Tessarin, as a memento looking back not only to 1883 but to Wagner's initial Venetian sojourn, in 1858–59, when he first met Tessarin.

13. This report, or whatever source it had, is presumably the origin of the idea that these words were Wagner's last, but there is no clear evidence for that attribution. On the somewhat blurred issue of just what the last words were, see addendum 9.

14. Which, of course, was not what did come to pass. See pp. 281–82.

15. Franco Faccio (1840–91) began his brilliant musical career as a composer, joining Boïto in spearheading a movement of supposed musical regeneration in Italy. And, also together with the latter, Faccio incurred the anger of Verdi. After unsuccessful operatic ventures, Faccio abandoned composing in favor of conducting, in which he established himself as the peer of Mariani and Mancinelli. In 1871 he became principal conductor at Milan's La Scala. Reconciled to Verdi, he conducted the Italian premiere of *Aïda* (1872) and the world premiere of *Otello* (1887). His mental breakdown at the end of 1889 forced his withdrawal from La Scala. During this period, he also conducted Milan's orchestra, of the Società del Quartetto, and it was under their auspices that the Wagner memorial concert described here took place. Primarily identified with Verdi and other Italian composers, he was by no means as much a Wagner champion as Mancinelli, but Faccio did prepare and conduct performances of *Lohengrin* and *Die Meistersinger* in Milan.

16. There is no evidence that these holy souvenirs were ever passed on to Bayreuth. One tradition asserts that much of what was taken, including the bed, was destroyed on Cosima's orders. But the Wagner museum of Wahnfried in Bayreuth still displays the small sofa on which the composer breathed his last (see fig. 33), which was, according to Perl and Glasenapp, carried off with the family luggage on February 16. On the taking of such relics, see the account of Perl, quoted on pp. 134–35.

Chapter Seven

1. A further point is that Perl's little book was known to, and used by, the Wagners' "house" biographer, Carl Friedrich Glasenapp, who presumably found many of Perl's details authentic. Through him they were thus passed on, as part of "official" documentation, to Panizzardi (who also used Perl directly), and thence into the working general accounts of Wagner's residence. Accordingly, the reader will have found some of Perl's accounts or details already subsumed into the narrative in chapter 3, even though most recent biographers of the composer have ignored her book and have thus benefited from it only indirectly.

Perhaps partly through the intermediacy of Glasenapp, however, Perl's little book was very much utilized by other early writers on Wagner. Henry Finck, in his *Wagner and His Works*, vol. 2, 438–52, depends heavily upon "Mr. Perl" [*sic*] with and without acknowledgment, in general and on explicit details, for his account of the composer's final stay in Venice and of his mortal day. Even more striking is the case of the English clergyman, amateur musician, adventurer, traveler, and writer, Hugh Reginald Haweis (1838–1901). In his large, rambling volume, *My Musical Life*, he devotes almost a third of it to a string of reflections on Wagner, including a section

(448–60) on the final stay and death in Venice. That segment is largely a pillaging of Perl's book, without any acknowledgment: in many places it descends to close paraphrases and almost direct translations of her original German. It is curious that so knowing a Wagner scholar as Stewart Spencer would, in his invaluable anthology *Wagner Remembered*, 274–76, use Haweis's description—at best, a thirdhand account—to represent Wagner's death in the final selection.

2. The original edition is now a rarity, but the German text has been reprinted in facsimile, as *Henry Perl: Richard Wagner a Venezia*, with Italian translation, plus annotations, and an insightful introduction (in both Italian and German) by Quirino Principe. To this supporting material I am indebted for much of my information on Perl. Her own work will be cited parenthetically hereafter in both text versions, with German/Italian page references in that sequence.

3. This report seems to be a confusion over an opera project that Wagner actually intended to call *Die Sieger* (The Victors). It was to deal not with Indian legends of Brahma but with the life of the Buddha. It was to draw not only on the Buddhist and Far Eastern thought with which Wagner had long been flirting but also the philosophy of Schopenhauer that Wagner had found deeply attractive. Wagner first sketched this libretto in 1856, and then worked on it fitfully during the years 1868–73. But he had long abandoned the project by his last years, and never produced any music for such a work. Nevertheless, the idea still seems to have continued to run through Wagner's mind to the end: see Gutman, *Richard Wagner*, 452–54.

Indeed, over the years, Wagner thought of making *Die Sieger* into a spoken drama, without music. This would have been one of several plays he thought about writing, again without music, on such separate subjects as Martin Luther and his marriage to Catherine Bora, and Frederick Barbarossa. (See Cosima, June 27, 1869, for example.) As the years passed, and his post-*Ring* efforts focused on *Parsifal*, Wagner came to realize he would never carry out these "conventional" theatrical projects. But the fact that he flirted all his life with such things perhaps attests to the childhood theatrical attractions fostered by his stepfather, the actor Ludwig Geyer.

But the ghost of *Die Sieger* seems to have haunted Wagner nearly to the end of his days. In his new book, *The Redeemer Reborn—Parsifal as the Fifth Opera of Wagner's Ring* (New York: Amadeus, 2007), Paul Schofield, a former Buddhist priest, has argued that Wagner's final masterpiece was actually infused with Buddhist themes and concepts of redemption that had originally been projected in the planned *Die Sieger*.

4. For Cosima's account, see p. 47, and n. 19 to chapter 8; for the newspaper report, pp. 83–84 and Norlenghi, p. 151. Comparison of all our accounts of these concerts, and of Wagner's dealings with Calascione, will be considered in the next chapter, p. 356, n. 19. See also Barker, "Forgotten Early Champion," 11–14.

5. The war pitting France and Piedmont against Austria, initiated in late April 1860.

6. He was actually working, of course, on *Tristan und Isolde*, not the *Ring*.

7. This account of the concert of April 22, 1882, differs on some points from the other existing accounts; see pp. 87; 355, n. 11.

8. In her diaries, Cosima traces a brief fascination that her son Siegfried developed for gondolas. On November 6, she notes that Richard was "particularly pleased by Fidi's rowing, amused by the gondolier's cries he hears from him." Three days later she records that "Fidi's gondolier calls provide us with a pleasant distraction on the journey." On November 15: "We ride home through the narrow canals, Fidi rows

and calls while Luigi [Trevisan, their gondolier] prompts him—'like Mephisto the astrologer,' says R.; but it makes us laugh heartily to see that, when it really matters, Luigi always calls out himself. The next day: 'Fido rows us home.' "

On a different occasion (December 18, 1882), Cosima reports that, in one of his humorous moods with the children, Wagner extended a musical pun he had first (November 27) made of the word *tombola* (the lottery) to fit the word *gondola* as well: ". . . that *gondola* is the theme of the Scherzo in [Beethoven's Ninth Symphony] when it is played softly on the strings, *tombola* when it is played by the timpani."

9. See also addendum 6.

10. Perl inserts here a note (*), giving an assessment of the causes of Wagner's death taken from Italian sources. This is discussed below, in relation to other "obituary" sources, in addendum 7. As to Wagner's awkward and compensatory walking posture, Cosima suggests how far back it may have begun: ". . . After lunch we go out together; he laughs over his 'fresh and stormy gait' when with me; if he had been alone, he says, he would just have slouched along, hands behind his back" (March 15, 1878).

11. The reference is to the *koryphaios*, the leader of the chorus, in ancient Greek drama. For Cosima's purposes, the word might be approximated today as "cheerleader."

12. The original event was described by Cosima in her diary entry for December 24, 1880. The graphic embodiment of it seems to have been among a number of portraits of the children that Joukowsky was working on the following spring (Cosima: May 14, 16, 1881). That summer Wagner was still after him to complete the group painting in oils despite "mistaken attempts at deception" (August 29). In the completed painting (see fig. 7), Joukowsky substituted himself for Pepino as Joseph. (Sadly, if inevitably, Rubinstein's piano playing left no trace.)

13. See p. 85.

14. On Wagner's extensive use of perfumes in his lodgings, see addendum 5.

15. But note a comment on the physician by Wagner, recorded by Cosima on January 17: "Dr. Keppler provides him with food for thought; he finds him quite pleasant but feels he has no eyes in his head; there are people who are just specialists, he says, otherwise not human beings at all." Two days before, on January 15, Cosima had noted that "R., feeling prejudiced against Dr. Keppler, engaged a Dr. Kurz, whose prescriptions did not, however, appeal to him, and then he sent for Dr. Keppler. Now the doctor, who was engaged to come 3 times a week, turns up, and R. falls, as he puts it, 'into his jaws.' "

16. For discussion of this passage, see p. 183.

17. For the full text of this passage, see addendum 5.

18. Cosima is more restrained and less positive in reporting the involvements that she and her husband had with the Carnival. The early stages of the festivities first appear in her diary entry for January 21, when, on a foggy day, the Wagner family went for lunch to the Cappello Nero restaurant on the Piazza San Marco. After the repast: "We wish to go home but are forced back by the crush, and from the restaurant we watch the masked procession, in which a cook keeps greeting R.; and R. replies. It is estimated that there are 20,000 people in the square; the children—who went off at R.'s bidding but then returned—watch the seething crowds with us, 'a black mass in which patches of flesh color emerge,' a strange, uncanny impression. As R. and I are riding home together, he talks about the sight and the impression,

both so sad. 'And yet,' he said, 'a person who does not try to make closer contact with the masses is not worth much!'"

The next day (January 22), Cosima observes that "yesterday was too much for him" and that a visit to the Piazza was limited to a brief session of sitting at the San Marco portal; still she adds: "He feels the outing yesterday was a success, and he says we should always just let him grouse properly."

Strolls in the Piazza/Piazzetta area are recorded for the next few days without any further reference to the festivities, until she mentions on January 28 that, after Wagner did some work, "we ride in wonderful weather to the Piazzetta, where preparations are being made for the masquerade." Two days later she noted that Wagner took a walk by himself: "He returns home much delighted with the sight of the lively lanes. . . ." But on February 2 she reports: "In glorious weather we ride to the Piazzetta, but the crowds milling around on account of the festival are repugnant to him. . . ."

Accounts of walking around the city again ignore any Carnival activities, until their actual climax on the evening of February 6. Wagner had already spent some time that day basking at the Doge's Palace, but then the family returned for the closing episode: ". . . at around 9 o'clock we set out to the Square for the Shrovetide celebrations. R. does this to please the children, who reward him with their gaiety. The impression is mixed; R. finds something touching about the procession carrying carnival to the grave, with its melody which he thinks to be an old one, but after going to the podium with the children, he returns to me in the Cappello Nero looking sad. He says poor artisans were hopping around there without really understanding why. But the midnight bells and the extinguishing of the flames produce another fine effect." Compare the descriptions by Cosima and Perl with that of Norlenghi, pp. 160–61. Also, compare Perl's description of Wagner's buoyant behavior with the parallel observations of Hermann Levi, quoted in pp. 337–38, n. 14.

19. See p. 109.

20. Cosima's corresponding diary entry is somewhat oblique, without reference to her own involvement: "At 2 o'clock my father takes his departure—R. claims frequently to have discerned in him a mood of sadness about himself. In connection with my father's life, R. wonders what would have become of him if things had continued as they were in Vienna (1856). Impossible to imagine." It would appear that Perl's is the only account to report the two men embracing at both the arrival and the departure of Liszt; a detail perhaps passed on by someone of the household staff.

21. As the reader might have noticed, eyewitness though she may have been, Perl slipped into one confused detail: the restaurant was not "Al Bianco Cappello" but "Il Cappello Nero," a clear difference between black and white!

22. In her entry for the following day, Cosima adds a detail: "R. has breakfast with Fidi [Siegfried], who worried me yesterday by suddenly disappearing, but R. was not disturbed by it even for a moment." At just what point in the day this occurred Cosima does not make clear, but this was fixed by Glasenapp in his account (see following note) as happening during Wagner's participation in the carnival finale. Curiously, in his *Erinnerungen* Siegfried makes no reference at all to this incident, or, in fact, to the carnival participation in general.

23. Glasenapp, *Das Leben*, vol. 6, 765–66.

24. See pp. 46–47. For Norlenghi's account of the February 7 excursion, see pp. 161–62. Unaware of Norlenghi, Glasenapp, *Das Leben*, vol. 6, 766, once more made a synthesis of the accounts by Perl and Cosima.

25. Glasenapp, *Das Leben*, vol. 6, 768–69.

26. For Norlenghi's report of still other incidents that afternoon, see, pp. 162–63.

27. For the full account of this episode, see addendum 6.

28. For these among other brief accounts, see addendum 8.

29. For the sorting out of Wagner's "last words," see addendum 9.

30. The speed in communicating the news of Wagner's death was the product of a technological revolution that occurred within the composer's own lifetime. That speed, and the significance that was attached to the event itself, are illustrated by the report published by the *New York Times* on February 14. Headed "DEATH OF RICHARD WAGNER," it began: "Without a word of preliminary warning the announcement was telegraphed all over the world last night of the sudden death, in Venice, of Richard Wagner." The article then continued with a very extensive survey of Wagner's life and musical works, running two long columns of fine print the full vertical span of a large-format page. It seems unlikely that an article of such length and detail would have been whipped up on the instant: one assumes it had been written in advance and held for its eventual use, as is common journalistic practice in handling the obituaries of prominent persons.

31. On other reactions by the grieving Luigi Trevisan, see p. 308; on the cat again, see p. 153.

32. According to Bürkel's letter to King Ludwig, quoted as our prologue, Cosima put her husband's beret upon her own head, presumably at the time of the sealing of the coffin. Ever eager to disparage Cosima in any way possible, Köhler, *Der Letzte der Titanen*, 809, trans. Spencer, 636, seems to suggest that she had appropriated Richard's hat as a symbol of gloating or succession. But, besides being a plausible gesture of final communion, it could also reflect a need to warm a chilly head just recently shorn of its long hair.

33. As pointed out by editor Principe, 254/265, n. 93, Perl has here mistakenly made two salon-carriages out of the two-car combination of the one salon-carriage and the funeral carriage.

34. Perl's report of Cosima's words—"It is shameful that I still live, were I to have died Richard would have immediately killed himself!"—tally with Bürkel's report of Cosima's self-reproach "that her pain did not kill her, inasmuch as she knew that the Master would not have survived her death so long." (Joukowsky suggests parallel sentiments in his letter of February 22, as quoted in addendum 8: p. 304.) Such allusions have been taken by some (e.g., Köhler, *Der Letzte der Titanen*, 801, trans. Spencer, 629) to suggest that the couple had some kind of pact: should one die, the other would commit suicide as a gesture of despairing devotion. On that count, what Perl quotes was an expression either of guilty weakness or of guilty betrayal. More likely, it was simply the feeling of a romanticized grief: "Isolde wanted to follow her Tristan," as Bürkel put it. Or perhaps it was just the practical thought that, were Cosima to die, Richard would be lost without her and would soon follow her, out of grief or neglect.

Nevertheless, the idea that Cosima should die when Richard did was even older than their marriage. The two had talked often, especially in their early years together, about death: particularly "union in death," usually with explicit reference to the example of Tristan and Isolde (e.g., July 25, 1871). Indeed, on March 15, 1869, while they were living together but not yet married, Cosima recalled a relevant anniversary of unspoken *Tristan*esque evocation: "Six years ago today R. came through Berlin, and then it happened that we fell in love; at that time I thought I should never see him again, we wanted to die together." Later that year (November

29), Cosima went so far as to end her entry quite explicitly to the point: "My single prayer: one day to die with Richard in the selfsame hour. My greatest pride: to have rejected everything in order to live for him. My finest happiness: his joy.—Without him the world is to me no better than a sty, as Cleopatra says."

Wagner himself encouraged the *Tristan* analogy, as Cosima records in a conversation they had about love on July 25, 1871: "Yes, love up to the point of complete union is just suffering, yearning," she quotes him as saying. To that she responds: "And complete union achieved only in death—the whole of *Tristan* is saying that; this is what I constantly feel, I feel myself as an obstacle which I long to burst through. And yet I want as an individual to be united with you in death—how can one explain this?" To which she has him reply: "Everything that is remains, what one already has persists, freed entirely from the conditions of its occurrence." . . . Almost three years later, now settled in Wahnfried, and amid endless assertions of self-sacrifice, Cosima returned (January 7, 1874) to the idea of joint death: ". . . Yesterday and today I put my whole being into a prayer: to die at the same time as Richard! To wander this earth only so long as my gaze can meet his, my hand hold his, my poor spirit look upon and grasp his spirit! R., to whom I state this quite simply, replies, 'We shall go on living together for a long time yet.'—" Even Richard could be caught up in the theme of union in death. A year later (January 17, 1875), Cosima reports: "R. declared yesterday that now, having acquired me after his 'beggar's life,' he knew for certain he would live to a ridiculously old age, and we would both die by euthanasia on the sofa in his room, which he had furnished for that purpose." The idea that Cosima could not outlive her husband seems even to have been taken up by others. She records a tribute given by a local dignitary during a gala concert in Bayreuth on December 26, 1878: ". . . in his speech he touched me with his reference to me: 'she who has no desire to live for an instant without her Richard.'"

Speaking, meanwhile, of Bürkel's letter, we note that it is the only source that reports Cosima's evasive determination to remain with her husband's body, even after she had been removed from the death chamber.

35. As is shown on pp. 162–63, Norlenghi parallels Perl's account of Frontali's visit, but with more personalized details; Norlenghi, on the other hand, fails to note the epilogue that Perl gives us, that Frontali was allowed to be one of the pallbearers. See also pp. 163; 361, n. 42.

By the way, who was the eighth pallbearer? Perl stipulates eight but names only seven. My guess would be Tessarin. There is nothing to confirm such a suggestion. But it is interesting that the novelist Kürenberg (280) reached the same conclusion.

36. See p. 103. As to the fate of the furniture taken from Venice, there is the clear survival of the sofa on which Wagner died, still on display at Wahnfried in Bayreuth (see figure 33). According to some reports, the remaining items were burned on Cosima's orders.

37. On what follows, see Spencer, "'Er starb,'" 66–67.

38. In volume 2 of his biography of Cosima, Du Moulin Eckart, 10, quotes a letter written from Bayreuth to Dr. Keppler by the banker and family friend Adolf von Gross, apparently in late February 1833, not long after Wagner's death—a letter now apparently no longer extant and documented only in this transcription. Gross reports to the doctor the desperate condition of Wagner's widow and the family's concern for her. He continues: "A few days past we read in all the newspapers what you find in the attached clipping. We hope that you put me in such a position that I might deny this. Frau Wagner and the children ask that nothing of this kind be pub-

lished. If you have set down these observations in writing, I ask that you have these sent to me under seal. I, as guardian of the children, would transmit what is entrusted to me at the later time when Siegfried attains majority."

In conjunction with Keppler's oblique allusion in his "autopsy report" to psychological causes for Wagner's heart attack, this passage has sometimes been taken as reflecting Keppler's knowledge of the supposed argument between Cosima and Richard over Carrie Pringle: thus Westernhagen, "Wagner's Last Day," 397; Köhler, *Der Letzte der Titanen*, 805–6, trans. Spencer, 635). Spencer now dismisses that interpretation (see addendum 2) and suggests that Gross was referring rather to the passage printed in *LGdV* on February 15 (see p. 91ff), or to other newspaper reports parallel to it or dependent upon it. These reports Gross would have regarded as a betrayal of the family's privacy in the days after Wagner's death.

But, as we will see below (p. 377, n. 1 to addendum 2), the novelist Kürenberg suggested that Keppler's supposed delicate statements and their supposed newspaper transmissions might relate to a dubious rumor that Wagner's death was brought on by the exertions of a dalliance with Betty Bürkel!

Chapter Eight

1. Norlenghi is nowhere mentioned by Jung, *Rezeption*, in her section "Das Problem des Wagnerismus" (429–47), as among the *wagneriani* in late nineteenth-century Italy; nor is he noted in Marion S. Miller's probing essay, "Wagnerism, Wagnerians, and Italian Identity." I am indebted to Professor Miller, however, for the information that Norlenghi was identified, if not as a faculty member of the Liceo Benedetto Marcello, at least as a *socio* or "associate" of the institution. He is listed as attending organizational convocations of the conservatory on August 30 and September 10 of 1876 (the year before its formal foundation): thus the archival *Il Conservatorio di Musica Benedetto Marcello di Venezia*, ed. Verardo, 203, 205. Such status would confirm Norlenghi's access to events and personnel at the Liceo.

Norlenghi's name and publication do not appear in conventional Wagner bibliographies, such as those in the *New Grove Dictionaries*, and his work is even less recognized than that of Perl and even Panizzardi. Panizzardi himself (*Wagner in Italia*) made little or no use of Perl, and was seemingly unaware of Norlenghi's book. In their historical chapters in *Il Conservatorio* (1977), Guglielmini Tieri and Pietro Verardo are rarities in drawing extensively upon Norlenghi. Among recent Wagner scholars, the only ones I notice using Norlenghi's book are: Carlo de Incontrera in his essay on Wagner's Italian visits, in *Wagner in Italia*, ed. Giancarlo Rostirolla (1982); and Stewart Spencer, in a passing reference in his " 'Er starb,' " 69, n. 50.

2. Something of the book's obscurity may have to do with scanty survival: in the initial pages a curt notice reports that the edition consists of only 300 copies. (I first discovered its existence by spotting the copy in the library of Gabriele D'Annunzio in his Villa Vittoriale degli Italiani on Lake Garda.) A year later Norlenghi delivered a preconcert lecture in Rome, which was published the year after that as *Ricordo wagneriano: Parole dette per la commemorazione di Riccardo Wagner al le Associazione artistico internazionale di Roma*. Supplemental to his major book, this lecture is summarized in addendum 14.

3. Arminius was a German tribal leader who became a trusted ally of the Romans under the rule of Augustus. But he turned on them, organizing a German rebellion and leading his forces in the notorious ambush of the Roman army under Varus at Teutoberg Forest in the year 9 AD. Three full legions were massacred in the battle and Varus committed suicide. The defeat destroyed all plans for extending or consolidating Roman control further into German territory. It is said that for years afterward the disaster gave Augustus nightmares from which he awoke screaming "Varus, give me back my legions!" Arminius continued a warrior's career for another ten years, to his death, by which time he had become a hero of legendary proportions among Germans. (Arminius was the Latin name by which the Romans knew him: it has been suggested that its native form may have been Hermann.) Norlenghi, obviously with a good education in the classics behind him, was apparently using "Arminio" as the ultimate symbol of German manhood and national identity.

4. As it happens, Norlenghi's recollection can be matched precisely with Cosima's testimony. To be sure, his remembrance of the timing was faulty, for the Wagners at no time went to the Lido in October. But they did go there on September 27, and Cosima's diary entry offers a fascinating and otherwise close counterpart to Norlenghi's picture.

The tutor Stein had taken the children in the morning out to the Lido, a point to which Cosima returns belatedly: "In the afternoon R. and I go to the Piazzetta, where R. has the idea of taking the steamer to the Lido to fetch the children. On the steamer R. was delighted by a dog, and he said, 'What a joy it is suddenly to see such a naïve creature before one's eyes!' We do find Siegf. and Stein, but the girls are unpunctual; we decide to say nothing to them and to play a joke on them, but at supper we discover that they were delayed by a horrible accident: a young lady was drowned, they saw it and also witnessed the despair of the father, husband, and brothers!—The evening passes in horrifying accounts of it."

Needless to say, the Wagners never noticed the admirer who was inspecting them; but it is interesting that they had not seen the drowning, and did not have it on their minds on the vaporetto, not learning of it until later.

5. See pp. 232–40.

6. See pp. 14, 15, 109. Also Barker, "Forgotten Early Champion," 11–13.

7. Cf. Glasenapp, *Das Leben*, vol. 5, 311–12.

8. Glasenapp, *Das Leben*, vol. 6, 687.

9. Ibid., 395.

10. Wagner's positive reaction to his encounter with them in 1858 has already been mentioned on pp. 11, 14, 16. At the beginning of the first family visit to Venice (September 19, 1876), Cosima reports "a serenade by the Società! Workers in the dockyard who delight us and regale us with songs, lighthearted, devout, and serious; I ask them for the '*Canzone del Tasso*,' which moves me greatly. Indescribable pleasure in this music, the soul of the people!" At the end of their second family stay, as they were leaving Venice on October 30, 1880, Cosima notes: ". . . The singers who had so often upset R. arrive, and this time they really please us and rouse our spirits as, singing all the while, they precede our gondola and accompany us as far as the station. Farewell Venice! Departure at 6 o'clock." The salon carriage is much better than expected. Wagner and his family seem to have become identified as celebrities to honor on departure—or did they by now commission these salutes? At any rate, Cosima describes a parallel scene when the family was leaving Venice, on April 29, 1882, at the end of their penultimate stay in the city: ". . . We leave the hotel [the

Europa?] at one o'clock, accompanied by the singers, a sight which draws onto all the bridges, and we leave Venice, after having once again inspected the *entresol* of the P. Vendramin. . . ." The singers had already been on the scene over a week before that. For April 21 she reports: ". . . at about 9 o'clock we go to Princess Hatzfeldt's; the singers are awaiting us below, and they lead us there amid singing, moonlight, and Bengal lights, and also take us home." Later on, however, during the final stay, such entertainers seem to been wearing out their welcome (or employment?). Reporting the evening events of December 12, 1882, Cosima notes an incident that preceded a presupper game with Dr. Keppler: ". . . Before which the singers came around, and R. (who no longer cares for them) remarked: 'On the other hand, they are a part of Venice.' " Indeed, Wagner's impatience had already become even harsher. Cosima reports, on September 18, 1882, immediately after their move into the Vendramin: "In the evening the singers appear; R. gives them a substantial gift, along with a request never to come again." That episode almost echoes the one Norlenghi has reported for 1876!

11. See p. 81 (newspapers) and pp. 109–10 (Perl). As can be observed, the newspaper reports say nothing about the presence of a Wagner daughter, or any difficulty in recognizing Wagner. Whatever the conflicting sources, the impression is given that at least Norlenghi had direct testimony from Calascione himself. As for Cosima, we might remember her very much more terse and casual: ". . . we go to St. Mark's Square; R. asks the military band for [Rossini's] *Gazza Ladra* Overture, which is then played, and very prettily (April 21, 1882)." See also Barker, "Forgotten Early Champion," 8–9.

12. See pp. 107, 119.

13. We see here another instance of the rumors about some new opera project attributed to Wagner at this point. Cf. Perl's reports, pp. 108; 348, n. 3; also, addendum 10. Perl was properly critical of the rumors, whereas Norlenghi seems willing to accept this.

14. See pp. 163–64, where Norlenghi, in the direct context of describing Wagner's death, fails to restate the claim that the composer died in the gondolier's arms.

15. While Perl notes Wagner's patronage of the Lavena café (see p. 46), Norlenghi gives the fullest vignette. It matches well with Cosima's frequent references to visiting it. For example: ". . . Toward 4 o'clock we go out, R., Fidi [Siegfried], and I; it cheers R. up to stroll through the arcades, and our short stop at Lavena's he also finds entertaining. There his attention is caught by a handsome tomcat, who sits motionless on the sweets counter watching the movement made by the glass flame on the ceiling. R. then talks about the goats he has just seen mentioned in the history of Persia—how perfect such an animal is! 'And then to turn it into a human being! It is a step backward, so to speak: how ugly the ape is, until the stage of genius is reached!' " . . . (November 15, 1882).

". . . In the afternoon we go to Saint Mark's Square; to the Merceria, which he calls Peking. He delights in the tower, the view of Saint Mark's, the horses [i.e., the famous bronze quadriga set on the loggia above the portal], and that brings us to the capture of Constantinople. Then we go into Lavena's, with whose proprietor R. enjoys conversing. An eclipse of the sun is being talked about (November 18, 1882)."

". . . In the afternoon we meet in Saint Mark's Square (at Lavena's, where he [R.] makes arrangements about quartets with a violinist; the latter asks him about Brahms and Dvořák! . . ." (November 19, 1882).

It is perhaps of some interest that Wagner preferred to patronize Lavena's on the north side of the Piazza San Marco, as against the more prestigious Florian's on the south side. The latter was the regular haunt of Venice's literati, a circle that Wagner may have deliberately chosen to avoid.

16. This episode has, of course, already been discussed, pp. 47 and 109, as well as in Barker, "Forgotten Early Champion," 12–13.

17. At this point, Norlenghi inserts a footnote [*]: "Maestro Angelo Tessarin, greatly talented Venetian musician, but who now lives in Milan, enjoyed for many years the good will of the great Master, who felt great affection for him, and greatly appreciated his talent. Even earlier Tessarin was, for these reasons, selected as music-master for the daughters." This would seem to be the only reference to Tessarin as a music teacher for the Wagner girls. On Tessarin (or Tesarion, or Tessarini), see p. 326, n. 20.

18. See p. 109. The issue of correct tempo in the interpretation of music was vital, as we see throughout these pages. It is one of the central themes on which he constantly discourses in his treatise *Über das Dirigiren* or "On Conducting," published in 1869 and included in his *Gesammelte Schriften und Dictungen von Richard Wagner* (6 vols., Leipzig, 1871–83), vol. 8, pp. 325–410, trans. Edward Dannreuther, 3rd ed. (London: William Reeves, 1911). For example: "The whole duty of a conductor is comprised in his ability always to indicate the right *tempo*. His choice of *tempi* will show whether he understands the piece or not. With good players, again, the true *tempo* induces correct phrasing and expression and conversely, with a conductor, the idea of appropriate phrasing and expression will induce the conception of the true *tempo*" (20). Wagner devotes much space to deploring the complete misunderstanding of many conductors, famous or not, as to the proper pacing of music, and he recurrently restates his point: "I am persistently returning to the question of *tempo* because, as I said above, this is the point at which it becomes evident whether a conductor understands his business or not" (34).

He goes on at particular length to illustrate painful encounters with conductors who ignored his precise instructions and showed little sympathy for both establishing and changing tempos.

19. ". . . he [R.] goes to the Piazzetta by himself in the morning and meets the children there. In the afternoon we arrange to meet in Saint Mark's Square, but I find him in Lavena's shop, having had a spasm. Riding in the gondola, he and the girls had heard strains of *Lohengrin*, he then tried to hurry, and that brought on the trouble! ... Hardly is the spasm over, however, when he beckons Tesarini and invites him and the music director to our house in the evening on account of the wrong tempi! ... But he then says to me, 'I ought to forget who I am, make no sudden movements, and turn into a boring donkey!' . . .—After supper (in which he eats almost nothing) he discusses the tempi with the musicians. . . ." (November 5, 1882). On this concert, see pp. 47, 109; also Barker, "Forgotten Early Champion," 11–12.

20. ". . . In the evening we are at Princess Hatzf.'s, where Lusch [Daniela] plays Marianne in *Die Geschwister*. The play itself once again moves R. to tears, but he feels that Lulu's portrayal should have been more naïve. The rest of the *soirée*, however, the introductions, etc, R. finds more than ever unbearable, though he very patiently takes it in good part. The presence of our dear Grosses is of help to him in this . . ." (December 10, 1882).

Cosima ignores the German consul Fiers in her report, and never mentions him in her diaries, but Norlenghi's reference to him as a participant in this little domestic production suggests that Fiers might have had some connection with the Wagner circle in Venice. We hear of him later identified as a family friend and as a source of information for a report by *LGdV* (February 17, 1883): see pp. 91, 99. On this *soirée*, see Pachl, *Siegfried Wagner*, 62.

21. Indeed, Cosima makes clear that Wagner disliked the Hatzfeldt gatherings, to which the gregarious Liszt went regularly, usually taking one or more of the daughters. On December 29, she reports "the accounts of Princess H.'s Thursdays upset him. He does not like anyone from his circle to go elsewhere."

22. This would presumably be the cat of which Luigi Trevisan told Perl: see p. 137. Wagner's favor to this cat is curious, since Wagner was an avid dog lover so much of his life.

23. See pp. 53–54; 85; 377, n. 11.

24. See pp. 318–19.

25. The four institutions that Norlenghi mentions were not *scuole* (charitable confraternities) but *ospedali*, or "foundling" asylums (conservatories) for orphaned children. The most recognizable of them today is the Ospedale della Pietà, now famous for employing Vivaldi, though that composer's absence from our writer's references testifies to the obscurity into which Vivaldi's reputation had sunk by the late nineteenth century.

By contrast with Vivaldi's long service at the Pietà, the four composers whom Norlenghi identifies with the *ospedali* had widely varying associations with them. The versatile and highly regarded Niccolò Jommelli, or Iommelli (1714–74), held diverse positions all around Italy and in Europe beyond. Of his very numerous operas, only four were written for Venice (1742, 1745, 1746, 1749), where he served as music director at the Ospedale degli Incurabili for only about three years (1743–46), and where he also composed some of his sacred music.

German-born Johann Adolph Hasse (1699–1783) was an even more cosmopolitan master who held posts and composed likewise numerous operas all around Europe, including Venice (1730, 1732, 1739, 1740, 1745, 1746, 1747, 1758). The report that he was appointed music master at the Incurabili in 1727 or 1728 is a myth, but he composed for that institution during the years 1733 and 1742 and he was officially *maestro di cappella* there in 1735–39, serving temporarily there again in 1757–60. He visited Venice repeatedly, and for the last ten years of his life took up permanent and final residence there, continuing his affiliations with the Incurabili and his composition of sacred works; he was buried in the church of San Marcuola.

Nicola Porpora (1686–1768) not only was another prolific composer of opera but also was famous as a teacher of singers. He is said to have been one of Hasse's teachers, and certainly was the latter's long-time rival in operatic activity; he was also later young Haydn's teacher. Venice was one of his recurrent bases: seven of his operas were written for it (1725, 1727, 1729, 1731, 1737, 1742), mostly for the Teatro S. Giovanni Crisostomo, and he rotated with Hasse as music director a the Incurabili (1726–35; 1736–38 while Hasse was in Dresden), and then at the Ospedale della Pietà (1741–42) and the Ospedaletto (1744–47).

It is not clear which Scarlatti Norlenghi refers to. Alessandro (1660–1725) was the principal figure in the emergence of Neapolitan opera, and worked mainly in Naples and Rome. He made only one visit to Venice, in 1707, where he produced two new operas. But his style enjoyed little success there, and he held no official post in the city. His son Domenico (1685–1757), most famous as a composer for the harpsichord, was sent job hunting to Venice in advance of his father's visit to the city in

1707. There are flimsy stories of Domenico's time there, including one of an encounter and contest with the traveling Handel. But Domenico found no real employment in Venice during his brief stay there. Indeed, neither father nor son ever had any proven association with any of the *ospedali* or any other institutions in Venice, beyond Alessandro's writing for the S. Giovanni Crisostomo Theater—thus making either of them a strange reference for Norlenghi.

26. Benedetto Marcello (1686–1739) was an amateur but gifted and productive composer born of an important Venetian noble family. He was expected to follow the career of public service for which Venetian patricians were destined, but he did not distinguish himself and ended his days buried in obscure posts. Details of his musical career have not survived, but he had a good training, as part of a wide cultural education, and he composed extensively in instrumental and vocal forms, if not opera. His most enduring music is his setting of fifty Psalms, in Italian translation, which were admired for generations after him, and which show his interest in Hebrew and early Christian liturgical elements, while his understanding of ancient literature and culture were reflected in critical writings that anticipate the later ideals of "classicism" to be identified subsequently with the composer Gluck and the art historian Winckelmann. He was also highly regarded as a vocal trainer: an early pupil was soprano Faustina Bordoni, subsequently Hasse's wife. Later in his life, in May 1728, amid serious personal crises—and in a further compromise of his social standing—Marcello married one of his voice students, Rosanna Scalfi, whose singing was highly admired.

27. It is difficult to know all that Norlenghi wished to comprehend within his rather general reference to the past glories of lyric theater in Venice, once opera's acknowledged capital. His reference suggests that he could have looked back already to the pioneering Claudio Monteverdi (1567–1643), who was born in Cremona, served the court of Mantua, and became *Maestro di Cappella* at San Marco, but who really founded the Venetian operatic tradition. Or to Monteverdi's disciple and successor, Francesco Cavalli (1602–76), whose productivity and success made Venice the first European center of opera. Of eighteenth-century operatic masters, he would presumably have ignored, or been ignorant of Vivaldi; but he surely would have thought of Baldassare Galuppi (1706–85), eventually another director at San Marco but one of the most prolific Venetian opera composers of his day, who often had as his librettist the great Venetian playwright Carlo Goldoni (1707–93). Besides his operatic labors and travels, as it happens, Galuppi also held posts at the Ospedale dei Mendicanti 1740–41, 1743–46), and, in concurrent terms (1762–64, 1768–85), at the Ospedale degli Incurabili and the great basilica of San Marco.

28. This would seem to be exactly the opposite of the perception that Perl (see p. 109) attributed to Wagner, that Italian musicians rushed tempos because Italian audiences were impatient and want the music to move along quickly.

29. Cf. Cosima, more cursorily: "In the afternoon R. receives Count Contin, founder and president of the Conservatoire, R. describes correctness of tempo as the alpha and omega of what should be taught" (December 11, 1882).

30. Obviously unaware of what was going on, Cosima simply says: "Before lunch R. visited the Conservatoire and its president" (December 12, 1882).

31. Cf. Cosima: "Unfortunately our lunch is somewhat delayed by my father, R. very vexed about it, since he had promised to go with my father to the Liceo. At supper he tells me that he had some spasms there. But when he says he must go again tomorrow, since they have no conductor, and notes my slight surprise, it bursts out

of him that on my birthday he is going to play his symphony to me! Great laughter from Loldi and Fidi (Eva in bed, Lusch with her grandpa at Princess Hatzfeldt's). He tells me all the difficulties he has been having at rehearsals, with missing parts, with Seidl's absence; now he has sent a telegram to Humperdinck in Paris, hoping to get him here for the occasion. It moves me to complete silence!" (December 14, 1882).

32. The first movement of Wagner's Symphony in C Major begins with a slow introduction, marked *Sostenuto e maestoso*, leading then to the main body, marked *Allegro con brio*, which opens with a distinct motto, a five-note figure. In this rehearsal, Wagner was humorously giving his players a clue to its shape by singing first the solmization syllables of those notes, and then fitting to them the call to action. Ironically, he mistakes the symbol for the fifth note, which should be ut instead of mi. Translating what Norlenghi shows into notation, his corrected illustration would appear thus:

Besides Norlenghi's observations in 1882, we have some earlier and quite extensive impressions of the composer's rehearsal behavior and general production preparation: *1876: Richard Wagner auf der Probe. Das bayreuther Tagebuch des Ballettmeisters und Hilfsregisseurs Richard Fricke* (Stuttgart: Akademischer Verlag Han-Dieter Heinz, 1983), or trans. George R. Fricke as *Wagner in Rehearsal, 1875–1876: The Diaries of Richard Fricke* (Stuyvesant, NY: Pendragon Stuyvesant, 1998); or the parallel observations of Heinrich Porges, *Wagner Rehearsing the "Ring": An Eye-Witness Account of the Stage Rehearsals of the First Bayreuth Festival*, trans. Robert L. Jacobs (Cambridge: Cambridge University Press, 1983). Further, we have the comments of Siegfried Wagner, *Erinnerung*, 32–35, in which he describes the performance of the Symphony as only the third time he heard his father conduct. A rare drawing of Wagner at a rehearsal is in figure 27.

33. For these rehearsals, see pp. 49–51. But note particularly Cosima's entry for December 20: "Then he goes off to rehearsal; on his return I go to see him, and he tells me—after saying that I should ask the children to tell me about it—that the rehearsal began very stormily because two players were absent and the others tried to make excuses for them! R. made a speech in French which had a great effect; after that, apparently, they played excellently, and altogether the players seem to be full of enthusiasm for R., they repeat his jokes to one another and understand him quite well. R. feels very happy in his *métier*, and it is only things coming from outside that he finds disagreeable—such as Herr Filippi from Milan, for example. This journalist was made to pay for it, and R. says he finds this type of person particularly repugnant, for they always feel they must write wittily, 'and it looks very odd when witty things are written about people like us!'"

From much later comes the recollection of Siegfried Wagner: "My father understood how to make the rehearsals for his Youth-Symphony very pleasant and jolly through little jokes with the Italian orchestra. Thus he was able to achieve everything he wanted as to precision of performance. His imperfect Italian also contributed to comic misunderstandings" (*Erinnerungen*, 35).

34. Note that Perl (p. 117) places this remark at the end of the concert itself, not the rehearsal. Her report is only partially anticipated by *LV*, February 14, 1883: see p. 90. With his contacts at the Liceo, Norlenghi surely heard about this directly from Frontali himself, which would give it weight. On the other hand, might Wagner have made the statement more than once?

35. For the rest of this passage and its context, see p. 51.

36. The confusions shared by Perl and Norlenghi over the date of the final concert are very strange: see pp. 115, 117–18. Cosima's testimony is irrefutable. Perl, who may have relied upon the newspaper misstatement for the concert date, apparently had some testimony from the musicians to cite, but Norlenghi was even closer to them, and drew upon them more extensively. The newspapers and our authors seem to be at odds as to the locale for the rehearsals and concert. These were held in the Fenice Theater complex, but not in the main auditorium: instead in the large Sala Apollonea, in the adjacent rooms by then used as the location of the Liceo Benedetto Marcello. The casual interchange of Liceo and La Fenice would have been common among locals at the time, and was automatically understood.

Note that Norlenghi's account of the rehearsals and the concert itself is reproduced in full in *Il Conservatorio di Musica Benedetto Marcello*, ed. Verardo, 51–52, n. 25.

37. This episode is reported nowhere else, and is difficult to square with Cosima's reports. It poses an immediate problem of dating: Wagner was never in Venice in 1881, the year Norlenghi states. He was there through October 1880, and in late April 1882, during both of which stays the pianist Josef Rubinstein was in attendance. Rubinstein did stay with the Wagners for about a month at the beginning of the final sojourn of (September 19–October 22), so a dating then is plausible. The Wagners socialized regularly with the Princess Hatzfeldt—whose name Norlenghi, or at least his proofreader, could never spell consistently—though mainly it was Cosima and the children who did so. Richard himself seems not to have liked being involved. One of the few times he did so was on the eve of their departure from their penultimate stay in Venice: "In the evening a farewell *soirée* at Princess H[atzfeldt]'s, at which R. feels ill at ease. He is embarrassed by Lusch's having gone somewhere else, and he tells me of his tendency to be jealous of his loved ones" (April 28, 1882).

During the stay in 1880, Wagner likewise did not participate in most visits to the Hatzfeldt palace. The one exception was one occasion that could possibly correspond with what Ruben told Norlenghi: "In the evening a pleasant hour at Princess Hatzfeldt's with all the children; while Rub. plays the *Msinger* Prelude, R. acts out the scene between Walther and Eva with Mimi [i.e., Contessa Marie Schleinitz]. When we return home, he tells me he cannot bear listening to his own music" (October 15, 1880).

The disparities vis-à-vis Norlenghi are obvious, however. Is it possible that, between them, Ruben and Cosima each remembered separate things that were, indeed, all part of one program? Then, too, Cosima makes no mention of invited guests. Of course, Cosima was clearly adept at forgetting or ignoring people and events in her entries, but it is unlikely she would have passed over some other event *chez* Hatzfeldt. At the least, if we can accept something of the Ruben/Norlenghi tale, disparities and all, it suggests that Wagner had at least met the artist Ruben before their socializing during the final visit: Cosima makes reference to him first only on November 25, 1882.

38. For comparison of Perl's account with Cosima's reference, see pp. 120–23; 123–25; 349–50, n. 18. In the course of Norlenghi's account that follows here, he speaks of this as Wagner's first encounter with the Venetian Carnevale. In point of

fact, Wagner had gone through it during his very first residence in Venice, in early 1859. Apparently its observance at that time was a shallow affair, and Wagner certainly showed no interest in it: see p. 19.

39. These are presumably the same victims on whose behalf was held the benefit concert of January 15, conducted by Mancinelli, on which see pp. 53–54, 85–87, 154, and 337, n. 11. The devastating floods referred to were presumably those that threatened the Wagners' passage to Venice the previous September.

40. Norlenghi adds the explanatory footnote: "A most lovely stroll along the Lagoon, where Venetians go by tradition on the first day of Quaresima [Lent]."

41. See pp. 125–26.

42. Cosima mentions Frontali by name only once in her diaries, in connection with rehearsals for the birthday concert in December. As mentioned (pp. 162–63), he could have been the unnamed violinist she and Wagner encountered at Lavena on November 19 (see n. 15 above), but that must remain supposition. Cosima says nothing about Wagner going out on Sunday February 11. She does state that he went out on the afternoon of Monday the twelfth with daughter Eva, and that he bought her some chocolate. That treat was regularly taken at Lavena's, which is just a few yards from the entrance to the Merceria, so the encounter with Frontali that Norlenghi reports then could possibly have happened, and have been left unmentioned by Wagner himself or unnoticed by Cosima. One assumes that Norlenghi had his information on these two anecdotes directly from Frontali himself. But Norlenghi's image of Wagner brooding morbidly over the lagoon on the trip home is pure fantasy. Cosima describes him as in a cheerful mood. Her account of that evening, Wagner's last, conveys an amiable and chatty scene that is not at odds with Norlenghi's picture. But then, how would he know about it?

Frontali played a key role in assembling the orchestra for Wagner's concert, perhaps partly on the basis of prior contacts through Liszt: *Il Conservatorio de Musica Benedetto Marcello*, ed. Verardo (40–41) preserves information about Frontali playing with Liszt in musicales at the Palazzo Malipiero, on the invitation of Daniela von Bülow and Ada Pinelli. It also reproduces (43) two of a set of drawings of scenes from the *Ring*, inscribed in Italian: "Dono della famiglia Wagner Venezia 1883." Not Wagner himself, be it noted, but his family, and most likely given after the composer's death—not only as a token of appreciation for his service as a pallbearer but perhaps even by way of consolation for his exclusion from the death scene: see pp. 134, 135, 137, 165. See also figure 26.

43. Norlenghi's own footnote (*): "A little boat that specifically serves youngsters to train themselves at the oar."

44. All this is discussed in addendum 10. For the earlier claim of Luigi and the dying Wagner, see pp. 149–50.

45. This is, I believe, the only report that Wagner was given morphine.

46. Though it is surely coincidental, it is interesting to note the parallel of Norlenghi's use of the Tristan/Isolde analogy with Ludwig von Bürkel's, in the letter given as our prologue.

47. Casamicciola is located on the northern slope of Monte Epomeo on the island of Ischia, off the Bay of Naples. Its Terme have long made it popular as swimming resort and as health spa famous for its mineral water. Town and resort were stricken in 1883 by a devastating earthquake that claimed some 1,700 lives. Its other claim to fame is that, in a villa nearby, Henrik Ibsen began writing his play *Peer Gynt* in 1867.

48. This reported gesture would seem to be one of the few attentions of any kind that the Wagner family paid to Venice and Italy after Richard's death.

Chapter Nine

1. On this theme, see the admirable survey by Miller, "Wagnerism, Wagnerians, and Italian Identity," 167–97. Her notes are rich in bibliography, but among background works that might be mentioned is Gaetano Mariani, *Storia della scapigliatura* (Rome, 1967).

2. On Giovannina Lucca, see pp. 29 and 330, n. 12; the difficulties she was to give Wagner's apostle, Angelo Neumann, will be sketched in chapter 10.

3. The *Lohengrin* premiere in Bologna, and Italian reactions to it, is treated at length by Panizzardi, *Wagner in Italia*, vol. 2, 7–61. See also Jung, *Rezeption* (see below, n. 5), 15–30.

4. Panizzardi, vol. 2, 35–40, gives Boïto's translation of Wagner's letter. For an English rendering, see the translation by William A. Ellis, *Richard Wagner's Prose Works*, vol. 5: *Actors and Singers* (London: Kegan Paul, Trench, Trübner & Co., 1896), 285–88.

5. Anna Laura Belina and Bruno Brizi, "Il melodramma e la musica strumentale," in *Storia della cultura veneta*, ed. G. Arnaldi and M. P. Storchi, vol. 7: *Dall'età napoleonica alle prima guerra mondiale* (Venice, 1986), 429–60: 456, 458. On the Venetian premiere of *Rienzi*, see Panizzardi, *Wagner in Italia*, vol. 2, 217–19.

The background is, of course, documented massively in Jung's *Rezeption*, with sources and data on each important Wagner premiere in Italian cities. Part 1 only of this study has been translated into Italian as "La fortuna di Wagner in Italia," in *Wagner in Italia*, ed. Rostirolla, 57–225; but its later sections (not included in the Italian version) are rich in discussions of nineteenth-century Italian musical life and the impact thereon of Wagner's opera—see especially the section "Das Problem des Wagnerismus," 429–47 (including discussion of "Die Gruppe der 'wagneriani'"). Conversely, see the other essays in Rostirolla's anthology (several of which were originally presented at a colloquium in 1969 and then published in 1972), especially Friedrich Lippmann's "Wagner e l'Italia," 247–86 (originally in German), and Agostino Zino's "Rassegna della critica wagneriana in Italia," 317–407. Also, Gualerzi and Roscioni, *Wagner in Italia, 1871–1971*, containing the detailed statistics for the earliest Italian productions. For an older discussion, there is the section "Antiwagneriani" in Panizzardi, *Wagner in Italia*, vol. 2, 153–72, on hostile critics. Meanwhile, there are some good comments on the Wagnerian inroad in Julian Budden's pungent chapter, "A Problem of Identity (Italian Opera 1870–90)," 271–75, in his *The Operas of Verdi*, vol. 3: *From Don Carlos to Falstaff* (London: Cassell and New York: Oxford University Press, 1981), 263–92.

6. Alfred Loewenbert, *Annals of Opera, 1597–1940* (Totowa, NJ: Rowman and Littlefield, 1943, 3rd ed., 1978); and Giuseppe Pugliese, "Two Centuries of Music at the Teatro La Fenice," 225, in the lavish *Gran Teatro La Fenice*, written with Giandomenico Romanelli, José Sasportes, and Patrizia Veroli (Cologne: Taschen-Evergreen, 1999), 191–272.

7. The fullest data on this institution is a volume celebrating its centenary, *Il Conservatorio di Musica Benedetto Marcello di Venezia, 1876–1976*, ed. Verardo, espe-

cially its historical chapters (rich in documentation), 15ff, 196ff. See also: Giovanni Distefano and Giannantonio Paladini, *Storia di Venezia, 1797–1977*, vol. 3. *Dalla Monarchia alla Repubblica* (Venice: Supernova-Grafiche Biesse, 1997), 336–37; Giovanni Morelli, "La musica," in *Storia di Venezia: L'ottocento e il novecento*, vol. 3: *Il novecento*, ed. Mario Isenghi (Rome: Enciclopedia Italiana, 2002), 2138ff.

8. See Barker, "Forgotten Early Champion," 3–7; also Morelli, "La musica," 2138; also, Verardo, *Il Conservatorio*, 27, 39.

9. The operatic and general performing picture of Venice as a backwater in the late nineteenth century should be softened by recognition of what was building there, well into the twentieth century. Venice was to emerge as a leading center in the study and revival of earlier music, especially Venetian. There were composers such as Ermanno Wolf-Ferrari (1876–1948) and especially Gian Francesco Malipiero (1882–1973) who were interested in reviving old forms, styles, and theatrical idioms of earlier Venetian days in their own musical works. And it was Malipiero himself—descendant of one of Venice's great noble families—who spearheaded the reassessment of Monteverdi's music by editing the first comprehensive modern edition of that great composer's works (published 1926–42). The revival of seventeenth- and eighteenth-century music led to the rediscovery of Vivaldi and other Venetians of his time. The generations that came of age in the Veneto after Malipiero included such modernists as Luigi Dallapiccola and, later, Giuseppe Sinopoli, who helped turn twentieth-century Venice into an important center for European avant-gardism, very much in the mainstream of musical internationalism, while making it also a point of contact with the cultural life of Eastern Europe after World War II—a long way from the cultural provincialism of a century before!

10. On this specific subject there is now: Robert C. Davis and Garry R. Marvin, *Venice, the Tourist Maze: A Cultural Critique of the World's Most Touristed City* (Berkeley: University of California Press, 2004). But see also the references given in n. 1 to chapter 4, especially the books by Plant, *Venice, Fragile City*; Norwich, *Paradise of Cities*; and Hibbert, *Venice*, 255–311.

11. Giorgio Pullini, "Il teatro fra scena e società," in Arnaldi-Storchi *Storia della cultura veneta*, vol. 6, 237–82: 247, suggests that what the Venetian public had been hearing, not only of Wagner but of late Verdi, was perceived as boring by significant elements of that public, conditioning them for the eventual emergence in the 1890s of the new idiom of verismo opera as a revitalized reassertion of Italian expression. Again, see the chapter in Budden's book, cited above in n. 5.

Chapter Ten

1. Not long before his death, Neumann produced his devout but eminently reasonable memoirs, titled *Erinnerungen an Richard Wagner*, and translated almost immediately into English by Edith Livermore as *Personal Recollections of Wagner*. Quotations made hereafter are based on the Livermore translation. The most concise discussion of Neumann's dealings with Wagner may be found in Milton E. Brener's *Richard Wagner and the Jews*: for their earliest contacts, 204–8. For a good sketch of the impresario's career of Wagner production, see the section "On the Road with Angelo Neumann," in Carnegy, *Wagner and the Art of the Theatre*, 123–30.

The photo portrait of Neumann, offered as our figure 37, includes a handwritten inscription to its recipient in April 1883. This inscription quotes four lines of

German poetry. I am indebted to Dr. Gudrun Föttinger of the Richard-Wagner-Museum, Bayreuth, for identifying their source as from the *Spätherbstblätter* of Emanuel von Giebel (1825–84). This *Sprüche 12* reads: "Wer da fährt nach grossen Ziel,/Lern' am Steuer ruhig sitzen,/unbekümmert, ob am Kiel/Lob und Tadel hoch auf spritzen!". Dr. Föttinger translates this as "If you are navigating towards an ambitious aim, you should learn to sit calmly and insouciantly at the rudder and not mind either praise or reproof splashing high on the keel."

2. In his memoirs, Neumann stated the date of their reconciliation as June 21, 1881, which Cosima's diary gives as Monday, June 20: she, of course, portrays the matter (May 29: "this Israelite affair") as Neumann seeking her husband's forgiveness, whereas Neumann understood it as Wagner's conciliating him.

On a very different picture of Wagner's behavior at the end of the Berlin *Ring* performances, see p. 366, n. 9. Generally on the Berlin *Ring* and the falling out of the two men, see Brener, *Wagner and the Jews*, 206–8, 257–63; also, Rose, *Wagner: Race and Revolution*, 128–34.

3. Neumann, *Erinnerungen*, 130–32; *Recollections*, 125–26; translation heavily revised, partly in accord with that in Curt von Westernhagen's *Wagner*, trans. Whittall, 567.

4. Supplementing Neumann's own account of the negotiations is Brener, *Wagner and the Jews*, 262–66.

An article printed in *La Gazzetta di Venezia* on April 10, 1883, just as the company's *Ring* production was about to be mounted in Venice, contains an interesting background account of the Neumann troupe's history for the benefit of local readers. One of its paragraphs contains some vivid suggestions, whatever their accuracy, of troubles at an early stage: "Sig. Angelo Neumann, who is director of the Bremen theater, conceived the idea of putting together and of bringing to balanced perfection an artistic company, complete in every part, bearing the name of *Teatro Riccardo Wagner*, in order to undertake with it an artistic pilgrimage. It was a colossal labor, and there came even a moment in which sig. Neumann decided to dissolve it, finding the burden beyond his powers. The artists and all the personnel implored him to pull back from that decision, and they made so much of it that sig. Neumann yielded to their pleas and the so-named Wagner Theater remained united."

5. Letter of March 9, 1882, in Strobel, ed., *König Ludwig II. und Richard Wagner*, vol. 3, 236.

6. Cf. Gutman, *Richard Wagner*, 414–15. See addendum 11.

7. Neumann, *Erinnerungen*, 271–73; *Recollections*, 259–61.

8. How seriously Neumann took the idea of a venture in the United States is not clear. But the idea certainly had a long if spotty history in Wagner's thinking. See addendum 12.

9. Neumann, *Erinnerungen*, 274; *Recollections*, 262. In contrast to Neumann's glowing account, we may note a report published in *LGdV* on January 30, 1883—no doubt with sensitivity to the idea of a *Ring* production in the Lagoon City—of reactions to the opening night of the tetralogy in Brussels: "The audience in the theater was crowded, and divided into three camps very clearly differentiated among them: the fanatics, the moderates, and the ignorant [*profani*]."

"The Wagnerians naturally received the opera with enthusiastic acclamations, with frantic ovations; the rowdy listened to the music with curiosity and resignation."

The outcome of *Rheingold*, as judged by the real audience, was rather cold.

10. Neumann, *Erinnerungen*, 295; *Recollections*, 279, Livermore's translation adjusted.

11. Neumann, *Erinnerungen*, 281–83; *Recollections*, 268–69 (each with a facsimile of the letter). Oberdan[k] was the Italian patriot and would-be assassin recently (on December 20, 1882) executed by the Austrians: see above, p. 336, n. 9.

12. Neumann, as in n. 10 above.

13. There is still frequent misunderstanding about the question of relating Neumann's *Ring* production at the Fenice to Wagner's residence in Venice and death there. For example, in the lavish volume *Gran Teatro La Fenice*, the usually knowing Giuseppe Pugliese could write (215): ". . . although Richard Wagner had died at the Palazzo Vendramin Calergi in Venice on 13 February 1883, it was too late at that point to cancel the Italian *tournée* of the Bayreuth Company [*sic*] (which had been organized by Angelo Neumann)."

14. Perl, 184–85/55.

Chapter Eleven

1. Neumann, *Erinnerungen*, 251–52; *Recollections*, 243; Livermore's translation revised.

2. Eugenio Pirani (1852–1939) was an eminent pianist and composer with an international career. In the early 1880s he appeared in a concert series in Heidelberg with the famous violinist Eugène Ysaÿe; in 1905 he took up residence for a while in New York City where he directed his own music school; he died in Berlin.

3. *Erinnerungen*, 315–16; *Recollections*, 296–97; Livermore's translation being a little free but not substantively objectionable.

4. Girolamo Alessandro Biagi (1819–97) had a varied career as an activist in the Risorgimento movement, as an opera composer, as a biographer (Rossini), and as a critic for Florence's *Nazione* and the *Nuova Antologia*; he was also author of a musical dictionary.

5. The Venetian-born writer and musician Angelo Zanardini (1820–98) originally studied law in Padua and served in the insurrectionist Manin government (1848–49). He turned to composing and produced several operas: one, *Amleto*, after Shakespeare, was performed in Venice in 1854. He settled in Milan where he composed other operas—one to a libretto by Enrico Panzacchi: see below n. 7. As a translator of librettos, he worked for both the Ricordi and Lucca firms. He became the most active translator into Italian of Wagner's librettos: on these see Jung, *Rezeption*, 405–9.

6. On this Christian interpretation by "Toni," see its reiteration on pp. 224; 369, n. 12.

7. Enrico Panzacchi (1840–1904), a poet, librettist, and professor of aesthetics at Bologna's Accademia di Belle Arti, was a burgeoning Wagnerite at this time; he had been one of the important Italian critics to report on the Bayreuth premiere of the *Ring*. In 1883 he made a Wagner presentation with Mancinelli (March 14), and he delivered a memorial oration for Wagner (March 16) in Bologna; later that year he published an important collection, *Riccardo Wagner. Ricordi e studi* (Bologna: Zanichelli). A selection of essays from that volume is included by Dario della Porta, *Il fenomeno Wagner* (Turin: Fògola Editore, 1983), 8–28. See also Panizzardi, *Wagner in Italia*, vol. 2, 131–36.

8. Rocco Pagliara (1857–1914) was a poet and lyricist—Tosti in particular made songs of his poems. He served as critic for *Il Mattino* in Naples, and he succeeded Florimo as the music librarian there.

9. This article includes a report of Wagner's reaction to Neumann's *Ring* production in Berlin, a report quite at odds with our documented accounts of that unhappy episode, as discussed above. Just where the Italian writer acquired his material is not clear, but his publication of it by *LGdV* made a promotional point to the Venetian readers, while allowing some conclusions of his own, all worth quoting: "Riccardo Wagner has supported in every fashion the most fervent undertaking of sig. Neumann, and certain testimony of it are the following words of his, offered on the final evening which concluded the cycle of performances at Berlin's Victoria Theater:

'If I were to let this moment pass in silence I would be the most ungrateful of men. Therefore, to you, my friends (*addressing the artists*), and to you, my protectors (*addressing the audience*), my most lively thanks for the proofs of sympathy and of lively interest that you have displayed to my work. At the time I conceived it and could bring it to completion, certainly I could not imagine the public of a great city that permeates its own lives with art, that is, follows its own taste and that wants to be entertained. Accordingly, I am so very much amazed at how felicitous a success is reported among you.

'From the outset, this work was intended only for a restricted circle of friends and followers, and therefore I initiated the project of Bayreuth. Now I recognize that I had been mistaken.

'Back in 1876 I observed with amazement that this musical work, that stood so far apart from others, had *been able to reach* so many and such warm patrons. At the time this most courageous man (*indicating sig. Neumann*) gave me notice of his proposal of wishing to give the Tetralogy at Berlin after Bayreuth, I could not deny him my assistance, and the success apparently proves that he had deserved it. And what has made me so greatly amazed is that artists who were not conditioned to my idiom were able to identify themselves with it so easily. Therefore I address my thanks to them, and also to you in particular, dear Neumann, that with so much courage you have brought to fulfillment an opera so difficult and risky. Likewise to you, my young friend Seidl, my lively thanks for having directed my opera so bravely and with so much enthusiasm.

'The proven profits taken so far by this company are very considerable, but likewise enormous are their expenses, so that in order to sing of his victory sig. Neumann needs to await the definitive closing of the box office.

'We predict, however, that the outcome matches his hopes. But we are firmly of the opinion that a traveling company of our own, precisely assembled, wisely directed, and cleverly administrated, with a repertoire of three or four Italian operas, would do much better business in Germany than what Wagner's Tetralogy has done in Germany itself.

'And with that we by no means intend to fail in the respect due to the memory of the illustrious German musician, but only to reaffirm a truth, well known by all and everywhere.'" Here, as in so many instances, our Venetian writers cannot escape nervous comparisons of Italian operatic values with German ones".

10. Neumann, *Erinnerungen*, 296–97; *Recollections*, 280–82, the Livermore translation slightly modified.

11. *Erinnerungen*, 299; *Recollections*, 283, which is slightly free. Curiously, while the Venetian critics later had some nasty things to say about Unger, they ignored his poor singing in their immediate reactions.

12. *Erinnerungen*, 300–301; *Recollections*, 284.

13. *E'una pensiero pietoso, che onera quegli egregi artisti.*

14. *Erinnerungen*, 301–2; *Recollections*, 284–85. For an evocative modern account, see Norwich, *Paradise of Cities*, 171–72.

15. *Erinnerungen*, 302; *Recollections*, 285–86, Livermore's translation slightly modified.

16. By this time, Mancinelli had developed considerable associations both with Wagner's music and with Wagner himself: see pp. 53–54; 330–31, n. 13; 337, n. 11. Accordingly, this episode seems strange at first. But Mancinelli's difficulties in preparing the Neumann concert may have arisen from working with unfamiliar musicians—singers and orchestra players used to Seidl and not willing to adapt to another maestro. In addition, Mancinelli was accustomed to conducting Wagner's operas in Italian translation, and he may have had problems working with German singers in their own language.

17. *Erinnerungen*, 305; *Recollections*, 288, slightly adapted.

18. *Erinnerungen*, 316–17; *Recollections*, 297–98—the Livermore translation is somewhat compressed, and is modified here.

19. *Erinnerungen*, 320; *Recollections*, 301.

20. *Erinnerungen*, 321; *Recollections*, 301–2.

21. *Erinnerungen*, 321–22; *Recollections*, 302.

22. *Erinnerungen*, 339–41; *Recollections*, 316–18.

Chapter Twelve

1. Neumann, *Erinnerungen*, 296; *Recollections*, 280, Livermore's translation slightly adapted.

2. A simple culling of such general reactions is provided by Jung, *Rezeption*, 171–80, or "La fortuna," 192–200. D'Arcais was, however, of particular importance in his time. Note Panizzardi's little essay, "Il wagnerismo di Francesco d'Arcais," in *Wagner in Italia*, vol. 2, 229–41.

3. For a very cursory summary, Panizzardi, *Wagner in Italia*, vol. 2, 161.

4. On Francesco Florimo, see p. 331, n. 14. As a passionate musical nationalist, devoted to Italian operatic traditions in general, Florimo saw Rossini as the transitional figure away from earlier Neapolitan dominance, with Bellini as the consolidating spirit whose work was completed by Donizetti and Verdi. Initially an outspoken opponent of Wagner's influence in Italy Florimo was, as has been seen above, drawn by personal contact with the German master to soften his original hostility.

5. See pp. 194–95.

6. Pierre Terrail de Bayard (c. 1473–1524) was a famous French soldier and commander who served valiantly in the Italian wars of Kings Charles VIII, Louis XII, and Francis I. He was particularly celebrated for his knightly spirit and nobility, winning the sobriquet of "the fearless and blameless knight (*Chevalier sans peur et sans reproche*)". Such was his reputation that the new King Francis I, having won his first victory at Marignano (1515) had himself dubbed a knight on the battlefield at the

hands of none other than Bayard. His name has thus become a byword for knightly bravery and grace.

7. Teresa Stolz (1834–1902) was Bohemian by birth and trained initially in Prague, then in Trieste. Her career was an international one, but was particularly focused on Italy, where she early became identified with Verdi roles. Her relationship with that composer was particularly close, if not also controversial; but he cast her as lead soprano in the Italian premieres of *Don Carlo* and *Aïda* as well as in the premiere of his *Requiem*. Retiring early (1877), she left behind a high reputation and vivid memories as a singer of power, deep feeling, but highly disciplined technique, regarded also as the quintessential Verdi dramatic soprano.

8. The concern by Italian critics of Wagner with the issue of "melody" as Italians understood it, and the supposed lack of melody in Wagner's music, was a major one, widely advanced: see Jung, *Rezeption*, 419–28.

9. Cf. Jung, 424, and also 440, for partial quotations.

10. The three composers to whom our critic refers had certainly shown significant awareness of Wagner and his techniques, though their assimilations of them had been variously limited. Boïto's *Mefistofele*, only sparingly influenced by Wagner, was first given in Milan in 1868 and then in its revised version in Bologna in 1875 (see below, n. 18). Amilcare Ponchielli (1834–86) achieved his true success with *La gioconda* in Milan in 1876. As for Giuseppe Verdi (1812–1901), it is worth recalling that, seemingly retired after his *Aïda* (1871), he was about to launch into the glorious epilogue to his career with his last two operas. Indeed, in the midst of preparations of Neumann's *Ring* in Venice, *LV* published, on March 27, 1883, a brief notice reporting that Verdi was at work on a new opera titled *Jago*. Shortly after, on April 1, it returned to the matter, this time with the projected opera's final title, *Otello*, a work to be premiered at La Scala in February 1887.

Meanwhile, Alfredo Catalani (1854–93), important precursor of the subsequent Italian verismo school of opera, was the most significant and substantial "Wagnerizer" among Italian composers of the moment. His third opera, *Dejanice* (with a libretto by Zanardini) had just received its premiere in Milan a month earlier (March 17, 1883), to be followed soon by his last two, *Edmea* (1886) and *La Wally* (1892). Only his tragically premature death would prevent him from showing what he might have done in achieving "the wedding of the schools."

Still to enter the scene were prime verismo exponents: Ruggiero Leoncavallo (1860–1941), with his first triumph, *I Pagliacci* (1892); one of Ponchielli's students, Pietro Mascagni (1863–1945), his breakthrough coming with *La cavalleria rusticana* (1890); and Umberto Giordano (1867–1948), reaching his first peak with his *Andrea Chenier* (1896). Wagnerian influence was moderately evident in the case of Mascagni, more so, perhaps, for Leoncavallo, and quite a bit with Giordano.

But the most significant fulfillment of the "wedding of schools" prophesy was, of course, that other Ponchielli disciple, Giacomo Puccini (1858–1924). His first opera, *Le villi*, had its first performance in Milan the year after Neumann's *Ring* in Venice, and the second, *Edgar*, followed in 1889; only with *Manon Lescaut* (1893), ten years after our Venetian critic's prediction, did Puccini enter into full maturity; *La Bohème* came three years after that, and Puccini was on his way to bringing the main line of Italian opera to its final climax. What Puccini achieved, of course, was to assimilate the Wagnerian orchestral palette and to master the reduction of set pieces into a continuing dramatic flow, without sacrificing the Italian love for rich lyricism and vocal display.

The foregoing sketch should make clear that the point at which the Neumann company brought the *Ring* to Venice was indeed a precariously transitional period in Italian operatic history. For discussions of Wagner's stylistic impact on Italian composers of the age, see Jung, *Rezeption*, 327–42 (on Verdi), 364–85 (including Boïto, Catalani, and Puccini).

11. It is interesting to note that the eminent Viennese critic, Eduard Hanslick (see n. 16 below), complained that the weakness of much of the *Ring* as drama is that it was mainly about gods and the like, instead of real human beings.

12. Again looking to Hanslick for comparison, it is curious that Vienna's critic found little or nothing of Christianity in Wagner's treatment at least of the *Nibelungenlied* material the composer used (as against the earlier Norse writings)—a striking contrast with the point made by "Toni" here, and, earlier, in his essay published by *LV* on April 9.

13. From our vantage point, it would seem that the German/Italian polarization would best have been represented by a Wagner/Verdi dichotomy. The choice instead of Rossini to stand for Italian style is an interesting commentary on how potent a national symbol that composer had become. (It also suggests that, for Italians brought up in the world of bel canto, the mature works of Verdi were still regarded as on the "modern" side and not yet fully digested.) The point is given some meaning by noting a report published by *LGdV* on November 1, 1882 (not long after Wagner had arrived in Venice for his final stay). Under the heading of *Cronaca franco-latina*, the Venetian journal passed on a report from a Parisian source: "In a concert at Marseilles, a piece by Wagner was played, and some people hissed. The majority applauded, and there was the cry: 'There is no more any fatherland, there are no more frontiers, long live Wagner!'—A little later, the orchestra played the overture to Rossini's *Cenerentola*. Then everybody hissed. The fatherland was rediscovered, and the frontiers were restored—southward."

14. See p. 365, n. 2.

15. Wolzogen's pamphlet was titled *Thematischer Leitfaden durch die Musik von R. Wagners Festspiel "Der Ring des Nibelungen"* (Leipzig, 1876). It was published in an English translation in 1882, just the year before Wagner's death and the Neumann tour in Italy. Wolzogen published a series of intensive studies on "Die Motive in Wagners 'Götterdämmerung'" in three very large articles in the *Musikalisches Wochenblatt* 8–10 (1877–79), and he also issued subsequent guides to two of Wagner's other operas: *Tristan und Isolde* in 1880 and *Parsifal* in 1882. By 1883, there had also been expositions of this subject in Italian, notably one by S. Farina in the issue of *Gazzetta Musicale di Milano* for April 1872.

The subject of recurrent motives in opera, which extends to other composers beyond Wagner, is complicated and too extensive for pursuit here. There are good articles on the concept, under the word "Leitmotif," by Arnold Whittall in *The New Grove Dictionary of Opera*, ed. Stanley Sadie (London and New York: Macmillan/Grove, 1992), vol. 2, 1137–41, and by Thomas S. Grey in *The Wagner Compendium: A Guide to Wagner's Life and Music*, ed. Barry Millington (London and New York: Thames and Hudson/Schirmer, 1992), 234–35. On their use in the tetralogy, perhaps the best treatment is still to be found in Robert Donnington's *Wagner's "Ring" and Its Symbols: The Music and the Myth* (London: Faber, 1963; 3rd ed., 1974). For the most recent reflections on the technique, see Carolyn Abbate, *Unsung Voices: Opera and Musical Narrative in the 19th Century* (Princeton: Princeton University Press, 1991); see also her chapter, "Opera as Symphony, a Wagnerian Myth," in the valuable collection *Analyzing Opera: Verdi and Wagner*, ed. Abbate and Roger Parker (Berkeley: University of California Press, 1989), 92–124.

16. Available in English in Henry Pleasant's collection and translation of the critic's reviews, *Vienna's Golden Years of Music, 1850–1900* (New York: Simon & Schuster, 1950), 139–74; second edition as *Eduard Hanslick: Music Criticisms, 1846–99* (Baltimore, MD: Penguin Books, 1963), 129–56. Among other points of comparison, be it noted that Hanslick had studied Wolzogen's treatise and was quite ready to discuss Wagner's use of leitmotifs.

17. See p. 154. Page citations here, as above, are made directly to the original edition.

18. This is, of course, the *Grosser Festmarsch* or *American Centennial March*, the potboiler that Wagner ground out at the beginning of 1876 purely to earn money, much needed toward the expenses of the first *Ring*, as already mentioned (see n. 14 to chapter 4). Wagner demanded, and was granted, a fee of $5,000, an extraordinary sum for the time. Norlenghi seems to have misunderstood its purpose. It was commissioned not for any labor festival, but by the American Centennial Committee, for the opening of a world's fair that was to celebrate the hundredth anniversary of American independence. It was first performed on May 10, 1876, in Philadelphia. To compose it, Wagner interrupted work on the composition of *Parsifal*, and he cordially hated the task. Cosima reports (February 16, 1876) that he showed her a sketch for a chorus of the Flower Maidens that was at the same time "an attempt to be American." Nevertheless, he seems to have been pleased with the results, for he spoke of it intermittently thereafter, he included it in performances, and he even played it a few times himself on the piano, or in duet with Rubenstein.

19. Boïto's *Mefistofele*, in its original form, was given a tumultuously hostile reception at its premiere at La Scala on March 5, 1868. In a drastically shortened and revised form, it was presented in several other cities (including Venice) and was then well received in Milan in 1881.

20. As has been seen (pp. 204–206), the Neumann company was unable to present its *Ring* production in Milan, during its brief performing stop there.

21. The pianist was, of course, Pirani: see p. 365, n. 2.

22. Norlenghi's efforts did not end with his little book on Wagner. For his second venture on Wagner commentary, see addendum 15.

Chapter Thirteen

1. There were, to be sure, Italian composers who died in Venice and were even buried there. There was the native Venetian Giovanni Gabrieli (1612), buried in the church of San Stephano. Born in Cremona and first employed in Mantua, the great Claudio Monteverdi was long employed and resident in Venice where he died (1643), to be buried in the church of the Frari. Burano-born Baldassare Galuppi (1785) was buried in San Vitale (location now lost). Domenico Cimarosa (d. 1801) was a Neapolitan; of two native Venetians, Ermanno Wolf-Ferrari (1948) was buried in the San Michele Cemetery, while Gian Francesco Malipiero (1973) died and was buried outside Venice, in Treviso. Almost unique as a non-Italian composer is Igor Stravinsky: true, he died in New York (1971), but his body was quickly conveyed to

Venice where he was buried, amid much-publicized ceremony, in the San Michele Cemetery—in the Orthodox section and, significantly, just down the lane from his old friend and patron, Sergei Diaghilev.

2. For an interesting survey of such memorials, see Aldo Andreolo and Elisabetta Borsetti, *Venezia recorda* (Venice: Le Altane, 1999), trans. Michael Gluckstein as *Venice Remembers: The Faces, Lives and Works of the Venetians and Non-Venetians Whom the City has Wished to Commemorate in Marble* (Venice: Le Altane, 2000).

3. See Miller, "Wagnerism, Wagnerians, and Italian Identity," 178–81.

4. The important affirmation of such a connection was made by the French writer Maurice Barrès in an essay, *La Mort de Venise* published in 1903. See Plant, *Venice, Fragile City*, 196, 198. But the connection had already been strongly shaped, to his own purposes, by Gabriele D'Annunzio, through his notorious novel *Il fuoco* (1900).

For extended studies on this theme, see: Werner Vortriede, "Richard Wagners Tod in Venedig," *Euphorion* 19 (1955), 334–59; Hellmuth Petriconi, "La Mort de Venise und Der Tod in Venedig," in his collection *Das Reich des Untergangs: Bermerkungen über ein mythologisches Thema* (Hamburg: Hoffmann und Campe, 1958), 67–95; Erwin Koppen's chapter, "Tödliches Venedig," in his *Dekadenter Wagnerismus: Studien zur europäischen Literatur des Fin de Siècle* (Berlin: Walter de Gruyter, 1973), 214–396; Giandomenico Romanelli, "Venezia nell'Ottocento: Ritorno alla vita e nascita del mito della morte," in *Storia di cultura veneta*, Vol. 6: *Dall'età napoleonica alla Prima Guerra Mondiale*, ed. Girolamo Arnaldi and Manlio Pastore (Vicenza: Neri Pozza, 1986), 749–66; Christiane Schenk, *Venedig im Spiegel der Décadance-Literatur des Fin de Siècle* (Frankfurt: Peter Lang, 1987).

5. The following presentations depends essentially upon accounts in the Venetian newspapers. The weaknesses of that dependence are in the limits of time and accessibility. Time has not allowed a year-by-year scouring, though my survey has been very extensive. Above all, many volumes for individual or sequential years have not been available for consultation. I particularly regret that I could not consult either journal for the year 1884.

6. Jung, *Rezeption*, 131–32, supplemented by Gualierzi and Roscioni, *Wagner in Italia (1871–1971)*.

The broader scope of the latter study sets forth in rich detail the data on the first century of the composer's operas in Italy. Simply in the picture it gives for Venice (and, unless stipulated otherwise, at La Fenice) during that time period is illuminating. Among other things, it reminds us anew that Venice and Italy shared the practice, common to most European countries until after World War II, of presenting operas in the local audience's language rather than the original tongue. The statistics make clear that Venice shared the Italian preference by far for *Lohengrin*. It became a comparative staple as an offering consistently in Italian (1861, 1889, 1898, 1906, 1911, 1912, 1933, 1944, 1967 in the Fenice; 1912 in the Teatro Rossini; 1920, 1923, 1924, and 1938 in the Teatro Malibran); Venice would not have the opera in the original German until well after 1972. As against fourteen *Lohengrins*, *Tristan* ran a poor second with only nine offerings, four of them in Italian (1909, 1922, 1940, 1947 [with Maria Callas]) but then five in German (1942, 1953, 1958, 1966, 1971), mostly with visiting companies. *Die Meistersinger* was given a sketchier round of five productions, mainly in Italian (1899, 1938, 1947, 1963) but also in German (1954). *Tannhäuser* fared no better, with four Italian productions (1887, 1900, 1914, 1925) and one in German (1969).

After Neumann's 1883 production, the four *Ring* operas returned in the reiterated German-language cycles at the Fenice in 1957 and 1968 by other visiting German companies. Of individual productions of the four in Venice, meanwhile, *Die Walküre* led with five, all in Italian (1899, 1909, 1920, 1939, 1949 [with Callas]), followed by *Siegfried* with three in Italian (1904, 1933, 1941) and one other in German (1963). *Götterdämmerung* had only two independent offerings, one in Italian (1933) and one in German (1953); while *Das Rheingold* was accorded but a single separate one (1912), in Italian. After its Italian introduction in 1914, *Parsifal* returned only in its first German production in Italy (1949), reappearing thus twice again (1963, 1970). As mentioned, *Der fliegende Holländer* reached Venice only in 1961. *Rienzi*, on the other hand, which the Fenice introduced to Italy in 1874, did not appear again on the Venetian stage, at least not before 1972.

It should be stressed, of course, that these figures apply only to the 1871–1971 century, and that productions thereafter would modify the larger picture of Venetian offerings. Nevertheless, that century's statistics alone suggest that Venice was not totally out of step with Wagner tastes in Italy in general (and even, in some ways, around Europe outside Germany). Houses larger than La Fenice—in such cities as Milan, Rome, and Bologna, for example—had the audiences and the facilities to present more Wagner operas. For its size and situation, Venice did comparatively well with the Wagner repertoire, even if it never became a notable center of Wagnerian music in Italy over the decades.

7. His career is treated more fully in Barker, "Forgotten Early Champion." It might be noted that his surname is the word for a musicial instrument once common in Neapolitan and south-Italian popular and folk music, a kind of simplified lute or theorbo. It was known as both the *calascione* and the *colascione*, or the *tiorba a taccone* ("heel-theorbo"), or even *colascione turchesco*. It bears some similarity to the Turkish *saz*, and, like the last-mentioned, it had three double-strings, on a long and straight neck, with a drop-shaped soundbox reminiscent of a mandolin. It apparently entered Neapolitan musical life by the early sixteenth century, either from Levantine contacts or from Moorish North Africa. The calascione was favored over the Arab-derived lute (specifically by the anti-Arab Spanish rulers) especially for accompanying singers in the popular *villanesche*. Thus, to some informed Italian ears or witty Neapolitan tongues, our bandmaster's name might be roughly equivalent to "Jacob Mandolin" or "Jake Ukulele."

8. See pp. 82–84, also Barker "Forgotten Early Champion," 9–11.

9. These two events were reviewed in detail by *LGdV* on the following day. The journal's writer made the point, among others, that Calascione's band was "among the foremost in Italy" and that the event "was a new confirmation of the merit of Calascione as a conductor." On the day after that, Sunday, February 15, the same journal used the occasion of the Wagner commemorations to reproduce—from the report on February 20, 1883, by its rival, *La Venezia*—of the letter that Dr. Keppler has written on behalf of Cosima Wagner to Angelo Tessarin, "il nostro concittadino," one of Wagner's earliest champions in Italy. (See p. 101.)

10. *LGdV*'s reviewer, on the following day, not only praised the performers but took occasion to recall Henry Perl's book, expressing hope for an Italian translation to appear.

11. *Il Gazzettino*, October 29, 1907.

12. See Kahan, *Music's Modern Muse*.

13. *LGdV*, January 12, 1902.

14. That plaque, in typical dedicatory style, reads "To Riccardo Wagner, died within these walls, 13 February 1883, Venice" (*A/Riccardo Wagner/Morto fra queste mura/Il XIII Febbraio MDCCCLXXXIII/Venezia*). See figure 17.

15. *LGdV*, February 14, 1902; Kahan, *Music's Modern Muse*, 125–26.

16. *LGdV*, February 14, 1903, treating the concert as essentially a society event, with particular attention devoted to the distinguished socialites in attendance.

17. Letters of September 3, and 5. See pp. 7–8. The German texts of these letters had just been published for the first time in Berlin, in 1904.

18. See pp. 36–37, and figure 11.

19. De Pury was Swiss, one of the local cultural circle whose company Wagner enjoyed at Posillipo that summer. Wagner sat for the painting on July 11, 1880, as Cosima reports in her diary. See p. 31 and figure 9.

20. *IG*, October 30, 1907. The *Lohengrin* episode occurred on November 5, 1882, and led to a personal meeting between Wagner and Calascione at the Vendramin: see pp. 47, 83–84, 109–10, 151. Wagner's request that the band play the Rossini overture was made earlier, on April 21, 1882, and the request was granted immediately, not two days later: see pp. 40; 81–82; 146; 355, n. 11. For a review of the sources, see Barker, "Forgotten Early Champion," 9–13.

21. Like Calascione, Carmelo Preite was not a native Venetian but a southerner, and had come up through the military. He was born on February 14, 1866, in Presiece (Lecce district), and trained in Naples. By 1884, he was director of a regimental band in Bergamo, until his selection as Calascione's successor in 1908. He was an excellent musician who emulated his predecessor's efforts to make the Venice band the finest in Italy. He was also a composer, of wider range than Calascione: he produced not only numerous arrangements for band but also original works, as well for orchestra, plus vocal and chamber music. He retired from his post with Venice's Banda Cittadina in March 1928, after twenty years of service, and moved to Milan. He remained active, however, and in 1936 he published an important treatise, *Istrumentazione per banda* (Milan: Hoepli). He died in Milan on March 30, 1958.

That Giuseppe Marasco did not automatically succeed Calascione may suggest that his role with the band had not been intended to be continuing. From 1883 to 1930, Marasco was the much-admired teacher of clarinet on the Liceo's faculty, producing generations of finely trained players of that instrument; he presumably found his identity in teaching (and some composing) rather than in a permanent position with the Banda Cittadina.

22. See pp. 295–96.

23. See pp. 309–10.

24. Schaper (1869–1956) was a Berlin sculptor famous in Germany for portraits of Goethe and of members of the German Imperial family.

25. Transcripts of both speeches are given by *LGdV*, whereas *IG*, quoting only the end of Thiem's address, summarizes the rest, while quoting fully Chiggiato's reply. Without any comment to the contrary, it is assumed that Thiem's discourse was given in Italian.

26. Both newspapers give virtually the same summary of the lecture.

27. Bortotti (1857–1925) was an established sculptor in his day, particularly known for treatment of religious subjects.

28. The most substantial was a long discourse by S. E. Rava, the government's Minister of Public Instruction, on the subject of "Venice and Civilization." It

expanded upon the important cultural role of Venice in the past, but as extended down to the present, and to serve as a bridge to the future. Dwelling on his own efforts to arrange government-financed restoration of Venetian monuments, he concluded: "As always—I might venture the prediction—the most zealous custody of artistic memories and the shared, active will of the Venetians and of all Italians will come together in the city that your wise chronicler has called *golden*. Golden in truth, for the sparkling crown of your palaces, for the silent mystery of your picturesque *lagunes*, for the inexpressible fascination of the serene dawns and the golden sunsets that in any season gave peace to the souls of artists, of scientists, of politicians and of poets, from Alverto [*sic*] Dürer to Riccardo Wagner, from Giorgio Byron to number upon number of souls of dreamers and workers" (*LGdV*, Sunday, April 25, 1909).

29. See figures 43–45. Nature has been adding its respective reflections. The Wagner bust stands open and fully visible. But, when last seen, in March of 2006 (figure 45), the Verdi bust was on the verge of being enveloped by the overly ambitious growth of a large boxwood tree behind it. One hopes that future maintenance will reestablish Verdi's full visibility!

30. The writer went on to use the opportunity to complain about the Commune's failure to rectify the very insufficient and unstable financial situation of the band players. He suggested it was time to consider the establishment of pensions for the players, one of the dreams of the late Calascione (with links to his hopes for expanding the repertoire), something on which all agree. "Politics divide us, and music unites us," he concluded.

31. Ettore Cadorin (1876–1952)—to give his correct name—was the son of the sculptor and engraver Vincenzo Cadorin (1854–1925), who had carved the wooden plaque in the Lavena Café in honor of Wagner's regular patronage there: see pp. 257–58 and figure 41.

Ettore himself had a remarkably diverse career. Born in Venice, he studied for a while in Rome. He then settled in Paris, where he worked through 1915. It was there he fulfilled the 1910 commission for the Wagner sculpture, as well as executing a terracotta statue of Isadora Duncan in the same year. Another work of this period destined for Venice was a bust of Benedetto Marcello, for the Conservatorio of his name. In 1915 Cadorin moved to the United States, to which he devoted the rest of his career. In 1931 he did work for the Capitol building in Washington. Settling in California, he sculpted a famous statue of the great Franciscan missionary, Junipero Serra. He died in Sonoma, California, slightly over a half-century ago.

32. "In questo palazzo/l'ultimo spiro di Riccardo Wagner/odono le anime/perpetuarsi come la marea/che lambe i marmi."

33. That would become: "XIII Febraio MDCCCLXXXIII/In Memoriam/MCMX."

34. This will be discussed in my subsequent study on the fictionalization of Wagner in Venice. For now, see Gino Damerini, *D'Annunzio e Venezia* [1943], rev. Giannantonio Paladini (Venice: Albrizzi, 1992), 84–85; Plant, *Venice: Fragile City*, 206–8.

35. *IG*, on the day after the ceremony, made a more color-conscious description of the location, incorporating again a by-now unstoppable inaccuracy: "The sculpture on the other side of the Canalazzo [from the band and attendants] stood out as white against the redness of the ancient brick, of which was constructed the wall that girdled the garden of that Palazzo Vendramin-Calergi, then of the Duca della Grazie, where Wagner lived, composed [*sic*] his *Tristano et Isotta*, and where he died on February 13, 1883."

36. See figure 42. Cf. Andreolo and Borsetti, *Venice Remembers*, 217–18. As the absence of D'Annunzio's name from the account of the dedication would indicate, the poet was not present himself for the occasion. See the reprinted edition of Gino Damerini, *D'Annunzio e Venezia*, 85.

Chapter Fourteen

1. See Plant, *Venice, Fragile City*, 271–78; Hibbert, *Venice*, 313–17. More generally on Italy in this period, see: Martin Clark, *Modern Italy, 1871–1982)* (London and New York: Longman, 1984), 180–202, which has good bibliographical references; Spencer M. Di Scala, *Italy: From Revolution to Republic, 1700 to the Present* (Boulder, CO: Westview Press, 1995), 193ff.

2. I recall attending an open-air performance of Beethoven's Ninth Symphony, opposite the facade of San Marco itself, in the Piazza crowded with thousands of people—a uniquely thrilling and uplifting experience.

3. It has been a serious handicap, and a deep regret, that the newspaper volumes for 1933 and 1934 have not been available to me.

4. In the published studies of the two dictators, their Venice meeting is usually dealt with cursorily. The fullest general account is by Santi Corvaja, *Mussolini nella tana del lupo*, trans. Robert L. Miller as *Hitler and Mussolini: The Secret Meetings* (New York: Enigma Books, 2001), 31–39. See also: Peter Neville, *Mussolini* (London and New York: Routledge, 2004), 123; Richard J. Bosworth, *Mussolini* (London: Arnold, 2002), 280–81; Richard Lamb, *Mussolini as Diplomat: Il Duce's Italy on the World Stage* (New York: Fromm International, 1999), 104–5; Jasper Ridley, *Mussolini* (New York: St. Martin's Press, 1997), 239–41; Denis Mack Smith, *Mussolini* (New York: Knopf, 1982), 184–85; Ivone Kirkpatrick, *Mussolini: A Study in Power* (Westport, CT: Greenwood Press, 1964), 290–91; Christopher Hibbert, *Benito Mussolini: A Biography* (London: Longman's, 1962), 77–78. See also: John Toland, *Adolf Hitler* (Garden City, NY: Doubleday, 1976), 325–28; William L. Shirer, *The Rise and Fall of the Third Reich: A History of Nazi Germany* (New York: Simon & Schuster, 1960), 217.

5. There is a story, which I have been unable to trace or verify, that during the ride down the Grand Canal Hitler attempted to show off his background as an art student. The story has it that Hitler pointed out one palazzo or monument after another, quite incorrectly, while his hosts cringed, unable to contradict him.

6. On this, the most recent study is Köhler's *Wagners Hitler*, trans. Taylor, 200. For a more balanced perspective, see Bryan Magee, *The Tristan Chord: Wagner and Philosophy* (New York: Holt, 2000), 361–80; more briefly, Ernst Hanisch, "The Political Influence and Appropriation of Wagner," in Müller and Wapnewski, *Wagner Handbook*, trans. Deathridge, 186–201, esp. 198–201.

7. See now Brigitte Hamann, *Winifred Wagner, oder, Hitlers Bayreuth* (Munich: Piper Verlag, 2002), abbreviated English trans., Alan Bence, *Winifred Wagner: A Life at the Heart of Hitler's Bayreuth* (London: Granta Books, 2005); as well as Spotts, *Bayreuth*. See also accounts by members of the younger Wagner generations, each with some strong perspectives: Friedelind Wagner and Page Cooper, *Heritage of Fire: The Story of Richard Wagner's Granddaughter* (New York and London: Harper, 1945); Gottfried Wagner (the composer's left-wing great-grandson), *Wer nicht mit dem Wolf heult* (Cologne: Verlag Kiepenheuer & Witsch, 1997), trans. Della Couling, *He Who Does not Howl with the Wolf: The Wagner Legacy, An Autobiography* (London: Sanctuary, 1998) or as *Twilight*

of the Wagners: The Unveiling of a Family's Legacy (New York: Picador, 1999); or Nike Wagner (the composer's ambitious great-granddaughter), Wagner Theater (Frankfurt: Insel, 1998), trans. Ewald Osers and Michael Downes, The Wagners: The Dramas of a Musical Dynasty (London: Weidenfeld & Nicolson, or Princeton University Press, 2000). And now, comprehensively, there is Jonathan Carr's The Wagner Clan.

8. Ernst Hanfstaengel, Unheard Witness (Philadelphia and New York: Lippincott, 1957), 243–44, 246–52. German-born but American-educated and with an American wife, he was on a visit to the United States to attend his class reunion at Harvard University when the visit he claimed to have fostered occurred in his absence. Supposedly, he had been frozen out of its actual planning, even by Hitler himself. When Hanfstaengel read the newspaper accounts of the Venice meeting, he tells us (256–57), he was furious at what he regarded as a hijacking of his idea. ". . . He [Hitler] misleads me for weeks, waits until my back is turned, and then takes up my suggestion when he knows I cannot be there to guide the conversation along the right lines. . . . We now know that he talked to Mussolini as if he were at a public meeting and that this first contact was a near fiasco. . . ."

The recent biography by Peter Conradi, Hitler's Piano Player: The Rise and Fall of Ernst Hanfstaengl, Confidant of Hitler, Ally of FDR (New York: Carroll & Graf, 2004), 139, follows "Putzi's" assertion that the Vendramin connection was used as bait in negotiations with Mussolini. Conradi also reports Hitler's initial indifference to the scheme (143–44), and plays down Hanfstaengl's supposed frustration at being frozen out of the Venice meeting (168–69).

9. Franz von Papen, Memoirs, trans. Brian Connell (New York: Dutton, 1953), 331–32. Von Papen's account is very brief and terse, claiming the initiative for the meeting entirely for himself, and never making the slightest reference to Hanfstaengel—much less to Wagner.

10. To hold the meeting in Rome would have involved making it a state visit, with King Vittorio Emmanuele III as the technical host. Mussolini clearly wanted the meeting to be a purely personal one between himself and the Führer. Cf. Elisabetta Cerruti, in her memoir Visti da vicino (Milan: Garzanti, 1951): "The meeting took place in Venice, city of dreams and, if I may add, of twisted diplomacy. Mussolini had probably picked Venice because it was the least 'official' Italian city and thought this would have given the visit less emphasis. However, any location would have conveyed enormous importance to the event." (Quoted by Corvaja, Hitler and Mussolini, 32.)

11. This idea seems to have been recognized in Hitler's third visit to Italy, in May 1938, in which the King was the official host. In the course of that stay, Hitler was treated to an outdoor performance of one act of Lohengrin in the Piazza di Siena on the grounds of the Villa Borghese. (Corvaja, trans. Miller, Hitler and Mussolini, 78.)

12. A clear example can be found in the section "Wagner a Venezia," of Guido Perocco's chapter, "Venezia nell'epoco romantico," in Civiltà di Venezia, Vol. 3: L'età moderna, ed. Perocco and Antonio Salvadori (Venice: La Stamperia di Venezia Editore, 1976), 1270–73. A classic antecedent would be the chapter "Wagner a Venezia" in the nostalgic mélange by Venetian antiquarian Gino Damerini, Amor di Venezia (Bologna: Nicola Zanichelli, 1920), 103–14.

13. On the basis of this film festival, a collection of essays was published in Venice that year, as edited by Ermanno Comuzio and Giuseppe Ghigi, under the title L'immagine in me nascota. R.W. Un itinerario cinematografico.

14. On this eccentric poem, Hommage à Wagner, see Elwood Hartmann, "Wagner and Mallarmé: Aesthetic Rivalry," in Wagner in Retrospect, ed. Leroy Shaw, Nancy

Cirillo, and Marion Miller (Amsterdam: Rodopi, 1987), 130–36; also Raymond Furness, *Wagner and Literature* (New York: St. Martin's Press, 1982), 60–61, n. 9. An English translation is given by Robert Greer Cohn, *Toward the Poems of Mallarmé* (Berkeley: University of California Press, 1965), 178–81, and this is also quoted by Hartmann in his n. 11.

15. *Itinerari Veneziani di Richard Wagner: Immagine d'epoca e foto di Mario Vidor* (Treviso: Bubolo e Naibo, 1995).

16. The organization's address is: c/o A.C.I.T.-Palazzo Albrizzi, 4118 Cannaregio, 30131 Venezia; e-mail: arwv@libero.it; telephone (for access to the Museo Richard Wagner) 39 041 2760407 or 39 349 5936990.

Addendum 1

1. See figure 35.
2. Gregor-Dellin, *Richard Wagner*, trans. Brownjohn, 308–10.
3. Wagner, *Richard Wagner an Mathilde Wesendonk*, trans. Ellis, *Wagner to Mathilde*, 288–91.
4. Ibid., 285–88.
5. Nike Wagner, *The Wagners: The Dramas of a Musical Dynasty*, trans. E. Osers and M. Downes (London: Weidenfeld & Nicolson, 2000), 90–91.
6. Wapnewski, "The Operas as Literary Works," in *Wagner Handbook*, ed U. Müller and P. Wapnewski, trans. John Deathridge, 1–94 (Cambridge, MA: Harvard University Press, 1992), 82–83.
7. Köhler, *Der Letzte der Titanen*, 572–74, 791–92, or trans. Spencer, 445–46, 621–22.
8. Further discussions of the Titian/*Meistersinger* issue by German scholars are cited by Werner Breig in *Wagner Handbook*, ed. Müller and Wapnewski, 466. But see especially Bernhard Schubert, "Wagners 'Sachs' und die Tradition des romantischen Künstlerselbstverständnis," *Archiv für Musikwissenschaft* 40 (1983): 212–53.
9. Cf. p. 25.

Addendum 2

1. See pp. 138–39; 352–53, n. 38, regarding controversy over Keppler's supposed statements. Note also that the novelist Kürenberg has related them and "the report of a newspaper in Venice" to a rumor of a possible dalliance instead with Betty Bürkel—a rumor he mentions and dismisses.
2. English translation by Stewart Spencer, pp. 64–65 of his article "'Er starb,—ein Mensch wie alle': Wagner and Carrie Pringle," in *Wagner* 25 (2004), 55–77. Much reduced excerpts from this entry are given by Westernhagen, p. 397 of his "Wagner's Last Day," *Musical Times* 120 (1979): 395–97. In his article, Spencer (55, n. 4), cites the assertion of Norbert Götz (2003) that Cosima's supposed guilt over her alleged responsibility for Wagner's fatal heart attack was itself her sole motivation for creating the Wagnerian "cult" of Bayreuth!
3. Jean Mistler, "La mort à Venise," in *Richard Wagner*, ed. Pierre Levallois (Paris, 1962), 213–32; 231; translation by Spencer in "'Er starb,'" 56, n. 9.

4. "Absturz aus Klingsors Zaubergarten," in supplement (August 1978) to the *Nordbayerischer Kurier*.

5. It is taken as fact by Gregor-Dellin, *Richard Wagner*, 798, 823, 837, 840, or trans. Brownjohn, 448, 508, 518, 521; by Millington, *Wagner*, 111–12; by Pachl, *Siegfried Wagner*, 63; and by Cotterill, *Wagner*, 141. It has been relished most recently, and most greedily, by Köhler, *Der Letzte der titanen*, 805–8, trans. Spencer, 633–35. Millington, in his article "Wagner" in *The New Grove Dictionary of Music and Musicians*, 2nd ed. (London, 2001), vol. 26, 940, at first accepted the Pringle story. But in his revision of that article in *The New Grove Guide to Wagner and his Operas* (Oxford: Oxford University Press, 2006), 27, Millington has conceded that the "legend" of the "fatal" argument with Cosima and the idea of an affair with Pringle has been shown by "recent research" to be without evidence.

6. See above, n. 2.

7. *Wagner, His Life and Music* (Naxos Books, 2007), 124: "On 13 February 1883, Wagner and Cosima had an almighty row about a young English singer called Carrie Pringle, one of the Flower Maidens in the recent *Parsifal*, who was planning a visit. Wagner returned to his desk, [. . .] He died shortly afterward." On the other hand, the whole Pringle affair is dismissed judiciously, if reluctantly, by Carr, *Wagner Clan*, 48, 54.

Addendum 3

1. See Walker, *Liszt*, vol. 3, 508–19; cf. Köhler, *Der Letzte der Titanen*, 801–3, trans. Spencer, 629–31.

2. The best and most recent treatment of Rubinstein and his relationship to the composer is now Brener's *Richard Wagner and the Jews*, 182–85, 206–9, 257. For short sketches, see Gutman, *Wagner*, 450–51; Aberbach, *The Ideas of Richard Wagner*, 288–90 (1st ed.), or 234–36 (2nd ed.); Rose, *Wagner: Race and Revolution*, 123–24.

3. Siegfried Wagner, *Erinnerungen*, 14–15; also translated by Stewart Spencer in his anthology, *Wagner Remembered*, 272–73.

4. *1876. Richard Wagner auf der Probe: Das Bayreuther Tagebuch des Ballettmeisters und Hilfsregisseurs Richard Fricke*, ed. Joachim Herz (Stuttgart: Akademischer Verlag Hans-Dieter Heinz, 1983), 81; see also 46, 54; or trans. George R. Fricke as *Wagner in Rehearsal, 1875–1876: The Diaries of Richard Fricke*, ed., James Deaville (Stuyvesant, NY: Pendragon Press, 1998), 58; also 36, 41.

5. The earliest and most massive biography, was that by Count Richard Du Moulin-Eckart, whose first volume ends abruptly with Wagner's death, as does Skelton's book. But Du Moulin-Eckart went on to produce a second volume, titled *Die Herrin von Bayreuth (1883–1930)*, and this stands as the most extended study. On a smaller scale, the book by Millenkovich-Morold, devotes the last two of its seven chapters (360–471) to the post-1883 years. Other studies cited above give only the briefest treatment to the post-1883 years. But important coverage of the later years can be found in a collection of documents with commentary, Dietrich Mack, ed., *Cosima Wagner, Das zweite Leben. Briefe und Aufzeichnungen 1883–1930* (Munich: R. Piper, 1980); but see Spotts, *Bayreuth*, 90–122. A good overview of her later career, as Bayreuth's "Queen of the Hill," is given by Carr, *Wagner Clan*, 55–64; his book in general provides extensive treatment of Wagner's children.

6. On Wagner's son, the most recent treatment is in Carr's *Wagner Clan*, 114–31. But the most thorough study of his life and compositions is Pachl's *Siegfried Wagner*, an earlier study, carried out under the auspices of his widow and Bayreuth resources is Kraft's *Der Sohn*.

Siegfried Wagner's operas avoid attempting to emulate those of his father, and instead extend the idiom of the "fairy tale opera" of his teacher, Humperdinck, while absorbing some musical currents of his time (i.e., Richard Strauss, even Impressionism). But, on his father's model, Siegfried did write his own librettos as well as the music. Biographer Pachl has suggested that there are autobiographical hints in the librettos, notably the fourteenth of them, *Rainulf und Adelasia*, Op. 14. Completed by 1923, but never performed in Siegfried's lifetime, the opera is set in the Norman Kingdom of southern Italy at the end of the twelfth century and reflects, among other things, the Wagners' connection with the noble Sicilian Gravina family. Pachl (308–9) speculates that the opera's antihero Rainulf "has a number of autobiographical traits," while at the same time evoking the character of Houston Stewart Chamberlain, Siegfried's brother-in-law. Pachl perceives Siegfried's resentment of his mother for favoring Chamberlain over himself, plus Siegfried's anger at Chamberlain for prompting Cosima to commit perjury in the dispute over Isolde's paternity.

7. For Siegfried's marriage, and his heiress, there is now Brigitte Hamann's *Winifred Wagner oder Hitlers Bayreuth* (Munich and Zurich: Piper, 2002); abbreviated English translation by Alan Bance, *Winifred Wagner—A Life at the Heart of Hitler's Bayreuth* (London: Granta Books, 2005). Carr, in *Wagner Clan* (131–243, 257–66), includes coverage of Winifred's rule at Bayreuth through the end of World War II, and then her "de-nazification trial."

8. The postwar history of the family and the festival is treated in the latter chapters of Carr's book (244–352). See also Spotts, *Bayreuth*.

9. There is an extensive account of Isolde von Bülow-Beidler's estrangement from her mother and the resulting legal battle in her son's essays (Beidler, *Cosima Wagner-Liszt*, 367–84). See also Carr, *Wagner Clan*, 127–28.

10. Carr, *Wagner Clan* (90–110), gives an interesting profile of Chamberlain.

Addendum 4

1. *The Letters of Giuseppe Verdi*, trans. Charles Osborne (New York: Holt, Rinehart & Winston, 1971), 219. Cf. Newman, *Life of Richard Wagner*, vol. 4, 714.

2. Trans. Edward Downes, in *Verdi: The Man in his Letters*, ed. Franz Werfel and Paul Stefan (New York: Fischer, 1942), 365.

3. Ibid., 343–45.

4. Mario Medici and Marcello Conati, eds., with Marisa Casati, *Carteggio Verdi-Boito*, 2 vols. (Parma: Istituto di Studi Verdiani, 1978), vol. 2, 421–22. At the time of this exchange, von Bülow had only two more years to live. On April 15, Verdi reported to Boïto the reply he had made, noting that he had sent both the original and a copy of the reply to Giulio Ricordi, who published both four months later in the *Gazzetta musicale di Milano*.

5. For example, see Jung, *Rezeption*, 330–42; Anna Amalie Abert, "Verdi e Wagner," in *Wagner in Italia*, ed. Giancarlo Rostirolla, 305–14; more comprehensively, Ernö Lendvai, *Verdi and Wagner* (Budapest, 1988).

Addendum 5

1. These recollections by Goldwag were recorded by Ludwig Karpath and published in 1906. The passages quoted are taken from the more extensive segments translated by Spencer in his *Wagner Remembered*, 149–53. A newly discovered letter written by Wagner in 1874 to the dressmakers Gaetano Ghezzi and his wife Charlotte Chaillon of Milan, stipulating with great detail the specifics of garments ordered for Cosima has been published and analyzed by Spencer in the *Wagner Journal* 1 (2007): 18–32, as part of a thorough review of the composer's dealings in feminine clothing: see below, n. 9. See also notes 2 and 3 on p. 18 of this Spencer article for bibliography on Wagner's letters to Goldwag, as well as Karpath's documentation of her recollections.

2. Westernhagen, *Wagner*, trans. Whittall, 469–70.

3. Newman, *Life of Wagner*, vol. 4, 689, n. 2. Cosima writes often in her diaries of the enjoyment she and Richard took in the fragrances of violets and roses, and their essences distilled into perfumes (e.g., September 9, 1873; October 8 and November 4 of 1878). On several occasions he made a point of giving her gifts of perfume: July 4, 1878, and January 1, 1879. On the latter occasion, Cosima even suggests that Wagner concocted perfumes himself: ". . . returning from his walk, he says to me, 'I have been performing rose miracles in your room.' In the morning he placed on my bureau a little bottle of 'Extract Richard Wagner,' which he brewed himself, and in the afternoon he pours a few drops of rose essence on my bouquet . . ."

4. A portion of this passage by Perl is given in English in the leaflet prepared by the Associazione Richard Wagner di Venezia to accompany its exhibit in the very room in the Palazzo Vendramin that housed the composer's Blue Grotto.

5. Köhler, *Last of the Titans*, trans. Spencer, 626–27.

6. Kürenberg, *Carneval der Einsamen*.

7. Later in the novel, well after the scene of the fire in the study (ch. 24), Kürenberg imagines the reactions of Henry Thode, when the latter visits the Vendramin in late January 1883, and can observe the Wagners' ostentatious "lifestyle" there: "The young, quiet scholar is astounded by the display of luxury at the all-evening family celebration. Carneval seems to have broken through the seams of the quarters, to have transformed the three *Einsame* [Liszt, Wagner, Cosima] into maskers, and the house into a holiday hall. He does not know that in Bayreuth, at the Villa Wahnfried, things are not much different. The salons of the *piano nobile* are filled with expensive flowers and plants in copper kettles, terra-cotta tubs, and marble basins, in crystal vases and clay pots. Arm-thick altar candles burn in prodigal quantity; champagne flows on into the waning night. In the tightly restricted circles of his intimates Wagner could dare to appear in his expensive garments, which otherwise only his study occasionally allowed. Specially favored by him at night, would be light-colored satin worked in gold, trimmed with fur, and bound by a filigreed sash, usually set with semiprecious stones; the design going back to Old German antecedents. It appears that Wagner during a single night—always according to his mood—repeatedly changes these robes; each garment has its own strongly scented, quite overpowering perfume. According to each choice of garment. Frau Cosima can determine Wagner's mood with certainty."

Kürenberg goes on to describe how Cosima, who on the street wore only severe black, at her husband's request adapted quite elaborate garb for the family circle. Between Cosima's jewelry and Richard's "many expensive rings with rubies, emeralds, and diamonds," Liszt is perceived as "a black exclamation point," wearing only a bishop's ring with a large amethyst set in diamonds. Joukowsky is made to brush aside so much gaudiness, especially amid Carneval: "Display of luxury is altogether fitting in this half-oriental, almost functionally Byzantine city" (217–18).

8. It is interesting to note that Kürenberg seems both to amplify the effect and to dilute slightly the credibility of the supposed eye- (and nose-)witness testimony on which he had depended. In a late section of his novel, he imagines drastic effort directed at the Blue Grotto on Cosima's specific instructions, carried out while Wagner's corpse was still in the Palazzo Vendramin: ". . . Hardly has the coffin been borne out into the hall that the entire interior decoration of the study—fabrics, garments, cushions, and roses—is dismantled. By evening there are no more tapestries on the walls, so that the piano and the furniture are left to stand in a bare, curtainless chamber. No stranger could claim to have truly seen with his own eyes the Holy-of-Holies on the *piano nobile.*

"So it happens that, become thus so veiled and sober, Richard Wagner's study in the Palazzo Vendramin-Calergi, down to the present day, can no longer give any concept of the that curious luxury that once reigned here. No remembrance still remains; there would be only a few wilted flowers on the naked staircase left behind here for the Wagner admirer" (279).

9. Köhler, *Letzte der Titanen,* 583–86, trans. Spencer, 454–56. Documentation for Wagner's extensive purchases of luxury garments has been gathered by L. Kusche, *Wagner und die Putzmacherin* (Wilhelmshaven, 1967), and is sampled in the citations of Sabor, *The Real Wagner,* 143–45. Most recently, in reviewing in detail Wagner's extensive and detailed ordering of feminine garments (specified as for Cosima), Stewart Spencer has touched cautiously, if with skepticism, on Wagner's fascination with feminine garments as suggesting a penchant for cross-dressing, in his article "Wagner and Gaetano Ghezzi," *Wagner Journal* 1 (2007): 24, 31–32. (This article prompted a flurry of quite inappropriate sensationalism in the popular press when it appeared.) In the process, Spencer repeats the understanding that Wagner required silks and satins in his garments because of his skin sensitivities (n. 52), as well as a part of his psychological need in transcending the mundane world in his quest for the higher, artistic reality to which he aspired—exactly what Perl argued. We might mention a suggestive reference in Cosima's diary entry for October 5, 1879: "After a good night R. gaily looks through my fashion journal in bed; he is always interested in costumes, but unfortunately we cannot help finding everything incomprehensibly ugly."

10. Ferdinand Praeger, a close friend who visited and observed the composer over the years, has left us vivid recollections in his memoir, *Wagner As I Knew Him* (London: Longmans, Green & Co., 1892), including the most fascinating picture of the composer's devotion to snuff. Praeger describes Wagner playing and singing snatches of Weber's music, regularly interrupted by large doses of snuff. "The snuff-taking scene of the evening is the deeper graven on my memory, because Wagner abruptly stopped singing, on finding his snuff-box empty, and got into a childish, pettish fit of anger. He turned to us in deepest concern, with 'Kein schnupf tabac mehr also Kein gesang mehr' (no more snuff, no more song); and though we had reached the small hours of early morn, would have someone start in search of this 'necessary adjunct.' When singing, the more impassioned he became, the more frequent the snuff-taking. Now, this practice of Wagner's, one cultivated from early manhood, in my opinion pointedly illustrates a phase in the man's character. He did not care for snuff, and even allowed the indelicacy of the habit, but it was that insatiable nature of his that yearned for the enjoyment of all the 'supposed' luxuries of life. It was precisely the same with smoking. He indulged in

this, to me, barbarous acquirement more moderately, but experienced not the slightest pleasure from it. I have seen him puffing from the mild and inoffensive cheroot, to the luxurious hookah—the latter, too, as he confessed, only because it was an Oriental growth, and the luxury of Eastern people harmonized with his own fondness for unlimited profusion. 'Other people find pleasure in smoking; then why should not I?' This is, briefly, the only explanation Wagner ever offered in defence of the practice—a practice which he was fully aware increased the malignity of his terrible dyspepsia" (251-52). Cosima has hinted how devoted to snuff Richard actually became. On November 12, 1879, during one of his illnesses, she observed how "run down R. looks. Whether it is due to pain, the fact that he is forbidden to take snuff, or the air in the room, only God knows,.." How his habit had affected his sense of smell was noted earlier (September 9, 1873): ". . . yesterday I had clumsily sprinkled my handkerchief so strongly with essence of violets that I was unwilling to take it out of my pocket; but R. had not smelled it, since his snuff always prevents him anyway!" We also have at least one graphic representation of Wagner in the act of taking snuff: see figure 27. There exists, too, a Viennese silhouette by Otto Bühler, showing Wagner offering snuff to an adoring Anton Bruckner. One reproduction of this may be found as illustration #4 in *Bruckner Remembered*, ed. Stephen Johnson (London: Faber and Faber, 1998).

Addendum 6

1. We have already noted the report of Wagner's failure, only nine days before his death, to bring off a joke on Hermann Levi: see p. 54. And there is also his wordplay on the "tombola," "gondola," and a Beethoven motive: see p. 349, n. 8; also his teasing of Cosima at table, as reported by Norlenghi, p. 162; and Norlenghi's account of Wagner's joking threat to the painter Reuben, for which see p. 159. Cosima herself constantly refers in her diaries to Wagner's boisterous good humor as a regular mood. On April 1, 1878, for example, she notes: "He [Richard] performs all kinds of April Fools' jokes with the children at lunch, much to his amusement." Wagner's humor could also have an ironic touch. For Sunday, December 31, 1882, Cosima records: ". . . At lunch he is in turn irritable and full of fun. When it is pointed out that the New Year starts on a Monday, he says, 'Then it is beginning well again,' and he tells of a man being led to execution who asked 'What day is it today?' 'Monday.' 'Ah, the week is starting well.'" Of course, Wagner could not know that there was a double irony in applying this quip to what would be his own last New Year.

2. Liszt and dancing are involved with another demonstration of Wagner's almost childlike playfulness. For January 10, 1883 (a month before his death), Cosima records the following: ". . . Around 6 o'clock my father plays to us the Andante from the A major Symphony [Beethoven's Seventh], and the Scherzo Allegretto from the F major [Beethoven's Eighth]; twice during the latter R. comes in dancing, which makes Fidi laugh a lot. . . ."

Siegfried later recalled this incident in his *Erinnerungen*: ". . . While Liszt himself, surrounded by my mother, the Princess Hatzfeldt, and some friends, played in the salon, we children listened in an adjoining chamber. Suddenly, in the Scherzo, we see our father enter and, unnoticed by Liszt and the listeners, dance in the most skillful and graceful fashion. One might well believe he was seeing a youth of twenty before him. It was difficult for us not to show our delight at such dancing in loud laughter. One thing is certain: Beethoven could not imagine his Scherzo being more beautifully danced, and Isadora Duncan could rightly refer back to my father when anyone reproached her for dancing to Beethoven." Cf. Pachl, *Siegfried Wagner*, 62–63. It could be observed, however, that Wagner, who often delivered opinions and comments on each of these two Beethoven Symphonies, had famously dubbed the Seventh as "the apotheosis of the dance."

Also interesting in this dancing story, as well as in the reports of Wagner's youthful appearance at the closing of Carnival, is the indication of Wagner making striking displays of physical vigor in the weeks before his death.

3. A curious and slightly parallel incident is recorded by Cosima on August 14, 1876, in the midst of the Bayreuth premiere of the *Ring*, attended by the German Emperor: "he [R.] is summoned to the Emperor, who praises everything highly, says jokingly that, if he were an orchestra player, R. would never have got him down (into the orchestra pit), regrets not being able to remain for more than the two performances, whereupon R. replies, 'Favor is not dependent on time and place.' The Grand Duchess [of Baden], however, says she is staying on. R.: 'Then you extend the favor.' The Emperor, jokingly: 'That was a dig.' He says goodbye, takes a step backward, does not notice the doorstep, stumbles so awkwardly that it takes all of R.'s strength to hold him; he is convinced that this backward fall would have meant the death of the Emperor! ..."

Addendum 7

1. See pp. 111–13, 116–18, 122, 123, 126.

2. For example, by Gregor-Dellin, *Richard Wagner*, 886; or in the Postscript to the publication of Cosima's Diaries, vol. 2, 1013–14, in Skelton's English translation.

3. As translated by Brownjohn in his English version of Gregor-Dellin, *Richard Wagner*, 551–52, very slightly modified.

4. The latest comments on all this may be found in Köhler, *Der Letzte der Titanen*, 795–97, trans. Spencer, 624–26; and in Spencer's own article, " 'Er starb,' " 64–65. There is a full discussion of Wagner's health, illnesses, and medical treatments by two physicians, Joachim Thiery and Dietrich Seidel, in their article titled " 'Ich behage mir nicht,' " 491–502, trans. Spencer, " 'I feel only discontent,' " 3–22. An important conclusion of their study (21–22) is that Keppler's report should be treated with critical caution, due to its transmission through Perl. As can be observed in the lengthy quotations from her book in chapter 7, Perl herself gives repeated comments on Wagner's health problems, undoubtedly derived in large part from Keppler. Indeed, as is discussed above, pp. 138–39, Perl may have written her book in part at the prompting of Keppler, as a vehicle for defending himself against accusations of malpractice in treating Wagner.

5. This digression is included as n. 31 to the latter-day edition of Perl's book: original German, 260; or Italian translation, 249–50.

6. At the end of his novel, Kürenberg looks ahead to the post-1883 lives of his characters and has this to say about the doctor: "The family physician Doctor Keppler will put all that he witnessed and collected into Journals. Sixty years ago [i.e., 1887] a newspaper in Venice gathered small extracts, inaccurate, translated, distorted, and treated sensationally. In this [Kürenberg's] book those notes of Doctor Friedrich Keppler are adapted [*verwandt*] in their entirety, and certainly without

arbitrary interpretation and malevolent misrepresentations" (283). Then, in his bibliography, Kürenberg gives three entries for Keppler: two are to notes or journals kept on Wagner's health and death, surviving in manuscript in private possession. The third gives us a distinct variant to "a newspaper in Venice": "Various publications in a German-language newspaper (cuttings), without location (probably Bozen) and date (probably 1883)." If a truly authentic body of Keppler's observations survives, it should certainly be brought to light and made accessible.

Addendum 8

1. See pp. 91–92 [*LGdV* account].
2. Given as our prologue, pp. xvi–xvii.
3. See pp. 128–29 [Perl account].
4. See pp. 163–64 [Norlenghi].
5. The original French text is in *Briefe hervorragender Zeitgenossen an Franz Liszt*, ed. La Mara, vol. 3: *(1836–86)*, no. 306, 398–99. The major part has also been translated by P. R. J. Ford and Mary Whittall, in Barth, Mack, and Voss, *Wagner: A Documentary Study*, 245. Barely a fortnight later, on March 5, Joukowsky wrote again to Liszt, this time from Munich to report on the state of things (ibid., no. 310, 404–6). In it Joukowsky speaks of pondering Liszt's *La lugubre gondola* "after having seen the gondola bearing the remains of the great deceased!" He reports that Cosima is well, and active with her children. He conveys three of her requests to Liszt: for Wagner's letters to him, for the manuscript score of his *Christus*, and to preserve with care and security the manuscript of Wagner's autobiography, lest it fall into the wrong hands and be published before the thirty-year delay after his death that Wagner had stipulated. There are other requests Joukowsky makes for himself, and conveys his own greetings along with those of Levi, who has joined him.
The "Porges" referred to is Heinrich Porges (1837–1900), a music journalist and editor, but also choral conductor. He served on the Bayreuth Festival's production team in 1876 and 1882. Porges was Jewish, and Wagner had mixed feelings about him.
6. I use the translation given by Geoffrey Skelton in the Postscript to his translation of *Cosima Wagner's Diaries*, vol. 2, 1014.
7. Lacking access to the original, I have translated this passage from the Italian version given by Panizzardi, *Wagner in Italia*, vol. 1, 229–30.
8. Siegfried Wagner, *Erinnerungen*, 35–36; also translated by Stewart Spencer in his anthology of texts, *Wagner Remembered*, 273–74. The actor mentioned by Siegfried is Tommaso Salvini (1829–1915) who was particularly celebrated in his day for his portrayal of Othello. Cosima records reference made to him on November 12, 1879, during family discussion of Shakespeare's *Othello*.
As to Cosima's musical talents, it should be noted that they were diverse, and constituted one of the bonds between them that he had with no other women in his life. In addition to her helping him with score editing and correction, and other such chores, they regularly played piano duets together (especially four-hand arrangements of chamber and orchestral works) through their marriage, particularly in its earlier years.

Addendum 9

1. Glasenapp, *Das Leben Richard Wagners*, vol. 6, 774. Among Wagner biographers who have accepted the "words of the watch" are: Panizzardi, *Wagner in Italia*, vol. 1, 231; Newman, *Life of Richard Wagner*, vol. 4, 712; Watson, *Richard Wagner*, 314; and Köhler, *Der Letzte der Titanen*, 793, trans. Spencer, 622.

2. See p. 102.

3. Jullien, *Richard Wagner: sa vie et ses oeuvres*, trans. Percival Hall, 353–54.

Addendum 10

1. Panizzardi, *Wagner in Italia*, vol. 2, 237.

Addendum 11

1. Wagner, *Selected Letters*, trans. and ed. Spencer and Millington, no. 480, 905.

2. Ibid., no. 481, 906; cf. Neumann, *Erinnerungen*, 139; trans. Livermore, 132.

3. See Millington's comments, Wagner, *Selected Letters*, 805–6.

4. Ibid., no. 489, 918. Again, see Gutman, *Richard Wagner*, 429. Wagner's awareness of the paradox of so many Jewish supporters is also conveyed by a discussion Cosima records on January 13, 1879: "Alone together again, R. and I discuss the curious attachment individual Jews have for him; he says Wahnfried will soon turn into a synagogue! ..." The following day, Cosima reports: "Lunch with the children, much fun regarding our pet Israelites, R. thinks the only feeling they have in regard to his compositions is how well he does things."

5. See the extensive section (429–57) in Léon Poliakov, *The History of Anti-Semitism*, vol. 3: *From Voltaire to Wagner*, trans. Miriam Kochan (London: Routledge and Kegan Paul, 1970; repr. Philadelphia: University of Pennsylvania Press, 2003). Somewhat dated now is Leon Stein, *The Racial Thinking of Richard Wagner* (New York: Philosophical Library, 1950); still useful is Jacob Katz, *The Darker Side of Genius: Richard Wagner's Anti-Semitism* (Hanover, NH: University Press of New England, 1986). A more up-to-date discussion, including cases of specific Jewish colleagues (Meyerbeer, Halévy, Tausig, Rubinstein, Porges, Neumann, Levi) is in Aberbach, *The Ideas of Richard Wagner* (2nd ed., 2003), 225–51. (The segment on Neumann, 238–42, should particularly be noted.) A skeptical study of the issue through the composer's operas themselves is Marc A. Weiner's *Richard Wagner and the Anti-Semitic Imagination* (Lincoln: University of Nebraska Press, 1995). Meanwhile, the connection of Wagner's racial ideas with his political thinking and evolution has been explored by Paul Lawrence Rose, in his two studies, *Revolutionary Antisemitism in Germany from Kant to Wagner* (Princeton: Princeton University Press, 1990), and *Wagner: Race and Revolution* (1992), with especially relevant material on "house Jews" and Jewish associates such as Neumann (119–34). A more recent analysis of the subject, and a particularly balanced one, may be found in the Appendix, "Wagner's Anti-Semitism," of Bryan Magee's *The Tristan Chord: Wagner and Philosophy* (New York: Holt, 2000), 343–80, including discussion of Hitler's relationship with Wagner's music. The latest consideration of the issue is the chapter "The Plastic Demon," in

Carr's *Wagner Clan*, 65–89. But the most comprehensive treatment of the subject, of course, is now Brener's *Richard Wagner and the Jews*: on interpretations of Wagner's anti-Semitism (especially Gutman's virulent hostility), see 286–91.

Addendum 12

1. Wagner, *Richard Wagner an Minna Wagner*, ed. Wolzogen, vol. 2, 58–59, trans. Ellis, vol. 2, 463.

2. Wagner, *Selected Letters*, ed. Spencer and Millington, 865–86.

3. Ibid., 889–90.

4. The fullest survey of Wagner's musings on a relocation in America has already been given in an extensive collation of quotations made by Sabor in *Real Wagner*, 226–38, to which this addendum is a somewhat more curtailed alternative. See also Joseph Horowitz, *Wagner Nights: An American History* (Berkeley and London: University of California Press, 1994), 19–24, 33; further, Westernhagen, *Wagner*, 488, 519–23, trans. *Whittall*, 517–18, 550–54; Gregor-Dellin, *Richard Wagner*, 788–89, trans. Brownjohn, 481–82; and Klaus Liepmann, "Wagner's Proposal to America," *High Fidelity* 25, no. 12 (December 1975): 70–72.

Addendum 13

1. A remote but amusing reflection of Seidl's standing is included in a little note by *LV* in one of its final announcements (April 14) of the *Ring* production about to begin. The journal takes note of the fact that Seidl's conducting had been warmly approved by Wagner himself, "and it is known that Wagner was not quick to give praise!"

2. Seidl's career in the United States is a central theme of Joseph Horowitz's book *Wagner Nights: An American History* (Berkeley and London: University of California Press, 1994). See also the same author's essay "Anton Seidl and America's Wagner Cult," in *Wagner in Performance*, ed. Barry Millington and Stewart Spencer (New Haven, CT: Yale University Press, 1998), 168–81. See figure 38.

Addendum 14

1. See pp. 154, 234–37.

2. It will be recalled that Hedwig Reicher-Kindermann, ill through much of the Neumann tour in Italy, died near its end, in Trieste. See pp. 206–207.

Addendum 15

1. Norlenghi, *Ricordo Wagneriano* (Venice: Luigi Fu Gennaro Favai, 1886).

2. To which, remembering Wagner's private musicale outside Palermo (see p. 38), we would have to add: "in public."

Selected Bibliography

Aberbach, Alan David. *The Ideas of Richard Wagner: An Examination and Analysis [of His Major Aesthetic, Political, Economic, Social, and Religious Thoughts]*. Lanham, MD: University Press of America, 1984; 2nd ed. 2003.

Barker, John W. "A Forgotten Early Champion of Wagner: Venetian Bandmaster Jacopo Calascione." *Journal of Band Research* 43 (2007–8): 1–37.

Barre's, Maurice. *La Mort de Venise* [1903], ed. Marie Odile Germain. Saint-Cyr-Sur-Loire: Christian Pirot, 1990.

Barth, Herbert, Dietrich Mack, and Egon Voss, eds. *Wagner: A Documentary Study*. New York: Oxford University Press, 1975.

Beidler, Franz Wilhelm. *Cosima Wagner-Liszt: Der Weg zum Wagner-Mythos*. Bielefeld: Pendragon, 1997.

Brener, Milton E. *Richard Wagner and the Jews*. Jefferson, NC: McFarland, 2006.

Carnegy, Patrick. *Wagner and the Art of the Theatre*. New Haven, CT: Yale University Press, 2006.

Carr, Jonathan. *The Wagner Clan: The Saga of Germany's Most Illustrious and Infamous Family*. New Haven, CT: Yale University Press, 2007.

Cotterill, Rowland. *Wagner*. Staplehurst, UK: Spellmount, 1996.

Deathridge, John, and Carl Dahlhaus. *The New Grove Wagner*. New York: Norton, 1984.

Dieckmann, Friedrich. *Richard Wagner in Venedig: Eine Collage*. Leipzig: Reclam Verlag, 1983.

Dippel, Paul Gerhardt. *Richard Wagner und Italien: Vom Zaubergarten zur Lagune*. Emsdetten: Verlag Lechte, 1966.

Du Moulin-Eckart, Richard Graf. *Cosima Wagner: Ein Lebens- und Charakterbild*. Vol. 1 [1837–83]. Vol. 2: *Die Herrin von Bayreuth*. Munich: Drei Masken Verlag, 1929, 1931. Vol. 1 only, trans. Catherine Ellis Phillips as *Cosima Wagner*. 2 vols. New York: Knopf, 1930.

Finck, Henry T. *Wagner and His Works: The Story of His Life, with Critical Comments*. 2 vols. New York: Scribner's, 1916.

Furness, Raymond. *Wagner and Literature*. New York: St. Martin's Press, 1982.

Glasenapp, Carl Friedrich. *Das Leben Richard Wagners*. 4th ed. 6 vols. Leipzig: Breitkopf und Härtel, 1905–11. Partial trans. of 3rd ed. (vols. 1–3; 4–6 rewritten), William Ashton Ellis, *Life of Richard Wagner*. London: Kegan Paul, Trench, Trübner, 1900–1908.

Gregor-Dellin, Martin. *Richard Wagner: Sein Leben, sein Werk, sein Jahrhundert.* Munich and Zurich: Piper, 1980. Abbreviated trans. J. Maxwell Brownjohn, *Richard Wagner: His Life, His Work, His Century.* New York: Harcourt Brace Jovanovich, 1983.

Gualerzi, G., and C. Marinelli Roscioni. *Wagner in Italia, 1871–1971.* Venice: Teatro La Fenice, 1972.

Gutman, Robert W. *Richard Wagner: The Man, His Mind, and His Music.* New York: Harcourt, Brace and World, 1968.

Haweis, Hugh Reginald. *My Musical Life.* London: Longmans, Green, 1912.

Hibbert, Christopher. *Venice: Biography of a City.* New York: Norton, 1989.

Incontrera, Carlo de. "I viaggi di Wagner in Italia." In *Wagner in Italia,* ed. Giancarlo Rostirola. Turin: Edizioni RAI, 1982, 9–54 plus 68 plates.

Ipser, Karl. *Richard Wagner in Italien.* Salzburg: Bergland-Buch, 1951.

Jullien, Adolph. *Richard Wagner: sa vie et ses oeuvres.* Paris: J. Rouam, 1886. Trans. Florence Percival Hall, *Richard Wagner: His Life and Works.* Philadelphia: Theodor Presser, 1910; reprs. 1974, 1981.

Jung, Ute. *Die Rezeption der Kunst Richard Wagners in Italien.* Regensburg: Gustav Bosse Verlag, 1974. Part 1 only, in Italian version, in *Wagner in Italia,* ed. Giancarlo Rostirola. Turin: Edizioni RAI, 1982, 57–225.

Kahan, Sylvia. *Music's Modern Muse: A Life of Winnaretta Singer, Princesse de Polignac.* Rochester, NY: University of Rochester Press, 2003.

Köhler, Joachim. *Der Letzte der Titanen—Richard Wagners Leben und Werke.* Munich: Claasen Verlag, 2001. Trans. Stewart Spencer, *Richard Wagner: The Last of the Titans.* New Haven, CT: Yale University Press, 2004.

———. *Friedrich Nietzsche und Cosima Wagner.* Berlin: Rowohlt Verlag, 1996. Trans. Ronald Taylor, *Nietzsche and Wagner: A Lesson in Subjugation.* New Haven, CT: Yale University Press, 1998.

———. *Wagners Hitler: Der Prophet und sein Vollstrecker.* Munich: Karl Blessing Verlag, 1997. Trans. Ronald Taylor, *Wagner's Hitler: The Prophet and his Disciple.* Cambridge and Oxford: Polity Press, 2000.

Kraft, Zdenko von. *Der Sohn: Siegfried Wagners Leben und Umwelt.* Graz and Stuttgart: Leopold Stocker Verlag, 1969.

Kürenberg, Joachim von [Eduard Joachim von Reichel]. *Carneval der Einsamen: Richard Wagners Tod in Venedig.* Hamburg: Robert Mölich Verlag, 1947.

Lauritzen, Peter, and Alexander Zielcke. *Palaces of Venice.* New York: Viking Press, 1978.

Lippert, Woldemar. *Richard Wagners Verbannung und Rückkehr, 1849–1862.* Dresden: Paul Aretz Verlag, 1927. Trans. Paul England, *Wagner in Exile, 1849–1862.* London: G. G. Harrap, 1930.

Marek, George R. *Cosima Wagner.* New York: Harper and Row, 1981.

Millenkovich-Morold, Max. *Cosima Wagner: Ein Lebensbild.* 2nd ed. Leipzig: Philipp Reclam, 1937.

Millington, Barry. *Wagner.* London: Dent, 1984.

———, ed. *The Wagner Compendium: A Guide to Wagner's Life and Music.* London: Thames & Hudson/New York: Schirmer Books, 1992.

Miller, Marion S. "Wagnerism, Wagnerians, and Italian Identity." In *Wagnerism in European Culture and Politics*, ed. David C. Large and William Weber. Ithaca, NY: Cornell University Press, 1984, 167–97.

Müller, Ulrich, and Peter Wapnewski, eds. *Richard Wagner-Handbuch*. Stuttgart: Alfred Kröner Verlag, 1986. Trans. John Deathridge, *Wagner Handbook*. Cambridge, MA: Harvard University Press, 1992.

Neumann, Angelo. *Erinnerungen an Richard Wagner*. Leipzig: L. Staackmann Verlag, 1907. Trans. Edith Livermore, *Personal Recollections of Wagner*. London: Archibald Constable, 1909.

Newman, Ernest. *The Life of Richard Wagner*. 4 vols. New York: Knopf, 1933–46.

Norlenghi, Giuseppe. *Ricordo Wagneriano: Parole lette per la commemorazione di Riccardo Wagner alla Associazione Artistica Internazionale di Roma*. Venice: Luigi Fu Gennaro Favai, 1886.

———. *Wagner a Venezia*. Venice: Ferd. Ongania, 1884.

Norwich, John Julius. *Paradise of Cities: Venice in the 19th Century*. New York and London: Doubleday, 2003.

Pachl, Peter P. *Siegfried Wagner: Genie im Schatten*. Munich: Nymphenburger, 1988.

Panizzardi, Mario. *Wagner in Italia*. Vol. 1: *Note biografiche*. Vol. 2: *Pagine di storia musicale*. Genoa, 1914–23.

Perl, Henry [= Henriette]. *Richard Wagner in Venedig. Mosaikbilder aus seinen letzten Lebenstagen. Mit einem Vorworte und unter Benuztung der Beobeachtungen des Herrn Dr. Friedrich Keppler*. Augsburg: Gebrüder Reichel, 1883; reprinted with Italian translation by Quirino Principe, *Richard Wagner a Venezia*. Venice: Marsilio, 2000.

Plant, Margaret. *Venice: Fragile City, 1797–1997*. New Haven, CT: Yale University Press, 2002.

Rose, Paul Lawrence. *Wagner: Race and Revolution*. New Haven, CT: Yale University Press, 1992.

Rostirolla, Giancarlo, ed. *Wagner in Italia*. Turin: Edizione RAI, 1982.

Sabor, Rudolph, ed. *The Real Wagner*. London: André Deutsch, 1987.

Schuh, Willi. *Renoir und Wagner*. Erlenbach and Stuttgart: Eugen Rentsch Verlag, 1959.

Skelton, Geoffrey. *Richard and Cosima Wagner: Biography of a Marriage*. Boston: Houghton Mifflin, 1982.

Sokoloff, Alice Hunt. *Cosima Wagner: Extraordinary Daughter of Franz Liszt*. New York: Dodd, Mead, 1969; or *Cosima Wagner: A Biography*. London: Macdonald, 1970.

Spencer, Stewart. "'Er starb, - ein Mensch wie alle': Wagner and Carrie Pringle." *Wagner* 25 (2004): 55–77.

———, ed. *Wagner Remembered*. London: Faber and Faber, 2000.

Spotts, Frederic. *Bayreuth: A History of the Wagner Festival*. New Haven, CT: Yale University Press, 1994.

Strobel, Otto, ed. *König Ludwig II und Richard Wagner: Briefwechsel*. 3 vols. Karslruhe: G. Braun Verlag, 1936–39.

Thiery, Joachim, and Dietrich Seidel. "'Ich behage mir nicht': Richard Wagner und seine Ärzte." *Münchener Medizinische Wochenscrift* 136 (1994): 491–502. Trans. Stewart Spencer, "'I Feel Only Discontent': Wagner and His Doctors." *Wagner* 16 (1995): 3–22.

Verardo, Pietro, ed. *Il Conservatorio di Musica Benedetto Marcello di Venezia, 1876–1976: Centenario della Fondazione.* Venice: Palazzo Pisani, 1977.

Wagner, Cosima. *Die Tagebücher, 1869–1883,* ed. Martin Gregor-Dellin and Dietrich Mack. 2 vols. Munich: Piper Verlag, 1976–77. Trans. Geoffrey Skelton, *Cosima Wagner's Daiaries, 1869–1883.* London: Harcourt Brace Jovanovich, 1978–80.

Wagner, Richard W. *Briefe,* ed. Hanjo Kesting. Munich: R. Piper, 1983.

———. *Briefe, 1830–1883,* ed. Werner Otto. Berlin: Henschelverlag Kunst und Gesellschaft, 1986.

———. *Das Braune Buch: Tagebuchaufzeichnungen, 1865 bis 1882,* ed Joachim Bergfeld. Zurich: Atlantis Verlag, 1975. Trans. George Bird, *The Diary of Richard Wagner, 1865–1882: The Brown Book.* Cambridge: Cambridge University Press, 1980.

———. *Mein Leben: Erste autentische Veröffentlichung,* ed. M. Gregor-Dellin. Munich: Paul List Verlag, 1963. Trans. Andrew Gray, *My Life,* ed. Mary Whittall. Cambridge: Cambridge University Press, 1983.

———. *Richard Wagner an Mathilde Wesendonk: Tagebuchblätter und Briefe, 1853–1871,* ed. W. Golther. Berlin: Verlag von Alexander Duncker, 1904. Trans. William Ashton Ellis, *Richard Wagner to Mathilde Wesendonk.* New York: Scribner's, 1905.

———. *Richard Wagner an Minna Wagner.* 2 vols. Berlin and Leipzig: Schuster und Loefflerm 1908. Trans. William Ashton Ellis, *Richard to Minna Wagner: Letters to his First Wife.* 2 vols. London: H. Grevel, 1909.

———. *Selected Letters of Richard Wagner,* trans. and ed. Stewart Spencer and Barry Millington. New York: Norton, 1988.

———. *Tagebuchblätter und Briefe an Mathilde Wesendonk, 1853–1871,* ed. R. Sternfeld. Berlin: Deutsche Buch-Gemeinschaft, n.d.

Wagner, Siegfried. *Erinnerung.* Stuttgart: J. Engelhorns Nachf., 1923.

Walker, Alan. *Franz Liszt.* Vol. 3: *The Final Years, 1861–1886.* New York: Knopf, 1996.

Watson, Derek. *Richard Wagner: A Biography.* New York: Schirmer, 1979.

Westernhagen, Curt von. *Wagner.* Zurich: Atlantis Verlag, 1968, 2nd enlarged edition, 1979. Trans. (from 2nd ed.), Mary Whittall, *Wagner: A Biography.* Cambridge: Cambridge University Press, 1978.

———. "Wagner's Last Day." *Musical Times* 120 (1979): 395–97.

Index

Eastman Studies in Music

"The Music of American Folk Song" and Selected Other Writings on American Folk Music
Ruth Crawford Seeger, edited by Larry Polansky and Judith Tick

Portrait of Percy Grainger
Edited by Malcolm Gillies and David Pear

Berlioz: Past, Present, Future
Edited by Peter Bloom

The Musical Madhouse
(Les Grotesques de la musique)
Hector Berlioz
Translated and edited by Alastair Bruce
Introduction by Hugh Macdonald

The Music of Luigi Dallapiccola
Raymond Fearn

Music's Modern Muse: A Life of Winnaretta Singer, Princesse de Polignac
Sylvia Kahan

The Sea on Fire: Jean Barraqué
Paul Griffiths

"Claude Debussy As I Knew Him" and Other Writings of Arthur Hartmann
Edited by Samuel Hsu, Sidney Grolnic, and Mark Peters
Foreword by David Grayson

Schumann's Piano Cycles and the Novels of Jean Paul
Erika Reiman

Bach and the Pedal Clavichord: An Organist's Guide
Joel Speerstra

Historical Musicology: Sources, Methods, Interpretations
Edited by Stephen A. Crist and Roberta Montemorra Marvin

The Pleasure of Modernist Music: Listening, Meaning, Intention, Ideology
Edited by Arved Ashby

Debussy's Letters to Inghelbrecht: The Story of a Musical Friendship
Annotated by Margaret G. Cobb

Explaining Tonality: Schenkerian Theory and Beyond
Matthew Brown

The Substance of Things Heard: Writings about Music
Paul Griffiths

Musical Encounters at the 1889 Paris World's Fair
Annegret Fauser

Aspects of Unity in J. S. Bach's Partitas and Suites: An Analytical Study
David W. Beach

Letters I Never Mailed: Clues to a Life
Alec Wilder
Annotated by David Demsey
Foreword by Marian McPartland

Wagner and Wagnerism in Nineteenth-Century Sweden, Finland, and the Baltic Provinces: Reception, Enthusiasm, Cult
Hannu Salmi

Bach's Changing World: Voices in the Community
Edited by Carol K. Baron

CageTalk: Dialogues with and about John Cage
Edited by Peter Dickinson

European Music and Musicians in New York City, 1840–1900
Edited by John Graziano

Schubert in the European Imagination, Volume 1: The Romantic and Victorian Eras
Scott Messing

Opera and Ideology in Prague: Polemics and Practice at the National Theater, 1900–1938
Brian S. Locke

Ruth Crawford Seeger's Worlds: Innovation and Tradition in Twentieth-Century American Music
Edited by Ray Allen and Ellie M. Hisama

Schubert in the European Imagination, Volume 2: Fin-de-Siècle Vienna
Scott Messing

Mendelssohn, Goethe, and the Walpurgis Night: The Heathen Muse in European Culture, 1700–1850
John Michael Cooper

Dieterich Buxtehude: Organist in Lübeck (includes CD)
Kerala J. Snyder

Musicking Shakespeare: A Conflict of Theatres
Daniel Albright

Pentatonicism from the Eighteenth Century to Debussy
Jeremy Day-O'Connell

Maurice Duruflé: The Man and His Music
James E. Frazier

Representing Non-Western Music in Nineteenth-Century Britain
Bennett Zon

The Music of the Moravian Church in America
Edited by Nola Reed Knouse

Music Theory and Mathematics: Chords, Collections, and Transformations
Edited by Jack Douthett, Martha M. Hyde, and Charles J. Smith

The Rosary Cantoral: Ritual and Social Design in a Chantbook from Early Renaissance Toledo
Lorenzo Candelaria

Berlioz: Scenes from the Life and Work
Edited by Peter Bloom

Beyond The Art of Finger Dexterity: Reassessing Carl Czerny
Edited by David Gramit

French Music, Culture, and National Identity, 1870–1939
Edited by Barbara L. Kelly

The Art of Musical Phrasing in the Eighteenth Century: Punctuating the Classical "Period"
Stephanie D. Vial

Beethoven's Century: Essays on Composers and Themes
Hugh Macdonald

Composing for Japanese Instruments (includes 2 CDs)
Minoru Miki
Translated by Marty Regan
Edited by Philip Flavin

Variations on the Canon: Essays on Music from Bach to Boulez in Honor of Charles Rosen on His Eightieth Birthday
Edited by Robert Curry, David Gable, and Robert L. Marshall

Wagner and Venice
John W. Barker

Richard Wagner had a longstanding love affair with the city of Venice. His sudden death there in 1883 also initiated a process through which Wagner and his reputation were integrated into Venice's own cumulative cultural image.

In *Wagner and Venice*, John Barker examines the connections between the great composer and the great city. The author traces patterns of Wagner's visits to Venice during his lifetime, considers what the city came to mean to Wagner, and investigates the details surrounding his death. Barker also examines how Venice viewed Wagner, by analyzing the landmark presentation of Wagner's Ring cycle two months after the composer's death, and by considering Venice's subsequent extensive Wagner celebrations and commemorations.

Throughout the volume, biographical detail from new and previously unavailable sources provides readers with a fresh interpretation of this seminal figure. Those already familiar with Wagner's life will find new information about, and insights into, the man and his career, while simultaneously discovering a neglected corner of Italian and Venetian cultural history.

John W. Barker is Emeritus Professor of History at the University of Wisconsin-Madison, specializing in medieval (including Venetian) history. He is also a passionate music lover and record collector, and an active music critic and journalist.

"It was in Venice that Wagner composed much of the second act of *Tristan und Isolde*, with its ecstatic love duet, and it was in Venice that he died two and a half decades later. Charting the composer's own love affair with La Serenissima over that period has been the quarter-of-a-century mission of John W. Barker, who sifts the plethora of eye-witness accounts with a forensic skill that brings to light all manner of fascinating documentary detail. A book to be relished by lovers of Wagner, of Venice, or of both."

—Barry Millington, Wagner scholar and author of *Wagner*, editor of *The Wagner Compendium*, and coeditor of *Selected Letters of Richard Wagner*

"A highly informative, smartly written book. Barker's *Wagner and Venice* is exhaustive in its research yet reads at times like a first-rate mystery, at other times like an intense romance novel about the special relationship between a man and a city. The copious illustrations and fifteen documentary addenda further enrich this study, which friends of Wagner (and Venice) will certainly want to add to their collections."

—James Deaville, associate professor of music at Carleton University, and coeditor of *Wagner in Rehearsal, 1875–1876: The Diaries of Richard Fricke*